READINGS IN THE MODERN THEORY
OF ECONOMIC GROWTH

READINGS IN THE MODERN THEORY
OF ECONOMIC GROWTH

EDITED BY JOSEPH E. STIGLITZ
AND HIROFUMI UZAWA

THE M.I.T. PRESS
Cambridge, Massachusetts, and London, England

Copyright © 1969 by
The Massachusetts Institute of Technology

Printed by HALLIDAY LITHOGRAPH CORPORATION.
Bound in the United States of America
by THE COLONIAL PRESS, INC.

Library of Congress catalog card number: 69-12758

PAPERS BY

Kenneth J. Arrow	Harvard University
D. G. Champernowne	Trinity College, Cambridge
Edward F. Denison	Brookings Institution
Evsey D. Domar	Massachusetts Institute of Technology
William Fellner	Yale University
R. F. Harrod	Christ Church, Oxford
J. R. Hicks	All Souls College, Oxford
Leif Johansen	University of Oslo
Lord Kahn	King's College, Cambridge
Nicholas Kaldor	King's College, Cambridge
Charles Kennedy	University of Kent at Canterbury
E. Malinvaud	Institut National de la Statistique et des Études Économiques
R. C. O. Matthews	Nuffield College, Oxford
James A. Mirrlees	Nuffield College, Oxford
Edmund S. Phelps	University of Pennsylvania
F. P. Ramsey	King's College, Cambridge
Joan Robinson	Newnham College, Cambridge
Paul A. Samuelson	Massachusetts Institute of Technology
R. M. Solow	Massachusetts Institute of Technology
T. W. Swan	Australia National University
James Tobin	Cowles Foundation for Research in Economics, Yale
Hirofumi Uzawa	University of Chicago
M. E. Yaari	Hebrew University

CONTENTS

Contents

Introduction

The primary object of the modern theory of economic growth is to explain, on the one hand, the movements in the output, employment, and capital stock of a growing economy and the interrelations among these variables, and on the other hand, to explain the movements in the distribution of income among the factors of production.

In the century after Malthus and Ricardo formulated their theories of growth, it appeared that some of the most important of their empirical predictions were not borne out; for instance, the share of landowners did not seem to be increasing, and population was not growing faster than output. In the intervening century, moreover, the importance of agriculture relative to manufacturing declined markedly. Thus, the empirical facts that the modern theory of growth attempts to explain are quite different from those which the classical theory confronted.

What are these "facts"? One of the most remarkable aspects of the modern theory of growth is that, even in the course of the last decade, as we have attempted to study actual growth processes with more sophisticated tools and concepts, the empirical laws to which economists once held so firmly have become more questionable. To mention but three examples: the constancy of the relative shares, the constancy of the capital output ratio, and the Harrod neutrality of technological change. Indeed, the importance of technological change in explaining the growth in output per man has been a subject of dispute, ranging from Solow's original estimate that $87\frac{1}{2}$ per cent of the growth in output per man was due to technological change[1] to Jorgenson and Griliches' more recent work in which they have suggested that almost none

[1] R. M. Solow, "Technical Change and the Aggregate Production Function," *REStat, 39* (August 1957), 312–320.

of the growth in output per man is attributable to technical change.[2]

Indeed, the lack of empirical information about many of the crucial aspects of growth models has led to proliferation of assumptions as well as to a number of disputes which will be settled only when further empirical evidence becomes available. At the same time, however, growth theory has provided a conceptual framework within which much more meaningful empirical research can take place, and it has, accordingly, generated a vast amount of econometric research into, for instance, production functions and technological progress. This volume is not concerned with the empirical aspects of the growth literature. But the discussions in this volume should point up the areas in which empirical research is badly needed.

In formulating a model of growth, specific assumptions about the nature of production, technical progress, consumption, and reproduction must be made. The economies which the modern theory of economic growth attempts to describe are essentially advanced, industrialized economies. Hence, capital and labor are the two inputs upon which attention is focused. Land, with few exceptions, is ignored, but technical progress is crucial. The analysis is conducted on a highly aggregative level. It is the consumption-investment decision and not the allocation among alternative investment or alternative consumption goods upon which the analysis has been primarily focused.[3] Alternative assumptions about reproduction have played a minor role in the theory. Usually, labor is assumed to grow exponentially.

In Part I of this volume, the basic growth models of Harrod, Domar, Tobin, Solow, and Swan are presented. Most of the other articles in this volume may be considered, in one way or another, as commentary on these basic papers. Part II focuses on the production function — in particular on the relationship between growth, capital, and technical change. Section A is concerned with the effects of technical progress on different factors of production. Section B considers the implications of the fact that newer machines are better than older machines because of technical progress. Section C considers a model where there is no choice of technique at any point of time, but where newer machines are better than older machines because of technical progress; and moreover, where the rate of technical progress depends on the level of investment. Section D discusses models where, although before the investment has been made there is a choice of alternative machines with alternative outputs per man, once the investment (machine) has

[2] D. Jorgenson and Z. Griliches, "The Explanation of Productivity Change," *REStud, 34* (July 1967), 249–284.

[3] Recently, however, some models which center on the allocation of investment have been investigated. See below, p. 124, and F. Hahn [69] and K. Shell and J. Stiglitz [70].

4

been made, the labor requirements per unit of output are fixed. Section E is concerned with the problem of forming a capital index, that is, a measure of the capital stock, when there are a number of different kinds of capital. Section F considers one special kind of durable asset, money, and its implications for growth.

Part III includes representatives of the Cambridge Growth and Distribution Theory. These differ from the neoclassical model presented in several crucial ways, which we discuss in detail in the introduction to that section.

Part IV, like Part II, is concerned with the nature of the production process. Here, however, the focus is on the different production functions for the consumption and investment goods sectors.

The models presented in the first four parts of the volume are descriptive models: they are concerned with positive as opposed to normative economics. In particular, the savings-investment decision, following the Keynesian tradition, has been made according to some behavioristic rule. In Part V the savings-consumption decision is made in a manner analogous to that in which the decisions about allocation of income among alternative commodities in the static consumers theory are made: the individual maximizes his intertemporal utility. In this way, the connection is made between planning and descriptive growth models.

It may be worthwhile to briefly summarize the major theoretical issues that have been raised by the alternative growth models.

1. *Momentary equilibrium.* Just as in the analysis of an ordinary static model, we first must determine how, at any point of time, the economy allocates its resources to different sectors and different individuals; to answer, in other words, the traditional economic questions of what is to be produced (in particular, how much of consumption goods and how much of investment goods), how it is to be produced, and for whom it is to be produced. For the simpler growth models, the answer to these questions is identical to the answers provided by the simple static models: given the production and consumption functions, it depends only on factor endowments (capital and labor), not on the previous history of the economy. For the more complicated models, however, it may depend on the previous history of investment or it may depend on whether in the previous period sales exceeded or fell short of anticipations.

One of the questions upon which growth theorists have focused in particular is, What are the conditions under which momentary equilibrium is unique? For if it is not unique, then the level of investment — and hence the growth path of the economy — may be indeterminate. Such indeterminancy plays a central role in the two-sector models discussed in Part IV.

Once momentary equilibrium in the first period is determined, then we can ask, What will the momentary equilibrium be like during the next period, and then during the period after? It is in this that growth models differ from static analysis — while static models focus on an isolated period, growth models focus on the sequence of equilibria over time.

2. *Steady states.* The easiest kind of sequence of equilibria to analyze are those for which the equilibrium each period is essentially identical to that of the previous period except in scale. We call such a path, along which certain of the variables are constant and others are growing at an exponential rate, a steady state path.

In a sense, steady states are the generalization to economies with growing population of the equilibrium analysis of stationary states. In a steady state, output, population, capital stock, consumption, and investment are all growing exponentially, while the capital-output ratio, interest rate, and consumption-investment ratio are constant. Because the proportions in which the different commodities are produced are constant (the consumption-investment goods ratio), steady states are often referred to as *balanced growth paths.*

Just as it is possible for there to exist more than one momentary equilibrium, so is it possible that there will exist more than one steady state path. Hence we usually are interested in finding out, Is there a *unique* balanced growth path? We are also interested in *characterizing the balanced growth paths.* In the steady state, what are the relationships among the various variables of the economy? Finally, we are interested in comparing different growth paths with different values of the exogenous variables, for example, with different savings rates or different rates of reproduction. In analogy to comparative statics, this is called *comparative dynamics.* It should be emphasized that these comparisons are not of the sort where we ask what would happen to a given economy if we changed the savings rate, but rather, if we look at two islands in balanced growth but with different savings rate, how will they differ in output per man, consumption per man, etc.

3. *Equilibrium and disequilibrium paths.* Broadly speaking, there are two kinds of nonsteady state dynamic paths. An *equilibrium path* is a path along which, if individuals have given expectations with respect to, for instance, the level of output, relative prices, etc., in the future, and they act according to those expectations, those expectations are in fact fulfilled. A *disequilibrium path* is a path along which people behave according to certain expectations, but those expectations are not (in general) fulfilled.

The assumption of an equilibrium path is also sometimes referred to as the perfect foresight assumption. It has played a crucial role in the dynamics of growth models; this is partly because many theorists feel somewhat queasy about assuming that individuals form their expectations in a particular way, and continue to believe in those expectations, in spite of the fact that they are (almost) never fulfilled.

Given the specific dynamic processes of the economy, one may ask several questions.

1. Given the economy's initial conditions, is its history completely determined? This is sometimes referred to as the question of *causality*. Note that causality and uniqueness of momentary equilibrium are separate problems. An economy which has a uniquely determined momentary equilibrium at all points of time is necessarily causal, but the converse is not necessarily true. There may be isolated points in the history of the economy in which the momentary equilibrium is not well determined, but since these are of infinitesimal duration, what happens during these moments is of no consequence, and the history may be well determined.

2. In particular, we are interested in the behavior of the economy asymptotically (i.e., in the very long run). If there is a unique balanced growth path to which the economy converges, then we say that the system is *globally stable*. We can also ask, if the economy is initially near a balanced growth path, does it converge to it? This is the question of *local stability*, which is of particular importance when there are many balanced growth paths. In that case, we may also be interested in whether the economy (a) converges to some growth path, (b) oscillates (in a limit cycle) around some growth path, or (c) has an ever increasing or decreasing capital-labor ratio.

It is apparent from what we have just said that steady states and the convergence to them have played a central role in the growth literature. Some criticism of this work has been directed to it on that account. This is not the place for evaluation of this controversy; time will undoubtedly be the final arbiter. But the motivations for studying steady states and stability include the following: (1) Most economic analysis consists of studying polar cases. Steady states are to growth theory what perfect competition and monopoly are to the theory of the firm. One can learn a great deal about the growth processes from studying these admittedly special cases. (2) If the economy converges with reasonable speed to the steady state, then the steady state becomes directly empirically relevant. How quickly the economy converges is a moot question.[4] (3) Historically, the knife-edge property of the Harrod-Domar model (see pp. 11–12), which showed that a full

---

[4] Although R. Sato's paper "Fiscal Policy in the Neo-Classical Growth Model: An Analysis of Time Required for Equilibrating Adjustment," *REStud* (February 1963), pp. 16–23, indicates that the economy converges very slowly, more recent work by students of Arrow and Kuh have indicated, not surprisingly, that this depends critically on the particular parameterization of the production process and the assignment of particular values to the parameters.

employment path was unstable was thought by many economists to be unrealistic, and their models have attempted to show how altering the Harrod-Domar assumptions could lead to stable growth paths (see Part I).

I

The Basic Aggregative Growth Models

INTRODUCTION

The modern theory of growth can conveniently be begun with Harrod's 1939 contribution, "An Essay in Dynamic Theory," elaborated at greater length in his book *Towards a Dynamic Economics*. The building blocks upon which Harrod constructed his model, in somewhat simplified form, were (1) the Keynesian multiplier (a constant fraction, s, of income, Y, is saved), (2) the accelerator (at any point of time there is a given required increment capital per unit increment in output, C); and (3) constant rate of growth of population (called the natural rate of growth) which sets a ceiling on the long run growth of output. Unlike Samuelson,[1] he was interested not in the cyclical effects of combining a multiplier with an accelerator, but in the long-run dynamics. The first question to which he addressed himself was, what rate of growth did a fixed s and C imply? If g is the equilibrium percentage change in output, $\Delta Y/Y$,[2]

$$g = \frac{\Delta Y}{Y} = \frac{\Delta Y}{\Delta K}\frac{\Delta K}{Y} = \frac{s}{C}.$$

[1] P. A. Samuelson, "Introduction between the Multiplier Analysis and the Principle of Acceleration," *REStat* (May 1939), pp. 75–78.
[2] Since savings equals investment, $sY = \Delta K$, and by definition $C = (\Delta K/\Delta Y)$. C may depend, however, on the rate of interest, the phase of the business cycle, etc.

It is the unique path along which producers will find that demand equals supply in all periods. This g is called the *warranted rate of growth*. If the warranted rate of growth was greater than the natural rate of growth, the unemployment rate would grow larger and larger. There was no reason for the two to be equal. This is his first important observation.

The other question to which he turned was the dynamic stability of the economy. He argued that the equilibrium (warranted) growth path of the economy was unstable: if the economy happened to grow (or was expected to grow) slightly slower than its equilibrium growth rate, there would be an excess of supply over demand, which would lead to further reductions in the rate of growth; the converse would be true if it grew (or was expected to grow) slightly faster than the warranted rate.[3] This instability has often been referred to as Harrod's knife-edge.[4]

The resolution of the two difficulties cited by Harrod constitutes the basic motif of the last two articles of this section. Before turning to them, however, we shall briefly discuss the contributions of Domar and Tobin. Domar was concerned with the first of the two questions which Harrod posed: that of the determination of the unique balanced growth path in an economy with a fixed savings rate and a fixed capital output ratio. Tobin's model differs from the other articles in this volume in several crucial ways. First, it is both a business cycle model and a growth model. Second, money and portfolio balance play crucial roles. Third, wage inflexibility is an essential part of the model. Only recently has the literature returned to the questions raised by Tobin. But one property of his model which has recurred throughout the past decade is the possibility of substitution of capital for labor. This allows for alternative "warranted" rates of growth.

Indeed, this substitutability between capital and labor plays the central role in the Solow formulation. Solow retains the Harrod assumptions of a constant rate of reproduction and a constant saving rate, but shows (1) because of the substitutability of factors for each other in production, by increasing the labor-capital ratio, the output-capital ratio can be increased, and hence the warranted rate can be made equal to the natural rate of growth; and (2) the economy converges to this capital-output ratio asymptotically, and the equilibrium path is stable.

The reason that the Solow model is stable and the Harrod unstable is not because Solow allows for the possibility of substitution of capital

---

[3] There are some important asymmetries between the two situations: factor endowments put an upper bound on the rate of expansion.

[4] There are a large number of alternative formal models attempting to capture the spirit of Harrod's model. See, for instance, the articles by Rose [8] and Jorgensen [7] and the chapters in W. J. Baumol, *Economic Dynamics: An Introduction* (New York: Macmillan, 1959) and G. Ackley, *Macroeconomic Theory* (New York: Macmillan, 1961).

for labor, but because of different assumptions about dynamic adjustments and the determination of aggregate output. While Solow assumes that output is determined by the factor supplies — the government, through monetary and fiscal policies, maintains full employment — Harrod assumes that entrepreneurs themselves determine the level of aggregate output (constrained, of course, by the factor supplies). Thus, while changes in output in the Solow model depend simply on changes in factor supplies (in the absence of technological changes), changes in output in the Harrod model depend on particular assumptions about entrepreneurial behavior and expectation formation.

Swan derived similar results in the context of a particular production assumption; he assumed that the aggregate production was of the Cobb-Douglas form, i.e., output was proportional to $K^\alpha L^{1-\alpha}$, where K is the capital stock and L is labor employed.

Solow and Swan have provided the basic outlines of the neoclassical resolution of Harrod's twin problems of the discrepancy between the warranted and the natural rates of growth, and the instability of the capitalist system. In Part III we will see the alternative resolution offered to the first problem by the Cambridge economists: that the savings propensities of different groups differ, and that by changing the distribution of income among these groups, the average savings rate of the economy may be changed. A few economists have offered still a third approach — that changes in the rate of population growth or the rate of technical change may serve to eliminate any discrepancy between the warranted and the natural rates of growth.

AN ESSAY IN DYNAMIC THEORY
R. F. Harrod

1. THE following pages constitute a tentative and preliminary attempt to give the outline of a " dynamic " theory. Static theory consists of a classification of terms with a view to systematic thinking, together with the extraction of such knowledge about the adjustments due to a change of circumstances as is yielded by the " laws of supply and demand." It has for some time appeared to me that it ought to be possible to develop a similar classification and system of axioms to meet the situation in which certain forces are operating steadily to increase or decrease certain magnitudes in the system. The consequent " theory " would not profess to determine the course of events in detail, but should provide a framework of concepts relevant to the study of change analogous to that provided by static theory for the study of rest.

The axiomatic basis of the theory which I propose to develop consists of three propositions—namely, (1) that the level of a community's income is the most important determinant of its supply of saving; (2) that the rate of increase of its income is an important determinant of its demand for saving, and (3) that demand is equal to supply. It thus consists in a marriage of the " acceleration principle " and the " multiplier " theory, and is a development and extension of certain arguments advanced in my *Essay on the Trade Cycle*.[1]

2. Attempts to construct a dynamic theory have recently been proceeding upon another line—namely, by the study of time lags between certain adjustments. By the introduction of an appropriate lag the tendency of a system to oscillate can be established. In these studies there is some doubt as to the nature of the trend on which the oscillation is superimposed. Supposing

---

[1] Especially in Ch. 2, secs. 4–5. The " Acceleration Principle " was there designated the " Relation." There is an objection to the use of the term acceleration in this connection. The study of the condition in which demand and supply are flowing at an unaltered rate has long been known as Static Theory : this implies that the equilibrium of prices and quantities resulting therefrom is regarded as analogous to a state of rest. By analogy, therefore, a steady rate of increase of demand, which is our first matter for consideration in dynamic theory, and a major effect of which is expressed by the " Relation," should be regarded as a velocity. Acceleration would be a rate of change in this.

However, the use of the expression Acceleration Principle in the sense of my relation is rapidly accelerating in current literature, and I reluctantly bow to the *force majeure* of usage.

Reprinted by permission of the author and publishers from *The Economic Journal*, XLIX (March 1939), 14–33; errata (June 1939), 377. London: Macmillan and Co. Limited, and New York: St. Martin's Press.

damping measures could be introduced, to counteract the oscillation caused by the lag, would the system be stationary or advancing ? And at what rate ? Dynamic theory in my sense may throw some light upon this.

Moreover it is possible, and this the following argument seeks to establish, that the trend of growth may itself generate forces making for oscillation. This, if so, would not impair the importance of the study of the effect of lags. But it may be that the attempt to explain the trade cycle by *exclusive* reference to them is an unnecessary *tour de force*. The study of the operation of the forces maintaining a trend of increase and the study of lags should go together.

3. The significance of what follows should not be judged solely by reference to the validity or convenience of the particular equations set forth. It involves something wider : a method of thinking, a way of approach to certain problems. It is necessary to " think dynamically." The static system of equations is set forth not only for its own beauty, but also to enable the economist to train his mind upon special problems when they arise. For instance, an economist may pose to himself the question, What would be the effect on the system of an increase of exports or of a labour-saving invention ? By reference to the static equations, he then proceeds to work out the new equilibrium position supposing the new higher level of exports to be maintained in perpetuity or the labour-saving invention to be incorporated in the productive technique once for all.

But let the question be : Suppose the level of exports begins and continues to increase steadily, or suppose its rate of increase to increase, or suppose labour-saving inventions begin to be made in a steady or growing stream; then the static method will not suffice. The static theorist may hope to reduce this supposed steady increase to a succession of steps up, each having the same effect. But if the following argument is correct, the effect on the moving equilibrium of advance may often be in the opposite direction to the effect on the static equilibrium produced by each of the steps considered singly. A new method of approach— indeed, a mental revolution—is needed.

Once the mind is accustomed to thinking in terms of trends of increase, the old static formulation of problems seems stale, flat and unprofitable. This is not to deny to static theory its own appropriate sphere. It will become apparent which kind of problem belongs to each branch of study.

4. I now propose to proceed directly to the Fundamental

Equation, constituting the marriage of the acceleration principle and the multiplier theory. This probably gives too much importance to the acceleration principle, and the necessary modification is introduced subsequently.

Let G stand for the geometric rate of growth of income or output in the system, the increment being expressed as a fraction of its existing level. G will vary directly with the time interval chosen —e.g., 1 per cent. per annum $= \frac{1}{12}$ per cent. per month. Let G_w stand for the warranted rate of growth. The warranted rate of growth is taken to be that rate of growth which, if it occurs, will leave all parties satisfied that they have produced neither more nor less than the right amount. Or, to state the matter otherwise, it will put them into a frame of mind which will cause them to give such orders as will maintain the same rate of growth. I use the unprofessional term warranted instead of equilibrium, or moving equilibrium, because, although every point on the path of output described by G_w is an equilibrium point in the sense that producers, if they remain on it, will be satisfied, and be induced to keep the same rate of growth in being, the equilibrium is, for reasons to be explained, a highly unstable one.

If x_0 is output in period 0 and x_1 output in period 1, $G = \frac{x_1 - x_0}{x_0}$. Since we suppose the period to be short, x_0 or x_1 may alternatively stand in the denominator.

x_0 and x_1 are compounded of all individual outputs. I neglect questions of weighting. Even in a condition of growth, which generally speaking is steady, it is not to be supposed that all the component individuals are expanding at the same rate. Thus even in the most ideal circumstances conceivable, G, the actual rate of growth, would diverge from time to time from G_w, the warranted rate of growth, for random or seasonal causes.

Let s stand for the fraction of income which individuals and corporate bodies choose to save. s is total saving divided by x_0 or x_1. This may be expected to vary, with the size of income, the phase of the trade cycle, institutional changes, etc.

Let C stand for the value of the capital goods required for the production of a unit increment of output. The unit of value used to measure this magnitude is the value of the unit increment of output. Thus, if it is proposed in month 1 to raise the output of shoes, so that in month 1 and all subsequent months output is one pair higher than in month 0, and the machine required to do this—neglecting all other capital that may be required—has a value 48 times the value of a pair of shoes, C per month $= 48$.

The value of C is inversely proportional to the period chosen. C per annum $= 4$ in this case.[1] The value of C depends on the state of technology and the nature of the goods constituting the increment of output. It may be expected to vary as income grows and in different phases of the trade cycle; it may be somewhat dependent on the rate of interest.

Now, it is probably the case that in any period not the whole of the new capital is destined to look after the increment of output of consumers' goods. There may be long-range plans of capital development or a transformation of the method of producing the pre-existent level of output. These facts will be allowed for in due course. For the moment let it be assumed that all new capital goods are required for the sake of the increment of output of consumers' goods accruing.

Reserving proof for the next paragraph, we may now write the Fundamental Equation in its simplest form[2] :—

$$G_w = \frac{s}{C} \quad . \quad . \quad . \quad . \quad . \quad . \quad 1$$

It should be noticed that the warranted rate of growth of the system appears here as an unknown term, the value of which is determined by certain " fundamental conditions "—namely, the propensity to save and the state of technology, etc. Those who define dynamic as having a cross-reference to two points of time may not regard this equation as dynamic; that particular definition of dynamic has its own interest and field of reference. I prefer to define dynamic as referring to propositions in which a rate of growth appears as an unknown variable. This equation is clearly more fundamental than those expressing lags of adjustment.

5. The proof is as follows. Let C_p stand for the value of the increment of capital stock in the period divided by the increment of total output. C_p is the value of the increment of capital per

[1] If a month is the unit, the number of shoes added per period is 1, if a year 144. The value of G per annum is 12 times as great as that of G per month, since the numerator of G per annum is 144 times as great and the denominator 12 times as great as the numerator and denominator respectively of G per month. The number of machines added per month is $1 \equiv 48$ shoes $\equiv 48$ units of increment of output. C per month $= 48$. The number of machines added per year is $12 \equiv 48 \times 12$ shoes. Thus the value in shoes of the annual increment of capital required to produce an annual increment of 144 shoes is 48×12 units. Therefore C per annum $= \dfrac{48 \times 12}{144} = 4 = \dfrac{1}{12}$ of C per month.

[2] Since the value of G_w varies directly and that of C inversely with the unit period chosen, and the value of s is independent of the unit, the validity of the equation is independent of the unit period chosen.

unit increment of output actually produced. Circulating and fixed capital are lumped together.

$$G = \frac{s}{C_p} \quad . \quad . \quad . \quad . \quad . \quad 1(a)$$

is a truism, depending on the proposition that actual saving in a period (excess of the income in that period over consumption) is equal to the addition to the capital stock. Total saving is equal to sx_0. The addition to the capital stock is equal to $C_p(x_1 - x_0)$. This follows from the definition of C_p. And so,

$$sx_0 = C_p(x_1 - x_0)$$

$$\therefore \frac{s}{C_p} = \frac{x_1 - x_0}{x_0} = G$$

G is the rate of increase in total output which actually occurs; C_p is the increment in the stock of capital divided by the increment in total output which actually occurs. If the value of the increment of stock of capital per unit increment of output which actually occurs, C_p, is equal to C, the amount of capital per unit increment of output required by technological and other conditions (including the state of confidence, the rate of interest, etc.) then clearly the increase which actually occurs is equal to the increase which is justified by the circumstances. This means that, since C_p includes all goods (circulating and fixed capital), and is in fact production minus consumption per unit increment of output during the period, the sum of decisions to produce, to which G gives expression, are on balance justified—*i.e.*, if $C = C_p$, then $G = G_w$, and (from $1(a)$ above)

$$G_w = \frac{s}{C}$$

This is the fundamental equation, stated in paragraph 4, which determines the warranted rate of growth. To give numerical values to these symbols, which may be fairly representative of modern conditions : if 10 per cent. of income were saved and the capital coefficient per annum (C) were equal to 4, the warranted rate of growth would be $2\frac{1}{2}$ per cent. per annum.

It may be well to emphasise at this point that no distinction is drawn in this theory between capital goods and consumption goods. In measuring the increment of capital, the two are taken together ; the increment consists of total production less total consumption. Some trade-cycle theorists concern themselves with a possible lack of balance between these two categories ; no doubt that has its importance. The theory here considered is more fundamental or simple ; it is logically prior to the considerations regarding lack of balance, and grasp of it is required as a preliminary to the study of them.

6. To use terminology recently employed by distinguished authorities, C_p is an *ex post* quantity. I am not clear if C should be regarded as its corresponding *ex ante*. C is rather that addition to capital goods in any period, which producers regard as ideally suited to the output which they are undertaking in that period. For convenience the term *ex ante* when employed in this article will be used in this sense.

The truism stated above, 1(*a*), gives expression to Mr. Keynes' proposition that saving is necessarily equal to investment—that is, to *ex post* investment. Saving is not necessarily equal to *ex ante* investment in this sense, since unwanted accretions or depletions of stocks may occur, or equipment may be found to have been produced in excess of, or short of, requirements.

If *ex post* investment is less than *ex ante* investment, this means that there has been an undesired reduction of stocks or insufficient provision of productive equipment, and there will be a stimulus to further expansion of output; conversely if *ex post* investment exceeds *ex ante* investment. If *ex post* investment is less than *ex ante* investment, saving is less than *ex ante* investment. In his *Treatise on Money* Mr. Keynes formulated a proposition, which has been widely felt to be enlightening, though experience has led him subsequently to condemn the definitions employed as more likely to be misconstrued than helpful. He said that if investment exceeded saving, the system would be stimulated to expand, and conversely. If for the definitions on which that proposition was based, we *substitute* the definition of *ex ante* investment given above, it is true that if *ex ante* investment exceeds saving, the system will be stimulated, and conversely. This truth may account for the feeling of satisfaction which Mr. Keynes' proposition originally evoked and the reluctance to abandon it at his behest. In many connections we are more interested in *ex ante* than in *ex post* investment, the latter including as it does unwanted accretions of stocks. Mr. Keynes' proposition of the *Treatise* may still be a useful aid to thinking, if we substitute for " Investment " in it *ex ante* investment as defined above.

7. Two minor points may be considered before we proceed with the main argument.

(i) It may be felt that there is something unreal in this analysis, since the increase in capital which producers will regard as right in period 1 is in the real world related not to the increase of total output in period 1, but to prospective increases in subsequent periods. This objection may be divided into two parts. (a) In view of the fact that much of the outlay of capital is connected with long-range planning, it may be held that the fundamental equation gives too much weight to the short-period effect of the acceleration principle. This objection is freely admitted and allowed for in the subsequent modification of the equation. (b) It may further be objected that even in the sphere in which the acceleration principle holds there must be some lag between the increased provision of equipment (and stocks?) and the increased flow of output which they are designed to support. There may be some force in this. But the point is deliberately neglected in this part of the argument, along with all questions of lags. The study of these lags is of undoubted importance, but a division of labour in analysis is indispensable, and in this case the neglect is necessary in order to get the clearest possible view of the forces determining the trend and its influence as such. Moreover, the lag referred to in this sub-heading (b) may properly be regarded as unimportant, since, in the event of a *steady* advance (G) being maintained, the difference between $x_1 - x_0$ and $x_2 - x_1$ will be of the second order of small quantities. In other words, it matters not whether we regard the increment of capital as required to support the increment of total output in the same period or in the one immediately succeeding it.

8. (ii) In the demonstration given above (paras. 6 and 7) reference was made to the distinction between the *ex post* and the *ex ante* increase of capital goods. No reference was made to the distinction between *ex post* and *ex ante* saving.[1] Suppose that G is not equal to G_w might not the discrepancy show itself on the other side of the equation, not in any divergence of C_p from C, but in *ex post* saving not being equal to *ex ante* saving?

I have no very clear view as to possible causes likely to operate in a systematic way to distort *ex post* from *ex ante* saving, or of the probable importance of such distortions. It is said, for instance, that in a time of rising prices, fixed-income classes will not adapt their modes of life simultaneously, and so may save less than they would be disposed to do had they clearly foreseen the impending rise. *Per contra* variable-income classes may not foresee their own rise of income, and so spend less than they would have been disposed to do.

---

[1] Be it noted that *ex ante* is here used of saving in a sense analogous to that defined in the expression *ex ante* investment; it is the saving which savers would choose to make in any period, were they able to adapt expenditure simultaneously with the changing circumstances of the period.

This question of the possible divergence of *ex post* from *ex ante* saving must be kept entirely distinct from that of the variations in s in the different phases of the trade cycle, which not only are admitted, but also play a part in the argument. s may vary because the level of income or of profit is abnormally swollen or depressed.

The neglect of these possible divergences has no importance for the argument, since they will have the same effect on growth as the divergences of C_p from C for which they may serve as substitute. Thus if G exceeds G_w, the right-hand side of the equation must exceed s/C. If the whole of this effect is found in C_p it will be *less* than C, and this is a stimulus to expansion.[1] Firms finding themselves short of stock or equipment will increase their orders. If, on the other hand, the whole of this effect is found in a divergence of *ex post* s from *ex ante* s, *ex post* s will be *greater* than *ex ante* s. Savers will find that they have saved more than they would have done had they foreseen their level of income or the level of prices correctly. Consequently they will be stimulated to expand purchases, and orders for goods will consequently be increased. Throughout the following pages the reader, whenever he finds a reference to the excess or deficiency of C_p compared with C, may substitute, if he prefers it, a supposed deficiency or excess of *ex post* saving compared with *ex ante* saving, without affecting the course of the argument.

9. We now come to a point of major importance, constituting the difference between the dynamic equilibrium (warranted rate of growth) and the static equilibrium. Normally the latter is stable and the former unstable. This gives a *prima facie* reason for regarding the dynamic analysis as a necessary propædeutic to trade-cycle study.

Some recent writers have been disposed to urge that the static equilibrium is not so stable as is sometimes claimed. Suppose that an increased output of a commodity, constituting a departure from equilibrium, is tried, so that its supply stands at a point at which the supply curve is above the demand curve. It is argued that, instead of a relapse at once occurring, reducing supply to the point of intersection of the supply and demand curves— this showing the stability of the old equilibrium—the upshot depends on how all parties now proceed. It is suggested that there may be a tendency to waltz round the point of intersection or, more broadly, that in the backward adjustment there may be

---

[1] The reader who is surprised that an excess of G over G_w is stimulating will find the explanation in the next paragraph.

wide repercussions disturbing the whole system. It is even held that the whole question of the stability of the static equilibrium, in the sense of the tendency of a relapse to it when a random departure occurs, is itself a dynamic problem, which cannot be looked after by the system of static equations. I have the impression that this type of criticism exaggerates the importance of this problem, and constitutes to some extent a failure to see the wood for the trees, and that on its own ground the theory of static equlibrium is well able to hold its own.

But when we look at the dynamic equilibrium, new vistas are opened. The line of output traced by the warranted rate of growth is a moving equilibrium, in the sense that it represents the one level of output at which producers will feel in the upshot that they have done the right thing, and which will induce them to continue in the same line of advance. Stock in hand and equipment available will be exactly at the level which they would wish to have them. Of course what applies to the system in general may not apply to each individual separately. But if one feels he has over-produced or over-ordered, this will be counterbalanced by an opposite experience of an equal importance in some other part of the field.

But now suppose that there is a departure from the warranted rate of growth. Suppose an excessive output, so that G exceeds G_w. The consequence will be that C_p, the actual increase of capital goods per unit increment of output, falls below C, that which is desired. There will be, in fact, an undue depletion of stock or shortage of equipment, and the system will be stimulated to further expansion. G, instead of returning to G_w, will move farther from it in an upward direction, and the farther it diverges, the greater the stimulus to expansion will be. Similarly, if G falls below G_w, there will be a redundance of capital goods, and a depressing influence will be exerted; this will cause a further divergence and a still stronger depressing influence; and so on. Thus in the dynamic field we have a condition opposite to that which holds in the static field. A departure from equilibrium, instead of being self-righting, will be self-aggravating. G_w represents a moving equilibrium, but a highly unstable one. Of interest this for trade-cycle analysis !

Suppose an increase in the propensity to save, which means that the values of s are increased for all levels of income. This necessarily involves, *ceteris paribus*, a higher rate of warranted growth. But if the actual growth was previously equal to the warranted growth, the immediate effect is to raise the warranted rate above the actual rate. This state of affairs sets up a depressing influence which will drag the actual rate progressively farther below the warranted rate. In this as in other cases, the movement of a dynamic determinant has an opposite effect on the warranted path of growth to that which it has on its actual path. How different from the order of events in static theory !

The reader may have some difficulty in the expression " stimulus to expansion." What is the significance of this, in view of the fact that some growth is assumed as a basic condition ? It must be remembered that the value of G depends on aggregates x_0 and x_1. These are sums of numerous quantities for which individuals are responsible. It must be supposed that at all times some individuals are jogging on at a steady level, others are risking an increase of orders or output, others are willy-nilly curtailing. G is the resultant of their separate enterprises. Some are in any event likely to be disappointed. If G is equal to G_w, it is to be supposed that the general level of enterprise undertaken in period 0, including in sum a certain increase over that in the preceding period, is found to be satisfactory. Those running short of stock balance those with surpluses. This justifies further action on similar lines, though the individuals increasing orders for stock in trade or planning new equipment in period 1 may not be identical in person with those doing so in period 0. If an expansive force is in operation, more individuals, or individuals having greater weight, will be induced by their trading position to venture increases than did so in the preceding period. Conversely if a depressing force is in operation.

The dynamic theory so far stated may be summed up in two propositions. (i) A unique warranted line of growth is determined jointly by the propensity to save and the quantity of capital required by technological and other considerations per unit increment of total output. Only if producers keep to this line will they find that on balance their production in each period has been neither excessive nor deficient. (ii) On either side of this line is a " field " in which centrifugal forces operate, the magnitude of which varies directly as the distance of any point in it from the warranted line. Departure from the warranted line sets up an inducement to depart farther from it. The moving equilibrium of advance is thus a highly unstable one.

The essential point here may be further explained by reference to the expressions over-production and under-production. The distinction between particular over-production and general over-production is well known. In the event of particular over-production, there will normally be a tendency to reduce production of the particular line, and so equilibrium will be restored. We may define general over-production as a condition in which a majority of producers, or producers representing in sum the major part of production, find they have produced or ordered too much, in the sense that they or the distributors of their goods find themselves in possession of an unwanted volume of stocks or equipment. By reference to the fundamental equation it appears that this state of things can only occur when the actual growth has been *below* the warranted growth—*i.e.*, a condition of general over-production is the consequence of producers in sum producing too little. The only way in which this state of affairs could have been avoided would have been by producers in sum producing more than they did. Over-production is the consequence of production below the warranted level. Conversely, if producers find that they are continually running short of stocks and equipment, this means that they are producing above the warranted level.

But the condition of over-production, or, as we should perhaps call it, apparent over-production, will lead to a curtailment of production or orders, or a reduction in the rate of increase on balance, and consequently, so long as the fundamental conditions governing the warranted rate are unchanged, to a larger gap between actual and warranted growth, and so to an intensification of the evils which the contraction was intended to cure.

It must be noted that a rate of growth lying on either side of the warranted rate is regarded here as unwarranted. If the actual rate exceeds the warranted rate, producers on balance will not feel that they have produced or ordered too much; on the contrary, they will be running short of stocks and/or equipment. Thus they will not feel that they have produced the warranted amount plus something; on the contrary, they will feel that everything which they have produced has been warranted, and that they might warrantably have produced something more. None the less, we define their production as unwarrantably large, meaning by that that they have produced in excess of the unique amount which would leave them on balance satisfied with what they had done and prepared to go forward in the next period on similar lines.

10. The foregoing demonstration of the inherent instability of the moving equilibrium, or warranted line of advance, depends on the assumption that the values of s and C are independent of the value of G. This is formally correct. The analysis relates to a single point of time. s is regarded as likely to vary with a

change in the size of income, but a change in the rate of growth at a given point of time has no effect on its size. C may also be expected to vary with the size of income, $e.g.$, owing to the occurrence of surplus capital capacity from time to time, but the same argument for regarding it as independent of the rate of growth at a particular point of time applies.

It may be objected, however, that this method of analysis is too strict to be realistic, since the discovery that output is excessive or deficient, and the consequent emergence of a depressing or stimulating force, takes some time, and in the interval required for a reaction to be produced an appreciable change in s or C may have occurred.

Consider this with reference to an experimental increase in G above a warranted level. According to the theory of instability, any such experiment will be apparently over-justified, stocks or equipment running short in consequence of it. Is it possible that if resulting changes in the values of s or C are taken into account, this doctrine will have to be modified?

In order to justify modifying the doctrine, it would be necessary to show that, in consequence of the experimental increase, s was substantially increased or C reduced. It is unlikely that C would be reduced. The capital coefficient may often stand below the level appropriate to the technological conditions of the age, owing to the existence of surplus equipment. If this were so, the higher rate of output consequent upon the experimental increase would tend to raise C. A smaller proportion of firms would come to find their capacity redundant, and a larger proportion would have to support a greater turnover by ordering extra equipment.

With saving the case is different. An expansion of activity might increase the proportion of income saved. What increase of saving is required for a modification of the instability theory?

This can be shown simply. Let x_e be an experimental increase of output above the warranted level. Let s_m stand for the fraction of the consequential income saved. The instability principle requires that

$$Cx_e > s_m x_e$$

$i.e.$, that

$$s_m < C$$

$$< \frac{s}{G_w}$$

This condition needs interpretation. Since C and G_w do not both appear in the equation, it is necessary to define the period by which G_w is measured. This should be done by reference to the reaction time mentioned above—namely, the time required for an undue accretion or depletion of capital goods to exert its influence upon the flow of orders. If this reaction time is six months, then G_w must be measured as growth per six months.

Thus the instability condition requires that the fraction of marginal income saved shall not be more than the fraction of total income saved multiplied by the total income and divided by the increment of warranted income per six months. Thus if the warranted growth is $2\frac{1}{2}$ per cent. per annum, or $1\frac{1}{4}$ per cent. per six months, the instability principle requires that the fraction of marginal income saved must be less than eighty times the fraction of average income saved. Supposing that the high figure of 50 per cent. is taken as the fraction of marginal income saved, the fraction of total income saved must be greater than five-eighths of 1 per cent. Thus for any normal warranted rate of growth and level of saving, the instability principle seems quite secure.

The force of this argument, however, is somewhat weakened when long-range capital outlay is taken into account. It will then appear that the attainment of a neutral or stable equilibrium of advance may not be altogether improbable in certain phases of the cycle.

11. It should be noticed that the instability theory makes the empirical verification of the acceleration principle more arduous. For it leads to the expectation that in the upward phase of the cycle the actual rate will tend to run above the warranted rate, and the accretion of capital to be less than that required by the acceleration principle; and conversely in the downward phase. Thus a finding that the volume of investment fluctuates less than is required by direct computation from the acceleration principle is consistent with the theory here set forth, in which, none the less, the acceleration principle is presented as a leading dynamic determinant.

12. It is now expedient to introduce further terms into our equation to reduce the influence of the acceleration principle. Some outlays of capital have no direct relation to the current increase of output. They may be related to a prospective long-period increase of activity, and be but slightly influenced, if at all, by the current increase of trade. Or they may be induced by new inventions calculated to cheapen production or change consumers' modes of spending their income, so that they are not related to increments of output, but are designed to revolutionise the methods for producing some portion of already existing output or to substitute one line of goods for another in the consumers' budget. There are doubtless numerous factors, including the

state of confidence and the rate of interest affecting the volume of such outlay. It may suffice for the purpose in hand to divide it into two parts.

One part, K, is conceived to be quite independent both of the current level of income and its current rate of growth. The other, expressed as a fraction of income, k, is conceived to vary with the current level of income, as distinct from its rate of growth. This seems a reasonable assumption. Long-period anticipations are bound to be influenced by the present state of prosperity or adversity : even public authorities are apt to reduce the volume of public works in a slump. Companies may relate their expenditure on long-range plans to the current state of their profit account.

Having regard to the principle that the total increase of capital is equal to the total saving in the period, our fundamental equation may be modified as follows :—

$$G_w = \frac{s - k - \dfrac{K}{x}}{C} \qquad . \qquad . \qquad . \qquad . \ (2)^1$$

$$\therefore \frac{s - k - \dfrac{K}{x_0}}{C_p} = \frac{x_1 - x_0}{x_0} = G$$

$$\therefore G_w = \frac{s - k - \dfrac{K}{x_0}}{C}$$

It must be noticed that C and C_p now stand not for the total increase of capital (desired and actual, respectively) per unit increment of output, but only for the net increase of capital after the capital represented by k and K has been subtracted.

It may be noticed that the larger the volume of outlay which will be sustained independently of the current rate of growth, the *smaller* is the warranted rate of growth. A larger part of savings being absorbed in such outlay, there will be a smaller part to be looked after by the acceleration principle.

13. In the following pages the expression **long-range capital** outlay will be used for the magnitude denoted by $xk + K$. This must not be supposed to cover all investment in durable fixed equipment; for much of that is related to, and directly governed by, the current output of consumption goods. It refers only to that part of the output of fixed equipment the production of which is not governed by the current demand for consumption goods.

If long-range capital outlay were large by comparison with that required to support the current increase in turnover of consumable

---

[1] $sx_0 = C_p(x_1 - x_0) + kx_0 + K$

goods, the peculiar conditions defined in § 10 for the invalidity of the instability principle might in certain circumstances be realised. For the fraction of total income saved *and* devoted to the finance of the increase of current output might be very small compared with the fraction of marginal income saved. It is not, however, to be supposed that it would normally be small enough to invalidate the instability principle. For, with normal growth at $2\frac{1}{2}$ per cent., saving at 10 per cent., marginal saving at 50 per cent. and the reaction time 6 months, this would mean that fifteen-sixteenths of capital would normally be devoted to long-range capital outlay and only one-sixteenth would be directly associated with the current increase of output (cf. § 10). But such a situation might well arise in certain phases of the trade cycle, especially when capital capacity was redundant and saving low. In that case a stable equilibrium of advance might for a time be achieved.

14. To complete the picture, foreign trade must be taken into account. It is reasonable to measure exports, including invisible exports and the earnings of foreign investments, in absolute terms. The value of income which may be earned in this way may be conceived to be independent both of the level of activity at home and of its growth (though in so far as the trade cycle is world-wide, its value will be *de facto* related to income). Let E stand for this value. Imports, on the other hand, are better taken as a fraction, i, of the current level of income. We then have, by parity of reasoning,

$$G_w = \frac{s + i - k - \dfrac{K}{x} - \dfrac{E}{x}}{C} \qquad . \qquad . \qquad . \quad (3)\,[1]$$

i need not be equal to $\dfrac{E}{x}$; the difference represents an international movement of capital. The influence of the various magnitudes on the warranted rate of growth is shown by the equation.

15. The fundamental dynamic equation has been used to demonstrate the inherent tendency of the system to instability. Space forbids an application of this method of analysis to the successive phases of the trade cycle. In the course of it the values expressed by the symbols on the right-hand side of the equation undergo considerable change. As actual growth departs

---

[1] The principle now is that saving plus income expended on imports must be equal to the increase of capital in the country plus income derived from abroad. This is deducible from the fact that income derived from the sale of home made goods to consumers at home is equal to the income devoted to their purchase. Thus :—

$$sx_0 + ix_0 = C_p(x_1 - x_0) + kx_0 + K + E$$

upwards or downwards from the warranted level, the warranted rate itself moves,[1] and may chase the actual rate in either direction. The maximum rates of advance or recession may be expected to occur at the moment when the chase is successful.

For the convenience of the reader who may be tempted to experiment with this tool, it must be observed that C is always positive. Being the total quantity of capital required in connection with increments (or decrements) of current output divided by the increment (or decrement) of that output, when the latter is negative the former is negative also, and the coefficient remains positive. C_p, on the other hand, may be negative; it is not negative whenever there is a depletion of capital goods, but only when the amount of capital goods outstanding is moving in the opposite direction to the level of total output.

The formula is not well adapted to dealing with the case of zero growth. But that matter is quite simple. Zero growth is only warranted when the amount of saving is equal to the amount required for long-range capital outlay. If the amount of saving exceeds this, there will be a tendency for output to decline, and conversely.

It may be well to make one point with regard to a downward departure from the warranted position of sufficient importance to outlive one reaction time and bring the system within the field where the centrifugal forces have substantial strength. The downward lapse will then continue until the warranted rate, determined by the values on the right-hand side of the equation, itself moves down. This will happen when the numerator falls or the denominator rises. But in a phase of declining rate of growth the capital coefficient is not in general likely to rise. And so long as there is still some positive growth, albeit at a declining rate, the fraction of income saved is not likely to fall. Therefore, once the rate of growth is driven downwards from the warranted level, the warranted level is not itself likely to fall, or the downward movement therefore to be checked until the rate of growth becomes negative and the level of income recedes. Now, if the actual rate is standing below the warranted rate, the centrifugal force will continue to operate, driving the actual rate progressively downwards, unless or until the warranted rate itself falls to a level as low as the actual rate. But, since the actual rate is now negative, this cannot happen until the numerator of the right-

---

[1] This idea is analogous to that propounded by Mr. D. H. Robertson that the " natural " rate of interest may be expected to vary in the different phases of the trade cycle. Cf. ECONOMIC JOURNAL, December 1934.

hand side of the equation becomes negative—that is, until saving falls below the level required for long-range capital outlay.

16. Alongside the concept of warranted rate of growth we may introduce another, to be called the natural rate of growth. This is the maximum rate of growth allowed by the increase of population, accumulation of capital, technological improvement and the work/ leisure preference schedule, supposing that there is always full employment in some sense.

There is no inherent tendency for these two rates to coincide. Indeed, there is no unique warranted rate; the value of warranted rate depends upon the phase of the trade cycle and the level of activity.

Consideration may be given to that warranted rate which would obtain in conditions of full employment; this may be regarded as the warranted rate " proper " to the economy. *Prima facie* it might be supposed healthier to have the " proper " warranted rate above than below the natural rate. But this is very doubtful.

The system cannot advance more quickly than the natural rate allows. If the proper warranted rate is above this, there will be a chronic tendency to depression; the depressions drag down the warranted rate below its proper level, and so keep its average value over a term of years down to the natural rate. But this reduction of the warranted rate is only achieved by having chronic unemployment.

The warranted rate is dragged down by depression; it may be twisted upwards by an inflation of prices and profit. If the proper rate is below the natural rate, the average value of the warranted rate may be sustained above its proper level over a term of years by a succession of profit booms.

Thus each state of affairs has its appropriate evils. There is much to be said for the view that it is better that the proper warranted rate should be lower rather than higher than the natural rate.

17. In order fully to grasp the dynamic principle, it is necessary to bear in mind that changes in fundamental conditions have opposite effects on the actual rate and the warranted rate. An increased amount of long-range capital outlay, an increase in the capital coefficient, an increase in the propensity to consume, and an increase in the active balance on international account, or a decline in the passive balance, are all properly thought to have a stimulating effect on the system. But they all tend, as may

readily be seen from the equation, to reduce the warranted rate. This paradox may be readily explained.

Suppose that one of these stimulants begins to operate when the actual rate is equal to the warranted rate. By depressing the warranted rate, it drags that down below the actual rate, and so automatically brings the actual rate into the field of centrifugal forces, driving it away from the warranted rate—that is, in this case, upwards. Thus the stimulant causes the system to expand.

It must not be inferred that these stimulants are only of temporary benefit. For it may be healthy for an economy to have its proper warranted rate reduced. This is likely to be so when its proper warranted rate is tending to be above the natural rate.[1] The long-run value of the stimulant can only be assessed if it is known whether, in its absence, the proper warranted rate is running above or below the natural rate.

It is often felt that a high propensity to save should warrant a great increase in the output of wealth, and this induces an extreme aversion to accept Mr. Keynes' view that excessive saving in the modern age is hostile to prosperity. The feeling is justified to the extent that higher propensity to save does, in fact, *warrant* a higher rate of growth. Trouble arises if the rate of growth which it warrants is greater than that which the increase of population and the increase of technical capacity render permanently possible. And the fundamental paradox is that the more ambitious the rate *warranted* is, the greater the probability that the actual output will from time to time, and even persistently fall below that which the productive capacity of the population would allow.

18. Policy in this field is usually appraised by reference to its power to combat tendencies to oscillation. Our demonstration of the inherent instability of the dynamic equilibrium confirms the importance of this. But there are two points to be noticed in this connection. 1. The nature of the measures suitable for combating the tendency to oscillate may depend on whether the natural rate is above or below the proper warranted rate. 2. In addition to dealing with the tendency to oscillation when it occurs, it may be desirable to have a long-range policy designed to

[1] This may be the most fundamental rational explanation of the common view that it is dangerous for an old country to be a large importer of capital. For this involves a high warranted rate of growth, and it is dangerous to have a high warranted rate when the natural rate is low. *Per contra* for a young country, whose natural rate is high, it is considered healthy and proper to have a large import of capital.

influence the relation between the proper warranted rate of growth and the natural rate.

If, in the absence of interference, the proper warranted rate is substantially above the natural rate, the difficulties may be too great to be dealt with by a mere anti-cycle policy. In the first place, there is the probability of a slump occurring before full employment is reached, since during the revival the warranted rate may be dangerously near the actual rate, and liable at any time to overpass it, thus generating depression. Secondly, there is an acute problem if the actual rate reaches the ceiling of full employment and is depressed to the natural rate, and therefore below the warranted rate. An attempt may then be made to drag down the warranted rate below its normal level by increasing public works (K). But the difficulty of the proper warranted rate being above the natural rate will be chronic, and this means that only by keeping in being a large and growing volume of public works can the slump be prevented. In fine, the anti-cycle policy has to be converted into a permanent policy for keeping down the proper warranted rate.

19. The ideal policy would be to manipulate the proper warranted rate so that it should be equal to the natural rate. If this could be achieved—but in fact only a rough approximation would be possible—an anti-cycle policy would none the less be an indispensable supplement. For the warranted rate is bound to be disturbed by the varying incidence of inventions and fluctuations in the foreign account. An anti-cycle policy would be necessary to combat the run-away forces which come into being as soon as a substantial change occurs in the warranted rate.

20. A low rate of interest makes for a low warranted rate of increase, by encouraging high values of K and C and, possibly also, by having a depressing influence on s. Since the effects of changes in the rate of interest are probably slow-working, it may be wise to use the rate of interest as a long-range weapon for reducing the warranted rate of growth, and to reserve *suitable* public works for use against the cycle. It is not suggested, however, that a low rate of interest has sufficient power of its own to keep down the warranted rate without the assistance of a programme of public works to be kept permanently in operation.

If permanent public works activity and a low long-term rate availed to bring the proper warranted rate into line with the natural rate, variations in the short-term rate of interest might come into their own again as an ancillary method of dealing with oscillations.

21. This essay has only touched in the most tentative way on a small fraction of the problems, theoretical and practical, of which the enunciation of a dynamic theory suggests the formulation. In the last paragraph it was implicitly hinted that our present situation is one of a relatively high proper warranted rate. The evidence for this comes from inside and outside the dynamic theory itself. According to the dynamic theory, the tendency of a system to relapse into depression before full employment is reached in the boom suggests that its proper warranted rate exceeds its natural rate. Outside evidence includes the known decline in the growth of population, which involves a decline in the natural rate. More controversial points are the tendency of a more wealthy population to save a larger fraction of its income (high value of s involves high warranted rate), and the tendency of modern progress to depress rather than elevate the value of C (low value of C involves high warranted rate).

The main object of this article, however, is to present a tool of analysis, not to diagnose present conditions.

R. F. HARROD

Christ Church, Oxford.

ERRATA

We have to apologise for four misprints in the ECONOMIC JOURNAL of March, 1939. In a note under "Current Topics" (page 178) concerned with the varied spellings of "autarky," that word was made to derive from the root ἀαρκεῖν. We need hardly point out that that should have read ἀρκεῖν. In Mr. Harrod's review of *Political Economy* by Nassau Senior, page 148, line 23, "ability" should read "utility." The other two both appear in Mr. Harrod's article, *An Essay in Dynamic Theory*. On page 18, line 3, equation 1(a), large S should read small s. On page 27, lines 18 and 19, namely

$$\therefore \frac{s - k - \dfrac{K}{x_0}}{C_p} = \frac{x_1 - x_0}{x_0} = G$$

$$\therefore G_w = \frac{s - k - \dfrac{K}{x_0}}{C}$$

belong to the footnote at the bottom of the page and should follow the equation therein set out.

CAPITAL EXPANSION, RATE OF GROWTH, AND EMPLOYMENT[1]

By Evsey D. Domar

I. INTRODUCTION

This paper deals with a problem that is both old and new—the relation between capital accumulation and employment. In economic literature it has been discussed a number of times, the most notable contribution belonging to Marx. More recently, it was brought forth by Keynes and his followers.

A thorough analysis of economic aspects of capital accumulation is a tremendous job. The only way in which the problem can be examined at all in a short paper like this is by isolating it from the general economic structure and introducing a number of simplifying assumptions. Some of them are not entirely necessary and, as the argument progresses, the reader will see how they can be modified or removed.

The following assumptions and definitions should be noted at the outset: (a) there is a constant general price level; (b) no lags are present; (c) savings and investment refer to the income of the same period; (d) both are net, i.e., over and above depreciation; (e) depreciation is measured not in respect to historical costs, but to the cost of replacement of the depreciated asset by another one *of the same productive capacity*;[2] (f) productive capacity of an asset or of the whole economy is a measurable concept.

The last assumption, on which (e) also depends, is not entirely safe. Whether a certain piece of capital equipment or the whole economy is considered, their productive capacities depend not only on physical and technical factors, but on the whole interplay of economic and institutional forces, such as distribution of income, consumers' preferences,

---

[1] This is a summary of a paper presented before a joint session of the Econometric Society and the American Statistical Association in Cleveland on January 24, 1946. It contains the logical essence of the argument with relatively little economic detail. I hope to develop the latter in a separate paper to be published in one of the other economic journals.

Many thanks for help and criticism go to my fellow members of the "Little Seminar": Paul Baran, Svend Laursen, Lloyd A. Metzler, Richard A. Musgrave, Mary S. Painter, Melvin W. Reder, Tibor de Scitovszky, Alfred Sherrard, Mary Wise Smelker, Merlin Smelker, and most of all to James S. Duesenberry.

[2] If the original machine worth $1,000 and producing 100 units is replaced by another one worth also $1,000, but producing 120 units, only $833.33 will be regarded as replacement, and the remaining $166.67 as new investment. A similar correction is made when the new machine costs more or less than the original one. The treatment of depreciation, particularly when accompanied by sharp technological and price changes, presents an extremely difficult problem. It is quite possible that our approach, while convenient for present purposes, may give rise to serious difficulties in the future.

Reprinted from *Econometrica*, 14 (April 1946), 137–147. Copyright 1946 by the Economic Society. By permission of the author and publishers.

wage rates, relative prices, structure of industry, and so on, many of which are in turn affected by the behavior of the variables analyzed here. We shall nevertheless assume all these conditions as given and shall mean by the productive capacity of an economy (or an asset) its total output when all productive factors are fully employed under these conditions.[3]

The economy will be said to be in equilibrium when its productive capacity P equals its national income Y. Our first task is to discover the conditions under which this equilibrium can be maintained, or more precisely, the rate of growth at which the economy must expand in order to remain in a continuous state of full employment.

II. THE PROBLEM OF GROWTH

The idea that the preservation of full employment in a capitalist economy requires a growing income goes back (in one form or another) at least to Marx. It has been fully recognized in numerous studies (recently made in Washington and elsewhere) of the magnitude of gross national product needed to maintain full employment. But though the various authors come to different numerical results, they all approach their problem from the point of view of the size of the labor force. The labor force (man-hours worked) and its productivity are supposed to increase according to one formula or another, and if full employment is to be maintained, national income must grow at the combined rate. For practical relatively short-run purposes this is a good method, but its analytical merits are not high, because it presents a theoretically incomplete system: since an increase in labor force or in its productivity only raises productive capacity and does not by itself generate income (similar to that produced by investment), the demand side of the equation is missing. Nor is the difficulty disposed of by Mr. Kalecki's method according to which capital should increase proportionally to the increase in labor force and its productivity.[4] As Mrs. Robinson well remarked, "The rate of increase in productivity of labor is not something given by Nature."[5] Labor productivity is not a function of technological progress in the abstract, but technological progress embodied in capital goods, and the amount of capital goods in

[3] It should undoubtedly be possible to work out a more precise definition of productive capacity, but I prefer to leave the matter open, because a more precise definition is not entirely necessary in this paper and can be worked out as and when needed.

[4] See his essay, "Three Ways to Full Employment" in *The Economics of Full Employment*, Oxford, 1944, p. 47, and also his "Full Employment by Stimulating Private Investment?" in *Oxford Economic Papers*, March, 1945, pp. 83–92.

[5] See her review of *The Economics of Full Employment*, *Economic Journal*, Vol. 55, April, 1945, p. 79.

general. Even without technological progress, capital accumulation increases labor productivity, at least to a certain point, both because more capital is used per workman in each industry and because there is a shift of labor to industries that use more capital and can afford to pay a higher wage. So if labor productivity is affected by capital accumulation, the formula that the latter should proceed at the same rate as the former (and as the increase in labor force) is not as helpful as it appears.

The standard Keynesian system does not provide us with any tools for deriving the equilibrium rate of growth. The problem of growth is entirely absent from it because of the explicit assumption that employment is a function of national income. This assumption can be justified only over short periods of time; it will result in serious errors over a period of a few years. Clearly, a full-employment level of income of five years ago would create considerable unemployment today. *We shall assume instead that employment is a function of the ratio of national income to productive capacity.* While this approach seems to me to be superior to that of Keynes, it should be looked upon as a second approximation rather than a final solution: it does not allow us to separate unused capacity into idle machines and idle men; depending upon various circumstances, the same ratio of income to capacity may yield different fractions of labor force employed.

Because investment in the Keynesian system is merely an instrument for generating income, the system does not take into account the extremely essential, elementary, and well-known fact that investment also increases productive capacity.[6] This *dual* character of the investment process makes the approach to the equilibrium rate of growth from the investment (capital) point of view more promising: if investment both increases productive capacity and generates income, it provides us with *both* sides of the equation the solution of which may yield the required rate of growth.

Let investment proceed at the rate I per year, and let the ratio of the potential net value added (after depreciation), i.e., of the productive capacity of the new projects to capital invested in them, i.e., to I, be indicated by s.[7] The net annual potential output of these projects will then be equal to Is. But the productive capacity of the whole econ-

---

[6] Whether every dollar invested increases productive capacity is essentially a matter of definition. It can safely be said that investment taken as a whole certainly does. To make this statement hold in regard to residential housing, imputed rent should be included in the national income. See also note 19.

[7] The use of the word "project" does not imply that investment is done by the government, or that it is always made in new undertakings. I am using "project" (in the absence of a better term) because investment can mean the act of investing and the result of the act.

omy may increase by a smaller amount, because the operation of these new projects may involve a transfer of labor (and other factors) from other plants, whose productive capacity is therefore reduced.[8] We shall define σ, the *potential social average investment productivity* as

$$(1) \qquad \sigma = \frac{\dfrac{dP}{dt}}{I}.$$

The following characteristics of σ should be noted:

1. Its use does not imply that other factors of production and technology remain constant. On the contrary, its magnitude depends to a very great extent on technological progress. It would be more correct to say that σ refers to an increase in capacity which accompanies rather than one which is caused by investment.

2. σ refers to the increase in *potential* capacity. Whether or not this potential increase results in a larger income depends on the behavior of money expenditures.

3. σ is concerned with the increase in productive capacity of the whole society, and not with the rate of return derived or expected from investment. Therefore σ is not affected directly by changes in distribution of income.

4. s is the maximum that σ can attain. The difference between them will depend on the magnitude of the rate of investment on the one hand, and the growth of other factors, such as labor, natural resources, and technological progress on the other. A misdirection of investment will also produce a difference between s and σ.

We shall make the heroic assumption that s and σ are constant.

From (1) it follows that

$$(2) \qquad \frac{dP}{dt} = I\sigma.$$

It is important to note that, with a given σ, dP/dt is a function of I, and not of dI/dt. Whether dI/dt is positive or negative, dP/dt is always positive so long as σ and I are positive.

Expression (2) showing the increase in productive capacity is essentially the supply side of our system. On the demand side we have the multiplier theory, too familiar to need any comment, except for an emphasis on the obvious but often forgotten fact that with any given marginal propensity to save, dY/dt is a function not of I, but of dI/dt. Indicating the marginal propensity to save by α, and assuming it to be constant,[9] we have the simple relationship that

---

[8] I am disregarding the external economies and diseconomies of the older plants due to the operation of the new projects.

[9] Over the period 1879–1941 the average propensity to save (ratio of net capital

(3)
$$\frac{dY}{dt} = \frac{dI}{dt}\frac{1}{\alpha}.$$

Let the economy be in an equilibrium position so that[10]

(4)
$$P_0 = Y_0.$$

To retain the equilibrium position, we must have

(5)
$$\frac{dP}{dt} = \frac{dY}{dt}.$$

Substituting (2) and (3) into (5) we obtain our fundamental equation

(6)
$$I\sigma = \frac{dI}{dt}\frac{1}{\alpha},$$

the solution of which gives

(7)
$$I = I_0 e^{\alpha\sigma t}.$$

$\alpha\sigma$ is the equilibrium rate of growth. So long as it remains constant, *the maintenance of full employment requires investment to grow at a constant compound-interest rate.*

If, as a crude estimate, α is taken at 12 per cent and σ at some 30 per cent, the equilibrium rate of growth will be some 3.6 per cent per year.[10a]

The reader will now see that the assumption of constant α and σ is not entirely necessary, and that the whole problem can be worked out with variable α and σ.

---

formation to national income) was fairly constant and approximately equal to some 12 per cent. See Simon Kuznets, *National Product Since 1869*, National Bureau of Economic Research (mimeographed, 1945) p. II–89 and the *Survey of Current Business*, Vol. 22, May, 1942, and Vol. 24, April, 1944. In a problem of cyclical character, an assumption of a constant propensity to save would be very bad. Since we are interested here in a secular problem of continuous full employment, this assumption is not too dangerous.

[10] The problem can be also worked out for the case when $P_0 > Y_0$.

[10a] After this paper was sent to the printer, I found a very interesting article by E. H. Stern, "Capital Requirements in Progressive Economies," *Economica*, Vol. 12, August, 1945, pp. 163–171, in which the relation between capital and output in the U. S. during 1879–1929 is expressed (in billions of dollars) as *capital* =3.274 *income* −3.55. My estimates gave roughly similar results. This would place s around 30 per cent, though this figure should be raised to account for the underutilization of capital during a part of that period. It is also not clear how the junking process (see p. 144) was reflected in these figures.

The average rate of growth of real national income over the period 1879–1941 was some 3.3 per cent. See Table V, p. 818, and Appendix B, pp. 826–827, in my paper, "The 'Burden' of the Debt and the National Income," *American Economic Review*, Vol. 34, December, 1944.

III. THE EFFECTS OF GROWTH

Our next problem is to explore what happens when investment does grow at some constant percentage rate r, which, however, is not necessarily equal to the equilibrium rate $\alpha\sigma$. It will be necessary to introduce two additional concepts: average propensity to save I/Y and the average ratio of productive capacity to capital P/K. To simplify the problem, we shall assume that

1. $I/Y = \alpha$, so that average propensity to save is equal to marginal.
2. $P/K = s$, i.e., the ratio of productive capacity to capital for the whole economy is equal to that of the new investment projects.

We shall consider first the special simple case $\sigma = s$, and then the more general case when $\sigma < s$.[11]

Case 1: $\sigma = s$. Since $I = I_0 e^{rt}$, capital, being the sum of all net investments, equals

$$(8) \qquad K = K_0 + I_0 \int_0^t e^{rt} dt = K_0 + \frac{I_0}{r}(e^{rt} - 1).$$

As t becomes large, K will approach the expression

$$(9) \qquad \frac{I_0}{r} e^{rt},$$

so that capital will also grow at a rate approaching r.

As $Y = (1/\alpha) I_0 e^{rt}$, the ratio of income to capital is

$$(10) \qquad \frac{Y}{K} = \frac{\dfrac{1}{\alpha} I_0 e^{rt}}{K_0 + \dfrac{I_0}{r}(e^{rt} - 1)},$$

and

$$(11) \qquad \lim_{t \to \infty} \frac{Y}{K} = \frac{r}{\alpha}.$$

Thus so long as r and α remain constant (or change in the same proportion) no "deepening" of capital takes place. This, roughly speaking, was the situation in the United States over the last seventy years or so prior to this war.

[11] It is also possible that, owing to capital-saving inventions in existing plants, $\sigma > s$. Formally this case can be excluded by falling back on the definition of depreciation given in note 2. This, however, is not a very happy solution, but the approach used in this paper will hardly offer a better one. I think, however, that α in our society is sufficiently high to make $\sigma > s$ in a continuous state of full employment more an exception than a rule.

Substituting $K = P/s$ into (11) we obtain

$$(12) \qquad \lim_{t \to \infty} \frac{Y}{P} = \frac{r}{\alpha s} \; .$$

Since in the present case $\sigma = s$,

$$(13) \qquad \lim_{t \to \infty} \frac{Y}{P} = \frac{r}{\alpha \sigma} \; .$$

The expression

$$(14) \qquad \theta = \frac{r}{\alpha \sigma}$$

may be called the *coefficient* of *utilization*. When the economy grows at the equilibrium rate, so that $r = \alpha\sigma$, $\theta = 100$ per cent and productive capacity is fully utilized. But as r falls below $\alpha\sigma$, a fraction of capacity $(1 - \theta)$ is gradually left unused.[12] *Thus the failure of the economy to grow at the required rate creates unused capacity and unemployment.*

Case 2: $\sigma < s$. As investment proceeds at the rate I, new projects with a productive capacity of Is are built. Since the productive capacity of the whole economy increases only by $I\sigma$, it follows that somewhere in the economy (not excluding the new projects) productive capacity is reduced by $I(s - \sigma)$. Therefore every year an amount of capital equal to $I(s - \sigma)/s$ becomes useless.

The problem can now be approached from two points of view. The amounts $I(s - \sigma)/s$, can be looked upon as capital losses, which are not taken into account in calculating income and investment.[13] In this case, I still indicates the rate of net investment, and all other symbols retain their old meaning, except that capital has to be redefined as the integral of investment *minus* capital losses: every year chunks of capital (over and above depreciation) are written off and junked. The annual addition to capital will then be

$$(15) \qquad \frac{dK}{dt} = I - \frac{I(s - \sigma)}{s} = I \frac{\sigma}{s} \, ,$$

and

$$(16) \qquad K = K_0 + I_0 \frac{\sigma}{s} \int_0^t e^{rt} dt = K_0 + I_0 \frac{\sigma}{sr} (e^{rt} - 1).$$

[12] It should be noted that if r, α, and σ are constant, θ is also a constant. Even though the economy fails to grow at the required rate, the relative disparity between its capacity and income does not become wider, because its capital also grows not at the $\alpha\sigma$ but at the r rate.

[13] These losses are not necessarily losses in the accounting sense. See note 14.

Also,

(17)
$$\lim_{t \to \infty} \frac{Y}{K} = \frac{r}{\alpha} \cdot \frac{s}{\sigma},$$

and

(18)
$$\lim_{t \to \infty} \frac{Y}{P} = \frac{r}{\alpha\sigma},$$

which is exactly the same result we had in (13).

The second approach consists in treating the amounts $I(s-\sigma)/s$ not as capital losses but as a special allowance for obsolescence. Net investment would then have to be defined not as I, but as $I\sigma/s$. Other symbols would have to be redefined accordingly, and the whole problem could then be reworked out in the same way as on pp. 142–143.

In a sense the choice between these two methods is a matter of bookkeeping; depending upon the character of the problem in hand, one or the other can be used, though I suspect that the second method can easily become misleading. The nature of the process will be the same whichever method is used. The fact is that, owing to a difference between s and σ, the construction of new investment projects makes certain assets (not excluding the new projects themselves) useless, because under the new conditions brought about by changes in demand, or a rise in the wage rates, or both, the products of these assets cannot be sold.[14] As stated on p. 140 the difference between s and σ is created either by misdirection of investment or by the lack of balance between the propensity to save on the one hand, and the growth of labor, discovery of natural resources, and technological progress on the other. So long as mistakes are made or this lack of balance exists, the junking process is inevitable.

From a social point of view, the junking process is not necessarily undesirable. In this country, where saving involves little hardship, it may be perfectly justified. But it may present a serious obstacle to the achievement of full employment, because the owners of capital assets headed for the junk pile will try to avoid the losses. So long as they confine themselves to changes in their accounting practices, no special consequences will follow. But it is more likely that they will try to accumulate larger reserves either by reducing their own con-

[14] To be strictly true, the statement in the text would require considerable divisibility of capital assets. In the absence of such divisibility, the expression "junking" should not be taken too literally.

The fact that these assets may still be operated to some extent or that their products are sold at lower prices or that both these conditions exist, does not invalidate our argument, because σ, being expressed in real terms, will be higher than it would be if the assets were left completely unused.

sumption or by charging higher prices (or paying lower wages). As a result, the total propensity to save may rise. This will be exactly the opposite measure from what is needed to avoid the junking process, and will of course lead to greater trouble, though I am not prepared to say to what extent capital owners will succeed in passing on these losses.

In so far as they are able to control new investment, they will try to avoid losses by postponing it. Consequently, the rate of growth may well be depressed below the required $\alpha\sigma$, and unused capacity will develop. Our present model does not allow us to separate unused capacity into idle capital and idle men, though most likely both will be present.[15] Because of humanitarian considerations, we are more concerned with unemployed men. But *unemployed capital is extremely important, because its presence inhibits new investment.*[16] It presents a grave danger to a full-employment equilibrium in a capitalist society.

IV. GUARANTEED GROWTH OF INCOME

In the preceding sections it was shown that a state of full employment can be maintained if investment and income grow at an annual rate $\alpha\sigma$. The question now arises as to what extent the argument can be reversed: suppose income is guaranteed to grow at the $\alpha\sigma$ rate; will that call forth sufficient investment to generate the needed income?

We are concerned here with a situation where spontaneous investment (i.e., investment made in response to changes in technique, shifts in consumers' preferences, discovery of new resources, etc.) is not sufficient, and therefore a certain amount of induced investment (made in response to a rise in income) is also required.[17] To simplify the argument, let us assume that spontaneous investment is absent altogether. It should also be made clear that the problem is treated from a theoretical point of view, without considering the numerous practical questions that the income guarantee would raise.

If an economy starts from an equilibrium position, an expected rise in income of $Y\alpha\sigma$ will require an investment equal to $Y\alpha\sigma/s$. As before, two cases have to be considered.

---

[15] The presence of unemployed men may be obscured by inefficient utilization of labor, as in agriculture.

[16] It is true that a given capital owner may often have a hard time distinguishing between capital idle because of $\sigma < s$, and capital idle because of $r < \alpha\sigma$. The first kind of idleness, however, is relatively permanent, and cannot be corrected by greater expenditures, while the second is temporary (it is hoped) and is due to poor fiscal and monetary policies.

[17] Cf. Alvin H. Hansen, *Fiscal Policy and Business Cycles*, New York, 1944, Part Three, and particularly p. 297.

1. If σ is equal or reasonably close to s, the resulting amount of investment of $Y\alpha$ will equal the volume of savings that will be made at that level of income, and equilibrium will be maintained.[18] *Thus a mere guarantee of a rise in income* (if taken seriously by the investors) *will actually generate enough investment and income to make the guarantee good without necessarily resorting to a government deficit.*

2. If σ is appreciably below s, investment will probably fall short of savings and equilibrium will be destroyed. The difficulty arises because a full-employment rate of investment in the face of a $\sigma < s$ makes the junking process (discussed on pp. 143–145) inevitable, while a mere guarantee of a rise in income, as a general rule, lacks the instrument to force the capital owners to discard their equipment. They will simply invest $Y\alpha\sigma/s$ instead of $Y\alpha$. Only if in the economy as a whole there is a considerable number of products the demand for which is highly elastic with respect to income, and therefore a good number of others the demand for which is negatively elastic with respect to income, will a larger amount than $Y\alpha\sigma/s$ be invested and a corresponding amount of capital junked. Of course, if the rise in income is accompanied by shifts in consumers' preferences, the appearance of new products, aggressive competition, and other changes, the junking process will be speeded up, but if these changes do take place they may give rise to spontaneous investment of their own and the guaranteed *rise* in income will not be important. Still, the assurance of a high and rising income is undoubtedly one of the best methods for encouraging investment.

As explained before, a substantial difference between s and σ simply indicates that with the available labor force and the current progress of technology, the maintenance of full employment under a given α requires the accumulation of capital at a faster rate than it can be used. As a general rule, this applies equally well to both private and public investment, though there may be special cases when, owing to the development of particular consumers' preferences (e.g., for vacations), or to technological reasons (e.g., need for power), or to institutional conditions (as in urban redevelopment), considerable need for public investment still exists.[19]

[18] There is a slight error in the magnitudes in the text because of the use of discontinuous functions.

[19] As soon as the government enters the picture we find ourselves in a maze of definitional problems. From the point of view of this paper, saving and investment should be understood in reference to the whole economy, including the government, and not to its private sector only. But which government expenditures should be regarded as investment? The difficulty is present in the private sector as well, except that there we can take refuge in formal definitions, which cannot be well applied to government. I leave the question open. Certainly, investment need not be limited to inventories, steel, and concrete.

I am not prepared to say whether we already are or shall soon be faced with a serious difference between s and σ, though I doubt that it was an important problem in the past, except perhaps for the short boom years. My own guess is that we shall be more concerned with the disparity between $\alpha\sigma$ and r, that is with the failure of income to grow at the required rate.

If, however, the difference between σ and s becomes serious and inhibits investment, or if the junking process proceeds at a faster rate than is deemed socially desirable, the society will have at its disposal two methods not mutually exclusive: (1) the reduction of the propensity to save, or (2) the speeding up of technological progress. I hope that the main emphasis will be placed on the latter.

This paper attempted to analyze the relation between investment, rate of growth, and employment. The analysis was carried out on a very abstract and simplified level—a procedure which may be justified at the beginning of an investigation, but which must be corrected later on. In general, there is no such a thing as an absolutely good or bad assumption: what may be safe in one kind of a problem can become fatal in another. Of the several assumptions made here, that regarding depreciation is likely to cause the greatest difficulties, but it is by no means the only one. I hope to develop the whole subject further at a later date.

The central theme of the paper was *the rate of growth*, a concept which has been little used in economic theory, and in which I put much faith as an extremely useful instrument of economic analysis. One does not have to be a Keynesian to believe that employment is somehow dependent on national income, and that national income has something to do with investment. But as soon as investment comes in, growth cannot be left out, because for an individual firm investment may mean *more* capital and *less* labor, but for the economy as a whole (as a general case) investment means *more* capital and *not less* labor. If both are to be profitably employed, a *growth* of income must take place.

Washington, D. C.

A DYNAMIC AGGREGATIVE MODEL[1]

JAMES TOBIN

Yale University

CONTEMPORARY theoretical models of the business cycle and of economic growth typically possess two related characteristics: (1) they assume production functions that allow for no substitution between factors, and (2) the variables are all real magnitudes; monetary and price phenomena have no significance. Because of these characteristics, these models present a rigid and angular picture of the economic process: straight and narrow paths from which the slightest deviation spells disaster, abrupt and sharp reversals, intractable ceilings and floors. The models are highly suggestive, but their representation of the economy arouses the suspicion that they have left out some essential mechanisms of adjustment.

The purpose of this paper is to present a simple aggregative model that allows both for substitution possibilities and for monetary effects. The growth mechanism in the model is not radically different from the accelerator mechanism that plays the key role in other growth models. But it is unlike the accelerator mechanism in that there is not just one tenable rate of growth. As in accelerator models, growth is limited by the availability of factors other than capital. But here these limitations do not operate so abruptly, and they can be tempered by monetary and price adjustments that the accelerator models ignore.

The cyclical behavior of the model is similar to the nonlinear cyclical processes of Kaldor, Goodwin, and Hicks.[2] But the cycle in the present model depends in an essential way on the inflexibility of prices, money wages, or the supply of monetary assets.

Furthermore, the model to be described here does not restrict the economic process to two possibilities, steady growth or cycles. An alternative line of development is continuing underemployment — "stagnation" during which positive investment increases the capital stock and possibly the level of real income. This outcome, like the cycle, depends on some kind of price or monetary inflexibility.

In Part I the structure of the model will be described, and in Part II some of its implications will be examined.

[1] I wish to acknowledge with gratitude helpful discussions of this subject with graduate students and colleagues at Yale University. In particular, Henry Bruton, Thomas F. Dernburg, William Fellner, Challis A. Hall, and Arthur Okun read the paper and made valuable comments. So did Robert M. Solow of M.I.T. But it is not their fault if I have failed to follow all their advice. The paper was written while I was holding a Social Science Research Council Faculty Fellowship.

[2] N. Kaldor, "A Model of the Trade Cycle," *Economic Journal*, L (March, 1940), 78–92; R. Goodwin, "The Nonlinear Accelerator and the Persistence of Business Cycles," *Econometrica*, XIX (January, 1951), 1–17, and "Econometrics in Business Cycle Analysis," in A. H. Hansen, *Business Cycles and National Income* (New York: W. W. Norton & Co., 1951), chap. 22; J. R. Hicks, *A Contribution to the Theory of the Trade Cycle* (Oxford: Oxford University Press, 1950).

I

The building blocks from which this model is constructed are four in number: (1) the saving function; (2) the production function; (3) asset preferences; and (4) labor-supply conditions.

THE SAVING FUNCTION

At any moment of time output is being produced at a rate Y, consumption is occurring at a rate C, and the capital stock, K, is growing at the rate $\dot{K}$, equal to $Y-C$. The saving function tells how output is divided between consumption and net investment:

$$\dot{K} = S(Y).\qquad (1)$$

This relationship is assumed to hold instantaneously. That is, consumption is adjusted without lag to the simultaneous level of output; any output not consumed is an addition to the capital stock. Whether or not it is a welcome addition is another matter, which depends on the asset preferences of the community, discussed below.

Of the saving function, it is assumed that $S'(Y)$ is positive and that $S(Y)$ is zero for some positive Y. Otherwise the shape of the saving function is not crucial to the argument. Variables other than Y—for example, W, total real wealth—could be assumed to affect the propensity to save without involving more than inessential complications.

THE PRODUCTION FUNCTION

The rate of output, Y, depends jointly on the stock of capital in existence, K, and the rate of input of labor services, N:

$$Y = P(K, N).\qquad (2)$$

The production function is assumed to be linear homogeneous. It follows that the marginal products are homogeneous functions of degree zero of the two factors; in other words, the marginal products depend only on the proportions in which the two inputs are being used. The real wage of labor, w, is equated by competition to the marginal product of labor; and the rent, r, per unit of time earned by ownership of any unit of capital is equated to the marginal product of capital:

$$w = P_N(K, N),\qquad (3)$$

$$r = P_K(K, N).\qquad (4)$$

If labor and capital expand over time in proportion, then output will expand in the same proportion, and both the real wage and the rent of capital will remain constant. If capital expands at a faster rate than labor, its rent must fall, and the real wage must rise.

A production function with constant returns to scale, both at any moment of time and over time, is a convenient beginning assumption. In judging the appropriateness of this kind of production function to the model, it should be remembered that, if it ignores technical improvement, on the one hand, it ignores limitations of other factors of production, "land," on the other. In the course of the argument the consequences of technological progress will be briefly discussed.

ASSET PREFERENCES

Only two stores of value, physical capital and currency, are available to owners of wealth in this economy. The own rate of return on capital is its rent, r, equal to its marginal product. Currency is wholly the issue of the state and bears an own rate of interest legally and permanently established. This rate will be assumed to be zero. The stock of currency, M, is exogenously determined and can be varied only by budget deficits or surpluses. The counterpart of this "currency" in the more complex asset structure of an actual economy is not money by the usual definition, which includes bank deposits corresponding to private debts. It is, for the United States, currency in circulation plus government debt plus the gold stock.[3]

If p is the price of goods in terms of currency, the community's total real wealth at any moment of time is

$$W = K + \frac{M}{p}. \qquad (5)$$

Given K, M, and p, the community may be satisfied to split its wealth so that it holds as capital an amount equal to the available stock, K, and as currency an amount equal to the existing real supply, M/p. Such a situation will be referred to as "portfolio balance."

Portfolio balance is assumed to be the necessary and sufficient condition for price stability ($\dot{p} = 0$). If, instead, owners of wealth desire to hold more goods and less currency, they attempt to buy goods with currency. Prices are bid up ($\dot{p} > 0$). If they desire to shift in the other direction, they attempt to sell goods for currency ($\dot{p} < 0$). These price changes may, in turn, be associated with changes in output and employment; but that depends on other parts of the model, in particular on the conditions of labor supply.

What, then, determines whether an

[3] This is the same concept developed in connection with discussions of the "Pigou effect"; see Herbert Stein, "Price Flexibility and Full Employment: Comment," *American Economic Review*, XXXIX (June, 1949), 725–26, and Don Patinkin, "Price Flexibility and Full Employment: Reply," *American Economic Review*, XXXIX (June, 1949), 726–28.

existing combination of K and M/p represents a situation of portfolio balance or imbalance? Portfolio balance is assumed in this model to be defined by the following functional relationship:

$$\frac{M}{p} = L(K, r, Y), \qquad (6)$$

$$L_K \gtreqless 0, \qquad L_r < 0, \qquad L_Y > 0.$$

Requirements for transactions balances of currency are assumed, as is customary, to depend on income; this is the reason for the appearance of Y in the function. Given their real wealth, W, owners of wealth will wish to hold a larger amount of capital, and a smaller amount of currency, the higher the rent on capital, r. Given the rent on capital, owners of wealth will desire to put some part of any increment of their wealth into capital and some part into currency. It is possible that there are levels of r (e.g., negative rates) so low that portfolio balance requires all wealth to be in the form of currency and that there is some level of r above which wealth owners would wish to hold no currency. But the main argument to follow in Part II concerns ranges of r between those extremes.

The assumption about portfolio balance has now been stated, and the reader who is more interested in learning its consequences than its derivation can proceed to the next section. But since this is the one of the four building blocks of the model that introduces possibly unconventional and unfamiliar material into the structure, it requires some discussion and defense.

The theory of portfolio balance implicit in most conventional aggregative economic theories of investment implies that rates of return on all assets must be equal. Applied to the two assets of the mythical economy of this paper, this theory would go as follows: Owners of wealth have a firm, certain, and unanimous expectation of the rate of price change, $\dot{p}_e$. This may or may not be the same as the actual rate of price change $\dot{p}$ at the same moment of time.[4] The rate at which a unit of wealth is expected to grow if it is held in the form of currency is, therefore, $-\dot{p}_e/p$. Similarly, owners of wealth have a firm and unanimous view of the rate at which wealth will grow if it is held as physical capital. This rate is r_e, the expected market rent, which may or may not be the same as r. Owners of wealth will choose that portfolio which makes their wealth grow at the fastest rate. If $-\dot{p}_e/p$ were to exceed r_e, they would desire to hold all currency and no capital; if r_e were greater than $-\dot{p}_e/p$, they would desire to hold all capital and no currency. Only if the two rates are equal will they be satisfied to hold positive amounts of both assets; and, indeed, in that case, they will not care what the mix of assets is in their portfolios. On this theory of asset preferences the relative supplies of the assets do not matter. Whatever the supplies, portfolio balance requires that the real expected rates of return on the assets be equal. In particular, if $r_e = r$ and $\dot{p}_e = 0$, equilibrium requires that $r = 0$.

Keynes departed from this theory in his liquidity-preference explanation of the choice between cash balances and interest-bearing monetary assets. He was able to show that, given uncertainty or lack of unanimity in the expectations of wealth owners, the rate of interest that preserves portfolio balance between cash and "bonds" is not independent of the supplies of the two kinds of assets. But he did not apply the same reasoning to the much more important choice between physical goods or capital, on the one hand, and monetary assets, on the other. His theory of investment was orthodox in requiring equality between the marginal efficiency of capital and the rate of interest.

The assumptions behind the portfolio-balance equation in the present model, equation (6), may be briefly stated. Each owner of wealth entertains as possibilities numerous values of both r_e and $-\dot{p}_e/p$, and to each possible pair of values he attaches a probability. The expected value of r_e, that is, the mean of its marginal probability distribution, is assumed to be r. The expected value of $-\dot{p}_e/p$ is assumed to be zero. In other and less precise words, the owner of wealth expects *on balance* neither the rent of capital nor the price level to change. But he is not sure. The dispersions of possible rents and price changes above and below their expected values constitute the risks of the two assets.

Owners of wealth, it is further assumed, dislike risk. Of two portfolios with the same expected value of rate of return, an investor will prefer the one with the lower dispersion of rate of return.[5] The principle of "not putting all your eggs in one basket" explains

[4] An individual may be assumed to know the historical course of prices $p(t)$ up to the present (for $t \lessgtr t_0$) and to expect a future course of prices $p_e(t)$ (for $\lessgtr t_0$). Presumably the expected course starts at the same price at which the historical course ends ($p[t_0]=p_e[t_0]$). But there is no reason that one should start with the same slope with which the other ends: $p'(t_0)$, referred to in the text as $\dot{p}$, is not necessarily the same as $p_e'(t_0)$, referred to in the text as $\dot{p}_e$.

[5] Risk aversion in this sense may be deduced from the assumption of generally declining marginal utility of income. Here, however, it is not necessary to go into the question of the usefulness of the concept of cardinal utility in explaining behavior under uncertainty.

why a risk-avoiding investor may well hold a diversified portfolio even when the expected returns of all the assets in it are not identical. For the present purpose it explains why an owner of wealth will hold currency in excess of transactions requirements, even when its expected return is zero and the expected return on capital is positive. It also explains why, given the risks associated with the two assets, an investor may desire to have more of his wealth in capital the larger is r. The higher the prospective yield of a portfolio, the greater is the inducement to accept the additional risks of heavier concentration on the more remunerative asset.[6]

LABOR SUPPLY

The behavior of the model depends in a crucial way on assumptions regarding the relations of the supply of labor to the real wage, to the money wage, and to time. It will be convenient, therefore, to introduce alternative assumptions in the course of the argument of Part II.

II

STATIONARY EQUILIBRIUM

The model would be of little interest if its position of stationary equilibrium were inevitably and rapidly attained, but, for the sake of completeness, this position will be described first. There are any number of combinations of labor and capital that can produce the zero-saving level of output. To each combination corresponds a marginal productivity of labor, to which the real wage must be equal; this marginal pro-

[6] There is an "income effect" working in the opposite direction. The portfolio-balance function, equation (6), assumes the substitution effect to be dominant.

ductivity is higher the more capital-intensive the combination. Suppose there is a unique relation between the supply of labor and the real wage. An equilibrium labor-capital combination is one that demands labor in an amount equal to the supply forthcoming at the real wage corresponding to that combination. The equilibrium absolute price level is then determined by the portfolio-balance equation. Given the rent and amount of capital in the equilibrium combination and the supply of currency, portfolio balance must be obtained by a price level that provides the appropriate amount of real wealth in liquid form.

BALANCED GROWTH

Proportional growth of capital, income, and employment implies, according to the assumed production function, constancy of capital rent, r, and the real wage, w. Maintenance of portfolio balance requires, therefore, an increase in M/p. Given the supply of currency, the price level must fall continuously over time. Balanced growth requires an expanding labor supply, available at the same real wage and at an ever decreasing money wage.

GROWTH WITH CAPITAL DEEPENING

In this model, unlike those of Harrod, Hicks, and others, failure of the labor supply to grow at the rate necessary for balanced growth does not mean that growth at a slower rate is possible. If the real wage must rise in order to induce additional labor supply, the rent of capital must, it is true, fall as capital grows. Portfolio balance requires, therefore, that a given increment of capital be accompanied by a greater price decline than in the case of balanced growth. But there is some rate of price decline that will preserve portfolio balance, even in the extreme case of completely inelastic labor supply. Although the rate of price decline per increment of capital is greater the less elastic the supply of labor with respect to the real wage and with respect to time, the time rate of price decline is not necessarily faster. The growth of income, saving, and capital is slower when labor is less elastic, and it takes longer to achieve the same increment of capital.

TECHNOLOGICAL PROGRESS AND PRICE DEFLATION

The preceding argument has assumed an unchanging production function with constant returns to scale. In comparison with that case, technological progress is deflationary to the extent that a more rapid growth of income augments transactions requirements for currency. But technological progress has offsetting inflationary effects to the extent that it raises the marginal productivity of capital corresponding to given inputs of capital and labor. Conceivably technical improvement can keep the rent on capital rising even though its amount relative to the supply of labor is increasing. This rise might even be sufficient to keep the demand for real currency balances from rising, in spite of the growth of the capital stock and of transactions requirements. At the other extreme, it is possible to imagine technological progress that fails to raise or even lowers the marginal productivity of capital corresponding to given inputs of the two factors. Progress of this kind contains nothing to counteract the deflationary pressures of a growing capital stock, declining capital rent, and increasing transactions needs.

MONETARY EXPANSION AS AN ALTERNATIVE TO PRICE DEFLATION

Growth with continuous price deflation strains the assumption that wealth owners expect, on balance, the price level to remain constant. The process itself would teach them that the expected value of the real return on currency is positive, and it would perhaps also reduce their estimates of the dispersion of possible returns on currency. This lesson would increase the relative attractiveness of currency as a store of value and thus force an ever faster rate of price decline.

An alternative to price deflation is expansion of the supply of currency. As noted above, monetary expansion cannot, in this model, be accomplished by monetary policy in the conventional sense but must be the result of deficit financing.[7] Assume that the government deficit $\dot{M}$ takes the form of transfer payments. Then equation (1) must be changed to read:

$$\dot{K} + \frac{\dot{M}}{p} = S\left(Y + \frac{\dot{M}}{p} \right). \qquad (7)$$

The normal result is that consumption will be a larger and investment a smaller share of a given level of real income. Thus, the greater is $\dot{M}$, the slower will be the rate of capital expansion. At the same time the growth of the currency supply meets growing transactions requirements and satisfies the desire of wealth owners to balance increased holdings of capital, possibly yielding lower rents, with enlarged holdings of liquid wealth.

[7] The implications of the approach of this paper concerning the effects of conventional monetary policy are left for discussion elsewhere. Clearly such a discussion requires the introduction of additional types of assets, including bank deposits and private debts.

That there is a time path of M compatible with price stability may be seen by considering the inflationary consequences of large values of $\dot{M}$. There is presumably a value of $\dot{M}$ large enough so that the desire of the community to save at the disposable income level $Y + \dot{M}/p$ would be satisfied by saving at the rate $\dot{M}/p$. Then the capital stock would remain constant, its marginal product would stay constant, and transactions requirements would remain unchanged. Portfolio balance could then be maintained only by inflation at the same rate as $\dot{M}/M$. Somewhere between this value of $\dot{M}$ and zero there is a rate of growth of the currency supply compatible with price stability.

WAGE INFLEXIBILITY AS AN OBSTACLE TO GROWTH

If the currency supply grows too slowly, the necessity that price deflation —probably an ever faster price deflation—accompany growth casts considerable doubt on the viability of the growth processes described above. This doubt arises from the institutional limits on downward flexibility of prices, in particular money wage rates, characteristic of actual economies. The purpose of this and the two following sections is to analyze the behavior of the system when money wage rates are inflexible.

For this analysis it is convenient to work with two relationships between the price level, p, and employment of labor, N. Both relationships assume a constant capital stock, K. The first, called the "labor market balance" (LMB) relation, gives for any level of employment, N, the price level, p, that equates the marginal productivity of labor to the real wage. Given the money wage, this p is higher for larger values

of N, because the marginal product of labor declines with employment with a given capital stock. This relation is shown in Figure 1 as curve LMB. The level of employment N_f is the maximum labor supply that can be induced at the given money wage. At that level of employment the money wage becomes flexible upward. If the money wage is raised or lowered, the LMB curve will shift up or down proportionately. If the capital stock is expanded, the LMB curve will shift downward, because an addition to capital will raise the marginal product of labor at any level of employment.

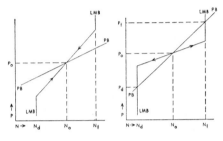

FIG. 1A.—Stable   FIG. 1B.—Unstable

The second relation between the same two variables, p and N, is the "portfolio balance" relation PB, also shown in Figure 1. As the name indicates, it shows for any level of employment the price level required for portfolio balance between the given stock of capital K and the given supply of currency M. Its slope may be either positive or negative. The marginal productivity of the given stock of capital, and hence the rent of capital, is greater the higher the volume of employment. Currency is thus a relatively less attractive asset at higher levels of employment; so far as this effect is concerned, the price level must be higher at higher levels of employment in order to reduce the real supply of currency. The transactions relation of demand for currency to the level of real income works, however, in the opposite direction. Whatever its slope, the *PB* curve will, for obvious reasons, shift upward if currency supply *M* is expanded, and downward if capital expands.

It is not possible to establish a priori which curve, *LMB* or *PB,* has the greater slope. The two possibilities are shown in Figures 1*A* and 1*B.* In Figure 1*A* the *LMB* curve has the greater slope; both curves are drawn with positive slopes, but the *PB* curve could equally well have a negative slope. In Figure 1*B* the *PB* curve has the greater slope. As indicated by the arrows, the intersection (p_0, N_0) is a stable short-run equilibrium in Figure 1*A* but an unstable one in Figure 1*B.* This follows from the assumption that $\dot{p}$ will be positive, zero, or negative, depending on whether wealth owners regard their currency holdings as too large, just right, or too small.[8] In Figure 1*B* (p_f, N_f) is a stable short-run equilibrium. And there may be another stable intersection (p_d, N_d). Here N_d would be a level of employment so low and, correspondingly, a real wage so high that the rigidity of the money wage breaks down.

Capital expansion shifts both the *LMB* and the *PB* curve downward. How does capital expansion affect the point (p_0, N_0)? The following results are proved in the Appendix: When the intersection (p_0, N_0) is an unstable point

[8] Employment has been assumed always to be at the point where the marginal product of labor equals the real wage. But the conclusions on the stability of (p_0, N_0) in the two parts of Figure 1 would not be altered if it were assumed instead that $\dot{N}$ is positive, zero, or negative depending on whether the marginal product of labor exceeds, equals, or is less than the real wage.

(Fig. 1*B*), capital expansion increases both N_0 and p_0. The *PB* curve shifts more than the *LMB* curve, and their intersection moves northeast. The qualitative effect of capital expansion may be depicted graphically by imagining the *PB* curve to shift downward while the *LMB* curve stays put. The same argument shows that capital accumulation moves a point like (p_f, N_f) or (p_d, N_d) in Figure 1*B* downward, while capital decumulation moves it upward. When the intersection (p_0, N_0) is a stable point (Fig. 1*A*), the argument of the Appendix indicates that capital expansion necessarily lowers p_0 but may either increase or decrease N_0; the intersection may move either southeast or southwest. It is, in other words, not possible to say which curve shifts more as a consequence of a given change in the capital stock.

These results permit consideration of the question whether growth with full employment of labor is compatible with a floor on the money wage rate. Except in the case where labor supply grows as rapidly as capital or more rapidly, the growth process brings about an increase of the real wage. A certain amount of price deflation is therefore compatible with rigidity of the money wage. But, according to the results reported in the previous paragraph, certainly in the unstable case and possibly in the stable case, too, the amount of price deflation needed to maintain portfolio balance is too much to enable employment to be maintained at a rigid money wage. Capital growth shifts the *PB* curve down more than the *LMB* curve. However, it is also possible in the stable case that the *LMB* curve shifts more than the *PB* curve, so that employment could be maintained and even increased while the money wage remains rigid and prices fall. But even this possibility depends on the assumption that wealth owners balance their portfolios on the expectation that the price level will remain the same. As noted above, it is only realistic to expect that a process of deflation would itself teach owners of wealth to expect price deflation rather than price stability. Such expectations would inevitably so enhance the relative attractiveness of currency as an asset that the process could not continue without a reduction of the money-wage rate.

WAGE INFLEXIBILITY AND
CYCLICAL FLUCTUATIONS

It is the situation depicted in Figure 1B that gives rise to the possibility of a cycle formally similar to those of Kaldor, Goodwin, and Hicks. Suppose the economy is at point (p_f, N_f). Capital expansion will sooner or later cause this point to coincide with (p_0, N_0) at a point like R in Figure 2. This day will be hastened by any inflation in the money-wage floor fostered by full employment; it may be that, once having enjoyed the money wage corresponding to (p_f, N_f) in Figure 1B, labor will not accept any lower money wage. Once R is reached, any further capital expansion will require a price decline that will push the real wage of labor, given that the money wage cannot fall, above its marginal productivity. Employers will therefore contract employment. But this does not obviate the necessity of price deflation. Indeed, it aggravates it, because the reduction of employment lowers the marginal productivity of capital. Balance cannot be restored both in the labor market and in wealth holdings until a level of employment is

reached at which the wage rate becomes flexible downward (N_d in Fig. 2).

The permanence of this "floor" equilibrium depends upon the saving function. If positive saving occurs at the levels of income produced by labor supply N_d, capital expansion will continue; and so also will price and wage deflation. Increase of employment then depends on the willingness of labor to accept additional employment at the low level to which severe unemployment has driven the money wage. Willingness to accept additional employment at this money wage may be encouraged by the

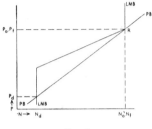

FIG. 2

increase in the real wage due to continued capital accumulation. A sufficient lowering of the money-wage rate demanded for increased employment would result in a situation like that represented by point S in Figure 3, and full employment could be restored.

Alternatively, the "floor" may correspond to a level of income at which there is negative saving. The gradual attrition of the capital stock will then move the PB curve up relative to the LMB curve. As capital becomes scarcer, its marginal product rises; and for both reasons its attractiveness relative to that of currency increases. Whatever happens to the money-wage terms on which labor will accept additional employment, the decumulation of capital will eventually lead to a position like S in Figure 3.

Once S is reached, any further reduction in the money wage, or any further decumulation of capital, will lead to an expansion of employment. But increasing employment only enhances the relative attractiveness of the existing stock of capital, causing the price level to rise and employment to be still further increased. As Figure 3 shows, the only stopping point is (p_f, N_f). Once N_f is reached, the money wage becomes flexible upward and follows the price level

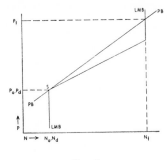

upward until portfolio balance is restored at the price level p_f. The cycle then repeats itself.

The floor in this model is provided by a level of employment so low, and a real wage correspondingly so high, that money-wage rates become flexible downward. The breakdown of money-wage rigidity may also be interpreted as a function of time; as Leontief has suggested, money-wage rigidity may not reflect any persistent "money illusion" on the part of workers and their organizations but only a lag in their perception of the price level to use in reckoning their real wage.[9] Trouble occurs at full employment, even when real wages

are increasing, because the time rate of price deflation becomes too fast in relation to this lag. Likewise, contraction of employment can be stopped and even reversed when money-wage demands have had time to catch up with what has been happening to the price level.

In this discussion of the floor it has been assumed that the rate of capital decumulation is controlled by the saving function. An interesting question arises when the saving function indicates dissaving at a rate higher than that at which the capital stock can physically decumulate. In the models of Goodwin and Hicks, in fact, the floor is the level of income at which dissaving equals the maximum possible rate of capital decumulation.

A physical limit on the rate of capital decumulation cannot really be handled within the framework of an aggregative model that takes account of only one industry, one commodity, and one price level. Such a model assumes that the output of the economy is essentially homogeneous and can equally well be consumed or accumulated in productive stocks, from which it can be withdrawn at will. If capital goods and consumers' goods are regarded as less than perfect substitutes, it is necessary to imagine that they have different price levels. Encountering a Goodwin-Hicks floor would then mean that the two price levels diverge. At any lower level of income the community would be unable to consume capital at the rate at which it wished to dissave. Consequently, the community would dissave from its holdings of currency. This would stop the fall in the price level of consumption

[9] W. Leontief, "Postulates: Keynes' *General Theory* and the Classicists," in S. E. Harris (ed.), *The New Economics* (New York: A. A. Knopf, 1947), chap. xix.

goods and make the Goodwin-Hicks floor an equilibrium level of employment and income. The price of capital goods would continue to fall as owners of wealth attempted to convert capital into either currency or consumption. This fall in the value of capital goods would restore portfolio balance—even though consumers' goods prices ceased to fall and money-wage rates remained rigid—by making capital a smaller proportion of the community's wealth.

With the model thus amended, the physical limit on capital decumulation provides a floor that will stop and eventually reverse a contraction even if the money-wage rate is intractable. But the contraction need not proceed to this extreme, if the wage-flexibility floor described above occurs at a higher level of employment and output.

WAGE INFLEXIBILITY AND STAGNATION

The cycle just described arises from the situation depicted in Figure 1B. But the situation of Figure 1A, where the LMB curve has an algebraically greater slope than the PB curve and the intersection (p_0, N_0) is a stable equilibrium, also is a possibility. In this case the intersection may move to the left as the capital stock increases. Growth of capital is accompanied by reduction of employment, so long as the money-wage rate is maintained. This process may end in a stationary equilibrium position if it entails such a reduction in output (or, if wealth is relevant to the saving function, such an increase in wealth) as to reduce saving to zero. But it is also possible that a process with positive saving, growth of capital, and increasing unemployment will continue indefinitely.

SUMMARY

The simple aggregative model that has been presented here differs from others used in discussions of growth and cycles in two main respects. The production function allows for substitution between capital and labor. The willingness of the community to hold physical capital depends on its rate of return and on the value of the liquid wealth held by the community. These two assumptions provide a link, generally absent in other models, between the world of real magnitudes and the world of money and prices. This link provides the model with some adjustment mechanisms ignored in other growth and cycle models. The following conclusions result:

1. Growth is possible at a great variety of rates and is not necessarily precluded when the labor supply grows slowly or remains constant.

2. The course of the price level as capital grows depends on (a) the accompanying rate of expansion of the labor force, (b) the rate at which the supply of currency is augmented by government deficits, and (c) the rate of technological progress. The first two factors are both inflationary. Technological progress has mixed effects. In the absence of monetary expansion and technological progress, price deflation is a necessary concomitant of growth even when the labor supply is increasing just as rapidly as capital. In these circumstances, therefore, growth with stable or increasing employment cannot continue if the money-range rate is inflexible downward.

3. Given wage inflexibility, the system may alternate between high and low levels of employment and, concur-

rently, between periods of price inflation and deflation. The ceiling to this cyclical process is provided by inelasticity of the labor supply. The floor may be provided either by the breakdown of the rigid money wage or by physical limits on the rate of consumption of capital. Alternatively, the system may "stagnate" at less than full employment, quite conceivably with capital growth and reduction of employment occurring at the same time. Whether the system behaves in this manner or with cyclical fluctuations depends on the relation between the conditions of portfolio balance and the rate of return on captial. The greater the shift in portfolios that owners of wealth wish to make when the rate of return on capital changes, the more likely it is that the system will have a cyclical solution.

APPENDIX

The equation of the labor-market-balance curve, for given K, is

$$pP_N (K, N) = w_0 , \qquad (1)$$

where w_0 is the rigid money-wage rate. The slope of this curve is

$$\left(\frac{dp}{dN}\right)_{LMB} = \frac{-p^2 P_{NN}}{w_0} . \qquad (2)$$

Since $P_{NN} < 0$, this slope is positive.

The equation of the portfolio-balance curve, for given K and M, is

$$M = pL (K, r, Y)$$
$$= pL (K, P_K [K, N], P [K, N]) . \qquad (3)$$

The slope of this curve is

$$\left(\frac{dp}{dN}\right)_{PB} = \frac{-p^2}{M} (L_r P_{KN} + L_Y P_N) . \qquad (4)$$

Since $L_r < 0$, $P_{KN} > 0$, and $L_Y > 0$, this slope may be either positive or negative.

The point (p_0, N_0) is determined by the intersection of (1) and (3). The problem is to find the changes in p_0 and N_0 associated with an increase in K.

Differentiating (1) and (3) with respect to K gives

$$\frac{\partial p_0}{\partial K}\left(\frac{w_0}{p_0}\right) + \frac{\partial N_0}{\partial K}(p_0 P_{NN})$$
$$ \qquad (5)$$
$$= - p_0 P_{NK} ,$$

$$\frac{\partial p_0}{\partial K}\left(\frac{M}{p_0}\right) + \frac{\partial N_0}{\partial K}(p_0 L_r P_{KN} + p_0 L_Y P_N)$$
$$\qquad (6)$$
$$= - p_0 L_K - p_0 L_r P_{KK} - p_0 L_Y P_K .$$

Equations (5) and (6) give the following solutions:

$$\frac{\partial p_0}{\partial K} = - \frac{p^2}{D} (P^2_{NK} L_r - P_{NN} P_{KK} L_r$$
$$\qquad (7)$$
$$- L_K P_{NN} + P_{NK} P_N L_Y - P_{NN} P_K L_Y) ,$$

$$\frac{\partial N_0}{\partial K} = - \frac{1}{D} (w_0 L_K + w_0 L_r P_{KK}$$
$$\qquad (8)$$
$$- M P_{NK} + w_0 L_Y P_K) ,$$

where

$$D = w_0 L_r P_{KN} - M P_{NN} + w_0 L_Y P_N . \qquad (9)$$

From (2), (4), and (9), it can be concluded that D will be positive, zero, or negative according as the slope of the LMB curve is greater than, equal to, or less than the slope of the PB curve. In the stable case (Fig. 1A), D is positive. In the unstable case (Fig. 1B), D is negative.

The production function is assumed to be homogeneous of degree one. Consequently,

$$P_N N + P_K K = P .$$

Differentiating this with respect to N and K gives

$$P_{NN} N + P_{KN} K = 0 , \qquad (10)$$

$$P_{NK} N + P_{KK} K = 0 . \qquad (11)$$

Using (10) and (11) in (7) gives

$$\frac{\partial p_0}{\partial K} = \frac{-p_0^2}{D}(P_{NN}L_K \qquad (12)$$

$$+ P_{NK}P_NL_Y - P_{NN}P_KL_Y).$$

Since P_{NN} is negative, this derivative has the opposite sign of D. Consequently, in the stable case it is negative, and in the unstable case it is positive.

Using (9), (10), and (11) in (8) gives

$$\frac{\partial N_0}{\partial K} = \frac{1}{D}\left(\frac{N}{K}D - w_0L_K - w_0L_Y\frac{Y}{K}\right), \quad (13)$$

where L_K and L_Y are positive. Consequently, if D is negative—the unstable case—$\partial N_0/\partial K$ must be positive. But if D is positive—the stable case—the derivative may have either sign.

A point like (p_f, N_f) represents the inter-section of the portfolio-balance curve (3) with a vertical labor-market-balance curve. To find out whether employment can be maintained at N_f when K is increased, it is necessary only to find $\partial w_0/\partial K$ for fixed N_f from (1) and (3). If this $\partial w_0/\partial K$ is negative, then maintenance of employment is not consistent with maintenance of portfolio balance unless the money-wage floor w_0 is lowered. If the derivative is zero or positive, then employment can be maintained or indeed increased even though the money-wage rate remains fixed or rises. Differentiating (1) and (3) with respect to K, for fixed N, gives:

$$\frac{\partial w_0}{\partial K} - \frac{\partial p_f}{\partial K}\left(\frac{w_0}{p_f}\right) = p_fP_{NK}, \quad (14)$$

$$\frac{\partial p_f}{\partial K}\left(\frac{M}{p_f}\right) = -p_fL_K \qquad (15)$$
$$- p_fL_rP_{KK} - p_fL_YP_K.$$

Therefore:

$$\frac{\partial w_0}{\partial K} = \frac{-w_0L_K - w_0L_rP_{KK} - w_0L_YP_K + MP_{NK}}{M/p_f}. \quad (16)$$

Comparing (8) and 16),

$$\left(\frac{\partial w_0}{\partial K}\right)_{N\text{const.}} = \frac{D}{M/p_f}\left(\frac{\partial N_0}{\partial K}\right)_{w_0\text{const.}}. \quad (17)$$

From the conclusions previously reached with the aid of (13), it follows that, when D is negative (unstable case), $\partial w_0/\partial K$ is negative. But when D is positive (stable case), $\partial w_0/\partial K$ may have either sign.

Correction: On article page 107, column 2, line 8 from the bottom of the page, the word possible should read: impossible. [The Editors.]

A CONTRIBUTION TO THE THEORY OF
ECONOMIC GROWTH

By Robert M. Solow

I. Introduction

All theory depends on assumptions which are not quite true. That is what makes it theory. The art of successful theorizing is to make the inevitable simplifying assumptions in such a way that the final results are not very sensitive.[1] A "crucial" assumption is one on which the conclusions do depend sensitively, and it is important that crucial assumptions be reasonably realistic. When the results of a theory seem to flow specifically from a special crucial assumption, then if the assumption is dubious, the results are suspect.

I wish to argue that something like this is true of the Harrod-Domar model of economic growth. The characteristic and powerful conclusion of the Harrod-Domar line of thought is that even for the long run the economic system is at best balanced on a knife-edge of equilibrium growth. Were the magnitudes of the key parameters — the savings ratio, the capital-output ratio, the rate of increase of the labor force — to slip ever so slightly from dead center, the consequence would be either growing unemployment or prolonged inflation. In Harrod's terms the critical question of balance boils down to a comparison between the natural rate of growth which depends, in the absence of technological change, on the increase of the labor force, and the warranted rate of growth which depends on the saving and investing habits of households and firms.

But this fundamental opposition of warranted and natural rates turns out in the end to flow from the crucial assumption that production takes place under conditions of *fixed proportions*. There is no possibility of substituting labor for capital in production. If this assumption is abandoned, the knife-edge notion of unstable balance seems to go with it. Indeed it is hardly surprising that such a gross

---

1. Thus transport costs were merely a negligible complication to Ricardian trade theory, but a vital characteristic of reality to von Thünen.

Reprinted by permission of the author and publishers from *The Quarterly Journal of Economics*, LXX (February 1956), 65–94. Cambridge, Mass.: Harvard University Press, Copyright 1956 by the President and Fellows of Harvard College.

rigidity in one part of the system should entail lack of flexibility in another. A remarkable characteristic of the Harrod-Domar model is that it consistently studies long-run problems with the usual short-run tools. One usually thinks of the long run as the domain of the neoclassical analysis, the land of the margin. Instead Harrod and Domar talk of the long run in terms of the multiplier, the accelerator, "the" capital coefficient. The bulk of this paper is devoted to a model of long-run growth which accepts all the Harrod-Domar assumptions except that of fixed proportions. Instead I suppose that the single composite commodity is produced by labor and capital under the standard neoclassical conditions. The adaptation of the system to an exogenously given rate of increase of the labor force is worked out in some detail, to see if the Harrod instability appears. The price-wage-interest reactions play an important role in this neoclassical adjustment process, so they are analyzed too. Then some of the other rigid assumptions are relaxed slightly to see what qualitative changes result: neutral technological change is allowed, and an interest-elastic savings schedule. Finally the consequences of certain more "Keynesian" relations and rigidities are briefly considered.

II. A Model of Long-Run Growth

There is only one commodity, output as a whole, whose rate of production is designated $Y(t)$. Thus we can speak unambiguously of the community's real income. Part of each instant's output is consumed and the rest is saved and invested. The fraction of output saved is a constant s, so that the rate of saving is $sY(t)$. The community's stock of capital $K(t)$ takes the form of an accumulation of the composite commodity. Net investment is then just the rate of increase of this capital stock dK/dt or $\dot{K}$, so we have the basic identity at every instant of time:

$$(1) \qquad\qquad \dot{K} = sY.$$

Output is produced with the help of two factors of production, capital and labor, whose rate of input is $L(t)$. Technological possibilities are represented by a production function

$$(2) \qquad\qquad Y = F(K,L).$$

Output is to be understood as net output after making good the depreciation of capital. About production all we will say at the moment is that it shows constant returns to scale. Hence the production function is homogeneous of first degree. This amounts to assuming that there is no scarce nonaugmentable resource like land. Constant returns to scale seems the natural assumption to make in a theory of growth. The scarce-land case would lead to decreasing returns to scale in capital and labor and the model would become more Ricardian.[2]

Inserting (2) in (1) we get

$$(3) \qquad \dot{K} = sF(K,L).$$

This is one equation in two unknowns. One way to close the system would be to add a demand-for-labor equation: marginal physical productivity of labor equals real wage rate; and a supply-of-labor equation. The latter could take the general form of making labor supply a function of the real wage, or more classically of putting the real wage equal to a conventional subsistence level. In any case there would be three equations in the three unknowns K, L, real wage.

Instead we proceed more in the spirit of the Harrod model. As a result of exogenous population growth the labor force increases at a constant relative rate n. In the absence of technological change n is Harrod's natural rate of growth. Thus:

$$(4) \qquad L(t) = L_0 e^{nt}.$$

In (3) L stands for total employment; in (4) L stands for the available supply of labor. By identifying the two we are assuming that full employment is perpetually maintained. When we insert (4) in (3) to get

$$(5) \qquad \dot{K} = sF(K,L_0 e^{nt})$$

we have the basic equation which determines the time path of capital accumulation that must be followed if all available labor is to be employed.

Alternatively (4) can be looked at as a supply curve of labor. It says that the exponentially growing labor force is offered for employment completely inelastically. The labor supply curve is a vertical

2. See, for example, Haavelmo: *A Study in the Theory of Economic Evolution* (Amsterdam, 1954), pp. 9–11. Not all "underdeveloped" countries are areas of land shortage. Ethiopia is a counterexample. One can imagine the theory as applying as long as arable land can be hacked out of the wilderness at essentially constant cost.

line which shifts to the right in time as the labor force grows according to (4). Then the real wage rate adjusts so that all available labor is employed, and the marginal productivity equation determines the wage rate which will actually rule.[3]

In summary, (5) is a differential equation in the single variable $K(t)$. Its solution gives the only time profile of the community's capital stock which will fully employ the available labor. Once we know the time path of capital stock and that of the labor force, we can compute from the production function the corresponding time path of real output. The marginal productivity equation determines the time path of the real wage rate. There is also involved an assumption of full employment of the available stock of capital. At any point of time the pre-existing stock of capital (the result of previous accumulation) is inelastically supplied. Hence there is a similar marginal productivity equation for capital which determines the real rental per unit of time for the services of capital stock. The process can be viewed in this way: at any moment of time the available labor supply is given by (4) and the available stock of capital is also a datum. Since the real return to factors will adjust to bring about full employment of labor and capital we can use the production function (2) to find the current rate of output. Then the propensity to save tells us how much of net output will be saved and invested. Hence we know the net accumulation of capital during the current period. Added to the already accumulated stock this gives the capital available for the next period, and the whole process can be repeated.

III. Possible Growth Patterns

To see if there is always a capital accumulation path consistent with any rate of growth of the labor force, we must study the differential equation (5) for the qualitative nature of its solutions. Naturally without specifying the exact shape of the production function we can't hope to find the exact solution. But certain broad properties are surprisingly easy to isolate, even graphically.

To do so we introduce a new variable $r = \dfrac{K}{L}$, the ratio of capital to labor. Hence we have $K = rL = rL_0e^{nt}$. Differentiating with respect to time we get

$$\dot{K} = L_0e^{nt}\dot{r} + nrL_0e^{nt}.$$

3. The complete set of three equations consists of (3), (4) and $\dfrac{\partial F(K,L)}{\partial L} = w$.

Substitute this in (5):

$$(\dot{r} + nr)L_0e^{nt} = sF(K, L_0e^{nt}).$$

But because of constant returns to scale we can divide both variables in F by $L = L_0e^{nt}$ provided we multiply F by the same factor. Thus

$$(\dot{r} + nr)L_0e^{nt} = sL_0e^{nt}F\left(\frac{K}{L_0e^{nt}}, 1\right)$$

and dividing out the common factor we arrive finally at

(6) $$\dot{r} = sF(r, 1) - nr.$$

Here we have a differential equation involving the capital-labor ratio alone.

This fundamental equation can be reached somewhat less formally. Since $r = \dfrac{K}{L}$, the relative rate of change of r is the difference between the relative rates of change of K and L. That is:

$$\frac{\dot{r}}{r} = \frac{\dot{K}}{K} - \frac{\dot{L}}{L}.$$

Now first of all $\dfrac{\dot{L}}{L} = n$. Secondly $\dot{K} = sF(K, L)$. Making these substitutions:

$$\dot{r} = r\frac{sF(K, L)}{K} - nr.$$

Now divide L out of F as before, note that $\dfrac{L}{K} = \dfrac{1}{r}$, and we get (6) again.

The function $F(r, 1)$ appearing in (6) is easy to interpret. It is the total product curve as varying amounts r of capital are employed with one unit of labor. Alternatively it gives output per worker as a function of capital per worker. Thus (6) states that the rate of change of the capital-labor ratio is the difference of two terms, one representing the increment of capital and one the increment of labor.

When $\dot{r} = 0$, the capital-labor ratio is a constant, and the capital stock must be expanding at the same rate as the labor force, namely n.

(The warranted rate of growth, warranted by the appropriate real rate of return to capital, equals the natural rate.) In Figure I, the ray through the origin with slope n represents the function nr. The other curve is the function $sF(r,1)$. It is here drawn to pass through the origin and convex upward: no output unless both inputs are positive, and diminishing marginal productivity of capital, as would be the case, for example, with the Cobb-Douglas function. At the point of intersection $nr = sF(r,1)$ and $\dot{r} = 0$. If the capital-labor ratio r^* should ever be established, it will be maintained, and capital and labor will grow thenceforward in proportion. By constant returns to

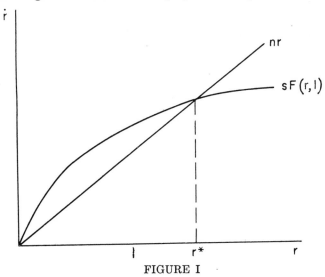

FIGURE I

scale, real output will also grow at the same relative rate n, and output per head of labor force will be constant.

But if $r \neq r^*$, how will the capital-labor ratio develop over time? To the right of the intersection point, when $r > r^*$, $nr > sF(r,1)$ and from (6) we see that r will decrease toward r^*. Conversely if initially $r < r^*$, the graph shows that $nr < sF(r,1)$, $\dot{r} > 0$, and r will increase toward r^*. Thus the equilibrium value r^* is *stable*. Whatever the initial value of the capital-labor ratio, the system will develop *toward* a state of balanced growth at the natural rate. The time path of capital and output will not be exactly exponential except asymptotically.[4] If the initial capital stock is below the equilibrium ratio,

4. There is an exception to this. If $K = 0, r = 0$ and the system can't get started; with no capital there is no output and hence no accumulation. But this

capital and output will grow at a faster pace than the labor force until the equilibrium ratio is approached. If the initial ratio is above the equilibrium value, capital and output will grow more slowly than the labor force. The growth of output is always intermediate between those of labor and capital.

Of course the strong stability shown in Figure I is not inevitable. The steady adjustment of capital and output to a state of balanced growth comes about because of the way I have drawn the productivity curve $F(r,1)$. Many other configurations are a priori possible. For example in Figure II there are three intersection points. Inspec-

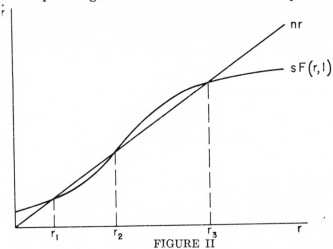

FIGURE II

tion will show that r_1 and r_3 are stable, r_2 is not. Depending on the initially observed capital-labor ratio, the system will develop either to balanced growth at capital-labor ratio r_1 or r_3. In either case labor supply, capital stock and real output will asymptotically expand at rate n, but around r_1 there is less capital than around r_3, hence the level of output per head will be lower in the former case than in the latter. The relevant balanced growth equilibrium is at r_1 for an initial ratio anywhere between 0 and r_2, it is at r_3 for any initial ratio greater than r_2. The ratio r_2 is itself an equilibrium growth ratio, but an unstable one; any accidental disturbance will be magnified over time. Figure II has been drawn so that production is possible without capital; hence the origin is not an equilibrium "growth" configuration.

Even Figure II does not exhaust the possibilities. It is possible

equilibrium is unstable: the slightest windfall capital accumulation will start the system off toward r^*.

that no balanced growth equilibrium might exist.[5] *Any* nondecreasing function $F(r,1)$ can be converted into a constant returns to scale production function simply by multiplying it by L; the reader can construct a wide variety of such curves and examine the resulting solutions to (6). In Figure III are shown two possibilities, together

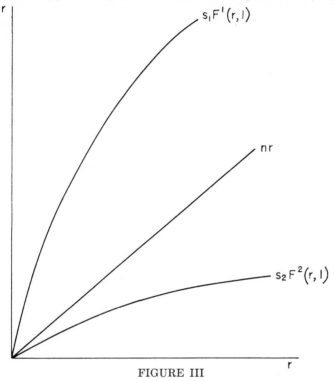

FIGURE III

with a ray nr. Both have diminishing marginal productivity throughout, and one lies wholly above nr while the other lies wholly below.[6] The first system is so productive and saves so much that perpetual full employment will increase the capital-labor ratio (and also the output per head) beyond all limits; capital and income both increase

5. This seems to contradict a theorem in R. M. Solow and P. A. Samuelson: "Balanced Growth under Constant Returns to Scale," *Econometrica*, XXI (1953), 412–24, but the contradiction is only apparent. It was there assumed that every commodity had positive marginal productivity in the production of each commodity. Here capital cannot be used to produce labor.

6. The equation of the first might be $s_1 F^1(r,1) = nr + \sqrt{r}$, that of the second

$$s_2 F^2(r,1) = \frac{nr}{r+1}$$

more rapidly than the labor supply. The second system is so unproductive that the full employment path leads only to forever diminishing income per capita. Since net investment is always positive and labor supply is increasing, aggregate income can only rise.

The basic conclusion of this analysis is that, when production takes place under the usual neoclassical conditions of variable proportions and constant returns to scale, no simple opposition between natural and warranted rates of growth is possible. There may not be — in fact in the case of the Cobb-Douglas function there never can be — any knife-edge. The system can adjust to any given rate of growth of the labor force, and eventually approach a state of steady proportional expansion.

IV. EXAMPLES

In this section I propose very briefly to work out three examples, three simple choices of the shape of the production function for which it is possible to solve the basic differential equation (6) explicitly.

Example 1: Fixed Proportions. This is the Harrod-Domar case. It takes a units of capital to produce a unit of output; and b units of labor. Thus a is an acceleration coefficient. Of course, a unit of output can be produced with *more* capital and/or labor than this (the isoquants are right-angled corners); the first bottleneck to be reached limits the rate of output. This can be expressed in the form (2) by saying

$$Y = F(K,L) = \min\left(\frac{K}{a}, \frac{L}{b}\right)$$

where "min (. . .)" means the smaller of the numbers in parentheses. The basic differential equation (6) becomes

$$\dot{r} = s \min\left(\frac{r}{a}, \frac{1}{b}\right) - nr.$$

Evidently for very small r we must have $\frac{r}{a} < \frac{1}{b}$, so that in this range $\dot{r} = \frac{sr}{a} - nr = \left(\frac{s}{a} - n\right)r$. But when $\frac{r}{a} \geq \frac{1}{b}$, i.e., $r \geq \frac{a}{b}$, the equation becomes $\dot{r} = \frac{s}{b} - nr$. It is easier to see how this works graphically. In Figure IV the function $s \min\left(\frac{r}{a}, \frac{1}{b}\right)$ is represented by a broken line: the ray from the origin with slope $\dfrac{s}{a}$ until r reaches the

value $\dfrac{a}{b}$, and then a horizontal line at height $\dfrac{s}{b}$. In the Harrod model

$\dfrac{s}{a}$ is the warranted rate of growth.

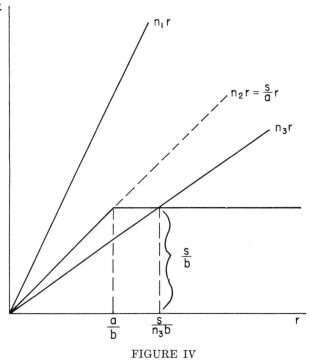

FIGURE IV

There are now three possibilities:

(a) $n_1 > \dfrac{s}{a}$, the natural rate exceeds the warranted rate. It can

be seen from Figure IV that $n_1 r$ is always greater than $s \min\left(\dfrac{r}{a},\dfrac{1}{b}\right)$,

so that r always decreases. Suppose the initial value of the

capital-labor ratio is $r_0 > \dfrac{a}{b}$, then $\dot{r} = \dfrac{s}{b} - n_1 r$, whose solution is

$r = \left(r_0 - \dfrac{s}{n_1 b}\right)e^{-n_1 t} + \dfrac{s}{n_1 b}$. Thus r decreases toward $\dfrac{s}{n_1 b}$ which is in turn less than $\frac{a}{b}$. At an easily calculable point of time t_1, r reaches

$\frac{a}{b}$. From then on $\dot{r} = \left(\frac{s}{a} - n_1\right) r$, whose solution is $r = \frac{a}{b} e^{\left(\frac{s}{a} - n_1\right)(t - t_1)}$.

Since $\frac{s}{a} < n_1$, r will decrease toward zero. At time t_1, when $r = \frac{a}{b}$

the labor supply and capital stock are in balance. From then on as the capital-labor ratio decreases labor becomes redundant, and the extent of the redundancy grows. The amount of unemployment can be calculated from the fact that $K = rL_0 e^{nt}$ remembering that, when

capital is the bottleneck factor, output is $\frac{K}{a}$ and *employment* is $b\frac{K}{a}$.

(b) $n_2 = \frac{s}{a}$, the warranted and natural rates are equal. If initially

$r > \frac{a}{b}$ so that labor is the bottleneck, then r decreases to $\frac{a}{b}$ and stays

there. If initially $r < \frac{a}{b}$, then r remains constant over time, in a sort

of neutral equilibrium. Capital stock and labor supply grow at a common rate n_2; whatever *percentage* redundancy of labor there was initially is preserved.

(c) $n_3 < \frac{s}{a}$, the warranted rate exceeds the natural rate. For-

mally the solution is exactly as in case (a) with n_3 replacing n_1.

There is a stable equilibrium capital output ratio at $r = \frac{s}{n_3 b}$. But

here capital is redundant as can be seen from the fact that the marginal productivity of capital has fallen to zero. The proportion of

the capital stock actually employed in equilibrium growth is $\frac{a n_3}{s}$.

But since the capital stock is growing (at a rate asymptotically equal to n_3) the absolute amount of excess capacity is growing, too. This appearance of redundancy independent of any price-wage movements is a consequence of fixed proportions, and lends the Harrod-Domar model its characteristic of rigid balance.

At the very least one can imagine a production function such that if r exceeds a critical value r_{max}, the marginal product of capital falls to zero, and if r falls short of another critical value r_{min}, the marginal product of labor falls to zero. For intermediate capital-labor ratios the isoquants are as usual. Figure IV would begin with a linear portion for $0 \leqq r \leqq r_{min}$, then have a phase like Figure I for $r_{min} \leqq r \leqq r_{max}$, then end with a horizontal stretch for $r > r_{max}$. There would be a whole *zone* of labor-supply growth rates which would lead to an equilibrium like that of Figure I. For values of n below this zone the end result would be redundancy of capital, for values of n above this zone, redundancy of labor. To the extent that in the long run factor proportions are widely variable the intermediate zone of growth rates will be wide.

Example 2: The Cobb-Douglas Function. The properties of the function $Y = K^a L^{1-a}$ are too well known to need comment here. Figure I describes the situation regardless of the choice of the parameters a and n. The marginal productivity of capital rises indefinitely as the capital-labor ratio decreases, so that the curve $sF(r,1)$ must rise above the ray nr. But since $a < 1$, the curve must eventually cross the ray from above and subsequently remain below. Thus the asymptotic behavior of the system is always balanced growth at the natural rate.

The differential equation (6) is in this case $\dot{r} = sr^a - nr$. It is actually easier to go back to the untransformed equation (5), which now reads

(7) $$\dot{K} = sK^a(L_0 e^{nt})^{1-a} .$$

This can be integrated directly and the solution is:

$$K(t) = \left[K_0{}^b - \frac{s}{n} L_0{}^b + \frac{s}{n} L_0{}^b e^{nbt} \right]^{\frac{1}{b}}$$

where $b = 1 - a$, and K_0 is the initial capital stock. It is easily seen that as t becomes large, $K(t)$ grows essentially like $\left(\dfrac{s}{n} \right)^{1/b} L_0 e^{nt}$, namely at the same rate of growth as the labor force. The equilibrium value of the capital-labor ratio is $r^* = \left(\dfrac{s}{n} \right)^{1/b}$. This can be verified by putting $\dot{r} = 0$ in (6). Reasonably enough this equilibrium ratio is larger the higher the savings ratio and the lower the rate of increase of the labor supply.

It is easy enough to work out the time path of real output from the production function itself. Obviously asymptotically Y must behave like K and L, that is, grow at relative rate n. Real income per head of labor force, Y/L, tends to the value $(s/n)^{a/b}$. Indeed with the Cobb-Douglas function it is always true that $Y/L = (K/L)^a = r^a$. It follows at once that the equilibrium value of K/Y is s/n. But K/Y is the "capital coefficient" in Harrod's terms, say C. Then in the long-run equilibrium growth we will have $C = s/n$ or $n = s/C$: the natural rate equals "the" warranted rate, not as an odd piece of luck but as a consequence of demand-supply adjustments.

Example 3. A whole family of constant-returns-to-scale production functions is given by $Y = (aK^p + L^p)^{1/p}$. It differs from the Cobb-Douglas family in that production is possible with only one factor. But it shares the property that if $p < 1$, the marginal productivity of capital becomes infinitely great as the capital-labor ratio declines toward zero. If $p > 1$, the isoquants have the "wrong" convexity; when $p = 1$, the isoquants are straight lines, perfect substitutability; I will restrict myself to the case of $0 < p < 1$ which gives the usual diminishing marginal returns. Otherwise it is hardly sensible to insist on full employment of both factors.

In particular consider $p = 1/2$ so that the production function becomes

$$Y = (a\sqrt{K} + \sqrt{L})^2 = a^2K + L + 2a\sqrt{KL}.$$

The basic differential equation is

$$(8) \qquad \dot{r} = s(a\sqrt{r} + 1)^2 - nr.$$

This can be written:

$$\dot{r} = s\left[(a^2 - n/s)r + 2a\sqrt{r} + 1\right] = s(A\sqrt{r} + 1)(B\sqrt{r} + 1)$$

where $A = a - \sqrt{n/s}$ and $B = a + \sqrt{n/s}$. The solution has to be given implicitly:

$$(9) \qquad \left(\frac{A\sqrt{r} + 1}{A\sqrt{r_0} + 1}\right)^{1/A} \left(\frac{B\sqrt{r} + 1}{B\sqrt{r_0} + 1}\right)^{-1/B} = e^{\sqrt{ns}\,t}$$

Once again it is easier to refer to a diagram. There are two possibilities, illustrated in Figure V. The curve $sF(r,1)$ begins at a height s when $r = 0$. If $sa^2 > n$, there is no balanced growth equilibrium: the capital-labor ratio increases indefinitely and so does real output per head. The system is highly productive and saves-invests enough at full employment to expand very rapidly. If $sa^2 < n$, there is a stable balanced growth equilibrium, which is reached according to the solution (9). The equilibrium capital-labor ratio can be found by putting $\dot{r} = 0$ in (8); it is $r^* = (1/\sqrt{n/s} - a)^2$. It can be further calculated that the income per head prevailing in the limiting state of growth is $1/(1 - a\sqrt{s/n})^2$. That is, real income per head of labor force will rise to this value if it starts below, or vice versa.

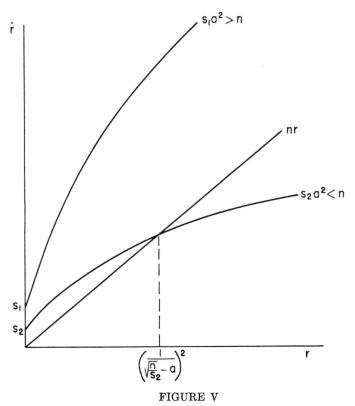

FIGURE V

V. Behavior of Interest and Wage Rates

The growth paths discussed in the previous sections can be looked at in two ways. From one point of view they have no causal significance but simply indicate the course that capital accumulation and real output would have to take if neither unemployment nor excess capacity are to appear. From another point of view, however, we can ask what kind of market behavior will cause the model economy to follow the path of equilibrium growth. In this direction it has already been assumed that both the growing labor force and the existing capital stock are thrown on the market inelastically, with the real wage and the real rental of capital adjusting instantaneously so as to clear the market. If saving and investment decisions are made independently, however, some additional marginal-efficiency-of-capital conditions have to be satisfied. The purpose of this section is to set out the price-wage-interest behavior appropriate to the growth paths sketched earlier.

There are four prices involved in the system: (1) the selling price of a unit of real output (and since real output serves also as capital this is the transfer price of a unit of capital stock) $p(t)$; (2) the money wage rate $w(t)$; (3) the money rental per unit of time of a unit of capital stock $q(t)$; (4) the rate of interest $i(t)$. One of these we can eliminate immediately. In the real system we are working with there is nothing to determine the absolute price level. Hence we can take $p(t)$, the price of real output, as given. Sometimes it will be convenient to imagine p as constant.

In a competitive economy the real wage and real rental are determined by the traditional marginal-productivity equations:

(10)
$$\frac{\partial F}{\partial L} = \frac{w}{p}$$

and

(11)
$$\frac{\partial F}{\partial K} = \frac{q}{p}.$$

Note in passing that with constant returns to scale the marginal productivities depend only on the capital-labor ratio r, and not on any scale quantities.[7]

7. In the polar case of pure competition, even if the individual firms have U-shaped average cost curves we can imagine changes in aggregate output taking place solely by the entry and exit of identical optimal-size firms. Then aggregate output is produced at constant cost; and in fact, because of the large number of relatively small firms each producing at approximately constant cost for small variations, we can without substantial error define an aggregate production function which will show constant returns to scale. There will be minor deviations since this aggregate production function is not strictly valid for variations in output smaller than the size of an optimal firm. But this lumpiness can for long-run analysis be treated as negligible.

One naturally thinks of adapting the model to the more general assumption of universal monopolistic competition. But the above device fails. If the industry consists of identical firms in identical large-group tangency equilibria then, subject to the restriction that output changes occur only via changes in the number of firms, one can perhaps define a constant-cost aggregate production function. But now this construct is largely irrelevant, for even if we are willing to overlook

The real rental on capital q/p is an own-rate of interest — it is the return on capital in units of capital stock. An owner of capital can by renting and reinvesting increase his holdings like compound interest at the *variable* instantaneous rate q/p, i.e., like $e^{\int_0^t q/p\,dt}$. Under conditions of perfect arbitrage there is a well-known close relationship between the money rate of interest and the commodity own-rate, namely

$$(12) \qquad i(t) = \frac{q(t)}{p(t)} + \frac{\dot{p}(t)}{p(t)}.$$

If the price level is in fact constant, the own-rate and the interest rate will coincide. If the price level is falling, the own-rate must exceed the interest rate to induce people to hold commodities. That the exact relation is as in (12) can be seen in several ways. For example, the owner of \$1 at time t has two options: he can lend the money for a short space of time, say until $t + h$ and earn approximately $i(t)h$ in interest, or he can buy $1/p$ units of output, earn rentals of $(q/p)h$ and then sell. In the first case he will own $1 + i(t)h$ at the end of the period; in the second case he will have $(q(t)/p(t))h + p(t + h)/p(t)$. In equilibrium these two amounts must be equal

$$1 + i(t)h = \frac{q(t)}{p(t)} h + \frac{p(t + h)}{p(t)}$$

or

$$i(t)h = \frac{q(t)}{p(t)} h + \frac{p(t + h) - p(t)}{p(t)}.$$

Dividing both sides by h and letting h tend to zero we get (12). Thus this condition equalizes the attractiveness of holding wealth in the form of capital stock or loanable funds.

Another way of deriving (12) and gaining some insight into its role in our model is to note that $p(t)$, the transfer price of a unit of capital, must equal the present value of its future stream of net

its discontinuity and treat it as differentiable, the partial derivatives of such a function will not be the marginal productivities to which the individual firms respond. Each firm is on the falling branch of its unit cost curve, whereas in the competitive case each firm was actually producing at locally constant costs. The difficult problem remains of introducing monopolistic competition into aggregative models. For example, the value-of-marginal-product equations in the text would have to go over into marginal-revenue-product relations, which in turn would require the explicit presence of demand curves. Much further experimentation is needed here, with greater realism the reward.

rentals. Thus with perfect foresight into future rentals and interest rates:

$$p(t) = \int\limits_{t}^{\infty} q(u)e^{-\int_{t}^{u}i(z)dz} \, du \, .$$

Differentiating with respect to time yields (12). Thus within the narrow confines of our model (in particular, absence of risk, a fixed average propensity to save, and no monetary complications) the money rate of interest and the return to holders of capital will stand in just the relation required to induce the community to hold the

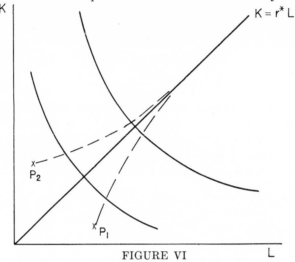

FIGURE VI

capital stock in existence. The absence of risk and uncertainty shows itself particularly in the absence of asset preferences.

Given the absolute price level $p(t)$, equations (10)–(12) determine the other three price variables, whose behavior can thus be calculated once the particular growth path is known.

Before indicating how the calculations would go in the examples of section IV, it is possible to get a general view diagrammatically, particularly when there is a stable balanced growth equilibrium. In Figure VI is drawn the ordinary isoquant map of the production function $F(K,L)$, and some possible kinds of growth paths. A given capital-labor ratio r^* is represented in Figure VI by a ray from the origin, with slope r^*. Suppose there is a stable asymptotic ratio r^*; then all growth paths issuing from arbitrary initial conditions approach the ray in the limit. Two such paths are shown, issuing from initial points P_1 and P_2. Since back in Figure I the approach of r to r^* was monotonic, the paths must look as shown in Figure VI. We see that if the initial capital-labor ratio is higher than the equilibrium value, the ratio falls and vice versa.

Figure VII corresponds to Figure II. There are three "equilibrium" rays, but the inner one is unstable. The inner ray is the dividing line among initial conditions which lead to one of the stable rays and those which lead to the other. All paths, of course, lead upward and to the right, without bending back; K and L always

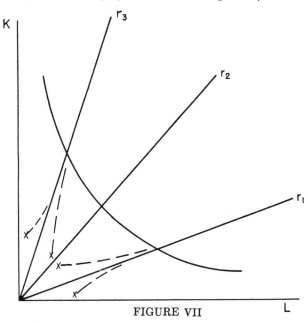

FIGURE VII

increase. The reader can draw a diagram corresponding to Figure III, in which the growth paths pass to steeper and steeper or to flatter and flatter rays, signifying respectively $r \to \infty$ or $r \to 0$. Again I remark that K and L and hence Y are all increasing, but if $r \to 0$, Y/L will decline.

Now because of constant returns to scale we know that along a ray from the origin, the slope of the isoquants is constant. This expresses the fact that marginal products depend only on the factor ratio. But in competition the slope of the isoquant reflects the ratio of the factor prices. Thus to a stable r^* as in Figure VI corresponds an equilibrium ratio w/q. Moreover, if the isoquants have the normal convexity, it is apparent that as r rises to r^*, the ratio w/q rises to its limiting value, and vice versa if r is falling.

In the unstable case, where r tends to infinity or zero it may be that w/q tends to infinity or zero. If, on the other hand, the isoquants reach the axes with slopes intermediate between the vertical and horizontal, the factor price ratio w/q will tend to a finite limit.

It might also be useful to point out that the slope of the curve $F(r,1)$ is the marginal productivity of capital at the corresponding value of r. Thus the course of the real rental q/p can be traced out in Figures I, II, and III. Remember that in those diagrams $F(r,1)$ has been reduced by the factor s, hence so has the slope of the curve. $F(r,1)$ itself represents Y/L, output per unit of labor, as a function of the capital-labor ratio.

In general if a stable growth path exists, the fall in the real wage or real rental needed to get to it may not be catastrophic at all. If there is an initial shortage of labor (compared with the equilibrium ratio) the real wage will have to fall. The higher the rate of increase of the labor force and the lower the propensity to save, the lower the equilibrium ratio and hence the more the real wage will have to fall. But the fall is not indefinite. I owe to John Chipman the remark that this result directly contradicts Harrod's position[8] that a perpetually falling rate of interest would be needed to maintain equilibrium.

Catastrophic changes in factor prices do occur in the Harrod-Domar case, but again as a consequence of the special assumption of fixed proportions. I have elsewhere discussed price behavior in the Harrod model[9] but I there described price level and interest rate and omitted consideration of factor prices. Actually there is little to say. The isoquants in the Harrod case are right-angled corners and this tells the whole story. Referring back to Figure IV, if the observed capital-labor ratio is bigger than a/b, then capital is absolutely redundant, its marginal product is zero, and the whole value of output is imputed to labor. Thus $q = 0$, and $bw = p$, so $w = p/b$. If the observed r is less than a/b labor is absolutely redundant and $w = 0$, so $q = p/a$. If labor and capital should just be in balance, $r = a/b$, then obviously it is not possible to impute any specific fraction of output to labor or capital separately. All we can be sure of is that the total value of a unit of output p will be imputed back to the

8. In his comments on an article by Pilvin, this *Journal*, Nov. 1953, p. 545.

9. R. M. Solow, "A Note on Price Level and Interest Rate in a Growth Model," *Review of Economic Studies*, No. 54 (1953–54), pp. 74–78.

composite dose of a units of capital and b units of labor (both factors are scarce). Hence w and q can have any values subject only to the condition $aq + bw = p, aq/p + bw/p = 1$. Thus in Figure IV anywhere but at $r = a/b$ either capital or labor must be redundant, and at a/b factor prices are indeterminate. And it is only in special circumstances that $r = a/b$.

Next consider the Cobb-Douglas case: $Y = K^a L^{1-a}$ and $q/p = a(K/L)^{a-1} = ar^{a-1}$. Hence $w/q = \dfrac{1 - a}{a} r$. The exact time paths of the real factor prices can be calculated without difficulty from the solution to (7), but are of no special interest. We saw earlier, however, that the limiting capital-labor ratio is $(s/n)^{1/1-a}$. Hence the equilibrium real wage rate is $(1 - a)(s/n)^{a/1-a}$, and the equilibrium real rental is an/s. These conclusions are qualitatively just what we should expect. As always with the Cobb-Douglas function the share of labor in real output is constant.

Our third example provides one bit of variety. From $Y = (a\sqrt{K} + \sqrt{L})^2$ we can compute that $\partial Y/\partial L = a\sqrt{\dfrac{K}{L}} + 1 = a\sqrt{r} + 1$. In the case where a balanced gr$\acute{o}$wth equilibrium exists (see end of section IV) $r^* = \left(\dfrac{1}{\sqrt{n/s} - a}\right)^2$; therefore the limiting real wage is

$$w/p = \dfrac{1}{\sqrt{n/s} - a} + 1 = \dfrac{1}{1 - a\sqrt{s/n}} .$$ It was calculated earlier that

in equilibrium growth $Y/L = \left(\dfrac{1}{1 - a\sqrt{s/n}}\right)^2$. But the relative share of labor is $(w/p)(L/Y) = 1 - a\sqrt{s/n}$. This is unlike the Cobb-Douglas case, where the relative shares are independent of s and n, depending only on the production function. Here we see that *in equilibrium growth* the relative share of labor is the greater the greater the rate of increase of the labor force and the smaller the propensity to save. In fact as one would expect, the faster the labor force increases the lower is the real wage in the equilibrium state of balanced growth; but the lower real wage still leaves the larger labor force a greater share of real income.

VI. Extensions

Neutral Technological Change. Perfectly arbitrary changes over time in the production function can be contemplated in principle, but are hardly likely to lead to systematic conclusions. An especially easy kind of technological change is that which simply multiplies the production function by an increasing scale factor. Thus we alter (2) to read

$$(13) \qquad Y = A(t)F(K,L).$$

The isoquant map remains unchanged but the output number attached to each isoquant is multiplied by $A(t)$. The way in which the (now ever-changing) equilibrium capital-labor ratio is affected can l e seen on a diagram like Figure I by "blowing up" the function $sF(r,1)$.

The Cobb-Douglas case works out very simply. Take $A(t) = e^{gt}$ and then the basic differential equation becomes

$$\dot{K} = se^{gt}K^a(L_0 e^{nt})^{1-a} = sK^a L_0^{1-a} e^{(n(1-a)+g)t},$$

whose solution is

$$K(t) = \left[K_0^b - \frac{bs}{nb+g}L_0^b + \frac{bs}{nb+g}L_0^b e^{(nb+g)t} \right]^{1/b}$$

where again $b = 1 - a$. In the long run the capital stock increases at the relative rate $n + g/b$ (compared with n in the case of no technological change). The eventual rate of increase of real output is $n + ag/b$. This is not only faster than n but (if $a > 1/2$) may even be faster than $n + g$. The reason, of course, is that higher real output means more saving and investment, which compounds the rate of growth still more. Indeed now the capital-labor ratio never reaches an equilibrium value but grows forever. The ever-increasing investment capacity is, of course, not matched by any speeding up of the growth of the labor force. Hence K/L gets bigger, eventually growing at the rate g/b. If the initial capital-labor ratio is very high, it might fall initially, but eventually it turns around and its asymptotic behavior is as described.

Since the capital-labor ratio eventually rises without limit, it follows that the real wage must eventually rise and keep rising. On the other hand, the special property of the Cobb-Douglas function is that the relative share of labor is constant at $1 - a$. The other essential structural facts follow from what has already been said: for example, since Y eventually grows at rate $n + ag/b$ and K at rate $n + g/b$, the capital coefficient K/Y grows at rate $n + g/b - n - ag/b = g$.

The Supply of Labor. In general one would want to make the supply of labor a function of the real wage rate and time (since the labor force is growing). We have made the special assumption that $L = L_0 e^{nt}$, i.e., that the labor-supply curve is completely inelastic with respect to the real wage and shifts to the right with the size of the labor force. We could generalize this somewhat by assuming that whatever the size of the labor force the proportion offered depends on the real wage. Specifically

$$(14) \qquad\qquad L = L_0 e^{nt} \left(\frac{w}{p} \right)^h .$$

Another way of describing this assumption is to note that it is a scale blow-up of a constant elasticity curve. In a detailed analysis this particular labor supply pattern would have to be modified at very high real wages, since given the size of the labor force there is an upper limit to the amount of labor that can be supplied, and (14) does not reflect this.

Our old differential equation (6) for the capital-labor ratio now becomes somewhat more complicated. Namely if we make the price level constant, for simplicity:

$$(6a) \qquad\qquad \dot{r} = sF(r,1) - nr - h\frac{\dot{w}}{w} .$$

To (6a) we must append the marginal productivity condition (10) $\dfrac{\partial F}{\partial L} = \dfrac{w}{p}$. Since the marginal product of labor depends only on r, we can eliminate w.

But generality leads to complications, and instead I turn again to the tractable Cobb-Douglas function. For that case (10) becomes

$$\frac{w}{p} = (1 - a)r^a$$

and hence

$$\frac{\dot{w}}{w} = a\frac{\dot{r}}{r} .$$

After a little manipulation (6a) can be written

$$\dot{r} = (sF(r,1) - nr)\left(1 + \frac{ah}{r}\right)^{-1},$$

which gives some insight into how an elastic labor supply changes things. In the first place, an equilibrium state of balanced growth still exists, when the right-hand side becomes zero, and it is still stable, approached from any initial conditions. Moreover, the equilibrium capital-labor ratio is *unchanged;* since $\dot{r}$ becomes zero exactly where it did before. This will not always happen, of course; it is a consequence of the special supply-of-labor schedule (14). Since r behaves in much the same way so will all those quantities which depend only on r, such as the real wage.

The reader who cares to work out the details can show that over the long run capital stock and real output will grow at the same rate n as the labor force.

If we assume quite generally that $L = G(t, w/p)$ then (6) will take the form

(6b) $$\dot{r} = sF(r,1) - \frac{r}{G}\left(\frac{\partial G}{\partial t} + \dot{w}\ \frac{\partial G}{\partial\left(\frac{w}{p}\right)}\right).$$

If $\dot{r} = 0$, then $\dot{w} = 0$, and the equilibrium capital-labor ratio is determined by

$$sF(r,1) = \frac{r}{G}\ \frac{\partial G}{\partial t}.$$

Unless $1/G\ \partial G/\partial t$ should happen always to equal n, as in the case with (14), the equilibrium capital-labor ratio *will* be affected by the introduction of an elastic labor supply.

Variable Saving Ratio. Up to now, whatever else has been happening in the model there has always been growth of both labor force and capital stock. The growth of the labor force was exogenously given, while growth in the capital stock was inevitable because the savings ratio was taken as an absolute constant. As long as real income was positive, positive net capital formation must result. This rules out the possibility of a Ricardo-Mill stationary state, and suggests the experiment of letting the rate of saving depend on the yield of capital. If savings can fall to zero when income is positive, it becomes possible for net investment to cease and for the capital stock, at least, to become stationary. There will still be growth of the labor force, however; it would take us too far afield to go wholly classical with a theory of population growth and a fixed supply of land.

The simplest way to let the interest rate or yield on capital influence the volume of savings is to make the fraction of income saved depend on the real return to owners of capital. Thus total savings is $s(q/p)Y$. Under constant returns to scale and competition, the real rental will depend only on the capital-labor ratio, hence we can easily convert the savings ratio into a function of r.

Everyone is familiar with the inconclusive discussions, both abstract and econometrical, as to whether the rate of interest really has any independent effect on the volume of saving, and if so, in what direction. For the purposes of this experiment, however, the natural assumption to make is that the savings ratio depends positively on the yield of capital (and hence inversely on the capital-labor ratio).

For convenience let me skip the step of passing from q/p to r via marginal productivity, and simply write savings as $s(r)Y$. Then the only modification in the theory is that the fundamental equation (6) becomes

$$(6c) \qquad \dot{r} = s(r)F(r,1) - nr .$$

The graphical treatment is much the same as before, except that we must allow for the variable factor $s(r)$. It may be that for sufficiently large r, $s(r)$ becomes zero. (This will be the case only if, first, there is a real rental so low that saving stops, and second, if the production function is such that a very high capital-labor ratio will drive the real return down to that critical value. The latter condition is not satisfied by all production functions.) If so, $s(r)F(r,1)$ will be zero for all sufficiently large r. If $F(0,1) = 0$, i.e., if no production is possible without capital, then $s(r)F(r,1)$ must come down to zero again at the origin, no matter how high the savings ratio is. But this is not inevitable either. Figure VIII gives a possible picture. As usual r^*, the equilibrium capital-labor ratio, is found by putting $\dot{r} = 0$ in (6c). In Figure VIII the equilibrium is stable and eventually capital and output will grow at the same rate as the labor force.

In general if $s(r)$ does vanish for large r, this eliminates the possibility of a runaway indefinite increase in the capital-labor ratio as in Figure III. The savings ratio *need* not go to zero to do this, but if it should, we are guaranteed that the last intersection with nr is a stable one.

If we compare any particular $s(r)$ with a constant saving ratio, the two curves will cross at the value of r for which $s(r)$ equals the old constant ratio. To the right the new curve will lie below (since I am assuming that $s(r)$ is a decreasing function) and to the left it will lie above the old curve. It is easily seen by example that the equilibrium r^* may be either larger or smaller than it was before. A wide variety of shapes and patterns is possible, but the net effect tends to be stabilizing: when the capital-labor ratio is high, saving is cut down; when it is low, saving is stimulated. There is still no possibility of a stationary state: should r get so high as to choke off

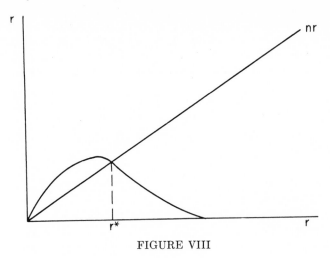

FIGURE VIII

saving and net capital formation, the continual growth of the labor force must eventually reduce it.

Taxation. My colleague, E. C. Brown, points out to me that all the above analysis can be extended to accommodate the effects of a personal income tax. In the simplest case, suppose the state levies a proportional income tax at the rate t. If the revenues are directed wholly into capital formation, the savings-investment identity (1) becomes

$$\dot{K} = s(1 - t)Y + tY = (s(1 - t) + t)Y.$$

That is, the effective savings ratio is *increased* from s to $s + t(1 - s)$. If the proceeds of the tax are directly consumed, the savings ratio is *decreased* from s to $s(1 - t)$. If a fraction v of the tax proceeds is invested and the rest consumed, the savings ratio changes to

$s + (v - s)t$ which is larger or smaller than s according as the state invests a larger or smaller fraction of its income than the private economy. The effects can be traced on diagrams such as Figure I: the curve $sF(r,1)$ is uniformly blown up or contracted and the equilibrium capital-labor ratio is correspondingly shifted. Non-proportional taxes can be incorporated with more difficulty, but would produce more interesting twists in the diagrams. Naturally the presence of an income tax will affect the price-wage relationships in the obvious way.

Variable Population Growth. Instead of treating the relative rate of population increase as a constant, we can more classically make it

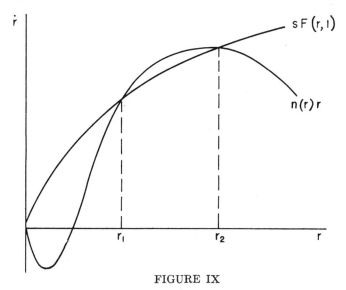

FIGURE IX

an endogenous variable of the system. In particular if we suppose that $\dot{L}/L$ depends only on the level of per capita income or consumption, or for that matter on the real wage rate, the generalization is especially easy to carry out. Since per capita income is given by $Y/L = F(r,1)$ the upshot is that the rate of growth of the labor force becomes $n = n(r)$, a function of the capital-labor ratio alone. The basic differential equation becomes

$$r = sF(r,1) - n(r)r.$$

Graphically the only difference is that the ray nr is twisted into a curve, whose shape depends on the exact nature of the dependence between population growth and real income, and between real income and the capital-labor ratio.

Suppose, for example, that for very low levels of income per head or the real wage population tends to decrease; for higher levels of income it begins to increase; and that for still higher levels of income the rate of population growth levels off and starts to decline. The result may be something like Figure IX. The equilibrium capital-labor ratio r_1 is stable, but r_2 is unstable. The accompanying levels of per capita income can be read off from the shape of $F(r,1)$. If the initial capital-labor ratio is less than r_2, the system will of itself tend to return to r_1. If the initial ratio could somehow be boosted above the critical level r_2, a self-sustaining process of increasing per capita income would be set off (and population would still be growing). The interesting thing about this case is that it shows how, in the total absence of indivisibilities or of increasing returns, a situation may still arise in which small-scale capital accumulation only leads back to stagnation but a major burst of investment can lift the system into a self-generating expansion of income and capital per head. The reader can work out still other possibilities.

VII. Qualifications

Everything above is the neoclassical side of the coin. Most especially it is full employment economics — in the dual aspect of equilibrium condition and frictionless, competitive, causal system. All the difficulties and rigidities which go into modern Keynesian income analysis have been shunted aside. It is not my contention that these problems don't exist, nor that they are of no significance in the long run. My purpose was to examine what might be called the tightrope view of economic growth and to see where more flexible assumptions about production would lead a simple model. Underemployment and excess capacity or their opposites can still be attributed to any of the old causes of deficient or excess aggregate demand, but less readily to any deviation from a narrow "balance."

In this concluding section I want merely to mention some of the more elementary obstacles to full employment and indicate how they impinge on the neoclassical model.[1]

Rigid Wages. This assumption about the supply of labor is just the reverse of the one made earlier. The real wage is held at some

1. A much more complete and elegant analysis of these important problems is to be found in a paper by James Tobin in the *Journal of Political Economy*, LXII (1955), 103–15.

arbitrary level $\left(\dfrac{\overline{w}}{p}\right)$. The level of employment must be such as to keep the marginal product of labor at this level. Since the marginal productivities depend only on the capital-labor ratio, it follows that fixing the real wage fixes r at, say, $\overline{r}$. Thus $K/L = \overline{r}$. Now there is no point in using r as our variable so we go back to (3) which in view of the last sentence becomes

$$\overline{r}\,\dot{L} = sF(\overline{r}L,L)\,,$$

or

$$\frac{\dot{L}}{L} = \frac{s}{\overline{r}}\,F(\overline{r},1).$$

This says that *employment* will increase exponentially at the rate $(s/r)F(\overline{r},1)$. If this rate falls short of n, the rate of growth of the labor force, unemployment will develop and increase. If $s/\overline{r}F(\overline{r},1) > n$, labor shortage will be the outcome and presumably the real wage will eventually become flexible upward. What this boils down to is that if $(\overline{w}/p)$ corresponds to a capital-labor ratio that would normally tend to decrease ($\dot{r} < 0$), unemployment develops, and vice versa. In the diagrams, $s/\overline{r}F(\overline{r},1)$ is just the slope of the ray from the origin to the $sF(r,1)$ curve at $\overline{r}$. If this slope is flatter than n, unemployment develops; if steeper, labor shortage develops.

Liquidity Preference. This is much too complicated a subject to be treated carefully here. Moreover the paper by Tobin just mentioned contains a new and penetrating analysis of the dynamics connected with asset preferences. I simply note here, however crudely, the point of contact with the neoclassical model.

Again taking the general price level as constant (which is now an unnatural thing to do), the transactions demand for money will depend on real output Y and the choice between holding cash and holding capital stock will depend on the real rental q/p. With a given quantity of money this provides a relation between Y and q/p or, essentially, between K and L, e.g.,

$$(15) \qquad \overline{M} = Q\left(Y, \frac{q}{p}\right) = Q(F(K,L), F_K(K,L))$$

where now K represents capital *in use*. On the earlier assumption of full employment of labor via flexible wages, we can put $L = L_0 e^{nt}$, and solve (15) for $K(t)$, or employed capital equipment. From $K(t)$ and L we can compute $Y(t)$ and hence total saving $sY(t)$. But this represents net investment (wealth not held as cash must be held as capital). The given initial stock of capital and the flow of investment determine the available capital stock which can be compared with $K(t)$ to measure the excess supply or demand for the services of capital.

In the famous "trap" case where the demand for idle balances becomes infinitely elastic at some positive rate of interest, we have a rigid factor price which can be treated much as rigid wages were treated above. The result will be underutilization of capital if the interest rate becomes rigid somewhere above the level corresponding to the equilibrium capital-labor ratio.

But it is exactly here that the futility of trying to describe this situation in terms of a "real" neoclassical model becomes glaringly evident. Because now one can no longer bypass the direct leverage of monetary factors on real consumption and investment. When the issue is the allocation of asset-holdings between cash and capital stock, the price of the composite commodity becomes an important variable and there is no dodging the need for a monetary dynamics.

Policy Implications. This is hardly the place to discuss the bearing of the previous highly abstract analysis on the practical problems of economic stabilization. I have been deliberately as neoclassical as you can get. Some part of this rubs off on the policy side. It may take deliberate action to maintain full employment. But the multiplicity of routes to full employment, via tax, expenditure, and monetary policies, leaves the nation *some* leeway to choose whether it wants high employment with relatively heavy capital formation, low consumption, rapid growth; or the reverse, or some mixture. I do not mean to suggest that this kind of policy (for example: cheap money and a budget surplus) can be carried on without serious strains. But one of the advantages of this more flexible model of growth is that it provides a theoretical counterpart to these practical possibilities.[2]

Uncertainty, etc. No credible theory of investment can be built on the assumption of perfect foresight and arbitrage over time. There are only too many reasons why net investment should be at

---

2. See the paper by Paul A. Samuelson in *Income Stabilization for a Developing Democracy*, ed. Millikan (New Haven, 1953), p. 577. Similar thoughts have been expressed by William Vickrey in his essay in *Post-Keynesian Economics*, ed. Kurihara (New Brunswick, 1954).

times insensitive to current changes in the real return to capital, at other times oversensitive. All these cobwebs and some others have been brushed aside throughout this essay. In the context, this is perhaps justifiable.

ROBERT M. SOLOW.

MASSACHUSETTS INSTITUTE OF TECHNOLOGY

Corrections: On article page 84, line 20, the first half of the equation should read:

$$w/p = \frac{a}{\sqrt{n/s} - a} + 1.$$

On article page 85, line 14 from the bottom should read: $n\,g/b$. This is not only faster than n, but even faster than $n + g$.

On article page 86, lines 2–4 should read: said: for example, since Y eventually grows at rate $n + g/b$ and K at rate $n + g/b$, the capital co-efficient K/Y is constant. On article page 86, Equation (6a) should read:

$$\dot{r} = sF(r,1) - nr - hr\,\frac{\dot{w}}{w}.$$

On article page 87, the equation at the top of the page should read: $\dot{r} = (sF(r,1) - nr)(1 + ah)^{-1}$. On article page 90, the equation at the foot of the page should read: $\dot{r} = sF(r,1) - n(r)r$. [The Editors.]

ECONOMIC GROWTH AND CAPITAL ACCUMULATION

T. W. Swan

1. *From Adam Smith to Arthur Lewis.*

"The design of the book is different from that of any treatise on Political Economy which has been produced in England since the work of Adam Smith." "The last great book covering this wide range was John Stuart Mill's *Principles of Political Economy.*" The first sentence is from Mill's preface, the second from the preface to Lewis' *The Theory of Economic Growth.* It would be rash to conclude from this sequence that one might keep up-to-date in economics by reading a new book every century. Lewis' remark is partly a warning that his book is about applications as well as theories, and partly a reminder that he is taking up an old theme of English economic thought. When Keynes solved "the great puzzle of Effective Demand", he made it possible for economists once more to study the progress of society in long-run classical terms—with a clear conscience, "safely ensconced in a Ricardian world."

The aim of this paper is to illustrate with two diagrams a theme common to Adam Smith, Mill, and Lewis, the theory of which is perhaps best seen in Ricardo: namely, the connexion between capital accumulation and the growth of the productive labour force. The neo-classical economists were in favour of productivity and thrift, but never found a way to make much use of them. Earlier views were much more specific: for example, Adam Smith's industry "proportioned to capital", Ricardo's Doctrine of Unbalanced Growth, Mill's "Irish peasantry, only half fed and half employed", now so familiar in the work of Harrod, Nurkse, or Lewis, and in a hundred United Nations reports. Nevertheless, our illustration takes a neo-classical form, and enjoys the neo-classical as well as the Ricardian vice.[1]

2. *An Unclassical Case.*

In the first instance, capital and labour are the only factors of production. In a given state of the arts, the annual output Y depends on the stock of capital K and the labour force N, according to the constant-elasticity production function $Y = K^a N^\beta$. With constant returns to scale, $a + \beta = 1$. The annual additon to the capital stock is

---

1. An appendix discusses some of the questions—especially those raised by Joan Robinson—concerning the role of Capital as a factor of production in the neo-classical theory. However, the appendix makes no attempt to discuss or defend the use of this or other concepts in a dynamic analysis, except by indicating some very artificial assumptions by which the main difficulties might be dodged.

Reprinted by permission of the publishers from *The Economic Record*, XXXII, No. 63 (November 1956), pp. 334–361. Published by the Melbourne University Press.

the amount saved[2] sY, where s is a given ratio of saving to output (or income.)

Therefore the annual relative rate of growth of capital is $s\dfrac{Y}{K}$. The symbols y and n stand for the annual relative rates of growth of output and labour respectively. In these terms the production function implies the basic formula for the rate of growth of output[3]:

$$(1)\ y = as\,\frac{Y}{K} + \beta n$$

Effective demand is so regulated (*via* the rate of interest or otherwise) that all savings are profitably invested, productive capacity is fully utilized, and the level of employment can never be increased merely by raising the level of spending. The forces of perfect competition drive the rate of profit or interest r and the (real) wage rate w into equality with the marginal productivities of capital and labour, derived from the production function:

$$(2)\ \ r = a\frac{Y}{K} \qquad (3)\ \ w = \beta\frac{Y}{N}$$

Thus the profit rate is proportional to output per unit of capital, $\dfrac{Y}{K}$, or the *output-capital ratio;* the wage rate is proportional to output per unit of labour, $\dfrac{Y}{N}$, or *output per head.* The relative shares of total profits and total wages in income are constants, given by the production elasticities a and β.

In Figure 1, look first at the three heavy lines. That rate of growth of capital $s\dfrac{Y}{K}$ is shown as a function of the output-capital ratio by a line through the origin with a slope equal to the saving ratio ($s = 10$ per cent).[4]

This may be called the *growth line* of capital. The resulting contribution of capital to the growth of output, $as\dfrac{Y}{K}$, is another line through the origin, of slope as ($a = 0.4$), and may be called the *contribution line* of capital.[5]

2. A given amount of saving, in terms of output, has a constant productive equivalent in terms of the capital stock. In Joan Robinson's language, the Wicksell effect is assumed to be zero. Part IV of the appendix argues that Joan Robinson is mistaken in her view that a rule can be laid down regarding the direction of the Wicksell effect.

3. The formula is obtained after logarithmic differentiation of the production function. All variables are treated as continuous functions of time, which is measured in years. For example, "annual output" is the instantaneous rate of output per annum. The words "growth", "rate of growth", etc. always refer to instantaneous relative rates of growth per annum, subject to instantaneous compounding.

4. Numerical plottings are used merely to help fix ideas.

5. According to the marginal productivity formula (2) above, $a_s\dfrac{Y}{K} = sr$. The rate of profit may therefore be read directly from Figure 1 by multiplying the contribution line of capital by 10.

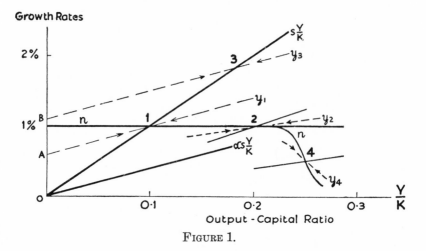

FIGURE 1.

The growth line of labour is horizontal, the rate of growth of the labour force being assumed for the present to be constant ($n = 1$ per cent). The distance OA on the vertical axis is βn ($\beta = 1 - a = 0 \cdot 6$), which is labour's contribution to the growth of output. Adding the contributions of capital and labour gives the growth line of output, y_1. Since $a + \beta = 1$, the geometry of the diagram implies that the three growth lines (of capital, labour, and output) must intersect at the same point (1), where growth in each case is 1 per cent per annum. The growth line of output is the intermediate between the growth lines of labour and capital, and divides the vertical distance between them in the proportion $a : \beta$. Anywhere west of (1) output is growing faster than capital, so the output-capital ratio is rising—moving eastward. Anywhere east of (1), capital is growing faster than output, so the movement of the output-capital ratio is westward. Only at (1) is there a resting-place. *At any other point the economy is always in motion towards (1)*,[6] as shown by the arrows on the line y_1.

The point (2) is another equilibrium point like (1), except that it corresponds with a saving ratio of 5 per cent, instead of 10 per cent at (1). The (unlabelled) continuous line is the new growth line of capital, with a slope through the origin of 5 per cent. The line y_2 is the new growth line of output, which if extended would meet the vertical axis at A as before. (The new contribution line of capital is not drawn.) At (2) economic growth is uniformly 1 per cent, just as at (1), because the three growth lines must still intersect somewhere on the horizontal line n. The given rate of growth of labour thus determines the equilibrium growth rate of the whole economy, while the saving ratio determines the output-capital ratio at which equilibrium will occur.

Suppose the economy is at (2), and that a thrift campaign suddenly raises the saving ratio from 5 per cent to 10 per cent. The growth line of output shifts from y_2 to y_1. Output per head begins to improve (as shown by the height of y_1 above n near (2)), and the wage rate rises in the same proportion. The output-capital ratio gradually sinks westward, and the profit rate sinks in the same proportion. The improvement of output per head continues at an ever-slackening pace down the slope of y_1, towards (1). At (1) output per head and the wage rate are higher than at (2), while the output-capital ratio and the profit rate are lower. These are permanent changes, but the rate of economic growth is faster only in the course of transition from (2) to (1).

Suppose next that the state of the arts, hitherto assumed constant, continually improves. "Neutral" technical progress contributes to the growth of output an annual m per cent beyond the contributions of capital and labour. In Figure 1 the distance AB on the vertical axis is m, at an assumed rate of $\frac{1}{2}$ per cent. The new growth line of output y_3 shows this amount added on top of y_1 (for a 10 per cent saving ratio), and it cuts the growth line of capital at the point (3). This will now be the equilibrium point. In some respects the transition from (2) to (1) is reversed by the introduction of technical progress, since the output-capital ratio and the rate of profit are both higher at (3) than at (1). But the main change is that output per head is not only permanently higher, but perpetually rising (as shown by the height of y_3 above n at (3)). Its rate of increase is actually greater than the m per cent contributed directly by technical progress, because the contribution of capital is also sustained by technical progress at a higher level (as shown by the height of y_1 above n at (3)).

The effect of a change in thrift, assuming constant technical progress, is not shown in the diagram. If another situation were depicted, combining the 5 per cent saving ratio of (2) with the

6. Figure 1 is in effect the "phase portrait" of a first-order differential equation in the variable $\frac{Y}{K}$ (cf. Andronow & Chaikin, *Theory of Oscillations,* Chapter IV). A similar device is used by R. M. Solow (*A Contribution to the Theory of Economic Growth,* Quarterly Journal of Economics, February, 1956). The approach to the point (1) along y, is asymptotic—i.e., (1) is reached only in infinity, the speed of travel towards it being directly related to the distance remaining to be travelled. (The time taken for $\frac{Y}{K}$ to move any given distance towards equilibrium is not revealed by the diagram, and can be discovered only by integrating the differential equation.) A point such as (1) is a *stable* equilibrium point because the growth line of capital cuts the growth line of labour (and so the growth line of output) from below. If over a certain range the saving ratio s were a decreasing function of $\frac{Y}{K}$, the growth line of capital might cut the growth line of labour from above, and this second intersection would be an *unstable* equilibrium point (the arrows would be directed away from it on either side).

$\frac{1}{2}$ per cent technical progress of (3), its equilibrium point would be found to lie well to the east of (3), but on exactly the same parallel of economic growth. So long as technical progress and the rate of growth of labour are taken as *data*, they jointly determine the equilibrium growth rate of output and capital.[7] After a transitional phase, the influence of the saving ratio on the rate of growth is ultimately absorbed by a compensating change in the output-capital ratio.

This conclusion is not really surprising. It is in fact the counterpart in our present unclassical model of the classical proposition that capital accumulation leads *ultimately* to the stationary state. A rise in the saving ratio does mean that the level of output per head is permanently higher at any time thereafter than it would have been otherwise. Further, the "transitional phase" is never literally completed; the "transitional" acceleration-deceleration of growth might be visible for centuries, depending entirely on the numerical assumptions. However, only extreme assumptions could produce such a result. It is at first sight disconcerting to find that "plausible" figuring suggests that even the impact effect of a sharp rise in the saving ratio may be of minor importance for the rate of growth: for example, the maximum amount added to the rate of growth, at the beginning of the transition from (2) to (1) in Figure 1, is only 0·4 per cent, though the thrift campaign doubles the saving ratio at a point where the yield on capital is 8 per cent.

To this anti-accumulation, pro-technology line of argument there are at least two possible anwers. First, the rate of technical progress may not be independent of the rate of accumulation, or (what comes to much the same thing) accumulation may give rise to external economies, so that the true social yield of capital is greater than any "plausible" figure based on common private experience.[8] This point would have appealed to Adam Smith, but it will not be pursued here. Second, the rate of growth of labour may

7. Equation (1) on page 335, with the addition of m per cent technical progress, becomes

$$(1') \quad y = \alpha s \frac{Y}{K} + \beta n + m$$

from which it follows that when $y = s \dfrac{Y}{K}$ (i.e., at an equilibrium point where the output-capital ratio is stationary) $y = \dfrac{\beta n + m}{1 - \alpha}$. For $\alpha + \beta = 1$ this is simply $y = n + \dfrac{m}{1 - \alpha}$.

8. In Figure 1, allowing for external economies, $\alpha + \beta$ would exceed unity and so y_1 would cut the growth line of capital above the level of n, just as y_3 does. If the external economies were concentrated on the side of capital (rather than labour), this elevation would take the form of a steeper slope for the contribution line of capital, which of course would no longer correspond with the rate of profit.

not be independent of the rate of accumulation. This is the distinctively classical answer.

In Figure 1 the sloping branch of the growth line of labour represents a situation in which the supply of labour is "elastic" in the vicinity of a certain level of output per head (and wage rate). This situation may be given a Malthusian interpretation, as the response of population to an improvement in the means of subsistence; it may be a situation of "disguised unemployment", with unproductive labour kept in reserve (by sharing with relatives, etc.) at a minimum living standard; it may be the result of Trade Union resistance or some other kind of institutional or conventional barrier, expressed in real terms; or it may reflect a potential supply of migrant labour, available if satisfactory living standards are offered. In any of these situations, "demand for commodities is not demand for labour" (if only Mill had understood his own doctrine) : the growth, or productive employment, of the labour force depends directly on the rate of accumulation. In the neighbourhood of the point (4), which is drawn for a saving ratio of 2 per cent, a higher saving ratio will evidently raise the rate of economic growth almost in proportion—and not only "transitionally", but in equilibrium as well. On the other hand, the wage rate and output per head (of *productively employed* labour) will not be much improved; nor will the rate of profit and the output-capital ratio suffer much decline.

This last fact is of course one of the reasons why capital accumulation appears so much more effective in raising the rate of economic growth when faster growth means primarily a faster expansion of productive employment, rather than a faster improvement of output per head. But the main reason is that accumulation is justly credited with the productive contribution of the additional labour that it "sets in motion."

It is now possible to look at Figure 1 in a new light. What is the maximum rate of labour growth consistent with the maintenance of a given standard of output per head? The answer (assuming no technical progress) is that for any such standard—i.e., at any given level of the output-capital ratio—the maximum rate of growth is directly proportional to the saving ratio. In fact, the growth line of capital $s\frac{Y}{K}$, wherever it lies, is the locus of all growth rates at which output per head is constant.

This is a more classical view of the problem, and also, unfortunately perhaps more relevant to many contemporary problems of population pressure and economic growth. However, to see its implications in either context, it is necessary to introduce a characteristic feature of the classical model—namely, the limited "powers of the soil".

3. *A Classical Case.*

A fixed factor of production, which may be called land, can be introduced very simply. Let its production elasticity be γ. Then, assuming constant returns to scale, $a + \beta + \gamma = 1$. However, since land is fixed in supply, it does not appear in the basic formula for the growth of output, $y = as\dfrac{Y}{K} + \beta n$, but makes its presence felt by reducing the sum of a and β below unity. With this interpretation, the former marginal productivity relationships for r and w remain unchanged, and there is now a third, of similar form, to determine the rent of land. a, β, and γ are now the constant relative shares of the three factors in income.

If Figure 1 were drawn for $a + \beta < 1$, the growth line of output would cut the growth line of capital below the horizontal growth line of labour. The only possible equilibrium with constant labour growth (and no technical progress) would be one in which output per head and the wage rate were perpetually falling. However, an answer can be given to the question: what rate of labour growth will maintain constant output per head? This condition can be expressed by putting $y = n$ in the formula repeated in the last paragraph, which gives $n = \dfrac{a}{1 - \beta} s \dfrac{Y}{K}$. In Figure 2 the constants are assumed to be $a = 0\cdot3$, $\beta = 0\cdot5$, $\gamma = 0\cdot2$ and $s = 10\%$. The coincident values of y and n that satisfy the condition of constant output per head are shown as a function of the output-capital ratio by the growth line $n_1 = y_1$, and this *locus classicus* is called the Ricardian line.

Along the Ricardian line labour is growing as fast as is compatible with a given living standard—keeping pace with the growth of output. Except at the origin, the growth line of capital lies above the Ricardian line, for capital must always grow faster than labour in order to sustain output per head in the face of continually diminishing returns on the land. But since capital is therefore also growing faster than output, the output-capital ratio is continually falling; the profit rate is falling in the same proportion, the wage rate is stable, while rent per acre is rising in proportion with output. As the output-capital ratio falls, the growth rate of labour and output gradually recedes down the slope of the Ricardian line, retreating from the unequal struggle against niggardly nature. In this manner the natural progress of society continues indefinitely towards the origin, where at last the growth line of capital and the Ricardian line intersect, at the point (1), in a stationary state.

If "long indeed before this period the very low rate of profit" has "arrested all accumulation", the change will have been seen in Figure 2 in the form of a decline in the saving ratio, reducing the

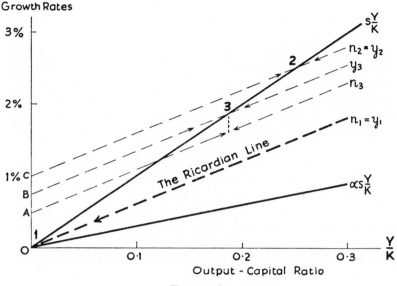

FIGURE 2.

slopes of the growth lines down to zero. On the other hand, a higher saving ratio would proportionally raise the growth rates at every point, but only temporarily interrupt the inevitable progress towards stationariness.

Suppose that this "gravitation . . . is happily checked at repeated intervals" by a constant rate of technical progress ($m = \frac{1}{2}$ per cent, as before). The new version of the Ricardian line $n_2 = y_2$ will lie above the old by the distance OC, which is $\dfrac{m}{1-\beta}$.[9] At the point (2) where the new line intersects the growth line of capital, technical progress is exactly balanced against diminishing returns, and output per head is constant with a growth rate of about $2\frac{1}{2}$ per cent. So instead of gravitating towards the origin, the economy if necessary levitates to this stable equilibrium point. Ricardo would no doubt object that if population is supposed to grow for ever at $2\frac{1}{2}$ per cent, it is very likely that at some point diminishing returns will set in with a violence not allowed for in our production function.

Given the proposition that at *some* standard of living (for the purpose of the foregoing argument it may be low or high) population will multiply fully in proportion with output, there is perhaps something to be said for the classical "law" of historically diminishing returns. It is in relation to the Malthusian postulate that the classical

9. This is obtained by putting $y = n$ in $y = \alpha s \dfrac{Y}{K} + \beta n + m$.

vision failed most signally. Suppose then that each generation demands samething better for its children: population is regulated so as to achieve, not a given living standard, but a progressive annual improvement of q per cent. The new element q affects the growth line of labour (now the locus of all labour growth rates consistent with q per cent improvement in output per head) exactly as if q were subtracted from the rate of technical progress, m.[10] Assuming q to be as little as $\frac{1}{4}$ per cent, the new growth lines n_3 and y_3 determine an equilibrium growth rate of labour of about $1\frac{1}{2}$ per cent at the point (3).

Growth lines such as n_1, n_2, and n_3 can be considered, not as time-paths which on various improbable assumptions the economy would follow towards an equilibrium point, but rather as a grid that divides the economic map into characteristic zones of improvement or determination in output per head. Every point on the map represents a particular conjunction of a labour growth rate with an output-capital ratio. In Figure 2, any point to the south and east of n_1 is a situation in which output per head is rising even if there is no technical progress. Between n_1 and n_3 output per head in the absence of technical progress would be falling, but with the assumed $\frac{1}{2}$ per cent technical progress it is rising by more than $\frac{1}{4}$ per cent. Between n_3 and n_2 the rise is less than $\frac{1}{4}$ per cent. A labour growth rate that strays to the north and west of n_2 incurs a decline in output per head, unless technical progress is greater than $\frac{1}{2}$ per cent.

A higher saving ratio, even though it does not change the growth rate at any of the so-called equilibrium points, swings the whole grid to the north and west. As a result, there is a larger area of desirable situations to the south and east of any given criterion of improvement, and a smaller area of undesirable situations to the north and west.

4. *The Harrod Model*

The model used above differs from Harrod's model of economic growth only in that it systematizes the relations between the "warranted" and "natural" rates of growth, and introduces land as a fixed factor.

Any point on the growth line of capital, $s\dfrac{Y}{K}$, is Harrod's warranted rate of growth $G_w = \dfrac{s}{C_r}$, since the output-capital ratio $\dfrac{Y}{K}$ at any given level is the reciprocal of Harrod's capital coefficient C_r. The corresponding point on the growth line of output is Harrod's natural rate of growth G_n. At an equilibrium point, where the two growth lines intersect, the warranted and natural rates of growth are equal.

10. The obtained by putting $y = n + q$ in the formula of the last footnote.

At any other point the wage rate and the profit rate are moving in such a way as to induce entrepreneurs to adjust the output-capital ratio in the direction which will bring the warranted and natural rates of growth together. Specifically, a reduction in the output-capital ratio (an increase in Harrod's C_r) always involves a decline in the rate of profit, and this automatically implies the appropriate movement of the wage rate.

Harrod envisages exactly the same mechanism of adjustment, *via* the "deepening" factor, d, which "may have a positive value because the rate of interest is falling". He argues that natural market forces cannot be expected to achieve the desired results, but does not despair that Keynesian policies may be successful. Nevertheless some of his readers seem to have been misled into the belief that in Harrod's model equality between the warranted and the natural rates of growth can occur only "by a fluke".[11] Harrod's own view is stated very clearly:

"Our aim should be to get such a progressive reduction in the rate of interest that $G_w\ C_r = s - d = G_n C_r$. If d is positive, C_r will increase through time, and may eventually become so great as to enable us to dispense with d. At that point interest need fall no further."[12]

The mechanism of Figures 1 and 2 merely makes explicit what this statement implies.

T. W. Swan

Australian National University,
Canberra.

APPENDIX: NOTES ON CAPITAL[1]

I   Joan Robinson's Puzzle.
II   The Wicksell Effect.
III   Åkerman's Problem.
IV   The Wicksell Effect in Reverse.

I. *Joan Robinson's Puzzle*

If we had to put up a scarecrow (as Joan Robinson calls it) to keep off the index-number birds and Joan Robinson herself, it would look something like this: Labour and Land are homogeneous man-

---

11. Joan Robinson, *The Accumulation of Capital*, p. 405.
12. *Towards A Dynamic Economics*, p. 96.

1. These notes are concerned with certain difficulties in the idea of Capital as a factor of production that were first seen by Wicksell and have now been greatly elaborated by Joan Robinson in two articles (*Review of Economic Studies* 1953-54, and *Economic Journal* 1955) and in her book, *The Accumulation of Capital*. See also the articles by D. G. Champernowne and R. F. Kahn, and by D. G. Champernowne, in the same number of *R.E.S.*, and by R. M. Solow in *R.E.S.* 1955-56. The criticism here ventured is in no sense a book review: it touches on only one aspect of a very important book, and in relation to the text above is best regarded as a face-saving gesture.

hours and acres respectively; Capital is made up of a large number of identical meccano sets, which never wear out and can be put together, taken apart, and reassembled with negligible cost or delay in a great variety of models so as to work with various combinations of Labour and Land, to produce various products, and to incorporate the latest technical innovations illustrated in successive issues of the Instruction Book; Output consists of goods (including meccano sets) that are all produced and sold at constant price-ratios amongst themselves, no matter how the rates of wages, rents, and profits may vary— e.g. they are all produced by similar (but continuously variable) combinations of Labour, Land, and Capital, with similar efficiency, and under similar competitive conditions; Saving = Investment = Accumulation is the current output of meccano sets, and can always be measured (by virtues of the constant price-ratios) at a constant value per meccano set in terms of peanuts or any other consumption product forgone: etc. With assumptions of this kind, the basic model of the text could be rigorously established in a form that would deceive nobody.

Fortunately, economists have usually been willing to hope that even very complicated aggregates like Output might somehow still contain, for some purposes, a rough kernel of meaning ''in an index-number sense''—a meaning not literally dependent upon the fantastic assumptions required to avoid all index-number ambiguities. Joan Robinson[2] has spoilt this game for us by insisting that the social Capital, considered as a factor of production accumulated by saving, cannot be given *any* operative meaning—not even in the abstract conditions of a stationary state.

2. The following passages are from the first of Joan Robinson's articles (*R.E.S.* 1953-54, pp. 81 and 82):

"The student of economic theory is taught to write $O = f(L, C)$ where L is a quantity of labour, C a quantity of capital and O a rate of output of commodities. He is instructed to assume all workers alike, and to measure L in man-hours of labour; he is told something about the index-number problem involved in choosing a unit of output; and then he is hurried on to the next question, in the hope that he will forget to ask in what units C is measured. Before ever he does ask, he has become a professor, and so sloppy habits of thought are handed on from one generation to the next. . . .

When we are discussing accumulation, it is natural to think of capital as measured in terms of product. The process of accumulation consists in refraining from consuming current output in order to add to the stock of wealth. But when we consider what addition to productive resources a given amount of accumulation makes, we must measure capital in labour units, for the addition to the stock of productive equipment made by adding an increment of capital depends upon how much work is done in constructing it, not upon the cost, in terms of final product, of an hour's labour. Thus, as we move from one point on a production function to another, measuring capital in terms of product, we have to know the product-wage rate in order to see the effect upon production of changing the ratio of capital to labour. Or if we measure in labour units, we have to know the product-wage in order to see how much accumulation would be required to produce a given increment of capital. But the wage rate alters with the ratio of the factors: one symbol, C, cannot stand both for a quantity of product and a quantity of labour time."

That there should be great difficulties in handling the concept of Capital in a process of change is not surprising. A piece of durable equipment or a pipe-line of work-in-progress has dimensions in time that bind together sequences of inputs and outputs jointly-demanded or jointly-supplied at different dates.[3] The aggregation of capital into a single stock at a point of time is thus the correlative of an aggregation of the whole economic process, not only in cross-section (which gives rise to the ordinary index-number problems), but also in time itself: in other words, the reduction of a very high-order system of lagged equations—in which each event, its past origins and its future consequences, could be properly dated and traced backward and forward in time—to a more manageable system with fewer lags. This second kind of aggregation introduces a further set of ambiguities, similar in principle to those of index-numbers, but as yet hardly investigated.[4] Our scarecrow assumptions dodge both sets of ambiguities—the first because all price-ratios within Output are held constant, the second because Capital, in the form of meccano sets, is both infinitely durable and instantaneously adaptable. This is an extreme of aggregation. From the idea of capital as a single stock there is in principle no sudden transition to "the enormous who's who of all the goods in existence"[5]. Between the two extremes lies an ascending scale of nth-order dynamic systems, in which capital like everything else is more and more finely subdivided and dated, with ascending degrees of (potential) realism and (actual) complexity. In fact, most of us are left at ground-level, on ground that moves under our feet.

In a stationary state, all the complexities of dating disappear. Related inputs and outputs, investments and returns, events and expectations, may be generations removed, but what happens at any time

3. Like the wool and mutton of Marshall's sheep (Wicksell, *Lectures,* Vol. 1, p. 260).

4. By what test should the (relative) success of a proposed scheme of aggregation be judged? Probably, by some measure of the degree of preservation of the dominant behaviour patterns which would be represented in the linear case by the larger roots of an appropriate high-order micro-system; surely not by the degree of "realism" of the scarecrow assumptions necessary to give literal validity to the low-order macro-system. In the present context, we are saved the trouble of trying to apply the suggested criterion by the fact that no appropriate micro-system is available (no one has yet set *Value and Capital* in motion, except under assumptions almost as rigidly fantastic as our own scarecrow). The puzzle may actually be easier if there are strong non-linear features (floors, ceilings, thresholds, etc.), since these sometimes lead to a limited number of highly charactertistic patterns of behaviour.

If the hands of a clock give a fair approximation to the even flow of time, in spite of the diminishing force exerted by the spring as it unwinds, our thanks are due to the discontinuous, non-linear mechanism of the escapement. This result is achieved at the price of an ambiguity—the finite intervals between ticks. Even the best clock is a mere scarecrow model of Time, and absurdly unrealistic from the viewpoint of the General Theory of Relativity. A bad clock that still ticks, or a good one wrongly set, may mean that its user misses the bus.

5. Joan Robinson, *R.E.S.* 1953-54, pp. 83-85.

is exactly repeated at any other time. No information is lost and no ambiguity created by aggregating all times into an eternal present; the shadows of past and future appear only in the form of profit steadily accruing at the ruling rate of interest on the time-consuming investment processes of which every moment has its share. Joan Robinson still insists that Capital cannot be given a meaning conformable with those neo-classical exercises in comparative statics for which the stationary state is expressly designed. In particular, Capital cannot be put into a production function from which, given the supplies of Labour and Land, under perfect-competition profit-maximization assumptions, the equilibrium rates of real wages, rent, and profit may be deduced in the form of marginal productivities. If this scheme is unworkable in a stationary state, it can hardly be sensible to retain it in a dynamic model (like that of our text).

From the various accounts given by Joan Robinson it is not easy to pick out the "basic fallacy" of the marginal productivity scheme. In the passage already quoted[6] she makes the novel suggestion that the production function itself works only if the stock of capital is measured by its value in wage-units, in which case it becomes useless for explaining the equilibrium factor-rewards. But it soon appears that, whatever may be the defects of the neo-classical production function, one geared to what Champernowne calls J.R. units can produce only mental and diagrammatic contortions. (Are there perhaps signs in *The Accumulation of Capital* of the reluctant beginnings of regret for this aberration?)

Frequently Joan Robinson seems to be explaining the factor-rewards by a widow's cruse type of distribution theory.[7] At first sight, it is not altogether clear whether she puts this forward as an independent explanation, or is merely exhibiting the other side of the double-entry national income accounts, which of course always balance in exact confirmation of the theory.[8] Before long, the reader begins

---

6. p. 344, note 2.

7. The widow's cruse theory of distribution is set out by Nicholas Kaldor (who calls it the Keynesian theory) in *R.E.S.* 1955-56. p. 94 ff. Briefly, the theory says that, given the ratio of investment to income, and given the propensities to save out of profits and wages respectively, the distribution of income between profits and wages must be such as to make the saving ratio equal the investment ratio. For examples see *The Accumulation of Capital* pp. 48, 75-83, 255, 271, 312, 331.

8. Consider the following example of widow's cruse reasoning (*The Accumulation of Capital,* p. 312):

"The relation of the rate of profit to the marginal product of investment is seen in its simplest form in the imagined state of bliss, where the highest technique known is already in operation throughout the economy and population is constant. The marginal product of investment is then zero. If there is no consumption out of profit (and no saving out of wages or rents) the rate of profit also is zero, and the wages and rent bill absorbs the whole annual output.

But if there is consumption out of profits (and no saving out of rent or wages) the rate of profit remains positive, for the prices of commodities (in

to understand that this profoundly arithmetical organon is not a rival economic calculus, but a subsidiary device that applies, as it were, only in blank spots on the map of economic calculation.[9] In Joan Robinson's world, the blanks are enlarged into great zones marked out by frontier-lines of technical discontinuity. Typically, all products are consumed in fixed proportions and capable of being produced by a single discontinuous "hierarchy of techniques"; each technique has its own fixed factor-proportions, which are rigidly unadaptable; techniques displace each other in profitability across iso-cost "frontiers" defined by well-separated critical sets of factor-rewards; any frontier applies uniformly and simultaneously to every industry throughout the economy.[10] Only at the frontier between two techniques is economic calculation, or the Principle of Substitution, fully effective. Within each zone (i.e. within the limits of the critical sets of factor-rewards along its frontiers) almost anything may happen.

The paradoxes and fabulous histories that enliven *The Accumulation of Capital* have their licence in these extremes of discontinuity. They are not the consequence of any special feature of Joan Robinson's view of capital or of the marginal calculus. When eventually

---

relation to money wages and rents) are such that their total selling value exceeds their total costs by the amount of expenditure out of profits. The total of real wages then falls short of total output by the amount of consumption of rentiers, that is, of purchase of commodities out of profit and rent incomes."

It is possible to clarify the two cases distinguished in these paragraphs. In a state of bliss with constant population investment is zero. Since therefore the amount saved has to be zero, any positive profit-saving propensity, whether unity or less, certainly precludes a positive amount of profits; so the second paragraph must refer only to a zero profit-saving propensity, as in effect its two sentences twice affirm (profits = selling value − (wages + rents) = consumption out of profits). Keeping the assumption of no saving out of wages or rents, the meaning of Joan Robinson's two cases may now be rendered as follows:

(i) If the capitalists save some part of any profits they may get, they get no profit, *either* because the rate of profit on capital employed is zero *or* because their saving propensity "multiplies" output itself down to zero (bliss becomes Nirvana).

(ii) If the capitalists consume the whole of any profits they may get, their profits equal the amount they consume, which is positive if they get any profits to consume. (The reason for this ham and eggs dictum is supplied by Kaldor, *R.E.S.* 1955-56, p. 95.)

The marginal productivity theory, on the other hand, infers that in a state of bliss the rate of profit is zero: capital has become a free good, and full employment output is blissfully consistent with zero profits. The true contribution of Kenesian theory is to point out that in these circumstances any positive saving propensity *out of wages or rents* is inconsistent with full employment output.

9. Just as the multiplier theory (to which the widow's cruse is closely related) applies when aggregate economic calculation is suspended by Keynesian unemployment.

10. Note how "realistic" it seems to allow for technical discontinuities (one thinks of coke-ovens, blast furnaces, etc.). The end-result in Joan Robinson's model is that the opportunities for substitution are limited in any situation to a single, universal choice between two techniques; and this restriction becomes the dominant feature of the economy as a whole. The "neo-classical vice of implicit theorising" has here its counterpart in the vice of *explicit realism*.

she considers a primitive agricultural economy in which continuous factor substitution is for once allowed,[11] her theory runs familiarly in terms of discounted products, following Wicksell. Again, when she indulges in some pronouncements concerning the nature of the factor of production and their marginal products, the substance of her thoughts is recognizable as that of the so-called Austrian view of the rôle of capital and time in production, more especially in the form which it was given by Wicksell.[12]

To find the kernel of Joan Robinson's meaning, it is best to go back to Wicksell,[13] to whose ideas she pays repeated and generous tribute. Part II of this appendix examines the problem from Wicksell's viewpoint. But first look again at the early Joan Robinson polemic against the neo-classical scheme (quoted on p. 344), and consider four comments:

1. The value of a stock of capital "in terms of product" is no more plausible than its value in J.R. units as an input to be fed into a production function. If Capital is to be treated, from a productive viewpoint, on all fours with Labour and Land, it must somehow be measured "in terms of its own technical unit",[14] in spite of the obvious difficulties. (In our scarecrow model, it is the *number* of meccano sets, along with the number of manhours and acres, that directly determines the volume of Output—not their value in terms of anything, although it happens that in our model the value of a meccano set in terms of product is constant.)

Joan Robinson is correct in so far as she is complaining that the neo-classical tradition contains no indication of how a "technical unit" for capital may be devised.

---

11. *The Accumulation of Capital*, pp. 291-292. "This . . . is purely a repetition of our former argument in a simpler setting."

12. *The Accumulation of Capital*, pp. 310-311. Cf. Wicksell, *Lectures*, p. 150.

13. If I were advising a student on a method of approach to *The Accumulation of Capital*, I would recommend the following preparations: (1) Re-read the whole of Wicksell's *Lectures*, Vol. 1. (2) Concentrate in particular on a full understanding of the discontinuous "exception" described by Wicksell in the last complete paragraph on page 177; this sets the stage for Joan Robinson's book. (3) Read the two articles by D. M. Bensusan-Butt, *Oxford Economic Papers*, September, 1954, and *American Economic Review*, September, 1954, for an analysis which in several respects anticipates Joan Robinson, but in terms of a much simpler, and also more flexible, model.

14. Wicksell, *Lectures*, p. 149. Wicksell rejected the possibility of employing such a unit, partly because he could see no way of combining the different kinds of "tools, machinery, and materials, etc." in a "unified treatment" (though he did not shrink from treating labour, land, and product as if each were homogeneous), and partly because he believed at the time that the Walrasian solution of the pricing of newly-produced capital goods involved "arguing in a circle". This latter problem, he thought, would still have to be solved before the "yield" of particular capital goods could be linked up with the rate of interest. Later (cf. *Lectures*, p. 226) he seems to have realised that this criticism was mistaken. The circularity that worried Wicksell (the fact that the rate of interest enters as a cost in the production of capital goods themselves) is merely another aspect of the mutual inter-dependence of all variables in the Walrasian system. For a similar example, see p. 357.

2. On the other hand, there is an ambiguity in her view that capital "measured in terms of product" goes naturally with a discussion of accumulation because "accumulation consists in refraining from consuming current output in order to add to the stock of wealth". What is the addition to the stock of wealth that is made by current accumulation? It is not the *change in the value* of the stock, measured in terms of product, but rather the *value of the change*, measured in terms of product, i.e. the (real) value of the current output not consumed, and so added to the stock. Only the latter element corresponds with the idea of accumulation, unless current output, income, saving, and investment are defined to include current revaluations of the pre-existing stock of capital goods—which is not the conventional usage.[15]

Joan Robinson apparently takes it for granted that the value of the capital stock in terms of product is the same thing as the cumulated value (the time-integral) of investment and saving in terms of product. The two measures may in fact diverge very widely, if there is any change in relative values between "capital goods" and "product": in the first measure, every such change is reflected in an immediate revaluation of the whole capital stock; in the second, the capital stock is recorded as a "perpetual inventory" accumulated by saving at original cost in terms of product. The first measure is certainly Wicksell's. The second is the neo-classical tradition—or rather the tradition of all the economists from Adam Smith to Keynes who have thought of current output as being divided between consumption on the one hand and additions to the capital stock (saving, investment, accumulation) on the other. In a stationary equilibrium, the two measures coincide: but they part company even for infinitesimal variations at the margin of a stationary state, if those variations involve any change in relative values between "capital goods" and "product."

3. A measure of the capital stock in its own technical unit—if that were feasible, as with meccano sets—is of course not the same thing as either of the two measures "in terms of product". When capital is measured in meccano sets, its marginal productivity—the rate of increase of product with respect to the number of meccano sets employed—does not correspond in equilibrium with the ruling rate of profit (the rate of interest), but with that rate multiplied

15. The value changes that accrue as "depreciation" are of course allowed for in the conventional definitions, but we are here concerned with quite a different issue. The relevant distinction is often made explicit in national income statistics in the form of an *inventory revaluation adjustment*. This adjustment is made only in respect of inventories, since revaluations of other capital assets are not included in the figures in the first place.

by the value of a meccano set in terms of product.[16] At the same time, the rate of increase in the number of meccano sets is the current rate of saving divided by the value of a meccano set. Thus for the purpose of any marginal calculation in which the value of a meccano set enters as a constant, Capital may be measured in terms of product (as the accumulation of saving), and its marginal productivity will then correspond with the rate of profit.

This is the *rationale* of the neo-classical procedure. Two elements of calculation are involved, and in both the value of a meccano set is correctly taken as constant: (a) a maximization process in which all prices, including the price of meccano sets, are treated in perfect competition as constant parameters, and (b) a marginal increment of accumulation—the translation of a small amount of product by saving into additional meccano sets—in which the "error" in measuring the capital stock arising from an associated marginal change in the value of a meccano set is confined to the marginal addition being made to the capital stock, and so is of "the second order of smalls". (The revaluation of the pre-existing stock, which occurs in the measure of capital in terms of product that Joan Robinson has in mind, is of a very different order.)

As soon as this point is accepted, it follows that the neo-classical procedure does not, after all, depend on the existence of a "technical unit" of capital—the meccano set—the value of which is in any case cancelled out. For marginal variations about the stationary equilibrium position—i.e. for all the purposes of the neo-classical theory— the natural unit of Capital is simply "an equilibrium dollar's worth" regardless of the physical variety of capital goods, and regardless of marginal value-changes or marginal adaptations of capital towards different physical forms.[17]

4. The foregoing argument is evidently quite symmetrical with respect to every factor and indeed every product: at the margin of a stationary state, Capital, Labour, Land, and Output can each be measured in terms of "an equilibrium dollar's worth". From the "tangency" and "convexity" conditions prevailing at the equilibrium point—by virtue of the first and second-order conditions of the economic maximization process—all valid theorems (as Samuelson might say) can then be deduced. In the given unit, aggregation is

16. To the profit-maximising, cost-minimising entrepreneur, the cost of the annual services of a meccano set, comparable with the real wage in terms of product which is the cost of the annual services of a unit of labour, is the annual interest bill on the price of a meccano set in terms of product.

17. This is essentially the familiar principle which Samuelson calls the Wong-Viner-Harrod envelope theorem (P. A. Samuelson, *The Foundation of Economic Analysis*, pp. 34, 66n, 243; also in *R.E.S.* 1953-54, p. 5). See also Marshall (rebuking J. A. Hobson), *Principles*, p. 409n.

itself quite superficial: the equalities and inequalities that hold for the aggregates at the equilibrium point hold uniformly in terms of "an equilibrium dollar's worth" of every possible subdivision of factor and product right down to the level of the individual firm. That is why the neo-classical theory often appears to be both aggregative and exact.

However, this achievement involves an inherent limitation, against which Joan Robinson has all along been tilting. The theory tells us something about the properties of an equilibrium point, but it gives no information in finite terms about one point in relation to any other point.[18] For instance, it does not enable us to "draw" the hypothetical isoquants of a production function combining (say) Capital and Labour. All we know, from the neo-classical or any similar theory, is certain curvative properties that must hold at any point that is capable of being an equilibrium point. Assuming one such point, we are entitled to draw an invisibly small segment of a curve with the known properties—a grin without a cat. Yet why should we expect a theory to produce even a hypothetical cat? The trouble is that if we were supplied with all the hypotheses or empirical data in the world, we should still be puzzled to draw the rest of the curve, because we should want each point on it to be a potential equilibrium point, whereas our unit—"an equilibrium dollar's worth"—is defined only for a single equilibrium point, and changes its character at any point separated by a finite distance from the first. It may do no harm to sketch in a metaphorical curve, provided the argument touches only a single equilibrium point and its immediate neighbourhood. On these terms, "comparative statics" is a misnomer: not different situations, but only "virtual" displacements at the margin of one situation, can be considered.

For structural comparisons "in the large" (e.g. as between two stationary states with different factor endowments), either the variables must be measurable in naturally homogeneous technical units (like meccano sets and manhours), or else some artificial means must be found to co-ordinate measurements made at different points. For the latter purpose, Champernowne has proposed the use of a *chain index*,[19] an approach which is entirely in keeping with the true character of aggregative analysis. Champernowne's chain index, as presented, looks like a rather *ad hoc* and specialized device to cope with Joan Robinson's difficulties. The next part of these notes is intended to show how a chain index of capital emerges naturally from the analysis of a simple problem considered by Wicksell.

18. In a footnote (*The Accumulation of Capital*, p. 414n.) Joan Robinson says something rather like this.
19. *R.E.S.* 1953-54, p. 112.

II. *The Wicksell Effect*

Joan Robinson finds extraordinary significance in Wicksell's demonstration that an increase in the social capital is partly "absorbed by increased wages (and rent), so that only the residue . . . is really effective as far as a rise in production is concerned".[20] "The amount of employment offered by a given value of capital depends upon the real-wage rate. At a lower wage rate there is a smaller value of a given type of machine."[21] To its discoverer, the *Wicksell effect* seemed mainly important as an obstacle to the acceptance of "von Thünen's thesis", the marginal productivity theory of interest. To Joan Robinson, "this point of Wicksell's is the key to the whole theory of accumulation and of the determination of wages and profits".[22]

To identify the Wicksell effect we may re-work very briefly his "point-input, point-output" case.[23] For Wicksell's grape-juice we substitute labour, imagining a productive process in which the application of an amount of labour N at a point of time results after a "period of production" t in a final output Q which is greater the longer the period of production allowed. Other variables are the real wage rate w, the value of capital in the form of goods-in-process K (both w and K measured in terms of product), and the competitive rate of interest or profit r. Interest is instantaneously compounded; e is the base of natural logarithms. Wicksell's main equations then appear as follows:

$$(1) \quad Q = Nf(t) \qquad (2) \quad w = \frac{Q}{N}\, e^{-rt} \qquad (3) \quad r = \frac{f'(t)}{f(t)}$$

$$(4a) \quad K = Nw \int_{o}^{t} e^{rx}\, dx = Nw\, \frac{e^{rt} - 1}{r}$$

$$(4b) \quad K = \frac{Q - Nw}{r}$$

Equation (1) is the production function, showing output per unit of labour as an increasing function $f(t)$ of the period of production. Equations (2) and (3) flow from (1) under perfect-competition profit-maximization assumptions: the wage rate is the discounted product per unit of labour, and the interest rate the (relative) "marginal productivity of waiting". Equation (4a) evaluates K from the cost side as the wages bill continuously invested in production and

20. *Lectures*, p. 268.
21. *The Accumulation of Capital*, p. 391.
22. *The Accumulation of Capital*, p. 396.
23. *Lectures*, pp. 172-181, and in particular pp. 178-180. In the following re-formulation, nothing material is changed. The reader is referred to Wicksell for further explanations. Where our symbols differ from his, the equivalents are: $\frac{Q}{N} = W, N = V_{o}, r = \rho$. Wicksell's "one hectolitre of grape-juice", which does not appear explicitly, is our N, but the change is only formal. Our numbering of the equations is not the same as Wicksell's. For the mathematics of this case, see R. G. D. Allen, *Mathematical Analysis for Economists*, pp. 248, 362, 403.

cumulated at compound interest over the period t; while (4b), using (1) and (2), shows that K is also the capitalized value of total profits $Q - Nw$. Using the second-order maximization condition upon $f(t)$, Wicksell proved that in equilibrium (for given N) increasing K necessarily means increasing w, decreasing r, and increasing t. In Joan Robinson's language, increasing t represents a higher ''degree of mechanization'', made profitable as w increases—the *Ricardesque effect*.

Differentiating (1) and (4a) or (4b) while holding N constant, Wicksell next derived a formula for the rate of increase of Q with respect to K. This formula can be expressed in four distinct ways:

$$\text{(5a)} \quad \frac{dQ}{dK} = r - K\left(\frac{r}{w}\frac{dw}{dK} + \left(\frac{rt}{1-e^{-rt}} - 1\right)\frac{dr}{dK}\right)$$

$$\text{(5b)} \quad = r + \left(K\frac{dr}{dK} + N\frac{dw}{dK}\right)$$

$$\text{(5c)} \quad = r + (K - Nwt)\frac{dr}{dK}$$

$$\text{(5d)} \quad = r - \left(\frac{K - Nwt}{wt}\right)\frac{dw}{dK}$$

The second term in these expressions is always negative—i.e. the ''marginal productivity of capital'' in this sense is always less than the rate of interest, part of the increase in K having been ''unproductively absorbed''. This is the Wicksell effect. Our four versions suggest that it is somewhat misleading to ascribe the ''absorption'' simply to increased wages. Version (a) shows the Wicksell effect from the viewpoint of the *cost* of the capital stock (4a), as the consequence of a higher wage rate only partly offset by a lower interest rate. Version (b), from the viewpoint of *capitalized profits* (4b), shows it as the consequence of a lower interest rate only partly offset by a higher wage rate. Versions (c) and (d) use the relation between r and w given in (2) to attribute the whole Wicksell effect on the one hand to a lower interest rate, and on the other hand to a higher wage rate. The multiplicity of explanations shows how treacherous is the idea of causation amongst interdependent variables.

Yet the different versions of the Wicksell effect have one common feature which is itself a complete explanation. To see this, we first write out the logarithmic total differential of (4a) and (4b), giving four alternative expressions for a (proprotional) change in the value of capital to parallel the four versions of (5):

$$\text{(6a)} \quad \frac{dK}{K} = \left[\frac{dN}{N} + \frac{rt}{1-e^{-rt}}\frac{dt}{t}\right] + \left[\frac{dw}{w} + \left(\frac{rt}{1-e^{-rt}} - 1\right)\frac{dr}{r}\right]$$

$$\text{(6b)} \quad = \left[\frac{Q}{Kr}\frac{dQ}{Q} - \frac{Nw}{Kr}\frac{dN}{N} \right] - \left[\frac{Nw}{Kr}\frac{dw}{w} + \frac{dr}{r} \right]$$

$$\text{(6c)} \quad = \left[\quad'' \quad\quad '' \quad \right] - \left[\frac{K - Nwt}{K}\frac{dr}{r} \right]$$

$$\text{(6d)} \quad = \left[\quad'' \quad\quad '' \quad \right] + \left[\frac{K - Nwt}{Krt}\frac{dw}{w} \right]$$

Here the terms are grouped by the square brackets into two columns. The first column shows the component of a change in the value of capital due to "productive" features (more labour, a longer period of production, greater output). The second column shows the component due to "financial" features (changes in the wage and interest rates). It is easy to verify that the different versions in each column are vertically equivalent: i.e. the "productive" component and the "financial" component of a change in K are respectively the same, whether considered (a) in terms of cost or (b) in terms of capitalization, and in the case of the "financial" element whether ascribed (c) to an interest change or (d) to a wage change. Let us make this distinction explicit by defining two synthetic variable, k and p, with the following properties at a certain equilibrium point:

$$\text{(7)} \quad kp = K$$

$$\text{(8a)} \; \frac{dk}{k} = \frac{dN}{N} + \frac{1 - e^{-rt}}{rt}\frac{dt}{t} \quad \text{(8b)} \frac{dp}{p} = \frac{dw}{w} + \left(\frac{rt}{1 - e^{-rt}} - 1 \right)\frac{dr}{r}$$

In these definitions, K is broken into two components which may be interpreted as a "quantity" k, and a "price" (in terms of product) p; $\frac{dk}{k}$ is identified with the first column of (6), and $\frac{dp}{p}$ with the second column. The stated properties cannot hold generally, because the product of the integrals of (8a) and (8b) is not, in general, K. Nevertheless the definitions involve no contradiction if they are restricted to a particular set of equilibrium values of w, r, and t—namely, those prevailing at the equilibrium point for which in any particular case the differentials in (5) or (6) are also calculated. We shall return in a moment to the question of integrating (8a) and (8b) so as to define k and p for other points.

Next we can put $dK = K\left(\frac{dk}{k} + \frac{dp}{p} \right) = pdk + kdp$ in (5a), and arrange the result as follows:

$$\text{(5a')} \; \frac{dQ}{pdk} = r + \frac{kr}{dk}\left(\frac{dp}{p} - \frac{dw}{w} - \left(\frac{rt}{1 - e^{-rt}} - 1 \right)\frac{dr}{r} \right)$$

According to the definition of $\frac{dp}{p}$ in (8b), the second term—which previously showed the Wicksell effect—is now identically zero: when the increment of capital is taken as $K\frac{dk}{k}$, or pdk ("the value of the change"), its marginal productivity corresponds with the rate of interest. The same result can of course be obtained by a similar substitution in the other three versions of (5). Here is the common feature of all four versions of the Wicksell effect, that the effect disappears when the marginal change in capital is measured so as to exclude

$K\frac{dp}{p}$, or kdp, which is the revaluation of the capital stock resulting from an associated marginal change in wage and interest rates. *The Wicksell effect is nothing but an inventory revaluation.*

The wage rate, previously given by (2) as the average product of labour discounted over the period of production, may now also be derived as the marginal productivity of labour. Differentiating (1), using (3), and substituting for dt from (8a), we obtain:

$$(9)\quad \frac{dQ}{Q} = e^{-rt}\frac{dN}{N} + (1 - e^{-rt})\frac{dk}{k}$$

By (1), (2), and (4b), the two coefficients in (9) are the proportional shares of wages and profits in output, $\frac{Nw}{Q}$ and $\frac{Kr}{Q}$, respectively. Therefore:

$$(10)\quad dQ = wdN + rpdk$$

Accordingly, when the quantity of capital k is held constant, $w = \frac{dQ}{dN}$.

The component pdk is the value at ruling prices (in terms of product) of an increment of capital goods, and so corresponds with the usual idea of investment, saving, or accumulation. It may be convenient to call $\frac{dQ}{pdk}$ ($=r$) the *marginal efficiency of investment*, reserving the term *marginal productivity of capital* for $\frac{dQ}{dk}$ ($=rp$). In relation to our earlier discussion, dk is an increment of capital measured "in terms of its own technical unit" (like meccano sets), while pdk is an increment measured in terms of "an equilibrium dollar's worth".

But we are now a step forward. The definitions of k and p in (7) and (8) can be recognized in their essential character as the differential definitions of *chain indexes* of quality and price, by which Divisia provided "an elegant logical justification" of Marshall's original invention of the chain index.[24] Thus although (8a) and (8b) cannot

24. Ragnar Frisch, *Econometrica* 1936, pp. 7-8. The elementary index-number formula used to construct each link of the chain will vary, as Frisch points out, "according as we choose the approximation principle for the steps of the numerical integration".

usually be integrated to give exact measures of k and p, such that $kp = K$ at every point, they can in principle be integrated numerically in successive small "links" (correcting the weights as each link is added) so as to form a consistent pair of chain indexes of the "quantity" and "price" of capital. With these indexes approximate structural comparisons "in the large" between different equilibrium situations may be made. The index k enters with N in the production function, while the index p measures for each point of the production function the amount of accumulation in terms of product necessary to achieve a given addition to k—in effect, converting "an equilibrium dollar's worth" at one point into its productive equivalent at another point.

This operation can most easily be visualized by considering a special case in which (8a) and (8b) lend themselves to exact integration—namely, the case in which the function $f(t)$ is of constant elasticity, and may be written $f(t) = t^a$. Then by (3) $rt = a$. The proportional share of profits in output is also now a constant, which it is convenient to write $1 - e^{-rt} = \beta$. Therefore (8a) and (8b) become

$$(8a') \quad \frac{dk}{k} = \frac{dN}{N} + \frac{a}{\beta} \frac{dt}{t} \qquad (8b') \quad \frac{dp}{p} = \frac{dw}{w} + \left(\frac{a}{\beta} - 1\right) \frac{dr}{r}$$

and in this form they give immediately the integrals

$$(a') \quad k = C_1 \, N t^{\frac{a}{\beta}} \qquad (b') \quad p = C_2 \, wr^{\left(\frac{a}{\beta} - 1\right)}$$

where C_1 and C_2 are constants of integration.[25] The production function (1) may now be expressed in terms of N and k, and its partial derivatives with respect to these factors of production will appear as w and rp:

$$(1') \quad Q = N^{1-\beta} \, k^{\beta} \qquad (2') \quad w = (1 - \beta)\frac{Q}{N} \qquad (3') \quad rp = \beta \frac{Q}{K}$$

Given the definitions of k and p in (a') and (b'), the new system is in all respects the equivalent of Wicksell's, as the reader may readily confirm by substitution. Although the wage rate w and the yield (or quasi-rent) of a unit of capital rp are derived from the new production function as the marginal productivities of labour and capital, it seems at first sight that in order to discover r we must know p, and vice-versa. However, in (b') there is another relation between

25 In order that k and p may satisfy (7) and (4), C_1 and C_2 must satisfy

$$C_1 \, C_2 = (e^a - 1) \, a^{-\frac{a}{\beta}}$$

It is convenient to choose units so that $C_1 = 1$. This choice accounts for the absence from (1') below of any explicit constant of integration.

w, r, and p, which enables r and p to be separately determined once the values of w and rp are given at any point of the production function.[26]

When the elasticity of $f(t)$ is not constant, this exact formulation in terms of k and p is no longer possible "in the large". Nevertheless the chain indexes of k and p are available as approximate measures, and they will play in principle the same role as k and p in the special case just considered.[27]

But why bother to show that with the help of chain indexes the neo-classical scheme can approximately mimic the solution of a highly artificial problem already obtained in an exact form by Wicksell? One answer is that Wicksell's analysis is exact only when K—the *value* of capital in terms of product—is taken as an independent variable. To consider the effect of a given amount of *accumulation*— the forgone consumption of a given amount of product—Wicksell too would have been driven to approximations and index-numbers. Another answer is that the elements which appear in our definitions of the indexes k and p are merely particular illustrations, drawn from Wicksell's model, of the "productive" and the "financial" attributes of capital goods that have to be distinguished in measuring their "quantity" and "price": index-number measurements may still be appropriate when capital does not take those particular forms which enabled Wicksell to specify its productive effect directly in terms of a period of time.

Wicksell himself thought of the period of production or period of investment as no more than a notional index of the time-aspect of capital—"a mathematical concept, without direct physical or psychic significance", but which "should, nevertheless, be retained as a concise general principle, reflecting the essence of productive capital".[28] If Joan Robinson will allow Wicksell in this spirit to draw a production function involving N, t, and (indirectly) K, she ought not to object if others prefer to draw one involving N, k, and (indirectly) p: for there is, as we have seen, a method by which one scheme may be translated into the other.

26. In this special case where the production function is such that the proportional share of each factor in output is constant, there is obviously no difficulty in extending the above analysis to cover any number of different factors of production. As far as I can see, the chain index approach in the general case also extends to any number of factors, provided that continuous adjustments in factor proportions are assumed to be possible. Champernowne (*R.E.S.* 1953-54, pp. 121-125, 132-135) shows that the chain index in general breaks down for more than two factors when techniques are discontinuous.

27. Of course a chain index is not necessarily a "better" approximation than some other kind of index-number. For the present purpose, however, the chain index in its Divisia formulation is very convenient, in that it shows a consistent way of making approximate measurements "in the large", while keeping the advantage of theoretical exactness "in the small".

28. *Lectures*, p. 184.

III. Åkerman's Problem

By the same method, Gustaf Åkerman's problem of durable capital equipment—as analysed by Wicksell in a celebrated essay[29]—can also be solved in accordance with the marginal productivity theory. Wicksell's analysis was mainly intended to refute Åkerman's claim that this could be done.

In the model which Wicksell developed for the purpose, capital consists of axes, which can be made more or less durable by putting more or less labour into their manufacture; the optimum life of an axe, n years, is chosen to maximize profits; the stock of axes in the stationary equilibrium is a "balanced equipment" with a uniform age distribution from o to n years; M labourers out of the total labour force A are occupied in replacing the nth part of the stock that wears out each year, while $A-M$ "free labourers" co-operate with the stock of axes to produce a (net) output π. K is the value of the stock of axes (in terms of product), l the wage rate, and ρ the rate of interest.[30]

K is evaluated by Wicksell in equation (15) p. 283. With one substitution from equation (4) p. 276, (15) becomes:

$$(15.1) \quad K = Mnl \left(\frac{1}{1 - e^{-\rho n}} - \frac{1}{\rho n} \right)$$

Here Mnl is the replacement cost of the whole stock of axes, while the bracketed expression can be recognized as the Champernowne-Kahn formula for the value of a "balanced equipment" as a proportion of its replacement cost.[31] Differentiating (15.1) as it stands, and

29. First published in Swedish in 1923, then republished in 1934 with the English edition of *Lectures*, Vol. 1, pp. 274-99). Until the Joan Robinson—Kahn—Champernowne papers of 1953-54, this essay seems to have been the only analysis available in English of the specific questions posed for (long-run) capital theory by durable, depreciable, capital equipment.

30. Wicksell's notation is preserved. In this case no attempt will be made to re-formulate Wicksell's model. Assuming that the interested reader will look up the original, we give the essentials of the argument with a minimum of incidental explanation.

31. Wicksell's derivation of (15) is explained by R. G. D. Allen, *Mathematical Analysis for Economists*, p. 405. The Champernowne-Kahn formula is derived by Champernowne and Kahn in four different ways (*R.E.S.* 1953-54, pp. 107-111). Joan Robinson reports in her preface that C. A. Blyth has derived it independently.

The underlying principle can be seen in graphical terms. The cost or value of a "machine" is equal to its future gross earnings discounted to the present moment. Given the prospective earnings at each point of its life, and given the rate of interest at which they are to be discounted, a curve showing the machine's value as a function of its age will fall from its starting-point at age o (replace-placement cost) down to zero at age n years when it falls to pieces. The average value of the machine *per year of life* is the area under the curve divided by n. A "balanced equipment" of such machines is of uniform age distribution from o to n, and so repeats in cross-section the life-history of a single machine. The average value *per machine* in a "balanced equipment" is therefore also the area under the curve divided by n. In the particular case when the earnings of a machine are at a constant rate throughout its life, the Champernowne-Kahn formula gives the ratio of this average value to the original value at age o.

then making a substitution from Wicksell's equation (9) p. 278, we obtain the logarithmic total differential of K:

$$(15.2) \quad \frac{dK}{K} = \left[\frac{dM}{M} + \frac{(1-\nu)\ (\nu + \phi(\nu))}{\nu + \phi(\nu) - 1} \frac{dn}{n} \right]$$
$$+ \left[\frac{dl}{l} + \left(\frac{1-\nu}{\nu + \phi(\nu) - 1} - \nu \right) \frac{d\rho}{\rho} \right]$$

The proportional change in the value of capital is split by the square brackets into a "productive" and a "financial" component, just as in (6a) of Part II. Again we identfy $\frac{dk}{k}$ with the first component, and $\frac{dp}{p}$ with the second. This time the distinction is easier to visualize. The "technical unit" of capital in which k is measured is in effect a *standard axe* (of given durability and age), while p is the value of such an axe, calculated at current wage and interest rates. This follows simply from the fact that the second component of (15.2) is the differential of (15.1) with respect to l and ρ, calculated as of constant M and n. In the present model the definition of a "standard axe" creates no index-number problems: Wicksell's constant elasticity formulae mean that the coefficients in (15.2) are constants, so that k and p can be obtained by direct integration as indexes with correct and constant weights at every point. Moreover, M is a constant proportion of the total labour force A (Wicksell, p. 287), and is therefore determined when A is taken as an independent variable.

The rest follows as in Part II—the Wicksell effect disappears, the production function[32] can be written in terms of A and k, etc. In fact, with an appropriate revision or re-interpretation of the various constants, our earlier equations (a'), (b'), (1'), (2'), and (3') will now serve as an exact representation in neo-classical form of Wicksell's analysis of Åkerman's problem.

IV. *The Wicksell Effect in Reverse*

One new feature emerges. In the model of Part II increasing K (or k) always means increasing p: the wage rate rises and the interest rate falls, but the net effect is necessarily a rise in the value of a unit of capital in terms of product. Thus the Wicksell effect is an apparent absorption of capital. However, in the model of Part III it turns out that the two components of (15.2) may very well be of

---

32. With k defined as above, it can be shown that the production function given by Wicksell in equation (17 *bis*) p. 287 is correctly reproduced by the integral of the following expression:

$$\frac{d\pi}{\pi} = \left(1 - \beta \frac{\nu + \phi(\nu) - 1}{\nu + \phi(\nu)} \right) \frac{dA}{A} + \beta \frac{\nu + \phi(\nu) - 1}{\nu + \phi(\nu)} \frac{dk}{k}$$

By Wicksell's assumptions, the coefficients are constants.

opposite sign. So long as the "convexity" conditions for profit maximization are satisfied, a higher wage rate and a lower interest rate must still accompany increasing K (or k), but the interest effect on p may now outweigh the wage effect.[33] The value of a "standard axe" may fall. *In this event the Wicksell effect goes into reverse.*

When Wicksell calculated $\frac{d\pi}{dK}$ he found again that by this measure Åkerman's and von Thünen's thesis was "not verified", but he found also that in his new model $\frac{d\pi}{dK}$ might actually exceed the rate of interest—i.e. he discovered the Wicksell effect in reverse. This phenomenon left Wicksell very puzzled, and caused him to admit that his previous explanation, in terms of the absorption of capital in increased wages, was "*not* general".[34]

Once it is realized that the Wicksell effect merely reflects a revaluation of the capital stock, it is no longer puzzling that it may go in either direction. When wages rise and interest falls, whether the value of a "standard axe" goes up or down in terms of product may be expected to turn (broadly speaking) on a comparison of the relative importance of the two factors for the axe on the one hand, and for the product on the other. In general, there is no presumption either way. But in Wicksell's previous models, before his analysis of Åkerman's problem, the product typically emerged only at the last and most "capitalistic" stage of production. In such models (as in Part II above) a higher wage rate and a lower interest rate must depress the final product, and elevate the goods-in-process at the earlier stages, in relative value. Hence Wicksell's surprise on finding himself at the age of 72 in a new world of durable capital equipment, in which this rule no longer applies.

33. Here we are looking at capital from the viewpoint of cost, as in (6a). It is possible as before to express $\frac{dp}{p}$ in terms of either the wage rate or the interest rate alone. For instance, corresponding with (6c), the second component of (15.2) may be written:

$$\frac{dp}{p} = -\left[\nu + \beta\,(1-\nu) - \frac{1-\nu}{\nu + \phi(\nu) - 1} \right] \frac{d\rho}{\rho}$$

The second-order maximization conditions imply that β and ν are each less than unity, and that the denominator of the third term is positive. But the sign of the sum within the brackets (which in (6c) is always positive) depends on the relative magnitudes of β and ν; it can be negative if β is small and ν neither very near unity nor very near zero.

34. pp. 292-293. It is interesting to note that Wicksell in these pages experimented with the possibility of adjusting his measure of the increase in capital, by deducting the effect of the rise in the wage rate, precisely as we have done in defining $\frac{dk}{k}$ and $\frac{dp}{p}$. He failed to reach the same conclusion only because he did not allow for the lower interest rate as well as for the higher wage rate.

What is more puzzling is why Joan Robinson thirty years later should write as if she and Wicksell were both back in the old world where capital was goods-in-process. Her rule that "at a lower wage rate there is a smaller value of a given type of machine" need not hold even for Wicksell's hand-made axe, far less for a typical machine, itself a capitalistic product.[35] The revaluation of a given machine in an opposite direction to the wage rate (in the same direction as the interest rate) is a reverse Wicksell effect, but there is nothing perverse about it[36], and in general it is just as likely to happen as its obverse, the original Wicksell effect.

Most puzzling of all is how the possibility of a shift in relative value between capital good and product *in an unpredictable direction* can become in Joan Robinson's hands "the key to the whole theory of accumulation and of the determination of wages and profits."

35. The influence of interest on the value of an axe is confined in (15.1) and (15.2) to the Champernowne-Kahn term of (15.1)—i.e. to the effect of the interest rate on the value of a "balanced equipment" of axes as a proportion of its replacement cost. The latter consists of labour cost alone. If axes were themselves made with the co-operation of capital, their replacement cost would also contain an interest element, and it would be much easier for the reverse Wicksell effect to occur.

36. The perverse case discussed by Joan Robinson, in which a higher wage rate and a lower interest rate make a *less* mechanized technique relatively profitable, has nothing to do with the direction of the Wicksell effect, though one might easily get the impression that Joan Robinson thinks it does (see *R.E.S.* 1953-54 pp. 95-96, 106, and *The Accumulation of Capital*, pp. 109-110, 147-148, 418). The perversity arises essentially from a failure over a certain range of the second-order ("convexity") conditions for profit maximization, as indeed Wicksell pointed out in his analysis of Åkerman's problem (pp. 294-297, especially the footnote on p. 295). Only in his earlier goods-in-process model would a reverse Wicksell effect imply the failure of those conditions, and so perversity.

II

Technical Progress

INTRODUCTION

Section A.   Theory of Technical Progress

The studies of the 1950's, by Kendrick[1] and Solow[2] among others, indicated that technological progress was an extremely important — perhaps the most important — determinant in the growth in output per man. The articles presented here investigate the character of technological progress. In the discussions of the role of technological change in the economy, four questions naturally arise.

1. How does technological change affect different factors? Traditionally, some technological changes are thought of as "labor saving," and some as "capital saving." Is there some way in which we can formalize these concepts?

2. What determines whether technological change is primarily "labor saving" or primarily "capital saving"?

3. What determines the rate of technical change?

4. How are changes in technique introduced into the economy?

We turn now to more detailed answers to these questions.

1. In the literature, several different definitions of a neutral technical

---

[1] J. G. Kendrick, *Productivity Trends in the United States,* National Bureau of Economic Research (Princeton, N.J.: Princeton University Press, 1961).

[2] R. M. Solow, "Technical Change and the Aggregate Production Function," *REStat, 39* (August 1957), pp. 312–320.

change have been proposed, reflecting in part the fact that different definitions may be useful in different situations. The interest in the factor "bias" of technological change is derived from the fact that depending on it steady state paths may not exist, for given savings assumptions, and the distribution of income may or may not be stable for given savings behavior.

Hicks, in the selection presented here, argues essentially for the following definition of neutrality, which is often referred to in the growth literature as Hicks neutrality: The ratio of the marginal products of the two factors must remain unchanged at the same capital-labor ratio. This is equivalent to a simple renumbering of the isoquants, and may formally be written as

$$Q = A(t)F(K,L).$$

It also implies that the distribution of income remains unchanged at the same capital-labor ratio. A labor-saving invention, then, in the Hicks classification scheme, reduces the marginal product of labor relative to that of capital at a fixed capital-labor ratio, and conversely for a capital-saving invention.

The alternative definition of neutrality, which is often referred to as Harrod neutrality, has played a more central role in the growth literature. The rate of interest must remain unchanged at the same capital-output ratio. (A capital-saving invention then reduces the rate of interest at a constant capital-output ratio.) This is equivalent to the distribution of income remaining unchanged at a constant capital-output ratio. It has often been alleged that technological change in fact is Harrod neutral, since we observe an "almost constant capital-output ratio with an almost constant rate of interest" (i.e., no marked secular trends). More recent empirical work has cast some doubt on the validity of these observations. Robinson discusses the Harrod definition in the second article in this section.

The importance of Harrod neutrality is that if and only if technological change is of that form can there be a balanced growth in the usual growth models. In fact, as Uzawa shows in the third article of this section, Harrod neutrality is equivalent to pure labor augmenting technological progress; the production function can be written

$$Q = F(K,\lambda(t)L).$$

This means that one worker under the new technology can do what λ workers could do under the old technology, irrespective of the capital stock. If we divide output and capital by *effective labor units* (λL), a growth model with technological change becomes equivalent to one without.

There are several ways of relating the Hicks and Harrod definitions. If capital augmentation is defined analogously to labor augmentation, that is, if units of capital under the new technology can do what μ units of capital could do under the old technology, the production function with both labor and capital augmentation can be written

$$Q = F(\mu K, \lambda L).$$

Then in Hicks neutrality, $\mu = \lambda$, while Harrod neutrality $\mu = 1$. If we use as the measure of bias of technological change the change in relative shares, then the Hicks definition measures the bias along a constant capital-labor ratio while the Harrod definition measures the bias along a constant capital-output ratio:

$$\left(\frac{\partial (F_K K)/(F_L L)}{\partial t}\right)_{\overline{K/L}} \gtreqless 0 \Longleftrightarrow \text{Hicks} \begin{cases} \text{labor-saving} \\ \text{neutral} \\ \text{capital-saving} \end{cases}$$

$$\left(\frac{\partial (F_K K)/(F_L L)}{\partial t}\right)_{\overline{K/Q}} \gtreqless 0 \Longleftrightarrow \text{Harrod} \begin{cases} \text{labor-saving} \\ \text{neutral} \\ \text{capital-saving} \end{cases}$$

2. Since Harrod neutrality (pure labor augmentation) plays such a central role in neoclassical growth theory, it was natural to enquire whether there was any economic reason to expect Harrod neutrality; in other words, what determines whether technological change is labor-augmenting or capital-augmenting. Fellner's article considers how wage expectations and factor market imperfections affect the "direction" of technical change. In his selection, Kennedy has postulated a model in which there is an invention possibilities schedule, giving trade-offs between labor and capital augmentation, which is assumed to be concave. He shows that if the rate of interest is constant, in a one-sector economy in the long run there would be Harrod-neutral technical change. Kennedy, following the Cambridge tradition, doubts the relevance of a production function; in a sense, his model can be viewed as assuming that at any point of time there is a single technique available (a fixed-coefficients production function). The innovation possibilities frontier gives the economy a choice of the coefficients for the next period. Samuelson [35] and Drandakis and Phelps [28], following in the neoclassical tradition, constructed a similar model but one in which there exists possibilities of substituting capital for labor. They showed that in such a model, if (a) competitive firms choose the amount of labor and capital augmentation that maximizes profits on expectations of constant wages and interest rates, even though these are constantly changing, (b) if the savings rate is constant, and (c) if the elasticity of substitution is less than unity, then asymptotically techno-

logical change is Harrod neutral.[3] But as Tobin[4] has commented, "The trouble is that the opportunity locus describing the terms of trade-off for the economy between labor augmentation and capital augmentation is a *deus ex machina*. How does the process work for the individual firm? What explains the concavity of the locus? What scarce resources determine its position? Why cannot it be moved by increasing these resources? Do they get paid, and if so, how does their payment affect the theory of distribution?"

3. Like the research into what determines the bias of technological change, the investigations into the determinant of the rate of change are at a very early stage. There are at least two broad classes of models that have been formulated. One focuses on technological change as a by-product to investment and production; this is described in more detail in the section on "Learning by Doing." The other has resources explicitly allocated to research, and includes the papers of Uzawa [37], Nordhaus [33], Phelps [34], and Atkinson and Stiglitz [27].

4. The final question of how technological change is introduced into the economy is one of the main themes of the next sections.

Sections B–E. Problems in Capital Theory

One of the main difficulties with the models presented in the first part of this book is their treatment of capital. In particular they assume that all machines are homogeneous. There are a number of ways in which capital goods differ from one another.

1. Machines built in different years may be different from each other because of technological change — new machines are generally better than old. In the first article reprinted in Section B, Solow suggests that new techniques are introduced into the economy through new machines, that technological progress is *embodied* in the new machines. Thus, it may be possible by increasing the savings rate to lower the average age of capital, and thus to increase the "average quality" of machines in use, and thus increase output per man. Phelps shows, however, that in the steady state, for a Cobb-Douglas production function, the average age is independent of the savings rate. But, in his comment, Matthews shows that this result is dependent on the special form of production function used; if the elasticity of substitution is less than one, average age is reduced, but if it is greater than one, it is increased. In the last article in this section, Denison suggests that, empirically, the whole problem of embodiment is unimportant. The empirical

[3] W. Nordhaus [33] has recently attempted to extend the analysis to economies where the choice of factor augmentation is based on intertemporal utility maximization.

[4] J. Tobin, in M. Brown, ed., *The Theory of Empirical Analysis of Production,* NBER (National Bureau of Economic Research), 1967, p. 52.

question of the importance of embodiment is, however, far from settled, and this remains one of the more active areas of empirical research at this time.

Not only are machines required to introduce new techniques, but, as a by-product of investment, knowledge is created. This process is what Arrow has called learning by doing, and is the subject of his article in Section C. His approach is similar to that taken by Kaldor [54] in his growth models. Kaldor calls the relationship between technological progress and investment the technological progress function.

2. Even if the "book of blueprints" from which the design of the machine is chosen remains unchanged from year to year, in different years different pages from the blueprint will be utilized; once the machine is built, its characteristics are fixed. In other words, the economy may face an unchanging *ex ante* production function, but machines built in different years will require, for instance, different amounts of labor per unit of output. Models which treat capital in this way are said to have *ex ante* substitutability and *ex post* fixed coefficients, or to be putty-clay models, as opposed to the Solow-Swan neoclassical production functions, which are said to have *ex post* and *ex ante* substitutability, or to be putty-putty models. The question of *ex post* substitutability is also referred to as the problem of malleability: once a machine has been constructed, can it change its form? Thus, before constructing a machine, an investor must form expectations of wage rates extending far into the future. The real wage will not be equal to the marginal product of labor on the *ex ante* production function, but it will equal the average output per man on the least efficient machine used in production. These questions are discussed in detail in the articles by Johansen and Solow in Section D.

3. In constructing an aggregate model, one ignores the heterogeneity of the commodities and types of capital goods which are actually produced in the economy. One hopes that the resulting simplification gains for one greater insight into the process of growth and capital accumulation, and the special assumptions made do not greatly affect the validity of the general results obtained. Over the years, however, it has been clear that many of the results of modern growth theory may not hold for more general models. Differences arise in the analysis of the comparative dynamics (comparisons of steady states) as well as in the analysis of stability.

One of the main properties of the one-sector model in comparing steady states is that economies with higher capital-labor ratios have higher output per man, lower interest rates, and — provided the rate of growth is less than the rate of interest — higher per capita consumption. This may not be true if there are many commodities and capital goods. First, assume that we were to use a value index of capital. Then since as capital accumulates, the price of capital relative to consumption, which is the usual numeraire, declines. It is possible that an economy with a higher output per man have a lower capital-labor ratio. This is known as the Wicksell effect. But more striking is the phenomenon, discovered by Champernowne in the article reprinted here, that it is possible for an economy to be in equilibrium at a low interest rate, using a given set of techniques and having a given capital stock, and to have the same capital stock and use the same techniques at a high interest rate, but to use a different set of techniques and to have a different stock of capital at an intermediate interest rate. But even when this reswitching of techniques does not occur, it is possible that equilibrium consumption per man declines as the rate of interest rises, even for rates of interest greater than the rate of growth.

More recently, Hahn [69] has suggested that the existence of two or more kinds of capital goods may in fact raise essentially new problems for the uniqueness of momentary equilibrium and the convergence to steady states along short-run perfect-foresight paths. Shell and Stiglitz [70] have shown, however, that at least under some simplified assumptions, on all short-run perfect-foresight paths not converging to balanced growth the relative price of the two capital goods becomes zero or infinite in finite time; that is, the only paths consistent with perfect foresight *forever* are stable. Moreover, they have suggested that if individuals have static expectations, the dynamic path is stable.

4. The capital goods differ in durability. Indeed, most of the literature has treated depreciation in a very unsatisfactory way. Most authors assume that machines depreciate exponentially, which may be a reasonable assumption for telephone poles but which is not for most machines. Johansen in his article in Section D has treated the polar case of fixed lifetime depreciation (the "one-horse shay" case). But the economic problem of the choice of durability of a machine has, with a few exceptions, been ignored in the growth literature. This seems to be quite important, if there are *ex post* fixed coefficients, since, in that case, the length of time which a machine is used is a variable. It would seem natural that if a machine is expected to be used for a shorter time, it should be made less durable than if it is expected to be used for a longer time. The paucity of the literature rather than the importance of the subject has dictated the omission of a section on these topics.

We have observed that capital goods differ from each other in at least four ways: (1) Newer machines are usually "better" than older machines; (2) even if before machines are constructed there are possibilities of substituting capital for labor, once the machine has been built, its labor requirements are fixed; machines built at different times, or even at the same time by different producers, will differ in their production characteristics; (3) machines in different industries are different; (4) machines differ in their durability. In most of the articles of this book, the concept of an "aggregate" capital stock is used. The articles in Section E attempt to clarify the conditions under which aggregation can take place. If the only differences are those resulting from technical change (type 1), then Fisher [57] and Diamond [56] have shown that if technical change is purely capital augmenting (that is, that one new machine is identical to two or more old machines in every way) then a capital aggregate can be formed. Champernowne, in the article included here, shows how a chain index of the capital stock can be formed, provided the underlying technology is not "perverse," that is, provided that output per man decreases as the rate of interest increases. Solow further clarifies the conditions under which aggregation can take place, providing a necessary and sufficient condition.

Section F. Money

Before leaving the discussion of the role of capital in growth models we briefly mention the recent studies in money and growth: like capital, money is a store of value; savings in money serves as at least a partial substitute for investment in capital. Tobin here examines a growth model in which a constant fraction of income is saved, and the money supply expands at a constant rate through transfer payments. Then since real savings is equal to investment in capital plus the increase in the real money supply, and since an increase in the real money supply increases savings by only a fraction of the money supply increase, a faster rate of increase of the money supply leads to a lower capital stock and output per man. Sidrauski [66] and Shell, Stiglitz, and Sidrauski [64] have also shown that such economies are unstable. Many questions are, however, still unanswered by these models, and the research is still at an early stage.

From *Theory of Wages*

J. R. Hicks

III

Under the assumption of competition, it inevitably follows that an invention can only be profitably adopted if its ultimate effect is to increase the National Dividend. For if it is to raise the profits of the entrepreneur who adopts it, it must lower his costs of production—that is to say, it must enable him to get the same product with a smaller amount of resources. On balance, therefore, resources are set free by the invention; and they can be used, either to increase the supply of the commodity in whose production the invention is used (if the demand for it is elastic), or to increase the supply of other commodities (if the demand for the first is inelastic). In either case, the total Dividend must be increased, as soon as the liberated resources can be effectively transferred to new uses.[1]

But although an invention must increase the total Dividend, it is unlikely at the same time to increase the marginal products of all factors of production in the same ratio. In most cases, it will select particular factors and increase the demand for those factors to a special extent. If we concentrate on two groups of factors, "labour" and "capital," and suppose them to exhaust the list, then we can classify inventions according as their initial effects are to increase, leave unchanged, or diminish the ratio of the marginal product of capital to that of labour. We may call these inventions "labour-saving," "neutral," and "capital-saving" respectively. "Labour-saving" inventions increase the

---

[1] For a fuller elaboration of this argument, see Wicksell, *Vorlesungen,* vol. i., pp. 195-207. Also Kaldor, "A Case against Technical Progress?" (*Economica,* May, 1932).

Reprinted from J. R. Hicks, *The Theory of Wages* (London: Macmillan & Co. Ltd., 1963, pp. 121–127) by the permission of St. Martin's Press, Inc., The Macmillan Company of Canada, Ltd., and Macmillan & Co. Ltd.

marginal product of capital more than they increase the marginal product of labour; "capital-saving" inventions increase the marginal product of labour more than that of capital; "neutral" inventions increase both in the same proportion.

A labour-saving invention, according to this definition, need not actually diminish the marginal product of labour, and consequently labour's absolute share in the Dividend. It may do so, if it is very labour-saving; there is nothing to prevent the ratio of marginal products being changed to such an extent as to make the absolute size of one lower than it was before.. But equally it may not. In every case, however, a labour-saving invention will diminish the relative share of labour. Exactly the same holds, *mutatis mutandis*, of a capital-saving invention.

It may be observed that the definition of a labour-saving invention just given is not identical with that given by Professor Pigou.[1] He supposes the technical change to take place in an industry which produces no wage-goods—*i.e.* none of whose products are bought by labourers. (This is, of course, a very unreal assumption if we interpret labour in the very wide sense which it has to be given in this discussion. The Attorney-General is a labourer.) However, taking this special case, he defines a labour-saving invention as one which diminishes the ratio of capital to labour employed in the rest of industry. Now if the ratio of capital to labour in the rest of industry is diminished, the marginal product of labour in terms of the products of the rest of industry (which is all that matters to labour) must be diminished. An extension of Professor Pigou's definition—and it cries out to be extended—would thus

[1] *Op. cit.*, p. 632.

make a labour-saving invention one which diminished the *absolute* marginal product of labour. Professor Pigou's case then becomes a useful illustration of this definition, but it is too limited to serve as a definition itself.

But even the extended Pigou definition appears on reflection rather unsatisfactory for our purposes. For if we were to call "labour-saving" inventions those which diminished the absolute marginal product of labour, and "capital-saving" inventions those which diminished the marginal product of capital, there would be a wide range of neutral inventions between—quite possibly including the great bulk of those inventions in which we are actually interested. But some of these "neutral" inventions would be more favourable to capital than labour and some the contrary. They would all increase both marginal products, but some would increase that of capital more than that of labour, and some the reverse. If we have any interest in relative shares, we do not want to leave this distinction in the dark. Thus it seems best to make the definition hinge upon relative shares; but it must of course be realised that any invention which is *very* labour-saving may diminish the absolute marginal product of labour; and similarly for capital.

Although this amendment of Professor Pigou's definition appears desirable, the definitions are still fairly close, and most of the things which he says about inventions can be perfectly well applied with the definition just given. In particular, there is no reason to question his view that inventions have a decided bias in the labour-saving direction. It is indeed difficult to find clear cases of important capital-saving inventions—wireless is, of course, the standard case, but beyond that, although there can be little doubt that capital-saving inventions occur, they are not easily identified. Obvious labour-saving inventions, on the other hand, are frequent. Not all those inventions popularly called labour-saving are labour-saving in the strict sense, but there can be little doubt that the great majority are.

This predominance of labour-saving inventions strikes one as curious. It may conceivably be the case that it is a mere "optical illusion"; labour-saving inventions cause more social friction than others, and so force themselves on the attention of the observer. There is probably some truth in this, but it hardly seems a sufficient explanation. It is also possible that the utilisation of fixed capital has a close relation to the particular kind of scientific knowledge which has been available for industry during the last two centuries: that it is to be connected with the special growth of mechanical and physical science. But this again does not seem very probable. For after all, wireless is the result of physics; and there seems no reason in the nature of physical enquiry why the growing complexity of industrial technique should not have been kept in check through the constant supersession of complex methods by simpler methods requiring less capital.

The real reason for the predominance of labour-saving inventions is surely that which was hinted at in our discussion of substitution. A change in the relative prices of the factors of production is itself a spur to invention, and to invention of a particular kind—directed to economising the use of a factor which has become relatively expensive. The general tendency to a more rapid increase of capital than labour which

has marked European history during the last few
centuries has naturally provided a stimulus to labour-
saving invention.

If, therefore, we are properly to appreciate the
place of invention in economic progress, we need to
distinguish two sorts of inventions. We must put on
one side those inventions which are the result of a
change in the relative prices of the factors; let us call
these "induced" inventions. The rest we may call
"autonomous" inventions. We shall expect, in practice, all or nearly all induced inventions to be labour-
saving; but there is no reason why autonomous inventions should be predominantly labour-saving.
There is no obvious reason why autonomous inventions
should incline, on balance, to one side more than to the
other. In the absence of special knowledge we may
reasonably assume a random dispersion. Then, since
induced inventions are mainly labour-saving, both
kinds taken together will give us a predominance of
labour-saving inventions—precisely what we appear to
find in practice. There is nothing therefore in observed
fact inconsistent with the hypothesis that autonomous
inventions are evenly distributed. But of course, this
even distribution will, at the most, be a long-run
affair; it is quite conceivable that scientific discovery
may tend to produce inventions with a bias in one
direction over quite long periods.

In order to complete this classification, one further
distinction must be drawn—within the field of induced
inventions. An induced invention is made as the
result of a change in relative prices; but it may be such
that its adoption depends upon the change in prices, or
it may not. Capital increases, let us say, and in consequence a labour-saving invention is made and

adopted. But either this invention would have paid before capital increased—and would therefore have been adopted if it had been known—or not. If it would not have paid under the old circumstances, then it is simply a cause increasing the facility of adjustment to a change in circumstances—*i.e.* increasing the elasticity of substitution. The elasticity of substitution is greater than it would have been in the absence of such an invention; consequently the possibility of capital increasing its relative share in the Dividend is greater. But so long as the invention is of this type the second rule about absolute shares still holds; it is quite certain that as a result of the whole change the absolute share of labour will be increased.

But it is certainly quite conceivable that a change in relative prices will stimulate invention to do more than this—to discover methods which, if they had been known, would have paid even before prices changed. Now induced inventions of this type (if they are labour-saving, as we may suppose generally to be the case) may reduce not only the relative share of labour, but also its absolute share. Such inventions as these are perhaps not very common, but there is little reason to doubt their occurrence; they are the only kind which are really dangerous to the real income of labour.

The classification of invention just made is a purely economic classification; there is no reason to suppose that it corresponds to any kind of scientific or technical division. At times when scientific and technical activity is great it will probably manifest itself in a large crop both of autonomous and induced inventions. In the dark ages of science, both autonomous and induced inventions will be rare. Further, although the kind of induced inventions just referred to (those which are induced by a change in prices, but do more than adjust technical methods to the new economic conditions) may occur at any stage of development, they are perhaps most likely to be important when the accumulation of capital has been proceeding for a long while, but many kinds of production have retained conservative methods, and have not benefited by technical progress.

The Classification of Inventions

Joan Robinson

In a discussion of the effect of changes in technique upon the position of long-period equilibrium, in my *Essays in the Theory of Employment*,[1] I made use of Mr. Hicks's classification of inventions, according to which an invention is said to be neutral when it raises the marginal productivities of labour and capital in the same proportion, and is said to be labour-saving or capital-saving according as it raises the marginal productivity of capital more or less than that of labour, the amounts of the factors being unchanged. I analysed the effect of an invention upon the relative shares of the factors in the total product, when the amount of capital is adjusted to the new technique (so that full equilibrium is attained, with zero investment), in terms of this classification of inventions and the elasticity of substitution, showing that, with a constant rate of interest, the relative shares are unchanged, in equilibrium, by an invention which is neutral in Mr. Hicks's sense provided that the elasticity of substitution is equal to unity, while if an invention is labour-saving or capital-saving in Mr. Hicks's sense, the relative shares are unchanged (in equilibrium, with a constant rate of interest) if the elasticity of substitution is correspondingly less or greater than unity.

Mr. Harrod [2] made some criticisms of my analysis which lead to the suggestion that it would be more convenient to use a classification in which an invention is said to be neutral when it leaves the relative shares of the factors unchanged, with a constant rate of interest, after the stock of capital has been adjusted to the new situation.[3] A method by which such a classification can be made is put forward in what follows. The argument is confined to the primitive stage at which it is assumed that there are only two factors of production, labour and capital, and that conditions of constant physical returns prevail. Draw AP_1 and AP_2, the average productivity curves of capital with a given amount of labour, before and after the invention, and the corresponding marginal productivity

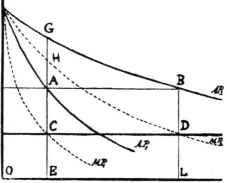

[1] Pp. 132–6.   [2] *Economic Journal*, June, 1937, p. 329.

[3] Mr. Harrod's criticisms were mainly concerned with the question of measuring the stock of capital. For our present purpose capital must be conceived in physical terms, that is, as a stock of capital goods, and it is most conveniently measured in terms of cost units. Two stocks of capital goods are said to be equal if they would cost the same sum to produce at a given date, in a given state of knowledge. An invention may introduce the knowledge of new types of capital goods, but it does not destroy the knowledge of the types of capital goods appropriate to the old technique ; the date for measuring capital must therefore be chosen after the invention has taken place, and the cost of each stock of capital goods must be measured on the basis of whatever may be the most efficient method of producing it. By this means the major difficulties presented by the conception of a given stock of capital are evaded, though some ambiguous cases would still remain.

Reprinted from V (February 1938), 139–142 of *Review of Economic Studies* by permission of *Review of Economic Studies* published by Oliver & Boyd Ltd., Edinburgh and London.
© 1938 The Economic Society.

curves, MP_1 and MP_2. The amount of capital employed with the constant amount of labour is measured on the x axis, and product per unit of capital on the y axis. In full equilibrium before the invention, the marginal product of capital, CE, is equal to the rate of interest, the amount of capital employed with the given amount of labour being OE. The average product of capital is AE. Total product is equal to $OE \times AE$, the income of capital to $OE \times CE$, and the income of labour to $OE \times AC$.

Now suppose that, when full equilibrium is restored after the invention, the amount of capital employed with the given amount of labour is OL and its marginal product DL, which is equal to CE, both being equal to the constant rate of interest. The average product of capital is now BL.

In the first position the ratio of the shares of labour and capital in the total product is AC : CE, and in the second position BD : DL. CE is equal to DL. Therefore the relative share of capital is increased or reduced by the invention according as BD is less or greater than AC. The relative share of capital is unchanged when, as in the diagram, BD is equal to AC.

Now, the elasticity of the curve AP_1 at A is equal to $\dfrac{AE}{AC}$[1] and the elasticity of the curve AP_2 at B is equal to $\dfrac{BL}{BD}$. Thus the share of capital is increased or reduced according as elasticity at B is greater or less than elasticity at A. In the diagram the two elasticities are equal and the share of capital is unchanged.

It thus appears that an invention which is neutral in the sense required by Mr. Harrod, that is, an invention which leaves the ratio of capital to product unchanged if the rate of interest is constant, raises the average productivity curve of capital iso-elastically.[2] A capital-saving invention, which reduces the ratio of capital to product, lowers the elasticity of the average productivity curve (at a given value of y); while a labour-saving, or more properly *capital-using*, invention, which increases the ratio of capital to product, raises the elasticity of the average productivity curve.

This classification of inventions lends itself more easily than that of Mr. Hicks's to realistic interpretation. An iso-elastic rise in the average productivity curve of capital means that there is a certain proportion, say k, such that if the amount of capital per unit of labour is increased by k, output also increases by k. Thus an invention which raises the average productivity curve iso-elastically, that is, a neutral invention in Mr. Harrod's sense, has the same effect as an increase in the supply of labour, in the ratio k, with unchanged technique. A neutral invention is thus seen to be equivalent to an all-round increase in the efficiency of labour. A capital-saving invention is one which improves efficiency in the higher stages of production relatively to efficiency at lower stages, and a capital-using invention is one which brings about a relative increase in efficiency in the lower stages. This corresponds to our general notions about the nature of inventions, wireless, for instance, being a capital-saving invention in this sense, and railways a capital-using one.

[1] See my *Economics of Imperfect Competition*, p. 36.
[2] Ibid., p. 42.

There is no inconsistency between this and my former method of analysis. The two concepts which I formerly used—the elasticity of substitution and the change, due to an invention, in the ratio of the marginal productivities of given amounts of the factors—merely represent two aspects of the productivity curves, and these aspects are equally well represented by the single concept of the change in the elasticity of the productivity curve brought about by an invention. The manner in which the two methods of analysis dovetail together can easily be seen.

Consider, for instance, the case in which an invention raises the average productivity curve of capital iso-elastically (so that the invention is neutral in Mr. Harrod's sense). In this case (with a constant rate of interest) the relative share of capital in the total product is unchanged by the invention ; it follows from my former analysis that if, in this case, the elasticity of substitution with the new technique is equal to unity, then the invention must be neutral in Mr. Hicks's sense, while if the elasticity of substitution is less or greater than unity, the invention must be capital-saving or labour-saving, to a corresponding extent, in Mr. Hicks's sense.

These relations can be demonstrated as follows : let GE be the average product of the original amount of capital, OE, with the new technique, and HE its marginal product. Then, with the new technique and the old amounts of the factors, total product is $GE \times OE$, and the income of labour is $GH \times OE$.

Now, if the elasticity of substitution is equal to unity over the relevant range, it follows that the ratio of the income of labour to the total product is independent of the amount of capital. Therefore $\frac{GE}{GH}$ is equal to $\frac{BL}{BD}$. Therefore the elasticity of the curve AP_2 at G is equal to its elasticity at B. But the elasticity of the curve AP_1 at A is also equal to the elasticity of AP_2 at B. Therefore the elasticity of AP_2 at G is equal to the elasticity of AP_1 at A. Therefore $\frac{GE}{GH}$ is equal to $\frac{AE}{AC}$. It follows that the marginal product of labour is raised by the invention (with a constant amount of capital) in the same proportion as total output, and the invention is neutral in Mr. Hicks's sense. Similarly, if the elasticity of substitution is less than unity, then $\frac{GE}{GH}$ is correspondingly greater than $\frac{AE}{AC}$ (as in the diagram) and the invention is labour-saving in Mr. Hicks's sense, while if the elasticity of substitution is less than unity, the invention is capital-saving, to a corresponding extent, in Mr. Hicks's sense.[1]

[1] This argument reveals an interesting property of the productivity function. The magnitude of the elasticity of substitution varies with the rate of change of the elasticity of the average productivity curve, being greater or less than unity according as the elasticity of the average productivity curve increases or decreases with an increase in the proportion of capital to labour.

Let $y = f(x)$ be the average productivity curve of capital, the amount of labour being constant.

The elasticity of the average productivity curve is $\frac{-f(x)}{xf'(x)}$. The rate of change of this

elasticity is $-\frac{x[f'(x)]^2 - f(x)[xf''(x) + f'(x)]}{[xf'(x)]^2}$. This is greater or less than zero, i.e. the elasticity

Thus there is no conflict between the system of analysis followed in my treatment of long-period equilibrium and the system suggested in this note, but the former is somewhat more cumbersome and less susceptible to realistic interpretation.

Cambridge. JOAN ROBINSON.

increases or decreases with an increase in the proportion of capital, according as

$$xf''(x)+f'(x) \gtrless \frac{x[f'(x)]^2}{f(x)},$$

or according as $xf''(x)+2f'(x) \gtrless \dfrac{f'(x)[f(x)+xf'(x)]}{f(x)}$ (1).

Now, the return per unit of capital is $f(x)+xf'(x)$, and the return per unit of labour is $-\dfrac{x^2}{L}f'(x)$, where L is the constant amount of labour.

It follows that the elasticity of substitution is

$$-x\left[\frac{2f'(x)+xf''(x)}{f(x)+xf'(x)} - \frac{2xf'(x)+x^2f''(x)}{x^2f'(x)}\right]$$

$$= \frac{f(x)[xf''(x)+2f'(x)]}{f'(x)[f(x)+xf'(x)]}$$

The elasticity of substitution is accordingly greater or less than unity according as

$$xf''(x)+2f'(x) \gtrless \frac{f'(x)[f(x)+xf'(x)]}{f(x)}$$

i.e. by (1) above, according as the elasticity of the average productivity curve increases or decreases with an increase in the proportion of capital.

Corrections: On the diagram on article page 139, add *H* at the intersection of the upper dotted line and line *GACE*. On article page 141, line 2 from the bottom line of text, the word less should read: greater. [The Editors.]

136

Neutral Inventions and the Stability of Growth Equilibrium[*]

Hirofumi Uzawa

1. *Introduction*

In criticising Hick's classification[1] of technical inventions, Harrod has proposed a new definition[2] of neutral inventions primarily intended for applications to the problem of economic growth. According to Harrod, a technical invention is defined as *neutral* if at a constant rate of interest it does not disturb the value of the capital coefficient. Harrod's classification has been discussed by J. Robinson [6] who showed graphically that a neutral invention is equivalent to " an all-round increase in the efficiency of labor " ([6], p. 140). The first part of the present article is concerned with precisely formulating Robinson's proposition and characterizing analytically those inventions that are neutral in Harrod's sense.

Harrod's definition of neutral inventions, as indicated above, has been introduced to handle the problem of economic growth. Recent contributions, however, in particular those of Solow [8] and Swan [9], are discussed for the case in which technical inventions are neutral in Hicks's sense.[3] In the second part of this article we consider a neoclassical growth model with neutral inventions in Harrod's sense, and prove the stability of the growth equilibrium in such a model. The aggregate production function underlying the model is assumed only to be subject to constant returns to scale and to diminishing marginal rates of substitution; the Cobb-Douglas condition, as is customarily imposed in recent literature, is not required.

2. *Neutral Inventions in Harrod's Sense*

It is assumed that there are two factors of production: capital and labor. Both are assumed to be composed of homogeneous quantities; K and L refer respectively to the capital stock and the labor forces in terms of physical units. The structure of production in each time period t (conveniently referred to as *year t*) is described by the *aggregate production function $F(K,L,t)$*, which specifies the maximum output Y produced by capital K and labor L in year t:

$$(1) \qquad\qquad Y = F(K,L,t).$$

Production is assumed to be subject to constant returns to scale; namely, the aggregate production function $F(K,L;t)$ is homogeneous of first degree:

[*] This work was in part supported by the Office of Naval Research under Task NR—047—004 at Stanford University.

[1] According to Hick's definition, introduced in [3], pp. 121-2, a technical invention is termed neutral if the ratio of the marginal product of capital to that of labor remains undisturbed at a constant capital-labor ratio.

[2] Harrod's criterion was first introduced in his review of Robinson's book [1]; see Kaldor [4], Hicks [3], Robinson [5], pp. 132-6, Harrod [2], pp. 22-27, and Robinson [7], pp. 131-3.

[3] Both Solow and Swan are concerned with the Cobb-Douglas production function case. The Cobb-Douglas production function is, as will be seen below, the only case in which Hicks's neutrality coincides with Harrod's neutrality. Hence, in Solow's and Swan's models, technical inventions are neutral in Harrod's sense also.

(2) $F(\lambda K, \lambda L; t) = \lambda F(K,L,t)$, for all $\lambda > 0$.

Hence, the output per head, to be denoted by y, is uniquely determined by the capital-labor ratio, to be denoted by k:

(3) $y = f(k,t)$,

where

(4) $y = Y/L$,

(5) $k = K/L$,

and

(6) $f(k,t) = F(k, 1, t)$.

We assume that production is subject to the neoclassical conditions; namely, the aggregate production function $F(K,L,t)$ is continuously differentiable with respect to $K.L,t$; capital is always productive, and the marginal rates of substitution are diminishing. The latter two conditions may be represented by

(7) $f_k(k,t) > 0$,

and

(8) $f_{kk}(k,t) < 0$,

where

$$f_k = \partial f/\partial k, \ f_{kk} = \partial^2 f/\partial k^2.$$

The Cobb-Douglas function

$$F(K,L,t) = A(t)K^{\alpha(t)} L^{1-\alpha(t)}, \ A(t) > 0, \ 0 < \alpha(t) < 1,$$

is the most familiar neoclassical production function.

For a given rate of interest r, the optimum capital-labor ratio in year t, to be denoted by $k(r,t)$, is determined as the one at which the marginal product of capital equals the rate of interest r:

(9) $f_k[k(r,t),t] = r$.

The corresponding optimum output per head $y(r,t)$ and capital-output ratio $x(r,t)$ are determined by

(10) $y(r,t) = f[k(r,r),t]$,

(11) $x(r,t) = \dfrac{k(r, t)}{y(r, t)}$.

The technical invention represented by the aggregate production function $F(K,L,t)$, or equivalently by $f(k,t)$, will be termed *Harrod neutral* if the optimum capital-output ratio $x(r,t)$ is independent of t.

Under the diminishing marginal productivity assumption (8), the definition of the Harrod neutrality may be rephrased as:

$F(K,L;t)$ is Harrod neutral if and only if the marginal product of capital f_k remains undisturbed at a constant capital-output ratio x.

3. *Robinson's Theorem on Neutral Inventions*

An analytical characterization of the Harrod neutrality is given by the following:

Robinson's Theorem: The technical invention represented by $F(K,L;t)$ is Harrod neutral if and only if the production function $F(K,L;t)$ is of the form:

(12) $$F(K,L;t) = G[K,A(t)L],$$

with a positive function $A(t)$.

Proof: By the assumptions (7) and (8), the relation (1) may be transformed into the one concerned with output per head y and capital-output ratio x:

(13) $$y = \varphi(x,t)$$

where

(14) $$k = xy.$$

The marginal product f_k of capital then can be expressed in terms of the function $\varphi(x,t)$ as follows:

Differentiating (11) and (12) with respect to x,y and k, we have

(15) $$dy = \varphi_x dx,$$

(16) $$dk = x\,dy + y\,dx.$$

Solving (15) and (16) with respect to dy and dk, we get

(17) $$\frac{\partial y}{\partial k} = \frac{\varphi_x}{\varphi + x\varphi_x}.$$

Hence $f(k,t)$ is Harrod neutral if and only if the right-hand side of (17) is independent of t; namely,

(18) $$\frac{\varphi_x}{\varphi + x\varphi_x} = c(x),$$

where $c(x)$ is a function of x only.

From (18), we have

(19) $$\frac{\varphi_x}{\varphi} = \frac{1}{\dfrac{1}{c(x)} - x}.$$

The relation (19) indicates that φ_x/φ is independent of t; hence the function $\varphi(x,t)$ is decomposable:

(20) $$\varphi(x,t) = A(t)\psi(x).$$

From (13) and (20), we have

(21) $$x = \psi^{-1}\left[\frac{y}{A(t)}\right],$$

where ψ^{-1} is the inverse function of ψ.

The relation (21), together with (14), implies

(22) $$\frac{k}{A(t)} = \frac{y}{A(t)}\psi^{-1}\left[\frac{y}{A(t)}\right];$$

hence,

(23) $$\frac{y}{A(t)} = g\left[\frac{k}{A(t)}\right], \text{ say.}$$

In view of (3) and (4), the relation (23) may be written as

$$Y = G[K, A(t)L],$$

where

$$G(K, L) = g(k)L.$$

On the other hand, let the condition (12) be satisfied. Then, for the function $y = f(k, t)$, we have

(24) $$y = f(k, t) = A(t)\, g\left[\frac{k}{A(t)}\right],$$

with $g(k) = G(K, L)/L = G(k)$.

Solving (24) with respect to y and x, we get

$$y = A(t)\, \psi(x)$$

for some $\psi(x)$. Hence

$$\frac{\varphi_x}{\varphi + x\varphi_x} = \frac{\psi'(x)}{\psi(x) + x\psi'(x)},$$

which is independent of t. Then, from (27), $\partial y/\partial k$ is independent of r; hence $F(K, L, t)$ of the form (12) is Harrod neutral.   Q.E.D.

It may be of some interest to compare Harrod's neutrality with Hicks's. According to Hicks [3], a technical invention is defined as *neutral* if the ratio of the marginal product of capital to that of labor remains unchanged at a constant capital-labor ratio. Such a technical invention may be termed *Hicks neutral*. It is possible to characterize the Hicks neutrality in terms of the aggregate production function $F(K, L, t)$; *namely, the technical invention represented by $F(K, L, t)$ is Hicks neutral if and only if $F(K, L)$ is decomposable*:[1]

(25) $$F(K, L, t) = A(t)\, F(K, L)$$

with some positive $A(t)$.

· *Corollary to Robinson's Theorem*: *The non-trivial technical invention represented by the aggregate production function $F(K, L.t)$ is both Harrod and Hicks neutral if and only if*

(26) $$F(K, L, t) = A(t)\, K^\beta\, L^{1-\beta},$$

with some positive $A(t)$ and $0 < \beta < 1$.

Proof: It suffices to show that the production function $y = f(k, t)$ is both Harrod and Hicks neutral if and only if

(27) $$y = A(t)\, k^\beta, \ A(t) > 0, \ 0 < \alpha < 1.$$

Let $f(k, t)$ be Harrod neutral. Then

(28) $$f(k, t) = B(t)\, g\left[\frac{k}{B(t)}\right],$$

with positive $B(t)$.

---

[1] This proposition is well-known; for an analytical proof, see, e.g., Uzawa and Watanabe [10].

On the other hand, the function $f(k,t)$ is Hicks neutral if and only if

(29)
$$\frac{\partial^2 \log f(k,t)}{\partial k \, \partial t} = 0, \text{ for all } k \text{ and } t.$$

Let the function $\psi(z)$ be defined by

(30)
$$\psi(z) = \log g(e^z);$$

hence,

(31)
$$\log f(k,t) = \log B(t) + \psi\left(\log \frac{k}{B(t)}\right).$$

Differentiating (31) with respect to k and t, we get

(32)
$$\frac{\partial^2 \log f(k,t)}{\partial k \, \partial t} = \frac{-B'(t)}{k \, B(t)} \psi''\left[\log \frac{k}{B(t)}\right].$$

From (32) and (29),

$$\psi''\left[\log \frac{k}{B(t)}\right] = 0, \text{ for all } k \text{ and } t.$$

Therefore,

$$\psi(z) = \alpha + \beta z;$$

hence

$$g(k) = e^\alpha k^\beta.$$

Q.E.D.

4. Stability of the Neoclassical Growth Equilibrium

In this section we shall show the stability of growth equilibrium in a competitive model of economic growth with neutral technical progress in Harrod's sense.

Among the many recent contributions to the neoclassical theory of eocncmic growth, the most important would probably be the one by Solow [8]; our formulation of a neo-classical growth model here is primarily based on Solow's.

We are concerned with an economy in which a homogeneous output is produced by capital and labor; any part of the output is either consumed by labor or accumulated as capital stock. For the sake of simplicity, it is assumed that capital never depreciates.

Let $K(t)$ and $L(t)$ be the capital stock and the labor force, respectively, and $Y(t)$ the rate of output, all in year t. The annual output $Y(t)$ is uniquely determined by capital stock $K(t)$ and labor force $L(t)$ in terms of the aggregate production function $F(K,L,t)$. It is assumed that the technical invention represented by $F(K,L,t)$ is always Harrod neutral; hence, by Robinson's theorem, the aggregate production function is of the form $F[K,A(t)L]$, where $A(t)$ may be referred to as the *efficiency of labor*. The function $F(K,L)$ satisfies all the neoclassical conditions.

In the neoclassical theory, both capital and labor markets are assumed *perfectly competitive*; hence the distribution of the annual output $Y(t)$ between capital and labor is determined by the marginal products of capital and labor. The return to capital $r(t)$ and the wage $w(t)$, in year t, are given by

(33)
$$r(t) = F_K[K(t), A(t) L(t)]$$

and

(34) $$w(t) = F_L[K(t), A(t) L(t)].$$

We have

(35) $$Y(t) = P(t) + W(t),$$

where $P(t)$ and $W(t)$ are respectively the shares of capital and labor in year t:

(36) $$P(t) = r(t) K(t),$$

(37) $$W(t) = w(t) L(t).$$

It is assumed for the sake of simplicity that labor does not save and capital does not consume. Then the neoclassical growth process may be described by the following system of differential equations:

(*)
$$\begin{cases} Y(t) = F[K(t), A(t) L(t)], \\ \dfrac{\dot{K}(t)}{K(t)} = F[(t), A(t) L(t)], \end{cases}$$

where

$$\dot{K}(t) = \frac{dK(t)}{dt}.$$

It is assumed that both the rate of growth in labor, $\dot{L}/L$, and the rate of increase in the efficiency of labor, $\dot{A}/A$, are exogenously given and constant:

(38) $$\frac{\dot{L}(t)}{L(t)} = \lambda > 0,$$

(39) $$\frac{\dot{A}(t)}{A(t)} = \mu > 0.$$

Let $y(t)$ and $k(t)$ be respectively the output per head and the capital-labor ratio in year t:

(40) $$y(t) = Y(t)/L(t),$$

(41) $$k(t) = K(t)/L(t).$$

The growth process may be transformed into the one with respect to $y(t)$ and $k(t)$:

(**)
$$\begin{cases} \dfrac{y(t)}{A(t)} = f\left[\dfrac{k(t)}{A(t)}\right], \\ \dfrac{k(t)}{k(t)} = f_k\left[\dfrac{k(t)}{A(t)}\right] - \lambda. \end{cases}$$

Let

$$z(t) = \frac{k(t)}{A(t)}.$$

Then

(42) $$\frac{\dot{z}(t)}{z(t)} = f_k[z(t)] - \lambda - \mu.$$

Since

$$f_{kk}(z) < 0, \text{ for all } z > 0,$$

the differential equation (42) is globally stable, and the equilibrium z^* is uniquely determined by

(43) $$f_k(z^*) = \lambda + \mu.$$

Therefore, for the solution $[y(t), k(t)]$ of the process (**), both $y(t)/A(t)$ and $k(t)/A(t)$ converge:

$$\lim_{t \to \infty} y(t)/A(t) = y^*, \text{ say,}$$

and

$$\lim_{t \to \infty} k(t)/A(t) = z^*.$$

Hence,

$$\lim_{t \to \infty} x(t) = x^*,$$

where

$$x(t) = k(t)/y(t), \ x^* = z^*/y^*.$$

The above observations lead us to the following:[2]

Euqilibrium Theorem: *Let the initial capital stock K^* and labor forces L^* satisfy*

$$f_k[K^*/A(0)L^*] = \lambda + \mu,$$

where λ is the rate of growth in labor, defined by (38), and μ is the rate of growth in the efficiency of labor, defined by (39). Then, for the solution $[Y^*(t), K^*(t), L^*(t)]$ to the neoclassical growth process (*), the capital-output ratio $x^* = K^*(t)/Y^*(t)$ remains constant, and the output per head $y^*(t) = Y^*(t)/L^*(t)$ increases at the same constant rate as the capital-labor ratio $k^*(t) = K^*(t)/L^*(t)$. The capital-output ratio x^* is uniquely determined and may be referred to as the equilibrium capital-output ratio of the process (*).

Stability Theorem:[3] *Let the growth equilibrium exist. Then the neoclassical growth process (*) is globally stable; namely, for the solution $[Y(t), K(t), L(t)]$ to the process (*) with arbitrary initial $K(0)$ and $L(0)$, the capital-output ratio $x(t) = K(t)/Y(t)$ converges to the equilibrium capital-output ratio x^*.*

University of California, Berkeley, and Stanford University.   H. UZAWA.

REFERENCES

[1] Harrod, R. F., " Review of Joan Robinson's *Essays in the Theory of Employment*," *Economic Journal*, Vol. 47 (1937), 326-330.

[2] Harrod, R. F., *Towards a Dynamic Economics*. London, Macmillan, 1948.

[3] Hicks, J. R., *The Theory of Wages*. London: Macmillan, 1932.

[4] Kaldor, N., " A case against technical progress? " *Economica*, Vol. 12 (1932), 180-196.

[5] Robinson, J., *Essays in the Theory of Employment*. London: Macmillan, 1937.

[1] If we measure the quantity of labor forces according to efficiency, then our stability theorem below is essentially reduced to the case without technical progress discussed by Solow [8].

[2] It has been pointed out by Professor Robert M. Solow that the stability of the neoclassical growth discussed here crucially hinges on the assumption that the balanced growth exists.

[6] Robinson, J., " The classification of inventions," *Review of Economic Studies*, Vol. 5 (1937-38), 139-142.

[7] Robinson, J., *The Accumulation of Capital*. Homewood: Richard D. Irwin, 1956.

[8] Solow, R. M., " A contribution to the theory of economic growth," *Quarterly Journal of Economics*, Vol. 70 (1956), 65-94.

[9] Swan, T. W., " Economic growth and capital accumulation," *Economic Record*, Vol. 32 (1956), 334-361.

[10] Uzawa, H., and Watanabe, T., " A note on the classification of technical inventions," Technical Report No. 85, Contract No. 225 (50), Applied Mathematics and Statistics Laboratories, Stanford University, 1960.

Corrections: On article page 118, Equation 10 should read:

$$y(r,t) = f[k(r,t),t].$$

On article page 120, line 15, (27) should read: (17). [The Editors.]

TWO PROPOSITIONS IN THE THEORY OF INDUCED INNOVATIONS

William Fellner

THIS note is intended to establish a presumption for the existence of an adjustment mechanism which in market economies directs inventive activity into more or less labour-saving (less or more capital-saving) channels, according as one or the other factor of production is getting relatively scarce on a macro-economic level. On the conventional static equilibrium assumptions for firms which are very small in relation to the economy, it would be inconsistent to assume the existence of such a mechanism. On these assumptions macro-economic resource-scarcities express themselves to the individual firms exclusively in the ruling factor prices, none of which is either " high " or " low " in relation to the marginal productivity of the resource. Consequently, the firm is not interested in whether any given product-raising or cost-saving effect is achieved by raising primarily the marginal productivity of the one or of the other factor of production. However, the point to be argued here is that this negative conclusion must be qualified significantly—indeed, loses its validity for pronounced scarcities—if we make the assumptions slightly more realistic.

The writer has presented a more detailed analysis of the problem at a conference on inventive activity, but while the note that follows here is less complete in several respects than the conference paper in question, it is more specific about some propositions whose relevance now seems greater to the writer than it did earlier.[1]

In Figs. 1 and 2 the simplifying assumption is made that labour and capital are the only factors of production. Each technology is defined by isoquants. Economies of scale are disregarded, since their effects on the preference for labour-saving versus capital-saving inventions is unpredictable (hence these economies may be viewed as having a random influence). The relative factor prices, which must be known before the iso-cost functions can be drawn, may be interpreted as " the real wage-rate " and " the interest rate," that is, as the money price of hiring workers, and as the cost of borrowing capital (or of renting capital goods of given money value), where the price of the final output is assumed as given. Sir Roy Harrod called my attention to the fact that, contrary to frequent

---

[1] The more detailed analysis, which was recently presented at a conference in Minneapolis, will be published in a volume of the National Bureau of Economic Research. Both propositions to be developed in this note below—the proposition concerning the " learning process " and the proposition concerning monopsonistic imperfections—are elaborations on hypotheses expressed in the writer's *Trends and Cycles in Economic Activity* (New York: Henry Holt, 1956). Professor H. A. J. Green has rightly pointed out that the presentation of these propositions in my *op. cit.* needed a more detailed explanation (see his excellent article in ECONOMIC JOURNAL, March 1960, pp. 57–73). The presentation of the first proposition (see Fig. 1, *infra*) has greatly benefited from discussions I had with Mr. Richard R. Nelson of the Rand Corporation.

Reprinted by permission of the author and publishers from the *Economic Journal*, LXXI, No. 282 (June 1961), 305–308. London: Macmillan and Co. Limited and New York: St. Martin's Press.

For more recent views on the theory of induced innovation, following the Kennedy-Samuelson discussions, see W. Fellner, "Technological Progress and Recent Growth Theories," *American Economic Review*, Dec. 1967, pp. 1–73–98.

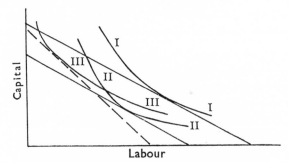

Fig. 1. Perfectly Competitive Factor Hiring.

Legend. All three isoquants of the firm relate to the identical quantity of output. The fully drawn straight lines are the iso-cost lines as of " now." Isoquant I describes the old technology. The firm must choose between making an effort to develop (acquire) "innovation" II or III. Given the factor-price ratios expressed by the present iso-cost lines, Technology II is superior to III. But if (as is the case in Western economies) a gradual increase in real wage-rates relative to interest rates is anticipated (see the broken iso-cost), then the firm expects that III will *in the future* become superior to II. Thus, whatever the length of the relevant periods is for which investment decisions are made, *it may be preferable to establish III rather than II*, provided that it is necessary to make a substantial allowance for the possibility that no further invention and innovation will become available during the subsequent periods. The argument gains in strength if II and III are nearly equivalent at present factor prices. Note that III is more " relatively labor-saving " than II. This is true on micro-economic grounds because for any given factor–price ratio the firm uses III with a smaller labour–capital ratio than II. Viewed macro-economically, III is more relatively labour-saving than II because if, given the macro-economic quantities of input, many firms use III the wage-rate is lower relative to the interest rate than if many firms use II. Hence the argument here points to a labour-saving bias in circumstances where real wage-rates are expected to rise relative to interest rates. As here drawn, innovation II could be defined as " neutral " and III as " labour-saving," but what matters for the argument is merely that III should be more labour-saving than II and that they should intersect.

practice, it is wrong to take it *generally* for granted that in models of this sort a change in money wage-rates relative to interest rates will lead to a change in the capital–labour ratio; yet I shall explain in a footnote why I believe that for my specific purpose this result may indeed by taken for granted.[1]

---

[1] The difficulty which in analysis of this sort needs to be watched is the following. If money wage-rates change (say, rise) *but the rate of interest does not change* (say, does not decline), then this does not *necessarily* provide an inducement for using methods of greater capital-intensity. The result may simply be that all prices, including those of the capital goods, rise in the same proportion as the money wage-rate, and hence the price of real " capital disposal," as well as the real wage-rate, stay unchanged. However, the reasoning in the present note will always imply assumptions on which it is legitimate to conclude that a change (say, a rise) in money wage-rates relative to interest rates does make it profitable to use methods of greater capital-intensity. This is because if the supply of capital rises relative to that of labour *along given production functions*, then interest rates do decline (and, of course, real as well as money wage-rates rise). If, on the other hand, the rise of the supply of capital relative to that of labour is accompanied by *technological progress*, then the rate of interest need not decline; yet even in this case unrealistic assumptions would have to be made with respect to extremely labour-saving innovations to arrive at the conclusion that real wage-rates will *not* rise. It seems quite appropriate to assume that in such circumstances a rise in money wage-rates expresses at the same time a rise in *real* wage-rates (say, with a constant price level); and if with a constant price level money and real wage-rates rise relative to interest rates, then this does make it profitable to use more capital-intensive methods of production.

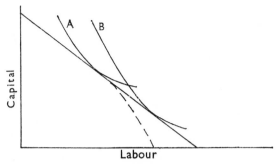

Fig. 2.   Monopsonistic Imperfection.

Legend.   Isoquants A and B relate to the same output.   Technology A is more relatively labour-saving than B (see Legend under Fig. 1).   The slope of the fully drawn iso-cost line expresses the factor–price ratios in the event of perfectly competitive factor hiring.   In this case A and B appear equally desirable to the firm.   Hence, both processes will be developed and used in the economy. However, if a " monopsonistic " imperfection raises the wage-rate relative to the rate of interest whenever the firm increases its labour input, A becomes superior to B.   The monopsonistic imperfection is here illustrated with the aid of an iso-cost line, which in the neighbourhood of the ordinate coincides with the fully-drawn line, but further down continues along the " broken " path.   Firms are here regarded as seeking (at a cost) innovation A or innovation B.

To save space I deduced the two central propositions of the argument in the Legends appearing under the two graphs.   In the text of this note I shall attempt to express the meaning of these two propositions briefly in more general terms.

The meaning of the first proposition (see Fig. 1) is that in some cases a preference may develop for inventions which are particularly factor-saving in the resource that is getting scarcer, because a *learning process* may induce atomistic firms to behave as if they were big enough to notice that *macro-economically* the factors of production are *not* in infinitely elastic supply. To be more specific, in Western economies, in which the supply of capital is expected to rise in a higher proportion than the supply of labour, a labour-saving invention which at present is inferior to a capital-saving invention may in due time become superior to the latter; and this is a macro-economic fact which the atomistic firm can *learn* by watching trends in factor prices. However, firms will, of course, give preference to a now inferior labour-saving invention over a now superior capital-saving invention only if they wish to make a substantial allowance for the possibility that no important further invention will be available for some time.   This is because for any given period the superiority or inferiority of an invention to the atomistic firm does not depend on whether the invention is relatively labour-saving or capital-saving.

The meaning of the second proposition (see Fig. 2) is that distortions or " market imperfections " of certain kinds may call forth market imper-fections of a different kind which counteract, or in some cases wholly neutralise, the initial distortion.   If, for example, the macro-economic capital–labour ratio is rising rapidly, and not enough labour-saving innovations are introduced, then after a sufficient decline of the profit rate this is apt to lead to a distortion which shows in the form of Keynesian Unemployment. This distortion results from imperfections—money-wage rigidities—such as prevent the Pigou–Patinkin process from going into effect. However, Keynesian Unemployment presupposes a low marginal efficiency of capital, and hence it may be interpreted as developing after an initial period in which labour is getting increasingly *scarce* relative to capital.[1] During this initial period a *counteracting* distortion (imperfection) is likely to develop, and this distortion may prevent the relative labour scarcity from turning into unemployment. The counteracting distortion is a consequence of the fact that in a situation of appreciably growing relative labour scarcity the individual firm is usually unable to hire additional labour of given qualities at unchanging wage-rates (an excess demand for labour of various kinds may exist for an extended period) and in these circumstances the individual firm does have reason to prefer labour-saving to capital-saving innovations. Technically, the reason is that in such circumstances even a small firm is in a quasi-monopsonistic position, since resources are not in infinitely elastic supply to the firm. If for this reason innovating activity becomes sufficiently slanted toward the labour-saving effect, the induced labour-saving slant may put an end to the relative labour scarcity and the phase of Keynesian Unemployment may thus be indefinitely postponed.

Similarly, if innovations become *too* labour-saving, and if for this or any other reason a relative shortage of *capital* develops,[2] the individual firm finds itself in a quasi-monopsonistic position in the capital market, and innovating activity may become directed into more capital-saving channels.

There is reason to assume that in those countries in which a genuine innovating process has originated, the character of innovating activity adjusted reasonably well to basic resource positions. I would like to suggest that this is unlikely to have been entirely the result of an historical accident.

WILLIAM FELLNER

Yale University.

[1] The type of unemployment with which the Keynesian theory is concerned has the " paradoxical " feature that it results indirectly from a labour supply which is *too small* to prevent the marginal efficiency of capital from falling to a critical level. It is this initial shortage of factors co-operating with capital which then turns into an excess supply of labour (because in the absence of the Pigou–Patinkin effect investment becomes insufficient to match savings at full employment). The other type of unemployment, which is usually attributed to the insufficiency of the capital stock (either because the labour supply is rising at a higher rate than the capital stock or because innovations become extremely labour-saving) does *not* have this " paradoxical " feature. This second type of unemployment may be explained directly with reference to the fact that given the size of the capital stock, the marginal productivity of the fully employed labour force would be smaller than the ruling wage-rate.

[2] Given a floor to real wage rates, such a shortage of capital can create the second type of unemployment discussed in the preceding footnote.

INDUCED BIAS IN INNOVATION AND THE THEORY OF DISTRIBUTION[1]

Charles Kennedy

PROFESSOR HICKS argued in the *Theory of Wages* that a fall in the price of capital relative to labour would induce inventions of a labour-saving type.[2] The late Mr. W. E. G. Salter has challenged this view for reasons given in the following quotation:

> " A second argument for assuming an inherent labour-saving bias arises out of the theory of induced inventions as set out by Hicks. This suggests that when labour becomes dearer relative to capital, the search for labour-saving techniques is stimulated. If one takes this to mean that new labour-saving designs are derived within the fold of existing knowledge, then this process is equivalent to the substitution within the designing process considered in Chapter II. It is simply a matter of words whether one terms new techniques of this character inventions or a form of factor substitution. If, however, the theory implies that dearer labour stimulates the search for new knowledge aimed specifically at saving labour, then it is open to serious objections. The entrepreneur is interested in reducing costs in total, not particular costs such as labour costs or capital costs. When labour costs rise any advance that reduces total cost is welcome, and whether this is achieved by saving labour or capital is irrelevant. There is no reason to assume that attention should be concentrated on labour-saving techniques, unless, because of some inherent characteristic of technology, labour-saving knowledge is easier to acquire than capital-saving knowledge." [3]

And he further summed up his general position in the concluding paragraph of the same chapter:

> " The above arguments make it difficult to accept any *a priori* reason for labour-saving biases sufficiently strong to explain the much greater increases in aggregate labour productivity compared to aggregate capital productivity. It therefore appears reasonable to place primary emphasis on the substitution induced by cheaper capital goods." [4]

Mr. Salter's reliance on substitution and his rejection of a theory of

[1] I am indebted to Dr. Ahmed of the University of Khartoum for having made clear to me, in an unpublished paper I have had the advantage of reading, the need for a reconsideration of the theory of induced bias in innovation.

[2] Macmillan, 1932, pp. 124 *et seq.*

[3] *Productivity and Technical Change*, Cambridge 1960, pp. 43–4.   [4] *Ibid.*, p. 44.

Reprinted with permission of author and publishers from the *Economic Journal, LXXIV* (September 1964), 541–547, published by Macmillan (Journals) Limited, London and St. Martin's Press, New York.

induced invention still leave some of the historical facts unexplained. While substitution as a result of cheaper capital goods is certainly adequate to account for the greater rise in aggregate labour productivity compared to aggregate capital productivity, it cannot explain the tendency, for advanced economies at any rate, towards constancy in distributive shares. This rough constancy of distributive shares requires in Mr. Salter's scheme an elasticity of substitution of unity, and there seems no *a priori* reason why it should take that particular value.[1]

One of the advantages of a theory of induced bias in innovation is that it can explain this constancy. The theory that will be presented below is both familiar and very simple, so simple in fact that those writers who have presented it have not thought it necessary to write more than a paragraph in explaining it.[2] However, in view of the controversy discussed above it may be desirable to set out the theory in more formal terms than have hitherto been used.

One of the reasons why Professor Hicks' theory of induced invention has not been developed as far as it might have been is that it was tied to changes in relative factor prices. This at once brought the theory up against the difficulty of drawing a sharp distinction between the substitution of capital for labour and labour-saving innovation. It will be argued below that changes in relative factor-prices are not essential for a theory of induced bias in innovation. Indeed, there is a good deal to be gained by presenting the theory in the first instance in a model in which relative factor prices do not change. Such a model is, of course, not to be regarded as realistic, since there is no doubt that technical progress in the capital-goods industries does lead to a secular fall in the price of capital goods relative to labour. There is, however, no great difficulty in later adapting the theory to take account of this fact.

Consider, then, a model in which technical progress takes place only in the consumption sector, the rate of interest is constant, labour is homogeneous, production functions are homogeneous of the first degree and there is perfect competition. These assumptions ensure that relative factor prices remain unchanged, and we can concern ourselves only with the nature of technical progress in the consumption sector. Assume further for simplicity that there is only one consumption product and two factors, labour and capital, the latter being measured in physical units. Let the total labour cost of producing one unit of product be L and the total capital cost be C. Denote the share of labour cost in total cost $\frac{L}{L+C}$ by λ and the share of capital cost $\frac{C}{L+C}$ by γ.

---

[1] It should be mentioned, however, that after a careful discussion Salter concludes finally that the constancy of distributive shares, though noteworthy, is not sufficiently marked or uniform to require a special hypothesis to explain it. *Ibid.*, Chapter X.

[2] E.g., Joan Robinson, *Accumulation of Capital* (Macmillan, 1956), p. 170, second complete paragraph.

In general, a technical improvement will reduce the amount of labour required to produce a unit of product in a certain proportion (p) and the amount of capital required in a proportion (q). Both p and q must obviously be less than one, but there is no reason for both to be positive— it is possible, for example, for a change that reduces labour requirements while increasing capital requirements still to be an improvement. An improvement will be labour-saving, neutral or capital-saving according as p is greater than, equal to or less than q.

It is reasonable to suppose that the entrepreneur will choose, or search for, the improvement that reduces his total unit cost in the greatest proportion. With constant factor prices, the proportionate reduction in unit costs (r) can be written:

$$r = \lambda p + \gamma q \ . \qquad . \quad . \quad . \quad . \quad . \quad (1)$$

Equation (1) suggests at once that the entrepreneur's choice of innovation, in so far as he has a choice, will not be a purely technological matter, but will be influenced by the economic weights λ and γ. If labour costs are high relative to capital costs ($\lambda > \gamma$) he will search, *ceteris paribus*, for a labour-saving innovation. If capital costs are high relative to labour costs he will search for a capital-saving innovation.

Even without further elaboration, the above argument would seem so indisputable that it is difficult to see how Mr. Salter, in the passage quoted above, persuaded himself otherwise. I believe he was misled by his own algebraic treatment. For he chose as his measure of technical progress the reduction in unit costs at constant prices or what we have denoted by r.[1] There is, of course, nothing improper in his choice of such a measure; but he then went on, so it seems to me, to regard r as independently given, rather than as something to be maximised.[2] It is this implicit treatment of r as an independent variable that has led him to reach a conclusion that conflicts with common sense. For if the reduction in unit costs is the same whatever the character of the innovation, then there is no reason why the entrepreneur should search for one type of improvement rather than another.

This same point may be approached in more formal terms as follows. It is clear that if the entrepreneur's choice of innovation is to be a determinate one there must be some restraint on the innovation possibilities, of the form

$$\phi(p, q) = 0 \qquad . \quad . \quad . \quad . \quad . \quad (2)$$

But there is no reason why this restraint should be the particular one

$$\lambda p + \gamma q = \text{constant} \ . \qquad . \quad . \quad . \quad . \quad (3)$$

as is implied by Salter's treatment of r as being independently given. Indeed, there is a very good reason why it should not be. In principle, the

---

[1] His T_r (defined on p. 31, *op. cit.*) is virtually the same as our r.
[2] Cf. especially *ibid.*, p. 39.

restraint on the innovation possibilities should be a purely technological one, and the introduction of the economic weights λ and γ into the restraint is therefore improper.

For further analysis, it will be useful to rewrite the restraint (2) in its explicit form

$$p = f(q) \qquad . \qquad . \qquad . \qquad . \qquad . \qquad (4)$$

and we shall take it that this function is quite independent of the economic weights λ and γ.

We then have a straightforward relative maximum problem. We are required to maximise r subject to the constraint $p = f(q)$. As a condition for a maximum we obtain, in the usual manner:

$$\frac{dp}{dq} = -\frac{\gamma}{\lambda} \qquad . \qquad . \qquad . \qquad . \qquad . \qquad (5)$$

In order to interpret this result, some discussion of the main characteristics of the innovation possibility function (4) is required. In the first place we should expect that

$$\frac{dp}{dq} < 0 \qquad . \qquad . \qquad . \qquad . \qquad . \qquad . \qquad (6)$$

Labour-reducing improvements are competitive with capital-reducing improvements; or, in other words, the greater the reduction in the labour required to produce a unit of output, the smaller will be the possible reduction in capital required. Indeed, after a certain point an increase in capital requirements will be necessary in order to make possible further reduction in labour requirements.

Secondly, it can be argued that

$$\frac{d^2p}{dq^2} < 0 \qquad . \qquad . \qquad . \qquad . \qquad . \qquad (7)$$

It is clear that for p to approach its upper limit of 1, even if this were at all possible, very large increases in the amount of capital would be required. Similarly, for q to approach 1, very large increases in labour would be required.

Graphically, the general shape of the innovation possibility function (4) can be thus shown as in Fig. 1.

It follows from (5), (6) and (7) above that the greater the share of labour costs in total costs, the more labour-saving will be the innovation chosen, or searched for, by the entrepreneur. The formal analysis merely confirms the conclusion already suggested by (1).

A bias in innovation will alter the weights λ and γ in the next period. However, on the assumption that the characteristics of the innovation possibility function (4) are the same in successive periods, equilibrium values

of the weights will be established.   Since, when $p = q$, there will be no
change in the weights from one period to the next, it follows from (5) that the
equilibrium values of the weights will be determined by the value of dp/dq
when $p = q$.   This particular value of dp/dq may be taken as an indicator of
the fundamental technological bias in innovation possibilities.   If, for
$p = q$, $-dp/dq$ is greater than one, we may say that there is a labour-saving
technological bias, which will result in a higher equilibrium value of γ
than of λ.

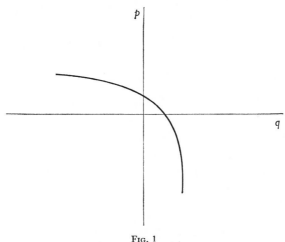

Fig. 1

The weights λ and γ stand not only for the share of the costs of a particular
factor in total costs but also for the distributive share of the different factors.
The analysis above has therefore established that in the long run the equilibrium values of the two distributive shares will be determined by the
characteristics of the purely technological innovation possibility function.
It is likely, moreover, that these equilibrium values will be stable ones, since
any departure from the equilibrium values will induce a bias in innovation
which will tend to restore the equilibrium values.[1]   The above theory of
induced bias in innovation explains the tendency to constancy in distributive
shares.

The analysis can easily be adapted to take care of the case in which technical progress takes place in the capital sector as well as in the consumption
sector.   It remains true that there will be determinate long-run equilibrium
values of the weights λ and γ, and that any departure from these equilibrium
values will induce a bias in innovation tending to restore them.   The main
difference arises from the fact that the equality of p and q will no longer

[1] Stability requires also a sufficient degree of curvature in the innovation possibility function.
If the curvature were insufficient it would be possible for the weights to oscillate in an extreme
manner from one period to the next.   The empirical evidence would not appear to support a belief
in any such tendency to extreme oscillation.

ensure constancy in the weights from one period to another, since the share
of capital costs in total costs is continuously being reduced by a fall in the
unit cost of producing capital goods brought about by technical progress in
the capital sector. If we denote the proportional fall in the unit cost of
producing capital goods by s, then it follows that in the consumption sector
the condition for equilibrium of the weights λ and γ is that

$$p = q + s$$

The equilibrium values of the weights will therefore depend on the value of
dp/dq when $p = q + s$. Since for a given innovation possibility function the
value of $-dp/dq$ is likely to be lower when p is greater than q than when p
is equal to q, it follows that technical progress in the capital sector is likely
to result in a higher equilibrium share going to labour than would be the case
if technical progress were confined to the consumption sector.

The system admits of a particularly simple solution in the case of the
much-analysed one-product model in which the single product can be used
equally well as consumption good or as capital good. In this case the
proportional fall in unit cost of capital goods (s) will be equal to the proportional fall in unit cost of the product (r) where

$$r = \lambda p + \gamma(q + s) \quad . \quad . \quad . \quad . \quad . \quad (8)$$

We therefore have

$$r = \lambda p + \gamma(q + r) \quad . \quad . \quad . \quad . \quad . \quad (9)$$

Since the condition of long-run equilibrium in distributive shares is that p
should equal $(q + r)$, and since also $\lambda + \gamma = 1$, it follows that for equilibrium

$$r = p = q + r$$

so that $q = 0$. We therefore have the result that the long-run equilibrium
distributive shares will be determined by the value of dp/dq when q is equal
to zero.[1]

Two features of the above theory are perhaps worthy of notice. In the
first place, it has not been found necessary to face the question of how far a
fall in labour requirements has been brought about by labour-saving
innovation rather than substitution of capital for labour as a result of the
cheapening of capital goods. Since this question is in principle unanswer-
able, there is some advantage in not having to ask it. It is, of course, true
that a fall in the price of capital goods will affect the choice of innovation,
but in our theory it has this effect as a result of its influence on the weights
λ and γ.

---

[1] This result is confirmed by the Harrod–Robinson analysis of neutral technical progress. In
the one-product model the capital–output ratio will remain constant only if the quantity of capital
rises *pari passu* with output.

In the second place it is a feature of the theory that the long-run equilibrium values of distributive shares are determined by the characteristics of the purely technological innovation possibility function.   In particular, the rate of interest has no bearing on the equilibrium solution.   It is true that it has been necessary to assume a constant rate of interest, because a change in the rate of interest would alter the relative factor prices, and thus the weights λ and γ in the short run.   But a change in the rate of interest, if permanently maintained, will have no effect on the long-run equilibrium values of the weights.

What started as a rather simple-minded theory of induced bias in innovation has turned out in the event to be a theory of distribution in its own right.   It has certain affinities with the marginal productivity theory of distribution—the slope of the innovation possibility function plays a somewhat similar role to that of the ratio of the marginal products in the latter theory.   It also shares some of the latter theory's weaknesses: an inability to take account of increasing returns to scale or of monopolistic elements in production.   At the same time, it has two important advantages over the marginal productivity theory.   First, it is dynamic in the sense of relying on innovation possibilities rather than on the characteristics of a static production function.[1]   Secondly, it has greater explanatory force, in that it can explain the rough historical constancy in distributive shares.   For these reasons those economists who still regard the marginal productivity theory as having something useful to say, may think that the theory outlined above is an improvement.   And it is even possible that it may commend itself to those who have already rejected the marginal productivity theory because of its unsatisfactory static features.

CHARLES KENNEDY

University of the West Indies,
Mona, Jamaica.

[1] Surprisingly enough, in view of the role that it has played in the above analysis, our innovation possibility function is really a disguised form of Kaldor's famous technical progress function (ECONOMIC JOURNAL, December 1957, pp. 595, *et seq.*).   Kaldor relates the proportional change in output per man-year to the proportional change in capital per man.   But it is, of course, possible to derive from these two variables the proportional change in output per unit of capital, and this means that if the technical progress function is known the innovation possibility function can be derived from it.

B. Vintage Model

Investment and Technical Progress

ROBERT M. SOLOW
Massachusetts Institute of Technology

1. Aggregate Production Functions and Technical Change

In a series of papers [1], [2], [3], [5], [7], [8], `[9] over the last few years, a number of authors have suggested an interesting and important proposition: that by far the larger part of the observed increase in output per head is a consequence of "technical progress" rather than of increased capital per head. The methods used are not all the same. In particular, some authors have made explicit use of an aggregate production function and others have on the surface avoided this device. Still, I think it fair to say that explicitly or implicitly the model underlying this work may be represented thus: $Q(t) = F(K(t), L(t); t)$ or more specifically

(1) $$Q(t) = B(t)f(K(t), L(t)) .$$

Here, Q, K, and L stand respectively for aggregate output and inputs of physical capital and labor services at time t. One may describe this as an aggregate production function shifting through time. The second and considerably more restrictive representation amounts to the assumption that shifts in the production function are "neutral" or "uniform." There is not much evidence for or against this assumption; since it is a great convenience it will be adopted without comment.

Three other specializations of (1) are sometimes made. The first is to postulate that the production function exhibits constant returns to scale, that is, that F or f is homogeneous of first degree in K and L. A nineteenth-century follower of Malthus and Ricardo would be inclined to believe that since land and other irreplaceable natural resources are implicitly being held constant, a tendency to diminishing returns would show itself. But over historical time few observers would claim to have found this the case, at least not in aggregates that give a heavy weight to manufacturing and other non-extractive industries. Against this, an even older tradition might expect to find increasing returns to scale, as a consequence of an ever-finer division of labor. A delicate empirical question arises here. Over long periods of time one observes a continuing trend increase in K and L. Presumably $B(t)$ is also an increasing function of time. Thus the effects of technical progress and of increasing returns to scale are confounded in the data. If K and L each double and Q increases by 110 per cent, the extra 10 per cent may be due to either effect or to both, and the time series do not provide enough independent variation to settle the allocation with confidence. Once again I will follow the dictates of custom and convenience and assume constant returns to scale.

Secondly, in [9] I stated my belief that the particular functional form adopted for f is a matter of no great consequence. Over the range of K/L actually observed in the United States almost any function of two variables with positive partial derivatives and the right curvature will do fairly well. The time-hallowed favorite is the constant-elasticity Cobb-Douglas function, and I adopt it in what follows. I think this is a safe procedure as long as it is taken frankly as an approximation and no deep distributive meaning is read into the results. My calculations could be carried out in principle with any choice of a production function; the Cobb-Douglas function enables me to carry them out in practice.

Finally, if we approximate $B(t)$ by an exponential, equation (1) is reduced to

$$(2) \qquad\qquad Q(t) = Be^{\lambda t}L(t)^{\alpha}K(t)^{1-\alpha} \ .$$

In this form the model has been used by Aukrust [2] on Norwegian, Niitamo [6] on Finnish, and Valavanis [11] on American data. My own earlier paper [9] can be interpreted in this way, as Aukrust has done, although my primary purpose at the time was to find a way to avoid the restrictive assumptions and to deal instead with (1) or something even more general. For the more complicated problem I want to treat now, I have not found any way to improve upon (2).

2. An Objection to the Usual Formulation

There are other criticisms that can be leveled against any attempt to interpret aggregate economic statistics in terms of (2). There are index-number problems involved in the measurement of each of the variables. In the same vein it may be argued that the aggregate production function is itself a dubious tool. Even waiving all this, it is true that the notion of time-shifts in the function is a confession of ignorance rather than a claim to knowledge; they ought to be analyzed further into such components as improvements in the skill and quality of the labor force, returns to investment in research and education, improvements in technique within industries, and changes in the industrial composition of input and output, etc.

But in this paper I want to take up only one difficulty with (2), a rather different one. It is an implication of (2) that "technical change" is peculiarly disembodied. It floats down from the outside. If K and L are held constant, equation (2) predicts that output will increase anyway, approximately exponentially at rate λ. If K and L both increase exponentially at rate γ, then output will simply increase at rate $\gamma + \lambda$. In particular, the pace of investment has no influence on the rate at which technique improves. It is as if all technical progress were something like time-and-motion study, a way of improving the organization and operation of inputs without reference to the nature of the inputs themselves. The striking assumption is that old and new capital equipment participate equally in technical change. This conflicts with the casual observation that many if not most innovations need to be embodied in new kinds of durable equipment before they can be made effective. Improvements in technology affect output only to the extent that they are carried into practice either by net capital formation or by the replacement of old-fashioned equipment by the latest models, with a consequent shift in the distribution of equipment by date of birth.

My objective is to reconstruct the model to make allowance for this aspect of reality.

3. An Alternative Model

To this end, it becomes necessary to distinguish capital equipment of different dates of construction or vintages. Let $K_v(t)$ represent the number of machines or units of capital of vintage v (i.e., produced at time v) still in existence at time $t \geq v$. At time t, the surviving stock of capital of vintage v will be worked by a certain quantity of labor, $L_v(t)$. If $L(t)$ is the total supply of labor, to be allocated over capital of all vintages, we have

$$(3) \qquad L(t) = \int_{-\infty}^{t} L_v(t)\, dv \, .$$

My assumption is that all technical progress is uniform and approximately exponential over time, and that capital goods at their moment of construction embody all the latest knowledge but share not at all in any further improvements in technology.[1] If $Q_v(t)$ stands for the output produced at time t using equipment of vintage v, then

$$(4) \qquad Q_v(t) = B e^{\lambda v} L_v(t)^{\alpha} K_v(t)^{1-\alpha} \, .$$

Thus the Cobb-Douglas function applies for output produced with capital of given vintage,[2] but it is also evident the multiplicative improve-

---

[1] It would not be difficult to allow simultaneously for a component of progress that does diffuse equally over old and new capital.

[2] One special feature of (4) depends critically on the multiplicative form of the Cobb-Douglas function. Suppose I write $Q_v(t) = B L_v(t)^{\alpha} [e^{\lambda t/(1-\alpha)} K_v(t)]^{1-\alpha}$. Formally, all technological progress appears as a steady improvement in the quality of capital goods at rate $\lambda/(1 - \alpha)$; this accounts for the important role this number will turn out to play. On the surface it seems that by grouping terms differently I could make it appear that only the quality of the labor force improves. But it is not really so. Shortly I shall require the marginal productivity of labor to be equal regardless of the vintage of the capital on which works. This condition reveals that labor is viewed as homogeneous. Of course I could *completely* reverse the roles of L and K, and then it would be legitimate to speak of sucessive generations of workers as more efficient than their forbears. Or if I were to treat B as a non-constant function of time, I could think of it as representing either pure know-how or improvement in the labor force, irrespec-

ment factor turns itself off the moment that the capital goods take shape.[3]

For $Q(t)$, the total output at time t, we have

(5) $$Q(t) = \int_{-\infty}^{t} Q_v(t)\, dv .$$

The quantity $K_v(v)$ stands for gross investment, the output of capital goods at time v. Call it $I(v)$. I shall make the simplest possible assumption about depreciation, that is, that capital goods are exposed to a constant force of mortality δ. Thus the average length of life of capital is $1/\delta$ and

(6) $$K_v(t) = K_v(v)e^{-\delta(t-v)} = I(v)e^{-\delta(t-v)} .$$

The picture is one of a continuum of capital goods of various vintages and corresponding productivity, subject to an exponential life table. At each moment of time the labor force is reshuffled over the existing capital goods. Total output is determined by integrating over all layers of capital stock.

If there is competition in the labor market, all homogeneous labor must receive the same wage regardless of the age of the capital on which it operates. Hence the allocation of labor to capital of various vintages must equalize the marginal productivity of labor in all uses. This will also have the effect of maximizing the output obtainable from the given total labor force and the given stock of capital goods. Naturally, this does not mean that the marginal product of labor is constant over time, but rather that it is a function of time and independent of v for each t. Let $m(t)$ be the marginal product of labor at time t; then from (4) we have

(7) $$m(t) = \frac{\partial Q_v(t)}{\partial L_v(t)} = \alpha B\, e^{\lambda v} L_v(t)^{\alpha-1} K_v(t)^{1-\alpha} .$$

Substitute for $K_v(t)$ from (6), solve for $L_v(t)$, and write $\sigma = \delta + \lambda/(1-\alpha)$; the result is

(8) $$L_v(t) = (\alpha B)^{1/(1-\alpha)} e^{-\delta t} m(t)^{1/(\alpha-1)} e^{\sigma v} I(v) = h(t) e^{\sigma v} I(v) .$$

If desired, $m(t)$ can then be determined from (3), since

(9) $$L(t) = (\alpha B)^{1/(1-\alpha)} e^{-\delta t} m(t)^{1/(\alpha-1)} \int_{-\infty}^{t} e^{\sigma v} I(v)\, dv = h(t) \int_{-\infty}^{t} e^{\sigma v} I(v)\, dv .$$

---

tive of date of birth. But all this is possible only because the production function is multiplicative. For other production functions that are homogeneous of first degree, one cannot translate a multiplicative shift of the whole function into improvement factors for individual inputs one at a time. (Of course, trivially a multiplicative shift can be thought of as an identical shift in all factors.)

[3] In a remarkable recent paper in *Econometrica* [4], Leif Johansen makes use of a rather similar formulation. But he also postulates that the ratio L_v/K_v is fixed at the moment capital is produced and is thereafter invariant. Thus the successive layers of old capital are operated under a fixed-proportion constraint, although the proportions themselves may vary from vintage to vintage. I am assuming that factor proportions are freely variable throughout the life of the equipment. The truth is no doubt somewhere in between.

Substitution of (8) in (4) and simplification yields $Q_v(t) = B e^{-\delta(1-\alpha)t} h(t)^\alpha e^{\sigma v} I(v)$ and, from (5), we have

(10) $$Q(t) = B e^{-\delta(1-\alpha)t} h(t)^\alpha \int_{-\infty}^{t} e^{\sigma v} I(v) \, dv \ .$$

Together, (9) and (10) give

(11) $$Q(t) = B e^{-\delta(1-\alpha)t} L(t)^\alpha J(t)^{1-\alpha} \ ,$$

where

$$J(t) = \int_{-\infty}^{t} e^{\sigma v} I(v) \, dv \ .$$

This is the equation that replaces the earlier formulation (2). The surface similarity hides some real differences, since $J(t)$ has a more complicated structure than the earlier $K(t)$. But a bit of similarity is regained when one remembers that in (2) the function $K(t)$ must represent net capital stock in the sense of machinery that is still in existence and productive. If we make the exponential life-table assumption, we have

(6′) $$K(t) = e^{-\delta t} \int_{-\infty}^{t} e^{\delta v} I(v) \, dv \ ,$$

and (2) and (11) will coincide when $\lambda = 0$ and differ otherwise, as differ they must.[4]

If an economy characterized by (2) and (6′) and one characterized by (11) and (6) have forever experienced the same rate of gross investment[5] and the same input of labor, and $\lambda \neq 0$, then of course the second economy will have a lower output than the first, and in general a different rate of growth of output. One curiosity does arise. If the two economies have both grown exponentially since the beginning of time, that is, if $L(t)$ and $I(t)$ have both been proportional to $e^{\gamma t}$, then while the second system will still have a lower output than the first, the outputs will remain in proportion and both will grow at the same rate, $\gamma + \lambda$.

---

[4] The reason why in working with (2) one could get along without an explicit assumption about depreciation has to do with application rather than with theory. For empirical experimentation with (2), one needs only a running estimate of net capital stock. The more complicated assumptions underlying (11) require in addition the vintage composition of the net stock of capital goods. Since such figures are not to be found in the usual sources, one has to create them by an assumption about depreciation. This is not so bad, since if the required figures *were* to be found in the usual sources, they would have been created in approximately this way. The most restrictive aspect of (6) is the assumption that δ is a constant, that technical change and the market itself do not influence the average durability of capital goods.

[5] This is not a wholly unambiguous notion. By the same rate of gross investment I mean the same physical output of "machines." But machines behave differently in the two economies and so must asset valuation. Production of identical numbers of machines may have quite different implications in value terms.

4. Estimation of λ

The empirical use of (2) is easy; all the parameters can be estimated by linear regression from time series of the logarithms of Q, K, and L. Purely statistical difficulties may arise if K and L have approximately exponential time paths, but at least implementation is straightforward. No such simple routine will work with (11), because time series of $J(t)$ are not to be had—in fact $J(t)$ is defined in terms of the unknown parameters. I have not found any elegant way of dealing empirically with (11). The experiment I report here involves taking outside estimates of α and δ and using the model (11) only for estimation of λ (and the inessential scale constant B).

From (11), we have

$$Q(t)^{1/(1-\alpha)} = B^{1/(1-\alpha)}e^{-\delta t}L(t)^{\alpha/(1-\alpha)}\int_{-\infty}^{t} e^{\sigma v}I(v)\,dv\;.$$

Designate the quotient $Q(t)^{1/(1-\alpha)} \div L(t)^{\alpha/(1-\alpha)}$ as $R(t)$. Then

$$R(t) = B^{1/(1-\alpha)}e^{-\delta t}\int_{-\infty}^{t} e^{\sigma v}I(v)\,dv\;,\qquad \frac{dR}{dt} = -\delta R + B^{1/(1-\alpha)}e^{(\sigma-\delta)t}I(t)\;,$$

so that

(12)
$$\frac{\dfrac{dR}{dt} + \delta R}{I(t)} = B^{1/(1-\alpha)}e^{\lambda t/(1-\alpha)}\;.$$

If we have any trial estimates of α and δ, it is possible[6] from time series of Q, L, and I to construct a series $(\Delta R + \delta R)/I$ to represent the left-hand side of (12). The logarithm of this series plotted against time should yield a straight line whose slope would be an estimate of $\lambda/(1 - \alpha)$.

5. An Empirical Application

I have used (12) to provide an estimate of λ for aggregate time series from the United States over the period 1919–53. Since this is meant as a preliminary exploration rather than as a definitive empirical study, I will not report the results or the data in detail but will limit myself to a summary of the conclusions. The basic sources of data were Kendrick's time series of real private gross national product and private man-hours employed [5], together with a series on real gross capital formation taken from Kuznets' still unpublished National Bureau of Economic Research study, *Capital Formation and Its Financing*. One difficulty is that the Kuznets

---

[6] In principle I could go one step further and estimate δ as well as λ from the data, using only an outside estimate of α. Differentiate (12), or better still the equation above it, once more with respect to time and use (12). The result is

$$\frac{d^2R}{dt^2} - \frac{1}{I}\frac{dI}{dt} = \delta\left[\frac{R}{I}\frac{dI}{dt} - \frac{dR}{dt}\right] + \frac{\lambda}{1-\alpha}\frac{dR}{dt}\frac{\delta\lambda}{1-\alpha}R\;.$$

But to use this as a regression equation would involve using a time series of second differences of R, and the results would almost certainly be worthless.

investment series includes government capital formation, although I did eliminate the "durable munitions" component. In dealing with (12), I used two values of α, 2/3 and 3/4, which bracket most of the previously published estimates. I used $\delta = .04$, which implies an average lifetime of twenty-five years for capital goods, and about this I have some serious qualms. Kuznets estimates the average life of equipment to be about twelve years and of buildings to be about fifty years. The relative weight of these two components in the capital stock varies slowly over time. A more difficult problem is presented by the fact that equipment is presumably much more subject to the risk of obsolescence than are buildings. Perhaps the best way to handle this is in terms of an aggregate production function that treats equipment and buildings as separately identifiable aggregates. But I have not done this yet.

The right-hand side of (12) is obviously positive, so the left-hand side is subject to the same condition. However, in the data the expression $\Delta R + .04R$ becomes negative in five of the thirty-five years. For those years, clearly, the model does not apply. The nature of the difficulty becomes clear when one notes that the bad years are 1920, 1930, 1932, 1933, and 1946. Thus it appears that the model fails badly in years when GNP declines substantially. This is confirmed by the fact that the figure for 1938, although not negative, is quite low. Now this kind of difficulty is not surprising. Any kind of aggregate production function can at most hope to provide an explanation of "capacity output." Or, to put it differently, a model like mine presupposes that capital equipment is never left idle (unless of course its marginal physical product has fallen to zero). But in fact over business cycles the phenomenon of excess capacity does appear. Within the model this might be characterized as a case of extraordinarily rapid retirement of capital, followed perhaps by a later compensating under-mortality as the excess capacity is drawn into use. This would have the effect of making the expression $\Delta R + \delta R$ at least more positive in the offending years.

The scatter diagrams (Figures 1 and 2) show a plot of the common logarithm of $(\Delta R + .04R)/I$ against calendar time for the case $\alpha=2/3$ and again for $\alpha=3/4$. The latter gives a slightly tighter fit, with a correlation of .72. The regression slope is .043, which implies $\lambda = .025$. The fit is not impressive, but it is at least fair and could probably be improved by careful rectification of the underlying data, and perhaps by an alternative choice of δ. It is tempting, having estimated λ from (12), to use the relation $B^{1/(1-\alpha)}e^{\lambda t/(1-\alpha)}I - \Delta R = \delta R$ to improve the trial value of δ, and then to iterate back and forth through successive approximations to λ and δ. In practice I found the first couple of values of δ to be fairly erratic, without much effect on λ. It seems preferable to wait for improvement of the data.

This value of λ is substantially larger than the .015 generally produced by empirical fits of model (2). The difference is in the direction one would expect, for in (11) the rate of increase of over-all productivity is slowed down by the drag of the older and less productive backlog of capital goods.

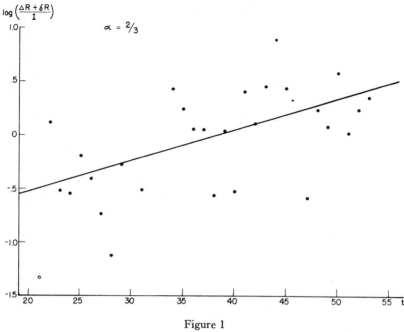

Figure 1

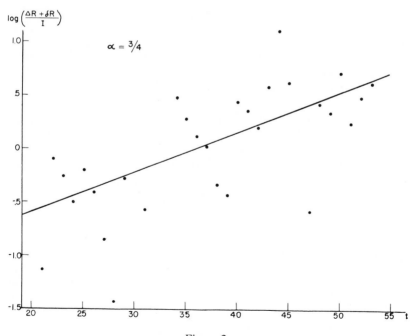

Figure 2

6. Economic Significance

When the aggregate production function (2) is estimated from time series for advanced economies, λ always comes out to be around .015 and α to be about .75. From this flows an important conclusion: that the possibility of speeding up economic growth by faster accumulation of capital is extremely limited. This follows because (2) implies

$$\frac{1}{Q}\frac{dQ}{dt} = \lambda + \alpha\frac{1}{L}\frac{dL}{dt} + (1-\alpha)\frac{1}{K}\frac{dK}{dt}\ .$$

If we take the numerical values suggested and assume the labor force to grow at 1 per cent per year and the capital–output ratio to be about 3,[7] output will grow at about 3 per cent per year if 10 per cent of the national product is invested. If the investment quota is doubled from 10 per cent to 20 per cent, the rate of increase of output rises only to just under 4 per cent. This seems like a meager reward for what is after all a revolution in the speed of accumulation of capital.

The alternative model developed in this paper redresses the balance somewhat and attributes greater importance to capital investment. The reason is, of course, that capital formation is a vehicle for carrying technical change into effect. A numerical illustration of this point will also suggest how deceptive it may be to traffic exclusively in exponential rates of growth, as many economists have come to do.

Let me make this last point first, and then proceed to a more useful comparison of the two models. In (2), suppose that both $L(t)$ and $I(t)$ have always grown exponentially at rate γ. Then Q has grown and will grow at rate $\gamma + \lambda$. Now turn to (11); make the same assumptions and precisely the same conclusions emerge. Output will grow in the form $e^{(\gamma+\lambda)t}$. *But,* in the first place, (2) yields an output that has a ratio of

$$\left(\frac{\sigma + \gamma}{\delta + \gamma}\right)^{1-\alpha} : 1\ .$$

to the output of (11). Thus the absolute gap in output between the two models itself grows exponentially, the ratio remaining fixed. As one would expect, (2) is more optimistic than (11), and possibly substantially more so. Since

$$\left(\frac{\sigma + \gamma}{\delta + \gamma}\right)^{1-\alpha} = \left(1 + \frac{\lambda}{(1-\alpha)(\delta + \gamma)}\right)^{1-\alpha}\ ,$$

we observe that the relative optimism of (2) increases in direct proportion to λ and in inverse proportion to γ, both of which conclusions confirm common sense.

In the second place, it seems to me that calculations of this kind may be quite misleading. It is not hard to generate paradoxes by juggling exponen-

---

[7] This is not quite legitimate. One cannot independently specify the production function, the rate of increase of the labor force, the rate of accumulation of capital, *and* the capital-output ratio. But to be more accurate would not change the flavor.

tials. If investment has been growing exponentially forever, then the capital stock is composed overwhelmingly of extremely new items. This is what enables (11) to make output grow at the same rate as (2): the drag of obsolete capital is relatively small. But the practical question is really a different one: if the rate of capital formation is stepped up now, how much will it influence output over the next decade?

Suppose that gross investment has always been constant, equal to I_0, up until $t = 0$, and that at $t = 0$ it jumps to and remains at $(1 + h)I_0$. For simplicity, assume that employment remains constant after $t = 0$. Then calculate the ratio of GNP at time t to GNP at time 0. From (2) we get

$$\frac{Q(t)}{Q(0)} = e^{\lambda t}[1 + h(1 - e^{-\delta t})]^{1-\alpha} .$$

From (11) we get

$$\frac{Q(t)}{Q(0)} = e^{\lambda t}[1 + h(1 - e^{-\sigma t})]^{1-\alpha} .$$

Remember that this is not the whole story. The $Q(0)$ derived fom (2) is itself larger than the $Q(0)$ derived from (11) in the ratio

$$\left(1 + \frac{\lambda}{(1 - \alpha)\delta}\right)^{1-\alpha} .$$

Let us put $\lambda = .015$, $\alpha = .7$, and $\delta = .05$, so that $\sigma = 10$, and ask what the picture is at $t = 10$. To make things substantial, imagine that $h = 1$, that is, that the historical rate of gross capital formation was suddenly doubled at $t = 0$. Then (2) would imply that $Q(10)/Q(0) = 1.28$, while (11) would make $Q(10)/Q(0) = 1.35$. If h were zero, that is, if the additional investment were not undertaken at all, the ten-year increase would be 16 per cent in both cases. Thus (2) suggests that the doubling of gross investment brought about an additional 12 per cent increase in output, while (11) attributes to the new capital formation a 19 per cent increase in output over a decade. The difference is not staggering, but neither does it seem to me negligible.

Similar calculations can be made for the hypothetical case in which investment has been constant until $t = 0$, at which time it begins to increase at 5 per cent per year. The results are not qualitatively different from the above. The $Q(t)/Q(0)$ ratios are about 1.19 and 1.25 respectively, and since as before the ratio would be 1.16 with no change in investment policy, we may say that (2) attributes a 3 per cent increase in output to the new capital formation, while (11) imputes 9 per cent.[8]

All this is with $\lambda = .015$, as in the earlier studies. Since my tentative empirical calculations suggest that λ is closer to .03, let me rework my first case above using this value. With $\lambda = .03$, σ becomes .15, with all

---

[8] Since $Q(t)/Q(0)$ is made up multiplicatively out of the "pure" λ effect and an investment effect, this additive decomposition must be interpreted as rough description, not as metaphysics. A decomposition in reverse order would lead to slightly different results.

other constants having the same value as before. Then the model (2) gives $Q(10)/Q(0) = 1.49$ and (11) gives $Q(10)/Q(0) = 1.61$. Now if $h = 0$, the ten-year increase in output would be 35 per cent. Thus (2) attributes to the doubling of gross investment an additional 14 per cent increase in output, while according to (11) the extra capital formation is responsible for a 26 per cent increase in output over the decade. In other words, (11) makes the extra capital formation and technical progress share almost equally in the increase of output. This somewhat understates the difference between the two models, since (11) asserts what (2) denies; that if gross investment were to fall to zero, technical progress would cease.

7. Valuation of Assets

The view of production developed here practically begs to be incorporated into a model of macroeconomic growth and fluctuation. That requires among other things a theory of savings, which in turn requires a definition of net income and some measurement of capital values. The introduction of technical progress and changes in the quality of capital goods makes the valuation problem just a bit more complicated. I do not propose to carry out the full program here, but I will take the first steps toward the distinction between net and gross output. The very first step, of course, has to be the valuation of durable assets. In another paper I intend to give a fuller treatment of these questions, using for the purpose a two-sector model in which the production of capital goods is sharply distinguished from the production of consumables.

To begin with, the gross rental per unit time earned by a piece of vintage v capital at time t will under competitive conditions settle at the marginal product of vintage v capital. On the assumption that for $t \geqq v$ the surviving stock of old capital is inelastically supplied to the market, the gross rental can be calculated from (4) and (6) to be

$$(13) \qquad r(v,\ t) = (1 - \alpha)[\alpha^{\alpha}Bm(t)^{-\alpha}e^{\lambda v}]^{1/(1-\alpha)} .$$

This value is expressed in terms of units of output, or in other words the price of a unit of output is one. At time t the only kind of capital commodity actually being constructed is vintage t capital. The value placed by the market on a unit of older capital will depend only on the rentals it is expected to earn over the indefinite future. Thus the second-hand price of a piece of equipment is inevitably a matter of anticipations about future earnings and therefore about future gross investment decisions. This last is true because the rentals earned by equipment will be influenced by the extent of competition from newer capital goods.

Suppose first that the market anticipates future rentals correctly. Then the value at time t of a unit of vintage v capital is

$$p_v(t) = \int_t^{\infty} r(v,\ u)e^{-\delta(u-t)-\rho(u-t)}\,du ,$$

166

where future rentals are discounted at the market interest rate ρ and by the allowance for depreciation δ. For simplicity, the interest rate is assumed to be constant. Were it to vary over time in a known way, the expression $\rho(u - t)$ would need to be replaced by

$$\int_t^u \rho(z)\,dz$$

in all that follows, with no fundamental change in results. Substitution in the present-value integral and use of (7)–(9) gives

$$(14) \qquad p_v(t) = (1 - \alpha)B\,e^{\lambda v/(1-\alpha)+(\delta+\rho)t}\int_t^\infty L(u)^\alpha J(u)^{-\alpha}e^{-[\delta(1-\alpha)+\rho]u}\,du\ .$$

Now at time t there exist $I(v)e^{-\delta(t-v)}$ units of vintage v capital, and the total value of this stock is

$$(15) \qquad A_v(t) = p_v(t)I(v)e^{-\delta(t-v)} = (1 - \alpha)B\,e^{\rho t}e^{\sigma v}I(v)\int_t^\infty (L/J)^\alpha e^{-[\delta(1-\alpha)+\rho]u}\,du\ .$$

Finally, the value of the complete stock of capital of all vintages at time t is obtained by integrating $A_v(t)$ over all vintages and is

$$(16) \qquad A(t) = (1 - \alpha)B\,e^{\rho t}J(t)\int_t^\infty (L/J)^\alpha e^{-[\delta(1-\alpha)+\rho]u}\,du\ .$$

We can make one important simplification in these formulas. If $I(t) > 0$, so that gross investment is actually occurring, the market value of a unit of brand new capital must also be equal to its cost of production. If the model is completely aggregated, so that a unit of new capital is simply a unit of output, then this market value must be unity. That is,

$$(17) \qquad p_t(t) = (1 - \alpha)B\,e^{(\sigma+\rho)t}\int_t^\infty (L/J)^\alpha e^{-[\delta(1-\alpha)+\rho]u}\,du = 1\ .$$

It follows that

$$(18) \qquad\qquad\qquad A(t) = e^{-\sigma t}J(t)\ .$$

This may be taken as a condition on the rate of interest.[9]

Substitution of (18) into (11) leads to a remarkable result:

$$Q(t) = B\,e^{\lambda t}L(t)^\alpha A(t)^{1-\alpha}\ ,$$

which is almost identical to (2). Thus if asset valuations faithfully reflected perfect foresight, the "homogeneous capital" model (2) would be accurate, provided the capital stock were measured not by a count of machines but by the real market value of the stock of capital.

---

[9] This equation places a very strong restriction on the gross investment over time that is consistent with a constant rate of interest. If we think of the rate of gross investment and the evolution of the supply of labor as determined by some other mechanism, then the rate of interest will change over time and all formulas should be amended as suggested earlier to accommodate a variable $\rho(t)$.

However, all this is under conditions of accurate foresight as to future rates of technological progress, labor-force growth, and gross capital formation. Any other assumption about the formation of expectations will naturally lead to different results but in the same straightforward way. For example, at the opposite extreme we can work out the consequences of the naive belief that at any time t, future gross rentals on each layer of the capital stock will remain exactly what they currently are. Let an asterisk denote values calculated under this assumption. Then

$$
p_v^*(t) = r(v,\ t) \int_t^\infty e^{-\delta(u-t)-\rho(u-t)}\ du = \frac{r(v,\ t)}{\rho + \delta}\ ,
$$

(19) $$A_v^*(t) = \frac{r(v,\ t)I(v)e^{-\delta(t-v)}}{\rho + \delta}\ ,$$

$$
A^*(t) = (1-\alpha)BL(t)^\alpha J(t)^{1-\alpha}e^{-\delta(1-\alpha)t}(\rho + \delta)^{-1} = (1-\alpha)\frac{Q(t)}{\rho + \delta}\ .
$$

One could have written down the last result without computation. Under the Cobb-Douglas assumption, gross rentals on capital of vintage v are $(1-\alpha)Q_v(t)$. Hence total gross rentals are $(1-\alpha)Q(t)$. Hence the present value of future rentals under the naive assumption is simply $(1-\alpha)Q(t)$ capitalized at the interest rate ρ and "discounted" for depreciation.

It is an implication of (19) that the capital–output ratio, defined as the value of the capital stock divided by the gross output $Q(t)$, is a constant, equal to $(1-\alpha)/(\rho + \delta)$. If $1-\alpha$ is taken to lie between 1/4 and 1/3, and ρ and δ taken to be numbers between .04 and .08 (remember that δ relates only to physical depreciation, not to obsolescence), then the implied capital–output ratio will be somewhere between 1.5 and 3, which seems reasonable.

Neither of the extreme hypotheses mentioned so far comes anywhere near the really difficult problems connected with the formation of anticipations. It is evident [from (9) and (13) if evidence is necessary] that future rentals on capital will depend on the growth of the labor force, on the accumulation of capital, and on the rate of technical change. At the very least the rate of accumulation of capital will be influenced by expected gross rentals on capital (and by the rate of interest). Therefore what gross rentals turn out to be depends in part on what they are expected to be, and so forth. Any theory of saving must take such effects into account; they provide an important link between the theory of capital and the theory of effective demand.

A still more difficult problem has to do with the valuation of durable assets immediately after some unexpected change in circumstances has occurred. My whole argument has been conducted on the assumption that the steady improvement in the quality of capital goods has always been going on and is confidently expected to go on in the future. Obviously, sudden and surprising changes in technology do occur, and when they do they occasion a sudden revaluation of the stock of capital. The precise nature of this response is an empirical question. Until one knows something about it, even the definition of net output is uncertain at such moments.

If this knotty problem is waived, a number of intermediate assumptions present themselves. One could suppose that capital assets are valued on the hypothesis that the momentary rate of change of gross rentals is extrapolated into the future, or that some more complicated process of averaging over the past combined with extrapolation into the future takes place. The first of these modifies (19) to replace $\rho + \delta$ by

$$\rho + \delta - \frac{1}{r(v,\ t)}\frac{\partial r(v,\ t)}{\partial t} = \rho + \delta - \alpha\left(\frac{L}{J}\left(\frac{\dot{L}}{L} - \frac{\dot{J}}{J}\right) + \delta\right).$$

8. Depreciation, Obsolescence, and Net Output

One consequence of any hypothesis about the valuation of assets is that it becomes possible to calculate the rate of depreciation and thus to distinguish between gross and net output. To the extent that there is a subjective or uncertain element in asset valuation, there must be a similar vagueness in the relevant measure of net output.

Suppose, as in the preceding section, that future investment, labor force, rentals, and asset values are forecast accurately. Then aggregate depreciation may be analyzed in the following way. From (18) the total change in the value of the stock of capital is

$$\frac{dA}{dt} = -\sigma A + e^{-\sigma t}\frac{dJ}{dt} = -\sigma A + I\ .$$

Part of the change in the value of the stock of capital is of course the current gross investment. For depreciation purposes this should be subtracted to leave

(20) $$\frac{dA}{dt} - I = -\sigma A = -\left(\frac{\lambda}{1-\alpha} + \delta\right)A\ .$$

The term δA clearly represents physical depreciation. If there were no technological progress, i.e., if $\lambda = 0$, then a fraction δ of the remaining stock of capital of each vintage would die in each period and total depreciation would be δA. This sounds peculiar. Even if there were no technical progress one might expect $p_v(t)$ to change over time, so that owners of vintage v capital would experience not only physical depreciation but also capital gains and losses. But in the present one-commodity model this cannot occur. If $\lambda = 0$, surviving machines of all vintages are interchangeable (this depends on the exponential life table assumed for machines; if machines had a finite lifetime an old machine would always be worth less than a new one). Since a new machine *is* also a unit of consumable output it must always bear a price of unity measured in consumption goods, and hence so must an old machine. This is grossly unrealistic, and one should clearly consider the case when capital gains and losses on durable equipment are possible even in the absence of innovation. But this problem is more naturally posed in a two-sector model and will be treated in a subsequent paper.

Within the narrow confines of this model, then, it is natural to label the remaining part of (20), $\lambda A/(1 - \alpha)$, as obsolescence. Under the assumptions made, obsolescence is a constant fraction of the value of the stock of capital.

By definition, net output is $Q(t) - \sigma A(t)$.

In a two-sector model, one would want to decompose aggregate depreciation into at least three parts. First would be physical depreciation, the change in the value of the existing stock of assets on the assumption that unit values were not changing. Second, one might define a different component consisting of capital gains and losses other than obsolescence. This might be calculated as the change in the value of the existing stock of assets if there were no physical mortality but unit values changed as they would change if λ were zero. The remainder one might interpret as pure obsolescence. A somewhat better decomposition might result from the answer to the following question: how would unit asset values change if λ were known to be about to fall to zero in the next instant and remain zero forever? But to provide an answer we would have to recalculate what the future allocation of labor to machines of various vintages would be (lumping together machines produced currently and in the future) and this might be complicated. In any case, it is hard to believe that realism is gained by asking what would occur were all technical progress to cease tomorrow.

Under the alternative assumption that gross rentals on machines of each vintage are expected to remain constant for all future time at whatever level they have reached in the present, subjectively assessed depreciation will consist entirely of physical mortality,[10] and so, from (19), will amount to

$$\delta A^*(t) = \frac{(1 - \alpha)\delta}{\rho + \delta} Q(t) \, .$$

This implies that subjectively estimated net product is a constant fraction of gross product, and that fraction is $(\rho + \alpha\delta)/(\rho + \delta)$.

9. A Brief Comment on Saving

The simplest sort of saving function one could graft to this or to any other aggregate production function would make gross saving a fraction s of gross output. On any assumption this elementary, it is easy to work out the time path of output compatible with full employment and the absence of excess capacity. I have done this for the older model (2) in [10, p. 81] (which contains an obvious arithmetical error). To do the same for (11)

---

[10] This is different from $(dA^*/dt) - I$. The difference reflects the fact that we are now working with a set of expectations that are perpetually being disappointed. What $(dA^*/dt) - I$ represents is this: it is the *ex post* change in the value of the capital stock, the change that takes place after the fact, when current expectations have been disappointed and the public has acquired the naive belief that the *new* rentals will endure forever.

requires only that we note $\dot{J} = e^{\sigma t}I$ and that therefore $\dot{J} = e^{\sigma t}sQ = e^{\sigma t}sBe^{-\delta(1-\alpha)t}L^{\alpha}J^{1-\alpha}$. Also see [4].

But there is nothing descriptive in such a procedure. It does not contribute much to an analysis of the volume of *ex ante* saving and investment to be expected under specified conditions. For this purpose one would require a theory of consumption behavior and a theory of investment (or of asset preferences). For the former, one might want to think in terms of net saving and net income; for the latter, one would certainly need to value the stock of capital and consider both depreciation and obsolescence. In either case it is instructive to see how central is the problem of asset valuation. The incorporation of technical progress does not alter the problem fundamentally but, by adding yet another source of uncertainty to the picture, it does point up the difficulty of finding any clear-cut rule that is both empirically acceptable and tractable. In the last two sections of this paper I have merely scratched the surface of this problem by exploring two extreme assumptions that have only tractability to recommend them.

REFERENCES

[1] ABRAMOVITZ, M. "Resource and Output Trends in the U.S. since 1870," *American Economic Review*, **46** (1956), 5-23.

[2] AUKRUST, O. "Investment and Economic Growth," *Productivity Measurement Review*, **16** (1959), 35-53.

[3] FABRICANT, S. *Basic Facts on Productivity Change*, New York: National Bureau of Economic Research, 1959.

[4] JOHANSEN, L. "Substitution versus Fixed Production Coefficients in the Theory of Economic Growth: A Synthesis," *Econometrica*, **27** (1959), 157-76.

[5] KENDRICK, J. "Productivity Trends: Capital and Labor," *Review of Economics and Statistics*, **39** (1956), 248-57.

[6] NIITAMO, O. "Development of Productivity in Finnish Industry, 1925-1952," *Productivity Measurement Review*, **15** (1958), 30-41.

[7] SCHMOOKLER, J. "The Changing Efficiency of the American Economy, 1869-1938," *Review of Economics and Statistics*, **34** (1952), 214-31.

[8] SCHULTZ, T. W. "Reflections on Agricultural Production, Output and Supply," *Journal of Farm Economics*, **38** (1956), 748-62.

[9] SOLOW, R. "Technical Change and the Aggregate Production Function," *Review of Economics and Statistics*, **39** (1957), 312-20.

[10] SOLOW, R. "A Contribution to the Theory of Economic Growth," *Quarterly Journal of Economics*, **70** (1956), 65-94.

[11] VALAVANIS, S. "An Econometric Model of Growth, U.S.A. 1869-1953," *American Economic Review*, **45** (1955), 208-21.

THE NEW VIEW OF INVESTMENT:
A NEOCLASSICAL ANALYSIS*

EDMUND S. PHELPS

In 1956 appeared the first in a series of papers[1] disputing the
traditional thesis that capital deepening is the major source of
productivity gains and conjecturing that we owe our economic
growth to our progressive technology.

Thesis and antithesis were synthesized by 1960. Investment
has been married to Technology.[2] In the new view, the role of
investment is to modernize as well as deepen the capital stock. Now
investment is prized as the carrier of technological progress.

No criticism is made here of this "new view" of the role of
investment. Nor is the need for accelerated investment, public and
private, questioned. This paper is concerned only with the logic
of certain conclusions which the new view has shown a tendency to
inspire. In what sense does its new role make investment more
important? What are the prospects of modernizing the capital

* I am grateful to Edwin Mansfield, Arthur M. Okun and Robert M.
Solow for their suggestions and comments on earlier drafts.

1. M. Abramovitz, "Resource and Output Trends in the United States
since 1870," *American Economic Review*, XLVI (May 1956). O. Aukrust,
"Investment and Economic Growth," *Productivity Measurement Review*, No.
16 (1959), pp. 35–53. S. Fabricant, *Basic Facts on Productivity Change*, Na-
tional Bureau of Economic Research (New York, 1959). John W. Kendrick,
"Productivity Trends: Capital and Labor," *Review of Economics and Statistics*,
XXXVIII (Aug. 1956). B. Massell, "Capital Formation and Technological
Change in United States Manufacturing," *Review of Economics and Statistics*,
XLII (May 1960). T. W. Schultz, "Reflections on Agricultural Production,
Output and Supply," *Journal of Farm Economics* XXXVIII (Aug. 1956).
R. Solow, "Technical Change and the Aggregate Production Function," *Review
of Economics and Statistics*, XXXIX (Aug. 1957).

2. PEP (Political and Economic Planning), *Growth in the British
Economy* (London: Allen and Unwin, 1960). R. Solow, "Investment and
Technical Progress," *Mathematical Methods in the Social Sciences, 1959*
(Stanford: Stanford University Press, 1960). U. N. Economic Commission for
Europe, *Economic Survey of Europe in 1958*, Chap. II (Geneva, 1959). U.S.
Joint Economic Committee, "The American Economy in 1961: Problems and
Policies," Council of Economic Advisers, *Hearings on the Economic Report
of the President, 1961*.

Reprinted by permission of the author and the publishers from *The Quarterly Journal of
Economics, LXXVIII*, 4 (November 1962) 548–567. Cambridge, Mass.: Harvard University Press.

stock through increased thrift? Does the new view of investment present any new reasons — should added ones be needed — for faster capital accumulation? The analysis is confined largely to invest-ment-thrift policies described by a fixed saving ratio. The final section presents estimates of the rate of return to investment as implied by certain new-view assumptions. The results of the inquiry are summarized at the conclusion of the paper.

THE BASIS OF INVESTMENT PESSIMISM

The empirical work cited above spans a great variety of analyt-ical methods and historical materials. One of the best known papers is that by Professor Solow.[3] A number of other investigators fol-lowed much the same approach.

That method postulates aggregate output, Q_t, to be a contin-uously differentiable function of capital, K_t, employment, N_t, and "time" (standing for the state of technology). If, further, technical progress is "neutral," then output is a separable function of time and the inputs, as follows:

$$(1) \qquad Q_t = A(t) \, F(K_t, N_t).$$

Such a production function implies that technical progress is or-ganizational in the sense that its effect on productivity does not require any change in the quantity of the inputs. Existing inputs are improved or used more effectively.

It follows that the growth rate of output is equal to the rate of technical progress plus a weighted average of the growth rates of the inputs. These weights are the elasticities of output with respect to capital and to labor. Assuming constant returns to scale, the weights add to one and we obtain

$$(2) \qquad \frac{\dot{Q}_t}{Q_t} = \frac{\dot{A}_t}{A_t} + a_t \frac{\dot{K}_t}{K_t} + (1 - a_t) \frac{\dot{N}_t}{N_t}$$

where a_t is the capital elasticity of output, that is $\dfrac{F_K(K_t, N_t) K_t}{Q_t}$.

There are two unknowns in equation (2), the rate of technical progress and the capital elasticity. Solow, and later Massell,[4] relied on an "outside" estimate of the capital elasticity and proceeded to focus on the rate of technical progress. Solow took capital's relative share of national income in year t as a measure of a_t and Massell, who assumed a_t was constant over time, used the average share going to capital. It is not known how close such approxima-

3. Solow, "Technical Change and the Aggregate Production Function," *op. cit.*

4. *Op. cit.*

tions are. The practice presumes pure competition (which is not strictly implied by the model) as well as constant returns to scale.

The results of this approach produced a wave of investment pessimism. From a study of U.S. time series it was concluded that less than one-third of the average growth rate of output per worker in the last quarter century could be credited to the increase in capital per worker which occurred.[5]

Of course, it does not follow from this conclusion that capital deepening is ineffectual. It might mean only that over the time period investigated little capital deepening took place.[6] For policy purposes, the effectiveness of additional investment is of greater interest. On this score too, however, the approach outlined above produces some gloomy results.

Consider the effect of doubling the (net) investment-income ratio from .09 to .18. If the capital-output ratio is about 3, then this increase in the saving ratio would in a year increase the capital stock by about 3 per cent (beyond what it would have increased otherwise). Now capital's share in (net) national income is less than one-third. Therefore, according to equation (2), the 3 per cent increase in the capital stock would increase (net) output by less than 1 per cent (and it would increase output even less if the capital-output ratio rose).[7] Solow has remarked of such a calculation: "This seems like a meager reward for what is after all a revolution in the speed of accumulation of capital."[8]

5. From equation (2) it is easy to derive the proportion of the growth rate of output per worker which is attributable to capital deepening. It is

$$\frac{a_t(k_t - n_t)}{q_t - n_t} = \frac{a_t(k_t - n_t)}{r_t + a_t(k_t - n_t)}$$

where k_t, n_t, q_t and r_t denote the (relative) growth rates of capital, labor, output, and technology respectively, at time t. If there is no capital deepening, meaning $k_t = n_t$, then the proportion is equal to zero. If there is no technical progress, the proportion is equal to one.

The Solow-Massell result is easy to explain. In the U. S. time series they employed, capital and output grew at approximately the same rate. But if k_t equals q_t then the proportion equals a_t. Their factor share data put a_t at about one-third (or less).

6. The current alarm over the decline since the early twenties in the capital-output ratio rests on just such a counterinterpretation.

7. H. Stein and E. Denison's remarkably pessimistic paper for the President's Commission on National Goals is based on calculations of this kind. E. F. Denison and H. Stein, "High Employment and Growth in the American Economy," in *Goals for Americans*, report of the President's Commission on National Goals (Englewood Cliffs, N.J.: Prentice-Hall, 1960).

8. Solow, "Investment and Technical Progress," *op. cit.*

THE NEW VIEW

Just when the reputation of investment seemed at low ebb came the first signs of a new tide. Critics of the research described contended that new technologies generally require new kinds of capital goods. Therefore without positive (gross) investment productivity could hardly be expected to grow at all. Furthermore, it was argued, the higher the rate of gross investment, the newer and hence more modern and "efficient" will the capital stock become. Proponents of this new view of investment were apt to assign as much weight to capital modernizing as to capital deepening.[9]

In 1961 the new view of investment was embraced by the new administration. The President's Economic Message to Congress in January, 1961 stated:

Expansion and modernization of the Nation's productive plant is essential to accelerate economic growth and to improve the international competitive position of American industry. Embodying modern research and technology in new facilities will advance productivity, reduce costs, and market new products.[1]

Expansion and modernization are put on equal footing and the latter is stressed. A statement by the Council of Economic Advisers before the Joint Economic Committee in March 1961 amplifies this view:

One of the reasons for the recent slowdown in the rate of growth of productivity and output is a corresponding slowdown in the rate at which the stock of capital has been renewed and modernized. . . As has been confirmed by more recent research, the great importance of capital investment lies in its interaction with improved skills and technological progress. New ideas lie fallow without the modern equipment to give them life. From this point of view the function of capital formation is as much in modernizing the equipment of the industrial worker as in simply adding to it. The relation runs both ways: investment gives effect to technical progress and technical progress stimulates and justifies investment.[2]

To clarify the meaning of this new notion and to lay the basis

9. Two of the earliest documents taking the new view are *Economic Survey of Europe in 1958, op. cit.*, and *Growth in the British Economy, op. cit.* They argue that rapid labor force growth — contrast Britain and Germany — will raise output per worker by stimulating gross investment. The stimulation required is not spelled out.

1. Message from the President of the United States relative to a Program to Restore Momentum to the American Economy, *New York Times*, Feb. 2, 1961.

2. *Op. cit.*, p. 338.

for the analysis to follow, we turn now to an important theoretical paper by Solow which adopts the new view.[3] The purpose of that paper is to show that such neoclassical concepts as aggregate capital and the aggregate production function (containing aggregate capital) can be modified to accommodate the new view.

Solow postulates an index of technology, $B(t)$, which advances neutrally and exponentially at the rate λ. The nature of the technology so indexed is such that at every point of time it affects the efficiency only of new capital goods. Every capital good embodies the latest technology at the moment of its construction but it does not participate in subsequent technical progress. Thus "capital" becomes a continuum of heterogeneous vintages of capital goods.

The output rate at time t, $Q_v(t)$, of capital equipment of vintage v is assumed to be given by a Cobb-Douglas function,

(3) $Q_v(t) = B_o\, e^{\lambda v}\, K_v(t)^a\, N_v(t)^{1-a}$

where $K_v(t)$ denotes the amount of equipment (in physical terms) of vintage v surviving at time t and $N_v(t)$ denotes the amount of labor employed on that equipment. Since technical progress is neutral, the elasticity parameter a is the same for all vintages.

Solow then shows that if labor is allocated efficiently over the various vintages (by equalizing labor's marginal productivity on all equipment), aggregate output — the sum of the homogeneous outputs of the various vintages — is given by:

(4) $Q_t = B_o\, J_t^a\, N_t^{1-a}$

where

$$J_t = \int_{-\infty}^{t} e^{\frac{\lambda}{a} v}\, K_v(t)\, dv.$$

The "J" variable might be called "effective capital." The integral adds up all the (surviving) capital goods like the conventional capital measure; but here the capital goods of older vintages (with their small v's) receive a smaller weight than new capital goods.

For comparison with the old-fashioned model, let us specialize (1) in the same way. If all technological progress is organizational, neutral and proceeding at the constant relative rate, then

(5) $Q_t = A_o\, e^{\mu t}\, K_t^a\, N_t^{1-a}$.

According to this classical view, old and new capital goods share alike in technical progress, so that "capital," K_t, is simply the sum of the homogeneous surviving capital goods. Hence (5) can be written:

3. Solow, "Investment and Technical Progress," op. cit.

$$(6) \qquad Q_t = A_o \left[\int\limits_{-\infty}^{t} e^{\frac{\mu t}{a}} K_v(t) \, dv \right]^a N_t^{1-a}$$

The encouragement drawn from the new view — as represented by (4) — as compared with the old view — represented by (6) is illustrated by the following example.

Suppose that existing machines are of just two vintages, v_1 (old) and v_2 (new), and that there are an equal number of machines of the two vintages.

According to (6) a 2 per cent increase in the number of machines of the current vintage, v_2, will bring about a 1 per cent increase in the value of K and of the bracketed expression in (6); we are weighting a 2 per cent and a zero increase equally.

Consider the case in equation (4). J is the weighted sum of the machines of the two vintages with the weight for the contemporary machines, namely $e^{\lambda v_2}$, being greater. Consequently a 2 per cent increase in the number of machines of current vintage will produce an increase of J in excess of 1 per cent. Here current investment increases output per man partly through affecting the average modernity of the capital stock.

What if we lengthen our view and ask what happens as the program of capital accumulation continues? Pretty soon we will be confronted by a changed situation; large investments today will present us with a large amount of old equipment in the future. Investment must grow in order to maintain a constant average age of capital. And as we shall see, there is (under certain plausible assumptions) an average age of capital such that no smaller average age is tenable for long. The modernizing effects of expanded investment are limited.

Suffice it to say that the long-run consequences of a change in investment policy are not so clear as the immediate effect, and both are deserving of study. True, in the long run we are dead but our children will have to live in it. Can we control to an important degree the modernity of the capital stock they will inherit? Do we owe the modernity (such as it is) of our present stock to our ancestors' thrift? What significance has the new view of investment for the long run? This is examined now.

A SIMPLE MODEL OF GROWTH

We shall confine our analysis to the implications for output growth and productivity of investment policies which make gross investment a fixed proportion of gross output. The choice of an investment policy is thus a matter of selecting the investment-output ratio s. Hence, where $I(t)$ denotes the rate of investment at t:

$$(7) \qquad I(t) = s\,Q(t).$$

Second, we assume that the labor force grows at the constant relative rate n:

$$(8) \qquad N_t = N_o\,e^{nt}.$$

Finally we assume that all capital goods depreciate exponentially at the rate δ per annum. Hence

$$(9) \qquad K_v(t) = I(v)\,e^{-\delta(t-v)}.$$

If we think of δ as a mortality rate, then the average lifetime of capital goods is $\frac{1}{\delta}$ years.

Now our purpose is to compare the relation between investment and growth under the new and old view. We can do this by comparing a pure new-view model with a pure old-view model. But the simplest approach is to examine a single model which, by a variation of parameters, can be made to represent either pure or a mixture of both.

Thus we shall work with the following "general" production function which is simply a blend of (4) and (6):

$$(10) \qquad Q_t = B_o\,e^{\mu t}\,J_t^a\,N_t^{1-a}$$

where, as before

$$J_t = \int_{-\infty}^{t} e^{\frac{\lambda}{a}v}\,K_v(t)\,dv$$

or, by virtue of (9)

$$J_t = e^{-\delta t} \int_{-\infty}^{t} e^{(\frac{\lambda}{a}+\delta)v}\,I(v)\,dv.$$

When we compare the new view to the old view we are comparing the behavior of the model with $\lambda > 0$, $\mu = 0$ against the behavior when $\mu > 0$, $\lambda = 0$. And if one believes in both kinds of technological progress then he can let $\lambda > 0$, $\mu > 0$ simultaneously.[4] (In that

---

4. It may be (and has been) objected that it cannot be assumed that the other parameters, a, δ and so forth, are invariant to the nature of the technology (i.e., whether it is the λ-type or μ-type). But we find no implication in the new view that the nontechnological parameters differ from their supposed or implied values under the old view. That is, "$\lambda > 0$, $\mu = 0$" implies nothing about δ and a; to the contrary, the postulate that the embodied or λ-type technical progress is "neutral" implies that a is independent of λ. Whether empirical estimates of a and δ would be affected depends upon the method of estimation. Under neoclassical conditions it is common practice to take capital's relative share as an estimate of a; this procedure is equally

case the efficiency of all capital goods may be said to rise at the rate $\dfrac{\mu}{a}$ except the efficiency of new capital goods which rises at the rate $\dfrac{\lambda+\mu}{a}$.)

Differentiating Q_t in (10) with respect to time yields (omitting the t subscript):

$$\begin{aligned}
(11) \quad \dot{Q} &= \mu\, Q \\
&+ a\, Be^{\mu t}\, J^{a-1}\, N^{1-a}\left[e^{\frac{\lambda}{a}t}\, I - \delta\, J \right] \\
&+ (1-a)Be^{\mu t}\, N^{-a}\, J^a\, \dot{N}
\end{aligned}$$

where we use $\dot{J}_t = e^{\frac{\lambda}{a}t}\, I_t - \delta\, J_t$.

Using (7), (8) and (9) (to express J^{a-1} in terms of Q and N) we obtain the following differential equation governing the growth path of output:

$$(12) \qquad \dot{Q} = c_1\, Q + c_2\, Q^{c_3}\, e^{c_4 t}$$

where
$$c_1 = \mu - a\delta + (1-a)n$$

$$c_2 = as\, B^{\frac{1}{a}}\, N_0^{\frac{1-a}{a}}$$

$$c_3 = \frac{2a-1}{a}$$

$$c_4 = \frac{\lambda+\mu+(1-a)n}{a}.$$

This equation can be solved for the path of output.[5] In the next section the long-run or asymptotic behavior of output will be considered.

INVESTMENT AND PRODUCTIVITY IN THE LONG RUN

These models have the convenient property[6] that, starting from the initial position, the path of growth will be asymptotic to a balanced-growth, "golden-age" equilibrium growth path along which path production, consumption, investment, and the capital stock

appropriate on the two views. One's assumptions about λ and μ would affect B_o, the technology index at $t = 0$; we return to this in a footnote *infra*.

5. For the solution we are indebted to a regrettably unpublished paper by Dernburg and Quirk, which analyzes an old-view Cobb-Douglas growth model. T. Bernburg and J. Quirk, "Per Capita Output and Technological Progress," Institute of Quantitative Research in Economics and Management, Purdue University (1960).

6. Dernburg and Quirk, *op. cit.* R. Solow, "A Contribution to the Theory of Economic Growth," this *Journal*, LXX (Feb. 1956). T. Swan, "Economic Growth and Capital Accumulation," *Economic Record*, XXXII (Nov. 1956).

(of all ages) all grow exponentially at the same rate. This "equilibrium" output path is denoted $\bar{Q}(t)$.

The limiting or asymptotic solution to equation (13) or (15) is

(13) $$\bar{Q}(t) = \bar{Q}_0 \, e^{\frac{c_4}{1-c_3}t} \, .$$

Thus the growth rate, g, tends in the long run to the constant $\dfrac{c_4}{1-c_3}$. In terms of the original parameters:

(14) $$g = \frac{\lambda + \mu}{1 - a} + n.$$

It will be noticed that the limiting growth rate is independent of the investment ratio. This is a well-known property of old-style Cobb-Douglas models.[7] It is not surprising to find this same property in the "new model," which allows $\lambda > 0$. Associated with this exponential growth pattern is a certain unchanging age distribution of capital. Capital which is $(t - v)$ years old will grow at the rate g like most everything else; the proportion of capital which is $(t - v)$ years old or less is constant over time. The fact that capitals of different vintages get different technical weights is immaterial in the determination of the exponential equilibrium growth rate.

Note also that the long-run growth rate depends only upon the total rate of technical change, say, $\Delta = \lambda + \mu$, not upon the nature of the change. The reason is that the efficiency of capital $(t - v)$ years old will, in exponential equilibrium, improve at the rate Δ in either (pure or any mixed) case.

What then is the relation between investment and productivity in the long run? The higher the investment ratio that society chooses the larger will be its capital stock (at every point of time) in the long run. Thus the *level* of the "equilibrium" exponential growth path which the economy approaches is a function of the investment ratio. In short, $\bar{Q}_0$, the equilibrium value of Q at "time zero" (chosen arbitrarily), is a function of s. This value is to be distinguished from the actual output at time zero, Q_0; the two will be equal only if the initial capital-output ratio happens to equal that ratio which the chosen s would have brought about.[8]

7. Solow, "A Contribution to the Theory of Economic Growth," *op. cit.*, and Swan, *op. cit.*

8. On the equilibrium path the "conventional" capital-output ratio is constant; both K and Q grow at the rate g. But if $\lambda > 0$, "effective" capital grows at the rate $g + \dfrac{\lambda}{a}$ and so the effective capital-output ratio rises.

The solution for the long-run growth path is:

$$(15) \qquad \overline{Q}_0 = \left[\frac{(1 - c_3) \, c_2}{c_4 - (1 - c_3) c_1} \right]^{\frac{1}{1-c_3}}$$

or, in terms of the original parameters

$$(16) \qquad \overline{Q}_0 = s^{\frac{a}{1-a}} \left[\frac{(1-a) \, B^{\frac{1}{a}} N_0^{\frac{1-a}{a}}}{\mu + \frac{\lambda}{a} + (1 - a) \, (n + \delta)} \right]^{\frac{a}{1-a}}.$$

What significance, we ask again, has the new view in relation to investment and productivity in the long run? From (16) one can see immediately that the elasticity of Q_0 with respect to s is $\frac{a}{1-a}$, independent of λ and μ. Whether one takes the new view or the old, it follows from this model that, in the long run, a 1 per cent increase in the investment ratio will yield asymptotically an output rate which is $\frac{a}{1-a}$ per cent in excess of what asymptotically it would otherwise have been (i.e., had the orginal investment ratio prevailed).

This result seems at first to contradict the little example of increased investment presented at the end of the "The New View" section. The explanation of the puzzle lies in the behavior of the average age — or more precisely, the age distribution — of capital. It has apparently been overlooked that, in exponential growth, the age distribution of capital depends upon the rate of growth and the rate of depreciation and upon nothing else. Since both rates are, in the long run, independent of the investment ratio, a once-for-all change in that ratio can have no permanent influence on the age distribution of capital. Consequently, in the long run, any increase in thrift must rely for its effectiveness upon the prosaic mechanism of capital deepening — of an equiproportionate deepening of capital of every age.

This is easily proved. Suppose the economy has been growing smoothly at the rate g, along the growth path corresponding to the chosen fixed investment ratio, for quite some time. If, say at $t = 0$ (for convenience only), we were to look at the distribution of capital equipment by age we could summarize our findings by the exponential curves in Figure I. In order to obtain the amount of capital of vintage v still in use at $t = 0$, $K_v \, (0)$, we have to multiply $I(v)$ by $e^{\delta v}$. This gives the lower curve.

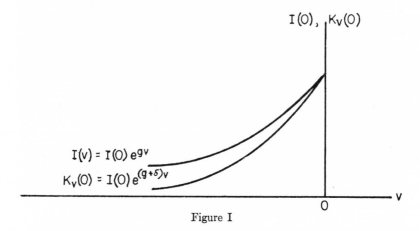

Figure I

To obtain the mean age and the other moments of the age distribution of capital, it is necessary to normalize the curve so that its area will equal 1. This requires dividing $K_v(0)$ by $I(0)/(g + \delta)$ for all v.[9] Thus we obtain the formula for the proportion of equipment of age v:

(17) $f(v) = (g + \delta)\, e^{(g+\delta)v}$.

It is clear that all the moments of the equilibrium age distribution of capital are independent of the quantity of capital and the rate of investment. The equilibrium mean age of capital, for example, is simply $\dfrac{1}{g+\delta}$[1]

Given the investment ratio, the mean age of capital depends in the long run only upon the rate of depreciation and the limiting rate of growth, and neither of these depend upon the investment ratio in this model.

9. $I(0)/(g + \delta)$ is the total area under the $K_v(0)$ curve, by the familiar "capitalization" formula.

1. Proof:

$$-\bar{v} = \int_{-\infty}^{0} (g + \delta)\, e^{(g+\delta)v}\,(-v)\, dv$$

$$= \frac{-v(g + \delta)e^{(g+\delta)v}}{g + \delta}\Bigg]_{-\infty}^{0} + \int_{-\infty}^{0} \frac{(g + \delta)e^{(g+\delta)v}}{(g + \delta)}\, dv$$

$$= 0 + \frac{e^{(g+\delta)v}}{g + \delta}\Bigg]_{-\infty}^{0}$$

$$= \frac{1}{g + \delta}$$

Therefore a once-for-all rise in the investment ratio can significantly "modernize" the capital stock only temporarily. Ultimately the average age (or modernity) of capital must settle back toward its equilibrium level. A permanent modernization of the capital stock (starting from equilibrium) would require the investment ratio to increase without limit, a policy which is not feasible (without foreign assistance at any rate).

Of course, actual economies are never found in dynamic long-run equilibrium because of fluctuations in investment. An upswing in investment is usually associated with a downswing in the mean age of capital. But it should be understood that when the mean age of capital exceeds its equilibrium value, a decline in the mean age is bound to occur eventually no matter what investment ratio society elects to adopt.[2] This leads us to digress briefly on the present mean age of capital in the United States and the direction in which it may be expected to move.

The Terborgh-Knowles estimates of the average age of capital, which end at 1957, together with the experience of the past five

2. When the economy is out of equilibrium, the basic model is likely to forecast a different limiting growth path (corresponding to a given investment ratio) for every different value of λ we should assign. If, for example, the mean age is below its equilibrium value then a new-view forecast, taking the eventual equilibrating increase in mean age into account, would predict a lower equilibrium path (whatever the investment ratio) than would an old-view forecast because the latter would attribute no significance to the eventual rise in the mean age of capital. This fact in no way invalidates the conclusions of this section concerning the long-run growth rate, the "investment elasticity" and the equilibrium mean age of capital, these relations being independent of the level of the equilibrium growth path.

A special case of some interest is that in which the economy has always traveled along the equilibrium path corresponding to the prevailing investment ratio. In this case the mean age of capital is in equilibrium and the value of λ will not affect the predicted equilibrium growth path corresponding to any investment ratio, because μ adjusts to satisfy (14) and B to satisfy (16).

Note that high λ implies high B. Let n, δ and s be recorded from direct observation and let a be estimated from relative shares. Then Δ can be estimated simply from (14). If we believe some of this Δ is λ then $\dfrac{\lambda}{a} + \mu$ rises so we have to make an upward adjustment of B in (16) in order that the model be able to explain the actual level of output $Q_0 = \overline{Q}_0$.

The adjustment of B makes sense because the implied old-view estimate of B is actually an estimate of the average level of technology embodied in all capital goods while the new view implies that the current level of technology is superior to the average. At time zero, the current (or best-practice) level of technology is measured by B.

years suggest that the mean age today is about 17.5 years.[3] Thus the postwar vintages comprise half the nation's capital. In 1975 the postwar investment boom will be working against a modern capital stock. Then all capital of vintages 1957 and earlier — particularly the heavy investments of 1946–57 — will be older than 17 years. Between now and 1975 we apparently require an increase in investment comparable to the postwar increase in order to avert an increase in the mean age of capital.

Yet such an acceleration of investment is not unlikely, even without an increase of the investment ratio. Due to the expected rise in the rate of increase of the labor supply, many observers anticipate full-employment growth at $4\frac{1}{2}$ per cent or more over the next decade — about 1 percentage point better than the postwar experience (in output and investment) to date.[4] Therefore if investment should keep pace with output over the future, the mean age of capital may well hold steady or even fall.

Still, the major impression drawn from a study of the Terborgh-Knowles series is the remarkable stability of the mean age of capital. It took a depression and a war to raise the average age from 16.5 (in 1930) to 21.2 years (in 1945). This suggests that, given the technical and demographic factors which determine the limiting growth rate, it would be very difficult to reduce by means of investment the mean age of capital by more than 3 or 4 years. And, as we have seen, according to the model here this gain could not be indefinitely maintained. Eventually the mean age would slip back up to its natural long-run level.

Investment and Productivity in the Short Run

The foregoing analysis has some significance for "positive economics." For example, a sustained improvement in the modernity of the capital stock of a country should be ascribed (proximately) not to the level (rate) nor to the rate of growth of its investment but to a rise of the rate of growth of investment. The improvement can be expected to be permanent only if there have been (or will be) technical and demographic changes causing a rise in the limiting growth rate of output (thus averting a future deceleration of investment).

3. See James Knowles, "The Potential Economic Growth in the United States," Study Paper 20, *Employment, Growth and the Price Level* (U. S. Congress, Joint Economic Committee, 1959), p. 26.

4. See, for example, *The Economic Report of the President, 1962* (Washington, U. S. Government Printing Office, 1962.)

The implications of the analysis for investment policy depend, of course, on the decision rules used by the policymaker. Many (all?) sensible rules will involve, among other things, the responsiveness of output *in the short run* to a policy of greater thrift and investment. The short run assumes considerable importance when we observe that our model economy approaches its limiting path only asymptotically. Even to get close to that path may take considerable time. It is worthwhile therefore to inquire into the speed with which the economy adjusts to a change in the equilibrium path brought about by a change in the investment ratio. It will be seen that the new view forecasts a faster transition from the old to the new equilibrium path.

This task requires the full solution of the differential equation in (12), for which we are indebted to the paper by Dernburg and Quirk.[5] The complete solution is:

$$(18) \qquad Q(t) = \left[(Q_o{}^{1-c_3} - \bar{Q}_o{}^{1-c_3}) e^{c_1(1-c_3)t} + \bar{Q}_o{}^{1-c_3} e^{c_4 t} \right]^{\frac{1}{1-c_3}}$$

where $\bar{Q}_0$ is given in equation (16).

Equation (18) implies that output will "approach" its equilibrium path, in the sense that $\dfrac{Q^t}{\bar{Q}^t} \to 1$ as $t \to \infty$, if and only if $c_1(1-c_3) - c_4 < 0$, in which case the model is said to exhibit *absolute stability*.[6] This stability condition can be seen more clearly if we look at equation (18) in the form

$$(18a) \qquad Q(t) = \bar{Q}(t) \left\{ 1 + \left[\left(\frac{Q_0}{\bar{Q}_0} \right)^{1-c_3} - 1 \right] e^{[c_1(1-c_3)-c_4]t} \right\}^{\frac{1}{1-c_3}}.$$

The condition $c_1(1 - c_3) - c_4 < 0$ means $\mu + \dfrac{\lambda}{a} + (1 - a)$ $(n + \delta) > 0$ which is assumed here. Thus the latter expression determines the rate of approach to equilibrium. Given n, δ and a, the larger $\mu + \dfrac{\lambda}{a}$ the faster is the approach. How does the new view affect it?

It is clear that if one were to start with a pure old-view model, with its rate of approach determined by $\mu + (1 - a)(n + \delta)$, and

5. *Op. cit.*
6. If only the limiting growth rate span (and not also the limiting path) is independent of initial conditions then the model possesses only "relative stability."

then proceeded to add $\dfrac{\lambda}{a}$ to this expression, as if λ measured a neglected source of technical progress, the result would be a faster implied rate of approach to equilibrium.

But λ and μ are not additive. An alteration of the model does not change the world but only the conception and estimation of its parameters. Suppose a pure old-view adherent, if one could be found, and a pure new-view supporter were dispatched out into the world to estimate the relevant parameters. Using conventional estimation procedures (based on neoclassical assumptions), they would return with identical estimates except for Δ (the rate of technical progress) and B (the level of technology), the latter fortunately being irrelevant to the question at hand.

A little reflection will indicate that the new view estimate of λ will exceed the old view estimate of μ if the mean age of capital has been steadily increasing and will fall short of the old-view estimate if the mean age has been steadily falling. A fluctuating mean age complicates the picture. In any event, the estimates could not be presumed to be equal unless the economy had happened to be in long-run equilibrium.[7]

Therefore, if the mean age of capital had been falling sharply, the estimate of λ might be smaller than the estimate of μ by a factor of a or more.[8] In this event, the old-view model would paint a more dynamic and adaptable economy than would the new-view model. It would predict a higher limiting growth rate (μ being larger than λ); and, with respect to the question posed in this section, it would imply a capacity to close a given disequilibrium more quickly and therefore to make the transition faster from a low equilibrium path to a higher one.

Circumstances are conceivable, therefore, in which a permanent increase in the investment ratio would appear — at least for a while — more attractive on the old view of the economy than on the new view. But it must be noted that when the economy has been out of equilibrium — and this is an essential part of those circumstances — the two models will imply different absolute levels of the equilibrium path corresponding to the prevailing investment ratio, and they will

7. For details of this argument, see the extended footnote of the section above concerning the long run.

8. It would be better to represent the new view by a mixed model allowing $\lambda > 0$. Then the μ estimate would be compared with the estimated sum of $\mu + \dfrac{\lambda}{a}$ in the new model.

imply different limiting growth rates. A rational investment policy may well take these factors into account together with the transition speed. Further, a wide discrepancy between the λ and μ estimates could only be temporary. As the economy approached long-run equilibrium, they would have to come together.

This last observation reminds us once again that the mean age of capital does not move sharply and that estimates of λ and μ (in alternative pure models utilizing the same data) do not differ much. Actually, estimates of λ tend slightly to exceed estimates of μ in the United States because of the secular upward trend in the mean age of capital in this country. In point of fact, then, a permanent increase in thrift does appear to be more effective in the new view than it does in the old view.

The Rate of Return on Current Investment

This paper has studied the effect on the path of output of a once-for-all increase in the investment ratio under alternative models. Presumably the purpose of such an increase would be to raise the time path of consumption (public and private). A higher consumption rate could be sustained in all future years.

But what if it were desired to increase only the consumption of a single future period? In this case clearly and perhaps more generally, the rate of return on investment would be a desideratum of investment policy.

The marginal productivity of investment, in the sense of $\frac{\partial Q}{\partial I}$, is determined in the old model by

$$(19) \qquad \frac{\partial Q}{\partial I} = a \frac{Q}{K} \qquad \text{(from (5))}$$

and the new model by

$$(20) \qquad \frac{\partial Q}{\partial I} = a \frac{Q}{J} \frac{\partial J}{\partial I} = a \frac{Q}{J} e^{\left(\frac{\lambda}{a}\right) t} \qquad \text{(from (4))}.$$

Since the assignment of the zero point is arbitrary, we can consider $\frac{\partial Q}{\partial I}$ only at $t = 0$ without loss of generality. Since all $v < t$ are then negative, old (surviving) capital goods will be assigned weights $e^{\frac{\lambda}{a} v}$ smaller than unity in J while all (surviving) capital goods receive unit weights in K. Hence $J < K$ (if there is any old capital) and the marginal product of investment is higher in the new view.

Some rough new-view estimates of the marginal product of investment in the United States may be of interest. The President's Council of Economic Advisers has compiled several time series of the fixed reproducible tangible capital in the business sector (excluding shelter and the output of government-owned enterprises) corresponding to different quality improvement rates of the λ type. A little manipulation of these data and the addition of corresponding inventory estimates by Goldsmith yield the following table: [9]

TABLE I
EFFECTIVE CAPITAL AND POTENTIAL OUTPUT
IN THE U. S. BUSINESS SECTOR 1954
(in billions of dollars)

	Definition	Excluding Inventories	Including Inventories
K	No improvement	543	643
J'	2% improvement rate [1]	412	512
J"	3% improvement rate [1]	369	469
Q	4% unemployment	301	301

Source: Council of Economic Advisers and R. W. Goldsmith, *op. cit.*

[1] The improvement rate corresponds to $\dfrac{\lambda}{a}$ in equation (4). Hence, if $a = .4$, 3% improvement implies $\lambda = 1.2\%$. This is small but not so implausible when it is recalled that the 3% is a correction for quality improvement not already reflected in the conventional K series. The competition by producers of outmoded equipment tends to depress the capital goods price index below its appropriate level for K calculations to the extent that old equipment will no longer be produced when inventories of them are depleted. Also, some quality improvements are usually taken into account in the deflation of investment expenditures. In addition, econometric models of the mixed variety will normally show some technical progress of the μ type.

Making use of (19), the following estimates of the marginal productivity of 1954 investment can be computed:

TABLE II
POTENTIAL MARGINAL PRODUCTIVITY OF 1954 INVESTMENT

	$a = .15$	$a = .25$	$a = .40$
K:	7.0%	11.7%	18.7%
J':	8.8%	14.7%	23.5%
J":	9.6%	16.0%	25.7%

9. Raymond W. Goldsmith, *The National Wealth of the United States in the Postwar Period* (Princeton: Princeton University Press, 1962), Statistical Appendix, Table A-39, Columns (2), (3) and (4).

The a values are for illustrative purposes only. They denote the elasticity of gross final potential business output with respect to effective business capital. Relative gross factor share data indicate that business before-tax quasi-rents as a ratio to business product at high levels of activity is somewhere between .25 and .40. This fact is a rough guide as to the value of a.

These marginal productivity estimates are equivalent to "gross earning" rates as defined by quasi-rents, aQ, divided by the market (equals replacement) value of the capital stock, J. This concept is gross of obsolescence and physical depreciation. To figure the *net* (social and private) *rate of return* to investment, we must deduct the annual proportionate decline in the real market value of the investment due to these causes.

By the net rate of return on investment we shall mean the marginal rate of transformation between next year's and this year's consumption *minus* one, subject to constancy of consumption possibilities in all subsequent periods. That is, let $-\dfrac{\partial C_1}{\partial C_0} - 1$, subject to $C_2, C_3, \ldots$ held constant, define the net rate of return on investment, where C_t denotes consumption t periods in the future.

Normalizing conveniently, and denoting the annual improvement factor by $\iota = \dfrac{\lambda}{a}$, we can write

$$P_0 = C_0 + I_0 = F(J_0, L_0)$$
$$P_1 = C_1 + I_1 = (1 + \mu)\, F\,(J_1, L_0) =$$
$$F\left(J_0(1 - \delta) + I_0, L_0 \right)$$
$$P_2 = C_2 + I_2 = (1 + \mu)^2\, F\,(J_2, L_2) =$$
$$F\left(J_1(1 - \delta) + (1 + \iota)I_1, L_0 \right)$$

where δ, μ and λ measure simple annual rates. For simplicity we have assumed a constant labor supply. By $F(J,L)$ we mean the Cobb-Douglas function but we use this notation for convenience.

The consumption possibilities beginning two periods hence will be unchanged by this year's and next year's investment (consumptions) if and only if capacity output two periods hence, P_2, is constant. But this requires that J_2 be constant. Hence we have the constraint:

$$J_2 = [J_0(1 - \delta) + I_0]\,(1 - \delta) + (1 + \iota)\,I_1 = \text{constant.}$$

Now if we consume less this year in order to invest more, we can consume more in the future for two reasons: We will get more P_1.

And we will need less I_1 — to the extent the I_0 does not wear out — to meet our fixed J_2 goal. Algebraically,

$$\frac{-\partial C_1}{\partial C_0} = \frac{\partial P_1}{\partial I_0} - \frac{\partial I_1}{\partial I_0}$$

$$= \frac{\partial P_1}{\partial I_0} + \frac{1 - \delta}{1 + \iota}.$$

Finally we obtain the net rate of return:

$$-\frac{\partial C_1}{\partial C_0} - 1 = \frac{\partial P_1}{\partial I_0} - \frac{\iota + \delta}{1 + \iota}.$$

$\frac{\partial P_1}{\partial I_0}$ is the marginal productivity of base year investment (here 1954). Evidently it is necessary to deduct from this the rates of "obsolescence," $\frac{\iota}{1+\iota}$, and "effective" depreciation, $\frac{\delta}{1+\iota}$, to obtain the net rate of return on investment. By applying this result to the marginal productivity estimates of Table II (and neglecting the lag between I_0 and the increase of capacity it creates) we obtain the illustrative rates of return in Table III.

TABLE III

POTENTIAL RATE OF RETURN ON 1954 INVESTMENT
NET OF OBSOLESCENCE AND 3% PHYSICAL DEPRECIATION

	$a = .15$	$a = .25$	$a = .40$
$K(\iota = 0)$	4.0%	8.7%	15.7%
$J'(\iota = 2\%)$	3.9%	9.8%	18.6%
$J''(\iota = 3\%)$	3.8%	10.2%	19.9%

The table shows that, with respect to the higher and more "reasonable" values of a, the new view yields higher estimates of the net rate of return on investment in the United States around 1954. But it is interesting and possibly important to note that this implication of the new view could not have been taken for granted on a priori grounds. Suppose that the 1954 capital stock had been so up-to-date that the J's differed little from K. Or suppose we believed that a was only .15 or less because we thought quasi-rents as a ratio to final output, while in the neighborhood of 25–40 per cent, contained a very large element of monopoly profit. In either case — Tables II and III verify the second case — the alternative marginal productivity estimates corresponding to different improvement factors would be much smaller and would *differ so little* among themselves that the *net* rates of return would be smaller the larger is the assumed rate of obsolescence!

SUMMARY

A growth model has been constructed which accommodates two types of technical progress. The first type can be implemented by existing capital while the second type needs to be embodied in new kinds of capital goods. Comparison of the solutions of the model corresponding to these two types reveals that:

(1) the limiting long-run growth rate depends on the rate of technical progress, not the type of progress;

(2) the elasticity of the limiting exponential growth path with respect to the investment ratio depends only on the capital elasticity of output, which is independent of the type of technical progress;

(3) no permanent, finite modernization of the capital stock can be achieved by increased thrift; in the model constructed here, the limiting equilibrium age distribution of capital depends only on the long-run rates of growth and depreciation and neither of these is affected by the fraction of income saved;

(4) the anticipated rise in the labor force growth rate in the United States will lead to a more modern stock, given a fixed investment ratio;

(5) normally, but not necessarily, the new-view model — which represents the second type of technical change — will paint a more adaptable economy, one faster to make the transition to the equilibrium growth path corresponding to a higher level of thrift;

(6) however, empirical estimates of the rate of technical progress (and other parameters of the model) might differ depending on which type of technical progress was assumed; in this event the two variants of the model will predict different limiting growth paths (corresponding to any investment ratio) and different limiting growth rates; this complicates at least the answer to the question of which "view" of technical progress offers the larger investment incentive;

(7) finally, the new view implies a higher estimate than does the old view of the "potential" net rate of return to 1954 United States business investment; however, this result need not hold in all countries nor in this country at all times; if the capital stock is sufficiently up-to-date or capital's income share sufficiently small, then the new-view implication that additional investment today would satisfy future capital requirements which would be "cheap" to fill with the super-investments of tomorrow will operate to reduce our estimate of the rate of return to present investment.

YALE UNIVERSITY

"THE NEW VIEW OF INVESTMENT": COMMENT*

R. C. O. MATTHEWS

It has been suggested by a number of recent writers that if part or all of technical progress requires to be embodied in new machines, a rise in the propensity to save may contribute to raising the level of output not only by raising the capital/labor ratio on machines of a given "vintage" but also by lowering the average age of machines, thus increasing the proportion of the capital stock that embodies the latest technology at any time. This view is disputed by Edmund S. Phelps in his article "The New View of Investment: a Neoclassical Analysis." [1] Phelps maintains that the average age of machines, once the economy is established on a path of steady growth, is independent of the propensity to save, s (defined as the ratio of gross saving to gross income). The purpose of the present note is to show that on the type of assumptions used by Phelps this conclusion is valid in an economically significant sense only if the elasticity of substitution (σ) between labor and capital is equal to unity (as it is in his model). It will be shown that in certain more general models a higher s will be associated with a lower average age of capital in steady growth, so long as $\sigma < 1$. If, however, $\sigma > 1$, a higher s will actually be associated with a higher average age of capital.

The idea that thrift may affect the level of output by lowering the average age of capital as well as by increasing the capital-intensity of production has been put forward largely because of doubts about whether there is much scope for varying the capital-intensity of production. It would appear, therefore, that the more interesting case in the present context is where $\sigma < 1$, which is the case where the validity of the idea will be shown to be upheld.

I

Phelps offers a proof [2] that the average age of the machines in existence under steady growth depends only on the rate of growth and the rate of depreciation. This proof is very general and does

* My thanks are due to F. H. Hahn for much help in the preparation of this note. In particular I am indebted to him for suggesting the proofs contained in footnotes (5) and (8). An earlier version was sent by the editor of the *Journal* to Professor Phelps for his observations, and I am grateful for these also.

1. This *Journal*, LXXVI (Nov. 1962), 548–67.
2. *Ibid.*, pp. 557–59.

not depend on any particular properties in the production function. However it does depend on machines being scrapped solely because of depreciation (which is assumed to proceed at an externally given rate) and not because of obsolescence. Now complete scrapping because of obsolescence is only a limiting case of a more general phenomenon, the withdrawal of labor from old machines. If the amount of labor per machine of a given vintage is a variable, the unweighted average age of all machines in existence is not a very meaningful measure of the average age of the capital stock. A more relevant measure is that obtained by weighting each machine by the amount of labor employed on it. (This distinction does not arise if technical progress is "disembodied," since the entire capital stock is then homogeneous, and the same amount of labor is employed with each machine, whatever its age.) Given that the unweighted average age is independent of s, it follows that the weighted average age will vary with s if the relative number of workers on machines of different vintages varies with s. This it in fact does unless σ is equal to unity. This may be seen as follows.

Phelps adopts the model suggested by Solow [3] in which a Cobb-Douglas production function applies to machines of each vintage. In the same spirit, but rather more generally, let us suppose that a constant-elasticity-of-substitution production function [4] applies to machines of each vintage,

$$Q_v = (a_v K_v{}^{-\beta} + b_v N_v{}^{-\beta})^{-\frac{1}{\beta}} \tag{1}$$

where K_v is the number of machines of vintage v, N_v is the amount of labor working on them, Q_v is the output from them, a_v and b_v are parameters and $\beta = (1 - \sigma)/\sigma$.

Suppose further that technical progress is exponential, Harrod-neutral, and wholly embodied. The general form of Harrod-neutral technical progress [5] is

$$Q(t) = f[K(t), A(t) N(t)]. \tag{2}$$

Therefore in the present case the production function for machines of any vintage v is

3. R. M. Solow, "Investment and Technical Progress," in *Mathematical Methods in the Social Sciences, 1959*, ed. K. J. Arrow, S. Karlin and P. Suppes (Stanford, California: Stanford University Press, 1960), pp. 89–104; *idem*, "Technical Progress, Capital Formation and Economic Growth," *American Economic Review, Papers and Proceedings*, LII (May 1962), 76–86.
4. K. J. Arrow, H. B. Chenery, B. Minhas, and R. M. Solow, "Capital-Labor Substitution and Economic Efficiency," *Review of Economics and Statistics*, XLIII (Aug. 1961), 225–50.
5. H. Uzawa, "Neutral Inventions and the Stability of Growth Equilibrium," *Review of Economic Studies*, XXVIII (Feb. 1961), 117–24.

$$Q_v = (aK_v{}^{-\beta} + e^{-\beta g v}\, bN_v{}^{-\beta})^{-\frac{1}{\beta}} \tag{3}$$

where a and b are the same for machines of all vintages, and g is the rate of technical progress.

Comparing the path of steady growth in two economies that differ only in s, the rate of growth of wages will be the same in both, but the economy with the higher s will have a higher wage at any point of time. The effect of differing levels of s can therefore be inferred from the effects of differing levels of the wage at any point of time.

We want to compare the labor/capital ratio on machines of the latest vintage, t, with the labor/capital ratio on machines of some earlier vintage still in use, v.

Differentiating (3) with respect to N_v and equating the result to the wage, w, we derive

$$\frac{N_v}{K_v} = a^{\frac{\sigma}{\sigma-1}}\, b^\sigma\, e^{-gv} \left[w^{\sigma-1}\, e^{-gv(\sigma-1)} - b^\sigma \right]^{\frac{\sigma}{1-\sigma}}. \tag{4}$$

This equation shows the labor/capital ratio on machines of vintage v at any time in terms of the wage prevailing at that time. Under steady growth, w rises exponentially. As can be seen from (4), this will cause N_v/K_v to fall over time, as is to be expected. (It may be noted that only if $\sigma < 1$ does N_v/K_v actually fall to zero, implying complete scrapping because of obsolescence.)

At any given time the wage is the same for workers employed on machines of all vintages. Hence the labor/capital ratio for machines of vintage t is the same as (4), only with t substituted for v. The ratio of the labor/capital ratios on the two different vintages is therefore given by

$$\frac{N_t/K_t}{N_v/K_v} = \left(\frac{w^{\sigma-1}\, e^{-gt(\sigma-1)} - b^\sigma}{w^{\sigma-1}\, e^{-gv(\sigma-1)} - b^\sigma} \right)^{\frac{\sigma}{1-\sigma}} e^{-(t-v)g}. \tag{5}$$

It can be seen that, with $t > v$, the ratio expressed in (5) varies directly with w if $\sigma < 1$ and inversely with w if $\sigma > 1$. This gives us the result we require, since under steady growth w depends on s. If $\sigma < 1$, a high s is thus associated with a relatively low amount of labor allotted to the old machines and hence with a relatively low weighted average age of machines. If $\sigma > 1$, the opposite holds. If $\sigma = 1$ (the Cobb-Douglas case), equation (5) gives an indeterminate result, but by applying the above procedure direct to the

Cobb-Douglas production function, the result is duly reached that the ratio of N_t/K_t to N_v/K_v is independent of w and hence of s.[6]

II

The same conclusion can be proved more simply in a case rather different from that dealt with by Phelps. This is the case considered by Salter [7] and others, where substitution between labor and capital is possible only *ex ante*, at the time when it is being decided what kind of machine should be built (the Marshallian long period) and is not possible *ex post*, once the machine has been built (the Marshallian short period). A machine of given vintage then continues to be operated with the same number of men (disregarding increased running costs due to physical deterioration) so long as it is operated at all, but it passes out of use altogether at a certain date when the rise in wages has reduced to zero the quasi-rents that it earns. The wage-bill on a machine of given vintage rises at the same rate as

6. In the more general case, where technical progress is not necessarily Harrod-neutral and σ is not necessarily constant, the results are somewhat less clear cut. With any linear homogeneous production function $Q = f(K,N)$, it can be shown that

$$\frac{dN}{N} = \frac{dK}{K} - \frac{\sigma}{\pi w} \tag{A1}$$

where π is the proportion of output going to capital. This expression may be used to compare the effect of a rise in s on the amount of labor employed at a given time on machines of two different vintages. In steady growth a rise in s will raise the stock of machines of all vintages in use by the same proportion, λ. Therefore

$$\frac{dN_v}{N_v} = \lambda - \frac{\sigma_v}{\pi_v w} \tag{A2}$$

and

$$\frac{dN_t}{N_t} = \lambda - \frac{\sigma_t}{\pi_t w}. \tag{A3}$$

The difference between the proportional changes in N_v and N_t due to a rise in s is given by

$$\frac{dN_t}{N_t} - \frac{dN_v}{N_v} = \frac{1}{w}\left(\frac{\sigma_v}{\pi_v} - \frac{\sigma_t}{\pi_t}\right). \tag{A4}$$

If this expression varies directly with w, a rise in s raises the weighted average age of capital; obversely if it varies inversely with w. Now in steady growth the share of the product going to capital, π, on machines of the latest vintage at the time they are built must remain constant over time. Whether π on any machine once it has been built rises or falls over time as w rises depends on whether $\sigma \gtrless 1$. If $\sigma_t = \sigma_v$, the effect of w on the weighted average age of capital depends on the relative magnitude of π_t and π_v and hence on whether $\sigma \gtrless 1$. This confirms the result already reached for the constant-elasticity-of-substitution Harrod-neutral case. If $\sigma_t \neq \sigma_v$, the result is more complicated, though it is still true that the weighted average age of capital is independent of w only in a special case.

7. W. E. G. Salter, *Productivity and Technical Change* (Cambridge, England: Cambridge University Press, 1960) and "Productivity Growth and Accumulation as Historical Processes," paper delivered at the International Economic Association's Congress on Economic Development, Vienna 1962.

the wage.   How long a time elapses before the quasi-rents on a
machine fall to zero, given the rate of increase of wages, varies
directly with the ratio of the wage-bill to the value of output when
the machine was new.   Let us assume that labor is paid the value
of its marginal product on new machines.   Then if $\sigma < 1$, a high w
at the time a machine is built means that the wage-bill is a high
proportion of the value of output on the machine; hence it means
an early scrapping date.   If $\sigma = 1$, the level of w does not affect the
proportion of the wage-bill to the value of output on the new machine, and the scrapping date is independent of w.   Finally if $\sigma > 1$,
a high w means a late scrapping date.   On steady growth assumptions the level of w at any time varies with the level of s, so the
above argument shows the effect of s on the scrapping date.

Putting this in symbolic terms, using Q_v, N_v, and g in the same
sense as before, with $w(t) = $ wage prevailing at time t, and $T = $ the
age of machines on the margin of scrapping, we have

$$Q_v - N_v\, w(v + T) = 0. \tag{6}$$

Under steady growth,

$$w(v + T) = w(v)\, e^{gT}. \tag{7}$$

Substituting (7) in (6) and solving for T,

$$T = \frac{1}{g} \log \left(\frac{Q_v}{w(v)N_v} \right). \tag{8}$$

The expression in parentheses in (8) is the reciprocal of labor's
share in the value of output of machines of vintage v at the time
they were built.   Whether this share, and hence the age at scrapping, T, is an increasing or diminishing function of $w(v)$ depends
on whether $\sigma \gtrless 1$.

To complete the argument, it is obvious that the average age
of the machines in use varies in the same direction as the age of
the machine that is on the margin of scrapping.

One way of interpreting this result intuitively is in terms of
the balance of advantages of new machines over old ones.   The
average age of equipment will be less, the greater the inducement to
scrap old machines and transfer their labor to new ones.   The inducement to scrap arises because the labor cost is lower on the
new machines than on the old ones, because of embodied technical
progress.   Anything that increases labor costs relatively to the value
of output on *both* old and new machines increases the relative advantage of new machines.   A high s means a high w at any time,
given steady growth.   Whether the high w means high labor costs

or low labor costs relative to the value of output depends on σ.

All this so far depends on the assumption that the wage of labor is equal to the value of labor's marginal product on new machines. This assumption is appropriate enough in the case considered in Section I. But it is open to criticism in the case where there is no *ex post* substitution. Amending it calls for some modification of the argument, and makes the conclusion less simple and no longer identical with that of Section I. The reasons for this are as follows.

With no *ex post* substitutability, the entrepreneur is committed to retaining the same labor force on a machine so long as he uses it at all. In deciding which of two machines (of equal value), with differing labor requirements and outputs, will yield the higher discounted stream of quasi-rents, he must therefore have regard to expected future wage rates. If he expects wages to stay constant, he will equate the marginal product of labor to the wage. But in a steady growth model, it is more appropriate to assume that he expects wages to grow at the steady-growth rate. The extra output to be had from the machine that uses more labor will stay constant over time, but the cost of the extra labor will rise. So the discounted stream of quasi-rents will be maximized by choosing a machine with labor requirements such that the marginal product of labor exceeds the wage prevailing at the time the machine is built. In another recent paper Phelps has worked out the consequences of such a model, still sticking to Cobb-Douglas.[8]

The assumption that wages are expected to rise does not invalidate equations (6)–(8). It is still true that the effect of s on T depends on the effect of s on labor's share on new machines, and may be either positive or negative. But it is no longer true that this share is constant with $\sigma = 1$. In the article cited, Phelps has shown that with $\sigma = 1$, a higher s under steady growth is associated with a *higher* T. It can be shown by an extension of his argument that in order for labor's share on new machines, and hence T, to be constant with respect to s, it is necessary that σ should be *below* unity (the exact value of σ depending on the rate of growth as well as the shape of the production function). σ has to be below this crucial value in order for a higher s to be associated with a lower T.[9]

8. "Substitution, Fixed Proportions, Growth and Distribution," *International Economic Review*, Vol. 4 (Sept. 1963). An earlier version appeared as Cowles Foundation Discussion Paper No. 133.

9. Use the same notation as before, but write Q and N (without subscripts) to denote the output and labor requirements respectively of a machine

The meaning of this result can be understood intuitively as follows. With no *ex post* substitution, a decision about the capital-intensity of new machines has to have regard to future factor prices as well as to present ones. The relevant wage is a weighted average of wages over the life of the machine. Since wages rise over time, a rather more capital-intensive method will be chosen than would be if *ex post* substitution were possible. Now the extent to which the entrepreneur is influenced by the future depends on the rate at which future quasi-rents are discounted. This rate, r, may be assumed equal to the rate of profit. Comparing steady rates, a higher s is associated with a lower r as well as with a higher w, and the lower r tends to cause more weight to be attached to the future. By its effect on r, a higher s increases the extent to which the absence of *ex post* substitution causes the capital-intensity chosen to exceed

of vintage v, $Q_N = \dfrac{\partial Q}{\partial N}$, r the rate at which future quasi-rents are discounted, and w the wage when the machine is built. Then the present value of the output of the machine over its life is given by

$$\frac{Q}{r}(1 - e^{-rT}).\tag{B1}$$

The present value of the cost of the labor employed with it over its life is likewise

$$\frac{Nw}{r - g}[1 - e^{(g-r)T}].\tag{B2}$$

Maximizing the excess of (B1) over (B2) leads to

$$Q_N = w\left(\frac{r}{r - g}\right)\left[\frac{1 - e^{(g-r)T}}{1 - e^{-rT}}\right].\tag{B3}$$

This shows the relationship between the wage and the marginal product of labor. A machine is scrapped when

$$Nwe^{gT} = Q.\tag{B4}$$

Substituting for w from (B3),

$$\frac{Q}{NQ_N} = e^{gT}\left(\frac{r - g}{r}\right)\left[\frac{1 - e^{-rT}}{1 - e^{(g-r)T}}\right].\tag{B5}$$

Expanding the right-hand side in Taylor series and ignoring terms of higher than second order, we have

$$\frac{Q}{NQ_N} = 1 + \frac{gT}{2 + T(g - r)}.\tag{B6}$$

Differentiating with respect to s,

$$\frac{\partial}{\partial s}\left(\frac{Q}{NQ_N}\right) = \frac{g}{[2 + T(g - r)]^2}\left(2\frac{\partial T}{\partial s} + T^2\frac{\partial r}{\partial s}\right).\tag{B7}$$

Now under Cobb-Douglas ($\sigma = 1$) the left-hand side is zero. Since $\dfrac{\partial r}{\partial s} < 0$, it follows that in this case $\dfrac{\partial T}{\partial s} > 0$. This is Phelps's result referred to in the text. The crucial case where $\dfrac{\partial T}{\partial s} = 0$ occurs when σ is sufficiently below unity to make

$$\frac{\partial}{\partial s}\left(\frac{Q}{NQ_N}\right) = \frac{gT^2}{[2 + T(g - r)]^2} \cdot \frac{\partial r}{\partial s}.\tag{B8}$$

This result is, of course, an approximation, based on the neglect of higher order terms in (B6).

the capital-intensity that would have been chosen if *ex post* substitution were possible. Hence, with Cobb-Douglas, instead of getting, for a given difference in w between two steady states, an exactly proportional difference in capital-intensity, leaving labor's share on new machines constant, what happens is that a higher w is associated with a lower r, more weight is given to the future (when labor will be dearer) and hence there is a somewhat *greater* than proportional difference in capital-intensity. The result is that labor's share on new machines is lower, and this leads to a longer T. There will be some value of σ lower than unity at which the above-noted effect of the fall in r will exactly offset the increase in labor's share that would otherwise have occurred, and so will leave labor's share and T unchanged.

The case where there is *ex post* substitutability and the case where there is no *ex post* substitutability but wages are expected to stay constant both lead to the same result ($\sigma = 1$ the watershed) because in both the entrepreneur need have regard only to present factor prices. In the case just considered the absence of *ex post* substitution causes the capital-intensity of production to be higher by an amount that varies with r and hence with s. The watershed value of σ is therefore below unity.

III

This note has been concerned with a limited issue: the effect of the propensity to save on the average age of capital under steady growth. No attempt has been made to work out the more general implications of vintage-capital models with elasticity of substitution not equal to unity. But even without working out a fully articulated model, it seems clear that dropping the Cobb-Douglas assumption does alter certain conclusions that may have a bearing on policy. One such is Phelps's conclusion that the magnitude of the increase in the level of steady-growth-income that can be brought about by a given increase in s is the same whether technical progress is embodied or disembodied.[1] That this conclusion does not hold generally is suggested by considering the limiting case where the scope for substituting capital for labor at the intensive margin is very small (σ approaches zero). If technical progress is completely disembodied, the benefit to income from a rise in s will then approach zero; more capital will be employed per man, but the gain to output will be very small. On the other hand, if technical progress is

1. *Ibid.*, p. 557.

embodied, the extra savings can be absorbed by earlier scrapping; the extent to which the average age of the capital stock is reduced does not approach zero, and the same will be true of the consequent increase in the level of income.

St. John's College
Cambridge

REPLY

E. S. Phelps and M. E. Yaari

Mr. Matthews is excessively generous to offer his constructive paper as a comment on "The New View of Investment." Nevertheless we accept the invitation to register some thoughts on Matthews's findings.

To begin with, the paper by Phelps contains some results which show that there are significant differences between the behavior of growth models which differ (in the postulates) only in respect to whether technical progress is of the embodied or disembodied type. These results are that "normally" the economy will make the transition from one golden age to another (corresponding to a given change of the saving ratio) faster if technical progress is embodied and, second, the rate of return to saving is "normally" greater when technical progress is embodied, keeping the appropriate set of "other things" equal.

Matthews's paper is concerned with another result which may, unfortunately, be more striking. This is that the responsiveness of *golden-age* or *balance-growth* output to a change of the saving ratio is the same whether progress is embodied or disembodied. The elasticity was shown to be equal to $a/1 - a$, where a is the elasticity of output from currently installed capital with respect to current investment. (In the old model this is just the elasticity of aggregate output with respect to aggregate capital and in the new model it is the elasticity of aggregate output with respect to aggregate "effective capital.")

In explanation of this result it was shown that since the mean age of capital (all capital in existence is used) depends in the golden age only on the golden-age rate of growth of capital and the latter is independent of the saving ratio — it is equal to the rate of technical progress (of whatever type) multiplied by $1/1 - a$ plus the rate of increase of the labor force — the effect of a rise of the saving ratio on the mean age of capital will tend to vanish as the new golden age path is approached. Because a golden age is approached for every fixed saving ratio, no permanent shortening of the mean age of capital is possible (for that would require that the saving ratio increase without limit which is infeasible).[1]

Now Matthews argues that the mean age of capital is not generally a satisfactory statistic. He studies instead the weighted mean age of capital, where the weight given to investment of a given age is equal to the fraction of the labor force which works with that investment. He then shows that, in the neoclassical case of *ex post* substitutability the same as *ex ante*, this weighted mean age is independent of the saving ratio (in a golden age) only if the production function exhibits a unitary substitution elasticity (Cobb-Douglas); the weighted mean age will fall or rise with an increase of the saving ratio according as the substitution elasticity is smaller or larger than unity.

This is a suggestive finding but its significance is not yet clear. The finding might suggest to the reader that the responsiveness of golden-age output to a change of the saving ratio is greater in the new model than in the old when the substitution elasticity is less than unity and vice versa when it is greater than unity. But is this true? Matthews refers to a later paper by Phelps in which the production function is Cobb-Douglas but there is no *ex post* substitutability between capital and labor. In that paper it is shown that while an increase of the saving ratio raises the age of the oldest capital in use (and hence increases the weighted mean age of capital) this rise is, up to a point, favorable to productivity, not detrimental as assumed by the enthusiasts for a young capital stock.[2] (The critical point is reached when the saving ratio obeys

---

1. Interest in the behavior of the mean age of capital in the "new" (Cobb-Douglas) is justified by the proposition, demonstrated in unpublished work by Richard Nelson of the RAND Corporation and others, that aggregate output, $Q(t)$, can be written as a Cobb-Douglas function of labor, $L(t)$, *conventional* (rather than "effective") capital, $K(t)$ multiplied by some coefficient which is a decreasing function of m, the mean age of capital:
$$Q(t) = A K(t)^a L(t)^{1-a} c(m).$$
2. This is as it should be: One can imagine an economy in which the operating life of capital goods is so small that productivity suffers from the crowding of labor around the few brand new machines available. If the operating life were increased, productivity would rise because the available labor would have more, albeit less modern, capital on which to work. But as the operating life is further lengthened, progressively older machines have to be dusted off and assigned a portion of the labor force, machines which are less efficient (more labor using per unit of output) than the new ones, so that eventually a finite operating life is reached such that any further lengthening of it will cause a net decline of productivity.

the Golden Rule of Accumulation.) This should warn us against assuming that a reduction of the weighted mean age of capital is necessarily a good thing.

Let us consider the first of Matthews's models in which *ex post* and *ex ante* substitutability are the same: (i) $L(t) = L(0)e^{\gamma t}$, (ii)

$$I(t) = sQ(t),\ (iii)\ Q(v,\ t) = [a\,I(v)^{-\rho} + \beta\,e^{-\rho\lambda v}\,L(v,\ t)^{-\rho}]^{-\frac{1}{\rho}},$$

(iv) $\displaystyle\int_{-\infty}^{t} L(v,\ t)\,dv = L(t)$, (v) $\displaystyle\int_{-\infty}^{t} Q(v,\ t)\,dv = Q(t)$ and (vi) labor is allocated (the $L(v,\ t)$ are chosen) so as to maximize $Q(t)$ for every t (efficiency requirement).

On the assumption that for some s there exists a golden-age solution, $Q(t) = \bar{Q}(t) = \bar{Q}(0)e^{gt}$ and $w(t) = \bar{w}(t) = \bar{w}(0)e^{mt}$, where $w(t)$ is the wage rate (marginal productivity of labor) at time t, we can show that if (and only if) $\rho > 0$ (meaning the substitution elasticity is less than unity) there is a finite operating life of capital goods, say z, which satisfies the equation $w(0) = \beta^{-\frac{1}{\rho}}e^{-\lambda z}$. From this relation, the golden-age assumption and the properties of the model listed above we can derive, making use of the fundamental growth equation,

$$\dot{Q}(t) = \frac{\partial Q(t,\ t)}{\partial I(t)}\,I(t) + w(t)\,\dot{L}(t),\quad \text{the following solution for}$$

golden-age output, $\bar{Q}(t)$, as a function of s and z:

$$(1)\quad \bar{Q}(t) = \frac{\gamma\beta^{-\frac{1}{\rho}}\,L(0)\,e^{(\gamma+\lambda)t}}{(\gamma + \lambda)e^{\lambda z} - s\,a^{-\frac{1}{\rho}}\left[\dfrac{\lambda\rho z}{e^{1+\rho}} - 1\right]^{\frac{1+\rho}{\rho}}},\ \rho > 0.$$

Our interest is in the response of $\bar{Q}(t)$ to a change of s, recognizing that z changes with s. A measure of this response is the total derivative,

$$\frac{d\bar{Q}}{ds} = \frac{\partial\bar{Q}}{\partial s} + \frac{\partial\bar{Q}}{\partial z}\cdot\frac{dz}{ds}.$$

It is easily seen that $\dfrac{\partial\bar{Q}}{\partial s} > 0$ for all $z > 0$. It can also be seen from the above relation between $\bar{w}(0)$ and z that an increase of s will decrease z provided $\bar{w}(0)$ increases with s; hence $\dfrac{dz}{ds} < 0$.

(This accords with Matthews's result that when the substitution elasticity is less than one the weighted mean age of capital falls with an increase of the saving ratio.) But what of the sign of $\dfrac{\partial \bar{Q}}{\partial z}$? Is it necessarily negative as Matthews suggests?

It is easily shown that

$$\frac{1}{\bar{Q}}\frac{\partial Q}{\partial z} = -\frac{\lambda\left\{(\gamma+\lambda)e^{\lambda z} - s\,a^{-\frac{1}{\rho}}\left[e^{\frac{\lambda\rho}{1+\rho}z} - 1\right]^{\frac{1}{\rho}}e^{\frac{\lambda\rho}{1+\rho}z}\right\}}{(\gamma+\lambda)e^{\lambda z} - s\,a^{-\frac{1}{\rho}}\left[e^{\frac{\lambda\rho}{1+\rho}z} - 1\right]^{\frac{1}{\rho}}\left[e^{\frac{\lambda\rho}{1+\rho}z} - 1\right]}.$$

The denominator must be positive if $\bar{Q}(t)$ is to be positive; this implies that $s\,a^{-\frac{1}{\rho}} < \gamma + \lambda$ for there to be a golden age. Further it can be shown that the numerator has the sign of the denominator. In particular, the quotient approaches λ very quickly. Hence the expression is everywhere negative (taking the minus sign into account). So Matthews is right in assuming that $\dfrac{\partial \bar{Q}}{\partial z} < 0$ in the neo-classical case when *ex post* equals *ex ante* substitutability.

None of this proves that the responsiveness of golden-age output to a change of the saving ratio is greater in this model (with $\rho > 0$) than in the old-style model where technical progress is disembodied. Consider the latter system which differs from the former in that $(iii)-(vi)$ are replaced with

> (iii') $Q(t) = [a\,K(t)^{-\rho} + \beta\,e^{-\rho\mu t}\,L(t)],$

> (iv') $\dot{K}(t) = I(t).$

It can be shown that if $s\,a^{-\frac{1}{\rho}} < (\gamma + \mu)$ then a golden age exists in which golden-age output is the following function of the saving ratio:

$$(2) \quad \bar{Q}(t) = \frac{(\mu+\gamma)\beta^{-\frac{1}{\rho}}L(0)e^{(\gamma+\mu)t}}{\left[(\gamma+\mu)^{-\rho} - s^{-\rho}a\right]^{-\frac{1}{\rho}}}.$$

Unfortunately we cannot compare $\dfrac{d\bar{Q}}{ds}$ from (2) with $\dfrac{dQ}{ds}$ from (1) because we lack the complete solution to the first model which would yield us the size of $\dfrac{dz}{ds}$. So it is for the present an open question whether golden-age output is more responsive to changes of the saving ratio when technical progress is embodied than when it is disembodied. Nevertheless any full-scale assault on this question should find Matthews's contribution an important foothold.

YALE UNIVERSITY

The Unimportance of the Embodied Question

Edward F. Denison

In a recent article in this journal, Moses Abramovitz noted that Robert M. Solow and I obtain different estimates of the effect on economic growth of alternative investment rates because of different appraisals of the importance of embodiment of new knowledge in capital goods. Abramovitz suggested "an issue of first-rate importance is, therefore, posed" [1, p. 773]. Recent literature seems to imply that the issue can be resolved by discovering what fraction of developments that can potentially raise productivity must be embodied in capital. I wish to suggest here that the whole embodiment question is of little importance for policy in the United States; that the issue is not usefully formulated in terms of the fraction of progress that is embodied; and that the right question can't be answered beyond a showing that it *is* unimportant.

The argument that the question was of no great consequence that was given in my *Sources of Economic Growth* may be stated as follows [2, pp. 234-37, 254-55]. The embodiment effect operates through the age distribution of the gross capital stock of business. This distribution can be summarized accurately enough by average age, provided weights of different types of capital goods (particularly structures and equipment) are held constant. Suppose then the growth rate of output per man is 1.6 per cent a year, of which .6 per cent is due to advances in knowledge (my estimates for the 1929-57 period). Suppose we can change the average age by one year from 1960 to 1970.[1] In so far as productivity-changing developments are embodied, we will then be working in 1970 with the technology that we would be using in 1971 if average age did not change. If nothing is embodied, the change in average age of capital will not affect output. If all advances of knowledge but not other productivity-affecting developments are embodied, 1970 output will be .6 per cent higher than if nothing is embodied and the 1960-70 annual growth rate .06 percentage points higher. If *everything* affecting output per man favorably or unfavorably is embodied, 1970 output will be 1.6 per cent higher as a result of the reduced age of capital and the annual growth rate .16 percentage points higher. If half of either is embodied, the amounts will be half as large. After 1970 the growth rate will be the same as otherwise unless the average age is again changed. Thus the most extreme assumptions yield annual growth rates, calculated over a ten-year period, that differ by .16 percentage points for each year that the average age of capital changes; thereafter, for as long as the new average age is maintained, the levels of national income differ by a constant 1.6 per cent.

The force of the calculations depends on the fact that average age is a

---

[1] If average age (and the rate at which knowledge advances) does not change between dates or assumed situations, the calculated growth rate is the same whether advances are or are not embodied in capital.

Reprinted from *The American Economic Review, LIV,* No. 2, part 1 (March 1964) pp. 90–94. Copyright American Economic Association 1964. By permission of the author and publishers.

variable that does not and can not vary much under normal conditions, so that one year is a big change. This is especially the case with equipment, for which the age level is short and observed variation small. Commerce Department calculations [5, p. 17] based on Bulletin F lives give an average age for equipment of 7.2 years in 1961 and a range of 1.5 years during the period since 1929. An alternate calculation based on assumed lives 20 per cent shorter gives an average age of 5.6 years and range of 1.2 years. Ranges even as large as these were possible only because of the extreme variation in gross capital formation due to the depression of the 'thirties and war.

Equipment, quite reasonably, is usually stressed, but some attention is given to structures. Their age is longer and the range greater. If structures and equipment are weighted by value of gross stock (surely the maximum weight that can be assigned to structures), based on an average of 1929 and 1961 weights in 1954 prices, extreme ranges of 2.6 and 3.6 years are given by the alternative estimates. Both extreme ranges include 1945. From 1929 to 1961 the change was only .3 years by one estimate and 1.0 years by the other.[2]

Such data illustrate how insensitive is the age of equipment, and even of plant and equipment, to big swings in the rate of gross investment. Edmund Phelps has also shown that average age is independent of the equilibrium (or average) level of capital formation and tends to return to an equilibrium point, so that sustained changes are hard to obtain [6]. This is borne out by the actual data.

The purpose of the present note is to argue that, though such calculations and considerations themselves assign no large importance to the embodiment question unless rates of technological progress well outside the bounds of experience are assumed, they overstate its significance by what I should judge to be an enormous amount. To speak of technological progress embodied in capital is simply to refer to changes in the quality of capital goods. The index of quality change in capital goods is the quotient of indexes of the quantity of capital goods when capital of different vintages is equated (1) by ability to contribute to production, and (2) by production cost at a common date.[3] Ordinary observation indicates that the amount of quality change in any time period must vary enormously among different types of equipment or structures, ranging from zero for many types of capital that aren't changed to huge amounts for a few types. The profitability of replacing any capital good (or complex of capital goods) before it is physically worn out depends directly upon the extent to which its quality falls short of the quality of its potential replacement. If an industry invests $50 million, profit maximization will lead it to replace those types of capital in which quality improvement (hence obsolescence) is greatest. An extra $10 million will go to capital in

---

[2] These average lives are computed from stock estimates derived by the perpetual inventory method. Lives were probably extended during the war, so the divergence between 1945 and more normal periods is probably understated.

[3] That is, quality change is the quotient of indexes of capital computed by methods 3 and 1 in the language of an earlier article [3], where the meaning of these indexes is specified more fully.

which quality improvement is smaller, and so on. Moreover, a particular type of capital good acquired for replacement will be applied first to uses where the gains from replacement are greatest. Also, the mix of capital goods, and consequently the average quality change, varies greatly among industries; hence so does the average profitability of replacement of capital. Industries in which average quality of new capital goods changes most will, other things equal, have the highest replacement rate. Any reasonable amount of gross investment in the economy will already provide for taking up those investment opportunities arising because quality change in capital goods is large: i.e., within firms and industries, large relative to all capital used; and, as among industries, large relative to the average industry.

It follows that if we suppose $50 billion of investment in the economy will embody 25 per cent more technological progress than $40 billion—an assumption which would be consistent with calculations made earlier based on average lives—we shall have a radical overestimate. Within ranges of gross investment worth talking about—that is, above some reasonable minimum, certainly above the point of no net capital formation—I should think the additional amount of technological progress that will be incorporated into production at a higher investment rate rather than a lower rate must be very small relative to the amount incorporated at the lower rate. We can legitimately take only a small fraction of the .16 previously computed as the difference between the 10-year growth rates if everything or nothing is embodied (given a one-year change in average age) because that calculation assumed quality change on incremental investment to be the same as on average gross investment. All the calculations I have seen on embodiment effects assume the same rate of quality improvement for all capital goods, hence are great overestimates.[4]

The same reasoning disputes the importance of the idea that a high rate of gross capital formation is necessary in order to get radically improved equipment into use quickly so that, with experience in its use, further technological advance will be accelerated. Any attention to rates of return will tell us that introduction of capital goods representing radical improvement over those previously available will be made at even a low rate of gross capital formation. There may be cases of radically improved capital goods whose merit is not obvious to potential buyers, so that attachment of a high risk premium makes their introduction marginal, but the point hardly deserves much weight.

I have explained why the embodiment question appears to me unimportant in the United States at present. The same reasoning shows it would not be helpful to know the fraction of "technological progress" that is, or must be, embodied. We are dealing not with a two-way classification but with a curve of rates of return. Some innovations (the purely unembodied) require no gross investment, and their introduction, if computed against capital cost (other costs may be involved), yields an infinite rate of return. Others (I suspect a great many) require some trifling readjustment of existing capital or insignificant capital expenditure to achieve a substantial continuing gain; these imply a near-infinite rate of return on capital if we compare the effects

<hr />

[4] In addition to Solow [7] and myself, I may refer specifically to W. A. Eltis [4] and Phelps [6].

of making or not making the capital expenditure, but will be made routinely with scarcely a thought to capital cost or total capital budget. In a two-way classification these are embodied, but the fact is of no significance. We then move down to those changes requiring appreciable investment, which must be expected to yield rates of return ranging from very high down toward zero.

If one seriously wished to measure the embodiment effects of having (say) $50 billion instead of $40 billion of gross investment a year, he would need (1) to specify the composition of the extra $10 billion in terms of types of capital goods; and (2) to measure the quality improvement in these capital goods. The first is difficult, the second, I have argued [3, pp. 229-34] and am convinced, impossible.

Calculations that assume (1) that quality improvement in capital is necessary for all productivity increase and (2) that quality improvement in (say) the first $40 billion of gross investment is no larger, per dollar, than in the next $10 billion, yield results that are, I believe, enormously too large. They are useful only because they yield such small numbers that we can deduce that the true figures must be insignificant under normal circumstances in the United States.

There is an important reservation to universal application of the conclusion that it makes little difference to analysis whether or not one takes account of embodiment effects. It' need not hold in countries where (or times when) capital goods are used much longer than in the present-day United States (hence have more room for variation) or their age distribution is greatly distorted and where (or when) tendencies toward equalizing rates of return are (or recently have been) extremely weak because of lack of competition or because of controls on investment. These conditions existed to a degree in the United States in the immediate postwar years, their effects on short-term productivity changes perhaps being important until around 1950. Because specific investment controls during the war and wartime demand patterns prevented the introduction of new capital in the industries serving postwar markets, at war's end there presumably was a significant backlog of high-yielding investment opportunities deriving from improvement in capital goods. This was reflected in a catching-up of productivity, particularly from 1948 to 1950. Opportunities deriving from previous improvement in capital goods are therefore significant in examination of the early postwar period. A one-year change in the true average age of equipment had a different effect then than in normal times; and the change recorded by the available capital stock estimates probably understates the change in average age that actually took place.[5]

EDWARD F. DENISON*

[5] Note, however, that if average age is understated in the immediate postwar period, the size of the gross stock is also understated.

* The author is a senior staff member of The Brookings Institution.

REFERENCES

1. MOSES ABRAMOVITZ, "Economic Growth in the United States: A Review Article," Am. Econ. Rev., Sept. 1962, 52, 762-82.
2. E. F. DENISON, The Sources of Economic Growth in the United States and the Alternatives Before Us. New York 1962.

3. ———, "Theoretical Aspects of Quality Change, Capital Consumption, and Net Capital Formation," *Problems of Capital Formation,* Nat. Bur. Econ. Research Stud. in Income and Wealth Vol. 19. Princeton 1957.
4. W. A. ELTIS, "Investment, Technical Progress, and Economic Growth," *Oxford Econ. Papers,* March 1963, *N.S. 15,* 32-52.
5. G. JASZI, R. C. WASSON AND L. GROSE, "Expansion of Fixed Business Capital in the United States," *Surv. Curr. Bus.,* Nov. 1962, *42,* 9-18.
6. E. S. PHELPS, "The New View of Investment: A Neoclassical Analysis," *Quart. Jour. Econ.,* Nov. 1962, *76,* 548-67.
7. R. M. SOLOW, "Technical Progress, Capital Formation and Economic Growth," *Am. Econ. Rev., Proc.,* May 1962, *52,* 76-86.

The Economic Implications of Learning by Doing

Kenneth J. Arrow

It is by now incontrovertible that increases in per capita income cannot be explained simply by increases in the capital-labor ratio. Though doubtless no economist would ever have denied the role of technological change in economic growth, its overwhelming importance relative to capital formation has perhaps only been fully realized with the important empirical studies of Abramovitz [1] and Solow [11]. These results do not directly contradict the neo-classical view of the production function as an expression of technological knowledge. All that has to be added is the obvious fact that knowledge is growing in time. Nevertheless a view of economic growth that depends so heavily on an exogenous variable, let alone one so difficult to measure as the quantity of knowledge, is hardly intellectually satisfactory. From a quantitative, empirical point of view, we are left with time as an explanatory variable. Now trend projections, however necessary they may be in practice, are basically a confession of ignorance, and, what is worse from a practical viewpoint, are not policy variables.

Further, the concept of knowledge which underlies the production function at any moment needs analysis. Knowledge has to be acquired. We are not surprised, as educators, that even students subject to the same educational experiences have different bodies of knowledge, and we may therefore be prepared to grant, as has been shown empirically (see [2], Part III), that different countries, at the same moment of time, have different production functions even apart from differences in natural resource endowment.

I would like to suggest here an endogenous theory of the changes in knowledge which underlie intertemporal and international shifts in production functions. The acquisition of knowledge is what is usually termed "learning," and we might perhaps pick up some clues from the many psychologists who have studied this phenomenon (for a convenient survey, see Hilgard [5]). I do not think that the picture of technical change as a vast and prolonged process of learning about the environment in which we operate is in any way a far-fetched analogy; exactly the same phenomenon of improvement in performance over time is involved.

Of course, psychologists are no more in agreement than economists, and there are sharp differences of opinion about the processes of learning. But one empirical generalization is so clear that all schools of thought must accept it, although they interpret it in different fashions: Learning is the product of experience. Learning can only take place through the attempt to solve a problem and therefore only takes place during activity. Even the Gestalt and other field theorists, who stress the role of insight in the solution of problems (Köhler's famous apes), have to assign a significant role to previous experiences in modifying the individual's perception.

A second generalization that can be gleaned from many of the classic learning experiments is that learning associated with repetition of essentially the same problem is subject to sharply diminishing returns. There is an equilibrium response pattern for any given

Reprinted from XXIX (June 1962), 155–173 of *Review of Economic Studies* by permission of *Review of Economic Studies* published by Oliver & Boyd Ltd., Edinburgh and London. © 1962 The Economic Society.

stimulus, towards which the behavior of the learner tends with repetition. To have steadily increasing performance, then, implies that the stimulus situations must themselves be steadily evolving rather than merely repeating.

The role of experience in increasing productivity has not gone unobserved, though the relation has yet to be absorbed into the main corpus of economic theory. It was early observed by aeronautical engineers, particularly T. P. Wright [15], that the number of labor-hours expended in the production of an airframe (airplane body without engines) is a decreasing function of the total number of airframes of the same type previously produced. Indeed, the relation is remarkably precise; to produce the Nth airframe of a given type, counting from the inception of production, the amount of labor required is proportional to $N^{-1/3}$. This relation has become basic in the production and cost planning of the United States Air Force; for a full survey, see [3]. Hirsch (see [6] and other work cited there) has shown the existence of the same type of " learning curve " or " progress ratio," as it is variously termed, in the production of other machines, though the rate of learning is not the same as for airframes.

Verdoorn [14, pp. 433-4] has applied the principle of the learning curve to national outputs; however, under the assumption that output is increasing exponentially, current output is proportional to cumulative output, and it is the former variable that he uses to explain labor productivity. The empirical fitting was reported in [13]; the estimated progress ratio for different European countries is about ·5. (In [13], a neo-classical interpretation in terms of increasing capital-labor ratios was offered; see pp. 7-11.)

Lundberg [9, pp. 129-133] has given the name " Horndal effect " to a very similar phenomenon. The Horndal iron works in Sweden had no new investment (and therefore presumably no significant change in its methods of production) for a period of 15 years, yet productivity (output per manhour) rose on the average close to 2% per annum. We find again steadily increasing performance which can only be imputed to learning from experience.

I advance the hypothesis here that technical change in general can be ascribed to experience, that it is the very activity of production which gives rise to problems for which favorable responses are selected over time. The evidence so far cited, whether from psychological or from economic literature is, of course, only suggestive. The aim of this paper is to formulate the hypothesis more precisely and draw from it a number of economic implications. These should enable the hypothesis and its consequences to be confronted more easily with empirical evidence.

The model set forth will be very simplified in some other respects to make clearer the essential role of the major hypothesis; in particular, the possibility of capital-labor sub-stitution is ignored. The theorems about the economic world presented here differ from those in most standard economic theories; profits are the result of technical change; in a free-enterprise system, the rate of investment will be less than the optimum; net investment and the stock of capital become subordinate concepts, with gross investment taking a leading role.

In section 1, the basic assumptions of the model are set forth. In section 2, the implications for wage earners are deduced; in section 3 those for profits, the inducement to invest, and the rate of interest. In section 4, the behavior of the entire system under steady growth with mutually consistent expectations is taken up. In section 5, the divergence between social and private returns is studied in detail for a special case (where the subjective rate of discount of future consumption is a constant). Finally, in section 6, some limitations of the model and needs for further development are noted.

1. THE MODEL

The first question is that of choosing the economic variable which represents " experience ". The economic examples given above suggest the possibility of using cumulative output (the total of output from the beginning of time) as an index of experience, but this does not seem entirely satisfactory. If the rate of output is constant, then the stimulus to learning presented would appear to be constant, and the learning that does take place is a gradual approach to equilibrium behavior. I therefore take instead cumulative gross investment (cumulative production of capital goods) as an index of experience. Each new machine produced and put into use is capable of changing the environment in which production takes place, so that learning is taking place with continually new stimuli. This at least makes plausible the possibility of continued learning in the sense, here, of a steady rate of growth in productivity.

The second question is that of deciding where the learning enters the conditions of production. I follow here the model of Solow [12] and Johansen [7], in which technical change is completely embodied in new capital goods. At any moment of new time, the new capital goods incorporate all the knowledge then available, but once built their productive efficiency cannot be altered by subsequent learning.

To simplify the discussion we shall assume that the production process associated with any given new capital good is characterized by fixed coefficients, so that a fixed amount of labor is used and a fixed amount of output obtained. Further, it will be assumed that new capital goods are better than old ones in the strong sense that, if we compare a unit of capital goods produced at time t_1 with one produced at time $t_2 > t_1$, the first requires the co-operation of at least as much labor as the second, and produces no more product. Under this assumption, a new capital good will always be used in preference to an older one.

Let G be cumulative gross investment. A unit capital good produced when cumulative gross investment has reached G will be said to have *serial number* G. Let

$\lambda(G) = $ amount of labor used in production with a capital good of serial number G,
$\gamma(G) = $ output capacity of a capital good of serial number G,
$x = $ total output,
$L = $ total labor force employed.

It is assumed that $\lambda(G)$ is a non-increasing function, while $\gamma(G)$ is a non-decreasing function. Then, regardless of wages or rental value of capital goods, it always pays to use a capital good of higher serial number before one of lower serial number.

It will further be assumed that capital goods have a fixed lifetime, $\bar{T}$. Then capital goods disappear in the same order as their serial numbers. It follows that at any moment of time, the capital goods in use will be all those with serial numbers from some G' to G, the current cumulative gross investment. Then

(1) $$x = \int_{G'}^{G} \gamma(G)dG,$$

$$(2) \qquad L = \int_{G'}^{G} \lambda(G)dG.$$

The magnitudes x, L, G, and G' are, of course, all functions of time, to be designated by t, and they will be written $x(t)$, $L(t)$, $G(t)$, and $G'(t)$ when necessary to point up the dependence. Then $G(t)$, in particular, is the cumulative gross investment up to time t. The assumption about the lifetime of capital goods implies that

$$(3) \qquad G'(t) \geqq G(t - \bar{T}).$$

Since $G(t)$ is given at time t, we can solve for G' from (1) or (2) or the equality in (3). In a growth context, the most natural assumption is that of full employment. The labor force is regarded as a given function of time and is assumed equal to the labor employed, so that $L(t)$ is a given function. Then $G'(t)$ is obtained by solving in (2). If the result is substituted into (1), x can be written as a function of L and G, analogous to the usual production function. To write this, define

$$\Lambda(G) = \int \lambda(G)dG,$$

$$(4)$$

$$\Gamma(g) = \int \gamma(G)dG.$$

These are to be regarded as indefinite integrals. Since $\lambda(G)$ and $\gamma(G)$ are both positive, $\Lambda(G)$ and $\Gamma(G)$ are strictly increasing and therefore have inverses, $\Lambda^{-1}(u)$ and $\Gamma^{-1}(v)$, respectively. Then (1) and (2) can be written, respectively,

$$(1') \qquad x = \Gamma(G) - \Gamma(G'),$$

$$(2') \qquad L = \Lambda(G) - \Lambda(G').$$

Solve for G' from (2').

$$(5) \qquad G' = \Lambda^{-1}[\Lambda(G) - L].$$

Substitute (5) into (1').

$$(6) \qquad x = \Gamma(G) - \Gamma\{\Lambda^{-1}[\Lambda(G) - L]\},$$

which is thus a production function in a somewhat novel sense. Equation (6) is always valid, but under the full employment assumption we can regard L as the labor force available.

A second assumption, more suitable to a depression situation, is that in which demand for the product is the limiting factor. Then x is taken as given; G' can be derived from (1) or (1'), and employment then found from (2) or (2'). If this is less than the available labor force, we have Keynesian unemployment.

A third possibility, which, like the first, may be appropriate to a growth analysis, is that the solution (5) with L as the labor force, does not satisfy (3). In this case, there is a shortage of capital due to depreciation. There is again unemployment but now due to structural discrepancies rather than to demand deficiency.

In any case, except by accident, there is either unemployed labor or unemployed capital; there could be both in the demand deficiency case. Of course, a more neo-classical model, with substitution between capital and labor for each serial number of capital good, might permit full employment of both capital and labor, but this remains a subject for further study.

In what follows, the full-employment case will be chiefly studied. The capital shortage case, the third one, will be referred to parenthetically. In the full-employment case, the depreciation assumption no longer matters; obsolescence, which occurs for all capital goods with serial numbers below G', becomes the sole reason for the retirement of capital goods from use.

The analysis will be carried through for a special case. To a very rough approximation, the capital-output ratio has been constant, while the labor-output ratio has been declining. It is therefore assumed that

$$(7) \qquad \gamma(G) = a,$$

a constant, while $\lambda(G)$ is a decreasing function of G. To be specific, it will be assumed that $\lambda(G)$ has the form found in the study of learning curves for airframes.

$$(8) \qquad \lambda(G) = bG^{-n},$$

where $n > 0$. Then

$$\Gamma(G) = aG, \Lambda(G) = cG^{1-n}, \text{ where } c = b/(1-n) \text{ for } n \neq 1.$$

Then (6) becomes

$$(9) \qquad x = aG[1 - \left(1 - \frac{L}{cG^{1-n}}\right)^{1/(1-n)}] \text{ if } n \neq 1.$$

Equation (9) is always well defined in the relevant ranges, since from (2'),

$$L = \Lambda(G) - \Lambda(G') \leqq \Lambda(G) = cG^{1-n}.$$

When $n = 1$, $\Lambda(G) = b \log G$ (where the natural logarithm is understood), and

$$(10) \qquad x = aG(1 - e^{-L/b}) \text{ if } n = 1.$$

Although (9) and (10) are, in a sense, production functions, they show increasing returns to scale in the variables G and L. This is obvious in (10) where an increase in G, with L constant, increases x in the same proportion; a simultaneous increase in L will further increase x. In (9), first suppose that $n < 1$. Then a proportional increase in L and G increases L/G^{1-n} and therefore increases the expression in brackets which multiplies G. A similar argument holds if $n > 1$. It should be noted that x increases more than proportionately to scale changes in G and L in general, not merely for the special case defined by (7) and (8). This would be verified by careful examination of the behavior of (6), when it is recalled that $\lambda(G)$ is non-increasing and $\gamma(G)$ is non-decreasing, with the strict inequality holding in at least one. It is obvious intuitively, since the additional amounts of L and G are used more efficiently than the earlier ones.

The increasing returns do not, however, lead to any difficulty with distribution theory. As we shall see, both capital and labor are paid their marginal products, suitably defined. The explanation is, of course, that the private marginal productivity of capital (more strictly, of new investment) is less than the social marginal productivity since the learning effect is not compensated in the market.

The production assumptions of this section are designed to play the role assigned by Kaldor to his " technical progress function," which relates the rate of growth of output per worker to the rate of growth of capital per worker (see [8], section VIII). I prefer to think of relations between rates of growth as themselves derived from more fundamental relations between the magnitudes involved. Also, the present formulation puts more stress on gross rather than net investment as the basic agent of technical change.

Earlier, Haavelmo ([4], sections 7.1 and 7.2) had suggested a somewhat similar model. Output depended on both capital and the stock of knowledge; investment depended on output, the stock of capital, and the stock of knowledge. The stock of knowledge was either simply a function of time or, in a more sophisticated version, the consequence of investment, the educational effect of each act of investment decreasing exponentially in time.

Verdoorn [14, pp. 436-7] had also developed a similar simple model in which capital and labor needed are non-linear functions of output (since the rate of output is, approximately, a measure of cumulative output and therefore of learning) and investment a constant fraction of output. He notes that under these conditions, full employment of capital and labor simultaneously is in general impossible—a conclusion which also holds for for the present model as we have seen. However, Verdoorn draws the wrong conclusion: that the savings ratio must be fixed by some public mechanism at the uniquely determined level which would insure full employment of both factors; the correct conclusion is that one factor or the other will be unemployed. The social force of this conclusion is much less in the present model since the burden of unemployment may fall on obsolescent capital; Verdoorn assumes his capital to be homogeneous in nature.

2. Wages

Under the full employment assumption the profitability of using the capital good with serial number G' must be zero; for if it were positive it would be profitable to use capital goods with higher serial number and if it were negative capital good G' would not be used contrary to the definition of G'. Let

$$w = \text{wage rate with output as numéraire.}$$

From (1') and (7)

$$(11) \qquad G' = G - (x/a)$$

so that

$$(12) \qquad \lambda(G') = b\left(G - \frac{x}{a}\right)^{-n}.$$

The output from capital good G' is $\gamma(G')$ while the cost of operation is $\lambda(G')w$. Hence

$$\gamma(G') = \lambda(G')w$$

or from (7) and (12)

$$(13) \qquad w = a\left(G - \frac{x}{a}\right)^{n}/b.$$

It is interesting to derive labor's share which is wL/x. From (2') with $\Lambda(g) = cG^{1-n}$ and G' given by (11)

$$L = c \left[G^{1-n} - \left(G - \frac{x}{a} \right)^{1-n} \right],$$

for $n \neq 1$ and therefore

(14) $wL/x = a \left[\left(\frac{G}{x} - \frac{1}{a} \right)^n \left(\frac{G}{x} \right)^{1-n} - \left(\frac{G}{x} - \frac{1}{a} \right) \right] / (1 - n)$ for $n \neq 1$,

where use has been made of the relation, $c = b/(1-n)$. It is interesting to note that labor's share is determined by the ratio G/x.

Since, however, x is determined by G and L, which, at any moment of time, are data, it is also useful to express the wage ratio, w, and labor's share, wL/x, in terms of L and G. First, G' can be found by solving for it from (2').

(15) $G' = \left(G^{1-n} - \frac{L}{c} \right)^{1/(1-n)}$ for $n \neq 1$.

We can then use the same reasoning as above, and derive

(16) $w = a \left(G^{1-n} - \frac{L}{c} \right)^{n/(1-n)} / b,$

(17) $\dfrac{wL}{x} = \dfrac{\left[\left(\dfrac{L}{G^{1-n}} \right)^{(1-n)/n} - \dfrac{1}{c} \left(\dfrac{L}{G^{1-n}} \right)^{1/n} \right]^{n/(1-n)}}{b \left[1 - \left(1 - \dfrac{L}{cG^{1-n}} \right)^{1/(1-n)} \right]}.$

Labor's share thus depends on the ratio L/G^{1-n}; it can be shown to decrease as the ratio increases.

For completeness, I note the corresponding formulas for the case $n = 1$. In terms of G and x, we have

(18) $w = (aG - x)/b,$

(19) $wL/x = \left(\frac{aG}{x} - 1 \right) \log \frac{G/x}{(G/x) - (1/a)}.$

In terms of G and L, we have

(20) $G' = Ge^{-L/b},$

(21) $w = \dfrac{aG}{be^{L/b}},$

(22) $wL/x = \dfrac{L}{b(e^{L/b} - 1)}.$

In this case, labor's share depends only on L, which is indeed the appropriate special case ($n=1$) of the general dependence on L/G^{1-n}.

The preceding discussion has assumed full employment. In the capital shortage case, there cannot be a competitive equilibrium with positive wage since there is necessarily unemployment. A zero wage is, however, certainly unrealistic. To complete the model, it would be necessary to add some other assumption about the behavior of wages. This case will not be considered in general; for the special case of steady growth, see Section 5.

3. PROFITS AND INVESTMENT

The profit at time t from a unit investment made at time $v \leq t$ is

$$\gamma[G(v)] - w(t) \ \lambda[G(v)].$$

In contemplating an investment at time v, the stream of potential profits depends upon expectations of future wages. We will suppose that looking ahead at any given moment of time each entrepreneur assumes that wages will rise exponentially from the present level. Thus the wage rate expected at time v to prevail at time t is

$$w(v) \ e^{\theta(t-v)},$$

and the profit expected at time v to be received at time t is

$$\gamma[G(v)] \ [1-W(v) \ e^{\theta(t-v)}],$$

where

(23) $W(v) = w(v) \ \lambda[G(v)]/\gamma[G(v)],$

the labor cost per unit output at the time the investment is made. The dependence of W on v will be made explicit only when necessary. The profitability of the investment is expected to decrease with time (if $\theta > 0$) and to reach zero at time $T^* + v$, defined by the equation

(24) $We^{\theta T^*} = 1.$

Thus T^* is the expected economic lifetime of the investment, provided it does not exceed the physical lifetime, $\bar{T}$. Let

(25) $T = \min (\bar{T}, T^*).$

Then the investor plans to derive profits only over an interval of length T, either because the investment wears out or because wages have risen to the point where it is unprofitable to operate. Since the expectation of wage rises which causes this abandonment derives from anticipated investment and the consequent technological progress, T^* represents the expected date of obsolescence. Let

$$\rho = \text{rate of interest.}$$

If the rate of interest is expected to remain constant over the future, then the discounted stream of profits over the effective lifetime, T, of the investment is

$$(26) \qquad S = \int_0^T e^{-\rho t} \gamma[G(v)] (1 - W e^{\theta t}) dt,$$

or

$$(27) \qquad \frac{S}{\gamma[G(v)]} = \frac{1 - e^{-\rho T}}{\rho} + \frac{W(1 - e^{-(\rho-\theta)T})}{\theta - \rho}.$$

Let

$$(28) \qquad V = e^{-\theta T} = \max (e^{-\theta \bar{T}}, W), \; \alpha = \rho/\theta.$$

Then

$$(29) \qquad \frac{\theta S}{\gamma[G(v)]} = \frac{1 - V^\alpha}{\alpha} + \frac{W(1-V^{\alpha-1})}{1-\alpha} = R(\alpha).$$

The definitions of $R(\alpha)$ for $\alpha = 0$ and $\alpha = 1$ needed to make the function continuous are:

$$R(0) = -\log V + W(1-V^{-1}), R(1) = 1 - V + W \log V.$$

If all the parameters of (26), (27), or (29) are held constant, S is a function of ρ, and, equivalently, R of α. If (26) is differentiated with respect to ρ, we find

$$dS/d\rho = \int_0^T (-t)e^{-\rho t} \gamma[G(v)] (1 - W e^{\theta t})dt < 0.$$

Also

$$S < \gamma[G(v)] \int_0^T e^{-\rho t}dt = \gamma[G(v)] (1 - e^{-\rho T})/\rho$$

$$< \gamma[G(v)]/\rho.$$

Since obviously $S > 0$, S approaches 0 as ρ approaches infinity. Since R and α differ from S and ρ, respectively, only by positive constant factors, we conclude

$$dR/d\alpha < 0, \; \lim_{\alpha \to +\infty} R(\alpha) = 0.$$

To examine the behavior of $R(\alpha)$ as α approaches $-\infty$, write

$$R(\alpha) = -\frac{(1/V)^{1-\alpha}}{(1-\alpha)^2} [(1 - \alpha)V + \alpha W]\left(\frac{1-\alpha}{\alpha}\right) + \frac{1}{\alpha} + \frac{W}{1-\alpha}.$$

The last two terms approach zero. As α approaches $-\infty$, $1 - \alpha$ approaches $+\infty$. Since $1/V > 1$, the factor

$$\frac{(1/V)^{1-\alpha}}{(1-\alpha)^2}$$

approaches $+\infty$, since an exponential approaches infinity faster than any power. From (28), $V \geq W$. If $V = W$, then the factor,

$$(1 - \alpha)V - \alpha W = \alpha(W - V) + V,$$

is a positive constant; if $V > W$, then it approaches $+\infty$ as α approaches $-\infty$. Finally,

$$\frac{1 - \alpha}{\alpha}$$

necessarily approaches -1. Hence,

(30) $R(\alpha)$ is a strictly decreasing function, approaching $+\infty$ as α approaches $-\infty$ and 0 as α approaches $+\infty$.

The market, however, should adjust the rate of return so that the discounted stream of profits equals the cost of investment, i.e., $S = 1$, or, from (29),

(31) $R(\alpha) = \theta/\gamma[G(v)]$.

Since the right-hand side of (31) is positive, (30) guarantees the existence of an α which satisfies (31). For a given θ, the equilibrium rate of return, ρ, is equal to $\alpha \theta$; it may, indeed be negative. The rate of return is thus determined by the expected rate of increase in wages, current labor costs per unit output, and the physical lifetime of the investment. Further, if the first two are sufficiently large, the physical lifetime becomes irrelevant since then $T^* < \overline{T}$, and $T = T^*$.

The discussion of profits and returns has not made any special assumptions as to the form of the production relations.

4. RATIONAL EXPECTATIONS IN A MACROECONOMIC GROWTH MODEL

Assume a one-sector model so that the production relations of the entire economy are described by the model of section 1. In particular, this implies that gross investment at any moment of time is simply a diversion of goods that might otherwise be used for consumption. Output and gross investment can then be measured in the same units.

The question arises, can the expectations assumed to govern investment behavior in the preceding section actually be fulfilled? Specifically, can we have a constant relative increase of wages and a constant rate of interest which, if anticipated, will lead entrepreneurs to invest at a rate which, in conjunction with the exogenously given rate of interest to remain at the given level? Such a state of affairs is frequently referred to as " perfect foresight," but a better term is " rational expectations," a term introduced by J. Muth [10].

We study this question first for the full employment case. For this case to occur, the physical lifetime of investments must not be an effective constraint. If, in the notation of the last section, $T^* > \overline{T}$, and if wage expectations are correct, then investments will disappear through depreciation at a time when they are still yielding positive current profits. As seen in section 2, this is incompatible with competitive equilibrium and full employment. Assume therefore that

(32) $T^* \leqq \bar{T};$

then from (28), $W = V$, and from (29) and (31), the equilibrium value of ρ is determined by the equation,

(33) $$\frac{1 - W^\alpha}{\alpha} + \frac{W - W^\alpha}{1 - \alpha} = \frac{\theta}{\rho},$$

where, on the right-hand side, use is made of (7).

   From (16), it is seen that for the wage rate to rise at a constant rate θ, it is necessary that the quantity,

$$G^{1-n} - \frac{L}{c},$$

rise at a rate $\theta(1 - n)/n$. For θ constant, it follows from (33) that a constant ρ and therefore a constant α requires that W be constant. For the specific production relations (7) and (8), (23) shows that

$$W = a \frac{\left(G^{1-n} - \dfrac{L}{c} \right)^{n/(1-n)}}{b} \cdot \frac{bG^{-n}}{a} = \left(1 - \frac{L}{cG^{1-n}} \right)^{n/(1-n)},$$

and therefore the constancy of W is equivalent to that of L/G^{1-n}. In combination with the preceding remark, we see that

(34) L increases at rate $\theta(1 - n)/n$, G increases at rate θ/n.

Suppose that

σ = rate of increase of the labor force,
is a given constant.   Then

(35) $\theta = n\sigma/(1-n)$,

(36)   the rate of increase of G is $\sigma/(1-n)$.

Substitution into the production function (9) yields

(37)   the rate of increase of x is $\sigma/(1-n)$.

From (36) and (37), the ratio G/x is constant over time.   However, the value at which it is constant is not determined by the considerations so far introduced; the savings function is needed to complete the system.   Let the constant ratio be

(38) $G(t)/x(t) = \mu$.

Define

$g(t)$ = rate of gross investment at time $t = dG/dt$.

From (36), $g/G = \sigma/(1 - n)$, a constant. Then

(39) $g/x = (g/G)(G/x) = \mu\,\sigma/(1 - n)$.

A simple assumption is that the ratio of gross saving (equals gross investment) to income (equals output) is a function of the rate of return, ρ; a special case would be the common assumption of a constant savings-to-income ratio. Then μ is a function of ρ. On the other hand, we can write W as follows, using (23) and (13):

(40) $W = a\,\dfrac{\left(G - \dfrac{x}{a}\right)^n}{b}\,\dfrac{bG^{-n}}{a} = \left(1 - \dfrac{x}{aG}\right)^n = \left(1 - \dfrac{1}{a\mu}\right)^n.$

Since θ is given by (35), (33) is a relation between W and ρ, and, by (40) between μ and ρ. We thus have two relations between μ and ρ, so they are determinate.

From (38), μ determines one relation between G and X. If the labor force, L, is given at one moment of time, the production function (9) constitutes a second such relation, and the system is completely determinate.

As in many growth models, the rates of growth of the variables in the system do not depend on savings behavior; however, their levels do.

It should be made clear that all that has been demonstrated is the existence of a solution in which all variables have constant rates of growth, correctly anticipated. The stability of the solution requires further study.

The growth rate for wages implied by the solution has one paradoxical aspect; it increases with the rate of growth of the labor force (provided $n < 1$). The explanation seems to be that under full employment, the increasing labor force permits a more rapid introduction of the newer machinery. It should also be noted that, for a constant saving ratio, g/x, an increase in σ decreases μ, from (39), from which it can be seen that wages at the initial time period would be lower. In this connection it may be noted that since G cannot decrease, it follows from (36) that σ and $1-n$ must have the same sign for the steady growth path to be possible. The most natural case, of course, is $\sigma > 0$, $n < 1$.

This solution is, however, admissible only if the condition (32), that the rate of depreciation not be too rapid, be satisfied. We can find an explicit formula for the economic lifetime, T^*, of new investment. From (24), it satisfies the condition

$e^{-\theta T^*} = W.$

If we use (35) and (40) and solve for T^*, we find

(41) $T^* = \dfrac{-(1-n)}{\sigma}\,\log\left[1 - \dfrac{1}{a\mu}\right]$

and this is to be compared with $\overline{T}$; the full employment solution with rational expectations of exponentially increasing wages and constant interest is admissible if $T^* \leq \overline{T}$.

221

If $T^* > \bar{T}$, then the full employment solution is inadmissible. One might ask if a constant-growth solution is possible in this case. The answer depends on assumptions about the dynamics of wages under this condition.

We retain the two conditions, that wages rise at a constant rate θ, and that the rate of interest be constant. With constant θ, the rate of interest, ρ, is determined from (31); from (29), this requires that

(42) W is constant over time.

From the definition of W, (23), and the particular form of the production relations, (7) and (8), it follows that the wage rate, w, must rise at the same rate as G^n, or

(43) G rises at a constant rate θ/n.

In the presence of continued unemployment, the most natural wage dynamics in a free market would be a decreasing, or, at best, constant wage level. But since G can never decrease, it follows from (43) that θ can never be negative. Instead of making a specific assumption about wage changes, it will be assumed that any choice of θ can be imposed, perhaps by government or union or social pressure, and it is asked what restrictions on the possible values of θ are set by the other equilibrium conditions.

In the capital shortage case, the serial number of the oldest capital good in use is determined by the physical lifetime of the good, i.e.,

$G' = G(t - \bar{T})$.   From (43),

$$G(t - \bar{T}) = e^{-\theta \bar{T}/n} G.$$

Then, from (1') and (7),

$$x = aG(1 - e^{-\theta \bar{T}/n}),$$

so that the ratio, G/x, or μ. is a constant,

(44) $\mu = 1/a(1 - e^{-\theta \bar{T}/n})$.

From (43), $g/G = \theta/n$; hence, by the same argument as that leading to (39),

(45) $g/x = \theta/na(1 - e^{-\theta \bar{T}/n})$.

There are three unknown constants of the growth process, θ, ρ, and W. If, as before, it is assumed that the gross savings ratio, g/x, is a function of the rate of return, ρ, then, for any given ρ, θ can be determined from (45); note that the right-hand side of (45) is a strictly increasing function of θ for $\theta \geq 0$, so that the determination is unique, and the rate of growth is an increasing function of the gross savings ratio, contrary to the situation in the full employment case. Then W can be solved for from (31) and (29).

Thus the rate of return is a freely disposable parameter whose choice determines the rate of growth and W, which in turn determines the initial wage rate. There are, of course, some inequalities which must be satisfied to insure that the solution corresponds to the capital shortage rather than the full employment case; in particular, $W \leq V$ and also the labor force must be sufficient to permit the expansion. From (2'), this means that the labor force must at all times be at least equal to

$$cG^{1-n} - c(G')^{1-n} = cG^{1-n}(1 - e^{-\theta(1-n)\bar{T}/n});$$

if σ is the growth rate of the labor force, we must then have (46)

(46) $\sigma \geq \theta(1 - n)/n,$

which sets an upper bound on θ (for $n < 1$). Other constraints on ρ are implied by the conditions $\theta \geq 0$ and $W \geq 0$ (if it is assumed that wage rates are non-negative). The first condition sets a lower limit on g/x; it can be shown, from (45). that

(47) $g/x \geq 1/a\bar{T};$

i.e., the gross savings ratio must be at least equal to the amount of capital goods needed to produce one unit of output over their lifetime. The constraint $W > 0$ implies an interval in which ρ must lie. The conditions under which these constraints are consistent (so that at least one solution exists for the capital shortage case) have not been investigated in detail.

5. DIVERGENCE OF PRIVATE AND SOCIAL PRODUCT

As has already been emphasized, the presence of learning means that an act of investment benefits future investors, but this benefit is not paid for by the market. Hence, it is to be expected that the aggregate amount of investment under the competitive model of the last section will fall short of the socially optimum level. This difference will be investigated in detail in the present section under a simple assumption as to the utility function of society. For brevity, I refer to the *competitive solution* of the last section, to be contrasted with the *optimal* solution. Full employment is assumed. It is shown that the socially optimal growth rate is the same as that under competitive conditions, but the socially optimal ratio of gross investment to output is higher than the competitive level.

Utility is taken to be a function of the stream of consumption derived from the productive mechanism. Let

$$c = \text{consumption} = \text{output} - \text{gross investment} = x - g.$$

It is in particular assumed that future consumption is discounted at a constant rate, βt so that utility is

(48) $$U = \int_{o}^{+\infty} e^{-\beta t}c(t)dt = \int_{o}^{+\infty} e^{-\beta t}x(t)dt.$$

$$- \int_{o}^{+\infty} e^{-\beta t}g(t)dt.$$

Integration by parts yields

$$\int_{o}^{+\infty} e^{-\beta t}g(t)dt = e^{-\beta t}G(t)\Big|_{o}^{+\infty} + \beta \int_{o}^{+\infty} e^{-\beta t}G(t)dt.$$

223

From (48),

(49) $U = U_1 - \lim\limits_{t \to +\infty} e^{-\beta t} G(t) + G(0),$

where

(50) $U_1 = \int\limits_0^{+\infty} e^{-\beta t}[x(t) - \beta\, G(t)]dt.$

The policy problem is the choice of the function $G(t)$, with $G'(t) \geq 0$, to maximize (49), where $x(t)$ is determined by the production function (9), and

(51) $L(t) = L_0 e^{\sigma t}.$

The second term in (49) is necessarily non-negative. It will be shown that, for sufficiently high discount rate, β, the function $G(t)$ which maximizes U_1 also has the property that the second term in (49) is zero; hence, it also maximizes (49), since $G(0)$ is given.

Substitute (9) and (51) into (50).

$$U_1 = \int\limits_0^{+\infty} e^{-\beta t} G(t) \left[a - \beta - a\left(1 - \frac{L_0 e^{\sigma t}}{c\,G^{1-n}}\right)^{1/(1-n)} \right] dt.$$

Let $\bar{G}(t) = G(t)\, e^{-\sigma t/(1-n)}.$

$$U_1 = \int\limits_0^{+\infty} e^{-\left(\beta - \frac{\sigma}{1-n}\right)t}\, \bar{G}(t) \left[a - \beta - a\left(1 - \frac{L_0}{c\,\bar{G}^{1-n}}\right)^{1/(1-n)} \right] dt.$$

Assume that

(52) $\beta > \dfrac{\sigma}{1-n};$

otherwise an infinite utility is attainable. Then to maximize U_1 it suffices to choose $\bar{G}(t)$ so as to maximize, for each t,

(53) $\bar{G} \left[a - \beta - a\left(1 - \dfrac{L_0}{c\,\bar{G}^{1-n}}\right)^{1/(1-n)} \right].$

Before actually determining the maximum, it can be noted that the maximizing value of $\bar{G}$ is independent of t and is therefore a constant. Hence, the optimum policy is

(54) $G(t) = \bar{G}\, e^{\sigma t/(1-n)},$

so that, from (36), the growth rate is the same as the competitive. From (52), $e^{-\beta t} G(t) \longrightarrow 0$ as $t \longrightarrow +\infty$.

To determine the optimal $\bar{G}$, it will be convenient to make a change of variables. Define

$$v = \left(1 - \frac{L_0}{c\,\bar{G}^{1-n}}\right)^{n/(1-n)}.$$

so that

(55) $\bar{G} = \left[\dfrac{L_0}{(1 - v^{(1-n)/n})} \right]^{1/(1-n)}.$

The analysis will be carried through primarily for the case where the output per unit capital is sufficiently high, more specifically, where

(56) $a > \beta.$

Let

(57) $\gamma = 1 - \dfrac{\beta}{a} > 0.$

The maximizing $\bar{G}$, or v, is unchanged by multiplying (53), the function to be maximized, by the positive quantity, $(c/L_0)^{1/(1-n)}/a$ and then substituting from (55) and (57). Thus, v maximizes

$$(1 - v^{(1-n)/n})^{-1/(1-n)} (\gamma - v^{1/n}).$$

The variable v ranges from 0 to 1. However, the second factor vanishes when $v = \gamma^n < 1$ (since $\gamma < 1$) and becomes negative for larger values of v; since the first factor is always positive, it can be assumed that $v < \gamma^n$ in searching for a maximum, and both factors are positive. Then v also maximizes the logarithm of the above function, which is

$$f(v) = - \frac{\log (1 - v^{(1-n)/n})}{1 - n} + \log (\gamma - v^{1/n}),$$

so that

$$f'(v) = \frac{v^{\frac{1}{n} - 2}}{n} \left[\frac{\gamma - v}{(1 - v^{(1-n)/n}) (\gamma - v^{1/n})} \right].$$

Clearly, with $n < 1$, $f'(v) > 0$ when $0 < v < \gamma$ and $f'(v) < 0$ when $\gamma < v < \gamma^n$, so that the maximum is obtained at

(58) $v = \gamma.$

The optimum $\bar{G}$ is determined by substituting γ for v in (55).

From (54), L/G^{1-n} is a constant over time. From the definition of v and (58), then,

$$\gamma = \left(1 - \frac{L}{cG^{1-n}} \right)^{n/(1-n)}$$

for all t along the optimal path, and, from the production function (9),

(59) $\gamma = \left(1 - \dfrac{x}{aG} \right)^n$ for all t along the optimal path.

This optimal solution will be compared with the competitive solution of steady growth studied in the last section. From (40), we know that

(60) $W = \left(1 - \dfrac{x}{aG} \right)^n$ for all t along the competitive path.

It will be demonstrated that $W < \gamma$; from this it follows that *the ratio G/x is less along the competitive path than along the optimal path.* Since along both paths,

$$g/x = [\sigma/(1-n)]\,(G/x),$$

it also follows that *the gross savings ratio is smaller along the competitive path than along the optimal path.*

For the particular utility function (48), the supply of capital is infinitely elastic at $\rho = \beta$; i.e., the community will take any investment with a rate of return exceeding β and will take no investment at a rate of return less than β. For an equilibrium in which some, but not all, income is saved, we must have

(61) $\rho = \beta.$

From (35), $\theta = n\sigma/(1-n)$; hence, by definition (28),

(62) $\alpha = (1-n)\beta/n\sigma.$

Since $n < 1$, it follows from (62) and the assumption (52) that (63)

(63) $\alpha > 1.$

Equation (33) then becomes the one by which W is determined. The left-hand side will be denoted as $F(W)$.

$$F'(W) = \frac{1 - W^{\alpha-1}}{1 - \alpha}.$$

From (63), $F'(W) < 0$ for $0 \geq W < 1$, the relevant range since the investment will never be profitable if $W > 1$. To demonstrate that $W < \gamma$, it suffices to show that $F(W) > F(\gamma)$ for that value of W which satisfies (33), i.e., to show that

(64) $F(\gamma) < \theta/a.$

Finally, to demonstrate (64), note that $\gamma < 1$ and $\alpha > 1$, which imply that $\gamma^\alpha < \gamma$, and therefore

$$(1-\alpha) - \gamma^\alpha + \alpha\,\gamma > (1-\alpha)(1-\gamma).$$

Since $\alpha > 1$, $\alpha(1-\alpha) < 0$. Dividing both sides by this magnitude yields

$$\frac{1-\gamma^\alpha}{\alpha} + \frac{\gamma-\gamma^\alpha}{1-\alpha} < \frac{1-\gamma}{\alpha} = \frac{\theta}{a}$$

where use is made of (57), (28), and (61); but from (33), the left-hand side is precisely $F(\gamma)$, so that (64) is demonstrated.

The case $a \leq \beta$, excluded by (56), can be handled similarly; in that case the optimum v is 0. The subsequent reasoning follows in the same way so that the correspondihg competitive path would have $W < 0$, which is, however, impossible.

6. SOME COMMENTS ON THE MODEL

(1) Many writers, such as Theodore Schultz, have stressed the improvement in the quality of the labor force over time as a source of increased productivity. This interpretation can be incorporated in the present model by assuming that σ, the rate of growth of the labor force, incorporates qualitative as well as quantitative increase.

(2) In this model, there is only one efficient capital-labor ratio for new investment at any moment of time. Most other models, on the contrary, have assumed that alternative capital-labor ratios are possible both before the capital good is built and after. A still more plausible model is that of Johansen [7], according to which alternative capital-labor ratios are open to the entrepreneur's choice at the time of investment but are fixed once the investment is congealed into a capital good.

(3) In this model, as in those of Solow [12] and Johansen [7], the learning takes place in effect only in the capital goods industry; no learning takes place in the use of a capital good once built. Lundberg's Horndal effect suggests that this is not realistic. The model should be extended to include this possibility.

(4) It has been assumed here that learning takes place only as a by-product of ordinary production. In fact, society has created institutions, education and research, whose purpose it is to enable learning to take place more rapidly. A fuller model would take account of these as additional variables.

REFERENCES.

[1] Abramovitz, M., " Resource and Output Trends in the United States Since 1870," *American Economic Review, Papers and Proceedings of the American Economic Associations*, 46 (May, 1956): 5-23.

[2] Arrow, K. J., H. B. Chenery, B. S. Minhas, and R. M. Solow, " Capital-Labor Substitution and Economic Efficiency," *Review of Economics and Statistics*, 43 (1961): 225-250.

[3] Asher, H., *Cost-Quantity Relationships in the Airframe Industry*, R-291, Santa Monica, Calif.: The RAND Corporation, 1956.

[4] Haavelmo, T. *A Study in the Theory of Economic Evolution*, Amsterdam: North Holland, 1954.

[5] Hilgard, E. R., *Theories of Learning*, 2nd ed., New York: Appleton-Century-Crofts, 1956.

[6] Hirsch, W. Z., " Firm Progress Radios," *Econometrica*, 24 (1956): 136-143.

[7] Johansen, L., " Substitution vs. Fixed Production Coefficients in the Theory of Economic Growth: A Synthesis," *Econometrica*, 27 (1959): 157-176.

[8] Kaldor, N., " Capital Accumulation and Economic Growth," in F. A. Lutz and D. C. Hague (eds.), *The Theory of Capiatl*, New York: St. Martin's Press, 1961, 177-222.

[9] Lundberg, E., *Produktivitet och räntabilitet*, Stockholm: P. A. Norstedt and Söner, 1961.

[10] Muth, J., " Rational Expectations and the Theory of Price Movements," *Econometrica* (in press).

[11] Solow, R. M., " Technical Change and the Aggregate Production Function," *Review of Economics and Statistics*, 39 (1957): 312-320.

[12] Solow, R. M., " Investment and Technical Progress," in K. J. Arrow, S. Karlin, and P. Suppes (eds.), *Mathematical Methods in the Social Sciences*, 1959, Stanford, Calif.: Stanford University Press, 1960, 89-104.

[13] Verdoorn, P. J., " Fattori che regolano lo sviluppo della produttività del lavoro," *L'Industria*, 1 (1949).

[14] Verdoorn, P. J., " Complementarity and Long-Range Projections," *Econometrica*, 24 (1956): 429-450.

[15] Wright, T. P., " Factors Affecting the Cost of Airplanes," *Journal of the Aeronautical Sciences*, 3 (1936): 122-128.

Stanford.   KENNETH J. ARROW.

On article page 157, line 18, the phrase At any moment of new time, should read: At any moment of time,. [The Editors.]

D. Models with *Ex Post* Fixed Coefficients

SUBSTITUTION VERSUS FIXED PRODUCTION COEFFICIENTS IN
THE THEORY OF ECONOMIC GROWTH: A SYNTHESIS

By Leif Johansen[1]

Most growth models are based either on the assumption of fixed production
coefficients for labour and capital or on the assumption of substitutability between factors. The present paper proposes a hypothesis which is a compromise
between these extremes, viz., that any *increment* in production can be obtained
by different combinations of *increments* in labour and capital inputs, whereas
any piece of capital which is already installed will continue to be operated by
a constant amount of labour throughout its life span. First, a "general
model" is presented. Next, the model is solved in different special cases. In
conclusion it is suggested that the proposed hypothesis would be particularly
appropriate in studying the introduction of new techniques and the relationship
between population growth, the rate of saving and "structural" unemployment.

1. INTRODUCTION

THE MODELS HITHERTO most widely applied in the theoretical analysis of
problems of economic growth can be classified in the following three groups:

(a) Models with a given capital coefficient, where the labour input does
not enter the analysis explicitly, but is treated rather vaguely in supplementary comments. The models of R. F. Harrod [9], Evsey D. Domar [3][2],
Hans Brems [2], Robert Eisner [5] and Ingvar Svennilson [22] exemplify
this class.

(b) Models with fixed production coefficients for labour input as well as
for the capital stock, or some other kind of strict complementarity. As
examples one might mention the analysis of D. Hamberg [8], the work on
long-range projections at the Central Planning Bureau in the Netherlands,
cf. e.g., P. J. Verdoorn [25], and furthermore the more disaggregated
analysis by Wassily Leontief [14], Oskar Lange [13] and other authors in
the field of input-output analysis.

(c) Models with explicitly expressed possibilities of substitution between
total labour input and capital stock in a traditional production function.
This type of model is exemplified by the publications of Jan Tinbergen [23],
Trygve Haavelmo [7], Robert Solow [19] and Stefan Valavanis-Vail [24].

Models belonging to any of these groups may, of course, contain important

---

[1] I am indebted to professor Trygve Haavelmo and Mr. Hans Jacob Kreyberg at
the University of Oslo, with whom I have discussed many of the problems analysed in
this paper. Mr. Kreyberg has also read through the manuscript and given useful criticism.

[2] See in particular the Foreword and Essay III: "Capital Expansion, Rate of
Growth, and Employment," (*Econometrica*, April 1946 pp. 137-147).

and realistic aspects and be well suited for certain objectives. I have, however, the feeling that many theorists, whether they apply models belonging to the group (a), (b) or (c), often have been working with a "guilty conscience"[3] regarding the realism of their assumptions. The purpose of this paper is to propose a kind of synthesis between the approaches in (b) and (c) above. The synthesis will be based on the following assumptions:

(1) Any gross[4] *increment* in the rate of production can be obtained by different combinations of *increments* in capital and labour input. We may perhaps express this in another way by saying that there are ex ante substitution possibilities between capital and labour, or that there are substitution possibilities *at the margin*.

(2) Once a piece of capital is produced and has been put into operation, it will continue to operate through all its life span in cooperation with a constant amount of labour input. We may perhaps express this by saying that there are no ex post substitution possibilities, or that there are no substitution possibilities between total labour input and existing capital stock.

Even if a more flexible framework may be imagined, I have the feeling that an analysis based on the assumptions (1) and (2) above will in most cases be more realistic than an analysis based on models belonging to any of the groups, (a), (b), or (c).

The idea may of course be applied at different levels of aggregation. We shall, however, as an illustration, apply it in a pure macro-analysis of growth problems.

In Section 2 the idea is worked out more precisely and included in a rather general model. In Sections 3, 4 and 5 the solution of the model is given and some special cases are discussed. Some concluding remarks are given in Section 6.

2. THE "GENERAL" MODEL

The model to be presented in this section is, of course, not general in any absolute sense. It is only general relative to the specializations discussed in Sections 3, 4 and 5.

The model will be characterized by the following properties:

(1) There are two factors of production, labour and capital, producing an output which may be used either for consumption or for accumulation.

(2) There are substitution possibilities ex ante, but not ex post, as explained in the introduction.

---

[3] Cf. Evsey D. Domar [3, p. 7].

[4] That means that we have not subtracted the decline in production caused by old capital being depreciated or scrapped.

(3) From the point of time when an amount of capital is produced, it will shrink according to a given function of its age. The labour input needed to operate the capital and the production achieved shrink proportionately. Even if other interpretations are possible, this is perhaps most easily accepted if we assume that each amount of capital consists of a certain number of identical pieces or units which are operated in the same way and retain their productive efficiency during their entire life time, and that there exists a "death rate table" for these capital units. As special cases, this assumption includes the case of capital of infinite duration and the case for which all capital units have the same finite life time.

(4) New production techniques can be introduced only by means of new capital equipment. This statement is not quite clearly expressed here, but will be clarified by the formulas below.[5]

(5) We assume either that net investment is a constant fraction of net income, or as an alternative, that gross investment is a constant fraction of gross income.[6]

(6) By computing the depreciation necessary to obtain the "net" concepts introduced by (5), a unit of capital is valued in proportion to its remaining life span.

(7) The total labour force is governed by an autonomous pattern of growth.

(8) There will always be full employment of labour and capital.

It is, of course, possible to analyse the effects of points (1) through (7) with some alternative instead of point (8). That will, however, not be done in this paper. At the end of this section, we shall comment on the interpretation of assumption (8).

---

[5] This assumption probably corresponds to the idea expressed by Ingvar Svennilson [21, p. 208] in the following form: "The volume of investment, whether it constitutes a net addition to the stock of capital or not, can therefore be said to measure the rate at which capital is being modernized." Cf. also [22, p. 325]: "Technical progress will, however, mean that old capital goods are eliminated and new ones substituted." Compare further K. Maywald [15]: "It is assumed that only the best production process is used in every unit of equipment added in the course of each year to the total capacity of the industry or economy concerned. Each unit of equipment represents the technological stage of development reached in its year of origin, until the very end of its serviceable life." A similar hypothesis is also crucial, for instance, for important parts of Paul A. Baran's growth analysis [1, cf. e.g., p. 21 and pp. 78-79], and for S. G. Strumilin's analysis [20, cf. in particular p. 175].

[6] These are the savings hypotheses most widely applied in growth analysis. In his Essay VII in [3] ("Depreciation, Replacement, and Growth," *The Economic Journal*, 1953), Domar employs both hypotheses, maintaining that the gross concept is the more "applicable to a centrally directed economy, where a part of total output is set aside for investment, while the net concept is the more applicable to capitalist countries."

The unknowns that enter the model are:

$x(t)$, the rate of production at time t;

$N(t)$, the total labour force at time t;

$K(t)$, the total stock of capital at time t;

$k(t)$, the rate of gross investment at time t, i.e., $k(t)dt =$ the amount of capital produced and put into operation during the time interval $(t, t + dt)$;

$n(t)$, the rate of allocation of labour to newly constructed capital, i.e., $n(t)dt$ is the labour input allocated to the operation of the capital $k(t)dt$;

$y(t)$, the rate of gross increase in production at time t, i.e. the rate of increase in $x(t)$ caused by $k(t)$ and $n(t)$;

$V(t)$, the value of the capital stock at time t;

$D(t)$, the rate of depreciation at time t; and

$I(t)$, the rate of net investment at time $t = k(t) — D(t)$.

The main problem now is to provide a formal representation of a production process with the desired properties.

We first introduce the function φ describing the effects on production of the gross investment and the labour input used with this investment:

$$(2.1) \qquad\qquad y(t) = \varphi(n(t), k(t), x(t), t).$$

If we now assume $\partial\varphi/\partial n > 0$ and $\partial\varphi/\partial k > 0$, $n(t)$ and $k(t)$ will be substitutable factors in the process which causes a certain gross rate of increase, $y(t)$, in production.

It is perhaps reasonable to assume φ to be homogeneous of degree one in n and k. We shall, however, not introduce this specialization in the "general" model.[7]

In (2.1) we have introduced $x(t)$ as an argument besides $n(t)$ and $k(t)$. The reason for this is the following: $n(t)$ and $k(t)$ in no way indicate the "pressure" on natural resources resulting from the rate of production. This pressure may, however, have important consequences. When the pressure is already high, a greater effort in the way of increases in labour

---

[7] There is no immediate connection between the question of homogeneity of φ in n and k and the question of homogeneity of an ordinary production function in N and K. The arguments raised in connection with the latter question are perhaps more relevant for the role played by the argument x in φ; cf. the following discussion of this point.

Under extremely simplifying conditions we may, however, relate the function φ to traditional microeconomic production functions in the following way. Suppose that any increase in total production is generated through establishment of new firms. Suppose further that all firms which are established simultaneously have identical production functions, the form of which is denoted by $\psi(\bar{n},\bar{k})$ where $\bar{n}$ and $\bar{k}$ stand for employment and capital per firm. In order to obtain a rate of gross increase y in

and capital may thus be required to obtain a certain increase in production. As this pressure is mainly generated through the extraction from nature of raw materials which are required in rather fixed proportion to the amount of production, $x(t)$ may perhaps be a satisfactory indicator of this so-called pressure. Arguments might, however, be raised in favour of also introducing the total stock of capital $K(t)$ and the total labour input $N(t)$ in (2.1), indicating that the *way* in which production is carried out may possibly influence the degree of pressure on natural resources.

The arguments above imply $\partial\varphi/\partial x \leq 0$.

By contrast, one might perhaps also argue that $\partial\varphi/\partial x > 0$ on the basis of "external economies."

The symbol t is introduced as a separate argument in (2.1) to take care of the possible increase in productivity through improvements in "know-how," discoveries of new natural resources, etc.

Let us now study the shrinkage in capital over time. We introduce a function $f(\tau)$ with the following interpretation : *If an amount $k(t)dt$ of capital is produced in the time interval $(t - dt,t)$, then an amount $f(\tau)k(t)dt$ of this capital will still be active at time $t + \tau$ ($\tau \geq 0$).* It follows that $f(\tau)$ is monotonically non-increasing and that $f(0) = 1$.

As stated above (property 3) we assume that production shrinks proportionately with capital. This is equivalent to saying that if $k(\tau)d\tau$ (in cooperation with $n(\tau)d\tau$) caused an increase, $y(\tau)d\tau$, in the rate of production in the time interval $(\tau, \tau + d\tau)$, then the rate of production originating from this capital at time t equals $f(t - \tau)y(\tau)d\tau$. It is then obvious that the total rate of production at time t may be obtained by integrating the output from all layers of capital, with due account for the shrinkage:

$$(2.2) \qquad x(t) = \int_{-\infty}^{t} f(t - \tau)y(\tau)d\tau.$$

---

total production, it is then necessary to establish m new firms per unit of time, where $y = m\psi\,(\bar{n},\bar{k})$. We have further $n = m\bar{n}$ and $k = m\bar{k}$ which give $y = m\psi\,(n/m, k/m)$. This defines y as a function of n, k and m. Assume now that there exists for each expansion line in the $(\bar{n},\bar{k})$ space an optimal size of the firm (defined by the scale coefficient being equal to unity). Assume further that firms always attain this size. Then m will be a function $m(n,k)$ of n and k, and it is easily seen that $m(n,k)$ must be homogeneous of degree one in n and k. By these assumptions we get y as a function only of the variables n and k:

$$y = m(n,k)\psi\left(\frac{n}{m(n,k)},\ \frac{k}{m(n,k)}\right),$$

and this function is homogeneous of degree one in n and k irrespective of the form and properties of the function ψ.

We have here for simplicity disregarded the arguments x and t in the production functions. The introduction of these arguments in ψ (for the reasons given in the text) does, however, in no way change the reasoning above.

The interpretation of $y(t)$ as the "gross" increase in $x(t)$ will now be clear. Suppose there is no shrinkage in capital, i.e., $f(\tau) \equiv 1$. Then $x(t) = \int_{-\infty}^{t} y(\tau)d\tau$ and consequently $\dot{x}(t) = y(t)$. We may therefore say that the increase $\dot{x}(t)$ consists of a gross increase $y(t)$ due to $n(t)$ and $k(t)$, while a deduction $y(t)—\dot{x}(t)$ is due to the shrinkage of the existing capital. If $f'(\tau)$ exists we have $\dot{x}(t) = y(t) + \int_{-\infty}^{t} f'(t—\tau)y(\tau)d\tau$ where $f' \leq 0$.

A reasonable condition on the function φ is that $\varphi(0,0,x,t) \equiv 0$ identically in x and t. If $n(t) = k(t) = 0$ for $t > \theta$, then we shall have $x(t) = \int_{-\infty}^{\theta} f(t—\tau)y(\tau)d\tau$ for $t \geq \theta$, and the only changes in $x(t)$ for $t > \theta$ will result from shrinkage in the existing capital. In this case, therefore, there will be no effect of increased "know - how" after the time θ. This illustrates the condition that the increased "know - how" in our model can be utilized only through the introduction of new capital equipment.

Let us now study the development of the labour input $n(t)$ available at any point of time to man the new capital equipment.

Our basic assumption is

(2.3) $N(t)$ is an exogenously given function of time.

This total labour force will be distributed over capital of different ages. Cooperating with the capital produced in the interval $(\tau, \tau + d\tau)$ will be the labour $n(\tau)d\tau$. At time t this will be reduced to $f(t — \tau)n(\tau)d\tau$. Accordingly, we have the following condition on the development of $n(t)$:

(2.4) $$\int_{-\infty}^{t} f(t — \tau)n(\tau)d\tau = N(t).$$

By a similar integration we obtain an expression for the total amount of capital:

(2.5) $$\int_{-\infty}^{t} f(t — \tau)k(\tau)d\tau = K(t).$$

In the traditional description of the production structure, x is related uniquely to N and K (and possibly also to t as a separate argument). In our approach it is, however, characteristic that it is in general *not* possible to derive any such unique relation which holds regardless of the development of $N(t)$ and $K(t)$. A necessary and sufficient condition for this possibility to exist is that φ be linear in n and k, and that x and t do not enter the function φ as separate arguments. (If the condition $\varphi(0,0,x,t) \equiv 0$ is abandoned, t may also enter φ. Then φ must be linear in n, k and any unique function of t).

The production model above recognizes fully the impossibility of changing at will the manning of capital equipment once constructed. There exists, however, another kind of rigidity which is not recognized above. To explain this rigidity, let us look at the capital equipment engaged in producing more capital equipment. This equipment is perhaps so constructed that it can produce only capital equipment designed to be manned in a definite way. For instance, a factory producing spinning-jennies may be equipped in such a way that it is only able to produce spinning-jennies which must be operated by a definite amount of labour. If this kind of rigidity is important, it will perhaps be difficult to realize the smooth adaption of capital equipment to the given $n(t)$-development which is implied by our model.[8] It would then perhaps be interesting to construct a model which would lie between the model presented here and one with no substitution possibilities.

Now for capital accumulation or savings. Different assumptions can be conceived of here. The possibility of *choice* open to society would make it desirable to investigate the consequences of various assumptions or to postulate some optimality criteria.[9] However, in order to conform to the most widely accepted models of growth on this point—where this paper does not attempt to make any contribution—I shall treat only the hypothesis of a fixed ratio of savings to income.

In order to define the "net" concepts, we need a rule for the valuation of capital. We then simply value a unit of capital proportionately to its remaining life span.

A newly produced unit of capital will on the average last

$$(2.6) \qquad T(0) = \int_0^\infty f(\tau)d\tau$$

periods. A unit of capital already η periods of age will on the average have

$$(2.7) \qquad T(\eta) = \frac{1}{f(\eta)} \int_\eta^\infty f(\tau)d\tau$$

periods left.[10]

We then say that a unit of capital η periods old is worth $T(\eta)/T(0)$ relative to a new one. By an integration similar to (2.5), we then get for the value of the total stock of capital

[8] Some rigidities of this kind must be implied by the analysis of Hans W. Singer [18], cf., e.g., p. 182: "The capital-intensive technology—which is the only now existing—. . ." and p. 183: "The absence of a technology which is at the same time modern (in the sense of incorporating the latest state of scientific knowledge) and yet in harmony with the factor endowment of under-developed countries must be classed as another major obstacle to economic development." Further, on p. 181: "In many respects, the technology of one hundred years ago would be preferable and would make their (the underdeveloped countries) economic development easier."

[9] Cf. on this point H. J. A. Kreyberg [12].

[10] Cf. Gabriel A. Preinreich [17, p. 220].

(2.8) $$V(t) = \frac{1}{T(0)} \int_{-\infty}^{t} j(t-\tau)T(t-\tau)k(\tau)d\tau$$

which gives

(2.9) $$V(t) = \frac{1}{T(0)} \int_{\tau=-\infty}^{t} k(\tau) \int_{\xi=t-\tau}^{\infty} j(\xi)d\xi d\tau.$$

By differentiation this gives

(2.10) $$I(t) = \dot{V}(t) = k(t) - \frac{1}{T(0)} K(t),$$

and for depreciation the familiar formula[11]

(2.11) $$D(t) = \frac{1}{T(0)} K(t).$$

A constant fraction a of savings applied to the net concepts then gives $I(t) = a(x(t) - 1/T(0) K(t))$, which can be written

(2.12) $$k(t) = ax(t) + \frac{1}{T(0)} (1-a)K(t).$$

If we want to operate with a constant savings quota applied to the gross concepts, we need only neglect the last term in (2.12).

Considering our model as a whole now, we recognize that (2.1), (2.2), (2.3), (2.4), (2.5), and (2.12) where $T(0)$ is defined by (2.6) constitute 6 equations containing the six time functions $y(t)$, $n(t)$, $k(t)$, $N(t)$, $K(t)$, $x(t)$. This will be referred to in the following sections as our "general model."

One may now ask how it is that we have obtained a determinate model without any reference to the behaviour of the producers? In fact we have substitution possibilities "at the margin," and certain assumptions are therefore necessary to explain this behaviour.

The answer to this question is that a certain behaviour is tacitly implied by our assuming that $n(t)$ and $k(t)$ are always absorbed.

One explanation may be that our model applies to a centrally planned economy which at any time chooses to construct new equipment in such a way that the disposable labour is absorbed.

Another explanation may be that our model applies to an economy where production is governed by the profit motive. In that case a certain development of wages and the interest rate is implied by our model, namely, that development which makes entrepreneurs choose to absorb both the flow of savings and the flow of disposable labour at all times. These time functions for wages and the interest rate might be linked to our model. Many kinds of rigidities may, however, operate to make such smooth adaption impossible.[12]

[11] Cf. e.g., Essay VII in Domar [3].

[12] Cf. Robert M. Solow [19], D. Hamberg [8] and the discussion by Pilvin, Harrod, and Domar.

If the wage rate and the the rate of interest should move with rather different time shapes, a special problem would arise in connection with old capital. Capital which is constructed for instance at a time when wages are rather low and interest rates rather high may at a time of higher wages and lower interest rates be so unprofitable in use that it is scrapped prematurely or left idle for a while. Such a development may also be reflected in the valuation of the capital stock. These problems, however, are not taken care of formally in our model.[13]

In the case of a profit-motivated production process, it might be interesting to reverse the point of view described above and accepted in our model. Instead of assuming full employment of labour and capital, and implying tacitly the necessary development of wages and interest, we might assume certain developments for wages and interest, perhaps related to monetary aspects of the economy, and try to compute the time function for the possible unemployment which might occur. Such an attempt will however not be made in this paper.

The model above looks rather unmanageable in its general form. In the following sections we shall therefore work out the solutions for some special cases which are quite near to hand. The reason for working out the solution for different cases—that is, with different forms of the production function φ and the shrinkage function f—is partly that it is not obvious what functional forms are most realistic, and partly that I find it rather difficult to work out the solution if I try to combine that form of the production function (and the introduction of new techniques) which I personally find most interesting with that form of the shrinkage function which I would prefer if I had to choose.[14]

3. THE CASE WITH CAPITAL OF INFINITE DURATION

Rather important simplifications of the model are obtained if we consider the case with capital of infinite duration, i.e., the case in which

$$(3.1) \qquad\qquad\qquad f(\tau) \equiv 1 \qquad\qquad\qquad \text{for } \tau \geq 0.$$

[13] The technical changes which result from increasing "know-how," may, of course, also influence the valuation of capital. It is, however, not obvious how this ought to be introduced in the model, and I have therefore chosen to disregard it.

[14] In correspondence Robert Solow has made the following comment on an ambiguity which is not discussed above: "There is a little ambiguity involved in treating the 'physical' nature of the capital good as changing over time but at the same time assuming that the same commodity can be consumed without change. This of course is simply an aggregation difficulty; in a more complete model consumption goods will be separate from capital goods. But then in a more complete model the treatment of capital goods becomes more straightforward too. As time goes on and technical change occurs, some capital goods will be affected, others not. And one would naturally introduce different capital-labour substitution possibilities for different (including older and newer) machines, with rigidity appearing as a limiting case."

In that case (2.2) gives

$$(3.2) \qquad\qquad x(t) = \int_{-\infty}^{t} y(\tau)d\tau.$$

Equation (2.4) gives

$$(3.3) \qquad\qquad \int_{-\infty}^{t} n(\tau)d\tau = N(t),$$

and (2.12) gives simply

$$(3.4) \qquad\qquad k(t) = ax(t)$$

as $T(0) = +\infty$.

In this case, there can, of course, exist costs of maintenance and repair. These costs must, however, be constant over time for every piece of capital. We can then define y and x net of these costs.

As a rather satisfactory form of φ we shall accept

$$(3.5) \qquad\qquad \varphi(n,k,x,t) = An^a k^b x^{-c} e^{\varepsilon t}$$

with a, b, c and ε constant. Here $a + b = 1$ is possibly a realistic hypothesis, but in general we shall not make this assumption. The coefficient c is most probably ≥ 0, but we might, as mentioned in the discussion of the "general" model, have $c < 0$ as a consequence of "external economies." ε is the relative increase in productivity per period as a result of increased "know - how," etc. In general, we shall therefore have $\varepsilon \geq 0$.

It is seen that both x and t have a neutral effect in φ in the sense that the marginal rate of substitution between n and k is not influenced by x and t.

Let us further assume an exponential growth of the labour force N, i.e.,

$$(3.6) \qquad\qquad N(t) = N_0 e^{\nu t}$$

where ν is constant.

By differentiating (3.3) we then obtain

$$(3.7) \qquad\qquad n(t) = \dot{N}(t) = n_0 e^{\nu t} \qquad\qquad \text{where } n_0 = \nu N_0.$$

By differentiating (3.2) we obtain $\dot{x}(t) = y(t)$. By means of (3.4), (3.5) and (3.7) we then get

$$(3.8) \qquad\qquad \dot{x} = [An_0^a a^b] x^{b-c} e^{(a\nu+\varepsilon)t}.$$

This is a Bernoullian differential equation[15] which can be solved to give

$$(3.9) \qquad\qquad x(t) = \left[\frac{An_0^a a^b(1-b+c)}{a\nu + \varepsilon} e^{(a\nu+\varepsilon)t} + C \right]^{\frac{1}{1-b+c}}$$

where C can be determined by means of $x(0)$. The solution is not valid for $a\nu + \varepsilon = 0$. We shall, however, disregard this special situation assuming $a\nu + \varepsilon > 0$.

[15] Cf. e.g., E. L. Ince [10, p. 22].

As t increases, it is here easily seen that the growth rate of $x(t)$ converges,

$$(3.10) \qquad \frac{\dot{x}(t)}{x(t)} \rightarrow \frac{a\nu + \varepsilon}{1-b+c} \quad \text{as } t \rightarrow +\infty.$$

If we divide the solution for $x(t)$ by $N(t)$, we obtain for production per head,

$$(3.11) \qquad \frac{x(t)}{N(t)} = \frac{1}{N_0} \left[\frac{A n_0^a a^b (1-b+c)}{a\nu + \varepsilon} e^{(\varepsilon - (1-a-b+c)\nu)t} + C e^{-(1-b+c)\nu t} \right]^{\frac{1}{1-b+c}}$$

(where $n_0 = \nu N_0$ according to (3.7)).

Here, of course, different cases may be discussed. We shall, however, consider only the case for which

$$(3.12) \qquad a > 0,\, b > 0,\, a+b \leq 1,\, c \geq 0,\, \varepsilon > 0,\, \nu > 0.$$

Then the last term within the bracket in (3.11) will vanish as t increases, and the solution will converge asymptotically,

$$(3.13) \qquad \frac{x(t)}{N(t)} \rightarrow \frac{1}{N_0} \left[\frac{A n_0^a a^b (1-b+c)}{a\nu + \varepsilon} \right]^{\frac{1}{1-b+c}} e^{\left[\frac{a\nu+\varepsilon}{1-b+c} - \nu \right] t}.$$

For the growth rate in (3.13) to be positive, it is necessary and sufficient that

$$(3.14) \qquad \nu < \frac{\varepsilon}{1-(a+b)+c} \left(= \frac{\varepsilon}{c} \text{ if } a+b = 1 \right),$$

where the right hand side is always positive under our assumptions (3.12). (3.14) illustrates how an upper bound is set for the population growth by the requirement that average production shall not decline, and how this bound is influenced by technical change (the numerator of (3.14)) and by the scale properties of the production function (the denominator of (3.14)).

The most remarkable feature of the solution above is perhaps that the asymptotic growth rates given in (3.10) and (3.13) are independent of the propensity to save a.[16] Let us illustrate this by assuming two countries which are similar in all respects except for a. Asymptotically both countries will then obtain the same relative rate of growth in production per head, x/N, (and of course also in total production, x). It is, however, seen by the way in which a enters (3.13) that this asymptotic curve will lie on a higher level—and therefore the absolute rate of growth be greater—in the country with the higher propensity to save. This also implies that if both countries start from the same initial position, the country with the higher propensity to save will start out with the higher relative growth rate "before the asymptote is reached."

[16] This feature is not, however, dependent on our special way of introducing substitution in the model. A similar conclusion can be obtained by means of models with substitution possibilities of the traditional kind.

4. THE CASE WITH EXPONENTIAL SHRINKAGE OF CAPITAL

Let us now assume that the capital shrinkage function f defined in Section 2 has the exponential form

$$(4.1) \qquad f(\tau) = e^{-\delta\tau}.$$

This would be the case if capital units are eliminated through "accidents," and for every unit of capital existing at a point of time t there exists a probability δdt that it will be destroyed by an accident in the time interval $(t, t + dt)$, where δ is a constant independent of the age of the capital unit.

For $x(t)$ we have then

$$(4.2) \qquad x(t) = \int_{-\infty}^{t} e^{-\delta(t-\tau)} y(\tau) d\tau,$$

and similarly for $N(t)$ and $K(t)$,

$$(4.3) \qquad \int_{-\infty}^{t} e^{-\delta(t-\tau)} n(\tau) d\tau = N(t)$$

and

$$(4.4) \qquad \int_{-\infty}^{t} e^{-\delta(t-\tau)} k(\tau) d\tau = K(t).$$

Since

$$(4.5) \qquad T(0) = \int_{0}^{\infty} e^{-\delta\tau} d\tau = \frac{1}{\delta},$$

the savings equation (2.12) reduces to

$$(4.6) \qquad k(t) = ax(t) + \delta(1 - a)K(t).$$

For the growth of the labour force we shall assume, as in the preceeding section, that $N(t) = N_0 e^{\nu t}$.

In this case it turns out to be rather difficult to solve the system if we apply the function (3.5) with $c \neq 0$. Let us therefore study the special case in which

$$(4.7) \qquad \varphi(n,k,x,t) = A n^a k^b e^{\varepsilon t}.$$

By differentiating (4.2) we now obtain

$$(4.8) \qquad \dot{x}(t) = y(t) - \delta x(t),$$

and similarly for $N(t)$ and $K(t)$. For $n(t)$ this now gives

$$(4.9) \qquad n(t) = n_0 e^{\nu t} \qquad\qquad \text{where } n_0 = N_0(\nu + \delta).$$

The labour force available for new capital at any time consists therefore of the growth in the total labour force plus the workers who are set free from old capital which is eliminated.

By means of the equation for $K(t)$ and (4.6) we obtain

$$(4.10) \qquad \dot{k}(t) = a\dot{x}(t) + \delta ax(t) - \delta ak(t).$$

By means of (4.7), (4.8) and (4.9) we then get the following differential equation for $k(t)$:

$$(4.11) \qquad \dot{k} = [aAn_0^a] \, e^{(a\nu+\epsilon)t} k^b - a\delta k.$$

This is a Bernoullian equation of a slightly more complicated form than (3.8). It is solved to give

$$(4.12) \qquad k(t) = \left[\frac{An_0^a a(1-b)}{a\nu + \epsilon + (1-b)a\delta} \, e^{(a\nu+\epsilon)t} + Be^{-(1-b)a\delta t} \right]^{\frac{1}{1-b}},$$

where B is determined by initial conditions.

If $\delta = 0$, and accordingly $k(t) = ax(t)$, it is easily seen that (4.12) corresponds to (3.9) for $c = 0$. In the case of $\delta \neq 0$, it is not so easy to obtain the solution for $x(t)$.

We see, however, that the last term in (4.12) tends to vanish for increasing t. Let us therefore consider only the asymptotic solution

$$(4.13) \qquad \bar{k}(t) = \left[\frac{An_0^a a(1-b)}{a\nu + \epsilon + (1-b)a\delta} \right]^{\frac{1}{1-b}} e^{\frac{a\nu+\epsilon}{1-b} t}$$

which shows a constant relative growth rate.[17] The corresponding solution for $x(t)$, which we shall denote $\bar{x}(t)$, is then more easily obtained by means of (4.8) when we insert for y from (4.7):

$$(4.14) \qquad \bar{x}(t) = Ge^{-\delta t} + He^{\frac{a\nu+\epsilon}{1-b} t},$$

where G is determined by initial conditions and H is given by

$$(4.15) \qquad H = \frac{(1-b) \, An_0^a \left[\dfrac{An_0^a a(1-b)}{a\nu + \epsilon + (1-b)a\delta} \right]^{\frac{b}{1-b}}}{a\nu + \epsilon + \delta(1-b)}.$$

Since the first term in (4.14) tends to vanish, we observe that $x(t)$ in this case will tend to increase with the same relative rate of growth as in the case studied in the perceeding section (for $c = 0$) regardless of δ (cf. (3.10)).

It is seen that under the conditions (3.12) $H > 0$. Furthermore, H is larger, the larger is a. The role played by δ is more complicated. This seems reasonable since δ not only represents the shrinkage in capital but also influences the accumulation of capital through (4.6) and, under our assumptions regarding the production process, also influences the speed with which new techniques can be introduced.[18]

---

[17] A discussion of the admissibility of this kind of approximation can be found in Hans Brems [2]. Cf. also Evsey Domar [3], Essay IX ("A Soviet Model of Growth"), pp. 231-32.

[18] Cf. the discussion of the influences of the average life time of capital in Domar [3, Essay VII].

The development of the average income x/N can be studied in a way similar to that in the preceeding section.

In the case discussed in this section, important simplification is obtained if we substitute for the net savings equation, (4.6), a gross savings equation,

(4.16) $k(t) = \beta x(t)$.

It is then rather easy to solve the system even if we retain the production function (3.5) with c not necessarily equal to zero. The solution is

(4.17) $x(t) = \left[C'e^{-(1-b+c)\delta t} + \dfrac{(1-b+c)An_0^a\beta^b}{a\nu + \varepsilon + (1-b+c)\delta} e^{(a\nu+\varepsilon)t} \right]^{\frac{1}{1-b+c}}$

where C' is determined by initial conditions. For $\delta = 0$, this solution clearly corresponds to (3.9). Since the first term in the bracket tends to vanish for increasing t when $\delta > 0$, a discussion of the long range development of x and x/N will follow lines similar to those of Section 3.

In this case δ also does not influence the asymptotic relative growth rate. But δ influences the *level* of the asymptotic development. It is possible for instance (remembering that $n_0 = N_0 (\nu + \delta)$ and considering N_0 as given) to demonstrate that if $a + b = 1$ and $c = 0$, we shall have the following situation: If $\varepsilon = 0$ this level will be higher the smaller is δ. But for $\varepsilon > 0$, it is possible that the level is higher the higher is δ. There will then exist a (positive) optimal δ which is larger, the larger is ε. This clearly illustrates the interrelations between δ and the speed with which new techniques are introduced within our production theory framework.

Similar cases will, of course, exist also under assumptions less restrictive than that $a + b = 1$ and $c = 0$.

What is said here is that if we have a sufficiently fast technical development, there will exist an optimal positive δ (which implies an optimal average life time for capital units) *even if we disregard the different costs of producing capital equipment with higher and lower δ*. If these cost differences are taken into account, a positive optimal value of δ will, of course, exist *a fortiori*. It would be interesting to extend our analysis in this direction in order to obtain rules for a rational selection of δ in different cases.[19]

5. THE CASE WITH A FIXED LIFE TIME FOR EACH UNIT OF CAPITAL

In this section we shall assume $f(\tau)$ to have the following form:

(5.1) $f(\tau) = \begin{cases} 1 \text{ for } \tau \leqq \theta, \\ 0 \text{ for } \tau > \theta. \end{cases}$

This means that every unit of capital has a finite life time θ, and that it retains its original productive capacity all through this life time.[20]

---

[19] Some elements for such an analysis might be found in S. G. Strumilin [20].

[20] This is the assumption adopted for instance by Domar [3, Essay VII] and by Hans Brems [2].

This further gives

(5.2) $T(0) = \theta.$

In this case it seems rather difficult to solve the system with production functions such as those applied in the preceeding sections. We shall therefore now have to be content with a linear and homogeneous function

(5.3) $\varphi(n,k,x,t) = an + bk,$

where a and b are constants.

It would perhaps be possible to add a term depending on t on the right hand side of (5.3). This would, however, not satisfy the restriction $\varphi(0,0,x,t) \equiv 0$ and would therefore not be altogether meaningful within the framework of our approach. At the end of this section we shall, however, briefly discuss the case in which a is not constant, but depends on t.

From (2.2), (2.4) and (2.5) we now get

(5.4) $x(t) = \int_{t-\theta}^{t} y(\tau)d\tau = aN(t) + bK(t),$

which means that there now exists a production function relating x uniquely to N and K. Formally our model in this case does not, therefore, differ from the more common growth models on this point. The concrete meaning underlying the relation is, however, still different from that of the more common production functions, as explained in Sections 1 and 2.

For the savings function we have

(5.5) $k(t) = ax(t) + \dfrac{1}{\theta}(1 - a)K(t).$

Assuming as before that $N(t) = N_0 e^{vt}$, we obtain for $n(t)$:

(5.6) $n(t) = n_0 e^{vt}$ where $n_0 = \dfrac{vN_0}{1-e^{-v\theta}}.$

Instead of the usual differential equations as were obtained in the preceeding sections, we now get a mixed difference-differential equation to solve:

(5.7) $\dot{k}(t) = \gamma[k(t) - k(t-\theta)] + aavN_0 e^{vt}$

where

(5.8) $\gamma = \dfrac{1}{\theta}[1 + a(\theta b - 1)].$

Such an equation may show many curious solutions, among them discontinuous ones. The discontinuous solutions are, however, less interesting, at any rate in growth analysis. We shall therefore restrict our discussion to continuous solutions.

The results of James and Belz [11] then imply that the solution of the homogeneous equation corresponding to (5.7) can be expressed as a sum of exponential expressions (with real and complex exponents).

Let us insert an expression $Ce^{\varrho t}$ for $k(t)$ in the equation obtained by disregarding the last term in (5.7). We then get the characteristic equation[21]

$$(5.9) \qquad\qquad \varrho = \gamma(1 - e^{-\varrho\theta}).$$

Let us first consider only the real solutions for ϱ, which are the most interesting from the point of view of growth analysis. At the end of this section we shall briefly comment on the complex solutions.

We observe first that $\varrho = 0$ is a solution of (5.9). The equation has however one more real solution if $\gamma\theta = [1 + a(\theta b - 1)] \neq 1$.[22] It is also easy to demonstrate that this solution will be a value $\varrho > 0$ if $\gamma\theta > 1$.

The latter case is, however, the more interesting from an economic point of view. The condition $\theta b > 1$, which assures $\gamma\theta > 1$, may in fact be obviously interpreted as the condition for the profitability of round-about production through the employment of capital, b representing the productivity of capital and θ its productive life time. We can therefore conclude that (5.9) has two real solutions, one equal to zero and one positive, so that we can write the solution for the homogeneous part of (5.7) as

$$(5.10) \qquad\qquad k^*(t) = C_1 + C_2 e^{\varrho t}$$

where ϱ now designates the positive root of (5.9) and C_1 and C_2 are arbitrary constants.

By adding the particular solution resulting from the last term in (5.7), we obtain the following solution for $k(t)$ (where we are still disregarding the complex solutions of (5.9)):

$$(5.11) \qquad\qquad k(t) = C_1 + C_2 e^{\varrho t} + \frac{a a \nu N_0}{\nu - \gamma(1 - e^{-\nu\theta})} e^{\nu t}.$$

For $x(t)$ we obtain by integrating $k(t)$ to give $K(t)$ and by inserting in (5.4):

$$(5.12) \qquad x(t) = C' + C'' e^{\varrho t} + a N_0 \left[1 + \frac{a b(1 - e^{-\nu\theta})}{\nu - \gamma(1 - e^{-\nu\theta})}\right] e^{\nu t}$$

where C' and C'' are constants which may be determined by means of initial conditions.[23]

For the average income we obtain

$$(5.13) \qquad \frac{x(t)}{N(t)} = \frac{1}{N_0} C' e^{-\nu t} + \frac{1}{N_0} C'' e^{(\rho - \nu)t} + a\left[1 + \frac{a b(1 - e^{-\nu\theta})}{\nu - \gamma(1 - e^{-\nu\theta})}\right].$$

If now $\nu > \varrho$, the first two terms of (5.13) tend to vanish, and the last term remains as a constant asymptote. In this case it is easy to demonstrate that $\nu > \gamma(1 - e^{-\nu\theta})$ so that the asymptotic value for the average income is greater than a, which is obviously reasonable.

[21] Our equation (5.9) is equivalent to equation (5.3) in Domar [3, Essay VII].
[22] If $\gamma\theta$ should be equal to one, $\varrho = 0$ would be a double root.
[23] If we require $K(t) \to 0$ for $t \to -\infty$, then $C' = C_1 = 0$.

If $\nu < \varrho$, the second term on the right hand side of (5.13) will dominate in the long run. It is easy to prove that C'' must in this case be positive, provided that $K(t) \to 0$ for $t \to -\infty$, and x/N will therefore *increase* in the long run.

The special case $\varrho = \nu$ shall not be discussed here. (5.13) does not give the general (real, continuous) solution in this case.

The values of C' and C'' might be discussed further with reference to initial conditions. This discussion is, however, tedious and will be omitted here.

As regards the dependence of the growth rate ϱ on the parameters of the model discussed in this section, I shall only mention that ϱ now depends essentially on the propensity to save, a, and is higher the higher is a. For different values of a we have then the following possibilities: For low values of a, $\varrho < \nu$ and average income tends to a stationary value. This level is higher, the higher is a. When a is above a certain critical value, average income will, however, tend to increase in the long run, and increase faster, the higher is a.

In addition to the real solutions discussed above, the characteristic equation (5.9) contains an infinity of complex solutions. By means of the results of Frisch and Holme [6] it is easily seen[24] that in our case (with $\theta b > 1$) these complex solutions will correspond to one cycle with a period in each of the intervals (the bounds included)

$$(5.14) \qquad \left(\frac{\theta}{j + \frac{1}{2}}, \frac{\theta}{j}\right) \qquad (j = 1,2,3,\ldots),$$

i.e., in the intervals $\left(\frac{2}{3}\theta, \theta\right)$, $\left(\frac{2}{5}\theta, \frac{\theta}{2}\right)$, $\left(\frac{2\theta}{7}, \frac{\theta}{3}\right)$, etc.

As regards the dampening or explosion of the fluctuations, I have not reached any really general result. It is, however, rather easy to demonstrate[25]

---

[24] Cf. Table 2, case $C > 1$. In our case, Frisch and Holme's parameters a and c are both equal to our γ, and their C equals $\gamma\theta - \mathrm{Log}_e \gamma\theta$, which is greater than 1 because we have assumed $\gamma\theta > 1$.

[25] I shall briefly give the proof by help of the results of Frisch and Holme [6]. Write $\varrho = \beta + ia$ (where a and β are of course not identical with the propensities to save used in the text). We further write $u = a\theta$ and $v = \beta\theta$. A necessary and sufficient condition for dampening is then $v < 0$. By Frisch and Holme's equation (25) we have

$$(\mathrm{i}) \qquad v = \mathrm{Log}_e\left(\gamma\theta \, \frac{\sin u}{u}\right)$$

where we have introduced our γ instead of Frisch and Holme's c. Now Frisch and Holme further state (p. 232) that the u's corresponding to the cyclic components in our case $[C = \gamma\theta - \mathrm{Log}_e\gamma\theta > 1$ since $\gamma\theta > 1]$ will lie in the intervals

$(\mathrm{ii}) \qquad\qquad 2j\pi \leqq u \leqq (2j + 1)\,\pi \qquad\qquad (j = 1,2,\ldots.),$

that means that 2π is a lower bound for any u. Since $\sin u \leqq 1$, $\gamma\theta < 2\pi$ then implies $\gamma\theta \sin u/u < 1$, which by (i) is sufficient for $v < 0$ and thus for dampening.

These results are in conformity with some results by Hans Neisser [16] and by Domar [4] in similar cases. Their analyses are however carried out in terms of pure difference equations.

that all the cycles are damped for acceptable values of γ and θ, a sufficient condition for dampening being that

(5.15) $$\gamma\theta < 2\pi, \quad \text{i.e., } \theta b < 1 + \frac{2\pi - 1}{a}.$$

With the interpretation of θb given above, it is very unlikely that this condition should not be fulfilled.

The possible relevance of the results in this section for business cycle analysis and for the question of interaction between growth and cycles shall not be discussed here.

In the case discussed in this section, it seems to be rather difficult to introduce increasing technical efficiency in a satisfactory way. We might, however, introduce a changing marginal productivity of labour by leting a be a given exponential function of time:

(5.16) $$\varphi(n,k,x,t) = a_0 e^{\lambda t} n + bk$$

where a_0 is the marginal productivity of labour at $t = 0$ and λ is the (constant) relative rate of increase in this productivity. This satisfies $\varphi(0,0,x,t) \equiv 0$. However it obviously represents a quite special non-neutral change in productivity.

The solution for $x(t)$ with the assumption (5.16) takes the form (5.12) where $\nu + \lambda$ is substituted for ν and $a_0 (1 - e^{-(\nu+\lambda)\theta})/(1 - e^{-\nu\theta})$ is substituted for a.

The solution for $x(t)/N(t)$ then takes the form

(5.17) $$\frac{x(t)}{N(t)} = Pe^{-\nu t} + Qe^{(\rho-\nu)t} + Re^{\lambda t}$$

where P, Q and R are constants. (This solution is not valid in the special case, $\varrho = \nu + \lambda$.) When $\lambda > \varrho - \nu$, so that the last term in (5.17) will dominate in the long run, it is easily seen that R (which is independent of the initial situation except for a_0) is positive.

6. CONCLUDING REMARKS

As stated in the introductory remarks and in Section 2 of this paper, I find the hypothesis of "ex ante" substitution possibilities, but no such possibilities "ex post," more realistic than the hypotheses about the production process most widely accepted in *theoretical* growth analysis. In fact, I have the feeling that the hypothesis applied in this paper is closer to the experience of many students of economic growth who approach these questions from a "practical" point of view, and it may possibly be helpful in removing some of the "guilty conscience" of some theorists in the field who rely either on fixed coefficients or on full substitutability in a "classical" sense.

In particular, I find the hypothesis outlined in this paper important when technical progress is to enter the analysis as a main factor.

Sections 3, 4 and 5 show that our hypothesis does not make our models unmanageable in cases where on points other than the substitution possibilities we rely on hypotheses usually applied in theoretical growth analysis.

It seems that the conclusions are in some respects more sensitive to shifts in the *form* of the production function than they are to the shift from the assumption of substitutability in the usual sense to our assumption of substitutability only "at the margin." If the study had been directed more specially towards such subjects as, say, the importance of the rate of investment for the possibilities of adopting new techniques, the importance of obsolescence in the process of growth, the relation between population growth and "structural" unemployment, etc., then the conclusions would depend more specifically on the choice of what kind of substitutability one assumes.

Institute of Economics, University of Oslo

REFERENCES

[1] BARAN, PAUL A.: *The Political Economy of Growth*, New York: Monthly Review Press, 1957.

[2] BREMS, HANS: "Constancy of the Proportionate Equilibrium Rate of Growth: Result or Assumption?" *The Review of Economic Studies*, Vol. XXIV, February, 1957, pp. 131-138.

[3] DOMAR, EVSEY D.: *Essays in the Theory of Economic Growth*, New York: Oxford University Press, 1957.

[4] ————: "Depreciation, Replacement and Growth–and Fluctuations," *The Economic Journal*, Vol. LXVII, December, 1957, pp. 655-658.

[5] EISNER, ROBERT: "Underemployment Equilibrium Rates of Growth," *The American Economic Review*, Vol. XLII, December, 1952, pp. 820-831.

[6] FRISCH, RAGNAR AND HARALD HOLME: "The Characteristic Solutions of a Mixed Difference and Differential Equation Occurring in Economic Dynamics," *Econometrica*, Vol. III, April, 1935, pp. 225-239.

[7] HAAVELMO, TRYGVE: *A Study in the Theory of Economic Evolution*. Contributions to Economic Analysis, Amsterdam: North-Holland Publishing Company, 1954.

[8] HAMBERG, D.: "Full Capacity vs. Full Employment Growth," *The Quarterly Journal of Economics* 1952. Discussion by HAROLD PILVIN, R. F. HARROD, and EVSEY D. DOMAR, *The Quarterly Journal of Economics* 1953.

[9] HARROD, R. F.: "An Essay in Dynamic Economics," *The Economic Journal* 1953.

[10] INCE, E. L.: *Integration of Ordinary Differential Equations*, London: Oliver and Boyd, 1956.

[11] JAMES, R. W., AND M. H. BELZ: "The Significance of the Characteristic Solutions of Mixed Difference and Differential Equations," *Econometrica*, Vol. 6, October, 1938, pp. 326-343.

[12] KREYBERG, H. J. A.: "Economic Growth and Economic Welfare," *Statsøkonomisk Tidsskrift*, 1956 (Reprint No. 4 from the Oslo University Institute of Economics. In Norwegian with an English summary).

[13] LANGE, OSKAR: "Some Observations on Input-Output Analysis," *Sankhya*, 1957.

[14] LEONTIEF, WASSILY et al.: *Studies in the Structure of the American Economy*, New York: Oxford University Press, 1953.

[15] MAYWALD, K.: "The Best and the Average in Productivity Studies and in Long-Term Forecasting," *The Productivity Measurement Review*, No. 9 (Reprint Series No. 132, University of Cambridge, Department of Applied Economics.)

[16] NEISSER, HANS: "Depreciation, Replacements and Regular Growth," *The Economic Journal*, Vol. LXV, March, 1955, pp. 159-161.

[17] PREINREICH, GABRIEL A. D.: "Annual Survey of Economic Theory: The Theory of Depreciation," *Econometrica*, Vol. 6, January, 1938, pp. 219-241.

[18] SINGER, HANS W.: "Problems of Industrialization of Under-Developed Countries," in LEON H. DUPRIEZ, ed.: *Economic Progress: Papers and Proceedings of a Round Table Held by the International Economic Association*. Louvain, 1955.

[19] SOLOW, ROBERT M.: "A Contribution to the Theory of Economic Growth," *The Quarterly Journal of Economics*, Vol. XLL, February, 1956, pp. 65-94.

[20] STRUMILIN, S. G.: "The Time Factor in Capital Investment Projects," (Translated from the Russian.) in *International Economic Papers No. 1*, London and New York, 1951.

[21] SVENNILSON, INGVAR: *Growth and Stagnation in the European Economy*, Geneva, ECE, 1954.

[22] ————: "Capital Accumulation and National Wealth in an Expanding Economy," in *25 Economic Essays in Honour of Erik Lindahl*, Stockholm: *Ekonomisk Tidskrift*, 1956.

[23] TINBERGEN, JAN: "Zur Theorie der Langfristigen Wirtschaftsentwicklung," *Weltwirtschaftliches Archiv*, 1942.

[24] VALAVANIS-VAIL, STEFAN: "An Econometric Model of Growth: U.S.A., 1869-1953," *The American Economic Review*, Vol. XLV, May, 1955, pp. 208-221.

[25] VERDOORN, P. J.: "Complementarity and Long-Range Projections," *Econometrica*, Vol. 24, October, 1956, pp. 429-450.

Substitution and Fixed Proportions in the Theory of Capital

Robert M. Solow

I have long since abandoned the illusion that participants in this debate actually communicate with each other. So I omit the standard polemical introduction, and get down to business at once.

1. Assumptions and Notation

Imagine an economy with two sectors. One sector produces standard bundles of consumer goods. Its inputs are labor and machines. Man-years of labor are all alike, but machines come in different " types ". Raw materials are ignored. The second sector of the economy produces machines of different types.

A machine, once produced, has a fixed capacity per year, and it must be operated by a crew of fixed size. There is absolutely no loss of generality in choosing machine-units so that a machine of any type has a capacity of exactly one unit of consumables per year. The quality that differentiates one type of machine from another is the size of the required crew. If a machine needs to be operated by λ men to realize its capacity, I shall say that it is of type λ. A machine of type λ, then, requires λ man-years of labor to produce one unit of consumables per year, and λ is fixed forever the day the machine is built.

All machines, regardless of types, are one-hoss shays of fixed life L. Other assumptions are possible but it will be seen later that, for the kind of application I have in mind, the assumption I have made is particularly easy to handle. It would be a genuine generalization of this model to extend it to cover different life-times for different machine-types, or to permit the lifetime to be one of the unknowns of the problem.

I shall assume that machines are built by unassisted labor. I regret having to do this, but it is an immense simplification and I do not believe that any matter of principle is involved. The trouble with having machines used in the machine-building sector is that I would be forced to specify the operating characteristics of each type of machine in the production of each type of machine. And an equilibrium situation could arise in which one type of machine is built for the consumer-goods sector, another type of machine to produce that kind of machine, another type of machine to produce machines to produce machines for the consumer-sector and on and on. An intermediate assumption would be that a machine of type λ is necessary to produce another machine of type λ but not necessary in the production of any other type of machine, sort of like Noah's Ark. But this situation reduces ultimately to the machine-produced-by-labor-alone situation, and so I might just as well make the simple assumption to start with.

Why should anyone ever choose to operate a machine requiring a larger crew in preference to one requiring a smaller? Obviously, because a machine requiring a smaller crew must itself be more costly to produce than a machine with a larger value of λ. Let $w(v)$ stand for the real wage (in terms of consumables) at time v; then the cost in con-

Reprinted from XXIV (June 1962), 207–218 of *Review of Economic Studies* by permission of *Review of Economic Studies* published by Oliver & Boyd Ltd., Edinburgh and London.
© 1962 The Economic Society.

sumables of producing a machine of type λ at this time v is $c(\lambda)w(v)$, where $c(\lambda)$ is the number of man-years of labor required to produce a machine of type λ. I ignore gestation periods, in the hope that it will be clear how they may be introduced.

I assume that λ can be varied continuously, so that calculus techniques are applicable. If only a discrete set of machine-types is conceivable, programming techniques could handle that situation without difficulty. The cost-function $c(\lambda)$ is downward-sloping: the more labor required to operate a machine, the less labor it takes to build it. Moreover, the marginal cost of reducing λ rises as λ falls; this plays the same role as all increasing-marginal-cost assumptions. Thus we have $c(\lambda) \geqslant 0$, $c'(\lambda) < 0$, $c''(\lambda) < 0$.[1] A natural choice for illustrative purposes is $c(\lambda) = c_0\lambda^{-\gamma}$. This choice presupposes that it is infinitely costly to build a machine with $\lambda = 0$ and that a machine of zero cost requires infinitely much labor to produce a unit of consumables. In effect this rules out the production of consumables either by labor alone or by machine alone, but my general line of argument does not depend on the properties of the particular illustrative cost function.

Let $I(v)$ be the *number* of machines built in period v, which is the same thing as the consumer-goods capacity installed in period v. For definiteness, I assume that this capacity can not be operated until period $v + 1$ and that it then survives through period $v + L$, whether or not it is used in the interim.

2. WAGE DETERMINATION

At any time t, history has left a stock of machines of perhaps L different types: $I(t-L)$ of type $\lambda(t-L)$, $I(t-L+1)$ of type $\lambda(t-L+1)$, ..., $I(t-1)$ of type $\lambda(t-1)$. Suppose the supply of labor to the consumer-goods sector is $L(t)$, determined exogenously and inelastic with respect to the wage rate (this assumption could be lifted).

Take an arbitrary wage-rate w (in terms of consumables, remember). At that real wage a machine of type λ earns a quasi-rent of $1-\lambda w$ if it is used to capacity, and zero if it is not used at all (less-than-capacity utilization is uninteresting). Hence, in general the quasi-rent is $[1-\lambda w]^+$ where $[x]^+$ stands for the larger of x and zero.

The existing stock of machines can offer employment to at most $\sum_{v=t-L}^{t-1} \lambda(v)I(v)$ workers. I shall assume that $L(t)$ never exceeds this amount, so that labor is never supplied in absolutely redundant quantity to the consumer-goods sector. (Old machines may be held in stand-by capacity, or some limited extra-manning of machines may be possible: both these possibilities are outside the model as I have stated it.) At any real-wage w, the demand for labor comes from all machines for which $\lambda w \leqq 1$. (I have been assuming that each vintage contains machines of only one type; uncertainty about the future might lead to building several types of equipment at the same time, but I do not pursue that line right now.) Let $V(t,w)$ be the set of vintages between $t-1$ and $t-L$ for which $\lambda(v)w \leqq 1$. Thus $V(t,w)$ is the set of vintages which can be operated profitably (or without loss) at time t with wage rate w. The demand for labor at the product-wage w is $\sum_{v \in V(t,w)} I(v)\lambda(v)$. It is

[1] If machines of different types can be operated independently, then concavity is automatic. For half a machine of type λ and half a machine of type λ' can produce one unit of output with a labor input of $\dfrac{\lambda + \lambda'}{2}$. If machines of type $\dfrac{\lambda + \lambda'}{2}$ are produced at all, it must be that $c\left(\dfrac{\lambda + \lambda'}{2}\right) \leqq \frac{1}{2}\, c(\lambda) + \frac{1}{2}\, c(\lambda')$.

[The third expression should read: $c''(\lambda) > 0$ here and at the bottom of page 215. The Editors.]

clearly a non-increasing function of w; indeed, it is a decreasing step-function. As w increases, the demand for labor falls suddenly as soon as a whole vintage is rendered unprofitable and then remains constant until another vintage is eliminated from consideration. The size of each drop in demand is the volume of employment offered by the machines of the marginal vintage.

Equilibrium in the labor market requires that $\sum_{v \varepsilon V(t,w)} I(v)\lambda(v) = L(t)$ and I assume that $w(t)$ is determined in that way. Such an equilibrium must exist (apart from a minor indeterminacy) because if $w > \dfrac{1}{\min\limits_{t-L \leq v \leq t-1} \lambda(v)}$, the demand for labor is zero, and if $w = 0$ the demand for labor exceeds the supply, by my non-rendundancy assumption.

At a sufficiently high real wage none of the existing machinery can break even, and so none of it operates and the demand for labor is zero. As the wage drops, eventually the least labor-intensive machinery in existence can be profitably operated and the demand for labor is fixed by the size of the stock and the associated labor-input coefficient. If the wage falls further, the demand for labor remains constant until another vintage can break even and add to employment (while the even less-labor-intensive machinery earns positive quasi-rents). And so on.

In summary, the current wage-rate in terms of product is determined by the historically-given stock of machines and the supply of labor to the consumer-goods sector. The wage-rate will probably change from period to period because (a) the supply of labor grows or declines; and (b) the stock of capital changes as an old vintage disappears, a new one appears, and the new vintage may differ in quantity and type from the old.

3. INVESTMENT POLICY

A complete analysis of this model would require a hypothesis about how the *volume* of investment—in the sense of the gross addition to capacity, $I(t)$—is determined. Indeed, to be quite tidy, I should have used that information in analyzing the labor market; the supply of labor to the consumer-goods sector is presumably the aggregate supply less what is demanded in the machine-building industry (and *vice-versa!*). But for present purposes I need not commit myself on this question; I can take the volume of investment as exogenous. I must, however, describe how it is determined what *type* of machine will be produced in each period.

The smaller the value of λ, the more profitable will a newly-constructed machine be during its lifetime, and the more expensive it will be to build right now. A rational choice of λ depends unavoidably on expectations about interest rates and about real wages throughout the lifetime of the machine. Concrete analytical results must rest on concrete assumptions about expectations. I shall assume that the interest rate ρ is confidently expected to remain at its present level, even though it has fluctuated in the past. Since real wages have a much more definite historical trend, at least three alternative assumptions present themselves. Let $\hat{w}(t,v)$ be the real wage expected for time t when the present moment is time $v \leq t$. Then, of course, $\hat{w}(v,v) = w(v)$. The three simplest assumptions are:

(a) $\hat{w}(t,v) = w(v)$

(b) $\hat{w}(t,v) = w(v) + [w(v) - w(v-1)] (t-v)$

$$(c) \quad \hat{w}(t,v) = w(v) \left(1 + \frac{w(v) - w(v-1)}{w(v-1)} \right)^{t-v} \text{ or } \frac{\hat{w}(t,v)}{w(v)} = \left(\frac{w(v)}{w(v-1)} \right)^{t-v}.$$

The first assumption is wholly static expectations. The second assumption extrapolates real wages linearly from the most recent experience. The third assumption extrapolates real wages exponentially from the most recent experience. Since this paper does not deal explicitly with technological change (though I hope it will be clear how one could do so), I shall limit myself to the case of static expectations, which brings with it a key simplification.

Consider an arbitrary choice of λ at time t. The expected quasi-rent (in terms of consumables) for period $t + k$ is $[1 - \lambda\hat{w}(t+k,t)]^+$. If the current (and therefore expected) interest rate is ρ, then the expected present-value of the real flow of net revenues over the lifetime of the machine is $\sum_{k=1}^{L} [1 - \lambda\hat{w}(t+k,t)]^+ (1+\rho)^{-k} - c(\lambda)w(t)$. Entrepreneurs will choose λ so that this present value is a maximum. And, under competitive conditions in credit markets, the rate of interest will seek a level which makes this present value equal to zero.

Now it can be seen why the assumption of static expectations about real wages is such a help. In any other case it is possible that the optimal decision is to build a machine now which is *expected* to become uneconomical before its physical lifetime is over. Then I must be sure to truncate the present-value sum to allow for the fact that the annual quasi-rent never becomes negative, because the machine shuts down. But with static expectations, a machine that now earns a positive quasi-rent is expected to do so throughout its life; and a machine that is now uneconomical to operate would be expected to remain so and would not be built. It should be clear that *in fact* a machine may be forced out of operation during its lifetime by a rise in real wages; it is only *ex ante* that this eventuality may be neglected.

The present value, to be maximized by entrepreneurs and annihilated by the market, is now

$$\sum_{k=1}^{L} [1 - \lambda w(t)] (1 + \rho)^{-k} - c(\lambda)w(t) = [1 - \lambda w(t)] \frac{1 - \frac{1}{(1 + \rho)^L}}{\rho} - c(\lambda)w(t)$$

The [ ]$^+$ has disappeared by virtue of static expectations. Let $\dfrac{1 - \dfrac{1}{(1+\rho)^L}}{\rho} = \varphi(\rho)$

it is the present value of an annuity of one unit of consumables for L years.

The first job is to maximize $(1 - \lambda w(t)) \varphi(\rho) - c(\lambda)w(t)$ with respect to λ. The condition is:

$$-w(t)\varphi(\rho) - w(t)c'(\lambda) = 0$$

or

(1) $$c'(\lambda) = -\varphi(\rho).$$

(For a maximum we should have $c''(\lambda) > 0$, confirming the marginal-cost condition specified earlier.) The interpretation of (1) is that it equates the marginal cost of reducing the labor requirements of a newly-built machine to the present value of the consequent expected gain in revenues. Note that this condition is *independent of the real wage*, for entirely classical reasons.

If the interest rate were treated as exogenous, the current value of $\rho(t)$ would determine $\lambda(t)$ from (1); $w(t)$ is determined by the market mechanism already described; $I(t)$ is exogenous; $L(t)$ is exogenous; we could go on to period $t + 1$ and repeat the process. But if ρ were exogenous there would very likely be a pure profit or pure loss in the machine-building industry. In the normal course of events this pure profit or loss would be eliminated by changes in the demand for credit and hence in interest rates or by changes in the rate of investment, hence in the stock of capital, hence ultimately in real wages. For capital-theoretic purposes I shall suppose that the interest rate adjusts to wipe out any pure profit or loss. Thus our second equilibrium condition is:

$$(2) \qquad\qquad (1 - \lambda w)\, \varphi\, (\rho) = c(\lambda)w.$$

The real wage does enter into this condition, so that ultimately λ does depend on w, *through the rate of interest*.

Equations (1) and (2) together imply:

$$(3) \qquad\qquad \frac{w\lambda}{1 - w\lambda} = -\frac{\lambda c'(\lambda)}{c};$$

so that in equilibrium the ratio of wages to quasi-rents for the newest machines in the consumer sector is equal to the absolute elasticity of the cost-function in machine building.

A neat special case occurs when $c(\lambda) = c_0 \lambda^{-\gamma}$, as suggested earlier. In particular, it is easily calculated that

$$(3') \qquad\qquad \lambda(t)w(t) = \left(1 + \frac{1}{\gamma}\right)^{-1}.$$

Earlier I introduced the set $V(t,w)$ of vintages capable of earning non-negative quasi-rents at time t if the product-wage is w. $V(t,w)$ is the set of v for which $\lambda(v)w(t) \leqq 1$. But from (3') this is the set of vintages v between t—1 and t—L for which $w(t) \geqq \left(1 + \frac{1}{\gamma}\right) w(v)$. Thus to calculate the structure of the demand for labor one need only keep track of the history of wage rates. Machines still in existence at time t remain viable so long as the wage rate has not increased by more than $100 \cdot \frac{1}{\gamma}$ per cent since the machine in question was first built.

3. Operation of the Model

How would an economy like this behave over time? In principle that is not a hard question to answer, but in practice it would require much too much calculation for pencil-

and-paper analysis. One way out is to consider only special types of situations—say, where $I(t)$ and $L(t)$ grow exponentially at the same rate—but this limitation forecloses some of the most interesting questions one might ask of the model. For instance, I would very much like to know how and how badly the results are distorted if one analyzes the history of a model like this one on the assumption that it possesses a homogeneous stock of real capital, or that the stock of capital is in some way heterogeneous but substitution possibilities remain essentially unimpaired through the life of capital goods.

There is another possibility. The calculations necessary to simulate the operation of this model are well adapted to modern computing machinery. It would be relatively simple to choose reasonable time paths for the exogenous inputs $I(t)$ and $L(t)$, and let the model generate the rest of its history step by step. A computing-machine record of this history could then be analyzed as if it consisted of observed data. It would also be possible to incorporate in the programming any determinate method of generating endogenously the time series of gross investment. Circumstances have prevented me so far from trying out this experiment, but I intend to do so shortly.

A simulation would go something like this. One starts at time zero with an arbitrary initial stock of capital $I(-L+1)$, $I(-L+2)$, . . . , $I(0)$, and its distribution of operating characteristics $\lambda(-L+1)$, $\lambda(-L+2)$, . . . , $\lambda(0)$. In addition, $I(1)$, $I(2)$, . . . , $I(N)$ and $L(1)$, $L(2)$, . . . , $L(N)$ are both given, presumably as time series fluctuating about trends. Find the smallest of $\{\lambda(0), \lambda(-1), . . .\}$, say $\lambda(v_1)$, and compute $\lambda(v_1)I(v_1)$. Compare this number with $L(1)$. If $\lambda(v_1)I(v_1) > L(1)$, $w(1) = \dfrac{1}{\lambda(v_1)}$; if by chance $\lambda(v_1)I(v_1) = L(1)$ there is a minor indeterminacy and $\dfrac{1}{\lambda(v_2)} \leqslant w(1) \leqslant \dfrac{1}{\lambda(v_1)}$; if $\lambda(v_1)I(v_1) < L(1)$, find the smallest of $\{\lambda(0), \lambda(-1), . . .\}$, not counting $\lambda(v_1)$, say $\lambda(v_2)$, and compare $\lambda(v_1)I(v_1) + \lambda(v_2)I(v_2)$ with $L(1)$, etc. Finally in this sequence of steps one must come (by non-redundancy) to a first vintage v_k such that $\sum\limits_{i=1}^{k} \lambda(v_i)I(v_i) \geq L(1)$ and then we can record $w(1) = \dfrac{1}{\lambda(v_k)}$. We also know which vintages of machinery will actually produce in period 1; they have been temporarily renumbered v_1, v_2, . . . , v_k and constitute the set $V(1, w(1))$. The total output of consumables is $Q(1) = \sum\limits_{i=1}^{k} I(v_i) = \sum\limits_{v(1,w(1))} I(v)$ (with a trivial modification if partial use of the v_k vintage exhausts the labor supply).[1]

The next step is to use equations (1) and (2) to fix $\lambda(1)$ and $\varphi(1)$. If we use the special constant-elasticity case for $c(\lambda)$, it follows from (3′) that $\lambda(1) = \dfrac{1}{w(1)\left(1 + \dfrac{1}{\bar{\gamma}}\right)}$. The special case version of (1) is:

(1′)
$$\lambda = \left[\frac{c_0\,\gamma}{\varphi(\rho)} \right]^{\frac{1}{1+\gamma}}$$

$$\varphi(\rho) = c_0\gamma\lambda^{-(\gamma+1)}.$$

[1] To be exact, $Q(1) = \sum\limits_{1}^{k-1} I(v_i) + \dfrac{L(1) - \sum\limits_{1}^{k-1} \lambda(v_i)\,I(v_i)}{\lambda(v_k)}$.

Thus it is easy to store $\lambda(1)$ and $\varphi(\rho(1))$. For some purposes it may be important to have $\rho(1)$ itself; it can be obtained from standard tables, or $\varphi(\rho)$ can be inverted by machine·

We now have all of the essentials and can go on to the next period. The stock of machines is modified by the disappearance of $I(-L+1)$ units of capacity of type $\lambda(-L+1)$ and the addition of $I(1)$ units of capacity of type $\lambda(1)$. This procedure can be iterated for N periods and the machine will then print out the time series for $I(t)$, $\lambda(t)$, $L(t)$, $Q(t)$, $w(t)$, $\varphi(\rho(t))$ and, if desired, $\rho(t)$.

There are other characteristics of the model economy that one might wish to compute and record for further analysis. One such is the real value of the stock of capital (measured in consumer goods). A minor question arises here as to " when " in the period the real stock of capital should be measured. For instance, one might choose to measure $K(1)$ *excluding* $I(1)$ on the grounds that the gross investment of period 1 is not available for productive purposes until period 2. Having made that decision, one must further decide whether to value $K(1)$ on the basis of the equilibrium wage rate for period 1 or for period 0. Suppose we use $w(1)$. Then $K(1)$ is the present value of expected future quasi-rents on all vintages, calculated as if the current wage $w(1)$ and the current interest rate $\rho(1)$ would endure forever. Thus

$$K(1) = \sum_{i=-L+1}^{o} [1-\lambda(i)w(1)]^{+} \; \frac{1 - \left[\dfrac{1}{1+\rho(1)}\right]^{i+L-1}}{\rho(1)} \qquad I(i) = \sum_{i=1}^{k} [1-\lambda(v_i)w(1)]I(v_i)$$

$$\frac{1 - \left[\dfrac{1}{1+\rho(1)}\right]^{v_i+L-1}}{\rho(1)}$$

Note that $K(1)$ is a *market value*, deflated by the price of consumables. Old machinery which is too labor-intensive to earn quasi-rents at the current wage is counted as zero because the current wage is expected to persist forever.

Other possibilities present themselves for deflating the stock of capital. The current cost (in consumables) of a machine of type λ is $c(\lambda)w(t)$, or $c(\lambda)w(1)$ in period 1. The capital stock can be deflated by a machinery-price index simply by dividing each term in the sum by $c(\lambda(i))w(1)$. An original cost or book value measure of the stock of capital is even easier to compute: it is

$$\beta(t) = \sum_{t-L}^{t-1} I(v)c(\lambda(v))w(v).$$

Deflated to constant prices of period t_0, it is

$$\beta^*(t) = \sum_{t-L}^{t-1} I(v)c(\lambda(v))w(t_0);$$

the reader may have other pet ideas.

For some purposes it would be interesting to have a record of distributive shares for this model. The gross product of the economy, measured in consumables, is $Q(t) + c(\lambda(t))w(t)I(t)$. Under my simplifying assumption, all of the gross product of the investment-sector is wages. Thus the share of wages in gross income is

$$\frac{w(t)L(t) + c(\lambda(t))w(t)I(t)}{Q(t) + c(\lambda(t))w(t)I(t)}.$$

The measurement of net national product depends on the treatment of depreciation: either conventional straight-line depreciation, or the value of physical retirements, or a more carefully computed loss in value of the existing stock of machines can be deducted from gross product and the wage share in net product calculated.

4. MARGINAL PRODUCTIVITY

Despite the absence of any *ex post* possibility of substituting " capital " for labor, this model behaves in an entirely neo-classical way. I illustrate by calculating the marginal productivity of labor and the marginal productivity of capital.

How much more output would be attainable if one more worker should present himself to the consumer-goods sector for employment? That depends on the type of machine available for him to work on. If my non-redundancy assumption holds, there will always be *some* machine available for him to work on. At any given wage rate, machines enter production in order of increasing labor-intensity, so to speak. An extra worker can be most profitably employed on the least labor-intensive idle machine. Suppose the labor force is such that all machines of vintages $v_1, v_2, \ldots, v_{k-1}$ are producing, and some of the machines of vintage v_k are producing, while some are idle. Then vintage v_k machines are " no-rent " machines in the classical Ricardian sense; therefore $1 - w\lambda(v_k) = 0$, or $w = \frac{1}{\lambda(v_k)}$. Now an additional worker will be employed on a previously-idle machine of vintage v_k. Since it takes $\lambda(v_k)$ workers to operate the machine at its full capacity of 1 unit of output, the marginal worker will add $\frac{1}{\lambda(v_k)}$ to the total output of consumables and this is the marginal productivity of labor. It happens to be equal to the real wage.

Of course, it might happen that the initial labor force is·just sufficient to man all the machines of vintages $v_1, v_2, \ldots, v_k$, but none of v_{k+1}. Then an extra worker will produce an extra product of $\frac{1}{\lambda(v_{k+1})}$ units of consumables; and the disappearance of one worker will reduce output by $\frac{1}{\lambda(v_k)}$ units of consumables. One may either distinguish between the upward and downward marginal products of labor, or else one may say that the marginal product of labor is between $\frac{1}{\lambda(v_{k+1})}$ and $\frac{1}{\lambda(v_k)}$. Precisely in the case now under discussion, the real wage can settle anywhere between $\frac{1}{\lambda(v_{k+1})}$ and $\frac{1}{\lambda(v_k)}$ (because within that range the whole labor force can be employed profitably, but vintage v_{k+1} can not bid profitably and generate an excess demand for labor). So even in this case one may say that the real wage equals the marginal productivity of labor. One may go further: the demand curve for labor is, as in the Marshallian case, the (stepwise) falling curve of the marginal productivity of labor.

Now how about the marginal product of " capital "? We are to add a machine and observe how much extra output can be generated. Add what type of machine? Suppose the marginal machine is of type λ^*; that is, given the stock of machines and the size of the labor force, all machines actually in use are of type $\lambda \leqslant \lambda^*$. Clearly, then, to add a machine of type $\lambda \geqq \lambda^*$ yields *no* extra output; for to man the new machines would require moving a worker from a pre-existing machine with which he is more productive to the new one with which he is less (or no more) productive. The best rearrangement is to leave things as they are, and the marginal productivity of a machine of type $\lambda \geqslant \lambda^*$ is zero. Consider adding one machine of type $\lambda < \lambda^*$. To operate it and produce one unit of output, the sector must free λ man-years of labor. The largest net increment of output is achieved if this labor is freed from operating marginal machines. To dispose of λ man-years of labor, $\frac{\lambda}{\lambda}*$ marginal machines must be idled, and their output, $\frac{\lambda}{\lambda}*$ units of consumables, ceases. The net gain in output is $\triangle Q = 1 - \frac{\lambda}{\lambda*}$, and this is the marginal physical productivity of a machine of type λ. [In general $\triangle Q = \left[1 - \frac{\lambda}{\lambda*} \right]^+ .$]

Since λ^* is the marginal or no-rent type of machine, we know that $\lambda^* w = 1$. Thus $\triangle Q = [1 - \lambda w]^+$, or the marginal physical product of a machine of type λ is precisely the quasi-rent it earns in production. We can also calculate the value of the marginal product of a machine of type λ *per dollar of cost*. The cost of a new machine of type λ is $c(\lambda)w$. For an infra-marginal machine, the marginal product per dollar invested is thus $\frac{1 - \lambda w}{c(\lambda)w}$, But from (2),

$$(4) \qquad \frac{1 - \lambda w}{c(\lambda)w} = \frac{1}{\varphi(\rho)} = \frac{\rho}{1 - \left(\dfrac{1}{1 + \rho} \right)^L}$$

If machines were infinitely durable, (4) would say that the marginal productivity of "capital" is equal to the rate of interest. It doesn't say exactly that because what has been computed is actually the *gross* marginal productivity of capital, with no allowance for depreciation. When we remember the annuity-formula origin of $\varphi(p)$, it is clear that (4) does say that the net marginal productivity of capital is equal in equilibrium to the rate of interest.

I offer one more example to show the neo-classical content of equations (1) and (2). From (1) it follows that

$$(5) \qquad \frac{d\lambda}{d\rho} = - \frac{\varphi'(\rho)}{c''(\lambda)}.$$

Now $c''(\lambda) < 0$, as already noted; calculation shows that $\varphi'(\rho)$ has the sign of $1 + (L+1)\rho - (1+\rho)^{L+1} = 1 + (L+1)\rho - [1 + (L+1)\rho + \ldots]$ and is therefore negative. An increase in the interest rate leads to the construction of new machines of higher (i.e., less mechanized) type.

From (1) and (2) together it can be shown that

$$(6) \qquad \frac{d\lambda}{dw} = \frac{\lambda c'(\lambda) - c(\lambda)}{(1 - \lambda w)c''(\lambda)} < 0.$$

257

An increase in the wage rate leads to the construction of new machinery of lower (i.e. more mechanized) type.

Note that these are *total* derivatives. I am not holding the interest rate constant and changing the wage. Equations (1) and (2) have three unknowns; λ, ρ, and w. There is only one degree of freedom. When I change w, I calculate the change in λ with ρ changing as it has to change to preserve the validity of (1) and (2). Indeed, (5) and (6) entail that $\frac{d\rho}{dw} < 0$: if the wage rate rises, the interest rate must fall, to insure that the most profitable kind of machine to build can continue to break even, no better and no worse. (This point is a crucial one for the long-standing discussion of the effect of wage rates on the use of machinery, and its revival in Shove's famous review of Hicks. It is not enough simply to say that a change in wage rates washes out in its effect on the use of machinery, so long as the interest rate stays constant. One must be sure one has a model in which it is *possible* for the interest rate to stay fixed while the real wage moves. The model I have been describing is not like that.)

5. TECHNOLOGICAL CHANGE

Throughout this discussion, the underlying technology has been assumed to be fixed. Actually the model is a very convenient one for the study of technical progress. The simulation procedure I have outlined can easily be modified to cover regular and expected or irregular and unexpected technological changes.

Shifts in technology can be divided into two kinds, which may be described as disembodied and embodied. Disembodied improvements in technique are purely organizational; they permit more output to be produced from unchanged inputs, with no investment required. Embodied improvements in technique permit an increased output from an " ultimately " smaller input, but require the construction of new capital goods before the knowledge can be made effective. Most casual students of the problem seem to believe that the major part of observed technological progress is the embodied type, but there is very little solid information on this point.

The treatment of disembodied technical change in the model of this paper would go as follows. In the consumer-goods sector, technical progress could increase the output producible by any or all types of existing machines, without any change in the required labor complement. If the increase in capacity were the same for all machines, the technical improvement may be described as uniform. A biased technical improvement would increase the capacity of a machine of type λ from unity to some number depending on λ. It should be clear that a once-over unexpected uniform increase in productivity in the consumer-goods sector would simply have the effect of increasing real wages in the same proportion, unless the increased income of the population resulted in a change in saving and investment habits. Should increases in productivity be regular, or at least fully expected, the expectation should be incorporated into the forward-looking decision about the choice of machine-type. In the machine-building sector, the distinction between disembodied and embodied innovations comes to nothing, because I have assumed machines to be made by labor alone.

Embodied technical progress requires a more complicated accounting, because improvements are assumed to affect only those machines constructed after a given date. But it is in other ways simpler to deal with. Since machines have to be kept track of by vintage as well as by type, there is no loss in *continuing* to measure machines in units of capacity.   So the output of a machine, new or old, is one unit of consumables per year. This done, one sees that λ is after all only an *index* of machine types; before or after a technical invention, machines can be assumed to run the gamut from a very small crew to a very large one.   A new machine of type λ may look very different—indeed, may be very different—from an old machine of type λ, but the catalog of types, of labor requirements per unit of output, remains the same.   It appears, then, that all embodied technological progress can be thought of as localized in the machine-building sector. Uniform technical progress at time t_0 occurs when it becomes possible *after* t_0 to produce a machine of type λ at a cost in man-years less than $c(\lambda)$, and less in the same proportion for all values of λ. Thus, for a once-over change $c(\lambda)$ would be replaced by $\alpha c(\lambda)$, with $0 < \alpha \leq 1$; for continuing technical progress $c(\lambda)$ would be replaced by $\alpha(t)c(\lambda)$ when $0 < \alpha(t) \leq 1$, and $\alpha(t)$ is a non-increasing function of time.   Biased technical progress occurs if the function $\alpha(t)$ describing the reduction in cost of a machine is a function of λ as well.   If highly-mechanized techniques are becoming cheaper relative to labor-intensive techniques then $\alpha(t,\lambda)$ will have the property $\dfrac{\partial^2 \alpha}{\partial \lambda \partial t} > 0$.

Once the model is enlarged to include technical change in this way, other analytica steps are necessary.   In the first place, the normal expectation becomes one of rising rea wages and the assumption of static expectations will have to be abandoned.   Second, one must assume that an expectation of more or less continuous technological progress will have an effect on rates of investment.   Third, even if machines lasted forever, a gap would open between reproduction cost and market value, as a result of expected or unexpected obsolescence.   The reader can think of other problems and analytical opportunities opened by the incorporation of technical change.

6.   CONCLUSIONS AND BRIEF NOTES ON LITERATURE

I have had two main objectives in setting up and analyzing this model.   One was to demonstrate that, even in the absence of *ex post* substitutability between labor and " capital ", the neo-classical categories of thought make sense and even the neo-classical theorems continue to hold.

The second objective is for a future paper.   I am anxious to perform the machine simulation sketched in Section 3, and curious about the results.   In particular, I am interested in the answer to the following question: suppose the model were allowed to run on the basis of exogenous inputs much like the commonly-used macroeconomic time series for the U.S.; and suppose the outputs of the model were analyzed in terms of the standard (" surrogate "?) production function involving labor, " capital ", and perhaps a time trend; we know that the " data " were generated by a different model, but I wonder whether the more conventional analysis will yield approximately accurate predictions about such important economic quantities as the rate of return to social saving.

In this connection, I would like to show how the model worked out in my paper fits into the " surrogate production function " framework described by my friend Paul Samuelson in his contribution to this symposium.

The first step is to eliminate λ from equations (1) and (2).   Under my assumptions, (1) can always be inverted to give λ as a function of ρ (this is because $c''(\lambda) > 0$).   Then λ can be eliminated from (2) and what is left is a single equation involving w and ρ.   I have already (in Section 4) proved that this equation defines w as a downward-sloping function of ρ (or *vice-versa*). This function is the Factor-Price Frontier of Samuelson's paper. The trick is to find that " conventional " production function which has the same Factor-Price Frontier, or at least a close approximation.

In the case of my constant-elasticity example, $c(\lambda) = c_0 \lambda^{-\gamma}$, it can be calculated that

$$
w = \frac{\varphi^{\frac{1}{1+\gamma}}}{(\gamma c_0)^{1+\gamma} + c_0 (\gamma c_0)^{\frac{-\gamma}{1+\gamma}}} = k\varphi^{\frac{1}{1+\gamma}}
$$

where of course φ stands for $\varphi(\rho)$. Suppose that machines last forever; then $\varphi(\rho) = \dfrac{1}{\rho}$ and

$$
w = k\rho^{-\frac{1}{1+\gamma}}
$$

What surrogate production function corresponds to this? You'll never guess—it's the Cobb-Douglas with labor-elasticity $\dfrac{1+\gamma}{2+\gamma}$ and $\dfrac{1}{2+\gamma}$. Naturally these surrogate elasticities do not correspond to the relative shares deduced in (3), $\dfrac{\gamma}{1+\lambda}$ and $\dfrac{1}{1+\gamma}$.

The reason is that I have assumed machines to be made by labor alone, while Samuelson assumes the machine/labor ratio to be the same in machine production as in the consumer-goods sector. And in addition, (3) refers only to the newest machines.

The model I have used in this paper has long played a part in what might be called conversational economics. Mrs. Robinson and I have discussed it in correspondence. But it has only lately been subjected to careful analysis, and never to my knowledge in the way I have treated it here. Leif Johansen's well-known 1959 paper works in a very similar framework, but largely in the context of " warranted growth ". I think he would agree that he slurs over precisely the capital-theoretic aspects I have stressed here.

A similar model has been used in discussions of planned economic development by Maurice Dobb (*Economic Growth and Planning*, 1960), Amartya Sen (*Choice of Techniques*, 1960), and in an interesting Yale Ph.D. thesis by Mr. T. N. Srinivasan (*Investment Criteria and Choice of Techniques of Production*, 1961).

Much good sense on a related and analogous problem is to be found in W. E. G. Salter's *Productivity and Technical Change*, 1960, chapters IV and V. It seems to be that an article by D. B. Butt some years ago is also relevant here, as is his recent *On Economic Growth*, 1960. Finally, I should mention again Paul Samuelson's paper in this symposium and, on the relation between wage rates and mechanization, his contribution to the Åkerman *Festchrift*. (1961).

Cambridge, Mass. and Washington, D.C.   Robert M. Solow.

The Production Function and the Theory of Capital : A Comment

D. G. Champernowne

I. INTRODUCTION

In her note on the Production Function, Joan Robinson has drawn attention to the difficulties inherent in any attempt to measure the quantity of capital in a community by a single number, and of the consequent dangers in teaching pupils to regard output as a function of the amounts of labour and capital employed. In an effort to avoid in time " sloppy habits of thought," she has adopted the position that " when we consider what addition to productive resources a given amount of accumulation makes, we must measure capital in labour units " and hence determined a method of measuring the quantity of capital under the equilibrium conditions of a simplified model : this threw light on the manner in which the factor ratio (quantity of capital available per employed person) affected the choice of productive technique, the rate of interest and the real wage rate, and hence the distribution of product between capital and labour. For brevity we shall refer to the labour-units of quantity of capital, which Joan Robinson uses, as J.R. units.

The present comments will be directed towards the following points.

(*i*) If we propose to regard output as a function of the quantities of labour and capital employed, it is not very convenient to measure capital in J.R. units because, if we do,

(*a*) The same physical stock of capital equipment and working capital, producing the same flow of consumption goods, can appear under two equilibrium conditions, differing only in respect of the rate of interest and rate of real wages, as two different amounts of capital.

(*b*) The wage-rate of labour and the reward per unit of capital will, in general, differ under perfect competition from the partial derivatives of output with respect to the quantities of labour and capital employed.

(*c*) Output per head may be negatively correlated with quantity of capital per head measured in J.R. units, despite the assumption of a given state of technical knowledge. This can lead to the paradoxical result that a reduction of the capital per head (in J.R. units) is required to increase productivity.

(*ii*) If we abandon J.R. units of capital and employ instead a straightforward chain-index of quantity of capital, then we can again obtain, in principle, a production function $O = f(L\ C)$ with the property that the social product O is distributed into shares $L\ \frac{\partial f}{\partial L}$ for labour and $C\ \frac{\partial f}{\partial C}$ for capital.

(*iii*) A clear and rigorous deduction of these results requires a careful statement of the assumptions underlying the model and the explicit exclusion of certain exceptional cases. The exceptional cases themselves are of some interest as indicating situations where the production function is no longer single-valued and in which some of Joan Robinson's conclusions are falsified.

(*iv*) The use of the chain-index for measuring capital facilitates the discussion of the case where a " continuous spectrum " of techniques is available. The distribution of O into $L\ \frac{\partial f}{\partial L}$ and $C\ \frac{\partial f}{\partial C}$ still holds in this case.

Reprinted from *XXI* (1953–1954) 112–135 of *Review of Economic Studies* by permission of *Review of Economic Studies* published by Oliver & Boyd Ltd., Edinburgh and London. © 1954 The Economic Society.

(*v*) The remaining sections of the article are concerned with the effects of relaxing the three simplifying conventions :

     (*i*) only stationary states are to be considered and compared ;
     (*ii*) there are no technical advances ;
     (*iii*) labour and capital are the only two factors employed.

(*vi*) An appendix giving particular arithmetical and algebraic examples throws light on the working of the general model.

II. CHOICE OF UNITS FOR MEASURING QUANTITY OF CAPITAL

In her introduction, Joan Robinson complains that the student of economic theory is taught to regard output as a function of the amounts of labour and capital, but is not taught in what units the quantity of capital is to be measured. Her own answer is that under the simplified conditions which she assumes, the quantity of capital should be measured in units of labour, and should be equated to the labour input which it costs, compounded at the ruling rate of interest : if the capital has already been used to produce output, an appropriate deduction from its cost should be made on this account.

There is nothing inconsistent in this method, but it is not the only possible method and it is inconvenient if we wish to regard output as a function of the quantities of labour and capital. Suppose, for example, that as described in Joan Robinson's section " Technique of Production," there exists a hierarchy of techniques, which may become profitable at various stages of capital development. To each such technique there will correspond a range of interest rates at which it can be fully competitive (given appropriate wage-rates) compared to all other techniques. It is thus possible to conceive two stationary states, each using one and the same technique, with identical amounts and composition of capital equipment, with identical labour input and product-output : yet, although both in equilibrium, they may have differing real wage-rates, and two different interest rates, each within the range over which the technique can be fully competitive. For purposes such that output is to be regarded as technically determined by the amounts of labour and capital employed, it would be convenient to regard the quantities of capital employed in these two stationary states as the same, because the capital stock, the labour input and the output stream are identical in the two states. Yet because the rate of interest differs in the two states, the quantities of capital as measured by J.R. units must differ also.

Conversely, it is easy to see that two equilibrium stationary states may exist, with different techniques, with the same labour input, but with different interest rates, and different outputs, which will appear, with J.R. units, to have equal amounts of capital as well as of labour. Thus, whilst on the one hand the same physical capital can be measured as two different amounts of capital, yet on the other hand, the same amounts of labour and capital may result in different outputs. The function giving output in terms of the factor inputs fails to be single-valued.

These difficulties arise from the index-number problem involved in measuring the quantity of capital. They result simply from the fact that mere difference in interest rates, without necessarily corresponding to any difference in the productive possi- bilities or physical characteristics of the stocks of capital available in two stationary states, can yet affect their cost measured in J.R. units. Hence, comparing the amounts of capital in a sequence of stationary states, we shall obtain a set of numbers reflecting differences of interest rates as well as differences relevant to productive potential. There is a close analogy to an attempt to compare quantities of production by an

262

index giving their money values in a sequence of stationary states with slightly different price systems.

It may be asked whether these inconveniences disappear when we consider not a sequence of discrete equipments but a continuous spectrum, with the appropriate rate of interest altering continuously as we pass down the spectrum. The answer is that the most glaring inconveniences do disappear, but the basic weakness of the method remains : differences in interest rates which are irrelevant to the production possibilities (although not to the profit possibilities) of two sets of capital equipment still are allowed to affect the comparison of their amounts of capital when measured in J.R. units. That the distortion that this involves may be so great as to contradict common sense is suggested by the following extreme example. Suppose that there is a continuous spectrum of basic equipments E_u, with u a continuous variable. If now instead of discussing stationary states, we think of a very slow progress with constant employment, but changing type of equipment providing an increasing output, we should not go very far wrong by supposing wages and interest rates to move through the stationary state values appropriate to the various types of equipment.

Suppose that constant replacement of worn-out equipment by types providing more output per head involves the withholding of some labour from producing consumption goods, then this situation is such as is normally described as one with positive net investment, and we can legitimately require that any proposed system of measurement may show the quantity of capital to be increasing.

In Appendix II, Section II, the following simple example is discussed in some detail. Each basic equipment E_u costs the work of 100 men spread evenly over one year ; when complete, the equipment E_u needs $100u$ men to work it and produces a uniform output flow at the rate of $100 (1 + 11u)^{\frac{1}{11}}$ units per annum : at the end of one year the equipment wears out. It is shown that if 1 per cent of the labour force is withheld from other activity and devoted to replacing worn-out equipments by a (larger) number of equipments needing less men to operate them in relation to those required to build them, then as u steadily decreases and the number of equipments increases, the rate of interest will fall, real wages will rise and the output of food will rise. If in this example we use the chain-index method described in Section III below, and in Appendix I, each equipment can be regarded as 100 units of capital, and the total quantity of capital will increase at a rate of K per cent per annum where K is the proportion that the annual net income bears to the value of all capital.

Now consider how this process appears when J.R. units are used for the measurement of capital. It is shown in the Appendix that an equipment of type E_u will at the time of its use contain approximately $1,000u/\log (1 + 10u)$ J.R. units of capital. If the total number of men employed is $100N$ then the total number of equipments of type E_u is approximately $\dfrac{N}{1 + u}$, so that the total number of units of capital is approximately $1,000Nu/(1 + u) \log (1 + 10u)$. Numerical calculation shows that if $u = 2.326$ initially and capital accumulation proceeds as described above, u will fall from 2.326 towards zero, and the quantity of capital measured in J.R. units will simultaneously *fall* from about $219N$ down to $100N$. Thus, in this example, a process of capital accumulation carried out by labour withheld from making consumption goods, and financed out of saving, appears when J.R. units are used as a steady *decrease* in the quantity of capital. This is an extreme example of the negative bias induced in measurement of net investment when J.R. units are used, and this bias is due to including a negative element reflecting a fall in the rate of interest.

Thus our warning against the incautious use of J.R. units is based not merely on considerations of convenience, but also on the danger that as soon as we draw approximate conclusions from a comparison of stationary states, about a process of very slow investment, their use may cause what plainly is *positive* net investment in the customary sense of these words to appear as *negative* net investment.

Another inconvenience arising from the use of J.R. units is that if the marginal productivity of labour is obtained by partial differentiation of the production function, it will in general be found to differ from the equilibrium wage of labour, when J.R. units of capital are used, despite whatever heroic assumptions of perfect competition may be adopted. This symptom again suggests that " keeping the amount of capital constant " in J.R. units does not correspond to what is usually understood by keeping the amount of capital constant.

A natural method by which to construct an index of quantity of capital in a historical sequence would be to form a chain index, increasing the index at each step by the proportion in which the cost of the capital at current wage and interest rates at the end of the step exceeded the cost of capital at the beginning of the step, calculated at the same wage and interest rates. By shortening the steps, the distortion due to choosing wage and interest rates at the *end* of each step could be made as small as we pleased.

The same method can be used to construct an index of quantity of capital in a sequence of stationary states, and provided these are arranged in an order so that the difference between one and the next is always a small step, the distortion due to the method can again be reduced to negligible proportions. The method has the advantage that changes of cost merely due to changes in the interest rate do not affect this measure of the quantity of capital.

The technique of constructing the index number is further explained in the following section and in Appendix I. It will suffice to say here, that to a statistician accustomed to the problem of sorting out quantities from price-changes, this measure of quantity of capital would probably seem the most satisfactory one (at any rate for comparison of states fairly close together in the sequence), and that the use of this measure removes the more glaring difficulties in the way of regarding aggregate output as a function of the amounts of labour and capital employed. In particular, we shall show in Section IV that the rewards per unit of the factors are once again given by the partial derivatives of the aggregate production function if stationary state conditions with perfect competition are assumed.

A development of the theory of capital using these units needs a careful statement of the simplifying assumptions underlying the model. This is attempted in the following section, which describes a " discrete " model closely similar to that discussed by Joan Robinson.

III. SIMPLIFYING ASSUMPTIONS FOR DISCONTINUOUS MODEL

In line with Joan Robinson, we shall assume :

(*i*) The output of consumption goods is homogeneous. We shall refer to these goods as food.

(*ii*) Food may be produced in a constant stream by any of a number of techniques, each of which employs a distinctive outfit of equipment, and a constant stream of labour, part of which may be devoted to maintaining or replacing the equipment.

(*iii*) Equipment is already complete at the moment when the food stream begins to flow, having been built up by a varying stream of labour during the past.

(*iv*) For each technique constant returns prevail, in the sense that the equipment outfit and the labour stream are infinitely divisible ; that when each is multiplied by any number λ, so also is the food output stream ; and that the outputs and inputs of the sum of two or more different equipment outfits is the sum of their individual outputs and inputs.

(v) At any level of food-wages of labour, the rate of interest will settle at the highest level which any employer can pay without making losses.

(vi) The conditions of the stationary state hold, in the sense that everyone believes that prices, wage-rates of labour and interest rates will remain fixed for ever and
    either this is true
       or we retain this as a convention in calculating our rates of interest in assumption (v).

It follows that at any given food-wage-rate of labour V, there will be a rate of profit R_{vs} associated with each equipment E_s, which an employer can earn on its capital-value if he builds E_s and uses it for producing food. By assumption (v), if the rate of food-wages of labour is V, competition will drive the rate of interest to the level $R(V) = \underset{s}{Max}\ R_{vs}$ of the greatest of the R_{vs}. We may call this the competitive rate of interest at V, and when food-wages are at V, only that (those) equipment(s) E_s for which $R_{vs} = R(V)$ will be built for use. We may call this (these) equipment(s) " competitive at V."

There may be equipments which are not competitive at any V : these we shall call ineffective equipments : equipments which for some V are competitive will be called effective equipments.

In order to avoid giving special attention to possible exceptional cases, we shall introduce the following further assumptions.

(vii) There exists a finite set of " basic " equipments $E_1, E_2, \ldots, E_n$, such that any effective set of equipment is composed of one or more of these basic equipments.

It follows from assumptions (iv) and (vii) that any equipment competitive at V is composed only of those basic equipments which are competitive at V.

(viii) There is never more than one food-wage-rate at which two given basic equipments are both competitive.

(ix) Every set of values of V for which a basic equipment is competitive is a closed connected set.

From among our basic equipments select those each of which are competitive at more than one food-wage-rate, and hence over a closed range of rates. It follows from assumption (viii) that these ranges do not overlap and from (v) that between them they cover the whole range of V from O to V_{max}, the level at which the competitive interest rate is zero. Hence the ranges of V fall into a natural order and we may number our selected basic equipments accordingly $E_1, E_2, \ldots, E_m$, letting E_1 be that which is competitive at zero food-wage and E_m that which is competitive at V_{max}.

We may denote by V_1 that V at which both E_1 and E_2 are both competitive, and in general by V_s that rate at which E_s and E_{s+1} are both competitive. We may denote by R_s the competitive rate of interest at V_s, namely $R(V_s)$.

We may describe any adjacent pair of equipments E_s and E_{s+1} as consecutive equipments.

At this point we part company with Joan Robinson and introduce a definition about quantity of capital which conflicts with any use of J.R. units.

DEFINITION.   The ratio of the quantities of capital in any two equipments which are both competitive at the same rate of interest (and food-wage-rate)[1] is equal to the ratio of their costs calculated at that rate of interest (and food-wage-rate).

[1] The reference to the food-wage-rate is not essential to the definition, but is included in order to facilitate the extension of the definition to the case with many factors employed.

Since this definition applies to every pair of consecutive equipments, it determines the amount of capital in every one of the selected basic equipments, save for an arbitrary multiplying constant. It does this without contradiction, since the assumptions ensure that none of them is competitive at the same rate of interest as is any other except the two adjacent to it in the sequence : moreover, any consecutive pair E_s and E_{s+1} compete at a unique rate of interest R_s. The definition also covers without ambiguity those basic equipments which are competitive at only one interest rate. To extend the measure to mixed equipments composed of more than one basic equipment we adopt the following definition :

DEFINITION. The quantity of capital in any mixed equipment is the total of the quantities in the basic equipments of which it is composed.

We refer to this method of comparing the amounts of capital in different effective equipments as the chain index method, because of the obvious analogy with a chain index of quantities. The extension of the definition to the case where basic equipments form a continuous spectrum, instead of a sequence, is discussed in Appendix I.

IV. THE EQUALITY OF MARGINAL PRODUCT AND REWARD

Let E and E' be any two equipments both competitive at the rate of interest $R(V)$. Let employer A employ quantities Y of E and Y' of E', but employer B use quantities $Y + y$ of E and $Y' - y$ of E'. Then the cost at food-wage-rate V and interest rate $R(V)$, of the total equipment of each employer is the same. Hence the interest paid by each employer is the same. Hence, interest rates being at the competitive level $R(V)$ proper to V, the difference in the two wage-bills must equal the difference between the values of the two product-flows, since under competition profits of each employer are zero. It follows that the extra product of the employer employing the more labour is just sufficient to pay the wages of that labour at the competitive rate, or in technical language the competitive wage of labour equals the marginal product of labour, the quantity of capital being held constant.

This may be expressed algebraically as :

$$w_x = \frac{\partial}{\partial x} f(x, z) \dots\dots\dots\dots\dots\dots\dots\dots\dots\dots\dots\dots\dots\dots\dots (4.1)$$

where w_x is the food-wage of labour,
     x is the amount of labour employed,
     z is the quantity of capital,
   $f(x, z)$ is the flow of product from these quantities of factors.

Now by our assumption (*iv*) of constant returns $f(\lambda x, \lambda z) = \lambda f(x, z)$ for all real λ and hence :

$$x \frac{\partial f}{\partial x} + z \frac{\partial f}{\partial z} \equiv f \dots\dots\dots\dots\dots\dots\dots\dots\dots\dots\dots\dots\dots\dots\dots (4.2)$$

Also under competition, by assumption (*v*) :

$$x\, w_x + z\, w_z = f \dots\dots\dots\dots\dots\dots\dots\dots\dots\dots\dots\dots\dots\dots\dots (4.3)$$

where w_z is the food-reward under competition of each unit of capital.

Hence $z w_z \equiv f - x\, w_x \equiv f - x\, \dfrac{\partial f}{\partial x} \equiv z\, \dfrac{\partial f}{\partial z}$

Hence $w_z \equiv \dfrac{\partial f}{\partial z}$ ....(4.4)

or in other words, the reward of each unit of capital is equal in value to its marginal social product.

Our method has thus the added convenience that it provides a means of expressing capital as a quantity and yet enabling us still to say that under perfect competition the two factors, labour and capital, are each paid according to their marginal productivity to society.

V. POSSIBLE ANOMALIES IN THE TWO--FACTOR MODEL

It may seem intuitively obvious that the function $f(x\, z)$ expressing output as a function of labour and capital must be single-valued. But our assumptions are not sufficient to ensure this.

Let $f(1, z) = \phi(z)$ then by our assumption of constant returns $f(x, z) = x\, \phi\left(\dfrac{z}{x}\right)$ so that a knowledge of $\phi(z)$ is sufficient for a knowledge of $f(x, z)$.

Contrary to intuitive expectation, our assumptions do not ensure that a graph of $\phi(z)$ is a single-valued curve sloping upwards to the right. For example, a graph of the form shown in Fig. 1 is quite possible.

The further assumption that is needed in order to eliminate this possibility is that of two equipments E_{s-1} and E_s (both competitive at R_{s-1}), E_s (that competitive at the lower range of interest) will have the higher productivity, i.e. the higher ratio of food output to labour input. Under this assumption a gradual fall in the rate of interest would entail increases both in productivity and in the quantity of capital per head. But although this may fit in well with our preconceived notions, there is no logical justification for the assumption. It is logically possible that over certain ranges of the rate of interest, a fall in interest rates and rise in food-wages will be accompanied by a *fall* in output per head and a *fall* in the quantity of capital per head.

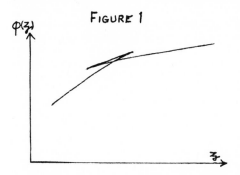

FIGURE 1

Suppose now, that instead of comparing stationary states, we are considering a sequence of states in time. If we conceive of the rise in food-wages and the accompanying fall in the rate of interest as being caused by a steady process of net investment, with all labour employed, it is interesting to consider what would happen next when a further rise in real wages and fall in the rate of interest would make competitive only equipment with lower productivity and employing *more* men per unit quantity, and thus requiring negative net investment. Presumably, the only way that investment could remain positive without a prolonged interval of disinvestment would be for food-wages to leap up and the rate of interest to leap down to levels where capital equipment even more productive than that in existence became competitive.

The fall in the rate of interest would be sufficient despite offsetting factors to cause a sudden increase in the (demand) value of existing capital equipment bringing windfall gains to its owners : on the other hand, the rise in wages would be sufficient, despite offsetting factors, to raise the replacement cost of existing equipment even more than its (demand) value, so that no more of it would be produced. During the switch to the new type of equipment it would no longer be true that the factor-rewards were equal to the values of their marginal products. A fuller discussion of this case is given in Appendix II.

A related inadequacy of our model arises in connection with our assumption (*ix*). This rules out the possibility that an equipment may be competitive over *two* ranges of the rate of interest, although not competitive over an intermediate range. This assumption is necessary in order to get neat results, and intuition suggests that the excluded case is unrealistic, but it is shown in the Appendix by simple numerical examples that there is no logical justification for the assumption : it is as easy to imagine a world featuring the excluded case as one free of it. If we drop assumption (*ix*) we admit again the possibility of two stationary states each using the same items of equipment and labour force, yet being shown as using different quantities of capital, merely on account of having different rates of interest and of food-wages.

VI. ACCUMULATION AND TECHNICAL PROGRESS

The model which we have so far discussed suffers from three serious limitations.

(*i*) It is confined to stationary states.
(*ii*) A given state of technical knowledge is assumed.
(*iii*) Labour and capital are the only two factors of production.

The concluding sections of the article will be concerned with the extension of the theory to the case where more than two factors are employed, but before advancing to this, it is worth while to consider what interest our results may have in spite of the two other limitations (*i*) and (*ii*).

Joan Robinson has pointed out that a rigorous discussion of the theory under conditions of steady increase in capital per head would be excessively complicated. However, the interest of a comparison of a sequence of stationary states is due to the presumption that this will give us a first approximation to a comparison of successive positions in a slow process of steady accumulation. This presumption is far stronger when we are considering a spectrum of basic equipments E_u, with u a continuous variable, than when the basic equipments form a discrete series E_s with s 1, 2, 3, ... n.

Provided that R, the rate of interest, is now regarded as the short-term rate, and employment is assumed constant, it is reasonable to expect that where the rate of net investment is of the first order of small quantities, then by using the stationary state analysis to provide snapshots of stages in a process of growth we shall incur errors only of the second order of small quantities. The result suggested by the above theory is that we may then regard output as determined by a function of the amounts of labour and capital employed, where capital itself is increasing at a rate equal to the net rate of saving measured in our units of capital. The rewards of the two factors at any stage may be found by the usual marginal rule : in particular, the investment will increase or decrease the relative share of capital according as the elasticity of substitution of capital for labour is greater or less than unity. On the other hand, it is worth noting that the *mere* knowledge of the production function, although it enables us to obtain the reward per unit of capital at each point, cannot of itself enable us to calculate the rate of interest at any point without further information.

It is reassuring to find that the orthodox analysis fits in so well with the new presentation, once a convenient method has been found for measuring the quantity of capital. But this does not mean that the new presentation adds nothing to the old. It shows that the form of the production function cannot be properly known until the whole history of the advancing economy is known : for it is only then that the quantity of capital can be appropriately measured. This capital must be a balanced outfit as regards age-distribution, and must include capital equipment under construction sufficient to enable the balanced outfit to be maintained. Similarly, the labour employed must include labour engaged in replacing and maintaining capital equipment. The appropriate definition of output is net output, i.e. output excluding maintenance and replacement of capital equipment : similarly, the appropriate concepts of saving and investment are net concepts, giving the excess of net output over consumption output, so that investment is equal in value to the rate of increase in the quantity of capital, as well as to the rate of saving. There is room for argument whether this concept of saving is the one that may most reasonably be regarded as a function of income, but this argument is quite distinct from any of the topics discussed in this article. It is, however, relevant to the question of the rate at which the accumulation of capital is likely to continue in any given model : this question we shall not pursue here.

In real life, the introduction of more productive capital equipment takes place most often because of advances in technical knowledge. Such investment lies outside the scope of the model so far discussed. The production function itself depends upon the state of technical knowledge, and the results we have obtained depend on the assumption that nobody expects technical advances to be made. New technical discoveries would involve a change in the whole production function and an entirely new theory is required to investigate the effects of this.

The difficulty of tracing the effects of technical advance in a model like ours lies in the need to decide which capital equipment after the change can be provided without further saving, and with constant employment, to replace the existing equipment as it wears out. The difficulty of this decision is due to the difference in the times required to build up different types of equipment.

These difficulties may be side-tracked by assuming the simple conditions of the model discussed above in Section II and again in Appendix II, Section II. Here each equipment costs the labour of 100 men spread over one year : it needs $100u$ men to operate it and produces $100\phi (u)$ tons of food over one year, at the end of which it wears out. It is easily shown that in this case the wage of labour is the slope of the curve relating $\phi(u)$ to u, and the relative share of labour is $\left(1 + \dfrac{1}{u}\right)$ times the slope of the curve relating $\log \phi(u)$ to $\log u$. Retaining the simplifying assumptions, we may represent a technical advance by a transference from the curve $\phi(u)$ to some higher curve $\psi(u)$: moreover, in virtue of our special assumptions, the effect of the advance will be a move from a point on the $\phi(u)$ curve to a point on the $\psi(u)$ with u unchanged. The new wage will be given by the slope of the $\psi(u)$ curve at this point and the new relative share of labour will be $\left(1 + \dfrac{1}{u}\right)$ times the slope at the corresponding point of the curve relating $\log \psi(u)$ to $\log u$.

Roughly speaking, we may regard capital-saving inventions as having the effect :

(a) $\psi(\theta u) \equiv \theta\phi(u)$ $\theta > 1$;

and inventions which economise labour in the using of equipment as having the effect :

(b) $\psi(\theta u) \equiv \phi(u)$ $\theta < 1$;

and inventions which economise labour equally in the building of equipment and in the use of equipment as having the effect :

(c) $\psi(u) \equiv \theta\phi(u)$ $\theta > 1$.

If for further simplicity we supposed $\phi(u)$ to have been such that the relative share of labour was insensitive to changes in the factor-ratio, this would be supposing that the slope of the curve relating log $\phi(u)$ to log u, was approximately proportionate to $\left(1 + \dfrac{1}{u}\right)$ It could then be shown that the effects of the three types of technical advance would be :

    (a) to increase wages but decrease labour's relative share ;
    (b) to increase wages and increase labour's relative share ;
    (c) to increase wages but leave the relative shares unchanged.

These results could most easily be obtained by considering the effects at given u, on the slope of the curve relating log $\phi(u)$ to log u, of a uniform shift of the curve ·

    (a) at 45 degrees upwards and to the right ;
    (b) to the left ;
    (c) upwards.

These results, whilst being suggestive and of some interest in their context, depend on the extra set of simplifying assumptions built into the model for this purpose : these assumptions exclude any differences in the construction-periods of different types of equipment. We shall not attempt to analyse the effects of technical advance when this assumption is relaxed.

The remainder of the article will be concerned with the removal of our other simplifying assumption that only two factors, labour and capital, are employed.

VII. EXTENSION OF THEORY TO CASE WHERE THREE FACTORS ARE EMPLOYED

It is possible to extend the above theory to the case where several homogeneous factors are employed with equipment, if we limit attention to the production function for the economy as a whole, and if the amounts employed of the homogeneous factors in the economy as a whole are fixed or in fixed proportions. In this case, we may define a composite factor, composed of the homogeneous factors, combined in the given fixed proportions, and regard output in the economy as a whole as a function of the amounts employed of the composite factor and of capital. It is possible to measure capital in such a manner that in any stationary state equilibrium, units of capital and units of the composite factor will be rewarded according to their marginal productivity.

The extension of the earlier theory is not quite so straightforward as might be supposed owing to the fact that the relative cost of two outfits of equipment will no longer depend only on the rate of interest, but also on the relative wage-rates of the various homogeneous factors. This complication is sufficiently serious to wreck any attempt to regard output as a function of the quantity of capital and the amounts of the homogeneous factors, *each* homogeneous factor being paid according to its marginal product.

The possibilities and limitations of the extended theory may be adequately illustrated by a consideration of the case where there are two homogeneous factors, labour and land.

We first amend our assumptions of Section II (*i*) to (*vi*) by inserting the words " and land " after " labour " whenever it occurs.

We now note, as a consequence of our assumptions, that at any pair (V, W) of food-wage-rates of labour and land there will be a rate of interest R_λ, $_{VW}$ which an employer can just afford on its capital cost if he builds E_λ and uses it for producing food. By assumption (*v*) if the food-wages of labour and land are (*V, W*) competition will drive the rate of interest to the level

$$R(V, W) = \underset{\lambda}{Max} R_{\lambda, VW} \quad \dots\dots\dots\dots\dots\dots\dots\dots\dots\dots\dots\dots\dots\dots(7.1)$$

of the greatest of the $R_{\lambda, VW}$. We may call this the competitive rate of interest at (*V, W*). When food-wages of labour and land are at (*V, W*) only that (those) equipment(s) E_{λ} will be built for which $R_{\lambda, VW} = R (V, W)$ we may call these equipments "competitive at (*V, W*)."

Equipments competitive at some (*V, W*) will be called effective, the others will be called ineffective.

We now introduce assumption (*vii*) unmodified. It follows from this assumption that any equipment competitive at *VW* is composed of basic equipments effective at *VW*.

We modify assumption (*viii*) to the form,

(*viii*) There is no closed region of finite area, of the plane of (*V, W*) throughout which two basic equipments are both competitive.

(*ix*) Every set of the values of (*V, W*) for which a basic equipment is competitive is a closed connected set

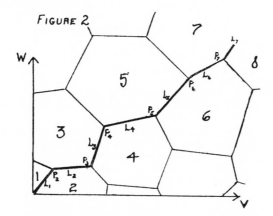

FIGURE 2

It is helpful at this stage to consider Fig. 2, showing which basic equipments are competitive at various wage-rates *V, W*.

Each cell of the diagram represents a region of (*V, W*) in which one particular basic equipment is competitive (the cells have for simplicity been drawn as hexagonal with straight sides, but, in general, the sides will be curved and the number of vertices may vary from cell to cell). If we imagine *R* rate of interest to be measured along a third axis, then we may regard the diagram as showing a lot of intersecting surfaces, only that with the highest *R*, appearing above each point (*V, W*). Where rents are high and wages low, the competitive equipment is likely to employ a high proportion of labour to land and vice versa : hence, if we divide the basic equipments into those with more men per acre, and those with less men per acre than the density laid down for the economy as a whole, the two types are likely to be separated on our diagram by a critical boundary such as that shown by the double line, those employing many men per acre lying above it.

It is clear that the only pairs of wage-rates which will allow a stationary state employing the required number of men per acre will be those corresponding to points on the critical boundary which we have just described. For only when (V, W) is any such point will it be possible to combine a basic equipment employing less than the required number of men per acre with one employing more than it, and thus to employ the correct number of men per acre in the economy as a whole.

Having found the critical boundary we may number off the basic equipments whose cells have edges along the boundary, odd numbers lying to one side, and even numbers to the other side of it. To each consecutive pair will correspond cells with a common edge along the critical boundary, and from such a pair we may construct a composite equipment employing the correct number of men per acre. Let the composite equipment composed of basic equipments E_s and E_{s+1} be called F_s, then the points (V, W) at which F_s is competitive form that segment of the critical boundary which joins the cells of E_s and E_{s+1}: call this segment L_s. Finally, let the point where L_{s-1} meets L_s be called P_s: then at the wage-rates (V, W) represented by P_s, both composite equipments F_{s-1} and F_s are competitive, and so is any combination of them.

From this point, the theory proceeds as in the case of two factors only. The composite equipments $F_1 \ldots F_{m-1}$ now take the place of the basic equipments $E_1, E_2 \ldots E_m$ of the two-factor theory. Analogously to that theory, we compare the quantities of capital in two consecutive composite equipments, by costing them at the factor-wages (VW) at which both are competitive, and at the rate of interest which is competitive at that rate. The composite equipment all employs the same number of men per acre, so we may measure men and land in terms of a composite factor embodying men and land in that proportion. When this is done output may be expressed as a function of quantity of capital and quantity of composite factor, and it follows by the same argument as before that in each stationary state, units of capital and units of the composite factor will each be paid according to their marginal productivity.

This extended theory is, however, limited by the fact that quantity of capital has been defined only for composite equipments and not for basic equipments. In any stationary state which does not employ land and labour in the specified proportions, the quantity of capital remains undefined. Hence, we cannot speak of the marginal productivity of labour, the quantities of land and capital being kept constant. Any attempt to define quantity of capital to cover these situations, and to develop a function relating output $f(x, y, z)$ to the quantities of labour, land and capital will fail to satisfy the hoped-for equations:

$$w_x \equiv \frac{\partial f}{\partial x} \qquad w_y \equiv \frac{\partial f}{\partial y} \qquad w_z \equiv \frac{\partial f}{\partial z} \quad \ldots\ldots\ldots\ldots\ldots\ldots\ldots(7.2)$$

where w_x, w_z, w_z denote the wage-rates of the three factors.

This failure springs from the fact that the ratio of the costs of two consecutive basic equipments E_s and E_{s+1} will *not* in general be the same at the wage-rates and competitive interest rates corresponding to the two points P_s and P_{s+1}, at *both* of which the two basic equipments are competitive. This divergence is associated with changes in the relative wage-rates of labour and land and to the fact that the two basic equipments embody different proportions of land and labour.

It is a matter of interest that the quantities of capital can still be compared as between the *odd*-numbered basic equipments—namely those employing *more* than the required number of men per acre. To compare the quantities of capital in basic equipment E_{2s-1} and E_{2s+1} we simply compare their costs in the only situation in which both are competitive, namely at the wage-rates and interest rates proper to P_{2s} : similarly, we may compare the quantities of capital in even-numbered basic equipments (those using *less* than the required number of men per acre). But we cannot satisfactorily compare the amount of capital in basic equipments using more than the required number of men per acre with that in those using less. To loosen the style let us call these two types of capital labour-using and land-using.

We can regard output as a function of four variables, namely the amounts of labour x, land y, labour-using capital z_1 and land-using capital z_2, provided we confine attention to those stationary states in which wage-rates and interest rates are at such levels that it would be *possible* to produce without loss, using the required number of men per acre. This may still allow considerable variation of the number of men employed per acre, as it includes the possibility of using either only land-using equipment or only labour-using equipment. Although there are four factors, there are from a technical point of view only three degrees of freedom in varying them, so that only a three-dimensional subset in the region (x, y, z_1, z_2) represent combinations of factors which are technically possible. When, therefore, we represent output as a function $O \equiv f(x, y, z_1, z_2)$ of technically possible combinations of the four factors, we cannot in general give meaning to the partial derivatives, and so we cannot say that each factor is rewarded according to its marginal product.

But an analogous proposition can be established, namely, that if $(\triangle x, \triangle y, \triangle z_1, \triangle z_2)$ represents any technically possible small variation in the amounts of the four factors, then :

$$\triangle f \equiv Wx \triangle x + Wy \triangle y + Wz_1 \triangle z_1 + Wz_2 \triangle z_2 \quad \dots\dots\dots\dots\dots\dots\dots (7.3)$$

where Wx, Wy, Wz_1, Wz_2 are the wage-rates of the four factors before the change. This proposition asserts that any combination of factors which has a productivity at the margin receives a wage-rate equal to that marginal product. This proposition will apply for example to appropriate combinations of any pair of the four factors.

The need for measuring capital by the two variables z_1 and z_2 arises from the fact that the wage-rates of labour-using capital and land-using capital will be in different ratio to one another in different stationary states.

VIII. EXTENSION OF THEORY TO THE CASE WHERE SEVERAL FACTORS ARE EMPLOYED

Even in the case where only land, labour and equipment were employed, a rigorous statement of the simplifying assumptions needed for clear-cut results has not been achieved. Many of our assumptions were packed into the drawing of Fig. 2, where we placed the numbered cells neatly along a corridor without thorough supporting discussion.

This topological device does not spring so readily to hand when we extend the discussion to the case where several factors are employed, and one can only suggest by analogy what results should be obtainable from a proper enlargement of the simplifying assumptions to that case.

If the quantities employed (or their proportions) of the homogeneous factors are fixed for the economy as a whole, we should still be able to express output as a function of the quantities employed of :

(*i*) a single composite factor,
(*ii*) capital,

and in such a way that both the composite factor and capital would, in each permissible stationary state, be rewarded according to its marginal product.

273

But if we wish to construct a function of output to cover cases where the quantities of homogeneous factors employed are *not* in the required proportions, we should have to represent capital by as many variables as there are homogeneous factors. In this case, marginal adjustments to the quantities of factors would in general involve combinations of them. It should be possible to prove that in each of certain permissible stationary states any such combination of factors would receive a wage-rate equal to its marginal productivity.

IX. ACKNOWLEDGMENT

I have been greatly helped in the writing of this article by criticism from Mrs. Robinson, Professor Kahn and Mr. Johnson, and by instruction from Mr. Kaldor. I need only add the customary rider that none of them bears any responsibility for the short-comings of the article.

APPENDIX I

THE CHAIN INDEX METHOD OF MEASURING CAPITAL

In Section IV a definition was given which determined the amounts of capital in each of a discrete series of selected basic equipments. This definition may be reformulated as follows : The unit of capital is so defined that where $C(s, R, V)$ denotes the cost per unit of capital, of equipment type E_s at interest rate R and wage-rate V, then for all s, V :

$$C(s, R_s\ V) = C(s + 1,\ R_s,\ V)$$

where R_s denotes that rate of interest at which both the consecutive equipments E_s and $E_s + 1$ are competitive.

When we consider a continuous spectrum of equipments E_u with u a continuous variable, we may adapt this definition as follows : Let $C(u, R, V)$ denote the cost per unit of capital of equipment of type E_u at rate of interest R and wage-rate V, the units of capital must be such that for all u and V,

$$\left\{ \frac{\partial}{\partial u}\ C(u, R, V) \right\}_{R\ =\ R_u} = 0$$

where R_u is the rate of interest at which E_u is competitive.

APPENDIX II

NUMERICAL EXAMPLES

I. SIMPLIFIED TWO-FACTOR MODEL WITH A FINITE SEQUENCE OF BASIC EQUIPMENTS

Suppose that there are N basic equipments $E_1, E_2 \ldots E_N$. Let x_s be the number of men required to operate and maintain E_s and let O_s be the annual food output produced by E_s. Let the cost of E_s consist of the expenditure of X_s man-years of labour during a short interval of time at T_s years before the food flow begins. If we define date of completion of the machine to be that at which the food flow begins, then the food cost of E_s at the date of completion is given by :

$$C_s = VX_s\ e^{RT_s} \dots\dots\dots\dots\dots\dots\dots\dots\dots\dots\dots\dots\dots\dots\dots\dots\dots\dots(1.1)$$

where R is the rate of interest and V the food-wage-rate.

274

Suppose that each E_s can be maintained permanently. The highest interest rate R_{vs} which can be afforded with E_s at wage-rate V is given by :

$$O_s = V\{ x_s + R_{vs}X_s e^{R_{vs}T_s} \} \dots\dots\dots\dots\dots\dots\dots\dots\dots\dots\dots (1.2)$$

(i) Numerical example involving no anomalies

Suppose that there are four basic equipments and that their technical coefficients $x_s \; O_s \; T_s \; X_s$ are those given in the following table.

s	x_s	O_s	T_s	X_s
1	4	10	0	20
2	3	9	1	17.193
3	2	7	2	14.920
4	1	4	4	10.054

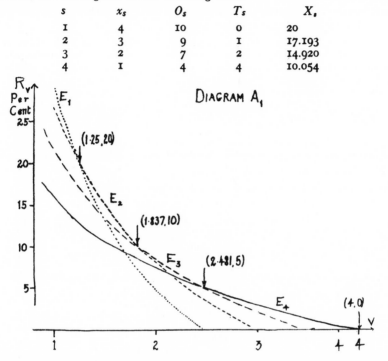

The values of R_{vs} calculated for formula (2) are shown for each equipment, for food wages in the range one to four tons of food per annum, in Diagram A_1. The competitive interest rate at each food-wage is shown by the envelope of the four curves. It can be seen from the diagram that for food-wages up to and including 1.25 tons of food per annum, equipment 1 is competitive : in the range 1.25 to 1.837 tons of food per annum, inclusive, equipment 2 is competitive : in the range 1.837 to 2.481 tons of food per annum, inclusive, equipment 3 is competitive : and in the range 2.481 to 4 tons of food per annum, inclusive, equipment 4 is competitive. At food-wages exceeding 4 tons per annum, the wage-bill would exceed the maximum national income technically possible.

We may distinguish two possible kinds of stationary state :

(i) Pure—employing only one basic type of equipment. The food-wage-rate may be at any level at which that basic equipment is competitive, and the rate of interest will be at the corresponding competitive level.

(*ii*) Mixed—employing some combination of a consecutive pair of equipments at the food-wage level at which both are competitive, and at the competitive level of the rate of interest.

In our model, just three mixed types of stationary state are possible :

(*i*) Employing a combination of E_1 and E_2 at a wage of 1.25 tons of food per annum and interest rate 20 per cent per annum.

(*ii*) Employing a combination of E_2 and E_3 at a wage of 1.837 tons of food per annum and interest rate 10 per cent per annum.

(*iii*) Employing a combination of E_3 and E_4 at a wage of 2.481 tons of food per annum and interest rate 5 per cent per annum.

To establish what quantity of capital is embodied in a unit of each of the four basic equipments we merely compare the costs in each consecutive pair at the rate of interest at which they compete. We find that at a rate of interest of 20 per cent the cost of items of equipments 1 and 2 are in ratio 20 : 21. At a rate of interest of 10 per cent, items of equipments of types 2 and 3 have costs in ratio 34.89 : 33.26. At a rate of interest of 5 per cent items of equipments of types 3 and 4 have costs in ratio 40.76 : 30.38. Accordingly, we take units of the four basic types of equipment to represent quantities of capital 20, 21, 20.16 and 14.96.

Food output may now be uniquely expressed in terms of the amounts $x\ z$ of labour and capital employed : we find it correctly given (in tons of food per annum) by

$f(x\ z) \equiv 1.250x + 0.25z$ where $5x \leqslant z \leqslant 7x$

$f(x\ z) \equiv 1.837x + 0.1661z$ where $7x \leqslant z \leqslant 10.08x$

$f(x\ z) \equiv 2.481x + 0.1011z$ where $10.08x \leqslant z \leqslant 14.96x$ ....(1.3)

The three forms of the equation correspond to the three mixed types of stationary state and they overlap at the two pure types with basic equipments 2 and 3.

In every stationary state of mixed type labour is paid a wage equal to $\frac{\partial f}{\partial x}$, the coefficient of x in the production function : and each unit quantity of capital earns $\frac{\partial f}{\partial z}$, the coefficient of z. In the pure types with basic equipments 2 and 3 the appropriate equation to use in calculating marginal productivity differs according to whether an increase or decrease is considered. In these pure types the factors are rewarded at rates within the closed ranges terminating in their two marginal productivities. In the pure state, with only equipment type 1, the marginal productivities give an upper limit to wage-rates and a lower limit to the reward of each unit of capital. In that with only type 4 they give a lower limit for wage-rates and an upper limit for the reward of each unit of capital.

Diagram A_2 (overleaf), which shows $\frac{f(x\ z)}{x}$ plotted against $\frac{z}{x}$ further illustrates the form of the production function in this example.

From our knowledge of $f(x\ z)$ we can calculate how labour's relative share of output varies with the quantity of capital employed per head. This brings out clearly the phenomena which Joan Robinson describes in connection with the Wicksell effect and the Ricardo effect.

Increases in labour's share only " take place " on the three occasions when the conditions are those of a pure stationary state : all increases of capital per head from one stationary state to another within the same mixed class involves an increase in output which accrues wholly to the owners of capital.

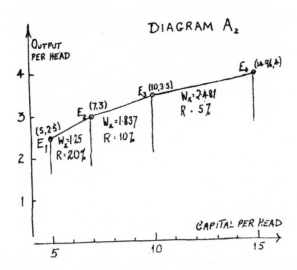

DIAGRAM A₂

(ii) Exceptional case

To illustrate the anomalies which may arise when food-wages and productivity vary inversely, consider the model represented by the following table, which superficially represents the normal example we have just discussed.

s	x_s	O_s	T_s	X_s
1	4	12	0	20
2	2	9	0	20
3	4	16	4	20.854
4	2	10	4	21.221

When we calculate the interest rates R_{vs} at which the four equipments can compete at various food-wage-rates, we find E_1 competitive above 20 per cent, E_2 in the range 10 to 20 per cent, E_3 in the range 5 to 10 per cent and E_4 at 5 per cent. Following our earlier procedure, we should argue that three mixed types of stationary state are possible, E_1 and E_2 ; E_2 and E_3 ; and E_3 and E_4 ; the three appropriate pairs of values of the food-wage and interest rate being (1.5, 20 per cent), (2.25, 10 per cent) and (3.034, 5 per cent).

In order to consider the production function, let us now assign a quantitative measure of capital as before. E_1 and E_2 may each count as 20 units ; E_2 and E_3 compete at 10 per cent and the ratio of their costs is then 20 : 31.11, so E_3 must be taken as 31.11 units. E_4 and E_3 at all rates of interest have their costs in the ratio 21.221 : 20.854 ; applying this ratio to 31.11, we find that E_4 must represent 31.657 units of capital.

We may now draw up a table showing for each of the four equipments, O_s the food output, x_s the number of persons employed, z_s the quantity of capital, and hence capital per head z_s/x_s, and output per head O_s/z_s.

We could construct a diagram[1] showing the output per head as a function of capital per head in the various possible stationary states ; the points for mixed types

---

[1] This diagram is not shown, but its main features would be the same as those of Fig. 1 above.

	Output	Employment	Quantity of capital	Capital per head	Output per head
s					
1	12	4	20	5	3
2	9	2	20	10	4.5
3	16	4	31.11	7.777	4
4	10	2	31.657	15.828	5

again being obtained by drawing straight lines to join the pair of points relating to the consecutive pair of equipments which are combined. We may also write down the production function $f(x\ z)$ as :

$$f(x, z) \equiv 1.5x + 0.3z \qquad 5x \leqslant z \leqslant 10x$$

$$f(x, z) \equiv 2.25x + 0.225z \qquad 7.777x \leqslant z \leqslant 10x$$

$$f(x, z) \equiv 3.034x + 0.124z \qquad 7.777x \leqslant z \leqslant 15.828x \quad \ldots\ldots\ldots\ldots\ldots (1.4)$$

These three forms corresponding to the three mixed types of stationary state, (E_1, E_2), (E_2, E_3) and (E_3, E_4).

This production function is triple-valued for those values of x and z such that $7.777x < y < 10x$. This is no paradox, since the function merely tells about various possible stationary states. The function preserves the property that each factor is paid a wage equal to its marginal product : thus $W_x = \dfrac{\partial f}{\partial x}$ and $W_z = \dfrac{\partial f}{\partial z}$ in all the mixed-type stationary states.

This triple-valued feature of the production function cannot be attributed to our method of measuring the quantities of capital per head in E_2 and E_3 : for any plausible method would ascribe more capital per head to E_2 than to E_3 : for example, Joan Robinson's method would give as large or larger a margin in the factor ratio.

It may again be objected that no employer in his senses would use E_3 and E_4 in the combination with the same factor ratio as E_2, since he could obtain higher output per head by using E_2 : the answer is that if wage-rates were at 3,034 tons of food per annum, then E_3 and E_4 could compete at 5 per cent, but E_2 could not. *At this interest rate of 5 per cent*, unit quantity of E_2 would cost considerably more than unit quantity of E_3 or E_4, and so much so as more than to offset the advantage in productivity.

Although the production function is quite satisfactory for describing possible stationary states it is in this case definitely inconvenient for illustrating a time-sequence. Suppose an economy, at constant employment, slowly, out of its saving, to have converted from E_1 to E_2 equipment. Wages have stood at 1.5 tons of food per annum and interest rates at 20 per cent. If, after the conversion, wages rise just above 2.25 tons of food and interest rates fall just below 10 per cent, E_3 will become the only competitive equipment, and E_2 will still be more nearly competitive than E_4. But any attempt to use E_3 must *lower* the national income and *decrease* the quantity of capital employed, on account of its lower productivity and lower factor ratio than E_2. The only way positive net investment and the rise in productivity can continue uninterrupted is for real wages to jump up to above 3.034 and interest rates fall below 5 per cent. If this is done, there will ensue a period of conversion from E_2 to E_4, and the economy will for a time be a mixture of E_2 and E_4. But such a mixture is certainly not possible in a stationary state, since there is no real wage-rate and rate of interest at which E_2 and E_4 are both competitive.

In our particular example we have assumed that the equipments never need replacement, but the same features of a multi-valued production can arise without this simplifying device. Suppose for the moment that the equipment needs renewal after a certain life, then if the rate of interest had been pushed down to the level at which E_4 is competitive, E_2 would fail by a considerable margin to be competitive. All E_2 would be replaced by E_4 as it fell due, and unless the life of E_2 was long, this would represent a tremendous demand on the investment industries—so that the capital per head could increase from 10 to 15.828 during one life-time of an E_2 equipment. This would take us far from the conditions of slow and gradual accumulation, to which our model, with its expectation of constant conditions, had a limited relevance.

The outcome of this discussion is that, although our method of measuring quantity of capital provides us with a production function satisfactory for describing the family of stationary states, formidable difficulties arise when we consider a sequence of states in time in a developing economy, unless we rule out cases in which a lowering of interest rates can cause the introduction of techniques with a *lower* productivity than those used up till then. A numerical example has shown that these cases cannot be ruled out merely on logical grounds.

To illustrate the case where assumption (*ix*) breaks down so that an equipment is competitive over each of two separated intervals of V, consider the position when, of our four equipments, only E_2 and E_3 have been invented. The condition that both E_2 and E_3 should be competitive at the interest rate R may be expressed :

$$\frac{x_2 + Re^{T_2R}X_2}{O_2} = \frac{x_3 + Re^{T_3R}X_3}{O_3} \qquad \dots\dots\dots\dots\dots\dots\dots(1.5)$$

so that substituting numerical values :

$$\frac{2 + 20R}{9} = \frac{4 + 20\,854Re^{4R}}{16}$$

Therefore $R\{\,320 - 187.686e^{4R}\,\} = 4$ $\qquad \dots\dots\dots\dots\dots\dots\dots\dots\dots(1.6)$

It may be verified that there are two positive solutions for R, namely $R = 0.3$ and $R = 0.0402$.

The corresponding food-wage-rates are 2.25 and 3.21. We find that for wage-rates below 2.25 E_2 is competitive, for wage-rates between 2.25 and 3.21 E_3 is competitive, and for wage-rates from 3.21 to 4.5 E_2 is competitive.

Moreover, since E_2 and E_3 are both competitive at $(V, R) = (2.25, 10$ per cent$)$ and also at $(3.21, 4.02$ per cent$)$, there are two possible bases for comparing the quantities of capital in E_2 and E_3. Counting E_3 as 31.11 units as before, the two possible methods ascribe to E_2 either 20 units or 25.4 units.

The formal solution is to regard E_2 as 20 units if it is used at a rate of interest of 10 per cent or over, and as 25.4 units if it is used at a rate of 4.02 per cent or less. This procedure has, however, little to recommend it, apart from its enabling one still to regard the factors as being rewarded according to their marginal productivity.

One final and somewhat fanciful remark may be made with reference to this example. Two mixed types of stationary state using E_2 and E_3 are possible, one at $(V\,R) = (2.25, 10$ per cent$)$ and one at $(3.21, 4.02$ per cent$)$. Both use the same equipment, but the question of which $(V\,R)$, and hence what income-distribution between labour and capital is fixed, is left in this model for political forces to decide. It is interesting to speculate whether more complex situations retaining this feature are ever found in the real world.

II. SIMPLIFIED TWO-FACTOR MODEL WITH CONTINUOUS SEQUENCE OF EQUIPMENTS

Consider a sequence of basic equipments E_u with u as a continuous variable. Suppose that to build any equipment E_u requires the work of 100 men spread over one year. Suppose that equipment E_u when completed requires $100u$ men to operate it and produces a flow of $100g(u)$ tons of food per annum, where $g(u)$ is a function of u. Suppose that the working life of each equipment E_u is one year, at the end of which it has no value.

At any rate of interest R and wage V the cost of any equipment E_u is :

$$K_R = 100 \, \frac{e^R - 1}{R} \, V \quad \dots\dots\dots\dots\dots\dots\dots\dots\dots\dots\dots\dots\dots\dots(2.1)$$

when new. By the formula for balanced equipment in the integrated case given in Champernowne and Kahn, it may be shown that the expression (2.1) also gives correctly the cost of the balanced set of equipment in equilibrium. Now this expression is the same for all u, and it follows (see Appendix I) that we can regard each equipment E_u as containing 100 units of capital, consistently with the chain-index method.

We are now in a position to write down the production function, for we know that the balanced equipment E_u represents 100 units of capital, employs $100u$ men for production and 100 men for replacement and produces an output stream of $100 \, g(u)$. Hence the production function must satisfy :

$$f \left(100 \, (1 + u), \, 100 \right) = 100 \, g(u) \quad \dots\dots\dots\dots\dots\dots\dots\dots\dots\dots\dots(2.2)$$

and since it must be homogeneous of degree one, it must be given in terms of the function $g(u)$ by :

$$f(x, y) = y \, g \left(\frac{x - y}{y} \right) \quad \dots\dots\dots\dots\dots\dots\dots\dots\dots\dots\dots\dots\dots\dots(2.3)$$

for those values of x and y which give to $u = \dfrac{x - y}{y}$ a value such that E_u is effective.

By the marginal principle, the wages of labour and capital are :

$$\left. \begin{aligned} &w_x = g'(u), \text{ the derivative of } g(u) \text{ where } u = \frac{x - y}{y} \\ &w_y = g(u) - (u + 1) \, g'(u) \end{aligned} \right\} \quad \dots\dots\dots\dots\dots(2.4)$$

Finally, the rate of interest R_u at which E_u is competitive is given, in virtue of (2.1), by :

$$g'(u) \{ u + e^{R_u} \} = g(u) \text{ whence } R_u = \log \left\{ \frac{g(u)}{g'(u)} - u \right\} \quad \dots\dots\dots\dots\dots(2.5)$$

Although each E_u contains the same amount of capital as measured by the chain index, they do not contain equal amounts of capital measured in J.R. units. The amount Q_u of capital in J.R. units in E_u is given by the condition (2.1) as

$$Q_u = 100 \, \frac{e^{R_u} - 1}{R_u}$$

which in virtue of (2.5) may also be written :

$$Q_u = 100 \, \frac{\dfrac{g(u)}{g'(u)} - u - 1}{\log_e \left\{ \dfrac{g(u)}{g'(u)} - u \right\}} \quad \dots\dots\dots\dots\dots\dots\dots\dots\dots\dots\dots(2.6)$$

It is possible for $Q_u/\mathrm{I} + u$ to decrease with decreases in u, even in cases where a decrease in u clearly involves an increase in productivity and in an increase in the proportion of the labour force devoted to replacing rather than operating equipment. That is to say, that a decrease in u involving what would ordinarily be understood as deepening or increased capital per head, will be shown as a reduction of the quantity per head of capital measured in J.R. units. As an example of this, consider the case where

$$g(u) = (\mathrm{I} + \mathrm{II}u)^{\frac{1}{11}} \quad \ldots\ldots\ldots\ldots\ldots\ldots\ldots\ldots\ldots\ldots\ldots (2.7)$$

then production per head is

$$\frac{(\mathrm{I} + \mathrm{II}u)^{\frac{1}{11}}}{\mathrm{I} + u} \quad \ldots\ldots\ldots\ldots\ldots\ldots\ldots\ldots\ldots\ldots\ldots (2.8)$$

which increases as u decreases, and the proportion $\dfrac{\mathrm{I}}{\mathrm{I} + u}$ of labour devoted to replacement increases. But the quantity of capital per head in J.R. units is by (2.6) :

$$\frac{Q(u)}{\mathrm{100}\,(\mathrm{I} + u)} = \frac{\mathrm{10}u}{(\mathrm{I} + u)\log(\mathrm{I} + \mathrm{10}u)} \quad \ldots\ldots\ldots\ldots\ldots\ldots\ldots (2.9)$$

and numerical calculation shows that this *decreases* from 2.19 to 1.00 as u decreases in the range 2.326 to 0, and the rate of interest meanwhile falls from 3.19 to 0. But production per head *increases* from 0.405 to 1.000 and capital per head, measured by the chain index, from 0.307 to 1.000.

It is evident that a variety of other forms for the function $g(u)$ could be chosen so as to demonstrate similar paradoxical results of measuring capital in J.R. units.

III. MODEL INVOLVING THREE FACTORS

In this model we shall allow five basic equipments E_1, E_2, E_3, E_4 and E_5. E_s will be supposed to cost at interest R, $\dfrac{X_s}{0.6 - R}$ units of labour, and $\dfrac{Y_s}{0.6 - R}$ units of land, as would happen, for example, if it had been built up by using $e^{-0.6t} X_s$ units of labour and $e^{-0.6t} Y_s$ units of land from the distant past $t = \infty$ up till $t = 0$. E_s will be supposed to employ x_s units of labour and y_s units of land permanently to produce a flow of O_s tons of food per annum.

The numerical values of these parameters are given in the following table :

s	x_s	y_s	O_s	X_s	Y_s
1	5	4	109.6	6	5
2	3	4	88	4	5
3	3	2	64	4	3
4	1	2	40	2	3
5	2	1	38	3	3

We shall suppose that in the economy as a whole the numbers of " men " and " acres of land " are equal. It will be seen that equipments 1, 3 and 5 are labour-using, whereas equipments 2 and 4 are land-using.

The values of $R_{s,\,vw}$ are given by such equations as the following :

$$\frac{R_{1vw}}{0.6 - R_{1vw}}\{6V + 5W\} + 5V + 4W = 109.6 \ldots\ldots\ldots\ldots\ldots\ldots\ldots (3.1)$$

By calculating various loci in the $V - W$ plane of the type $R_{svw} = R_{s'vw}$ and by making a few auxiliary calculations we may construct the following diagram, which shows in which regions of the $V - W$ plane (i.e. for what factor-wage combinations) the various basic equipments are competitive.

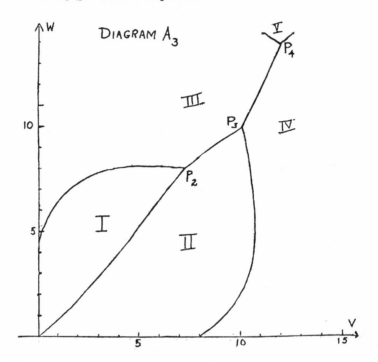

An equipment employing one man per acre can be obtained by the appropriate blend of a labour-using (odd-numbered) equipment, with a land-using (even-numbered) equipment.

The only combinations of factor-rewards VW for which this is possible are at points along the zig-zag corridor in the diagram which runs between consecutive pairs of the five equipments.

In the example only four of the pairs of equipments (E_1, E_2), (E_2, E_3), (E_3, E_4) and (E_4, E_5) can be suitably married : let us call these married couples F_1, F_2, F_3 and F_4.

Then we can construct a table for F_1, F_2, F_3 and F_4 similar to the table above.

s	x_s	y_s	O_s	X_s	Y_s
1	8	8	197.6	10	10
2	6	6	152	8	8
3	4	4	104	6	6
4	3	3	78	5	6

The equipments F_1 and F_2 will be competitive only at the point where equipments E_1, E_2 and E_3 are all competitive : this point is the point P_2 in the diagram, namely

(7.2, 8) and the competitive rate of interest is 20 per cent. Similarly, F_2 and F_3 are both competitive at P_3, namely (10, 10) with competitive interest rate 10 per cent. Finally, F_3 and F_4 are both competitive at P_4, namely (12, 14) with competitive interest zero.

At P_2 and rate of interest 20 per cent, F_1 and F_2 have costs of 380 and 304 tons of food.

At P_3 and rate of interest 10 per cent, F_2 and F_3 have costs of 320 and 240 tons of food.

At P_4 and zero rate of interest F_3 and F_4 have costs of 260 and 240 tons of food.

Hence, counting F_1 as 38 units of capital,
we must count F_2 as 30.4 units of capital,
F_3 as 22.8 units of capital,
and F_4 as 21.05 units of capital.

Counting one man with one acre as one unit of composite factor, and letting η and ζ represent the amounts employed of composite factor and capital, we can obtain the following production function for stationary states employing F_1, F_2, F_3, F_4 or pairs of them under competitive conditions.

$$f(\eta\zeta) = 15.2\eta + 2\zeta \quad \text{for } 4.25\eta \leqslant \zeta \leqslant 5.07\eta$$
$$f(\eta\zeta) = 20\eta + 1.05\zeta \quad \text{for } 5.07\eta \leqslant \zeta \leqslant 5.72\eta$$
$$f(\eta\zeta) = 26\eta \quad \text{for } 5.72\eta \leqslant \zeta \leqslant 7.1\eta$$

and in the mixed-type stationary states the composite factor and capital will be paid at rates equal to the marginal productivities as calculated from the appropriate one of the above three equations.

Returning now to the problem of evaluating the quantities of capital in each of the five basic equipments, we note that E_1 and E_3 only compete at P_2 with $R = 20$ per cent : under these conditions their costs are 208 and 132 and E_2 and E_4 only compete at P_3 with $R = 10$ per cent : under these conditions their costs are 130 and 100 and E_3 and E_5 only compete at P_4 with $R = 0$: under these conditions their costs are 150 and 130.

Hence, arbitrarily choosing E_1 and E_2 to represent 20 and 18 units of capital respectively, we find E_3, E_4 and E^1 represent 12.7, 10 and 11 units of capital respectively.

We may construct the following table :

s	x	y	z_1	z_2	O	y/x	z_1/x	z_2/x	O/x
2	5	4	20	0	109.6	0.8	4	0	21.92
1	3	4	0	18	88	1.33	0	6	29.33
3	3	2	12.7	0	64	0.67	4.23	0	21.33
4	1	2	0	10	40	2.0	0	10	40
5	2	1	11	0	38	0.5	5.5	0	19

It is now possible to express output as a function of three variables, x, z_1, z_2, representing the amounts used of labour, labour-using capital and land-using capital, it being assumed that the technically necessary amount of land is provided. The function is :

$$f(x, z_1, z_2) = 32.08x - 2.54z_1 - 0.46z_2$$
$$f(x, z_1, z_2) = 13.333x + 1.891z_1 + 2.667z_2$$
$$f(x, z_1, z_2) = 28.2x - 1.67z_1 + 1.18z_2$$

$$\left.\begin{array}{l} 24 - 4z_2/x \leqslant 6z_1/x \leqslant 24.8 - 4.13z_2/x \\[4pt] 24.8 - \dfrac{6z_1}{x} \leqslant 4.13\dfrac{z_2}{x} \leqslant 41.7 - 10\dfrac{z_1}{x} \\[4pt] 41.3 - 4.13\dfrac{z_2}{x} \leqslant 10\dfrac{z_1}{x} \leqslant 58.7 - 5.87\dfrac{z_2}{x} \end{array}\right. (3.2)$$

Consider, for example, the second equation. This relates to mixed stationary states using basic equipments 2, 3 and 4. The partial derivatives are 13.333, 1.891 and 2.667.

13.333 is the marginal productivity not merely of labour, but of labour plus the extra land needed to increase labour without altering the amount of either labour-using capital or land-using capital. It is, in fact, the marginal product of " one man and one-third of an acre." Similarly, 1.079 is the marginal product of " one unit of labour-using capital and 0.891 acres," whereas 2.667 is the marginal product of " one unit of land-using capital and one-sixth of an acre." Under competition, the wages paid for these three combinations of factors will in these stationary states be paid at rates equal to 13.333, 1.891 and 2.667.

The reason that the marginal productivities of some of these factors can be negative is that the adoption of such factors involves using less land, so that it is worth while employing them although it lowers product flow, in order to save rent. Thus the factor combination with negative productivity is always one involving a negative amount of land.

It can be verified that in our example the combined wage-rate of each factor combination is, in fact, equal to its marginal productivity as given by the appropriate regression coefficient in equations (3.2).

Oxford.   D. G. CHAMPERNOWNE.

The Production Function and the Theory of Capital

Robert M. Solow

INTRODUCTION

In her paper with the above title[1] Mrs. Robinson was annoyed at many of the practices of academic economists. We have reason to be grateful for her annoyance, for she seems to have written her article the way an oyster makes pearls—out of sheer irritation. Perhaps her main target is the custom of regarding output as a function of inputs of labor and " capital ". She tells us that the student—the English student, at least—is told that output is a kind of index-number, labor is a quantity of homogeneous man-hours, and then he is hustled away from the scene of the crime before he thinks to ask in what units " capital " is measured.

In the spirit of natural history I would like to record that the routine in at least some American classrooms is slightly different, if no more enlightening. If I write $Q = f(L,C)$, I simply assume that there exists only one kind of physically homogeneous capital good, and C, like L, is measured in unambiguous physical units. Of course, it's not true that only one kind of capital good exists, but then there's also more than one kind of labor, and anyhow this is neither the student's first nor last course in economic theory. All that matters is that it be made clear what part of the theory holds true in the general case.[2] I would go one step further. For many purposes it is remarkably useful to assume that there exists only one physical commodity which can either be consumed or used as capital in the production of more of itself. Then Q and C are measured in the *same* units except that Q is a flow and C is a stock. This simple but fruitful model of capital accumulation was one of the legacies to economics left by Frank Ramsey.[3] But this is by the way.

After having remarked on the degree of fakery involved in the notion of " capital " in general (for example : the composition of the capital stock changes as more is accumulated), Mrs. Robinson goes on to suggest a way of measuring " capital " by the cost of its component machines, buildings, etc., in labor units including interest accrued during the period of construction. This has a faintly archaic flavor. It doesn't seem to bother her much that on this definition two physically identical outfits of capital equipment can represent different amounts of " capital ". It wouldn't bother me either except that from the point of view of *production* two identical plants represent two identical plants.

It does bother Mr. Champernowne, and he recognizes the matter for what it is—a kind of index-number problem.[4] He gives a straightforward solution in this spirit. However, even Champernowne's chain-index can't dispel all the difficulties, as he points out.[5]

This leads me to ask : why does there have to be a useful concept of capital-in-general at all ? True, one feels that if God had meant there to be more than two factors of production, He would have made it easier for us to draw three-dimensional diagrams. But apart from this, as Mrs. Robinson remarks : " When an event has occurred we are thrown back upon the who's who of goods in existence, and the ' quantity of capital ' ceases to

---

[1] *Review of Economic Studies*, No. 55, p. 81.
[2] Sometimes it can be subtly suggested that the general case is really quite easy—this is known as Subscriptmanship. Sometimes it is even true.
[3] In his " A Mathematical Theory of Saving," *Economic Journal*, 1927.
[4] *Review of Economic Studies*, No. 55, p. 112, where some other paradoxes are mentioned.
[5] *Ibid.*, pp. 118, 121, 123.

Reprinted from XXIII (1955–1956) 101–108 of *Review of Economic Studies* by permission of *Review of Economic Studies* published by Oliver & Boyd Ltd., Edinburgh and London.

have any other meaning."[1]   Perhaps we should never have left the " who's who of goods in existence " in the first place.   I do not contend that dispensing with the notion of the " quantity of capital " will make the theory of capital any easier.   In fact it will make it harder.   But the real difficulty of the subject comes not from the physical diversity of capital goods.   It comes from the intertwining of past, present and future, from the fact that while there is something foolish about a theory of capital built on the assumption of perfect foresight, we have no equally precise and definite assumption to take its place. (It is clear from the context that I am not here concerned with capital as abstract purchasing power uncommitted to specific form).

In this paper I want to tackle the question from a slightly different angle : under what conditions can a consistent meaning be given to the quantity of capital ?   Suppose we have a production function which relates the output of a single commodity to inputs of labor (assumed homogeneous) and the services of several kinds of capital goods.   When if ever can the various capital inputs be summed up in a single index-figure, so that the production function can be " collapsed " to give output as a function of inputs of labor and " capital-in-general " ?   It will be seen that this is sometimes possible, but only in a very narrow class of cases.

CONDITIONS FOR COLLAPSING THE PRODUCTION FUNCTION

Formally, suppose we have a production function $Q = F(L, C_1, C_2)$ where Q is a single output, L an input of a single grade of labor, and C_1 and C_2 are inputs of the services of two distinct kinds of capital equipment (there could be more types of capital involved, but the argument would be the same).   The question is : when can we write, identically :

(1) $$Q = F(L, C_1, C_2) \equiv H(L, K)$$
         $$K \equiv \phi(C_1, C_2)$$

That is to say, when can we collapse the production function from one having three variables to one having only two ?   If this can be done, we would seem to have a right to call K an index of the quantity of capital.   For the purposes of production any pattern of inputs C_1 and C_2 are equivalent so long as they yield the same value of the index K.

At first glance it may seem as if a wide class of production functions can be treated in this way.   One consequence of equation (1) can be drawn immediately.   Calculate the marginal rate of substitution of C_1 for C_2, i.e., the ratio of their marginal physical productivities.   We find :

(2) $$\frac{MPP_1}{MPP_2} = \frac{\partial F/\partial C_1}{\partial F/\partial C_2} \equiv \frac{\frac{\partial H}{\partial K} \cdot \frac{\partial \phi}{\partial C_1}}{\frac{\partial H}{\partial K} \cdot \frac{\partial \phi}{\partial C_2}} \equiv \frac{\partial \phi/\partial C_1}{\partial \phi/\partial C_2}, \text{ which is to be independent of } L;$$

for the last ratio depends only on C_1 and C_2, and hence it and the first ratio must be *independent of L*.   We have in (2) a *necessary* condition for the collapsibility of the production function (1) : the marginal rate of substitution of one kind of capital good for another must be independent of the amount of labor in use.

Here is one implication of the existence of an index of the quantity of capital.   Are there any others ?   At this point we can appeal to a neat theorem of Leontief's[2] which,

---

[1] The next sentence reads : " Then only that part of the theory of value which treats of the short period, in which the physical stock of capital equipment is given, has any application."   This I doubt, but there is no time to go into it now.

[2] *Econometrica*, Vol. 15, No. 4, 1947, p. 364, Proposition I.   Leontief's results would enable us to handle the case where there are also several grades of labor and the problem is simultaneously to find indices of the quantity of labor and the quantity of capital.   But there seems to be no point in complicating the exposition.

applied to this situation, asserts that the answer is No.   The necessary condition just stated is also *sufficient*.   The invariance of the intra-capital substitution possibilities against changes in the labor input is equivalent to the possibility of finding an index of the quantity of capital.

There are two things to be noted about this condition.   It is natural, and it is stringent. If it is to be possible to reduce the two (or more) capital dimensions to one, it must be true that what happens in those dimensions does not depend on where we are along other axes, such as labor.   If a little C_1 could replace a lot of C_2 when we use a little labor and vice versa when we use a lot of labor, then clearly no single " average " of the amount of C_1 and C_2 would contain all the information we need.   There would then be no possibility of defining *universally* equivalent bundles of C_1 and C_2.

Secondly, condition (2) will not often be even approximately satisfied in the real world. The examples which come to mind where it will hold often turn out to be cases where the types of capital equipment are homogeneous in all but name : brick buildings and wooden buildings, aluminium fixtures and steel fixtures.   But note that it is not satisfied for one-ton trucks and two-ton trucks ; technical substitution possibilities will depend on the number of drivers available.   And there is no special reason at all why the condition should hold for totally different species of equipment like bulldozers and trucks.   In such cases no quantity of capital-in-general can be consistently defined.

There is, however, a whole class of situations in which the condition may be expected to hold and this possibility throws a new light on the meaning of the condition itself. It could be that the process of production described by F should have two stages such that *first* something called K is literally manufactured out of C_1 and C_2 alone, and *then* this substance K is combined with labor to manufacture the final output Q.   In this case the index function ϕ is actually a production function itself.   Obviously the inputs of C_1 and C_2 play no special role themselves ; only their yield of K matters ultimately.   For example, we can imagine C_1 and C_2 to be two kinds of equipment for generating electricity which is then used in further production.   Even though electric power is not itself a stock, generating capacity would be an index of the capital inputs.

In this interpretation it is useful to know whether the index-function ϕ and the collapsed function H have the characteristics we usually associate with production functions.   In the next section it will be shown that they do.

PROPERTIES OF THE INDEX FUNCTIONS

Theorem : Suppose that the underlying production function F exhibits constant returns to scale with respect to L, C_1 and C_2, and obeys the generalized law of diminishing returns to variable proportions, i.e., has properly convex equal-output surfaces.   Then exactly the same properties will characterize the index-function ϕ and the collapsed production function H.

This means that in (1) it is always possible to regard the index of the quantity of capital as the " output " of a production process which uses capital goods to produce capital-in-general.   Moreover the final output will be a well-behaved function of other inputs and the input of capital-in-general.

To begin with we can differentiate (1) to yield :

(3)
$$\frac{\partial F}{\partial L} = \frac{\partial H}{\partial L} \; ; \; \frac{\partial F}{\partial C_1} = \frac{\partial H}{\partial K} \frac{\partial \phi}{\partial C_1} \; ; \; \frac{\partial F}{\partial C_2} = \frac{\partial H}{\partial K} \frac{\partial \phi}{\partial C_2}$$

Since the marginal productivities calculated from F are positive (or at least not negative), we deduce that the marginal productivities calculated from ϕ have the same sign as the marginal productivity of K in the collapsed function H.   These can all be chosen to be positive.

Next I want to show that ϕ can be taken to be homogeneous of first degree. From (2) the identity can be extracted :

$$\frac{\partial F/\partial C_1}{\partial F/\partial C_2} = \frac{\partial \phi/\partial C_1}{\partial \phi/\partial C_2}$$

The right-hand side is, except for sign, the slope of equal-K contours of ϕ. The left-hand side, a ratio of marginal productivities of a constant-returns-to-scale function, depends only on ratios of all inputs, say C_2/C_1 and L/C_1. But this ratio is independent of L, and hence depends *only* on C_2/C_1. This means that the isoquants of ϕ all have the same slope along any ray from the origin. The numbering of such " homothetic " isoquants can then always be chosen so as to make ϕ homogeneous of degree one.

Once we know F and ϕ to be homogeneous of degree one it is an easy matter to prove the same of H :

(4) $tH(L, K) = tF(L, C_1, C_2) = F(tL, tC_1, tC_2) = H(tL, tK)$

It remains only to show that ϕ and H have correctly-shaped isoquants. They do, but I relegate the proof to a footnote.[1]

A CORRESPONDING PRICE-INDEX

Imagine that the production function is such that a consistent index of the quantity of capital (services) can be defined. It is natural to wonder whether one can speak of the " price " of capital-in-general. This price index should have the following properties. First, it should depend only on the prices of the various capital goods themselves. Second, under constant returns to scale one would expect the price index of capital-in-general to equal the " cost of production " of the capital index :

(5) $p_K K = p_1 C_1 + p_2 C_2$

where C_1, C_2 and K are related by the index-production function ϕ. Finally, one can think of the cost-minimization process as broken down into stages. In the first stage the prices p_L and p_K are quoted and cost-minimization, subject to the production constraint H, leads to a preferred capital-labor ratio K/L. In the second stage the prices p_1 and p_2 are quoted and cost-minimization, subject to the production constraint ϕ, leads to a preferred ratio C_1/C_2. One would like this two-stage process to lead to the same result as straightforward cost minimization, given prices p_L, p_1, p_2, and subject to the production constraint F. What this amounts to is that one might expect the price-index of K to be such that it makes no difference whether or not the " production " of K is vertically integrated with the production of Q.

---

[1] Suppose $K = \phi(C_1, C_2) = \phi(C_1', C_2') = K'$. Then since F has convex isoquants $H(L, K) + H(L, K')$

$= 2H(L,K) = F(L, C_1, C_2) + F(L, C_1', C_2') \leq F(2L, C_1 + C_1', C_2 + C_2') = 2F(L, (C_1 + C_1')/2, (C_2 + C_2')/2)$

$= 2H(L,\phi(C_1 + C_1')/2,(C_2 + C_2')/2))$. Hence $\phi\left(\dfrac{C_1 + C_1'}{2}, \dfrac{C_2 + C_2'}{2}\right) \geq \phi(C_1, C_2) = \phi(C_1', C_2')$, q.e.d.

My original proof of the convexity of the $H(L, K)$—isoquants was heavily infected with second derivatives. My colleague Paul Samuelson has shown me the following direct proof. We have to show that if $H(L, K) = H(L', K')$, then $H(L, K) \leq H(L + L')/2, (K + K')/2)$. If $K = \phi(C_1, C_2)$, choose $C_i' = mC_i$, so that $K' = mK = \phi(C_1', C_2') = m\phi(C_1, C_2)$. Then, using the convexity of F, $H(L, K) = H(L', mK) =$

$F(L, C_1, C_2) = F(L', mC_1, mC_2) \leq F\left(\dfrac{L + L'}{2}, \dfrac{1 + m}{2} C_1, \dfrac{1 + m}{2} C_2\right) = H\left(\dfrac{L + L'}{2}, \dfrac{1 + m}{2} K\right) = H\left(\dfrac{L + L'}{2}, \dfrac{K + K'}{2}\right)$

All this can easily be accomplished. There are several ways of getting at the desired price-index. One possibility is to use (5) directly for $K = 1$ after expressing C_1 and C_2 as functions of p_1 and p_2. Another way is as follows. The minimum-cost conditions for F and for H can be written out :

$$(6) \qquad \frac{1}{p_L}\frac{\partial F}{\partial L} = \frac{1}{p_L}\frac{\partial H}{\partial L} = \frac{1}{p_1}\frac{\partial F}{\partial C_1} \equiv \frac{1}{p_1}\frac{\partial H}{\partial K}\frac{\partial \phi}{\partial C_1} = \frac{1}{p_2}\frac{\partial F}{\partial C_2} = \frac{1}{p_2}\frac{\partial H}{\partial K}\frac{\partial \phi}{\partial C_2} = \frac{1}{p_K}\frac{\partial H}{\partial K}.$$

From this it is apparent that we must have

$$(7) \qquad p_K = p_1 \div \frac{\partial \phi}{\partial C_1} = p_2 \div \frac{\partial \phi}{\partial C_2}.$$

Both $\partial\phi/\partial C_1$ and $\partial\phi/\partial C_2$ are monotonic functions of C_2/C_1 alone ; hence we can eliminate C_2/C_1 between these two equations and what is left is p_K as a function of p_1 and p_2 alone. It is easily verified, from Euler's Theorem, that the condition (5) will hold. And the way (7) was derived from (6) tells us that two-stage and straightforward cost-minimization must lead to identical results. A competitive entrepreneur " buying " K at the price p_K would in effect make all the same decisions as one buying C_1 and C_2 at prices p_1 and p_2.

This result, together with the earlier-proved convexity of $H(L, K)$, justifies the statement : under the strong assumptions required, there is a perfectly definite and consistent sense in which it can be said that the relative factor-price ratio p_K/p_L is a decreasing function of the ratio of capital to labor K/L.

EXAMPLES

Take first the Cobb-Douglas production function :

$$Q = L^u C_1^v C_2^w \qquad\qquad u + v + w = 1$$

It is obviously collapsible since we can rewrite it :

$$Q = L^u K^{v+w}$$

$$K = C_1^{\frac{v}{v+w}} C_2^{\frac{w}{v+w}}.$$

It is easily verifiable that the marginal rate of substitution of C_1 for C_2 is $(v/w)(C_2/C_1)$ which is indeed independent of L. Equally clearly, Q is a constant-returns-to-scale function of L and K, and similarly for K as a function of C_1 and C_2. Both H and ϕ are Cobb-Douglas functions themselves and so their isoquants have the right convexity. K, the index of the quantity of capital, is a kind of weighted geometric mean of the two capital inputs, but this is because the Cobb-Douglas function has just that kind of structure.

As for the price-index, equations (7) yield in this case, after some manipulation :

$$P_K = (v + w)\left(\frac{p_1}{v}\right)^{\frac{v}{v+w}}\left(\frac{p_2}{w}\right)^{\frac{w}{v+w}}$$

which has all the required properties.

For a second example consider the production function :[1]

$$Q = (\sqrt{L} + a\sqrt{C_1} + b\sqrt{C_2})^2$$

---

[1] Similar remarks apply to production functions of the general class of " means " $Q = f^{-1}[f(L) + f(C_1) + f(C_2)]$, further restricted to be homogeneous of first degree.

It can then be collapsed into :

$$Q = (\sqrt{L} + \sqrt{K})^2$$

$$K = (a\sqrt{C_1} + b\sqrt{C_2})^2$$

The marginal rate of substitution of C_1 for C_2 is $(a/b)\sqrt{C_2/C_1}$, which does not involve L. Again H and K have all the desired properties of homogeneity and convexity. The price index calculation leads to :

$$p_K = \frac{p_1 p_2}{a^2 p_2 + b^2 p_1} = \frac{1}{\dfrac{a^2}{p_1} + \dfrac{b_2}{p_2}}$$

a kind of weighted harmonic mean of the individual capital-goods prices.

This is perhaps the place to mention a curious duality relation which seems to have no apparent economic interpretation. Notice that in these two examples, and in fact in general, the price-index p_K comes out as a homogeneous function of degree one of p_1 and p_2. (This, by the way, is natural : double the component prices and you double the index.) Moreover it has all the same convexity properties as a production function. Now suppose we replace p_K by K, p_1 by C_1, and p_2 by C_2. Then the price index is transformed into a quantity-of-capital-index like the ϕ we have been talking about. Now find the price-index that corresponds to this new ϕ-index. It turns out to be the old ϕ-index ! So price and quantity indices come in pairs : if the function A as a quantity index has the function B for a price index, then B as a quantity index has A as a price index. In my second example, if we find the price index that corresponds to :

$$K \doteq \frac{C_1 C_2}{a^2 C_2 + b^2 C_1}$$

it turns out to be :

$$p_K = (a\sqrt{p_1} + b\sqrt{p_2})^2$$

Apart from the comforting thought that at this late date no one should be surprised to find price-quantity dualities, I have no explanation to offer.

A LINEAR PROGRAMMING MODEL

Both Mrs. Robinson and Mr. Champernowne carry on their discussion in terms of discrete " activities " or processes. Everyone who invents linear programming these days seems to be charmed by it. I have used old fashioned production functions simply because the problem seemed more manageable in those terms. I have not proved similar theorems for the discrete case, but I have little doubt they are true. In any case, I conclude by showing how the parallel problem can be formulated.

Consider activities A, B, C, D, . . ., such that activity A produces a unit of output with inputs a_0 of labor, a_1 of C_1, and a_2 of C_2. Activities B, C, D, . . . are similar. If x_a units of output are produced with activity A, x_b with B, etc., then total output Q will be $x_a + x_b + x_c + x_d, \ldots$, and the total inputs of L, C_1, and C_2 respectively will be :

$$a_0 x_a + b_0 x_b + c_0 x_c + d_0 x_d \ldots = L$$

$$a_1 x_a + b_1 x_b + c_1 x_c + d_1 x_d \ldots = C_1$$

$$a_2 x_a + b_2 x_b + c_2 x_c + d_2 x_d \ldots = C_2$$

Now look at it the other way round. Given total inputs L, C_1, and C_2 how should output be allocated among the activities to yield the maximum output ? This is a garden variety linear programming problem, namely :

$$\text{Maximize } x_a + x_b + x_c + x_d + \ldots$$

subject to the constraints :

$$
\begin{aligned}
a_0 x_a + b_0 x_b + c_0 x_c + d_0 x_d + \ldots &\leq L \\
(8) \qquad a_1 x_a + b_1 x_b + c_1 x_c + d_1 x_d + \ldots &\leq C_1 \\
a_2 x_a + b_2 x_b + c_2 x_c + d_2 x_d + \ldots &\leq C_2
\end{aligned}
$$

Methods of solving problems like this are now well-known. By whatever method of solution, we must finally wind up with a maximal total output Q. Varying the total inputs we repeat the process and in this way trace out a production function :

$$Q = G(L, C_1, C_2)$$

This production function is not very different from the smooth neo-classical type. It will exhibit constant returns to scale and the usual non-increasing returns as proportions vary. The main difference is that its equal-output surfaces will consist of planar pieces, joined at edges and vertices. This possibility of corners means that marginal rates of substitution are not always well-defined.

One can still ask whether this production function can be collapsed into one involving only two independent variables. The answer is, in general, certainly not. There are some obvious sufficient conditions. For instance, if the only efficient activities are some which use up only C_1 and C_2, and others which use up only L, then trivially the production function can be decomposed. The constraints (8) will then appear in partitioned-matrix form as :

$$
\begin{pmatrix} A & O \\ O & C \end{pmatrix}
\begin{pmatrix} X_1 \\ - - \\ X_{11} \end{pmatrix}
\leq
\begin{pmatrix} L \\ - - \\ C_1 \\ C_2 \end{pmatrix}
$$

where A has one row, C has two, and each has as many columns as there are activities in its group. The output of the second group of activities will serve as an index of the inputs C_1 and C_2.

Rather more generally, suppose the constraints can be written :

$$
(9) \qquad
\begin{pmatrix} A & O \\ O & C \\ B & -D \end{pmatrix}
\begin{pmatrix} X_1 \\ - - \\ X_{11} \end{pmatrix}
\leq
\begin{pmatrix} L \\ - - \\ C_1 \\ C_2 \\ - - \\ O \end{pmatrix}
$$

where B and D have only a single row. Now the activities of the second group do not produce final output directly at all. Instead they use up C_1 and C_2 to " produce " a fictitious output—previously called K—which is fed into the first group of activities, along with L, to produce the final output Q. In this set-up Q is equal to the sum of the activity levels of first-group activities only. In this set up it is also possible to summarize C_1 and C_2 in a single number, namely the output of the fictitious intermediate K. Linear programming problem (9) breaks down into two problems.

First, maximize $K = DX_{11}$ subject to

$$CX_{11} \leqq \begin{pmatrix} C_1 \\ C_2 \end{pmatrix}$$

Then, maximize $Q = \Sigma X_1$ subject to :

$$\begin{pmatrix} A \\ B \end{pmatrix} (x_1) \leqq \begin{pmatrix} L \\ K \end{pmatrix}$$

The set-up (9) may very likely also be *necessary* for the collapsibility of the production function, in which case it plays the role of Leontief's theorem. In the theory of linear programming the concept of the " dual variable " plays the part of a marginal productivity. A marginal rate of substitution or price ratio would correspond to a ratio of dual variables. The dual problem to (9) is to minimize $Lu_0 + C_1u_1 + C_2u_2 + 0 \cdot u_3$ subject to :

$$\begin{pmatrix} A' & O' & B' \\ O' & C' & -D' \end{pmatrix} \begin{pmatrix} u_0 \\ \overline{u_1} \\ u_2 \\ \overline{u_3} \end{pmatrix} \gtreqless \begin{pmatrix} 1 \\ 1 \\ \vdots \\ \overline{0} \\ 0 \\ \vdots \end{pmatrix}$$

The second group of constraints require that u_1 and u_2 bear a fixed ratio to u_3 and hence to each other. Thus the marginal rate of substitution between C_1 and C_2 is determined independently of u_0 and hence of L. Thus the possibility of rewriting the production conditions in the very special form (9) would appear to be equivalent to the possibility of defining a single index of capital inputs.

I conclude that discreteness is unlikely to help matters. Only in very special cases will it be possible to define a consistent measure of capital-in-general. Some comfort may be gleaned from the reflection that when capital-labor ratios differ widely we hardly need a subtle index to tell us so, and when differences are slight we are unlikely to believe what any particular index says.

Cambridge, Mass.   ROBERT M. SOLOW.

MONEY AND ECONOMIC GROWTH[1]

By James Tobin

In non-monetary neo-classical growth models, the equilibrium degree of capital intensity and correspondingly the equilibrium marginal productivity of capital and rate of interest are determined by "productivity and thrift," i.e., by technology and saving behavior. Keynesian difficulties, associated with divergence between warranted and natural rates of growth, arise when capital intensity is limited by the unwillingness of investors to acquire capital at unattractively low rates of return. But why should the community wish to save when rates of return are too unattractive to invest? This can be rationalized only if there are stores of value other than capital, with whose rates of return the marginal productivity of capital must compete. The paper considers monetary debt of the government as one alternative store of value and shows how enough saving may be channeled into this form to bring the warranted rate of growth of capital down to the natural rate. Equilibrium capital intensity and interest rates are then determined by portfolio behavior and monetary factors as well as by saving behavior and technology. In such an equilibrium, the real monetary debt grows at the natural rate also, either by deficit spending or by deflation. The stability of the equilibrium is also considered.

1. The purpose of this paper is to discuss the rôle of monetary factors in determining the degree of capital intensity of an economy. The models I shall use in discussing this question are both aggregative and primitive. But I believe they serve to illuminate the basic points I wish to make. At any rate, I have taken the designation of this talk as a "lecture" as a license to emphasize exposition rather than novelty and sophistication. And my subject falls naturally and appropriately in the tradition of Irving Fisher of my own university.

Fisher and Keynes, among others, have drawn the useful and fruitful analytical distinction between choices affecting the disposition of income and choices affecting the disposition of wealth. The first set of choices determines how much is saved rather than consumed and how much wealth is accumulated. The second set determines in what forms savers hold their savings, old as well as new. Considerable economic discussion and controversy have concerned the respective rôles of these two kinds of behavior, and their interactions, in determining the rate of interest.

---

[1] This is the Fisher Lecture that was presented at the Joint European Conference of the Econometric Society and The Institute of Management Sciences in Zürich, September 11, 1964.

Reprinted from *Econometrica* (October 1965), pp. 671–684. Copyright 1965 by the Econometric Society.

2. Most models of economic growth are nonmonetary. They offer no place for significant choices of the second kind—portfolio choices. They admit only one type of asset that can serve wealth owners as a store of value, namely reproducible capital. It is true that some of these models, particularly disaggregated variants, may allow savers and owners of wealth to choose between different kinds or vintages of capital. But this is the only scope for portfolio choice they are permitted. Different questions arise when monetary assets are available to compete with ownership of real goods. I shall proceed by reviewing how the intensity and yield of capital are determined in a typical aggregative nonmonetary model of economic growth, and then indicating how their determination is modified by introducing monetary assets into the model.

3. In a nonmonetary model of growth and capital accumulation, so long as saving continues it necessarily takes the form of real investment. And so long as saving and investment augment the capital stock faster than the effective supplies of other factors are growing, nothing prevents the yields on capital investment from being driven to zero or below. Of course, low or negative yields may cause people to reduce or discontinue their saving or even to consume capital. This classical reaction of saving to the interest rate may help to set an upper limit to capital deepening and a lower bound to the rate of return on capital. But clearly this kind of brake on investment causes no problems of underemployment and insufficiency of aggregate demand. Increased consumption automatically replaces investment.

4. I can illustrate in Figure 1 the manner in which saving behavior determines capital intensity and the rate of interest in a nonmonetary growth model. (For the basic construction of the diagram I am indebted to my Yale colleague, John Fei, but he is not responsible for my present use of it.)

In Figure 1 the horizontal axis measures capital intensity k, the quantity of capital (measured in physical units of output) per effective manhour of labor. The significance of the term "effective" is to allow for improvements in the quality of labor inputs due to "labor-augmenting" technological progress. Thus, if a 1964 manhour is equivalent as input in the production function to two manhours in the base period, say 1930, then k measures the amount of capital per man half-hour 1964 or per manhour 1930.

The vertical axis measures various annual rates. Curve AA' represents y, the average annual product of capital. Since output and capital are measured in the same physical units, this variable has the dimension, pure number per year. It is the reciprocal of the famous capital-output ratio. In accordance with usual assumptions about the production function, y is shown to decline as capital intensity k becomes deeper.

Curve MM' represents the corresponding marginal product of capital. In

Figure 1 this becomes zero or negative for sufficiently intense use of capital. There are, of course, some technologies—Cobb-Douglas, for example—in which this cannot occur.

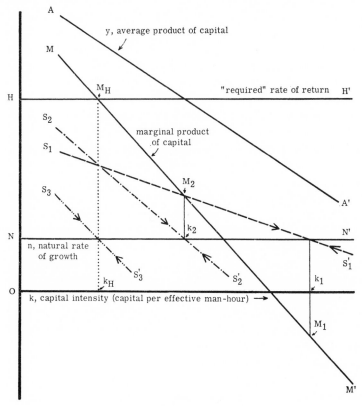

FIGURE 1

For present purposes it will be convenient to regard the average product y, shown by AA', and the corresponding marginal product of capital MM', as referring to output net of depreciation. If depreciation is a constant proportion δ of the capital stock, the average gross product of capital would simply be $y + \delta$, and the marginal gross product would likewise be uniformly higher than MM' by the constant δ.

Even after this allowance for depreciation, the yield on durable capital relevant to an investment-saving decision is not always identical with the marginal product of capital at the time of the decision. The two will be identical if the marginal product is expected to remain constant over the lifetime of the new capital. But if it is expected to change because of future innovations or because of future capital deepening or capital "shallowing" in the economy, the relevant marginal efficiency

295

of current new investment is a weighted average of future marginal products. I shall, however, ignore this distinction in what follows and use the marginal product in Figure 1 as at least an indicator of the true rate of return on capital. For the most part I shall be concerned with equilibrium situations where the two are stationary and therefore identical.

A curve like $S_1 S_1'$ reflects saving behavior. It tells the amount of net saving and investment per year, per unit of the existing capital stock. Therefore it tells how fast the capital stock is growing. In Harrod's terminology, this is the "warranted rate of growth" of the capital stock. The particular curve $S_1 S_1'$ is drawn so that its height is always the same proportion of the height of $A_1 A_1'$. This represents the common assumption that net saving is proportional to net output.

The effective labor force, in manhours, is assumed to grow at a constant rate n, independent of the degree of capital intensity. The "natural rate of growth" n depends on the natural increase in the labor force and on the advance of labor-augmenting technology. This conventional growth-model assumption is indicated in Figure 1 by the horizontal line NN'.

5. So much for the mechanics of Figure 1. Now what determines the development and ultimate equilibrium value, if any, of capital intensity? A rate of growth of capital equal to n will just keep capital intensity constant. If the "warranted" rate of growth of capital exceeds the "natural" rate of growth of labor n, then capital deepening will occur. If capital grows more slowly than labor, k will decline. These facts are indicated in the diagram by the arrows in curve $S_1 S_1'$. With the saving behavior assumed in $S_1 S_1'$, the equilibrium capital intensity is k_1. The corresponding stationary marginal product is M_1. To emphasize the point suggested above, M_1 in the diagram is negative.

A different kind of saving behavior is depicted by $S_2 S_2'$. Here the ratio of net investment to output declines with k. This decline could be the result of one or both of two factors which have played a rôle in the theory of saving. One factor is that capital deepening lowers the yield on saving and therefore increases the propensity to consume. The other is that capital deepening implies an increase in wealth relative to current income; according to some theories of consumption, this should diminish the saving ratio quite apart from any accompanying decline in the rate of return. With saving behavior $S_2 S_2'$, the ultimate equilibrium has a capital intensity k_2 and a marginal product M_2.

6. The theory of interest sketched in Section 5 is classical. The rate of return on capital, in long-run equilibrium, is the result of the interaction of "productivity" and "thrift," or of technology and time preference. To dramatize the conflict of this theory and monetary theories of interest, I shall begin with an extreme case—so extreme that the crucial monetary factor is not even specified explicitly.

Some growth models assume a lower limit on the marginal product of capital of quite a different kind from the limit that thrift imposed in Section 5. Harrod, for example, argues that investors will simply not undertake new investment unless they expect to receive a certain minimum rate of return. Savers, on the other hand, are not discouraged from trying to save when yields fall to or below this minimum. The result is an impasse which leads to Keynesian difficulties of deficient demand and unemployment. In Harrod's model these difficulties arise when the warranted rate of growth at the minimum required rate of profit exceeds the natural rate. The rate of saving from full employment output would cause capital to accumulate faster than the labor force is growing. Consequently, the marginal product of capital would fall and push the rate of return on investment below the required minimum.

In Figure 1, suppose HH to be the required minimum. Then, correspondingly, k_H is the maximum capital intensity investors will tolerate. Yet the saving behavior depicted in the diagram would, if it were actually realized, push marginal product toward M_1 and capital intensity toward k_1, given saving behavior $S_1 S_1'$ (or M_2 and k_2, given saving behavior $S_2 S_2'$). It is this excess of *ex ante* S over I which gives rise to the Keynesian difficulties.

The opposite problem would arise if there were a *maximum* return on investment *below* the equilibrium return (M_1 or M_2) to which saving behavior by itself would lead. At this maximum, the warranted rate of growth would fall short of the natural rate. So long as actual yields on investment exceeded the critical maximum, investment demand would be indefinitely large. In any event it would exceed saving.

The consequences of this impasse in Harrod's model are less clear than the events that follow the deflationary or Keynesian impasse. At this stage the two cases lose their symmetry, though it is possible for output to fall short of the technologically feasible, when *ex ante* investment is less than *ex ante* saving, it is not possible for output to surpass its technological limits in the opposite case. Presumably an excess of *ex ante* investment is an "inflationary gap," and its main consequence is a price inflation which somehow—for example, through forced saving—eliminates the discrepancy. But this only makes the point that monetary assets had better be introduced explicitly. For it is scarcely possible to talk about inflation in a nonmonetary model where there is no price level to inflate.

7. I have spoken of Harrod's model, but I have the impression that the concept of a required rate of profit plays a key rôle in other theories of growth, notably those of Mrs. Robinson and Mr. Kaldor. Indeed I understand one of the key characteristics of their models—one of the reasons their authors consider them "Keynesian" growth models in distinction to classical models of the type sketched in Section 5 above—is that they separate the investment decision from saving behavior.

A minimal rate of return on capital (a required rate of profit) cannot exist in a vacuum, however. It must reflect the competition of other channels for the placement of saving. For a small open economy, a controlling competitive rate might be set by the yield available on investment abroad. This would, however, leave unexplained the existence of such a limit for a closed economy, whether a national economy or the world as a whole. In any case the growth models under discussion are closed economy models.

In a closed economy clearly the important alternative stores of value are monetary assets. It is their yields which set limits on the acceptable rates of return on real capital and on the acceptable degree of capital intensity. To understand these limits, both how they are determined and how they may be altered, it is necessary to introduce monetary assets into the model explicitly. It is necessary to examine the choices of savers and wealth owners between these assets and real capital. I continue, I remind you, to make the useful distinction between saving-consumption choices, on the one hand, and portfolio choices on the other. The choices I am about to discuss are portfolio choices; that is, they concern the forms of saving and wealth rather than their total amounts.

8. The simplest way to introduce monetary factors is to imagine that there is a single monetary asset with the following properties:

(a) It is supplied only by the central government. This means that it represents neither a commodity produced by the economy nor the debts of private individuals or institutions.

(b) It is the means of payment, the medium of exchange, of the economy. And it is a store of value by reason of its general acceptability in the discharge of public and private transactions.

(c) Its own-yield (i.e., the amount of the asset that is earned by holding a unit of the asset a given period of time) is arbitrarily fixed by the government. This may, of course, be zero but is not necessarily so.

Furthermore, it will be convenient for expository reasons to introduce money in two stages, avoiding in the first stage the complications of a variable value of money, a variable price level. Suppose, to begin with, that the value of money in terms of goods is fixed. The community's wealth now has two components: the real goods accumulated through past real investment and fiduciary or paper "goods" manufactured by the government from thin air. Of course the non-human wealth of such a nation "really" consists only of its tangible capital. But, as viewed by the inhabitants of the nation individually, wealth exceeds the tangible capital stock by the size of what we might term the fiduciary issue. This is an illusion, but only one of the many fallacies of composition which are basic to any economy or any society. The illusion can be maintained unimpaired so long as the society does not actually try to convert all of its paper wealth into goods.

9. The simplest kind of two-asset portfolio behavior is the following: If the yields of the two assets differ, wealth owners will wish to place all of their wealth

in the asset with the higher yield. If they are the same, wealth owners do not care in what proportions they divide their wealth between the two assets. Evidently, if there are positive supplies of both assets, they can be willingly held in portfolios only if the two yields are equal. On this assumption about portfolio behavior, it is easy to see how the institutionally determined rate of interest on money controls the yield of capital. In particular, it is this rate of interest which is the minimal rate of profit that leads to the deflationary impasse discussed in Section 6 above.

At the same time, we can see two ways in which government policy can avoid this impasse. Returning to Figure 1, suppose that HH is the yield on money and therefore the minimal yield acceptable to owners of capital. The corresponding capital intensity is k_H. One measure the government could take is to reduce the yield on money, say to M_1. Such a reduction might—and in Figure 1 it does—entail a negative rate of interest on money, reminiscent of the "stamped money" proposals of Silvio Gesell. Manipulation of interest rates on monetary assets within more normal limits is, in more realistically complex models, accomplished by the usual instruments of central banking.

Alternatively, the government could channel part of the community's excessive thrift into increased holdings of money. Thus, let us now interpret $S_1 S_1'$ to measure the amount by which the public wishes to increase its total wealth relative to its existing holdings of capital. This leads to the Harrod impasse if all the saving must take the form of capital. But if only part of it goes into capital accumulation, if in particular the rate of increase of the capital stock can be lowered to $S_3 S_3'$, then all will be well. Equilibrium capital intensity will be k_H, consistent with maintaining the marginal product of capital at the required level HH. This can be done if the government provides new money to absorb the saving represented by the difference between $S_1 S_1'$ and $S_3 S_3'$.

The only way for the government to achieve this is continuously to run a deficit financed by issue of new money. The deficit must be of the proper size, as can be

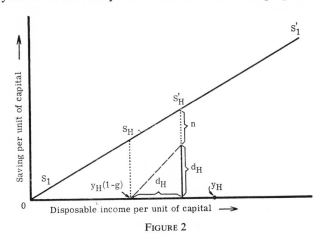

FIGURE 2

illustrated by Figure 2. Here saving is measured vertically, and output and income horizontally. Both are measured in proportion to the capital stock, as in Figure 1. y_H is the output per unit of capital corresponding to the required equilibrium capital intensity k_H. Government purchases of goods and services are assumed to be a fraction g of output. Consequently, $y_H(1-g)$ is output available for private use, and if the budget is balanced it is also the disposable income of the population. Taking $S_1 S_1'$ as the function relating saving to disposable income, S_H is the amount of private saving, (relative to the capital stock) when the budget is balanced. By assumption, however, this is too much investment—it causes the warranted rate to exceed the natural rate. Now n is the natural rate of growth; it is therefore the "right" amount of investment relative to the capital stock. A deficit of d_H (per unit of capital) will do the trick. It increases disposable income to $y_H(1-g)+d_H$, and this raises total saving to S_H'. But of this, d_H is acquisition of government debt, leaving only n for new tangible investment.

The arithmetic is simple enough: Since

(1) $S = s[y(1-g)+d] = d+n$,

(2) $\dfrac{d}{y} = \dfrac{s(1-g)-n/y}{1-s}$ gives the required deficit as a fraction of income.

On these assumptions about portfolio choice, the size of the government debt, here identical to the stock of money, does not matter. The deficit must absorb a certain proportion of income, as given in (2). But since wealth owners will hold money and capital in any proportions, provided their yields are in line, the size of the cumulated deficit is immaterial.

The opposite case would correspond to Harrod's inflationary impasse. Just as there is a deficit policy that will resolve the deflationary impasse, so there is a surplus policy that will remedy the opposite difficulty. In this case a balanced budget policy would leave the yield on capital so high that no one wants to hold money. To get the public to hold money it is necessary to increase capital intensity and lower the marginal product of capital. But a higher capital intensity takes more investment relative to output. To achieve a higher investment ratio, the resources that savers make available for capital formation must be supplemented by a government budget surplus. The mechanics of this can be seen by operating Figure 2 in reverse.

10. The portfolio behavior assumed in Section 9 is too simple. A more realistic assumption is that the community will hold the two assets in proportions that depend on their respective yields. There is a whole range of rate differentials at which positive supplies of both assets will be willingly held. But the greater the supply of money relative to that of capital, the higher the yield of money must be relative to that on capital. I shall not review the explanations that have been offered

for this kind of rate-sensitive portfolio diversification. One explanation runs in terms of risk-avoiding strategy where one or both yields are imperfectly predictable. Other explanations are associated with the specific functions of money as means of payment. Yield differentials must compensate for the costs of going back and forth between money and other assets. They must also offset the value of hedging against possible losses in case of unforeseen and exigent needs for cash.

The demand for money, presumably, depends also on income. Other things equal (i.e., asset yields and total wealth), more money will be required and less capital demanded the higher the level of output.

11. One implication of the assumption about portfolio behavior made in Section 10 can be stated very simply. Capital deepening in production requires monetary deepening in portfolios. If saving is so great that capital intensity is increasing, the yield on capital will fall. Given the yield on money, the stock of money per unit of capital must rise. Provided the government can engineer such an increase, capital deepening can proceed. There is a limit to this process, however. As in the previous cases discussed, there is an equilibrium capital intensity. Monetary deepening cannot push capital intensity beyond this equilibrium because the deficit spending required would leave too little saving available for capital formation.

In such an equilibrium, the shares of money and capital in total wealth must be constant so that their yields can remain constant. To maintain the fixed relation between the stocks, money and capital must grow at the same rate. That is, new saving must be divided between them in the same ratio as old saving.

Let $m(k, r)$ be the required amount of money per unit of capital when the capital intensity is k and the yield of money is r. We know that m is an increasing function of r: more money is demanded when its yield is higher. At the moment, we are taking r as fixed. I take m to be also an increasing function of k because an increase in k lowers the yield of capital. It is true that an increase in k also lowers y and therefore reduces the strict transactions demand for means of payment. But I assume the yield effects of variations in capital intensity to be the more powerful.

Let w (for "warranted") be the rate of growth of the capital stock, and let d represent, as before, the deficit per unit of existing capital. Then, constancy of amount of money per unit of capital at $m(k, r)$ requires that $d = m(k, r)w$. Assuming as before that saving is a constant proportion of disposable income, the basic identity is essentially the same as (1) above:

$$S = s(y(1-g) + d) = d + w .$$

Using the fact that $d = m(k, r)w$, we have

(3) $\qquad w(k, r) = \dfrac{sy(k)(1-g)}{1+(1-s)m(k, r)}.$

In equilibrium $w = n$: the warranted and natural rates must be equal. The equilibrium degree of capital intensity is the value of k that equates $w(k, r)$ in (3) to n.

I have written w and y in (3) as functions of k as a reminder that these variables, as well as m, depend directly or indirectly on capital intensity. Since y is a decreasing and m an increasing function of k, it is clear that w declines with k. Moreover, the amount by which w in (3) falls short of the hypothetical w for $m=0$ $(sy(1-g))$ increases with k.

This analysis may be presented diagrammatically, following the format of Figure 1. In Figure 3, $S_1 S_1'$ reflects, as before, the balanced budget $(d=0)$ saving function, with saving a constant fraction of disposable income. This would be the warranted rate of growth of capital if m were zero. $W_1 W_2'$ represents for every capital intensity the warranted rate of growth of capital, assuming that the stock of money is adjusted to that capital intensity and maintained in that adjustment by deficit spending. The intersection of $W_1 W_2'$ with NN', the natural rate of growth, gives the equilibrium capital intensity k_1. As before, the equilibrium yield on capital is M', its marginal product at k_1. This yield, however, is not necessarily equal to the yield on money r.

The curve $W_1 W_2'$ is drawn for a particular yield on money $\bar{r}_1$. Lowering the yield on money, say to $\bar{r}_2$, would shift the curve to the right, to $W_2 W_1'$—increasing equilibrium capital intensity and lowering the equilibrium rate of return on capital.

12. I turn now to the more interesting and realistic case where the value of money in terms of goods is variable. Its variability has two important consequences. The real value of the monetary component of wealth is not under the direct control of the government but also depends on the price level. And the real return on a unit of money—a favorite concept of Fisher—consists not only of its own-yield but also of the change in its real value.

Once again, we may ask whether there is an equilibrium capital intensity and, if so, how it is determined. The analysis of Section 11 tells us that there is an equilibrium capital intensity associated with a stable price level. But this requires a particular fiscal policy that maintains through deficit spending of the right magnitude just the right balance between stocks of money and capital. Now what happens when fiscal policy is determined independently so that a stable price level cannot necessarily be maintained?

In particular, suppose that a balanced budget policy is followed and the nominal stock of money remains constant. Real capital gains due to deflation play the same rôle as deficits did in Section 11. That is, they augment real disposable income and they absorb part of the propensity to save. Therefore, we can use the same apparatus as before, illustrated in Figure 3, to find the equilibrium capital intensity.

There is, however, one important difference. In the equilibrium the real stock of money must be increasing as fast as the capital stock, namely at the natural rate n. In the present instance this can happen only if the price level falls at rate n. If so, the real return on money r is not simply the nominal yield $\bar{r}$ but $\bar{r}+n$. Consequently the demand for money will be larger than if prices were expected to remain stable.

Equilibrium will require a greater stock of money per unit of capital and a lower capital intensity if deflation is substituted for money creation. This is indicated in Figure 3 where $W_3 W_3'$ is the curve corresponding to a yield on money n points higher than the yield behind $W_1 W_2'$.

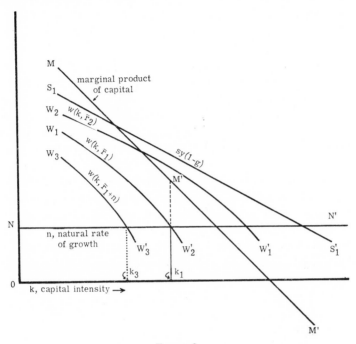

FIGURE 3

13. It is natural to ask whether there are symmetrical *equilibrium* situations in which a budget surplus or inflation is called for. The most obvious symmetrical case occurs when the natural rate of growth of the effective labor force is negative. But this is not a very interesting case of "growth."

The Harrod inflationary impasse, discussed above, would mean that at the hypothetical equilibrium capital intensity and rate of profit achievable when 100 per cent of saving goes into capital formation there is zero demand for money. Any money in existence, therefore, would have to be wiped out by surpluses or price increases; but these would be temporary rather than permanent.

One might, I suppose, imagine the public to desire a negative monetary position, i.e., to be net debtors to the government. Then there would be an equilibrium in which the public's net debt to the government grows in real value at the natural rate, thanks either to budget surpluses (with which the government acquires IOU's from its citizens) or to price inflation. In either case capital formation exceeds normal saving because the public saves extra either through taxes and the government

budget or through the necessity to provide for the increased real burden of its
debt to the government.

A negative monetary position is not as far-fetched as it sounds, if "money" is
interpreted in a broad sense to connote the whole range of actual fixed-money-
value assets, not just means of payment. It is quite possible, then, for the government
to be a net creditor over this entire category of assets, while still providing a circulating medium of exchange.

14. So far only the existence of an equilibrium path of the kind described in
Section 12 has been discussed. Its stability is something else again. I can only sketch
the considerations involved.

What happens when the community is thrown out of portfolio balance either by
some irregularity in technological progress, labor force growth, saving behavior,
change in yield expectations, or portfolio preferences? If the result of the shock
is that the public has too much capital and too little money for its tastes, goods
prices will fall faster or rise more slowly than before. In the opposite case, the
public will try to buy capital with money and will push prices up faster or retard
their decline.

Evidently there are two effects, at war with each other. One we might call the
Pigou effect, the other the Wicksell effect. The Pigou effect is stabilizing. Consider
the case of a deflationary shock. The accelerated decline in prices, by augmenting

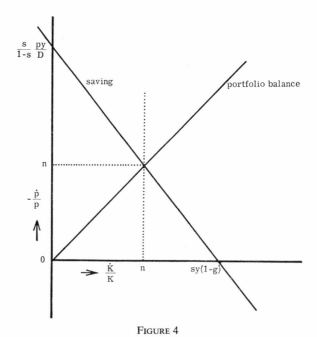

FIGURE 4

the real value of existing money balances, helps to restore portfolio balance. Moreover, by increasing total real wealth it retards the flow of saving into capital formation. The Wicksell effect is destabilizing. An accelerated decline in prices means a more attractive yield on money and encourages a further shift in portfolio demand in the same direction as the original shock.

There is no *a priori* reason why one effect should be stronger than the other in the neighborhood of equilibrium. In the model under discussion, the Pigou effect will eventually win out, but only after what may be a prolonged period of deflation, zero or negative capital formation, and retarded growth.

Figure 4 concerns the question of stability. Here the vertical axis measures the rate of price deflation, $-\dot{p}/p$, and the horizontal axis the rate of capital accumulation, $\dot{K}/K$. On each axis the natural rate of growth n is shown. On the horizontal axis, a rate of capital accumulation larger than n means capital deepening and a decline in yield, while capital accumulation at a rate slower than n means the opposite. It is assumed that a balanced budget policy is being followed so that the nominal stock of money is constant. The real value of this stock increases at the rate of deflation. It is, furthermore, assumed that existing real money balances and capital are in equilibrium; that is, their relative supplies are adjusted to the prevailing rate of profit on capital and to a real rate of return on money equal to n, the natural rate. The 45° line from the origin, labelled "portfolio balance," shows the combinations of price deflation and capital formation that will, preserve portfolio balances at the existing rates of return. The negatively sloped line labelled "saving" shows the combination of $-\dot{p}/p$ and $\dot{K}/K$ that exhausts saving, assuming once again the saving behavior of Figure 2. The values of the intercepts on both axes are indicated. On the horizontal axis, $sy(1-g)$ is the rate of capital growth if all saving goes into capital. On the vertical axis, $s/(1-s) \cdot py/D$ (where D is the nominal stock of money per unit of capital) measures a rate of price deflation at which the entire propensity to save would be satisfied by capital gains on monetary assets. The "saving" line crosses the "portfolio balance" line at the point (n, n). This is another representation of the equilibrium of Section 12. At this point, new saving will be divided so as to maintain both portfolio balance and capital intensity.

But suppose the rate of deflation were to exceed n. The point describing the division of saving would move to the northeast along the saving line. This means that the yield on money is higher—too high for the initial portfolio balance. Portfolio behavior may not reflect this rise in yield at once, since it will take time for the new rate of deflation to register in expectations and for wealth owners to try to adjust to new expectations.

Meanwhile, the yield on capital will be rising because capital accumulation is falling short of the natural rate. Moreover, via the Pigou effect the price decline is increasing the stock of money relative to the stock of capital. These two effects take time and increase in strength with time. They tend to satisfy or offset the increased demand for money due to the rise in yield on money, but they may do so too little and too late. If so, the rate of deflation will increase even further, and the point describing the course of the economy moves even further northeast on the saving curve. But the further it moves and the longer this process goes on, the smaller becomes capital's share in wealth and the higher its yield. The stabilizing effects become stronger, destabilizing effects weaker. As the ratio of income to money stock (py/D) declines, the vertical intercept of the saving line moves down. That is, the rate of deflation that would divert all saving away from capital formation becomes smaller and smaller. So the yield on money declines, the yield on capital rises, while the relative supplies are moving in the opposite direction. Eventually the rate of deflation will fall to n again, and we know that this is compatible with balanced growth.

This mechanism contains some cyclical possibilities. The cycle would be one in prices and in the composition of output as between consumption and investment. More realistic is the familiar possibility which I do not consider here, i.e., that downward stickiness of money wages prevents or limits deflation and substitutes underproduction and underemployment. In that case, capital formation is shut off, not because saving is diverted into government deficits or into real capital gains on monetary assets but because saving is curtailed by reduction of income and employment. The interruption of capital formation and growth is qualitatively the same either way, but the real losses of welfare during the process are of course much greater when employment rather than prices bears the brunt of adjustment.

15. In classical theory, the interest rate and the capital intensity of the economy are determined by "productivity and thrift," that is, by the interaction of technology and saving propensities. This is true both in the short run, when capital is being accumulated at a rate different from the growth of the labor force, and in the long-run stationary or "moving stationary" equilibrium, when capital intensity is constant. Keynes gave reasons why in the short run monetary factors and portfolio decisions modify, and in some circumstances dominate, the determination of the interest rate and the process of capital accumulation. I have tried to show here that a similar proposition is true for the long run. The equilibrium interest rate and degree of capital intensity are in general affected by monetary supplies and portfolio behavior, as well as by technology and thrift.

Cowles Foundation for Research in Economics, Yale University

III

Cambridge Growth and Distribution Theory

INTRODUCTION

One of the liveliest of debates in theoretical economics in the postwar period has been the controversy between the Cambridge Growth and Distribution Theory, represented in the articles collected in this part, and the neoclassical growth theory, of which most of the other articles in this volume are examples. One of the difficulties in this debate is that on neither side is there universal agreement: the growth theories of Kaldor and Robinson are perhaps as different as those of Robinson and Solow. Consequently, no statement of what separates the two schools will ever be acceptable to all the members of either one. Nonetheless, it may be worthwhile to try to summarize some of the basic differences. We shall first list the differences in the components of the models, and then indicate what implications these have for the total model.

First, the Cambridge economists believe that the aggregate savings ratio depends on the distribution of income. For instance, a higher proportion of profits are saved than of wage income (Kaldor).[1]

Neoclassicists maintain, on the other hand, that the aggregate savings

---

[1] One of the implications of this is, of course, that workers save a different proportion of their wage income than of their return from their previous savings. What Kaldor has in mind is some kind of corporate savings. Pasinetti [87] believes that workers save the same fraction of their interest income as of their wage income, but that there are pure capitalists, who save a higher fraction.

ratio is independent of the distribution of income. They believe, for instance, that individuals can see through the corporate guise, and can accordingly take compensating action for the high savings rates of corporations. Most neoclassicists would probably not hold firmly to any simple savings rule; they would argue that individuals save to maximize their intertemporal utility (the life cycle hypothesis).[2]

This is an illustration of one of the fundamental philosophical differences between the two schools. The neoclassicists are committed to an economic theory derived from some kind of rational behavior, while the Cambridge economists believe that individuals are not so calculating — in particular in a world of imperfect competition and uncertainty — and that rules of thumb are used. Hence, the most useful approach to descriptive economics is to construct behavioristic models, models in which individuals behave according to some rules, such as that a certain fraction of profits is saved. We shall see this difference arise again below in discussing, for instance, investment behavior.[3]

Second, the Cambridge economists object to the neoclassical production function. In particular, they object to the concept of a capital aggregate. Capital consists of a number of different types of machines, each with its own labor and other raw material requirements, and each used in producing different commodities. There is, as we noted in Part II, in general, no way in which one can aggregate these machines. Robinson refers to these alternative methods of production as the "Book of Blueprints"; essentially, she prefers an activity analysis approach to the study of production.

Most neoclassical economists probably agree that in general it is impossible to form a capital aggregate. They take on this issue in a pragmatic line; as Solow has said in his review of Hicks' *Capital and Growth*,[4] "I have never thought of the macroeconomic production function as a rigorously justifiable concept. In my mind it is either an illuminating parable, or else a mere device for handling data, to be used so long as it gives good empirical results, and to be abandoned as soon as it doesn't, or as soon as something better comes along." Whether or not it is an illuminating parable is, of course, the crucial question, and the answer will probably depend on the purpose at hand.[5]

[2] If the future is uncertain, the problem becomes technically difficult, but the hypothesis is that individuals maximize their expected intertemporal utility.

[3] Neoclassicists accuse the Cambridge school of *ad hoc*-ery, while the Cambridge economists accuse the neoclassicals of formulating irrelevant or tautological theories. It is interesting that on the next question to which we turn, the production function, Cambridge takes a much more purist line.

[4] R. M. Solow, "Review of *Capital and Growth*," *AER, 56* (December 1966), 1257–1260.

[5] Perhaps it should be pointed out that the problems of capital aggregation are not in substance that much different from the problems of aggregating different kinds of labor.

A third major difference in the two theories is in the investment function. In neoclassical models this is essentially nonexistent. Given the labor force, there is a full employment level of output. Since a certain fraction, s, of output is saved, the level of investment required to sustain full employment is immediately determined. The government, through monetary and fiscal policy, takes actions to ensure that the level of investment does in fact take place.

In Cambridge, the theory of the determination of investment has followed much more in the Keynesian tradition. At any point of time, the level of investment is fixed; the elasticity of investment to variations in monetary and fiscal policy during this period may be negligible. Investment is determined by entrepreneurs, on the basis of expectations, the present capital stock, etc. How entrepreneurs form their expectations is extremely complex, and (even if determinable) essentially unknown; and since the interaction between all these variables is itself extremely complex, some Cambridge theorists (notably Robinson) prefer to summarize all of this by saying that "animal spirits" determine the level of investment. On the other hand, Kaldor, in his growth models, and in particular in the Kaldor-Mirrlees article, shows explicitly how, under some behavioristic rules of thumb, such as a fixed time horizon, firms determine the level of investment.

If investment is determined, the economy, in a Cambridge model, maintains over the long run full or near full employment by varying the distribution of income. Since workers consume a higher proportion of their income than capitalists, by changing the distribution in favor of workers when investment is low and conversely when investment is high, full employment can be maintained. It is for this reason that the different savings propensities are so crucial for the Cambridge theory.

Thus, the full employment condition, with the differing savings propensities, determines in the Cambridge model the distribution of income. For instance, consider a Cambridge model with workers consuming all and capitalists saving s_c of their profits; for labor to be fully employed, and labor growing at the rate n, capital must be growing at the rate n (in the steady state); thus, $K = s_c rK$ or $r = n/s_c$. The choice of technique — if any choice is available — is then determined in the usual cost minimizing manner: a technique is chosen for which the marginal product of capital is equal to the rate of interest (with relevant inequalities for a nondifferentiable production function).

In the neoclassical model, on the other hand, distribution of income plays no part in determining either the long-run or short-run equilibrium of the system; in the long run, for instance, in the Solow model, the savings rate divided by the rate of growth is equal to the capital-output ratio. Corresponding to any capital-output ratio there is a marginal product of capital and a marginal product of labor — the greater the capital-output ratio, the smaller the marginal product of capital and the greater that of labor. And factor prices are then set equal to their marginal products. This is how the distribution of income is determined.

Although this difference in causality — whether the marginal product determines the rate of profit or the rate of profit determines the marginal product of capital — is one over which there has been a great deal of discussion, it is one of little deep significance. If, for example, there had been some savings out of wages, in the Cambridge model, then distribution and marginal products would have had to be determined simultaneously. The same thing can be said for the neoclassical model. If there is only a slight difference between savings rates out of wages and out of profits, then both distribution and marginal products would have had to be determined at the same time.[6]

One of the objections raised by Cambridge to the neoclassical model is that its distribution theory depends on marginal products, and marginal products are not well defined in discrete technologies; that is, instead of having a differentiable production function, the economy has a finite number of alternative techniques available. This objection is also not of deep significance since from activity analysis it is known that shadow prices can still be assigned to the different factors. The problem of defining the marginal products arises, of course, at the corners — at the points at which we switch from one technique to another. There is then a lower limit and an upper limit on the marginal products. As the number of techniques available gets large, this difference becomes negligible. The problem appears to be important only if one works with a model in which there is only one — or only a few — techniques available. But since there are usually many techniques available this is hardly a serious problem, particularly if we have a vintage model, where machines built in different years have different characteristics.

Moreover, in the more complicated technologies discussed in Part II,

---

[6] Recently, Pasinetti has formulated a model in which even though workers save a positive amount, the rate of profit is just the rate of growth divided by the savings propensity of capitalists. He postulates a two-class economy: capitalists, who do no work and who save a constant fraction s_c of their income; and workers, who save a smaller fraction of their income (which consists of the return from previous savings and wages). If the labor force L is growing exponentially at the rate n, then if K_c is capitalists' capital, $k_c = K_c/L$, and r the rate of profit, $\dot{K}_c = s_c r K_c$, or $\dot{k}_c = s_c r k_c - n k_c$ (where $\dot{x} = dx/dt$). Thus in long-run equilibrium $r = n/s_c$. But as Meade [86] and subsequently Samuelson and Modigliani [90] pointed out, if the savings rate of workers is sufficiently high (greater than the share of capital times the savings propensity of capitalists) there exists no balanced growth path with both classes. The only balanced growth path has only workers and no capitalists. Whether this is empirically relevant has been the subject of some debate (see [85], [88], and [89]).

with possibilities of substitution between capital and labor before the machine is constructed but not afterward, the differences between the two schools become further blurred, since, as we have already noted, in this case the real wage is equal not to the marginal product of labor along the *ex ante* production function, but to the average output per worker on the least efficient machine used.

The really important difference between the two theories does not lie in the theoretical purity each side insists upon — for where it is to their advantage, each side is willing to compromise — but on the determination of investment in the economy. Does savings with proper government intervention determine investment, that is, is investment sufficiently elastic that it can be made equal to desired savings, at full employment,[7] or does the distribution of income adjust savings to investment?

[7] Kaldor, in his growth models, has stressed one further point, which until recently had been more or less lacking from neoclassical growth models — the interaction between technological progress and production (his technological progress function). See Arrow's model of "Learning by Doing," pp. 210–228.

EXERCISES IN THE ANALYSIS OF GROWTH

By R. F. KAHN

THE development in the last few years of theories of economic growth has introduced new concepts and called on unfamiliar tools. In this-lecture I intend no more than to take out for an airing a few of the concepts to which Mrs. Robinson and others have introduced us and to try out the edge of a few of the tools. I am not attempting to build up a theory of growth and still less to arrive at any conclusions.

I will begin with the fundamental identity, based on treating income as divided between capitalists' incomes and wages. At any and every moment of time there is a simple relationship between the rate of growth in the value of the stock of capital and the ratio to that value of the stock of capital of the current incomes of the capitalists. This relationship involves the proportion of capitalists' incomes which is saved and the proportion of wages which is saved. The only other factor which enters into the relationship of identity is the ratio of the value of the stock of capital to the value of output, but this drops out if only a small proportion of wages is saved.[1]

What is necessary for this simple relationship to be generally valid is that *income* should be defined in a suitable manner, so that the excess of income over consumption is the same thing as the rate of change in the

---

[1] Let α be the proportion saved out of capitalists' incomes and β out of wages.

Then investment = saving

$$= \text{capitalists' saving} + \text{wage-earners' saving}$$
$$= \alpha \, (\text{capitalists' incomes}) + \beta \, (\text{wages})$$
$$= \alpha \, (\text{capitalists' incomes}) + \beta \, (\text{total income} - \text{capitalists' incomes})$$
$$= (\alpha - \beta) \, (\text{capitalists' incomes}) + \beta \, (\text{value of output}).$$

It follows that the rate of growth of the value of the stock of capital, which is measured by

$$\frac{\text{investment}}{\text{value of stock of capital}},$$

is identically equal to

$$(\alpha - \beta) \, \frac{\text{capitalists' incomes}}{\text{value of stock of capital}}$$
$$+ \beta \, \frac{\text{value of output}}{\text{value of stock of capital}}.$$

The form of this relationship was established and used by Mr. Kaldor in his 'Model of Economic Growth' (*Economic Journal*, Dec. 1957, p. 611). It is used by Professor Champernowne in his 'Capital Accumulation and Full Employment' (*Economic Journal*, June 1958, p. 218). As I have reproduced it here it must, however, be regarded for the present purely as an identity.

If $\alpha = 1$ and $\beta = 0$, the rate of growth becomes identically equal to the ratio of capitalists' incomes to the value of capital. This is the simplified form in which Mrs. Robinson had presented the relationship in her *Accumulation of Capital* (p. 76).

R. F. Kahn, "Exercises in the Analysis of Growth," *Oxford Economic Papers* N.S. 11 (June 1959) pp. 143–156. By permission of the Clarendon Press.

value of the stock of capital. This requires that the owner of a piece of capital equipment should include in his income any increase in its value which, after due deduction of depreciation, arises apart from any physical work conducted on it by way of improvement (and that he should deduct any fall in its value apart from depreciation). As a corollary, the relationship, if it is to be valid, requires that any such changes in the value of capital equipment are included in investment, which has to be defined as the rate of change in the value of capital and not in any sense as the value of the change in the amount of capital.

The same kind of relationship could be expressed in terms of alternative definitions of income provided that the rate of growth of the stock of capital was appropriately defined. For example, if we follow ordinary social accounting procedure, investment is measured by the cost of additions to the stock of capital and income does *not* include additions to the value of existing capital equipment which result, say, from a rising price level or from improving profit expectations. For the relationship to hold, the rate of growth would then have to be defined as the rate of expenditure on additions to the stock of capital (less depreciation, with the logical problems therein involved) divided by the value of the stock of capital.

The magnitude of the capitalists' savings coefficient depends on the definition of income which is adopted—unless capitalists do not consume at all, in which case the coefficient is always unity. And the natural choice of definition turns on the extent and manner in which increments in the value of capital influence capitalists' consumption.

This problem of definition is considerably eased if all values are measured in terms of consumption goods rather than money. This convention I will adopt, and when, for example, I speak of 'wage-rates' I shall mean 'real wage-rates'. The implications of an expectation of rising prices are not, however, by this device entirely eliminated and I shall have to return to the problem.

On whatever set of definitions the relationship is based, I have said nothing so far which imbues it with any causal force. It is purely an identity—a glorified version of the identity between savings and investment, which I claim to be a useful instrument for detecting error against those detractors who contemptuously dismiss it as a 'truism' or, more contemptible still, a 'tautology'. Our glorified version of the Keynesian identity would be as consistent, so far as anything emerges from what I have stated so far, with a system of ideas under which the rate of growth of capital was derived from the rate of profit as with a system under which the rate of profit is derived from the rate of growth. Also the identity is valid irrespective of any technical or other conditions—it does not require that the character of technical progress should conform to any particular pattern, and it is independent of the behaviour of the labour force and of employment and unemployment.

It is to be observed, however, that the relationship is not expressed in terms of the *rate of profit*. It is expressed in terms of the ratio of capitalists' incomes to the value of the stock of capital. It is the *current* incomes of capitalists which enter into the relationship. The rate of profit, on the other hand, if properly defined, is a matter of *expected* capitalists' incomes. At least this is what the rate of profit should signify if the term is used in the context of investment decisions, and in particular if it is regarded as having any correlation of a technical character with the stock of capital.

Let me now take one step forward and inquire what the position is if for some reason or other I can postulate that the rate of growth of capital is constant over a long period of time and that expectations are consistently such as, in the broad, to be realized, so that conditions of long-period equilibrium prevail. It follows from the relationship that if the proportion of wages saved is small, the ratio of capitalists' incomes to the value of capital is constant through time. Such a case is not only consistent with the assumption that capitalists' incomes are *expected* to grow at the same rate as the value of capital, but is highly congenial to the assumption that, in the broad, capitalists' expectations turn out to be justified. Then my postulate results in a rate of profit which is constant through time. And indeed it is only when the rate of profit is constant through time that it. can be uniquely defined and unambiguously measured.

So far I have—for fun, as it were, without offering any justification— postulated a constant rate of growth of capital and I have shown that the same conditions which underlie the postulate, whatever they may be, will establish a rate of profit which is also constant. The only other *assumption* is that the two savings coefficients are constant and that for wage-earners the saving coefficient is small. Now I want to take another step forward and make a set of assumptions about technical progress. The assumptions are heroic. I do not make them because I believe in their validity in practice. The reason why I make them is that, for my own part, I desire to learn to walk before I try to run. First of all, I assume that the stage of technical knowledge can at any moment of time be represented by a production function which indicates the technical character of the new plant which it is decided to produce, and the character of its intended utilization. Given the production function, the choice of technique depends on expectations over the prospective lifetime of the plant of the relationship between the price of the particular product and the cost of producing it. With a rate of profit which is constant through time there is a unique relationship between the rate of profit and the techniques which are being adopted at any moment of time, in the sense of higher rates of profit being associated with lower degrees of mechanization.

In the second place, I assume that the state of technical knowledge at each moment of time, as depicted in the production function, and the development of technical knowledge, as depicted by the movement of the production function through time, are independent factors, and in particular do not depend on the rate of accumulation of capital. In the third place, I assume that the progress through time of technical development is neutral: this means that if the conditions are such as to entail a constant rate of profit the rate of growth of output per head will be the same at earlier stages in the process of production as at later stages; that this condition holds good for every rate of profit within the relevant range; and that this uniform growth of productivity proceeds at the same rate for all rates of profit within the relevant range. All this is entailed in assuming neutral technical progress.

With these assumptions I now want to combine the postulate of a constant rate of profit, entailing a constant rate of growth of the value of capital if conditions of long-period equilibrium are assumed, in which expectations are realized in the broad and in particular in which on the average equipment is used in the manner intended. The ratio of the value of capital to the value of output will then be constant through time. And the relative shares of capitalists' and wage-earners' incomes will remain constant.[1]

The magnitude of this constant capital-output ratio will depend on the technical conditions of production, whereas the relationship between the rate of profit and the rate of growth of capital depends only on the savings coefficients. For any given technique, the capital-output ratio depends on the relative prices of capital-goods and consumption-goods. This depends on the wage-rate and the rate of profit, in the sense that a higher wage-rate by itself results in a higher capital-output ratio and a lower rate of profit by itself in a lower ratio. Which effect is the stronger depends on the time pattern of the application of labour in the productive process.[2] The result of technical substitutibility between capital and

[1] Since the ratio of the value of output to the value of capital is constant, the relationship which establishes consistency between a constant rate of growth of capital and a constant rate of profit no longer turns out on β, the proportion saved out of wages, being small.

The relationship can also be expressed in terms of the share of capitalists' incomes in total income and the share of investment in output, as has been done by Mr. Kaldor ('L'évolution capitaliste à la lumière de l'économie Keynésienne', *Économie Appliquée*, p. 268; also *Review of Economic Studies*, vol. xxiii, no. 2, p. 95). If the rate of growth of the value of capital is constant and the capital-output ratio is constant, then the share of investment in output is constant.

[2] See I. M. D. Little, 'Classical Growth', *Oxford Economic Papers*, June 1957, pp. 158 and 175.

labour is, taken by itself, that a lower rate of profit means a higher capital-output ratio—the greater the technical substitutibility (the wider the choice of technique at a given stage of technical development) the stronger this tendency will be.

Given the rate of profit, the wage-rate, which plays a part in determining the capital-output ratio, depends on the magnitude of the capital-output ratio and on the value of output per head. The fact that these various magnitudes depend on one another does not mean that the equation involved will not provide a solution. What it does mean is that the wage-rate, and the distribution of income, are related to the technical character-istics of the productive processes, as well as to the rate of growth and the savings coefficients—to which alone the rate of profit is related.[1] Even therefore when the rate of growth can be isolated as an independent factor —a matter which I shall have to deal with—it is only the rate of profit which can be imputed solely to it and to the savings coefficients. If we are interested in how wages and the distribution of income are determined, the technical conditions have to be brought in.

One statement that it is, however, possible to make about a state of constant growth with neutral technical progress is that the distribution of income remains constant through time.

A further such statement is that output per man employed, and the wage-rate, both grow at a rate equal to the rate of technical progress, irrespective of the rate of growth of capital. On the other hand, the aggregate of real wages grows with aggregate output at a rate equal to the rate of growth of capital.

The reconciliation lies in the behaviour of employment. This increases at a rate equal to the excess of the rate of growth of capital over the rate of technical progress. If the two are equal, employment remains constant. If the rate of technical progress exceeds the rate of growth of capital, employment diminishes.

I have said nothing so far about the labour force or, as I shall put it, population. The relation between the behaviour of employment and the behaviour of population determines the behaviour of unemployment.[2] I therefore make a further assumption. I assume that if population changes at all it grows (or diminishes) at a constant rate. And to match this assumption I assume also that the rate of technical progress is constant.

Then if the rate of growth of capital is equal to the rate of technical progress *plus* the rate of growth of population, the proportion of unem-

---

[1] If the wage-earners' savings coefficient is small.

[2] For the sake of simplicity, I assume that the unemployed subsist at the expense of the standard of living of those who are employed.

ployment will remain constant. If at any stage there is full employment, there is full employment continuously.

I have now, as a result of a succession of postulates and assumptions, arrived at Mrs. Robinson's Golden Age[1] of equilibrium growth with full employment. Her picturesque phrase provides, I think, a convenient method of identification, provided that the emotive undertones remain subdued. We must guard against any suggestion that the Golden Age is an ideal. Mrs. Robinson herself points out that a higher rate of accumulation than seems to be called for to secure a Golden Age with given technical conditions is likely itself to alter the conditions, and in particular the rate of technical progress: 'the pressure of scarcity of labour, driving up wage-rates, would induce more inventions to be made, and hasten the diffusion of improvements already known'. In other words, Mrs. Robinson is pointing out the unreality of the heroic assumptions, as I have described them, about technical progress. Moreover, we must be careful not to exclude, as a possibly more desirable alternative, a higher rate of growth of consumption, obtained at the expense of a temporarily lower current level of consumption, as a result of a higher rate of growth of capital and consequent progression to higher degrees of mechanization. In other words, we have to consider Mr. Little's *platinum age*[2] as a possibly more desirable alternative to Mrs. Robinson's Golden Age.

A further reason for guarding against the implication that a Golden Age represents some kind of ideal is that any particular Golden Age is based on given thriftiness of capitalists and of wage-earners. A higher proportion of incomes saved, on the part of either or both, would mean that, given the state and growth of technical knowledge and given the growth of population, the Golden Age would have built into it a lower rate of profit, so as to secure the correct relationship with an unchanged rate of growth of capital (equal to the rate of technical progress *plus* the rate of growth of population).[3] This lower rate of profit would, at each moment of time, go with a higher degree of mechanization than in the Golden Age adjusted to the lower level of thriftiness, and it would go with a larger total output, with a larger output of consumption goods, and with a higher wage-rate.

There is a practical reason why it is important to consider the implications of the degree of thriftiness. In the usual models of economic growth,

---

[1] Joan Robinson, op. cit., p. 99.

[2] See I. M. D. Little, loc. cit., p. 172.

[3] A cursory inspection of the relationship, as set out in my first footnote, might suggest that the capitalists' and wage-earners' savings coefficients, α and β, pull in opposite directions on the rate of profit called for by a given rate of growth. But this is illusory. The expression can be redeployed so that the factor $(\alpha - \beta)$ no longer occurs, and it should be borne in mind that the reciprocal of the capital-output ratio must exceed the rate of profit if wages are not to be negative.

such as Mrs. Robinson's Golden Age, the State is left out of the picture
and in particular there is no room for saving by the State. Now, an
economy might be developing as a Golden Age, but, thriftiness being low,
the methods of production are often so primitive, as a result of scarcity
of capital, that the word 'golden' is a mockery. The practical question
which then arises is whether the economy would not be in a happier
condition if the State were contributing to saving out of the proceeds of
higher taxes. For the purpose of analysis one can regard such State
saving as assimilated into the simpler model which disregards it. For
in so far as it is financed by taxation of profits its effects are the same as
those of a higher capitalists' savings coefficient; in so far as it is financed
by indirect taxation, it is equivalent in its effects to those of higher savings
coefficients for both capitalists and wage-earners, to the extent of their
consumption of the taxed commodities.[1]

I must now emphasize that what is involved in this line of exercise is
a comparison of the Golden Ages between which there exists a stated
difference but which in other respects are subject to the same conditions.
It is one thing to *correlate* two characteristics involved in such a comparison, such as the savings coefficients on the one hand and on the other
hand the rate of profit and the degree of mechanization—but it would be
quite another thing, for which justification would have to be produced,
to regard the one as causatively determining the other.

This brings me to the more fundamental question what process of
causation might be held conceptually responsible for the establishment and
persistence of any particular Golden Age. The simplest case to conceive
is that in which for a long time in the past the underlying conditions have
operated in a constant and uniform manner and the Golden Age appropriate
to them has in fact existed. A tranquil past breeds expectations based on
past experience. The constant rate of profit is, as a matter of expectation,
firmly based on experience. The structure of capital—and in particular
the proportions in which specialized equipment is divided between what is

---

[1] The beneficial influence on the wage-rate associated with a higher degree of thrift is
the larger, the smaller is the effect (expressed algebraically) in causing the capital-output
ratio to be higher. This effect is smaller

  (i) the smaller is the substitutibility of capital and labour;
  (ii) the smaller is the effect of a higher wage-rate, and the larger is the effect in the
       opposite direction of a lower rate of profit, on the prices of particular kinds of capital-
       goods in terms of consumption-goods.

If these factors operate with sufficient strength, higher thrift will benefit wages to such
a degree that even though practised entirely by wage-earners, their standard of living is on
the average actually higher, in each state of technical knowledge, despite the higher thrift.

It then follows equally, under such conditions, that indirect taxes devoted to State saving,
even if confined to commodities consumed by wage-earners, will actually entail *higher* real
wage-rates (and that taxation of wages, devoted to State saving, will entail wages which are
higher by more than the amount of the taxes paid out of them).

designed for making consumption-goods, for making capital-goods for making consumption-goods, and for making capital-goods for making capital-goods—is such as to result in a flow of capital-goods the value of which grows at the same rate as the value of the total stock of capital. As Mrs. Robinson puts it, entrepreneurs 'desire to accumulate at the same proportional rate as they have been doing over the past'.

This explanation is, however, too general. It justifies a state of equilibrium growth at *any* conceivable rate—what the rate happens to be being a matter of historical accident. It might be a rate less than the rate of technical progress, so as to result in steadily diminishing employment even though the population was constant or growing. And, as I have already indicated, the rate of growth may exceed the rate of technical progress, and employment may therefore be growing, but there may nevertheless be unemployment. It seems to me convenient to be able to describe such a state of equilibrium growth which has all the attributes of a Golden Age other than that of full employment. I suggest that it be called a Bastard Golden Age.

I now want to inquire whether there is any mechanism which can be said to determine the existence of a Golden Age proper, with a determined rate of growth, as opposed to a Bastard Golden Age with a rate of growth dependent on historical accident. What mechanism is there which is brought into operation at the point of full employment ? Clearly we do not need to look beyond the familiar Keynesian rationalization of the classical processes of thought. The decision to invest depends not only on the prospective profit but on a comparison of that profit with the cost of financing the investment or, if the finance is available from internal sources, with the yield which could be secured by using it on the financial and capital markets. In simple terms any Golden Age, whether bastard or legitimate, must have had built into it a rate of interest which matches the rate of profit, and which discourages capitalists from embarking on projects likely to yield less than the Golden Age rate of profit. This rate of interest is not to be conceived in any simple sense. It is simply a phrase used for convenience to sum up the state of finance. The risks of enterprise must be allowed for. The fact that in a Golden Age capitalists' expectations are realized *in the broad* does not exclude the risks involved in the vagaries of technical processes and of consumers' behaviour. For these reasons the risk-free rate of interest would even in a Golden Age lie below the rate of profit, with which yields on ordinary shares are more comparable since they involve the same kind of risks as physical investment. Imperfections of the financial and capital markets are also likely to be important factors limiting investment. To meet the requirements of a Golden Age it is only necessary to assume either that the number of capitalists grows at the Golden Age rate of growth or that the limits on the finance available to each expand on the average at the same rate of growth.

The possibility of a Bastard Golden Age turns on the absence of any progressive tendency towards the easing of the state of finance, and, more particularly, towards a lowering of rates of interest and of yields on ordinary shares. If, for example, money wage-rates tend to fall progressively under the pressure of unemployment or the quantity of money tends to rise faster than money wages or the monetary authority in the face of unemployment deliberately makes credit progressively cheaper, there will be such a progressive tendency and this will undermine the equilibrium of a Bastard Golden Age. In the absence of unemployment, on the other hand, there need be no such progressive easing of the state of finance. And with full employment any momentary tendency for investment to rise above the equilibrium rate will result in money wages being forced up under the pressure of unsatisfied demand for labour, until investment is pushed back to the Golden Age equilibrium rate. The rate of growth of a legitimate Golden Age, which grows in such a way as to maintain full employment, can thus be based on some idea of determinacy and not just historical accident.

Once the rate of growth is tethered in this way so that it can be inferred from the rate of technical progress and the rate of growth of population, it is possible to say that the rate of profit is *determined* by the rate of growth and by the savings coefficients.

Looked at in this way a statement that thrift has no influence on the rate of growth of capital is devoid of significance. If the rate of growth is determined in such a way as to secure full employment, it must match the growth of technical knowledge and population, and that is what it has to be equal to.

Thrift is important, however, because it determines the real wage-rate in a Golden Age, with given technical conditions at each stage and given rates of neutral technical progress and growth of population. In a certain sense growth is easier if at each stage the real wage-rate is higher—in the sense that a smaller sacrifice is called for from wage-earners. In this sense thrift is helpful to the process of growth.

This brings me to the 'inflation barrier'.[1] So far I have assumed that any real wage will be tolerated, no matter how low, and that only the approach to full employment will bring into operation a financial check resulting from the inflationary pressure on money wages of an unsatisfied demand for labour. It may be, however, that real wages which fail to reach a certain limit are unacceptable, in the sense that any attempt to enforce such real wages, even with the existence of unemployment, will

[1] Joan Robinson, op. cit., p. 48.

bring into operation an inflationary movement of money wages such as will result in a check on investment through its effect on the state of finance. Or the real wage may lie below the subsistence level. The inflation barrier is the minimum real wage-rate which will be tolerated without provoking reactions inconsistent with a state of equilibrium growth. To that minimum real wage-rate there corresponds, given the technical and thriftiness conditions, a particular Bastard Golden Age, with a rate of growth just sufficiently low to secure this minimum real wage-rate for those employed.[1] In such a Bastard Golden Age, the rate of growth is limited by the operation of the inflation barrier. Thrift can now be regarded as an influence on the rate of growth. It is the real wage-rate which is independently determined and greater thriftiness means a higher rate of growth and a less rapid increase of unemployment.

The inflation barrier may be in operation for a time even though the Golden Age real wage would be perfectly acceptable to the wage-earners. It may be that on account of the character of the development of the system back in history, unemployment still prevails and that the maximum possible rate of equilibrium growth is such as to bring the real wage-rate to the minimum and the inflation barrier into operation. Any higher rate of growth would bring inflationary forces into operation against itself; while any lower rate would be inconsistent with equilibrium because the state of finance would progressively ease, as a result of the existence of unemployment for which the inflation barrier was not responsible. Full equilibrium will therefore demand a Bastard Golden Age with a rate of growth greater than the legitimate Golden Age rate. Unemployment will progressively diminish until, with full employment in sight, there is no longer a valid basis for this Bastard Golden Age. The speed with which the position of full employment is attained will depend on the operation of the inflation barrier—the higher the minimum real wage-rate the lower the speed will be. It is shortage of capital which is the cause of such unemployment and the remedying of the shortage depends on the readiness of those who are in employment to make a temporary sacrifice on their real wage-rate.[2] And of course thrift here again operates as an influence

---

[1] To make equilibrium growth possible, it must be assumed either that there is no technical progress, so that the real wage-rate is constant, or that the minimum real wage-rate which constitutes the inflation barrier rises, as a matter of human progress and the development of ideas about minimum standards, at the same rate, purely by way of coincidence, as the rate of technical progress.

Professor Champernowne introduces the inflation barrier in terms purely of a minimum rate of growth of the minimum real wage-rate, the absolute level at any stage of development being apparently immaterial (loc. cit., p. 224).

[2] It is realistic to conceive of the inflation barrier to operate, as I do here, in terms of a minimum real wage-rate. It would be more logical but less realistic, to conceive it to operate in terms of the standard of living of those employed, after allowance for the support of the unemployed, or, better still, of the average standard of living of all the potential wage-earners, including the unemployed.

on the rate of growth—the greater the savings propensities, the more rapidly will the shortage of capital be overcome and unemployment be eliminated.

I now want to say something about the relation between profits and investment. In ordinary short-period economics, we are in the habit of associating higher profits with greater investment. This association involves two entirely different meanings of the word 'profit' and two different processes of cause and effect. The word 'profit' is often loosely used to signify what I have called capitalists' current incomes. In that sense high profits are caused by high investment—purely as a current phenomenon. But if the emphasis is on 'rate of profit', then it is the expectation of capitalists' incomes which is the subject of the association with the rate of investment, and the causation is the other way round: high investment is caused by high profits. In dealing with problems of non-equilibrium growth, such as I am not attempting, the difference between the two concepts of profit, and between the two types of causation, should be kept firmly in mind. With equilibrium growth the future is like the present. But although the rate of profit is the same viewed in current terms as in terms of expectations, the nature of the causation is still important.

If two different Golden Ages are compared, with the same savings coefficients but different rates of growth, the higher rate of growth is associated with the higher rate of profit.[1] This higher rate of profit is to be attributed to the higher rate of growth of capital rather than the other way round.

Indeed, in all these cases of equilibrium growth—Bastard as well as legitimate Golden Ages—the rate of growth of capital is inferred from factors other than profits: from rates of technical progress and population growth, from the minimum real wage-rate which constitutes the inflation barrier, and from pure historical accident. The reason why the causation does not operate the other way round as well is that a state of equilibrium growth requires a state of finance which has been built into the equilibrium system, in such a way that the deterrent influence on investment of the difficulty and cost of financing investment, and of the attraction of alternative methods of laying out financial resources, just matches the stimulating influence of profit expectations. The rate of interest, and all that goes with it in the financial sphere, has accommodated itself to the rate of profit and neither the rate of profit nor the rate of interest can be regarded as independent influences on investment.

This leads to the question what happens if the appropriate rate of

[1] Once again wage-earners' thrift is taken to be small.

profit is too low to be matched by the terms on which finance can be made available. There is in practice a minimum—a bottom-stop—below which it is difficult, or impossible, for the rate of interest to be forced down by monetary means.[1] Even if any particular minimum is likely to be broken down after long experience of consistently very low rates of interest, it is relevant that negative rates of interest are not conceivable and that the risk premium has to be added on to the rate of interest before the rate of profit is matched against it. If finance cannot become sufficiently easy to match the Golden Age rate of profit, and if other methods of stimulating investment are excluded, then the Golden Age is not possible.

Mr. Kaldor has pointed out that an expectation of rising prices can in such a situation provide a basis for a Golden Age and save the economy from the decay which is the alternative. If we continue to calculate our values in terms of consumption-goods rather than money, we must represent such an expectation as a lowering of the 'real' rate of interest corresponding to any particular money rate of interest bottom-stop, leaving the Golden Age rate of profit and rate of growth unaffected. If, on the other hand, we prefer to think in terms of the money rate of interest, then the rate of profit and rate of growth must be evaluated in money rather than in real terms and they will both be greater by reason of the rising prices.

Or rather this will be so if income is defined so as to include the increase in the value of capital equipment resulting from the rise in prices. If, on the other hand, the normal social accounting definition of income is employed, it makes no difference to the evaluation of the rate of growth whether prices are rising or not. And it makes no difference to the ratio of capitalists' current incomes to the value of the stock of capital. But this ratio is not a rate of profit which can be set against the rate of interest. As the prospective change in the value of capital equipment is left out of the account, the return from a given amount of current investment measured in money of current purchasing power is an annuity, the elements of which are progressively greater, on account of the expected rise in prices, as they attach to more distant points of time in the future. By reason of the expectation of rising prices, the rate of profit in the relevant sense exceeds the ratio of capitalists' current incomes to the value of the stock of capital.

Profit expectations and the rate of interest are not, in ordinary short-period economics, the only influences on investment. Having decided that neither of them has any influence on the rate of long-period equilibrium growth, I go on to ask myself about the part played in a Golden Age by

[1] See Keynes, *General Theory*, p. 309.

Keynes' 'animal spirits'—'a spontaneous urge to action rather than inaction. . . . If the animal spirits are dimmed . . . enterprise will fade and die.'[1]

High animal spirits can usefully be considered in four different aspects:

(i) They promote the growth of scientific knowledge. In this aspect they take a part in contributing to the rate of growth of the Golden Age.

(ii) They promote the exploitation of scientific knowledge, i.e. its conversion into technical knowledge. This is a more important way in which again they promote technical progress, and the growth of the Golden Age.

(iii) They promote an optimistic view of the future. In this aspect high animal spirits are incompatible with the conditions of a Golden Age, in which the prospect of the future is strictly determined by knowledge of the present and the past.

(iv) On the basis of given expectations, high animal spirits strengthen the urge to invest. In this aspect high animal spirits are in no sense incompatible with the conditions of a Golden Age. But they exert no influence on the rate of growth, their effect being rendered nugatory by reason of the terms on which finance is available. The stronger the animal spirits the higher has to be the rate of interest, and the tighter generally have to be financial conditions, while the rate of profit is unaffected.

In conclusion, I want to emphasize what I have *not* been doing in this lecture. I have talked about Golden Ages. But I have only touched on the question whether a system which is in Golden Age equilibrium is likely to stay there. And I have not discussed at all the really important question whether a system which is not in Golden Age equilibrium will tend to move towards the Golden Age.

Equally, I have not discussed what would be entailed in a movement, if it could be contrived, out of one Golden Age into another, within some definite limited period of time—or out of a Bastard Golden Age into a legitimate Golden Age. For example, I indicated that, other things being the same, if two Golden Ages differed only in respect of thrift, the one with the higher thrift was the preferable one, and that it was possible that even though the extra thrift was entirely at the expense of the wage-earners, the actual standard of wage-earners' consumption might be higher as a result of it. But when one speaks of a Golden Age being preferable in that sort of sense, it means that it would be preferable to be in it. But to be in it involves *having* been in it for a long time past, and

---

[1] Keynes, *General Theory*, pp. 161–2.

enjoying the legacy of the past in terms of the accumulated stock of capital and the degree of mechanization. The desirability of a movement from the one Golden Age to the other, and the manner in which it might be smoothly negotiated, is one of the important and difficult problems of economic growth. What I have said in this lecture is intended as no more than prolegomena to the solution of the real problems.

Alternative Theories of Distribution

Nicholas Kaldor

According to the Preface of Ricardo's Principles, the discovery of the laws which regulate distributive shares is the " principal problem in Political Economy ". The purpose of this paper is to present a bird's eye view of the various theoretical attempts, since Ricardo, at solving this "principal problem ". Though all attempts at classification in such a vast field are necessarily to some extent arbitrary, and subjective to the writer, in terms of broad classification, one should, I think, distinguish between four main strands of thought, some of which contain important sub-groups. The first of these is the Ricardian, or Classical Theory, the second the Marxian, the third the Neo-Classical or Marginalist Theory and the fourth the Keynesian. The inclusion of a separate " Keynesian " theory in this context may cause surprise. An attempt will be made to show however that the specifically Keynesian apparatus of thought could be applied to the problem of distribution, rather than to the problem of the general level of production ; that there is evidence that in its early stages, Keynes' own thinking tended to develop in this direction—only to be diverted from it with the discovery (made some time between the publication of the *Treatise on Money* and the *General Theory*) that inflationary and deflationary tendencies could best be analysed in terms of the resulting changes in output and employment, rather than in their effects on prices.

The compression of a whole army of distinguished writers, and schools of thought, between Ricardo and Keynes (Marx aside) under the term of Neo-Classical or Marginalist Theory is harder to justify. For apart from the marginalists proper, the group would have to include such " non-marginalists " or quasi-marginalists (from the point of view of distribution theory) as the Walrasians and the neo-Walrasians,[1] as well as the imperfect competitionists, who though marginalist, do not necessarily hold with the principle of Marginal Productivity. But as I shall hope to show, there are important aspects which all these theories have in common,[2] and which justifies bringing them under one broad umbrella.

Ricardo prefaced his statement by a reference to the historical fact that " in different stages of society the proportions of the whole produce of the earth which will be allotted to each of these (three) classes under the names of rent, profit and wages will be essentially *different*."[3] To-day, a writer on the problem of distribution, would almost be inclined to say the opposite—that " in different stages of (capitalist) society the proportions of the national income allotted to wages, profits, etc., are *essentially similar* ". The famous " historical constancy " of the share of wages in the national income—and the similarity of these shares in different capitalist economies, such as the U.S. and the U.K.—was of course an unsuspected feature of capitalism in Ricardo's day. But to the extent that recent empirical research tends to contradict Ricardo's assumption about the variability of relative shares, it makes the question of what determines these shares, more, rather than less, intriguing. In fact no hypothesis as regards the forces determining distributive

---

[1] By the term " neo-Walrasians " I mean the American " linear programming " and " Activity analysis " schools, as well as the general equilibrium model of von Neumann (*Review of Economic Studies*, 1945-46, Vol. XIII (1)) whose technique shows certain affinities with Walras even though their basic assumptions (in particular that of the " circularity " of the production process) are quite different. From the point of view of distribution theory however, the approach only yields a solution (in the shape of an equilibrium interest rate) on the assumption of constant real wages (due to an infinitely elastic supply curve of labour) ; it shows therefore more affinity with the classical models than with the neo-classical theories.

[2] With the possible exception of the " neo-Walrasian " group referred to above.

[3] Preface (my italics).

Reprinted from XXIII, No. 2 (1956), pp. 83–100 of *Review of Economic Studies* by permission of *Review of Economic Studies* published by Oliver & Boyd Ltd., Edinburgh and London.
© 1956 The Economic Society.

shares could be intellectually satisfying unless it succeeds in accounting for the relative stability of these shares in the advanced capitalist economies over the last 100 years or so, despite the phenomenal changes in the techniques of production, in the accumulation of capital relative to labour and in real income per head.

Ricardo's concern in the problem of distribution was not due, or not only due, to the interest in the question of distributive shares *per se*, but to the belief that the theory of distribution holds the key to an understanding of the whole mechanism of the economic system—of the forces governing the rate of progress, of the ultimate incidence of taxation, of the effects of protection, and so on. It was through " the laws which regulate distributive shares " that he was hoping to build what in present-day parlance we would call " a simple macro-economic model ".[1] In this respect, if no other, the Ricardian and the " Keynesian " theories are analogous.[2] With the neo-Classical or Marginalist theories, on the other hand, the problem of distribution is merely one aspect of the general pricing process ; it has no particular theoretical significance apart from the importance of the question *per se*. Nor do these theories yield a " macro-economic model " of the kind that exhibits the reaction-mechanism of the system through the choice of a strictly limited number of dependent and independent variables.

I. THE RICARDIAN THEORY

Ricardo's theory was based on two separate principles which we may term the " marginal principle " and the " surplus principle " respectively. The " marginal principle " serves to explain the share of rent, and the " surplus principle " the division of the residue between wages and profits. To explain the Ricardian model, we must first divide the economy into two broad branches, agriculture and industry and then show how, on Ricardo's assumptions, the forces operating in agriculture serve to determine distribution in industry.

The agricultural side of the picture can be exhibited in terms of a simple diagram (FIG. 1), where Oy measures quantities of " corn " (standing for all agricultural produce) and Ox the amount of labour employed in agriculture. At a given state of knowledge and in a given natural environment the curve p—Ap represents the product per unit of labour and the curve p—Mp the marginal product of labour. The existence of these two *separate* curves, is a consequence of a declining tendency in the average product curve—i.e., of the assumption of diminishing returns. Corn-output is thus uniquely determined when the quantity of labour is given :[3] for any given working force, OM, total output is represented by the rectangle $OCDM$. Rent is the difference between the product of labour on " marginal " land and the product on average land, or (allowing for the intensive, as well as the extensive, margin) the difference between average and marginal labour productivity which depends on the elasticity of the p—Ap curve, i.e., the extent to which diminishing returns operate.

The marginal product of labour (or, in classical parlance, the " produce-minus-rent ") is not however equal to the wage, but to the sum of wages and profits. The rate of wages is determined quite independently of marginal productivity by the supply price of labour

---

[1] " Political Economy " he told Malthus " you think is an enquiry into the nature and causes of wealth —I think it should rather be called an enquiry into the laws which determine the division of the produce of industry amongst the classes who concur in its formation. No law can be laid down respecting quantity, but a tolerably correct one can be laid down respecting proportions. Every day I am more satisfied that the former enquiry is vain and delusive, and the latter only the true objects of the science." (Letter dated 9 Oct., 1820, Works (Sraffa edition) vol. VIII, pp. 278-9.)

[2] And so of course is the Marxian : but then the Marxian theory is really only a simplified version of Ricardo, clothed in a different garb.

[3] This abstracts from variations in output per head due to the use of more or less fixed capital relative to labour—otherwise the curves could not be uniquely drawn, relative to a given state of technical knowledge. As between fixed capital and labour therefore the model assumes " fixed coefficients ' ; as between labour and land, variable coefficients.

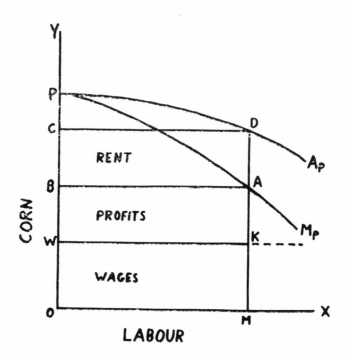

which Ricardo assumed to be constant in terms of corn. In modern parlance, the Ricardian hypothesis implies an infinitely elastic supply curve of labour at the given supply price, OW.[1] The demand for labour is not determined however by the p—Mp curve, but by the accumulation of capital which determines how many labourers can find employment at the wage rate OW. Hence the equilibrium position is not indicated by the point of intersection between the p—Mp curve and the supply curve of labour, but by the aggregate demand for labour in terms of corn—the " wages fund ".[2] As capital accumulates, the

---

[1] The basis of this assumption is the Malthusian theory of population, according to which numbers will increase (indefinitely) when wages are above, and decrease (indefinitely) when they are below, the " subsistence level ". In Ricardo's hands this doctrine had lost its sharp focus on a biologically determined quantum of subsistence to which the supply price of labour must be tied ; he emphasized that habits of restraint engendered in a civilized environment can permanently secure for labour higher standards of living than the bare minimum for survival. Yet he retained the important operative principle that in any given social and cultural environment there is a " *natural* rate of wages " at which alone population could remain stationary and from which wages can only deviate temporarily. The hypothesis of an infinitely elastic supply curve of labour thus did not necessarily imply that this supply price must be equal to the bare minimum of subsistence. Yet this assumption was inconsistent with another (implied) feature of his model discussed below, that wages are not only *fixed* in terms of " corn " but are entirely (or almost entirely) *spent* on corn.

[2] Total wages depend on—and are " paid out of "—capital simply because production takes time, and the labourers (unlike the landlords) not being in the position to afford to wait, have their wages " advanced " to them by the capitalists. This is true of fixed as well as circulating capital, but since with the former, the turnover period is relatively long, only a small part of annual wages is paid out of fixed capital ; the amount of circulating capital was therefore treated as the proper " wages fund ". Despite his analysis of the effect of changes in wages on the amount of fixed capital used relative to labour, i.e., on the proportions of fixed and circulating capital employed in production (Professor Hayek's celebrated " Ricardo effect ") for the purpose of his distribution theory this ratio should be taken as given, irrespective of the rate of profit.

labour force will grow, so that any addition to the total wage fund, through capital accumulation—the *agricultural* wages fund is indicated by the area $OWKM$—will tend to be a horizontal addition (pushing the vertical line KM to the right) and not a vertical one (pushing the horizontal line WK upwards).[1]

For any given M, profits are thus a residue, arising from the difference between the marginal product of labour and the rate of wages. The resulting ratio, $\frac{\text{Profits}}{\text{Wages}}$, determines the rate of profit per cent on the capital employed ; it is moreover *equal* to that ratio, on the assumption that the capital is turned over once a year, so that the capital employed is equal to the annual wages-bill. (This latter proposition however is merely a simplification, and not an essential part of the story).

In a state of equilibrium, the money rate of profit *per cent* earned on capital must be the same in industry and in agriculture, otherwise capital would move from one form of employment to the other. But it is the peculiarity of agriculture that the money rate of profit in that industry cannot diverge from the rate of profit measured in terms of that industry's own product, *i.e.*, the corn-rate of profit. This is because in agriculture both the input (the wage outlay) and the output consist of the same commodity, " corn ". In manufacturing industry on the other hand, input and output consist of heterogeneous commodities—the cost per man is fixed in corn, while the product per man, in a given state of technical knowledge, is fixed in terms of manufactured goods. Hence the only way equality in the rate of profit in money terms can be attained as between the two branches is through the prices of industrial goods becoming dearer or cheaper in terms of agricultural products. The money rate of profit in manufacturing industry therefore depends on the corn-rate of profit in agriculture,[2] the latter on the other hand, is entirely a matter of the margin of cultivation, which in turn is a reflection (in a closed economy and in a given state of technical knowledge) of the extent of capital accumulation. Thus " diminishing fertility of the soil," as James Mill put it, " is the great and ultimately only necessary cause of a fall in profit ".

To make the whole structure logically consistent it is necessary to suppose, not only that wages are fixed in terms of " corn " but that they are entirely spent on " corn ", for otherwise any change in the relation between industrial and agricultural prices will alter real wages (in terms of commodities in general) so that the size of the " surplus ", and the rate of profit on capital generally, is no longer derivable from the " corn rate of profit "—the relationship between the product of labour and the cost of labour working on marginal land. Assuming that (" corn ") agricultural products are wage-goods and manufactured products are non-wage goods (i.e., ignoring that *some* agricultural products are consumed by capitalists, and *some* non-agricultural products by wage-earners), the whole corn-output (the area $OCDM$ in the diagram) can be taken as the annual wages fund, of which $OWKM$ is employed in agriculture and $WCDK$ in the rest of the economy. Any increase in $OWKM$ (caused, *e.g.*, by protection to agriculture) must necessarily lower the rate of profit (which is the source

---

[1] The feature which the modern mind may find most difficult to swallow is not that capital accumulation should lead to a rise in population but that the reaction should be taken as something so swift as to ignore the intervening stage, where the increase in the wages fund should raise the rate of wages rather than the numbers employed. The adjustment of population to changes in the demand for labour would normally be treated as a slow long-run effect whereas changes in the demand for labour (caused by capital accumulation) may be swift or sudden. Ricardo however conceived the economy as one which proceeds at a more or less steady rate of growth in time, with the accumulation of capital going on at a (more or less constant) rate ; while he conceded that *changes* in the rate of capital accumulation will temporarily raise or lower wages, he assumed that the rate of population growth itself is adapted to a certain rate of capital accumulation which had been going on for some time.

[2] The analytical basis for this conclusion, given above, was never, as Sraffa remarks, stated by Ricardo in any of his extant letters and papers though there is evidence from Malthus's remarks that he must have formulated it either in a lost paper on the Profits of Capital or in conversation (cf. *Works*, Vol I., Introduction, p. xxxi.).

of all accumulation) and thus slow down the rate of growth.[1] Similarly all taxes, other than those levied on land, must ultimately fall on, and be paid out of, profits, and thus slow down the rate of accumulation. Taxation and agricultural protection thus tend to accelerate the tendency (which is in any case inevitable—unless *continued* technical progress manages to shift the *p—Ap* and *p—Mp* curves to the right sufficiently to suspend altogether the operation of the Law of Diminishing Returns) to that ultimate state of gloom, the Stationary State, where accumulation ceases simply because " profits are so low as not to afford (the capitalists more than) an adequate compensation for their trouble and the risk which they must necessarily encounter in employing their capital productively ".[2]

II THE MARXIAN THEORY

The Marxian theory is essentially an adaptation of Ricardo's " surplus theory ". The main analytical differences are :— (1) that Marx paid no attention to (and did not believe in) the Law of Diminishing Returns, and hence made no analytical distinction between rent and profits ; (2) that Marx regarded the supply price of labour (the " cost of reproduction " of labour) as being fixed, not in terms of " corn ", but of commodities in general. Hence he regarded the share of profits (including rent) in output as determined simply by the surplus of the product per unit of labour over the supply price (or cost) of labour—or the surplus of production over the consumption necessary for production.[3]

There are important differences also as between Marx and Ricardo in two other respects. The first of these concerns the reasons for wages being tied to the subsistence level. In Marx's theory this is ensured through the fact that at any one time the supply of labour—the number of workers seeking wage-employment—tends to exceed the demand for labour. The existence of an unemployed fringe—the " reserve army " of labour—prevents wages from rising above the minimum that must be paid to enable the labourers to perform the work. Marx assumed that as capitalist enterprise progresses at the expenses of pre-capitalistic enterprise more labourers are released through the disappearance of the non-capitalist or handi-craft units than are absorbed in the capitalist sector, owing to the difference in productivity per head between the two sectors. As long as the growth of capitalist enterprise is at the cost of a shrinkage of pre-capitalist enterprise the increase in the supply of wage labour will thus tend to run ahead of the increase in the demand for wage labour.

Sooner or later, however, the demand for labour resulting from accumulation by capitalist enterprise will run ahead of the increase in supply ; at that stage labour becomes scarce, wages rise, profits are wiped out and capitalism is faced with a " crisis ". (The crisis in itself slows down the rate of accumulation and reduces the demand for labour at any given state of accumulation by increasing the " organic composition of capital," so that the " reserve army " will sooner or later be recreated.)

The second important difference relates to the motives behind capital accumulation. For Ricardo this was simply to be explained by the lure of a high rate of profit. Capitalists accumulate voluntarily so long as the rate of profit exceeds the minimum " necessary compensation " for the risks and trouble encountered in the productive employment of capital. For Marx however, accumulation by capitalist enterprise is not a matter of choice

---

[1] The evil of agricultural protection is thus not only that real income is reduced through the transfer of labour to less productive employments, but that owing to the reduction in the rate of profit, industrial prices fall in terms of agricultural prices ; income is thus transferred from the classes which use their wealth productively to classes which use it unproductively.

[2] Ricardo, *Principles*, p. 122 (Sraffa Edition).

[3] Ricardo himself abandoned in the *Principles* the idea that wages *consist* of corn (to the exclusion of manufactures) but whether he also abandoned the idea that the agricultural surplus is critical to the whole distribution process through the fixity of wages in terms of *corn only* is not clear. (Cf. Sraffa, *op. cit.*, pp. xxxii-xxxiii.)

but a necessity, due to competition among the capitalists themselves. This in turn was explained by the existence of economies of large scale production (together with the implicit assumption that the amount of capital employed by any particular capitalist is governed by his own accumulation). Given the fact that the larger the scale of operations the more efficient the business, each capitalist is forced to increase the size of his business through the re-investment of his profits if he is not to fall behind in the competitive struggle.

It is only at a later stage, when the increasing concentration of production in the hands of the more successful enterprises removed the competitive necessity for accumulation—the stage of " monopoly capitalism "—that in the Marxian scheme there is room for economic crises, not on account of an excessive increase in the demand for labour following on accumulation but on account of an insufficiency of effective demand—the failure of markets resulting from the inability of the capitalists either to spend or to invest the full amount of profits (which Marx called the problem of " realising surplus value ").

Marx has also taken over from Ricardo, and the classical economists generally, the idea of a falling rate of profit with the progressive accumulation of capital. But whereas with the classicists this was firmly grounded on the Law of Diminishing Returns, Marx, having discarded that law, had no firm base for it. His own explanation is based on the assumed increase in the ratio of fixed to circulating capital (in Marxian terminology, " constant " to " variable " capital) with the progress of capitalism ; but as several authors have pointed out,[1] the law of the falling rate of profit cannot really be derived from the law of the " increasing organic composition " of capital. Since Marx assumes that the supply price of labour remains unchanged in terms of commodities when the organic composition of capital, and hence output per head, rises, there is no more reason to assume that an increase in " organic composition " will yield a lower rate of profit than a higher rate. For even if output per man were assumed to increase more slowly than (" constant " plus " variable ") capital per man, the " surplus value " per man (the excess of output per man over the costs of reproduction of labour) will necessarily increase faster than output per man, and may thus secure a rising rate of profit even if there is diminishing productivity to successive additions to fixed capital per unit of labour.

While some of Marx's predictions—such as the increasing concentration of production in the hands of large enterprises—proved accurate, his most important thesis, the steady worsening of the living conditions of the working classes—" the immiseration of the proletariat "[2]—has been contradicted by experience, in both the " competitive " and " monopoly " stages of capitalism. On the Marxian model the share of wages in output must necessarily fall with every increase in output per head. The theory can only allow for a rise of wages in terms of commodities as a result of the collective organisation of the working classes which forces the capitalists to reduce the degree of exploitation and to surrender to the workers some of the " surplus value ".[3] This hypothesis however will only yield a constant share of wages on the extremely far-fetched assumption that the rate of increase in the bargaining strength of labour, due to the growth of collective organisation, precisely keeps pace with the rate of increase in output per head.

---

[1] Cf. in particular, Joan Robinson, *An Essay in Marxian Economics*, pp. 75-82.

[2] It is not clear, in terms of Marx's own theoretical model, why such a progressive immiseration should take place—since the costs of reproduction of labour appear to set an *absolute* limit to the extent to which labour can be exploited. Some parts of *Das Kapital* could however be construed as suggesting that wages can be driven below the (long run) reproduction cost of labour, at the cost of a (long run) shrinkage in the labour force : and with the increasing organic composition of capital, and the rise of monopolies, the demand for labour may show an equally declining tendency.

[3] Marx himself would have conceived a reduction in the " degree of exploitation " in terms of a reduction in the length of the working day rather than a rise in real wages per day. In fact both have occurred side by side.

III THE NEO-CLASSICAL THEORIES

(A) MARGINAL PRODUCTIVITY

While Marx's theory thus derives from Ricardo's surplus principle, neo-classical value and distribution theory derives from another part of the Ricardian model : the " marginal principle " introduced for the explanation of rent (which explains why both Marx and Marshall are able to claim Ricardo as their precursor). The difference between Ricardo and the neo-classics is (1) that whereas Ricardo employed the " principle of substitution " (or rather, the principle of " limited substitutability "—which is the basic assumption underlying all " marginal " analysis) only as regards the use of labour relative to land, in neo-classical theory this doctrine was formalized and generalized, and assumed to hold true of any factor, in relation to any other ;[1] (2) whereas Ricardo employed the principle for showing that a " fixed " factor will earn a surplus, determined by the gap between the average and marginal product of the variable factor, neo-classical theory concentrated on the reverse aspect—i.e., that any factor variable in supply will obtain a remuneration which, under competitive conditions, must correspond to its marginal product. Thus if the total supply of *all* factors (and not only land) is being taken as given, independently of price, and all are assumed to be limited substitutes to one another, the share-out of the whole produce can be regarded as being determined by the marginal rates of substitution between them. Thus in terms of our diagram, if we assumed that along Ox we measure the quantity of any particular factor of production, x, the quantities of all the others being taken as fixed, p—Mp will exhibit the marginal productivity function of the variable factor. If the actual employment of that factor is taken to be M, AM will represent its demand price per unit, and the rectangle $OBAM$ its share in the total produce. Since this principle could be applied to any factor, it must be true of all (including, as Walras and Wicksell have shown, the factors owned by the entrepreneur himself) hence the rectangle $BCDA$ must be sufficient, and only just sufficient, for remunerating all other factors but x on the basis of their respective marginal productivities. This, as Wicksteed has shown[2] requires the assumption that the production function will be homogeneous of the first degree for all variables taken together—an assumption which he himself regarded as little more than a tautology, if " factors of production " are appropriately defined.[3] From the point of view of the theory, however, the *appropriate* definition of factors involves the elimination of intermediate products and their conversion into " ultimate " or "original" factors, since only on this definition can one assume the properties of divisibility and variability of coefficients. When factors are thus defined, the assumption of constant

---

[1] As well as of any particular commodity in the sphere of consumption. The utility theory of value is really Ricardian rent-theory applied to consumption demand. In fact, as Walras has shown, limited substitutability in consumption might in itself be sufficient to determine distributive shares, provided that the proportions in which the different factors are used are different in different industries. His solution of the problem of distribution, based on " fixed coefficients " of production (intended only as a first approximation) is subject however to various snags since the solution of his equations may yield negative prices for the factors as well as positive ones and it cannot be determined beforehand whether this will be the case or not. If the solution of the equations yields negative prices the factors in question have to be excluded as " free goods "; and the operation (if necessary) successive repeated until only factors with positive prices are left. Also, it is necessary to suppose that the number of different " factors " is no greater than the number of different " products " otherwise the solution is indeterminate.

[2] *The Co-ordination of the Laws of Distribution* (1894).

[3] *Ibid.*, p. 53 " We must regard every kind and quality of labour that can be distinguished from other kinds and qualities as a separate factor ; and in the same way, every kind of land will be taken as a separate factor. Still more important is it to insist that instead of speaking of so many £ worth of capital we shall speak of so many ploughs, so many tons of manure, and so many horses or footpounds of power. Each of these may be scheduled in its own unit." Under these conditions it is true to say that " doubling all factors will double the product ", but since these " factors " are indivisible in varying degrees, it does not mean that the production function is a linear and homogeneous one in relation to incremental variations of output. Also a change in output may be associated with the introduction of *new* factors of production.

returns to scale is by no means a tautology ; it is a restrictive assumption, which may be regarded, however, as being co-extensive with other restrictive assumptions implied by the theory—i.e., the universal rule of perfect competition, and the absence of external economies and diseconomies.

The basic difficulty with the whole approach does not lie, however, in this so-called " adding-up problem " but in the very meaning of " capital " as a factor of production.[1] Whilst land can be measured in acres-per-year and labour in man-hours, capital (as distinct from " capital goods ") cannot be measured in terms of physical units.[2] To evaluate the marginal product of labour it is necessary to isolate two situations containing identical " capital " but two different quantities of labour, or identical amounts of labour and two differing quantities of " capital ", in precise numerical relationship.[3]

Marshall, without going into the matter in any detail, had shown in several passages that he was dimly aware of this ; and in carefully re-defining marginal productivity so as to mean " marginal *net* productivity " (*net* after deduction of all associated expenses on other " factors ") he shied away from the task of putting forward a general theory of distribution altogether.[4]

In fact, in so far as we can speak of a " Marshallian " theory of distribution at all, it is in the sense of a " short period " theory, which regards profits as the " quasi-rents " earned on the use of capital goods of various kinds, the supply of which can be treated as given for the time being, as a heritage of the past. The doctrine of the " quasi-rent " assimilates capital as a factor of production to Ricardian land : the separate *kinds* of capital goods being treated as so many different kinds of " land ". Here the problem of the measurement of capital as a factor of production does not arise : since, strictly speaking, no kind of change or reorganization in the stock of intermediate products is permitted in connection with a change in the level or composition of production. It was this aspect of Marshall which, consciously or sub-consciously, provided the " model " for most of the post-Marshallian Cambridge theorizing. Prices are equal to, or determined by, marginal prime costs ; profits are determined by the difference between marginal and average prime costs ; prime costs, for the system as a whole, are labour costs (since raw-material costs, for a closed economy at any rate, disappear if all branches of industry are taken together) ; ultimately therefore the division of output between profits and wages is a matter depending on the existence of diminishing returns to labour, as more labour is used in conjunction with a *given* capital equipment ; and is determined by the elasticity of labour's average productivity curve which fixes the share of quasi-rents.

Marshall himself would have disagreed with the use of the quasi-rent doctrine as a distribution theory, holding that distributive shares in the short period are determined by long-period forces.[5] Clearly even if one were to hold strictly to the assumption that " profit margins " are the outcome of short-period profit-maximisation, this " short-

---

[1] For a general equilibrium system, capital goods cannot be regarded as factors of production *per se* (in the manner suggested by Wicksteed) otherwise the same things are simultaneously treated as the parameters and the unknowns of the system.

[2] Measurement in terms of value (as so many £'s of " capital ") already assumes a certain rate of interest, on the basis of which services accruing in differing periods in the future, or costs incurred at differing dates in the past, are brought to a measure of equivalence.

[3] The product of the " marginal shepherd " is the difference, in terms of numbers of sheep, between 10 shepherds using 10 crooks and 11 shepherds using 11 slightly inferior crooks, the term " slightly inferior " being taken to mean that the 11 crooks in the one case represent precisely the same amount of " capital " as the 10 crooks in the other case. (Cf. also, Robertson, " Wage Grumbles," in *Economic Fragments*, 1931.)

[4] " The doctrine that the earnings of a worker tend to be equal to the net product of his work, has by itself no real meaning ; since in order to estimate the net product, we have to take for granted all the expenses of production of the commodity on which he works, other than his own wages ". Similarly, the doctrine that the marginal efficiency of capital will tend to equal the rate of interest " cannot be made into a theory of interest, any more than a theory of wages, without reasoning in a circle ". (Cf. *Principles*, 8th edition, Book VI, ch. I, paras 7-8.)

[5] Cf., in particular, *Principles*, 8th edition, Book V, ch. V, and 6, and Book VI, ch. VIII, paras. 4.

period " approach does not really get us anywhere : for the extent to which diminishing returns operate for labour in conjunction with the capital equipment available to-day is itself a function of the price-relationships which have ruled in the past because these have determined the quantities of each of the kinds of equipment available. The theory does not therefore really amount to more than saying that the prices of to-day are derived from the prices of yesterday—a proposition which is the more true and the more trivial the shorter the " day " is conceived to be, in terms of chronological time.

For the true neo-classical attempt to solve the general problem of distribution we must go to Wicksell who thought that by integrating the Austrian approach to capital with Walrasian equilibrium theory he could provide a general solution, treating capital as a two-dimensional quantity, the product of time and labour. The " time " in this case is the investment period or waiting period separating the application of " original " factors from the emergence of the final product, and the marginal productivity of capital the added product resulting from an extension of " time ". This attempt, again, came to grief (as Wicksell himself came near to acknowledging late in life[1]) (i) owing to the impossibility of measuring that period in terms of an " average " of some kind ;[2] (ii) owing to the impossibility of combining the investment periods of different " original " factors in a single measure.[3]

In fact the whole approach which regards the share of wages and of profits in output as being determined by the marginal rate of substitution between Capital and Labour—with its corollary, that the constancy of relative shares is evidence of a unity-Elasticity of Substitution between Capital and Labour[4]—is hardly acceptable to present-day economists. Its inadequacy becomes evident as soon as it is realized that the "marginal rate of substitution " between Capital and Labour—as distinct from the marginal rate of substitution between labour and land—can only be determined once the rate of profit and the rate of wages are already known. The same technical alternatives might yield very different " marginal rates of substitution " according as the ratio of profits to wages is one thing or another. The theory asserts in effect, that the rate of interest in the capital market, (and the associated wage rate in the labour market) is determined by the condition that at any lower interest rate (and higher wage rate) capital would be invested in such " labour-saving " forms as would provide insufficient employment to the available labour ; whilst at any higher rate, capital would be invested in forms that offered more places of employment than could be filled with the available labour.

Quite apart from all conceptual difficulties, the theory focuses attention on a relatively unimportant feature of a growing economy. For accumulation does not take the form of " deepening " the structure of capital (at a given state of knowledge) but rather in keeping pace with technical progress and the growth in the labour force. It is difficult to swallow a theory which says, in effect that wages and profits are what they are for otherwise there would be too much deepening or too little deepening (the capital/output ratios would be either too large or too small) to be consistent with simultaneous equilibrium in the savings-investment market and in the labour market.

---

[1] Cf. the concluding passage of his posthumous contribution to the Wieser Festschrift. *Die Wirtschafts-theorie der Gegenwart* (1928) Vol. III, pp. 208-9 ; also his Analysis of Akerman's Problem, reprinted in *Lectures*, Vol. I, p. 270.

[2] Since owing to compound interest, the weights to be used in the calculation of the average will themselves be dependent on the rate of interest.

[3] For a more extended treatment cf. my articles on capital theory in *Econometrica*, April 1937 and May 1938 ; also Joan Robinson, The Production Function in the Theory of Capital, *Review of Economic Studies*, Vol. XXI (1953-54) p. 81, and *Comment* by D. G. Champernowne, *ibid* page 112.

[4] Cf. Hicks, *The Theory of Wages* (1932) ch. VI, passim.

(B) The " Degree of Monopoly " Theories of Distribution

Monopoly profit was always regarded as a distinct form of revenue in neo-classical theory, though not one of any great quantitative importance since the mass of commodities was thought of as being produced under competitive conditions. But the modern theories of imperfect competition emphasised that monopoly profit is not an isolated feature. Profits in general contain an *element* of monopoly revenue—an element that is best defined as the excess of the actual profit margin in output over what the profit margin would have been under perfectly competitive conditions. Under Marshallian " short-period " assumptions the perfectly-competitive profit margin is given by the excess of marginal cost over average prime costs. The additional monopoly element is indicated by the excess of price over marginal cost. The former, as we have seen, is a derivative of the elasticity of labour's productivity curve where capital equipment of all kinds is treated as given. The latter is a derivative of the elasticity of demand facing the individual firm. The novel feature of imperfect competition theories is to have shown that the increase of profit margins due to this element of monopoly need not imply a corresponding excess in the rates of profit on capital over the competitive rate ; through the generation of excess capacity (i.e., the tendency of demand curves to become " tangential " to the cost curves) the latter may approach a " competitive " or " normal " rate (as a result of the consequential rise in the capital/output ratio) even if the former is above the competitive level.

Kalecki[1] built on this a simplified theory of distribution, where the share of profits in output is shown to be determined by the elasticity of demand alone. This was based on the hypothesis that in the short period, labour and capital equipment are largely " limitational " and not " substitutional " factors, with the result that the short-period prime cost-curve is a reverse —L shaped one (prime costs being constant up to full capacity output). In that case marginal costs are equal to average prime costs ; the ratio of price to prime costs (and hence, in a closed economy, the ratio of gross profits to wages) is thus entirely accounted for by the elasticity of the firm's demand curve.

On closer inspection, however, the elasticity of the demand curve facing the individual firm turned out to be no less of a broken reed than its counterpart, the elasticity of substitution between factors. There is no evidence that firms in imperfect markets set their prices by reference to the elasticity of their sales-function, or that short-period pricing is the outcome of any deliberate attempt to maximize profits by reference to an independent revenue and a cost function. Indeed the very notion of a demand curve for the products of a single firm is illegitimate if the prices charged by different firms cannot be assumed to be independent of each other.[2]

In the later versions of his theory Kalecki abandoned the link between the " degree of monopoly " and the elasticity of demand, and was content with a purely tautological approach according to which the ratio of price to prime costs is *defined* simply as the " degree of monopoly ". Propositions based on implicit definitions of this kind make of course no assertion about reality and possess no explanatory value. Unless the " degree of monopoly " can be defined in terms of market relationships of some kind (as, for example, in terms of the " cross-elasticities " of demand for the products of the different firms)[3] and an attempt is made to demonstrate how these market relationships determine

---

[1] The original version appeared in *Econometrica*, April 1938. Subsequent versions appeared in *Essays in the Theory of Economic Fluctuations* (1938) ch. I, *Studies in Economic Dynamics* (1943) ch. 1, and *Theory of Dynamic Economics* (1954) Part 1.

[2] The theory of the " kinked " demand curve is in fact no more than a recognition of the fact that the demand curve of the firm (in the sense required for the purpose of deriving price from the postulate of profit maximisation) is non-existent. Since the position of the " kink " *depends* on the price, it cannot *determine* the price ; it thus leaves the profit margin completely undetermined.

[3] The " cross-elasticities " of demand indicate the degree of interdependence of the markets of different firms and are thus inversely related to monopoly power in the usual sense of the word.

the relation between prices and costs, the theory does not provide a hypothesis which could be affirmed or refuted.

There is no need, of course, to follow Kalecki in the attempt to lend spurious precision to the doctrine through implicit theorizing—a vice which afflicts all theories which we grouped together as " neo-classical " in varying degrees. Fundamentally, the proposition that the distribution of income between wages and profits depends on market structures, on the strength or weakness of the forces of competition, is not a tautological one ; it asserts *something* about reality (which may in principle be proved false) even if that " something " cannot be given a logically precise formulation. Just as the positive content of the marginal productivity theory can be summed up by the statement that the rate of profit on capital (and the margin of profit in output) is governed by the need to prevent the capital/output ratio from being either too large or too small, the positive content of the " degree of monopoly " theory can be summed up in the sentence that " profit margins are what they are because the forces of competition prevent them from being higher than they are and are not powerful enough to make them lower than they are " Unfortunately neither of these statements gets us very far.

Dissatisfaction with the tautological character and the formalism of the " marginal revenue-equals-marginal cost " type of price theory led to the formulation of the " full cost " theories of pricing,[1] according to which producers in imperfect markets set their prices independently of the character of demand, and solely on the basis of their long run costs of production (including the " normal " rate of profit on their own capital). If these theories asserted no more than that prices in manufacturing industry are *not* determined by the criterion of short-run profit-maximization, and that profit margins can be fairly insensitive to short-period variations in demand,[2] (the impact effect of changes in demand being on the rate of production, rather than on prices) they would provide a healthy antidote to a great deal of facile theorising. When, however, they go beyond this and assert that prices are determined quite independently of demand, they in effect destroy existing price theory without putting anything else in its place. Quite apart from the fact that a " full cost " theory is quite unable to explain why some firms should be more successful in earning profits than others, the level of the " normal profit " on which the full cost calculations are supposed to be based is left quite undetermined. The very fact that these full cost theories should have received such widespread and serious consideration as an alternative explanation of the pricing process is an indication of the sad state of vagueness and confusion into which the neo-classical value theory had fallen.

---

[1] Cf. Hall and Hitch, *Oxford Economic Papers*, 1939 ; P. M. S. Andrews, *Manufacturing Business* (1949).

[2] This, I believe, was the intention of the original Hall-Hitch article. Cf. Marshall, *Principles*, Book VI, ch. VIII, paragraph 4 : " We see then that there is no general tendency of profits on the turnover to equality ; but there may be, and as a matter of fact there is, in each trade and in every branch of each trade, a more or less definite rate of profits on the turnover which is regarded as a " fair " or normal rate. Of course these rates are always changing in consequence of changes in the methods of trade ; which are generally begun by individuals who desire to do a larger trade at a lower rate of profit on the turnover than has been customary, but at a larger rate of profit per annum on their capital. If however there happens to be no great change of this kind going on, the traditions of the trade that a certain rate of profit on the turnover should be charged for a particular class of work are of great practical service to those in the trade. Such traditions are the outcome of much experience tending to show that, if that rate is charged, a proper allowance will be made for all the costs (supplementary as well as prime) incurred for that particular purpose, and in addition the normal rate of profits per annum in that class of business will be afforded. If they charge a price which gives much less than this rate of profit on the turnover they can hardly prosper ; and if they charge much more they are in danger of losing their custom, since others can afford to undersell them. This is the " fair " rate of profit on the turnover, which an honest man is expected to charge for making goods to order, when no price has been agreed on beforehand ; and it is the rate which a court of law will allow in case a dispute should arise between buyer and seller." Cf. also Kahn, *Economic Journal*, 1952, p. 119.

IV THE KEYNESIAN THEORY

Keynes, as far as I know, was never interested in the problem of distribution as such. One may nevertheless christen a particular theory of distribution as " Keynesian " if it can be shown to be an application of the specifically Keynesian apparatus of thought and if evidence can be adduced that at some stage in the development of his ideas, Keynes came near to formulating such a theory.[1] The principle of the Multiplier (which in some way was anticipated in the *Treatise* but without a clear view of its implications) could be alternatively applied to a determination of the relation between prices and wages, if the level of output and employment is taken as given, or the determination of the level of employment, if distribution (i.e., the relation between prices and wages) is taken as given. The reason why the multiplier-analysis has not been developed as a distribution theory is precisely because it was invented for the purpose of an employment theory—to explain why an economic system can remain in equilibrium in a state of under-employment (or of a general under-utilization of resources), where the classical properties of scarcity-economics are inapplicable.   And its use for the one appears to exclude its use for the other.[2] If we assume that the balance of savings and investment is brought about through variations in the relationship of prices and costs, we are not only bereft of a principle for explaining variations in output and employment, but the whole idea of separate " aggregate" demand and supply functions—the principle of "effective demand "—falls to the ground ; we are back to Say's Law, where output as a whole is limited by available resources, and a fall in effective demand for one kind of commodity (in real terms) generates compensating increases in effective demand (again in real terms) for others.   Yet these two uses of the Multiplier principle are not as incompatible as would appear at first sight : the Keynesian technique, as I hope to show, can be used for both purposes, provided the one is conceived as a short-run theory and the other as a long-run theory—or rather, the one is used in the framework of a static model, and the other in the framework of a dynamic growth model.[3]

[1] I am referring to the well-known passage on profits being likened to a " widow's cruse " in the *Treatise on Money*, Vol. I, p. 139.   " If entrepreneurs choose to spend a portion of their profits on consumption (and there is, of course, nothing to prevent them from doing this) the effect is to *increase* the profit on the sale of liquid consumption goods by an amount exactly equal to the amount of profits which have been thus expended . . . Thus however much of their profits entrepreneurs spend on consumption, the increment of wealth belonging to entrepreneurs remain the same as before.   Thus profits, as a source of capital increment for entrepreneurs, are a widow's cruse which remains undepleted however much of them may be devoted to riotous living.   When on the other hand, entrepreneurs are making losses, and seek to recoup these losses by curtailing their normal expenditure on consumption, i.e., by saving more, the cruse becomes a Danaid jar which can never be filled up ; for the effect of this reduced expenditure is to inflict on the producers of consumption-goods a loss of an equal amount.   Thus the diminution of their wealth, as a class is as great, in spite of their savings, as it was before."   This passage, I think, contains the true seed of the ideas developed in the *General Theory*—as well as showing the length of the road that had to be traversed before arriving at the conceptual framework presented in the latter work.   The fact that " profits ", "savings" etc. were all defined here in a special sense that was later discarded, and that the argument specifically refers to expenditure on consumption goods, rather than entrepreneurial expenditure in general, should not blind us to the fact that here Keynes regards entrepreneurial incomes as being the resultant of their expenditure decisions, rather than the other way round—which is perhaps the most important difference between " Keynesian " and " pre-Keynesian " habits of thought.
[2] Although this application of Keynesian theory has been implicit in several discussions of the problem of inflation. (Cf. *e.g.* A. J. Brown, *The Great Inflation*, Macmillan, 1955.)
[3] I first thought of using the Multiplier technique for purposes of a distribution theory when I attempted the ultimate incidence of profits taxation under full employment conditions in a paper prepared for the Royal Commission on Taxation in 1951.   The further development of these ideas, and particularly their relationship to a dynamic theory of growth, owes a great deal to discussions with Mrs. Robinson, whose forthcoming book, *The Accumulation of Capital*, contains a systematic exploration of this field.   I should also like to mention here that I owe a great deal of stimulus to a paper by Kalecki, " A Theory of Profits " (*Economic Journal*, June-Sept. 1942) whose approach is in some ways reminiscent of the " widows' cruse " of Keynes' *Treatise* even though Kalecki uses the technique, not for an explanation of the share of profits in output, but for showing why the *level* of output and its fluctuations are peculiarly dependent on entrepreneurial behaviour. (In doing so, he uses the restrictive assumption that savings are entirely supplied out of profits.)   I have also been helped by Mr. Harry Johnson and Mr. Robin Marris, both in the working out of the formulae and in general discussion.

We shall assume, to begin with, a state of full employment (we shall show later the conditions under which a state of full employment will *result* from our model) so that total output or income (Y) is given. Income may be divided into two broad categories, Wages and Profits (W and P), where the wage-category comprises not only manual labour but salaries as well, and Profits the income of property owners generally, and not only of entrepreneurs ; the important difference between them being in the marginal propensities to consume (or save), wage-earners' marginal savings being small in relation to those of capitalists.[1]

Writing S_w and S_p for aggregate savings out of Wages and Profits, we have the following income identities :

$$Y \equiv W + P$$
$$I \equiv S$$
$$S \equiv S_w + S_p.$$

Taking investment as given, and assuming simple proportional saving functions $S_w = s_w W$ and $S_p = s_p P$, we obtain :

$$I = s_p P + s_w W = s_p P + s_w(Y-P) = (s_p-s_w)P + s_w Y$$

Whence
$$\frac{I}{Y} = (s_p-s_w)\frac{P}{Y} + s_w \quad \dots \dots \dots \dots \dots \dots \quad (1)$$

and
$$\frac{P}{Y} = \frac{1}{s_p - s_w}\frac{I}{Y} - \frac{s_w}{s_p - s_w} \quad \dots \dots \dots \dots \dots \dots \quad (2)$$

Thus, given the wage-earners' and the capitalists' propensities to save, the share of profits in income depends simply on the ratio of investment to output.

The interpretative value of the model (as distinct from the formal validity of the equations, or identities) depends on the " Keynesian " hypothesis that investment, or rather, the ratio of investment to output, can be treated as an independent variable, invariant with respect to changes in the two savings propensities s_p and s_w. (We shall see later that this assumption can only be true within certain limits, and outside those limits the theory ceases to hold). This, together with the assumption of " full employment ", also implies that the level of prices in relation to the level of money wages is determined by demand : a rise in investment, and thus in total demand, will raise prices and profit margins, and thus reduce real consumption, whilst a fall in investment, and thus in total demand, causes a fall in prices (relatively to the wage level) and thereby generates a compensating rise in real consumption. Assuming flexible prices (or rather flexible profit margins) the system is thus stable at full employment.

The model operates only if the two savings propensities differ and the marginal propensity to save from profits exceeds that from wages, i.e. if :

and
$$s_p \neq s_w$$
$$s_p > s_w$$

The latter is the stability condition. For if $s_p < s_w$, a fall in prices would cause a fall in demand and thus generate a further fall in prices, and equally, a rise in prices would be cumulative. The degree of stability of the system depends on the *difference* of the marginal propensities, *i.e.*, on $\dfrac{1}{s_p - s_w}$ which may be defined as the " coefficient of sensitivity of income distribution ", since it indicates the change in the share of profits in income which follows upon a change in the share of investment in output.

---

[1] This may be assumed independently of any skewness in the distribution of property, simply as a consequence of the fact that the bulk of profits accrues in the form of company profits and a high proportion of companies' marginal profits is put to reserve.

If the difference between the marginal propensities is small, the coefficient will be large, and small changes in $\frac{I}{Y}$ (the investment/output relationship) will cause relatively large changes in income distribution $\frac{P}{Y}$; and *vice versa*.

In the limiting case where $s_w = 0$, the amount of profits is equal to the sum of investment and capitalist consumption, *i,e,* :

$$P = \frac{1}{s_p} I.$$

This is the assumption implicit in Keynes' parable about the widow's cruse—where a rise in entrepreneurial consumption raises their total profit by an *identical* amount—and of Mr. Kalecki's theory of profits which can be paraphrased by saying that " capitalists earn what they spend, and workers spend what they earn."

This model (*i.e.*, the " special case " where $s_w = 0$) in a sense is the precise opposite of the Ricardian (or Marxian) one—here wages (not profits) are a residue, profits being governed by the propensity to invest and the capitalists' propensity to consume, which represent a kind of " prior charge " on the national output. Whereas in the Ricardian model the ultimate incidence of all taxes (other than taxes on rent) fall on profits, here the incidence of all taxes, taxes on income and profits as well as on commodities, falls on wages.[1] Assuming however that $\frac{I}{Y}$ and s_p remain constant over time, the share of wages will also remain constant—*i.e.*, real wages will increase automatically, year by year, with the increase in output per man.

If s_w is positive the picture is more complicated. Total profits will be reduced by the amount of workers' savings, S_w; on the other hand, the sensitivity of profits to changes in the level of investment will be greater, total profits rising (or falling) by a greater amount than the change in investment, owing to the consequential reduction (or increase) in workers' savings.[2]

The critical assumption is that the investment/output ratio is an independent variable. Following Harrod, we can describe the determinants of the investment/output ratio in terms of the rate of growth of output capacity (G) and the capital/output ratio, v :

$$\frac{I}{Y} = Gv \quad \ldots \ldots \ldots \ldots \quad (3)$$

---

[1] The ultimate incidence of taxes can only fall on profits (on this model) in so far as they increase s_p, the propensity to save out of *net* income after tax. Income and profits taxes, through the " double taxation " of savings, have of course the opposite effect : they reduce s_p, and thereby make the share of *net* profits in income larger than it would be in the absence of taxation. On the other hand, discriminatory taxes on dividend distribution, or dividend limitation, by keeping down both dividends and capital gains, have the effect of raising s_p. (All this applies, of course, on the assumption that the Government *spends* the proceeds of the tax—*i.e.*, that it aims at a balanced budget. Taxes which go to augment the budget surplus will lower the share of profits in much the same way as an increase in workers' savings.)

[2] Thus if $s_p = 50\%$, $s_w = 10\%$, $\frac{I}{Y} = 20\%$, $\frac{P}{Y}$ will be 15% ; but a rise in $\frac{I}{Y}$ to 21% would raise $\frac{P}{Y}$ to 17·5%. If on the other hand $s_w = 0$, with $s_p = 50\%$, $\frac{P}{Y}$ would become 40%, but an increase in $\frac{I}{Y}$ to 21% would only increase $\frac{P}{Y}$ to 42%. The above formulae assume that average and marginal propensities are identical. Introducing constant terms in the consumption functions alters the relationship between $\frac{P}{Y}$ and $\frac{I}{Y}$, and would reduce the *elasticity* of $\frac{P}{Y}$ with respect to changes in $\frac{I}{Y}$.

In a state of continuous full employment G must be equal to the rate of growth of the " full employment ceiling ", *i.e.*, the sum of the rate of technical progress and the growth in working population (Harrod's " natural rate of growth "). For Harrod's second equation :

$$\frac{I}{Y} = s$$

we can now substitute equation (1) above :

$$\frac{I}{Y} = (s_p - s_w) \frac{P}{Y} + s_w.$$

Hence the " warranted " and the " natural " rates of growth are not independent of one another ; if profit margins are flexible, the former will adjust itself to the latter through a consequential change in $\frac{P}{Y}$.

This does not mean that there will be an *inherent* tendency to a smooth rate of growth in a capitalist economy, only that the causes of cyclical movements lie elsewhere—not in the lack of an adjustment mechanism between s and Gv. As I have attempted to demonstrate elsewhere[1] the causes of cyclical movements should be sought in a disharmony between the entrepreneurs' *desired* growth rate (as influenced by the degree of optimism and the volatility of expectations) which governs the rate of increase of output capacity (let us call it G') and the natural growth rate (dependent on technical progress and the growth of the working population) which governs the rate of growth in output. It is the excess of G' over G— not the excess of s over Gv—which causes periodic breakdowns in the investment process through the growth in output capacity outrunning the growth in production.[2]

Problems of the trade cycle however lie outside the scope of this paper ; and having described a model which shows the distribution of income to be determined by the Keynesian investment-savings mechanism, we must now examine its limitations. The model, as I emphasized earlier, shows the share of profits $\frac{P}{Y}$, the rate of profit on investment $\frac{P}{vY}$, and the real wage rate $\frac{W'}{L}$, as functions of $\frac{I}{Y}$ which in turn is determined independently of $\frac{P}{Y}$ or $\frac{W}{L}$. There are four different reasons why this may not be true, or be true only within a certain range.

(1) The first is that the real wage cannot fall below a certain subsistence minimum. Hence $\frac{P}{Y}$ can only attain its indicated value, if the resulting real wage exceeds this minimum rate, w'. Hence the model is subject to the restriction $\frac{W}{L} \geqslant w'$, which we may write in the form :

$$\frac{P}{Y} \leqslant \frac{Y - w'L}{Y} \qquad \cdots \cdots \cdots \cdots \quad (4)$$

---

[1] *Economic Journal*, March 1954, pp. 53-71.

[2] $\frac{I}{Y}$ will therefore tend to equal $G'v$, not Gv. It may be assumed that taking very long periods G' is largely governed by G but over shorter periods the two are quite distinct, moreover G itself is not independent of G', since technical progress and population growth are both stimulated by the degree of pressure on the " full employment ceiling ", which depends on G'. The elasticity of response of G to G' is not infinite however : hence the greater G', the greater will be G (the *actual* trend-rate of growth of the economy over successive cycles) but the greater also the ratio $\frac{G'}{G}$ which measures the strength of cyclical forces.

(2) The second is that the indicated share of profits cannot be below the level which yields the minimum rate of profit necessary to induce capitalists to invest their capital, and which we may call the " risk premium rate ", r. Hence the restriction :

$$\frac{P}{vY} \geqslant r \quad . \quad . \quad . \quad . \quad . \quad . \quad . \quad . \quad . \quad . \quad . \quad (5)$$

(3) The third is that apart from a minimum rate of profit on capital there may be a certain minimum rate of profit on turnover—due to imperfections of competition, collusive aggreements between traders, etc., and which we may call m, the " degree of monopoly " rate. Hence the restriction :

$$\frac{P}{Y} \geqslant m \quad . \quad . \quad . \quad . \quad . \quad . \quad . \quad . \quad . \quad . \quad (6)$$

It is clear that equations (5) and (6) describe *alternative* restrictions, of which the higher will apply.

(4) The fourth is that the capital/output ratio, v, should not in itself be influenced by the rate of profit, for if it is, the investment/output ratio Gv will itself be dependent on the rate of profit. A certain degree of dependence follows inevitably from the consideration, mentioned earlier, that the value of particular capital goods in terms of final consumption goods will vary with the rate of profit,[2] so that, even with a *given technique* v will not be independent of $\frac{P}{Y}$. (We shall ignore this point). There is the further complication that the relation $\frac{P}{Y}$ may affect v through making more or less " labour-saving " techniques profitable. In other words, at any given wage-price relationship, the producers will adopt the technique which maximizes the rate of profit on capital, $\frac{P}{vY}$; this will affect (at a given G) $\frac{I}{Y}$, and hence $\frac{P}{Y}$. Hence any rise in $\frac{P}{Y}$ will reduce v, and thus $\frac{I}{Y}$, and conversely, any rise in $\frac{I}{Y}$ will raise $\frac{P}{Y}$. If the sensitiveness of v to $\frac{P}{Y}$ is great, $\frac{P}{Y}$ can no longer be regarded as being determined by the equations of the model ; the *technical* relation between v and $\frac{P}{Y}$ will then govern $\frac{P}{Y}$ whereas the savings equation (equation (2) above) will determine $\frac{I}{Y}$ and thus (given G) the value of v.[3] To exclude this we have to assume that v is invariant to $\frac{P}{Y}$,[4] *i.e.* :

$$v = \bar{v} \quad . \quad . \quad . \quad . \quad . \quad . \quad . \quad . \quad . \quad . \quad . \quad . \quad . \quad . \quad . \quad . \quad (7)$$

---

[1] Where L = labour force.

[2] Cf. p. 90 above. In fact the whole of the Keynesian and post-Keynesian analysis dodges the problem of the measurement of capital.

[3] This is where the " marginal productivity " principle would come in but it should be emphasized that under the conditions of our model where savings are treated, not as a constant, but as a function of income distribution, $\frac{P}{Y}$, the sensitiveness of v to changes in $\frac{P}{Y}$ would have to be very large to overshadow the influence of G and of s_p and of s_w on $\frac{P}{Y}$. Assuming that it is large, it is further necessary to suppose that the value of $\frac{P}{Y}$ as dictated by this technical relationship falls within the maximum and minimum values indicated by equations (4)-(6).

[4] This assumption does not necessarily mean that there are " fixed coefficients " as between capital equipment and labour—only that technical innovations (which are also assumed to be " neutral " in their effects) are far more influential on the chosen v than price relationships.

If equation (4) is unsatisfied, we are back at the Ricardian (or Marxian) model. $\frac{I}{Y}$ will suffer a shrinkage, and will no longer correspond to Gv, but to, say, αv where $\alpha < G$. Hence the system will not produce full employment ; output will be limited by the available capital, and not by labour ; at the same time the classical, and not the Keynesian, reaction-mechanism will be in operation : the size of the " surplus " available for investment determining investment, not investment savings. It is possible however that owing to technical inventions, etc., and starting from a position of excess labour and underemployment (*i.e.*, an elastic total supply of labour) the size of the surplus will grow ; hence $\frac{I}{Y}$ and α will grow ; and hence α might rise above G (the rate of growth of the " full employment ceiling ", given the technical progress and the growth of population) so that in time the excess labour becomes absorbed and full employment is reached. When this happens (which we may call the stage of *developed* capitalism) wages will rise above the subsistence level, and the properties of the system will then follow our model.

If equations (5) and (6) are unsatisfied, the full employment assumption breaks down, and so will the process of growth ; the economy will relapse into a state of stagnation. The interesting conclusion which emerges from these equations is that this may be the result of several distinct causes. " Investment opportunities " may be low because G' is low relatively to G, *i.e.*, the entrepreneurs' expectations are involatile, and/or they are pessimistic ; hence they expect a lower level of demand for the future than corresponds to potential demand, governed by G. On the other hand, " liquidity preference " may be too high, or the risks associated with investment too great, leading to an excessive r. (This is perhaps the factor on which Keynes himself set greatest store as a cause of unemployment and stagnation.) Finally, lack of competition may cause " over-saving " through excessive profit margins ; this again will cause stagnation, unless there is sufficient compensating increase in v (through the generation of " excess capacity " under conditions of rigid profit margins but relatively free entry) to push up Gv, and hence $\frac{I}{Y}$.

If however equations (2)-(6) are all satisfied there will be an inherent tendency to growth and an inherent tendency to full employment. Indeed the two are closely linked to each other. Apart from the case of a developing economy in the immature stage of capitalism (where equation (4) does not hold, but where $\gamma < G$), a tendency to continued economic growth will only exist when the system is only stable at full employment equilibrium— *i.e.* when $G' \geqslant G$.

This is a possible interpretation of the long-term situation in the " successful " capitalist economies of Western Europe and North America. If G' exceeds G, the investment/output ratio $\frac{I}{Y}$ will not be steady in time, even if the *trend* level of this ratio is constant.

There will be periodic breakdowns in the investment process, due to the growth in output capacity outrunning the possible growth in output ; when that happens, not only investment, but total output will fall, and output will be (temporarily) limited by effective demand, and not by the scarcity of resources. This is contrary to the mechanics of our model, but several reasons can be adduced to show why the system will not be flexible enough to ensure full employment in the short period.

(1) First, even if " profit margins " are assumed to be fully flexible, in a downward, as well as an upward, direction the very fact that investment goods and consumer goods are produced by different industries, with limited mobility between them, will mean that profit margins in the consumption goods industries will not fall below the level that ensures full utilization of resources in the consumption goods industries. A *compensating* increase

in consumption goods production (following upon a fall in the production of investment goods) can only occur as a result of a transfer of resources from the other industries, lured by the profit opportunities there.

(2) Second, and more important, profit-margins are likely to be inflexible in a downward direction in the short period (Marshall's " fear of spoiling the market ") even if they are flexible in the long period, or even if they possess short period flexibility in an upward direction.[1]

This applies of course not only to profit margins but to real wages as well, which in the short period may be equally inflexible in a downward direction at the *attained* level, thus compressing $\frac{I}{Y}$, or rather preventing an *increase* in $\frac{I}{Y}$ following upon a rise in the entrepreneurs' desired rate of expansion G'. Hence in the short period the shares of profits and wages tend to be inflexible for two different reasons—the downward inflexibility of $\frac{P}{Y}$ and the downward inflexibility of $\frac{W}{L}$—which thus tend to reinforce the long-period stability of these shares, due to constancy of $\frac{I}{Y}$, resulting from the long period constancy of Gv and $G'v$.

We have seen how the various " models " of distribution, the Ricardo-Marxian, the Keynesian and the Kaleckian are related to each other. I am not sure where " marginal productivity " comes in in all this—except that in so far as it has any importance it does through an extreme sensitivity of v to changes in $\frac{P}{Y}$.

Cambridge.   NICHOLAS KALDOR.

---

[1] Cf. the quotation from Marshall, note 2, page 93 above.
[2] This operates through the wage-price spiral that would follow on a reduction in real wages ; the prevention of such a wage-price spiral by means of investment rationing of some kind, or a " credit squeeze ", is thus a manifestation of downward inflexibility of $\frac{W}{Y}$.

From *Essays in the Theory of Economic Growth*

Joan Robinson

A MODEL OF ACCUMULATION

CLOSED AND OPEN MODELS

CONSIDER the most familiar piece of economic analysis : on the plane surface of the page of a text-book two curves are drawn, representing the flow of supply of a commodity per unit of time and the flow of demand for it, each as a function of price. They cut at the point E, where price is OP (on the y axis) and quantity traded OQ (on the x axis). We are accustomed to say that this represents a stable position of equilibrium if, at prices above OP, the supply curve lies to the right of the demand curve. What does this stability of equilibrium mean ? Clearly it means that E is a possible, and the only possible, position of equilibrium in the situation depicted by the curves. Does it mean any more than that ? It is often said that the picture shows that when price is above OP, it tends to fall towards E, and when it is below, to rise towards E. But this is by no means either clear or convincing.

First of all, falling and rising are movements in time, and there is no time on the plane surface of the diagram. Time may be conceived to lie at right-angles to the page but nothing in the picture tells us what happens when we move off the sheet.

Moreover, if price is anywhere but OP, it shows that expectations are not being fulfilled. Equilibrium means that the market price has settled at the supply price of the quantity being sold ; sellers are offering the quantity OQ in the expectation of selling at this price. If the price has recently risen above what was expected, it may very well have caused expectations to be revised in a way that will send it higher. Or if it has been falling, it may very well be going, not towards OP, but past it.

Now a pendulum is brought into the argument. The point E is said to be like the vertical position of a pendulum. The

Reprinted from Joan Robinson, *Essays in the Theory of Economic Growth* (London: Macmillan & Co., Ltd., and New York: St. Martin's Press, 1964), pp. 22–59. Reprinted by permission.

pendulum may be said to be *tending* towards the vertical even at those moments when it is moving away from it.

This metaphor can be applied to a market in which there is a clear concept in the minds of dealers as to what the equilibrium position is. In such a case it is true to say that price is always *tending* towards equilibrium even if it never settles there, and that, once settled, it will return to the equilibrium position after any chance displacement. For, in this case, dealers believe that profit is to be made by selling when price is above *OP* and buying when it is below.

How could they come by a belief that *OP* is the equilibrium price ? From experience. But the experience of each one is the result of how the others behave. The curves in the diagram are nothing but a statement of how buyers and sellers are assumed to behave.

What meaning can we attach to the conception of a position which is never reached at any particular moment of time but yet which exists only in virtue of the fact that the parties concerned believe, at each moment of time, that it will be reached in the future ?

The way out of this puzzle is to recognise that there are two kinds of economic argument, each of which is useful in analysis provided that it is not stultified by being confused with the other.

Logical and Historical Time

One kind of argument proceeds by specifying a sufficient number of equations to determine its unknowns, and so finding values for them that are compatible with each other (as above, the supply curve and the demand curve determine compatibility of price with quantity traded). The other type of argument specifies a particular set of values obtaining at a moment of time, which are not, in general, in equilibrium with each other, and shows how their interactions may be expected to play themselves out.

The first type of argument is not confined to stationary equilibrium relations. The equations may determine a path through time—say a continuous accumulation of capital, or a particular pattern of fluctuations. But the time through which

23

such a model moves is, so to speak, logical time, not historical time.

To take a familiar example, in a model applicable to a pure competitive private-enterprise economy, the equations may show constant employment; a relation between value of capital per man and value of output per man (values being reckoned in terms, say, of a basket of commodities—that is, goods sold to consumers[1]) that implies a rate of profit on capital falling as the total value of capital increases; and a relation between savings and profits that implies a rate of accumulation falling as the total value of capital increases. This describes a process in which capital is continually increasing at a decelerating rate. The model is following a path in logical time approaching in one direction a 'future' state with some limiting value of the rate of profit and in the other a 'past' state of indefinitely rapid growth.[2]

Drawing the movement with 'time' from left to right across the page and the rate of output of commodities vertically, there is a ceiling showing the output compatible with zero accumulation (equilibrium in the stationary state corresponding to our equations) and a curve asymptotic to it representing the path that the model follows as the value in terms of commodities of the stock of capital goods grows.

We can if we like chop the curve into lengths and present a number of sections in the same 'period', each with a different value of capital. That with the smallest value of capital is accumulating fastest 'today', but by the time it reaches the value of capital which one above it enjoys 'today', it will have slowed down to the rate of accumulation that that economy is experiencing 'today'. Each is following the same path from an indefinitely remote past towards a future that it will never reach.

Now, it is a nonsense question to ask: Is such a path stable, so that if the economy were displaced by some chance event, it would return to the path again? The reason why it is a nonsense question is as follows. Equilibrium implies that each

---

[1] Services sold to consumers are left out of the argument, for simplicity.
[2] Cf. my 'Accumulation and the Production Function', *Collected Economic Papers*, vol. ii, and *Economic Journal*, September 1959.

24

firm has arranged its affairs so as to maximise its own profits. This requires that firms carrying out accumulation should have sufficient foresight to pick in advance the forms in which investment will be embodied suitably to the market situations that will be met with in the relevant 'future'. (In general, more mechanised techniques and longer processes of production are chosen at a lower rate of profit.) If, at any moment, the actual position were appreciably off the prescribed path, they would not have made the right choices ; equality between the expected and the actual level of profits would not obtain. But if this has happened, we are in a world where it is liable to happen. A world in which expectations are liable to be falsified cannot be described by the simple equations of the equilibrium path. The out-of-equilibrium position is off the page, not in the same era of logical time as the movement along the path.

A large part of traditional economic argument is concerned with relations between prices, outputs, the rate of profit and so forth, in an economy existing in the conditions that prevail at the ceiling ; that is, in a stationary state. The argument consists of comparing the stationary states belonging to different sets of equations ; marginal productivity, comparative costs, profit-maximising monopoly price and many other familiar concepts, belong to this department of analysis.

There is much to be learned from *a priori* comparisons of equilibrium positions, but they must be kept in their logical place. They cannot be applied to actual situations ; it is a mortal certainty that any particular actual situation which we want to discuss is not in equilibrium. Observed history cannot be interpreted in terms of a movement along an equilibrium path nor adduced as evidence to support any proposition drawn from it.

A model applicable to actual history has to be capable of getting out of equilibrium ; indeed, it must normally not be in it. To construct such a model we specify the technical conditions obtaining in an economy and the behaviour reactions of its inhabitants, and then, so to say, dump it down in a particular situation at a particular date in historic time and work out what will happen next. The initial position contains, as well as physical data, the state of expectations of the characters

25

concerned (whether based on past experience or on traditional beliefs). The system may be going to work itself out so as to fulfil them or so as to disappoint them.

In a model depicting equilibrium positions there is no causation. It consists of a closed circle of simultaneous equations. The value of each element is entailed by the values of the rest. At any moment in logical time, the past is determined just as much as the future. In an historical model, causal relations have to be specified. Today is a break in time between an unknown future and an irrevocable past. What happens next will result from the interactions of the behaviour of human beings within the economy. Movement can only be forward.

An initial position might happen to be in near-enough equilibrium (at least we can imagine it to be so for the sake of argument) in the sense that no one in the economy who has any power to change his behaviour (to alter prices, purchases, techniques of production or what not) desires to do so. Then it is not nonsense to ask whether the position is stable, in the sense that a chance departure from it would quickly be reversed. (In this sense the equilibrium position in the market for a commodity is stable when dealers have a clear view of what the equilibrium price for that commodity is.)

An economy may be in equilibrium from a short-period point of view and yet contain within itself incompatibilities that are soon going to knock it out of equilibrium. (For instance, an expectation that the prices ruling in a seller's market are going to last may be inducing investment in productive capacity that will bring the seller's market to an end.) Or it may be in equilibrium also from a long-period point of view so that the position will reproduce itself, or expand or contract in a smooth, regular manner over the future, provided that no external disturbance occurs. The path that the model then follows appears exactly like the equilibrium path, but it is still an historical, causal story that has to be told—the economy follows the path because the expectations and behaviour reactions of its inhabitants are causing it to do so.

When the initial conditions are not in equilibrium, the model depicts how their interactions will play themselves out

26

over the next future. When a disturbance occurs on the equilibrium path, the model depicts how the economy responds to it. In reality, disturbing events occur on disequilibrium paths. The resulting turbulence is beyond the skill of model builders to analyse. Historical analysis can be made only in very general terms. When the analysis leads to results that are contradicted by experience the model must be re-examined to see whether there was some error in its construction or only some ill-considered application of it in the analysis.

The vice of the 'vulgar economics' that dominated academic teaching before Keynes (and still flourishes in some fields) was in drawing practical conclusions from equilibrium analysis.

When we compare equilibrium positions, that with a larger labour force has more employment—because full employment is specified as a characteristic of equilibrium; no causal mechanism is specified to show how an increase in the labour force raises the demand for labour in organised industry. When we compare points on an equilibrium path, that with the fastest rate of growth has the highest ratio of saving to consumption ; this does not mean that thriftiness is propitious to accumulation. In equilibrium, the rate of interest cannot be greater than the rate of profit on investment, for if it were, decumulation would be going on. This does not mean that a fall in the rate of profit produces an equivalent fall in the rate of interest. When we compare short-period situations, in competitive conditions, with the same physical equipment, that with the lower level of employment has the higher level of real wages per man hour, for, if it were not, the competitive prices cannot be ruling. This does not mean that raising wages causes unemployment.

On all these points, when challenged by Keynes, orthodox economists started looking round for causal relations that would establish the theorems that had been illegitimately deduced from equilibrium analysis. A bastard generation of theorems emerged—such as that, with unemployment, money-wage rates fall so that, provided the quantity of money is not reduced, the rate of interest is lowered, and (an unstated proviso, which has only to be stated to appear ridiculous) if expectations of profit in money terms are unaffected by the fall in prices, investment will increase. In these theorems (which continue to proliferate)

27

Keynesian causal relations are fitted into an arbitrary set of assumptions fixed up so as to lead to the results once believed to be established by equilibrium analysis.

A curious feature often found in the exposition of these pseudo-causal models is that equilibrium lies in the future. It is admitted that the economy today is not in an equilibrium position, but it is tending towards equilibrium and will get there in due course. There was evidently some influence in the past that prevented equilibrium from being reached so far, but the future is going to be different.[1]

It is also characteristic of the pseudo-causal models to throw up puzzles about the correct method of measurement of the quantities that enter into them. In concrete reality (as opposed to imaginary equilibrium conditions) the entities described as the amount of employment, the available labour force, the level of prices, the quantity of money, and so forth, are not sharply demarcated at the edges and are immensely complex in their internal structure. They can be presented, as Keynes used to put it, in a who's who of detailed items ; to express them as a number of homogeneous units we have to adopt some kind of convention, and each convention gives a different number for the same concrete situation. In a causal model the entities are of this vague and complex nature ; when simple measures are used, their conventional basis is frankly exposed. There is room for discussions about which convention is more in accord with common sense, but there is no meaning in a discussion about which is the correct one.[2]

In concrete reality an overall rise or fall in prices, employment, interest rates, or what not, is accompanied by relative changes in particular markets and regions, so that the pattern alters with the level. In a causal model these complications have to be recognised. When we are concerned with such a strong overall movement that any reasonable index would show

---

[1] A striking example of this kind of theorem is in Hicks, 'A "Value and Capital" Growth Model', *Review of Economic Studies*, June 1959, where correct foresight about the future is enjoyed today, but has not been enjoyed about today in the past.

[2] This point is clearly brought out in the account of Index Numbers in Chapter 8 of Keynes' *Treatise on Money*. What is there said about price indices applies, *mutatis mutandis*, to problems of measurement of all economic entities.

28

pretty much the same change, the shifting pattern may be neglected, but when the relative changes are important they play a part in the causal story itself.

In a pseudo-causal model in which there is a mechanism relating the quantity of money and the level of wages in such a way as to make the system tend towards a state of full employment, the money-wage rate, the level of prices, the rate of interest, the quantity of money and the rate of profit, must have precise meanings, for those are the entities which constitute the mechanism. How to match up these simple postulated entities with complex reality is an insoluble problem. But this is only to be expected, for the entities were not derived in the first place from contemplating reality ; they were hastily summoned out of their setting in a closed model only to try to recapture for equilibrium theory the position that Keynes had demolished.

The Rate of Profit

In a closed model applicable to a competitive economy in stationary equilibrium the rate of profit on capital (which may be zero) is that which is compatible with zero accumulation. Competition implies that the rate of profit is uniform throughout the economy. With given technical conditions and given money-wage rates, this determines the price of every commodity and of each component of the stock of capital goods. It thus determines the real-wage rate in terms of any basket of commodities and the cost of labour to each employer in terms of his own product. The rate of profit obtainable on each round of reinvestment of gross profit on replacement of capital goods is identical with the rate obtained on past investments.

In reality the situation today is not necessarily that which was expected when the relevant decisions were made in the past. The current rate of profit—that is, the ratio of current gross profits, minus depreciation, to the value of the stock of capital at current replacement costs—is not identical with the rate of profit which is expected to be realised on investments currently being made.

Both the realised rate of profit and the expected rate are vague and complex entities. The realised rate of profit is vague because there are various conventions that can be used to assess

29

it. The expected rate is vague because of uncertainty. Both are complex because each is an amalgam of the variegated experience of a large number of firms.

The view which the firms take of what is properly to be regarded as current profit has an influence upon the distribution which they make to rentiers, and so influences effective demand for commodities (that is, goods and services sold to the public). It also has an important influence upon expectations and so affects investment plans.

In constructing an historical model it is necessary to distinguish between the current and the expected rate of profit, and to specify what is assumed to be the connection between them. When an historical model is imagined to be following a smooth path on which the rate of profit expected on investment has been constant for some time, and has in fact been realised, we may suppose that its inhabitants hold very confident expectations that the rate of profit on investments now being made will be equal to that realised in the past. Such a path will be stable if small discrepancies between realised and expected profits do not change expectations. Investment decisions are then not affected by chance changes in current receipts (there is no 'accelerator') and accumulation continues smoothly on its path until some basic change in conditions or some major chance event upsets it.

Where experience has been very varied, confident expectations cannot be held. In such conditions there is a propensity for present experience to be overweighted in the formation of expectations; a chance change in current receipts then has an effect on investment decisions. The model follows a different course according as investment is assumed to be governed by the expectation that the current situation, whatever it may be, will continue indefinitely, that change will continue in the same direction, or that a departure from the average of past experience will reverse itself, partially or wholly, after a time.

The Quantity of Capital

The problem of measurement of a stock of capital has given a great deal of trouble. This has arisen from the habits of thought inculcated by pseudo-causal models. From the proposition

30

that, in equilibrium conditions with identical technical possibilities, a larger ratio of 'capital' to labour is associated with a lower rate of profit and higher real wages, the pseudo-causal theorem is deduced that accumulation of capital tends to lower the rate of profit. It therefore becomes a matter of the greatest importance to determine what is meant by 'capital' in the equilibrium proposition.

When we take the proposition in its own setting, in a closed model, the meaning of 'capital', though somewhat complicated, is quite unambiguous.

In any one stationary position the stock of capital goods is being reproduced continuously, item by item, so that the who's who of physical capital goods is unchanged in quantity, specification and age composition. A uniform rate of profit rules throughout the economy and there is a constant level of money-wage rates, so that all prices are determined; and the value of the stock of capital, whether in terms of money, commodities or labour time, is perfectly unambiguous.

A favourite exercise in stationary equilibrium analysis is to compare positions which have access to exactly the same technical knowledge but which exist in equilibrium with different rates of profit. (An economy which is in stationary equilibrium with a lower rate of profit has more thrifty capitalists.) Where the rate of profit is lower the real-wage rate is higher.

Generally speaking (apart from certain cranky cases[1]) in the economy with a lower rate of profit more mechanised techniques of production have been selected. There is a different who's who of capital goods in each economy. A given difference in the rate of profit is associated with a smaller difference in real wages, the more responsive is technique to differences in real wages (the easier in a technical sense is the 'substitution of capital for labour').

Comparing two stationary equilibrium positions with different rates of profit, the who's who of capital goods may have few or no items in common, and there is no presumption that the more mechanised technique requires machines that weigh more (though there is a presumption in favour of longer

[1] See my *Accumulation of Capital*, p. 109.

31

life). This has given rise to all the trouble. There is no physical measure that reflects the difference in the capital/labour ratio. Nor is there any direct measure in terms of value. With a different rate of profit the pattern of relative prices is different, and there is no common measure of the value in terms of money or of commodities to apply to the two stocks of capital goods. A measure in terms of labour-time makes more sense, for there is a general presumption that a more mechanised technique involves a greater quantity of labour-time embodied in the stock of equipment. But even this measure is not free from ambiguities, for the time pattern of production has to be taken into account; in equilibrium the cost of production of capital goods includes interest at a rate equal to the ruling rate of profit on the capital goods required to produce them. Man-hours alone are not an adequate measure. Nevertheless, the stock of capital goods is whatever equilibrium requires it to be. The difficulty is only about how to describe it.

The simplest method is to assume a uniform money-wage rate in the economies to be compared, and to draw up a schedule showing what the cost of each stock of capital goods would be at a uniform rate of profit. On this basis we can draw a *productivity curve* showing the permanently maintainable flow of output per head of commodities and the money (that is, wage unit) value of capital per head at each rate of profit. On any one curve the various degrees of mechanisation are shown in ascending order, that with a higher output per head requiring a higher capital/labour ratio. For each economy we pick out the technique of production in use there from the productivity curve corresponding to the rate of profit ruling there. Technique and rate of profit determine output per man employed and profit per man employed. They therefore entail the real-wage rate. We can now see for each economy the value of capital in terms of labour-time and in terms of commodities.[1]

There is no difficulty about this analysis so long as no conclusions are drawn from it. Economies with different rates of profit must exist either at different dates or in different regions. Between two dates technical knowledge has altered. Between two regions there are differences in natural and human resources.

[1] *Op. cit.* pp. 411-16 for diagrams illustrating the above.

32

The comparison of different economies with the same technical possibilities and different rates of profit is an exercise in pure economic logic, without application to reality.

In an historical model, the stock of capital goods at some base date is taken to be simply whatever it happens to be. It can be valued at historic cost or at current reproduction cost, or in terms of its prospective earning power discounted at whatever is considered to be the appropriate rate of interest. Each measure (unless, by a strange fluke, perfect equilibrium obtains) is vague and complex, and each gives a different result. This is certainly a very tiresome state of affairs for both private and social accountants, but it cannot be amended by pretending that it is not so.

Aggregation

A model which took account of all the variegation of reality would be of no more use than a map at the scale of one to one.[1] In order to examine large, overall movements within an economy or to compare economies each considered as a whole, we have to divide into broad groups the inhabitants, the organisations, the incomes and the products — workers and capitalists, firms and households, wages and profits, consumption goods and means of production and so forth. For a first sketch we may simplify the model by assuming a group homogeneous within itself — all workers alike, all firms alike, a single consumption good and so forth. In doing so, we must be careful not to make a simplification in such a way that the model falls to pieces when it is removed. For instance, we can measure a flow of output of consumer goods in adjacent periods of time or adjacent countries, for there is a large element of physically identical items in each output, and the rest can be measured in terms of it, on the basis of ruling market prices. This procedure may conceal serious flaws in a measure to be used in discussions of welfare or the standard of life of the population concerned, but it will serve, in a rough and ready way, for discussions of productivity provided that the common element in production is a substantial proportion of the whole. (It would not serve to compare the physical productivity of labour amongst, say, the

[1] Cf. Lewis Carroll, *Sylvie and Bruno*, p. 169.

33

Eskimos and the Trobriand Islanders.) For the reasons mentioned above, a similar measure of physical stocks of capital goods is not available.

A highly aggregated model is useful only for a first sketch of the analysis of reality, but it is much easier to fill in the details in the outline drawn by a simple model than it is to build up an outline by amassing details. The essays in this volume are concerned only to contribute towards clearing up the outline, which has fallen into much confusion in modern times.

CHOOSING A MODEL

To build up a causal model, we must start not from equilibrium relations but from the rules and motives governing human behaviour. We therefore have to specify to what kind of economy the model applies, for various kinds of economies have different sets of rules. (The *General Theory* was rooted in the situation of Great Britain in the 1930's; Keynes was rash in applying its conclusions equally to mediaeval England and ancient Egypt.) Our present purpose is to find the simplest kind of model that will reflect conditions in the modern capitalist world. Whether pure competitive *laisser-faire* capitalism ever existed is open to doubt; it certainly does not today. But we cannot understand the objectives and effects of national policies until we understand the operation of the 'free' economy that they attempt to modify. Our model, therefore, depicts a system in which production is organised by individual firms and consumption by individual households, interacting with each other without any overriding control.

The independent elements in the model must correspond with the features of reality which are given independently of each other, either by the brute facts of nature or by the freedom of individuals within the economy to decide how they will behave. In an uncontrolled capitalist economy, firms are free, within wide limits, to decide upon the amount and form of the investment that they will carry out, on price policy and on the proportion of profits distributed to shareholders. Property-owning families (rentiers, for short) have a fairly wide freedom,

34

and workers' families a limited freedom, to decide upon their
rate of expenditure for consumption. Owners of property have
freedom to decide the form in which their wealth shall be held.
Trade unions influence the level of money wages. Banks influence the supply of money. Starting from any initial situation
the interactions of the independent elements in behaviour with
each other and with the physical, technical conditions in which
they operate, determine the level and movement of employment,
outputs, prices, interest dates, real incomes and so forth, as time
goes by.

The determinants of equilibrium may thus be grouped
under these headings :

(1) Technical conditions
(2) Investment policy
(3) Thriftiness conditions
(4) Competitive conditions
(5) The wage bargain
(6) Financial conditions.

These determinants govern the flow of output, cost and price
of each kind of product, and so the rate of profit on capital and
the real wages per unit of labour.

In a state of equilibrium, the stock of capital goods must
already be that which is appropriate to the expected level of
costs and prices, in the sense that no firm can see any advantage
in changing the form in which its capital is embodied, or has
any desire to alter the amount of employment it is planning to
offer ; for equilibrium to persist it must turn out that expectations were correct. Equilibrium, in this sense, involves past
history. For an historical model, we want to be able to start in
any position, whether equilibrium or not, and discuss what will
happen next. To the above list of determinants, therefore, we
must add :

(7) The initial stock of capital goods and the state of expectations formed by past experience.

The Determinants

These seven elements are in the main independent of each other.
Under any head a change may be made without, so to say, asking

35

permission from any of the others. In economic affairs, however, causation is always circular, and no element is completely independent of what is happening to the rest.

We now consider what are the characteristics of the determinants to be postulated for a model designed to discuss, in very general terms, the growth of a pure private-enterprise economy, and what are the cross-connections between them.

Technical conditions.—The numbers and quality of the labour force, with its propensity to grow through time; the state of the industrial arts, with their propensity to be improved; and the supplies of natural resources, are, obviously, the most important determinants of production, but for the kind of analysis with which we are now concerned, in the main they must be taken simply as given. There are, however, cross-connections which have a very great influence on growth, between the level of investment and technical conditions ; investment in education and training may have an influence upon the character of the labour force ; investment in research has an influence on the growth of technical knowledge. Moreover, the same motives which make firms eager to grow, are likely to make them eager to increase productivity, especially in conditions of scarcity of labour ; and the same motives which make them compete with each other, make them eager to find ways of reducing costs.

To rule out a group of complications which require separate treatment we postulate an economy in which there are no scarce natural resources.[1]

Investment policy.—In setting up a model it is convenient to draw sharply distinctions which in reality are blurred by many border-line cases. In discussing consumption and accumulation it is convenient to postulate an economy in which there are no border-line cases between firms and households (such as peasant families) and no border-line cases between saving and spending (such as buying a house). Investment in productive capital, then, is entirely governed by decisions of firms.

The question of what governs the rate of accumulation that firms undertake is one on which there is no agreed doctrine in orthodox economics.[2] The formal structure of the *General Theory* embodies the proposition that the rate of investment

[1] See below, p. 74.   [2] Cf. p. 13.

36

tends to be such as to equate the marginal efficiency of capital
to the rate of interest ; this, it must be admitted, was in the
nature of a fudge. For a scheme of investment to be undertaken,
the profit expected from it must exceed its interest-cost by a
considerable margin to cover the risk involved. The prospective rate of profit on the finance to be committed can be reduced
to equality with the relevant rate of interest only by subtracting
a risk premium equal to the difference between them. To say
that the required risk premium is low or high is then no more
than saying that the propensity to invest is high or low.

Keynes did not take his own formalism seriously : 'Most,
probably, of our decisions to do something positive, the full
consequences of which will be drawn out over many days to
come, can only be taken as a result of animal spirits — of a
spontaneous urge to action rather than inaction, and not as the
outcome of a weighted average of quantitative benefits multiplied
by quantitative probabilities. Enterprise only pretends to itself
to be mainly actuated by the statements in its own prospectus,
however candid and sincere. Only a little more than an
expedition to the South Pole, is it based on an exact calculation
of benefits to come. Thus if the animal spirits are dimmed and
the spontaneous optimism falters, leaving us to depend on
nothing but a mathematical expectation, enterprise will fade
and die.'[1]

It is not only a matter of the innate characteristics of human
nature but also of the kind of behaviour that is approved by
society. Capitalism develops the spirit of emulation ; without
a competitive urge to grow, modern managerial capitalism could
not flourish. At the same time there are costs and risks attached
to growth that keep it within certain bounds. To attempt to
account for what makes the propensity to accumulate high or
low we must look into historical, political and psychological
characteristics of an economy ; with that sort of inquiry a model
of this kind cannot help us. It seems reasonably plausible,
however, to say that, given the general characteristics of an
economy, to sustain a higher rate of accumulation requires a
higher level of profits, both because it offers more favourable
odds in the gamble and because it makes finance more readily

[1] *General Theory*, pp. 161-2.

37

available. For purposes of our model, therefore, the 'animal spirits' of the firms can be expressed in terms of a function relating the desired rate of growth of the stock of productive capital to the expected level of profits.

Thriftiness conditions.—The simplest assumption to make about the relations between income and saving is that used by von Neumann; there are two classes of income, profits and wages; all wages are spent and all profits saved. At the other extreme, the distinction between classes of income is completely ignored and saving is taken to be whatever proportion of total net income individuals, taken one with another, desire to make it. The first approach makes saving depend entirely upon the type of income concerned. The second makes it depend entirely on individual preferences. The first appears more cogent. Our model leans towards it, but admits some element of the second.

The most important distinction between types of income is that between firms and households. Decisions concerning saving are made by both. The firms normally retain from gross profits something more than what they regard as the proper depreciation allowances required to keep their pre-existing capital intact. Since our model reflects the view that the central mechanism of accumulation is the urge of firms to survive and to grow, we may suppose that this policy in respect to distribution of dividends is framed in the interest of the firm as such rather than of the shareholders.[1] The firm has to balance the consideration that retained profits provide finance without any obligations attached to it, against the consideration that the market for its shares on the stock exchange depends very much upon the amount of dividends that it is expected to pay. In this respect each one is subject to some extent to the behaviour of the others, for if a convention is established that it is the safe

---

[1] The code of proper behaviour recommended by the Institute of Directors is as follows:

> Boards who settle their dividend policy by asking the question 'How little can we pay in order to keep the shareholders quiet?' fail to understand what their responsibilities are. The question *should* be 'What is the proper amount we need retain in the long-term interests of the company?'

Standard Board Room Practice. Prepared by a Special Committee. Published by the Institute of Directors.

38

and reputable thing to distribute no more than a particular proportion of profits, the market cannot penalise any one for adhering to the convention.

The amount of interest that firms are paying at any moment is the result of the terms on which finance was raised in the past.

The ratio of net saving by firms to their profits, then, depends on three sets of factors—the procedures that they use in calculating depreciation ; the structure of their indebtedness, with the interest obligations attached to it ; and their policy in respect to dividends.

Households may be divided into those of pure rentiers, using that term in a wide sense to include shareholders (since there are no scarce natural resources in the model, and no government, the only form of income-yielding property is the obligations of the firms) ; those whose income is entirely derived from earnings ; and those whose income is partly earned and partly derived from property.

The latter class will be gradually growing if wage earners are saving enough to leave some property to their heirs. For many of the problems with which we shall be concerned it lightens the argument very much, without making any essential difference to it, if we assume that there is no net saving, on balance, from earned income. We also rule out social security payments and unemployment allowances. Workers as a whole live from the earnings of those who are employed.

Rentiers' families must have saved in the past, otherwise they would not be rentiers. Along with their wealth, they inherit the desire to preserve and augment it. Their propensity to save may be influenced by the distribution of wealth amongst them, by the age composition of families, by the return to be expected on placements, by prospects of changing prices, by the selections of commodities offered to them, the skill of salesmen in luring expenditure from them, and so forth, but for our purpose here it is sufficient to express it simply as the proportion of receipts that they regard it as normal and proper to save.

The normal proportion of total profits saved, then, depends upon two factors — the proportion of profits distributed by the firms and the proportion of their receipts that rentiers save. The proportion of profits saved being given, the ratio of saving

39

to total net income depends upon the ratio of total profits to total income.

Savings equal to investment.—In Marshall's scheme of thought the rate of accumulation of capital in an economy was governed by the propensity to save of the households composing it. In the *General Theory* the rate of accumulation depends upon the decisions of firms concerning investment. This change of view on the mechanism of a capitalist economy gave rise to a confused controversy over the meaning of the proposition that saving is equal to investment.

This proposition can be interpreted as an accounting identity. When Y is the net income of a year, C value of consumption, I value of net investment and S of net saving, then to say

$$Y = I + C$$
$$Y = S + C$$
$$\therefore \ S = I,$$

is merely to lay out the headings for a set of columns of statistics. Net income and net investment must be defined in such a way as to be consistent with each other. Net saving is the excess of net income, so defined, over consumption, and this is identical with net investment. Any excess of value of net investment over saving by households is not only equal to the amount of undistributed profit but is actually identical with it, for what is counted as net undistributed profit is that part of net investment which is not covered by borrowing.

When the proposition is treated as a statement of equilibrium conditions, it means that whatever the rate of investment may be, the level and the distribution of income must be such as to induce the firms and households, between them, to wish to carry out saving at an equal rate. Whatever the capital/income ratio may be, the level of prices relatively to money wages is such, in equilibrium conditions, as to provide sufficient profits to call forth a rate of saving equal to the rate of net investment. That is to say that the rate of profit on capital is such as to make saving per unit of capital equal to the rate of accumulation.[1]

[1] This is true even when we do not make the convenient assumption of no net saving from earned incomes ; even if all households saved the same proportion of their receipts, there would still be additional saving represented by the retained profits of firms. Thus the ratio of saving to capital would still be an increasing function of the rate of profit.

40

A third way of taking the proposition about saving and
investment is to follow the consequences of a change in the level
of investment. When there is a higher level of outlay (money
wages being constant) on gross investment, in one year than
the last, there will follow an increase in the level of activity
and the level of prices (relatively to money wage rates) which
is at first less than is appropriate to the increase in gross investment; for the rise of profits takes some time to be reflected in
greater dividends, and expenditure takes some time to be
readjusted to changes in income. At any point in the process,
saving and investment must be equal in the truistic sense, and
at no point need they be equal in the equilibrium sense.

There may be a cross-connection between the thriftiness
conditions and the rate of accumulation in so far as distribution
policy of firms may be influenced by their investment plans. In
so far as a higher rate of accumulation is associated with reduced
distribution, it has a weaker effect in raising the rate of profit.

Competitive conditions.—The contrast between monopolistic
and competitive prices is usually conducted in terms of static
equilibrium analysis (or in that strange kind of analysis in which
equilibrium will be attained in the future). It is not to our
purpose to attempt a dynamic theory of monopoly, but it is
important to observe that there is no necessary connection
between monopoly in the market sense and the rate of growth.
Some firms with a strong hold over particular markets may be
full of 'animal spirits' and grow by continually opening up new
lines. Some near-enough competitive industries may have
sunk into a lethargic state of live-and-let-live, and have little
urge to expand. Comparing one economy with another, that
in which there is a large number of monopolistic firms, or in
which prices are regulated by agreements between groups of
firms, is not necessarily less dynamic or growing more sluggishly.
On the other hand, monopolies, especially in lines of production
which require a heavy minimum investment in long-lived plant,
cannot but be anxious to avoid excess capacity. A cautious
investment policy, from the point of view of the economy as a
whole, is equivalent to a low state of 'animal spirits'.

However that may be, there is another aspect to monopolistic
behaviour. A single firm or a price-fixing group which has a

41

strong hold over the supply of a particular commodity which has no close substitutes finds demand inelastic to price. It is likely, then, to find it advantageous to keep profit margins high. Given the total flow of demand in money terms, this means that there is so much the less demand in other markets and more competitive firms have to be content with lower profit margins. The total of profits cannot be increased by raising prices, unless at the same time effective demand is increased.

An all-round rise of profit margins would not increase total profits unless it was preceded by a corresponding increase in gross investment or in distribution to rentiers (and if it were, the same increase in profit margins would have come about automatically in competitive market conditions). Its effect is to reduce sales ; more or less the same gross profit is earned in a smaller volume of output, with lower real wages, less employment and under-utilisation of plant. Conversely, a cut in margins increases the real-wage rate without reducing profits.

Market behaviour is also important in connection with the reaction of prices to different kinds of unforeseen change. In particular, a fall in effective demand produces a greater fall in prices and a smaller fall in output the more closely does price policy correspond (with given technical conditions) to the ideal of perfect competition.

The wage bargain.—For a large part of the argument it will be convenient to assume money-wage rates constant. There are two kinds of situations, however, in which money-wage rates must be free to rise. The first is when there is an excess demand for labour, in the sense that plant is available to carry out the investment decisions of firms and to meet the demand for commodities that investment is generating, but there are not enough hands to man it. The second is when (given technical conditions) the rate of investment, together with the consumption of rentiers that it generates, is at such a level as to depress the real wage below what workers are willing to accept (or below the level at which they can work efficiently), so that an irresistible demand for higher money wages makes itself felt.[1]

Finance.—There are two aspects of finance which we must take into account. The first is the structural pattern of the

---

[1] Cf. p. 13 above.

42

relation between the distribution of the urge to accumulate of firms and the distribution of borrowing power. This largely depends upon legal conditions (it was revolutionised by the institution of limited liability), the organisation of financial institutions, the attitude of rentiers towards risk and so forth. For purposes of our model it is best treated, along with the 'animal spirits' of the firms, as an element in the propensity to accumulate of the economy.

The second aspect of finance is the general level of interest rates, which, with any one structure of financial institutions and pattern of distribution of borrowing power, may be higher or lower according to the relation between the supply and demand for placements of various kinds, including the supply of money.

Our model is intended to represent pure private enterprise, but it is impossible to imagine a capitalist economy without an organised monetary system. But monetary systems are national and monetary policy is bound up with the problems of the balance of payments and exchange rates. A model of a closed system in which monetary policy, via the interest rate, controls the level of investment, is a kind of day-dream that economists delight in, but our model is not designed to pander to this indulgence.[1] We therefore chose assumptions which give monetary policy a very minor role.

Replacements are normally financed entirely, and net investment to a considerable extent, from gross retained profits. Firms are able to raise additional finance by selling bonds and equities to rentiers, and by borrowing from banks at the ruling rate of interest.

Rentiers hold their wealth in the form of obligations of the firms or in bank deposits.

The banks allow their total lending (and therefore the supply of money) to increase gradually, at a constant rate of interest, as total wealth increases ; but when there is a sharp rise in the

[1] In some passages in the *General Theory* Keynes indulged in this day-dream, but his main concern was, on the theoretical plane, to demonstrate that in a closed system the rate of interest could be controlled (a demonstration that was necessary because of the confusion between the rate of interest and the rate of profit that was then prevalent) and, on the practical plane, to protest against the policy of sacrificing home employment to the balance of payments. It was for these reasons that interest rates play such a prominent part in his argument.

43

demand for money such as occurs in inflationary conditions, they raise the rate of interest to a level which checks investment.[1]

These assumptions are intended to reduce the importance of monetary policy in the operation of the model to a minimum, except as a stopper to inflation.

Equilibrium Relations

When the composition of the stock of capital in existence is in harmony with the rate of growth that firms are prepared to carry out, so that an overall rate of gross investment per annum, rising from year to year at a steady rate, would bring about the same overall rate of growth of the stock of capital (maintaining the appropriate proportion between equipment for producing equipment and equipment for producing consumer goods); and when the expectations of firms about the future are in line with current experience, the expected rate of profit (the marginal efficiency of investment) being the same in all lines; then our model is in a state of internal equilibrium for the time being. (This does not guarantee that the current growth rate can continue to be realised: situations where it can and cannot continue will be discussed below.)

The whole position, in real terms, is then determined by the rate of accumulation which is being carried out.

In such an equilibrium position there is a normal price for each kind of output, which is governed by its cost of production and marketing, including in cost notional interest at a rate equal to the rate of profit on investment. The price policy of firms is such as to establish the normal capacity operation of plant. There is then an interlocking system of prices in terms of wage units, each output paying for the labour that it requires, the intermediate products which enter into it (including amortisation of plant) and interest on the capital employed in

[1] Interest and dividends paid to rentiers constitute net income for the recipients; interest paid to banks represents their gross receipts. In general, different amounts will return to the firms as demand for consumption goods from rentiers' outlay and from the outlays of banks via the expenditure of their employees. This sets up some complications which it is not worth while to explore. We rule them out by assuming that the saving out of interest is the same for the banking sector as for rentiers when the rate of interest is at its normal level, while, when the rate has been raised to check inflation, the whole of the additional interest receipts of the banks are saved.

44

producing and selling it. When the stock of capital is valued at normal prices, the rate of profit on capital is then equal to the rate of profit on investment.

The distribution of profits by firms and the expenditure of rentiers are in their normal relation to current profits. Profit per annum is equal to the value of net investment plus the value of rentier consumption. The rate of profit on capital is determined by the ratio of net investment to the stock of capital (the rate of accumulation) and the proportion of profits saved. The level of wages in terms of commodities is determined by the technical conditions and the rate of profit.

The level of prices in terms of money is determined by the level of money-wage rates, which is arbitrarily given. The rate of interest is arbitrarily determined by the banking system, and the stock of money is adjusted to the level of money wages and prices in such a way as to establish it.

When the expectations entertained in the relevant past about what the current situation would be are turning out to have been correct, the forms in which investment has been embodied are appropriate to the current position. At the moment when investment decisions are made, firms are often presented with a choice of alternative methods of production. In our model, profits are desired for the sake of growth rather than growth for the sake of profits, but firms are still conceived to be attempting to 'maximise profits' in the sense that, in respect to particular choices, they prefer a more profitable to a less profitable alternative. Thus, if there are a variety of techniques, already known, for carrying out a particular line of production, investment plans are assumed to be designed to embody the technique which promises the highest rate of profit on the finance committed (which may consist of new investment or a reincarnation of the capital recovered, through amortisation, from an earlier investment). Thus a condition for the internal equilibrium of the system to be realised is that no firm is making use of one technique where another would be yielding a higher rate of profit.[1]

---

[1] This condition can be stated in terms of traditional marginal productivity concepts—equilibrium entails that the marginal net product of labour to an employer is not less than the wage in terms of product, and the marginal

45

Short-period Equilibrium

The above position depends upon the assumption that the initial conditions are in harmony with the determinants of the system. When initial conditions are not in harmony we cannot make use of the notion of a rate of profit which is uniform throughout the system and we cannot value output and the stock of capital at normal prices. We have to fall back upon the who's who of physical products.

We measure the flow of output of commodities in 'baskets' of representative composition, and we divide the stock of capital equipment into two sectors—plant designed for the production of commodities to be sold to consumers and basic plant which can be used either for producing itself or for producing plant for the commodity sector.

Now consider the situation with given stocks of plant of each kind, with a rate of gross investment going on, decreed by decisions of the firms that have already been taken, and with a flow of receipts of rentiers determined by the profits of the recent past.

Employment in gross investment is then given. Employment in the production of commodities is determined by the flow of sales (and the flow of sales expected over the near future, which governs the flow of reproduction of work in progress); the flow of sales is governed by the flow of demand in money terms coming from households and the price policy of firms.

If the short-period situation that we are examining is one in which there has been a fall of effective demand in the recent past, firms may be working plant below designed capacity and still charging the 'full cost' prices at which they were earlier able to sell their normal capacity output. But let us suppose that competition (in the short-period sense) is sufficiently keen to keep prices at the level at which normal capacity output can be sold. If the situation is one in which demand is higher than was expected, a seller's market prevails

productivity of investment to a firm is not less than the rate of profit, but it is to be observed that the marginal products are evaluated at a given set of prices. This line of argument does not apply to the comparison between techniques chosen at different rates of profit. Cf. above, p. 32.

46

and capacity is being strained, but there is not very much play in it. Thus we may say that employment in the production of commodities is more or less closely determined by the available plant.

The flow of expenditure on the purchase of commodities is equal to the flow of outlay on wages *plus* a certain part (determined by distribution policy and the thriftiness of rentiers) of the net profits enjoyed by the firms in the recent past.

The price level of commodities per 'basket' is this total flow of expenditure divided by the rate of output of baskets in physical units.

This price, with the ruling money-wage rate, determines the real wage in terms of the consumption good and the total amount of gross profit from sales.

We have to consider how the situation in which the firms find themselves influences their plans for the future. This involves the whole question of the mechanism of fluctuations in a private-enterprise economy. At this stage in the argument we assume that expectations are based upon a simple projection of the current situation. On the basis of prices and wages ruling today, firms calculate the rate of profit to be expected on investment.

The central mechanism of our model is the desire of firms to accumulate, and we have assumed that it is influenced by the expected rate of profit. The rate of investment that they are planning for the future is, therefore, higher the greater the rate of profit on investment (estimated on the basis of current prices). Valuing the existing stock of capital on the basis of the same rate of profit, we can then express their plans in terms of a rate of accumulation.

The double-sided relationship between the rate of profit and the rate of accumulation now appears. The accumulation going on in a particular situation determines the level of profits obtainable in it, and thus (on the basis of the type of expectations which we have postulated) determines the rate of profit expected on investment. The rate of profit in turn influences the rate of accumulation. The rate of profit generated by a particular situation may be such as to induce a rate of accumulation greater or less than that which is actually taking place.

47

The Desired Rate of Accumulation
The first question to be discussed is the relation between the
rate of profit *caused* by the rate of accumulation and the rate of
accumulation which that rate of profit will *induce*, which may
be found in the short-period situations which the chances and
changes of history throw up.   The various possible relations
can be mapped out in a diagram.

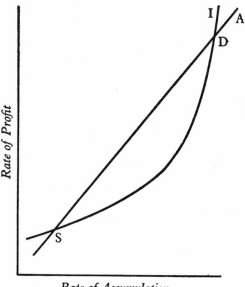

Rate of Accumulation

The *A* curve represents the expected rate of profit on investment as a function of the rate of accumulation that generates it.
The *I* curve represents the rate of accumulation as a function of
the rate of profit that induces it.
When the firms find themselves in a situation (to the right
of *D* in the diagram) such that the rate of accumulation going
on is higher than that which would be justified by the rate of
profit that it generates, the investment plans being drawn up
will bring a lower rate of accumulation into operation in the
immediate future.   The ratio of basic to commodity-sector
plant is unduly high and further investment in it does not

appear profitable ; the plans which the firms are now making will cause the ratio to fall.

When the current rate of accumulation is less than would be justified by the rate of profit that it is generating (the position lying between *S* and *D* in the diagram) the firms are planning to increase the rate of accumulation (unless there is some impediment to prevent them). The ratio of basic to commodity-sector plant is too low and (allowing for the replacements falling due) there is a higher ratio of basic plant in current investment than in the existing stock.

When the current rate of accumulation is at a level too low to generate profits sufficient to maintain even such a low rate, and any further fall would further increase the deficiency (the situation depicted by points below *S* in the diagram), the economy has fallen below its stalling speed and is heading towards even greater ruin and decay than it now suffers.

The point *D* represents a rate of accumulation which is generating just the expectation of profit that is required to cause it to be maintained.[1] This may be conveniently described as the *desired* rate of accumulation, in the sense that it is the rate which makes the firms satisfied with the situation in which they find themselves.[2]

The fact that the desired and the actual rate of accumulation coincide in a particular short-period situation does not by itself guarantee that they will continue to do so. There may be

---

[1] There is no logical necessity for the basic determinants to be such as to make all three types of situation possible. (1) The *A* curve may lie above the *I* curve all the way. There is then no limit to the desired rate of growth ; some physical obstacle has to be brought into the story to prevent the economy from exploding. (2) The *A* curve may lie above the *I* curve all the way below *D*. There is no intersection at *S* and no level of investment below which recovery towards *D* is impossible. (3) There may be an intersection at *S* but not at *D*. Then all possible rates of accumulation are divided between those below the stalling speed, which lead to ruin, and those above, which lead to explosive acceleration. (A case in which the *A* curve does not lie above the *I* curve anywhere in the positive quadrant of the diagram is impossible, for such an economy is not viable.)

[2] This concept is very similar to Harrod's *warranted rate of growth* and has a similar role in the analysis. Harrod, however, has never removed the ambiguity as to whether the firms are supposed to be content with the stocks of productive capital that they are operating or with the rate at which it is growing. To avoid confusion, it seems better to use a different term from his. Cf. below, pp. 33-5.

49

influences within the existing situation which will cause changes in the immediate future.

First, there is a lag between the receipt of profits and the rentiers' expenditure to which they give rise, so that a part of the current purchases of consumption goods are being made out of incomes derived from the distribution of profits of an earlier period. When the level of profits has not been growing smoothly, this is liable to cause wobbles in the relation between the current rate of accumulation and the current proceeds from the sale of consumption goods.

Second, past rates of accumulation leave fossils in the present structure of the stock of plant. When accumulation has been erratic in the past, the age composition of the stocks of the two kinds of plant will not be in a state of balance appropriate to the rate of accumulation that is now going on. From one short period to the next, the relation between current gross investment and net accumulation is then liable to be upset by a larger or smaller quantity of renewals falling due. Thus, having attained the desired rate of accumulation at one moment, the firms may be tipped off it at the next.

Before discussing such disturbances we will consider the development of the economy as it can be imagined to take place in tranquil conditions.

In a long run of time without disturbing events, the desired rate of accumulation (under the assumption about expectations that we are now making) will become established, if technical conditions permit. When accumulation has been going on for a sufficient time at the desired rate, the structure of the stock of productive capital has become more or less completely adjusted to requirements. Plants are divided between the sectors in near enough the proportions appropriate to the rate of accumulation which is taking place and the accompanying rate of consumption. The age-composition of the stock of plant, also, is a close approximation to that appropriate to the rate of growth; each generation is larger than the last in more or less exact proportion to the growth rate of the economy. A rate of gross investment growing from year to year at the growth rate then generates net investment growing at very nearly the same rate, and so an almost perfectly steady proportionate growth in the

50

physical stock of each kind of plant and working capital. Profit expectations are realised and so confirmed. The system is in a close approximation to the state of internal equilibrium described above, and remains in it while tranquillity continues to prevail.

DESIRED AND POSSIBLE GROWTH

We have been discussing the desired rate of accumulation for the firms as a whole which arises from the interaction of their individual plans under the proviso that there is no impediment to prevent them from growing as fast as they wish. We have said nothing about the availability of labour.

There are many interesting questions to discuss in relation to the influence upon the labour force of the age-composition of the population, the level of education and so forth, but we shall not enter into them here. We simply postulate a certain rate of growth of population, which may be zero, and assume that the available supply of labour grows with it, without any change in personal efficiency. The actual efficiency of labour, however, depends upon the state of technical knowledge. The formal analysis of technical progress is discussed below.[1] Here we shall merely assume that innovations are occurring throughout the economy in such a way as to be near-enough neutral on balance—that is, in such a way that the value of capital in terms of wage units per man employed does not alter appreciably when accumulation is going on at such a pace as to keep the rate of profit constant.

The rate of technical progress (the all-round rise in output per head that it produces) depends very much upon demand and supply of labour. When firms can see profitable markets expanding around them but cannot get hands, they set about trying to find labour-saving devices. (Since this occurs just as much in the production of equipment and intermediate products as in the final processes of production of commodities there is no reason why it should not be neutral on balance.) Without this stimulus innovations are more sluggish, and when there is a

[1] See p. 88 *et seq.*

51

surplus of labour, workers (with much support from public opinion) put up a resistance against the 'machines that take the bread out of their mouths'.

On the other hand, technical progress does go on even when there is massive unemployment. In practice it is not possible to distinguish sharply between 'autonomous' innovations due to the growth of knowledge, 'competitive' innovations due to the struggle between firms and 'induced' innovations due to the scarcity of labour, though in a rough-and-ready way the kind of situations that produce them can be observed.

For our present purposes it is sufficient to say that the desired rate of growth may fall short of the rate compounded of the growth of the labour force and the growth of output per head due to autonomous and competitive innovations ; a desired rate that is high relatively to the growth of the labour force may call forth the innovations that it needs ; or it may be so high that it cannot be satisfied and has to be restrained.

We now proceed to confront the desired rate of growth (resulting from the 'animal spirits' of the firms) with the rate of growth made possible by physical conditions (resulting from the growth of population and technical knowledge).[1]

I used the phrase 'a golden age' to describe smooth, steady growth with full employment (intending thereby to indicate its mythical nature). Corresponding nicknames may be given to other possible phases of growth.

A Golden Age

With a desired rate of accumulation equal to the possible rate, compounded of the rate of growth of population and of output per head, starting with near full employment and a composition of the stock of plant appropriate to the desired rate of accumulation, near full employment is maintained. This is a golden age.

The firms in our model are assumed (at this stage in the argument) to judge the future profitability of investment by current receipts, which implies that passing events, temporarily

[1] The following argument owes much to Harrod's distinction between the *warranted* and the *natural* rates of growth, but there are some important differences between his model and ours.

52

raising or lowering current receipts, produce the effect of an 'accelerator', one way and the other, on their investment plans; for the moment, however, we assume that conditions are sufficiently tranquil (and have been tranquil for a long enough past) to make such disturbances negligible; a steady rate of accumulation then rolls smoothly on its way. In so far as technical progress is raising output per head, the real-wage rate is rising equally. The rate of profit on capital remains constant. Techniques of production are chosen, at each round of gross investment, of the degree of mechanisation appropriate to the rate of profit, and gross profit margins are compatible with normal utilisation of plant.

From the point of view of the firms, *equilibrium* may be said to prevail, since the desired rate of accumulation is being realised. From the point of view of the overall demand and supply of labour *harmony* may be said to prevail. On the other hand, the position cannot be called an *optimum*; for the level of real wages depends partly upon the thriftiness conditions, so that there is an element in the situation of a conflict of interests between workers and rentiers. (A golden age in which there was no consumption out of profits would be an optimum, within the technical possibilities, from the point of view of the workers; the real-wage rate would be as high as was compatible with continuous full employment and the surplus accruing to capitalists would be no more than the necessary cost of maintaining it.[1])

A Limping Golden Age

A steady rate of accumulation of capital may take place below full employment. The stock of plant has the composition appropriate to the desired rate of accumulation, but there is not enough of it to employ the whole labour force.

The limp may be of various degrees of severity. When output is growing less fast than output per head, the level of employment in organised industry is falling as time goes by.

When output is rising faster than output per head, employment is increasing. It may be increasing faster than the labour force is growing (so that the system is heading towards full

---

[1] See below, p. 120 *et seq.*

53

employment) or more slowly so that the ratio of non-employed to employed workers is growing.

A Leaden Age

A growing ratio of non-employment means a falling standard of life for the workers all round, unless real wages for those employed are rising sufficiently rapidly to compensate for the rising ratio of mouths to employed hands (a somewhat implausible situation) or the opportunities for self-employment are sufficiently favourable.[1] When Malthusian misery checks the rate of growth of population, then, in the absence of technical progress, a situation might be reached in which the rate of accumulation and the rate of growth of the labour force were equal, the ratio of non-employment being great enough to keep the latter down to equality with the former.[2]

A Restrained Golden Age

We now turn to the more cheerful scene where, even with induced technical progress, it is impossible to maintain as high a rate of growth as firms are willing and anxious to carry out.

With a stock of plant appropriate to the desired rate of accumulation (which exceeds the rate of growth of population) and full employment already attained, the desired rate of accumulation cannot be realised, because the rate of growth of output per head (even with the stimulus of scarcity of labour) is not sufficient to make it possible.

There are two different ways in which it may be held in check.

When the firms desire to employ more labour than there is, a scramble for hands may lead to rising money-wage rates and consequently rising prices and a rising demand for credit to finance production. According to our assumptions, the rate of interest would then be pushed up to the point at which investment is checked. The demand for labour is thus prevented from exceeding the available supply.

---

[1] Cf. p. 19.

[2] This situation is different from that depicted by the 'iron law of wages'. In that case the growth of numbers is limited by a low level of real wages for those employed. Here it is limited as a result of the low rate of accumulation.

If the composition of the stock of plant had become adjusted to the physically possible rate of accumulation, leaving a sufficient margin of unemployment to prevent wages from rising, a sufficiently exact control of credit may be imagined to keep accumulation down to that level. (This is an aspect of the day-dream referred to above.[1]) If growth were kept down to the possible rate with a reserve of non-employed labour, the system could hardly be said to be in a state of internal equilibrium. The firms would always be straining to do more investment than they can. Any chance relaxation of credit would set them first increasing the stock of basic plant and then eating into the margin of non-employment, thus starting an inflation which would then be jerked to a halt. A golden age restrained by financial control, therefore, cannot be credited with short-period stability.

There is another way in which the desire to accumulate may be checked. When the scarcity of labour sets in, if the firms are under the influence of the fellow-feeling described by Adam Smith, they refrain from bidding up wage rates and trying to entice workers from each other. Each then has its own share of the labour force. If they realise the situation, they refrain from building plants that they will be unable to man. The desired rate of accumulation is then tailored to fit the possible rate. Or it may happen that each has built up productive capacity in the hope of getting hands, and, on the average, productive capacity is under-utilised. This situation may be kept alive by continual changes of fortune, each firm from time to time being lucky enough to get the labour it requires. The under-utilisation of plant reduces the rate of profit on capital. Overall steady growth would be established when the rate of profit expected (on the basis of average experience) is such that the rate of accumulation that it induces is brought down to the possible rate. In this case also short-period stability can hardly be supposed to prevail.

The type of restraint which is in force may be supposed to react upon the choice of technique. When the restraint operates simply by keeping the rate of interest at a level which dampens the desire to grow, there is no reason why the choice of technique

[1] P. 43.

55

should not be that appropriate to the ruling rate of profit. When the restraint operates by rationing of credit, firms may aim at less mechanised techniques than they would choose if they were untrammelled, though this will tend to increase the overall scarcity of labour and cause under-capacity working for lack of hands. When the restraint operates through monopsony in the labour market (so that each firm has its own group of workers and does not attempt to recruit any more) the techniques chosen are likely to be more mechanised than that which would maximise profits, and the rate of profit on capital is pushed down to such a level as to reduce the desired rate of growth to fit the actual rate that is being realised.

A Galloping Platinum Age

So far, we have considered situations in which the composition of the stock of capital is already adjusted to the rate of growth that is going on, so that the ratio of plant for producing plant to plant for producing commodities is such that it can maintain itself. Such a stock of capital does not drop from heaven. It has to be built up by a process of accumulation. We now examine the manner in which this process might develop.[1]

Let us suppose that 'animal spirits' are high, and a large mass of non-employed labour is available, but the desired rate of growth cannot be attained because of lack of basic plant to produce plant. The investment industries are experiencing a seller's market and a large part of investment is devoted to enlarging the investment sector; as it grows, more labour is employed and the ratio of gross investment to the output of commodities rises as the process goes on. Consequently the rate of profits is rising. Unless technical progress is sufficiently rapid, the real-wage rate is falling.

In so far as the rate of profit has an influence upon the choice of technique, less mechanised methods of production are chosen at each round of gross investment, which causes employment to increase all the faster. If this gallop is not interrupted either by reaching full employment or striking the

[1] Ian Little ('Classical Growth', *Oxford Economic Papers*, June 1957) used the expression 'platinum age' for what we call, below, a 'creeping platinum age', in which the rate of accumulation is decelerating. It is convenient to use his metal also for an accelerating process.

56

minimum acceptable real-wage rate, it proceeds until the stock of basic plants has been brought to the ratio to consumption-sector plants appropriate to the desired rate of accumulation.

A Creeping Platinum Age

The reverse situation, in which the ratio of basic plant is too high for the physically possible rate of growth, does not appear to be a plausible one, but it has some scholastic interest.

To simplify the argument, let us suppose that there are no new inventions and discoveries, so that techniques are changed only by way of adaptation to changes in profits and wages. When the story begins full employment has already been reached, the rate of accumulation is at a peak, the rate of profit is high and techniques of a low degree of mechanisation are being installed. The labour force is not growing fast enough to keep up with employment offered by the growing stock of plant. To check the scarcity of labour that threatens, the rate of interest is raised and a brake is imposed upon accumulation ; the consequent fall in the rate of profit brings the desired rate of accumulation down. Labour is released from investment and becomes available to the commodity sector. A sufficiently skilful operation of the financial machine may be conceived to raise the rate of interest in such a way as to bring down the rate of accumulation gradually without causing unemployment. At each moment, then, the narrowing gap between the rate of profit and the rate of interest is just sufficient to call forth a rate of investment, which, together with the demand for commodities that it generates, just absorbs the whole labour force. As the rate of profit falls, more mechanised techniques are chosen at each round of investment.

The process continues until the rate of accumulation has come down approximately to equality with the rate of growth of the labour force. The stock of capital is then gradually adjusted to the technique appropriate to the rate of profit corresponding to that rate of accumulation.

Thus the path which the model follows resembles the path through logical time of an equilibrium model with a decelerating rate of accumulation, falling rate of profit, falling marginal efficiency of investment and rising real-wage rate, approaching

57

asymptotically to a stationary state. There is an important difference, however. Our model is never exactly in equilibrium at any point on its path, for the technique of production chosen at each round of investment is that appropriate to the rate of profit expected on the basis of a projection of current prices, whereas in the equilibrium model techniques are chosen in the light of correct foresight of the movement of prices over the lifetime of each kind of capital good.[1]

A Bastard Golden Age

We must now consider another type of limit upon the rate of accumulation. Inflationary pressure, bringing financial checks into operation, may arise when there is no scarcity of labour— indeed a great mass of non-employment—if the real-wage rate refuses to be depressed below a particular level. A higher rate of accumulation means a lower real-wage rate. When the desired rate of accumulation is greater than the rate which is associated with the minimum acceptable real wage, the desire must be checked. A situation in which the rate of accumulation is being held in check by the threat of rising money wages due to a rise in prices (as opposed to rising money wages due to a scarcity of labour) may be described as a bastard golden age.[2]

The rate of accumulation may be less or greater than the rate of growth of population, so that non-employment is increasing or diminishing. (In the latter case the system is heading towards a legitimate golden age.)

A bastard golden age sets in at a fairly high level of real wages when organised labour has the power to oppose any fall in the real-wage rate. Any attempt to increase the rate of accumulation, unless it is accompanied by a sufficient reduction in consumption out of profits, is then frustrated by an inflation-

---

[1] Those who make pseudo-causal models to simulate the equilibrium path are somewhat casual in specifying the mechanism that produces the required result. For instance, Meade (*A Neo-classical Theory of Economic Growth*, p. 3.) merely postulates that monetary policy keeps the prices of consumption goods constant, while money-wage rates are such as to ensure full employment. He dodges the problem of foresight by making capital goods perfectly versatile. In his story the rate of interest *falls* with the rate of profit.

[2] Cf.R. F. Kahn, 'Exercises in the Analysis of Growth', *Oxford Economic Papers*, June 1959.

58

ary rise in money-wage rates. In such a situation, the rate of accumulation is limited by the 'inflation barrier'.

A low-level bastard golden age is seen when the real-wage rate is at the minimum level tolerable. (A low-level bastard golden age might have the same standard of life as obtains in a leaden age, but the mechanism of the system is different. In a leaden age the slow rate of accumulation keeps the standard of life to the minimum; in the bastard golden age the minimum standard of life sets a limit to the rate of accumulation.)

A Bastard Platinum Age

When technical progress is going on, the amount of labour required to produce the minimum acceptable real wage for a given team of men is gradually falling. Then a constant level of real wages is compatible with a rise in the ratio of gross investment to consumption. Thus acceleration of accumulation can take place without causing inflation.

Summary

In golden ages the initial conditions are appropriate to steady growth. In true and limping golden ages the actual realised growth rate is limited only by the desired rate. (In a true golden age, the possible rate coincides with the desired rate and near full employment has already been reached.) In a restrained golden age, the realised growth rate is limited by the possible rate, and kept down to it. In a leaden age the possible rate is held down by the realised rate. In a bastard golden age the possible rate is limited in a different way—that is, by real wages being at the tolerable minimum. Both in a limping golden age and a bastard golden age the stock of capital in existence at any moment is less than sufficient to offer employment to all available labour. In the limping golden age the stock of equipment is not growing faster for lack of 'animal spirits'. In the bastard age it is not growing faster because it is blocked by the inflation barrier.

In platinum ages the initial conditions do not permit steady growth and the rate of accumulation is accelerating or decelerating as the case may be.

59

A New Model of Economic Growth

Nicholas Kaldor and James A. Mirrlees

1. The purpose of this paper is to present a " Keynesian " model of economic growth which is an amended version of previous attempts put forward by one of the authors in three former publications.[1] This new theory differs from earlier theories mainly in the following respects:

(1) it gives more explicit recognition to the fact that technical progress is infused into the economic system through the creation of new equipment, which depends on current (gross) investment expenditure. Hence the " technical progress function " has been re-defined so as to exhibit a relationship between the rate of change of gross (fixed) investment per operative and the rate of increase in labour productivity on *newly installed* equipment;

(2) it takes explicit account of obsolescence, caused by the fact that the profitability of plant and equipment of any particular " vintage " must continually diminish in time owing to the competition of equipment of superior efficiency installed at subsequent dates; and it assumes that this *continuing obsolescence is broadly foreseen by entrepreneurs* who take it into account in framing their investment decision. The model also assumes that, irrespective of whether plant and equipment has a finite physical life-time or not, its *operative* life-time is determined by a complex of economic factors which govern the rate of obsolescence, and not by physical wear and tear;

(3) in accordance with this, the behavioural assumptions concerning the investors' attitudes to uncertainty in connection with investment decisions and which are set out below, differ in important respects from those made in the earlier models;

(4) account is also taken, in the present model, of the fact that some proportion of the existing stock of equipment disappears each year through physical causes—accidents, fire, explosions, etc.—and this gives rise to some " radioactive " physical depreciation in addition to obsolescence;

(5) since, under continuous technical progress and obsolescence, there is no way of measuring the " stock of capital " (measurement in terms of the historical cost of the surviving capital equipment is irrelevant; in terms of historical cost *less* accrued " obsolescence " is question-begging, since the allowance for obsolescence, unlike the charge for physical wear and tear etc., depends on the share of profits, the rate of growth, etc., and cannot therefore be determined independently of all other relations), the model avoids the notion of a quantity of capital, and its corollary, the rate of capital accumulation, as variables of the system; it operates solely with the value of current gross investment (gross (fixed) capital expenditure per unit of time) and its rate of change in time. The macro-economic notions of income, income per head, etc., on the the other hand are retained.

---

[1] Cf. N. Kaldor, "Alternative Theories of Distribution," *Review of Economic Studies*, 1955-56, (reprinted in *Essays on Value and Distribution*, pp. 228-236). " A Model of Economic Growth," *Economi c Journal*, December 1957 (reprinted in *Essays in Economic Stability and Growth*, pp. 256-300) and " Capit al Accumulation and Economic Growth " (presented in Corfu, September 1958 and published in *The Theory of Capital*, Macmillan, 1961, pp. 177-220). N. Kaldor's ideas in connection with the present model were worked out during his tenure as Ford Research Professor in Economics in Berkeley, California.

Reprinted from XXIX (June 1962) 174–192 of *Review of Economic Studies* by permission of *Review of Economic Studies* published by Oliver & Boyd Ltd., Edinburgh and London.

2. The present model is analogous to the earlier models in the following main features:

(1) like all " Keynesian " economic models, it assumes that " savings " are passive—the level of investment is based on the volume of investment decisions made by entrepreneurs, and is independent of the propensities to save; it postulates an economy in which the mechanism of profit and income generation will create sufficient savings (at any rate within certain limits or " boundaries ") to balance the investment which entrepreneurs decide to undertake;

(2) the model relates to an isolated economy with continuous technical progress, and with a steady rate of increase in the working population, determined by exogeneous factors;

(3) the model assumes that investment is primarily *induced* by the growth in production itself, and that the underlying conditions are such that growth-equilibrium necessarily carries with it a state of continuous full employment. This will be the case when the purely ' endogeneous ' growth rate (as determined by the combined operation of the accelerator and the multiplier) which is operative under conditions of an unlimited supply of labour, is appreciably higher than the " natural rate of growth," which is the growth of the " labour potential " (i.e., the *sum* of the rate of growth of the labour force and of (average) labour productivity). In that case, starting from any given state of surplus labour and under-employment, continued growth, as determined by these endogenous factors, will necessarily lead to full employment sooner or later; and once full employment rules, continued growth involves that the accelerator-multiplier " mechanism becomes " tethered " (through variations in the share of profits and through the imposition of a quasi-exogeneous growth rate in demand) to the natural rate of growth.

3. In a situation of continuing full employment the volume of investment decisions for the economy as a whole will be governed by the number of workers who become available, per unit period, to " man " new equipment, and by the amount of investment per operative. It may be assumed that each entrepreneur, operating in imperfectly competitive markets, aims at the maximum attainable growth of his own business (subject as we shall explain below, to the maintenance of a satisfactory rate of return on the capital employed) and for that reason prefers to maintain an appreciable amount of excess capacity so as to be able to exploit any chance increase in his selling power either by increasing his share of the market or by invading other markets. However, when gross investment per period is in excess of the number of workers becoming available to " man " new equipment, the degree of excess capacity must steadily rise; hence whatever the desired relationship between capacity and output, sooner or later a point will be reached when the number of workers available for operating new equipment exerts a dominating influence (via the mechanism of the accelerator) on the volume of investment decisions in the economy.[1]

We shall assume that the equipment of any given vintage is in " limitational " relationship to labour—i.e. that it is not possible to increase the productivity of labour by reducing the number of workers employed in connection with already existing equipment (though it is possible that productivity would, on the contrary, be *reduced* by such a reduction, on account of its being associated with a higher ratio of overhead to prime labour). This does not mean that the equipment of any vintage requires a fixed amount of labour to keep it in operation. The latter would assume the case not only of " fixed coefficients " but of complete indivisibility of the plant and equipment as well.

---

[1] We may assume that for the average, or representative, firm, sales grow at the same rate as production in the economy as a whole. But there will always be of course the exceptional firms who grow at a higher rate, and sub-average firms who grow at a lower rate. Investment in all cases serves the purpose of keeping productive capacity in some desired relationship with expected sales.

Writing n_t for the number of workers available to operate new equipment per unit period and i_t for the amount of investment per operative on machines of vintage t, and I_t for gross investment in fixed capital

$$i_t \equiv \frac{I_t}{n_t} \tag{1}$$

We shall use the symbols Y_t for the gross national product at t, N_t for the working population, and y_t for output per head, so that

$$y_t \equiv \frac{Y_t}{N_t}$$

4. We shall assume that " machines " of each vintage are of constant physical efficiency during their lifetime, so that the growth of productivity in the economy is entirely due to the infusion of new " machines " into the system through (gross) investment.[1] Hence our basic assumption is a technical progress function which makes the annual rate of growth of productivity per worker *operating on new equipment* a function of the rate of growth of investment per worker, i.e., that

$$\dot{p}_t/p_t = f(\dot{i}_t/i_t) \text{ with } f(0) > 0, f' > 0, f'' < 0 \tag{2}$$

This function is illustrated in Figure 1. It is assumed that a constant rate of investment per worker over time will itself increase productivity per worker; but that the rate of growth of productivity will also be an increasing function of the rate of growth of investment per worker, though at a diminishing rate.[2]

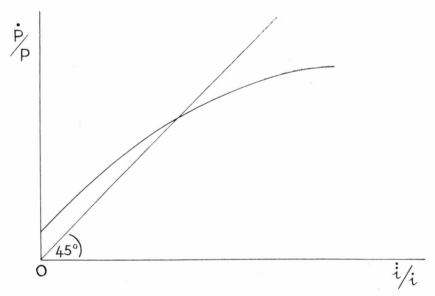

[1] It is probable that in addition to " embodied " technical progress there is some " disembodied " technical progress as well, resulting from increasing know-how in the use of existing machinery. On the other hand it is also probable that the physical efficiency of machinery declines with age (on account of higher repair and maintenance expenditures, etc.); our assumption of constant physical efficiency thus implies that these two factors just balance each other.

[2] It should be noted that the " technical progress function " in this model relates to the rate of growth of output per man-hour of the workers operating newly installed equipment (the equipment resulting from the investment of period t), *not* to the rate of growth of productivity in the economy in general (though in

Both output per operative and investment per operative are measured in terms of money values deflated by an index of the prices of " wage goods " (i.e., consumption goods which enter into the wage-earners' budget). This means that changes in the prices of equipment goods in terms of wage-goods (and also of such consumption goods which only enter into consumption out of profits) will in general cause shifts in the f-function. Provided, however, that there is a reasonably stable trend in the prices of these latter goods in terms of wage goods, we can still conceive of the function as stable in time for any particular value of I_t/Y_t in money terms, and the system may still possess a steady growth equilibrium with a constant (equilibrium) value of I_t/Y_t. A full demonstration of this would require, however, a fully fledged 2-sector model in which the technical progress functions of the consumption goods sector and the capital goods sector, the distribution of employment and of savings between the two sectors, etc., are all treated separately. Since this would go far beyond the scope of this paper, it is better to assume, for the present purposes, that the rate of technical progress, as measured by productivity growth, is the same in all sectors, and hence that relative prices remain constant; bearing in mind, however, that the model could probably be extended to cover a wider range of possibilities.

5. With regard to the manner in which entrepreneurs meet risk and uncertainty, we shall make two important assumptions. In the first place we shall assume that entrepreneurs will only invest in their own business in so far as this is consistent with maintaining the earning power of their fixed assets above a certain minimum, a minimum which, in their view, represents the earning power of fixed assets in the economy in general. This is because, if the earnings of a particular firm are low in relation to the capital employed, or if they increase at a lower rate than the book value of the fixed assets, fixed assets will take up an increasing proportion of the total resources of the firm (including its potential borrowing power) at any given rate of growth, with the result that the financial position of the firm will become steadily weaker, with enhanced risks of bankruptcy or take-over bids. Hence we may assume that the sum of the expected profits anticipated from operating the equipment during its anticipated period of operation (or lifetime), T, will earn after full amortisation, a rate of profit that is at least equal to the assumed rate of profit on new investment in the economy generally. Hence for any particular investor

$$i_t \leqslant \int_t^{t+T} e^{-(\rho+\delta)(\tau-t)} (p_t - w_\tau^*) d\tau \qquad (3)$$

where ρ stands for what the entrepreneur assumes the general rate of profit to be, w_τ^* for the expected rate of wages which is a rising function of future time[1] and δ is the rate of " radioactive " decay of machines (we take it that the investor assumes his machine is an average machine).[2]

full steady growth equilibrium, as we shall see, the two will correspond to each other); and to the rate of growth of gross investment per worker from year to year, not the rate of accumulation of capital (which may not be a meaningful or measurable quantity). It is plausible that, with technical progress, the same investment per operative should yield a higher output per operative in successive years; and that this rate of growth will be enhanced, within limits, when the value of investment per operative is increasing over time.

[1] In a golden age equilibrium, the inequality (3) should be replaced by an equality, and since all the variables will be determined independently by the other equations, (3) can then be taken as determining the rate of profit on investment. Cf. p. 180 below.

[2] Our equation (3) thus postulates conditions under which the amount of " finance " available to the firm is considerably greater than its fixed capital expenditure, so that the firm is free to vary its total investment expenditure per unit of time; and that it will adopt projects which pass the tests of adequacy as indicated by (3) even though it could earn a higher *rate* of profit on projects involving a smaller volume of investment and yielding a smaller *total* profit. (In other words we assume that the firm is guided by the motive of maximising the rate of profit on the shareholders' equity, which involves different decisions from the assumption of maximizing the rate of profit on its fixed investment.)

In the second place, under conditions of continuing technical progress, the expectations concerning the more distant future (whether in regard to money wages or in regard to the prices—or demands—of the particular products produced by a firm, both of which are projected in w_τ^*) are regarded as far more hazardous or uncertain than the expectations for the near future, where the incidence of unforeseeable major new inventions or discoveries is less significant. Hence investment projects which qualify for adoption must pass a further test—apart from the test of earning a satisfactory rate of profit—and that is that the cost of the fixed assets must be " recovered " within a certain period—i.e., that the gross profit earned in the first h years of its operation must be sufficient to repay the cost of investment. Hence

$$ i_t \leqslant \int_t^{t+h} (p_t - w_\tau^*) \, d\tau \tag{4} $$

We shall assume, for the purposes of this model, that (3) is satisfied whenever (4) is satisfied—hence in (4) the $=$ sign will apply, i.e., the undiscounted sum of profits over h periods must be equal to i_t. There is plenty of empirical evidence that the assumption underlying (4) is a generally recognised method of meeting the uncertainty due to obsolescence in modern business, though the value of h may vary with the rate of technical progress, and also as between different sectors. (In the U.S. manufacturing industry h is normally taken as 3 years; but in other sectors—e.g., public utilities—it is much higher.)[1]

7. It is assumed, as in the earlier Keynesian growth models, that the savings which finance business investment come out of profits, and that a constant proportion, s, of *gross* profits are saved.[2] Hence (dividing income into two categories, profits and wages, which comprise all forms of non-business income) the share of (gross) profits, π_t, in the gross national product will be given by the equation

$$ \pi_t = \frac{1}{s} \frac{I_t}{Y_t} \tag{5} $$

which, in virtue of equation (1), reduces to

$$ \pi_t = \frac{r}{s} \frac{i_t}{y_t} \tag{5a} $$

[1] The assumptions represented by these two equations should be contrasted with the assumptions made in " Capital Accumulation and Economic Growth," according to which

$$ \frac{P}{K} = r + \rho $$

$$ \rho = \xi(v) \quad (\xi' > 0) $$

where P/K the rate of profit, r the money rate of interest, ρ the risk premium, v the capital/output ratio. ρ was assumed to be a rising function of v, because v reflects the ratio of fixed to circulating capital, and investment in the former is considered far more risky or " illiquid " than investment in the latter. The present assumptions are not inconsistent with the former hypothesis concerning the higher returns demanded on fixed investments; but they also take into account that the " riskiness " of the investment in fixed capital will be all the greater the longer the period over which the cost of the investment is ' recovered ' out of the profits—a matter which depends not only on the capital/output ratio (or rather, the investment/output ratio) but also on the share of gross profits in output. " Gross profits " should for this purpose be calculated net of other charges, including a notional interest charge on the ' liquid ' business assets, (i.e., the investment in circulating capital associated with the investment in fixed capital).

[2] Savings out of wages are ignored—i.e., they are assumed to be balanced by non-business (personal) investment (i.e., residential construction). The assumption that business savings are a constant proportion of *gross* profits (after tax) is well supported by data relating to gross corporate savings.

where r is defined by

$$r_t = {}^{n_t}/N_t,$$

where N_t is the total labour force at time t and n_t, as earlier defined, is the number of workers available to operate new equipment per unit period.

We shall assume that once equipment is installed the number of workers operating it will only fall in time by the physical wastage of equipment, caused by accidents, fires, etc. —until the whole of the residual equipment is scrapped on account of obsolescence. Writing δ for the rate of (radioactive) depreciation per unit period, and $T(t)$ for the age of the equipment which is retired at t (i.e., the lifetime of equipment as governed by obsolescence), we have the following relationship for the distribution of the labour force:

$$N_t = \int_{t-T}^{t} n_\tau\, e^{-\delta(t-\tau)}\, d\tau \tag{6}$$

and for total output

$$Y_t = \int_{t-T}^{t} p_\tau\, n_\tau\, e^{-\delta(t-\tau)}\, d\tau \tag{7}$$

Since output Y_t is divided into two categories of income only, wages and profits, the residue left after profits is equal to the total wages bill. Writing w_t for the rate of wages at t, we further have

$$Y_t\, (1 - \pi_t) = N_t\, w_t \tag{8}$$

Finally, since equipment will only be employed so long as its operation more than covers prime costs, the profit on the oldest yet surviving machinery must be zero. Hence

$$p_{t-T} = w_t \tag{9}$$

We shall assume that population grows at the constant rate λ, hence

$$\dot{N}_t = \lambda\, N_t \tag{10}$$

We shall also assume that businessmen anticipate that wages in terms of output units will rise in the foreseeable future at the same rate as they have been rising during the past l periods.

Hence the expected wage rate at a future time T will be

$$w_T^* = w_t \left(\frac{w_t}{w_{t-l}}\right)^{\frac{T-t}{l}} \tag{11}$$

Finally, the model is subject to two constraints (or "boundary conditions") which are known from earlier models:

$$w_t \geqslant w_{min}$$

$$\pi \geqslant m$$

In other words, the wage rate resulting from the model must be above a certain minimum, (determined by conventional subsistence needs) and at the same time the share of profits resulting from the model must be higher than a certain minimum (the so-called " degree of monopoly " or " degree of imperfect competition ").

8. The above system gives 10 independent equations (regarding (3) only as a boundary condition) which are sufficient to determine the 10 unknowns; I_t, i_t, n_t, p_t, w_t, w^*_t, π_t, T, y_t, N_t, given the parameters, s, h, δ and λ, and the function f.

We shall investigate whether this system yields a solution in terms of a steady growth (or golden age) equilibrium where the rate of growth of output per head is equal to the rate of growth of productivity on new equipment and both are equal to the rate of growth of (fixed) investment per worker, and to the rate of growth of wages ; i.e., where

$$\dot{p}/p = \dot{y}/y = \dot{i}/i = \dot{w}/w ;$$

and where the share of investment in output I/Y, the share of profits in income π, and the period of obsolescence of equipment, T, remain constant.   Finally we shall show that there is a unique rate of profit on investment in a steady growth equilibrium.

The assumptions about the technical progress function imply that there is *some* value $\dot{p}/p$ (let us call it γ) at which

$$\dot{p}/p = \dot{i}/i = \gamma$$

Equilibrium is only possible when this holds.

If we integrate equation (4) using (11), we see that

$$i_t = hp_t - w_t \frac{e^{vh} - 1}{v},$$

where v is the expected rate of growth of w.   Hence p could only grow faster than i in the long run if w was growing faster than p: that would imply a continuous reduction in T, which would lead to unemployment and stagnation before T fell to h (at which point the rate of profit would be negative).   On the other hand, p cannot grow more slowly than i in the long run, since w cannot fall below w_{min} (and there would in fact be a inflation crisis before that point was reached).

It is clear too that, so long as $\dot{w}/w$ does not diverge too far from $\dot{p}/p$, $\dot{i}/i$ would increase if it were less than $\dot{p}/p$, and decrease if it were greater than $\dot{p}/p$.   For if $\dot{p}/p$ were less than γ, it would breed, by equation (4), a rate of growth of investment, $\dot{i}/i$ that would require higher $\dot{p}/p$, and so on, until the equilibrium position is reached.   A similar mechanism would be at work if $\dot{p}/p$ were greater than γ.   Thus the equilibrium would in general be stable; but instability cannot be excluded, and a movement away from equilibrium would be possible in either of the two ways described above.   For example a downward drift of the technical progress function might allow the rate of growth of p to fall off, and remain below the rate of growth of w (which reflects the rate of growth of y over the recent past) sufficiently long until with falling investment, unemployment and stagnation set in.[1] Conversely an upward shift in the technical progress function might lead to an inflationary situation at which investment, by one means or another, would be compressed below that indicated by (4) and (13).

---

[1] For example, a slowing down of technical progress in the late 1920's may have been responsible for that " sudden collapse of the marginal efficiency of capital " which led to the crisis and stagnation of the 1930's.

Hence, excluding the case where $\dot{p}/p$ is significantly different from $\dot{w}/w$, when

$$\frac{\dot{p}}{p} \begin{array}{c} > \\ < \end{array} \frac{i}{i}$$

there will be a convergent movement until (12) is obtained.

9. It will be convenient to deduce two further relations from the above equations. The first one relates to n_t, the amount of labour available for new equipment: it is obtained by differentiating (6) with respect to t.

$$n_t = \dot{N}_t + \delta N_t + n_{t-T}\left(1 - \frac{dT}{dt}\right) e^{-\delta T} \tag{13}$$

This equation says that n_t will be composed of three elements: (i) the growth in working population, $\dot{N}_t$; (ii) the labour released by physical wastage of equipment all vintages, which is δN_t; (iii) and finally the labour released by the retirement of obsolete equipment.

Differentiating equation (7) in the same way we obtain

$$\dot{Y}_t = p_t n_t - p_{t-T} n_{t-T}\left(1 - \frac{dT}{dt}\right) e^{-\delta T} - \delta Y_t$$

Substituting w_t for p_{t-T} in accordance with (9) and using (13) this becomes

$$\dot{Y}_t = p_t n_t - w_t (n_t - \dot{N}_t - \delta N_t) - \delta Y_t$$

Dividing both sides by $Y_t = N_t y_t$ we obtain

$$\frac{\dot{Y}_t}{Y_t} = r \frac{p_t}{y_t} - \frac{w_t}{y_t} (r - \lambda - \delta) - \delta$$

Using

$$\frac{\dot{Y}_t}{Y_t} = \frac{\dot{y}_t}{y_t} + \lambda$$

and re-arranging we finally obtain

$$\frac{\dot{y}_t}{y_t} + \lambda + \delta = r\frac{p_t}{y_t} - (r - \lambda - \delta)\frac{w_t}{y_t}. \tag{14}$$

10. In order that entrepreneurial expectations should be fulfilled, it is necessary that wages should grow at constant rate in time, β.

$$\frac{\dot{w}_t}{w_t} = \beta \text{ (constant)} \tag{15}$$

We shall now proceed to demonstrate that when β is constant, T will also be constant, provided that $\gamma < \frac{s}{h} - \lambda - \delta$.

It follows from (9) that

$$\frac{\dot{w}_t}{w_t} = \frac{\dot{p}_{t-T}}{p_{t-T}}\left(1 - \frac{dT}{dt}\right)$$

Hence

$$1 - \frac{dT}{dt} = \frac{\beta}{\gamma}, \text{ a constant.}$$

Integrating with respect to t we obtain

$$T = T_o + \left(1 - \frac{\beta}{\gamma}\right)t \tag{16}$$

where T_0 is the lifetime of equipment at some initial date, $t = 0$.

Substituting (16) into (13) and remembering that $r_t = n_t/N_t$, we obtain

$$r_t = \lambda + \delta + r_{t-T}\, e^{-(\lambda+\delta)T}\, \frac{\beta}{\gamma} \tag{17}$$

In order to show that, in a state of steady growth equilibrium $T = T_0$ and $\beta = \gamma$, we shall first consider the cases where $\beta \neq \gamma$.

(i) When $\gamma < \beta$, clearly steady growth cannot continue since entrepreneurs' profits would become negative sooner or later.

(ii) when $\gamma > \beta$, it follows from equation (16) that T becomes indefinitely large with time (and perhaps this is enough to dispose of this case, since for most goods there may be a maximum physical lifetime, quite apart from obsolescence). In any case this implies, in accordance with (17), that r ultimately tends to $\lambda + \delta$; and since w/y must tend to zero, so that the share of profits, π, tends towards unity,

$$i/y \text{ tends to } \frac{s}{\lambda + \delta}. \tag{18}$$

Also from (4) :

$$i/p \text{ tends to } h.$$

Hence from (14) :

$$\dot{y}/y \text{ tends to } \frac{s}{h} - \lambda - \delta.$$

(18) shows that y ultimately grows at the same rate as i, which grows at the rate γ.

Therefore

$$\gamma = \frac{s}{h} - \lambda - \delta \tag{19}$$

which implies, in Harrod's terms, that the " natural rate " (here, $\gamma + \lambda + \delta$) is equal to what the " warranted rate " would be if wages were zero and profits absorbed the whole output (since then s would equal the proportion of Y saved, and $h = i/p$).

11. It is easy to see that in fact the rate of growth of output per head cannot in the long run be greater than this quantity $\frac{s}{h} - \lambda - \delta$. By (5), i/y can rise no higher, ultimately, than s/r; hence by (4), even if (as might happen ultimately) the wage rate were negligible in relation to output per head, p/y could not be greater than $s/(rh)$. Turning to equation (14), we see that it implies the inequality

$$\dot{y}_t/y_t + \lambda + \delta \leqq r.\frac{s}{rh} = \frac{s}{h}.$$

Hence there can be no steady growth equilibrium unless

$$\gamma \leqq \frac{s}{h} - \lambda - \delta.$$

Normally we would not expect to have to worry about this constraint, for the quantity s/h will be large—especially when we remember that h will be small when there is a high rate of growth. If it is asked what would happen if the equilibrium growth rate given by the technical progress function really did fail to satisfy this inequality, the answer must be that the wage rate would be driven down to its minimum level and entrepreneurs would then find themselves unable to invest as much as the prospects would warrant: the equality (4) would become an inequality again. The rest of the discussion will be carried on under the assumption that the equilibrium rate of growth γ does satisfy this inequality.

We can see that, quite apart from the unrealistic value of γ implied by equation (19), equilibrium with $\gamma > \beta$ is a freak case; the slightest shift in γ would either render equilibrium impossible, or make it possible only with $\beta = \gamma$.

12. (iii) It is clear from the above that steady growth equilibrium will involve

$$\beta = \gamma$$

in which case it also involves a constant T.
(17) has now become

$$r_t = \lambda + \delta + r_{t-T}\, e^{-(\lambda+\delta)\,T},$$

where T is constant, so that r_t will tend to the equilibrium value

$$r = \frac{\lambda + \delta}{1 - e^{-(\lambda+\delta)T}} \tag{20}$$

From equation (5)

$$y_t = w_t + \frac{r}{s}\, i_t,$$

so that, since r is constant in equilibrium, y_t also grows at the equilibrium growth rate γ. It is convenient to write this last equation as

$$\frac{r}{s}\,\frac{i}{y} + \frac{w}{y} = 1 \tag{21}$$

In equilibrium, expectations are fulfilled, so that $w_t{}^* = w_t$. Since $w_t = w_0\, e^{\beta t} = w_0\, e^{\gamma t}$ (where w_0 is the wage rate at some initial time), the integral in equation (4) can be evaluated, so that

$$i_t = h p_t - \frac{e^{\gamma h} - 1}{\gamma}\, w_t,$$

which we can write

$$\frac{1}{h}\,\frac{i}{y} + \frac{e^{\gamma h} - 1}{\gamma h}\,\frac{w}{y} - \frac{p}{y} = 0 \tag{22}$$

(14) can now be rewritten

$$(r - \lambda - \delta)\,\frac{w}{y} - r\,\frac{p}{y} = -(\gamma + \lambda + \delta) \tag{23}$$

Equations (21), (22), (23) can be treated as three simultaneous equations for $\dfrac{i}{y}$, $\dfrac{w}{y}$, and $\dfrac{p}{y}$

(which are all constant in a state of steady growth).

Now equation (9) provides an equation for T:

$$e^{\gamma T} = \frac{p}{w} = \frac{p/y}{w/y}. \tag{24}$$

Using the values of $r, \dfrac{p}{y}, \dfrac{w}{y}$ found by solving (21), (22) and (23), we obtain:

$$e^{\gamma T} = \frac{1 - \dfrac{h(\gamma + \lambda + \delta)}{s} \cdot \dfrac{e^{\gamma h} - 1}{\gamma h} + \dfrac{\gamma}{r}}{1 - \dfrac{h(\gamma + \lambda + \delta)}{s}} \tag{25}$$

And from (20), since $e^{\gamma T} = [e^{-(\lambda + \delta)T}]^{-\gamma/(\lambda + \delta)}$

$$e^{\gamma T} = \left[1 - \frac{\lambda + \delta}{r}\right]^{-\frac{\gamma}{\lambda + \delta}} \tag{26}$$

(25) and (26) determine T and r simultaneously in terms of the parameters λ, δ, h, s, and the steady growth rate γ (which was determined by the technical progress function).   Equation (20) is not valid when $\lambda + \delta = 0$.   In that case we go back to equation (6); integration gives

$$r T = 1, \tag{27}$$

which replaces (26) in this particular case.

13.   Although (25) and (26) are rather cumbersome equations, numerical solution for particular values of the parameters presents no particular difficulty.   Once T and r are calculated, simultaneous solution of (23) and (24) yields the values of $\dfrac{p}{y}$ and $\dfrac{w}{y}$ (the share of wages).   Then $\dfrac{i}{y}$ is found from (22).   A demonstration of the existence of a unique meaningful solution to the equations is given in the Appendix.

If capital stock were valued at historic cost, without any allowance for reduction in value through obsolescence, we should have

$$K = \int_{t-T}^{t} i_\tau \, n_\tau \, e^{-\delta(t-\tau)} \, d\tau,$$

and

$$Y = \int_{t-T}^{t} p_\tau \, n_\tau \, e^{-\delta(t-\tau)} \, d\tau, \tag{28}$$

so that the aggregate capital-output ratio,

$$\frac{K}{Y} = \frac{i}{p},$$

since this latter is constant.

However, when obsolescence is *foreseen* the knowledge of the share of profits, π, and of the historical cost of invested capital as shown by (28), does not enable us to calculate either net profits or the rate of profit on capital.   The value of capital at any one time will be lower than K_t by the accrued provision made for obsolescence, and the appropriate obsolescence provision — which must take into account the annual reduction in the profits earned on equipment of a given vintage, as well as the retirement of equipment when it becomes T years old—cannot be calculated without knowing the capital on which the profit is earned, which in turn cannot be known without knowing the rate of profit.

14.   In a state of fully-fledged golden age equilibrium, where (1) expectations are (in general) fulfilled and the expected profit on new investments is therefore the same as the realised profit, and (2) the rate of profit earned on all investment will be the same, the inequality (3) above can be replaced by an equality and regarded as an additional equation determining ρ (since i_t, p_t, w_t and T are all determined by the other equations of the system.)

$$i_t = \int_0^T e^{-(\rho+\delta)\tau} (p_t - W_{t+\tau}) \cdot d\tau \tag{3a}$$

ρ is constant, so the familiar relation

$$\gamma + \lambda = \rho\,\sigma, \tag{29}$$

where σ is the proportion of *net* profits saved, holds; for it is easy to check that the value of capital—in terms of output to come—grows at the equilibrium growth rate $\gamma + \lambda$, and that ρ defined by (3a) is equal to the ratio of net profit to the stock of capital.   In general, of course, σ depends on ρ, and is best calculated from the relation (29).   But when $s = 1$, *i.e.*, when all (gross) profits are invested, σ must also be equal to unity, so that the rate of profit is equal to the rate of growth of output: $\rho = \gamma + \lambda$.   On the face of it, it is not clear that this value of ρ satisfies (29): yet it must do.   To show that it does, we use the fact that total output,

$$Y_t = \int_0^T p_{t-\tau}\, n_{t-\tau}\, e^{-\delta\tau}\, d\tau,$$

$$= p_t\, n_t \int_0^T e^{-(\gamma+\lambda+\delta)\tau}\, d\tau.$$

Thus, when we put $\rho = \gamma + \lambda$ in the right hand side of (3a), we get:

$$\frac{y_t}{r_t} - w_t \int_0^T e^{-(\lambda+\delta)\tau} d\tau.$$

This last integral $= \dfrac{1 - e^{-(\lambda+\delta)T}}{\lambda + \delta} = \dfrac{1}{r}$, by equation (20).   Hence the right hand side of equation (3a) is equal to $(y_t - w_t)/r$, which is equal to i_t when $s = 1$ (by equation (21).)

If $s \neq 1$, we must find ρ from equation (3a). If we perform the integration (which we can do, since p and w are growing exponentially), we get the following relation, which can be solved numerically for $\rho + \delta$:

$$\frac{i}{y} = \frac{1 - e^{-(\rho+\delta)T}}{\rho + \delta} \frac{p}{y} - \frac{1 - e^{-(\rho+\delta-\gamma)T}}{\rho + \delta - \gamma} \frac{w}{y}. \tag{30}$$

Outside a golden age equilibrium a rate of profit on investment does not exist except in the sense of an *assumed* rate of profit, based on a mixture of convention and belief, which enables entrepreneurs to decide whether any particular project passes the test of adequate profitability.

15. *Some Numerical Results*

The following are the solution of the equations for various arbitrarily selected values of the parameters.[1]

For $s = 0.66$:

h years	$\lambda + \delta\%$	$\gamma\%$	T years	r	$\pi\%$	$I/Y\%$	i/p	$\rho+\delta\%$
3	2	2	8·03	·135	8·0	5·3	·367	21·7
		2·5	8·15	·133	10·1	6·7	·459	22·1
		3	8·27	·131	12·2	8·1	·551	22·4
	4	2	8·68	·136	8·9	5·9	·401	23·0
		2·5	8·82	·135	11·2	7·5	·501	23·4
		3	8·97	·133	13·5	9·0	·601	23·7
4	2	2	11·20	·100	11·2	7·5	·672	17·0
		2·5	11·44	·098	14·1	9·6	·839	17·3
		3	11·68	·096	17·1	11·4	1·006	17·6
	4	2	12·54	·101	12·9	8·6	·759	18·2
		2·5	12·84	·100	16·3	10·9	·948	18·6
		3	13·15	·098	19·8	13·2	1·136	18·9
5	2	2	14·69	·078	14·6	9·7	1·080	14·1
		2·5	15·10	·077	18·5	12·3	1·348	14·4
		3	15·53	·075	22·4	14·9	1·615	14·7
	4	2	17·13	·081	17·8	11·9	1·267	15·4
		2·5	17·71	·079	22·5	15·0	1·579	15·7
		3	18·34	·077	27·4	16·4	1·888	16·0

[1] We are indebted to Mr. D. G. Champernowne for programming these calculations, and to the Director of the Mathematical Laboratory of Cambridge University for making the computer available.

Some representative values for different s:

s	h	$\lambda+\delta\%$	$\gamma\%$	T	r	$\pi\%$	$I/Y\%$	i/p	$\rho+\delta\%$
·33	3	2	2	20·66	·059	20·4	6·8	·955	30·6
			2·5	21·26	·058	25·6	8·5	1·169	30·8
·50	4	4	2	19·98	·073	20·7	10·3	1·207	21·7
			2·5	20·66	·071	26·2	13·1	1·490	22·0
			3	21·42	·070	31·8	15·9	1·765	22·3
	5	2	2	22·61	·055	22·2	11·1	1·655	17·0
			2·5	23·47	·053	28·1	14·0	2·038	17·3
			3	24·41	·052	34·1	17·0	2·407	17·6
1·00	4	4	2·5	6·08	·185	7·7	7·7	·387	6·5
			3	6·22	·182	9·4	9·4	·474	7·0
	5	2	2·5	7·28	·148	9·0	9·0	·561	4·5
			3	7·49	·144	11·1	11·1	·691	5·0
		4	2·5	8·20	·143	10·4	10·4	·662	6·5
			3	8·44	·140	12·7	12·7	·812	7·0

For the U.S. in the 1950's, reasonable values of the parameters are $\gamma = 2$ to $2\frac{1}{2}\%$, $\lambda + \delta = 2 - 4\%$, $s = \cdot66$, $h = 4$ to 5 years. The average lifetime of equipment in manufacturing industry has been estimated at 17 years. π as indicated by the ratio of gross corporate profit after tax to the gross income originating in corporations after corporation tax has been 21%, and the ratio of business fixed capital to business gross product around 1·5. These, as the table shows, are close to the results of the model when $s = \cdot66$, $h = 5$, $\lambda + \delta = 4\%$, and when γ is $2 - 2\cdot5\%$.[1]

The rate of profit on investment, on the other hand, appears rather high. However it must be remembered that our equation (3) derives the rate of (net) profit from the stream of gross profit *after* tax, and not (as is usually done) from the gross profit before tax. This involves a smaller provision for obsolescence, and consequently a higher net profit, than in the usual method of calculation. It also implies that in " grossing up " for tax, the relevant rate is the effective tax charge on profits before depreciation, and not the rate of tax on profits net of depreciation. Hence, if the tax on corporation profits is one third of gross profits before tax, a rate of net profit (net of tax) of 12·5 per cent (assuming $\lambda = 1\%$, $\delta = 3\%$) corresponds to a rate of net profit *before* tax of 18·5 per cent.[2]

It can be seen from the figures, too, that π and i/p are quite sensitive to changes in the technical progress function (i.e. in γ), and highly sensitive to changes in s and h, but stable

[1] It should be borne in mind, of course, that no allowance was made in the model for net investment in working capital (inventory accumulation) which would affect the values of T, π, I/Y and i/p, but the effect of which can be subsumed in h. Equally, the model assumes that government savings and investment are equal—i.e., that there is no financial surplus or deficit arising out of government operations, and that personal savings and personal investments (mainly in housing) are equal.

[2] U.S. estimates put the average rate of profit on (business) investment 16 per cent before tax and 8 per cent after tax.

for changes in λ and δ. T is only sensitive to changes in s and h, but *not* to γ. These results may sound surprising at first. One would expect T to be inversely related to γ, and one would also expect r ($= n_t/N_t$) to be positively correlated with $(\lambda + \delta)$. However, a rise in γ leads to a rise in i/p, and hence of π, which more than compensates for the rise in γ in determining the associated change in T; a rise in $(\lambda + \delta)$ reduces (as between one steady growth equilibrium and another) the amount of labour released through obsolescence in relation to the current labour force (since the labour force T years ago was that much smaller, when λ is larger; and of the equipment built T years ago so much less survives to be scrapped when δ is larger) so that it compensates for the increase in $(\lambda + \delta)$, leaving the value of r pretty much the same.

16. *General Conclusions*

The model shows technical progress—in the specific form of the rate of improvement of the design, etc., of newly produced capital equipment—as the main engine of economic growth, determining not only the rate of growth of productivity but—together with other parameters—also the rate of obsolescence, the average lifetime of equipment, the share of investment in income, the share of profits, and the relationship between investment and potential output (*i.e.*, the " capital/output ratio " on new capital).

The model is Keynesian in its mode of operation (entrepreneurial expenditure decisions are primary; incomes, etc., are secondary) and severely *non*-neo-classical in that technological factors (marginal productivities or marginal substitution ratios) play no role in the determination of wages and profits. A " production function " in the sense of a single-valued relationship between *some* measure of capital, K_t, the labour force N_t and of output Y_t (all at time t) clearly does not exist. Everything depends on past history, on how the collection of equipment goods which comprises K_t has been built up. Thus Y_t will be greater for a given K_t (as measured by historical cost) if a greater part of the existing capital stock is of more recent creation; this would be the case, for example, if the rate of growth of population has been accelerating.

Whilst " machines " earn quasi-rents which are all the smaller the older they are (so that, for the oldest surviving machine, the quasi-rents are zero) it would be wrong to say that the position of the marginal " machine " determines the share of quasi-rents (or gross profits) in total income. For the total profit is determined quite independently of the structure of these " quasi-rents " by equation (5), i.e., by the factors determining the share of investment in output and the proportion of profits saved and therefore the position of the " marginal " machine is itself fully determined by the other equations of the system. It is the macro-economic condition specified in (5), and not the age-and-productivity structure of machinery, which will determine what the (aggregate) share of quasi-rents will be.

This technical progress function is quite consistent with a technological " investment function ", i.e., a functional relationship (shifting in time) between investment per worker and output per worker.[1] However, owing to anticipated obsolescence and to uncertainty, it would not be correct to say that the " marginal product " of investment, dp_t/di_t, plays

---

[1] On the relationship of a technical progress function and a production function c.f. John Black, " The Technical Progress Function and The Production Function," *Economica*, May 1962. Whilst it is possible to make assumptions under which a technical progress function is merely one way of representing an (ex-ante) production function of constant elasticity which shifts at some pre-determined rate in time, the postulate of a technical progress function is also consistent with situations in which the rate of technical progress does not proceed at some pre-determined rate (where the shift of the " curve " is bound up with the movement *along* the " curve ") and where therefore one cannot associate a unique production function with a given " state " of knowledge.

a role in determining the amount per man. Since the profitability of operating the equipment is expected to diminish in time, the marginal addition to the stream of profits (which we may call the " marginal value productivity ") will be something quite different from the marginal product in the technological sense, and unlike the latter, it will not be a derivative of a technological function alone but will depend on the whole system of relationships. Further, owing to the prevailing attitude to uncertainty, it would not even be correct to say that " profit-maximising " will involve adding to investment per man until the marginal increment in anticipated profits, discounted at the ruling rate of interest or at some " assumed " rate of profit becomes equal to the marginal addition to investment. Whenever the desire to recover the cost of investment within a certain number of years—owing to the greater uncertainty of the more distant future—becomes the operative restriction (as is assumed in equation (4)), investment per man will be cut short before this marginal condition is satisfied.

The inequality (3) together with equation (4) enables us to specify an investment function in terms of the parameters of the system which determine both n_t and i_t without regard to the relationship between the expected rate of profit on investment and the rate of interest. In previous " Keynesian " models the existence of an independent investment function was closely tied to the postulate of some relationship between the " marginal efficiency " of investment and—an independently determined—rate of interest. This was a source of difficulty, since it either caused such models to be " over-determined "[1] or else it required the postulate that the capital/output ratio (or the amount of investment per worker) itself varied with the excess of the rate of profit over the money rate of interest[2]. The weakness of this latter approach has been that it assigned too much importance to the rate of interest. So long as one could assume that the rate of interest was a constant, determined by some psychological minimum (the " pure " liquidity preference of Keynesian theory), this did not matter very much. But it was unsatisfactory to rely on the *excess* of the rate of profit over the rate of interest as an important element—determining the chosen capital/output ratio and through that, the other variables—considering that this excess is under the control of the monetary authorities; if the authorities were to follow a policy of keeping the money rate of interest in some constant relationship to the rate of profit—which they may be easily tempted to do—this would have endowed them with an importance in the general scheme of things which is quite contrary to common experience.

The present model, by contrast allows the money rate of interest to move up and down, without the slightest effect on investment decisions, provided such movements do not violate certain constraints.[3] This is in much better accord with the oft-repeated assertions of business men (both in the U.K. and the U.S.) that the rate of interest has *no* influence on their investment decisions at least as far as investment in fixed capital is concerned.

Finally there is the question how far the postulate of a " technical progress function " as specified in (2) implies some restraint on the *nature* of technological change. Every change in the rate of investment per worker implies a change in the extent to which new ideas (" innovations ") are actually exploited. Since the " capital saving " innovations— which increase the output/capital ratio as well as the output/labour ratio—are much more profitable to the entrepreneur than the " labour-saving " ones that yield the same rate of

---

[1] Cf. R. C. O. Matthews, " The Rate of Interest in Growth Models," *Oxford Economic Papers*, October 1960, pp. 249-268.

[2] Cf. Kaldor, " Capital Accumulation and Economic Growth," *op. cit.*, pp. 217.

[3] For it must still remain true, of course, that the expected rate of profit on (fixed) investment must exceed the rate of interest by more than some minimum compensation for the " illiquidity " or other risks.

increase in labour productivity, clearly the former are exploited first and the balance of technological change will appear more "capital-using" (all the less "capital-saving") the greater the rate of increase in investment per man. There is therefore always *some* rate of increase in investment per worker which allows output per man to grow at the same rate as investment per man and in that sense takes on the appearance of "neutral" technical progress; to assume that this rate of increase in investment per man remains unchanged over time implies also assuming that the relative importance of "capital saving" and "capital using" innovations in the total flow of innovations remains unchanged. To assume this is really implied in the assumption that the rate of technical progress is *constant*; since a growing incidence of "capital saving" innovations is the same thing as an upward drift in the technical progress function, and *vice versa*. Therefore the only sense in which the technical progress function postulates some "neutral" technical progress is the sense in which "unneutral" technical progress necessarily involves either a continuous acceleration or deceleration in the rate of increase in productivity for any given value of i/i.

The main "practical" conclusion for economic policy that emerges from this model is that any scheme leading to the accelerated retirement of old equipment (such as a tax on the use of obsolete plant and equipment) is bound to accelerate for a temporary period the rate of increase in output per head $\dot{y}/y$, since it will increase n_t (the number of workers "available" for new machines) and hence I_t; and will thus involve a reduction in p_t/y_t. A more permanent cure, however, requires stimulating the technical dynamism of the economy (*raising* the technical progress function) which is not only (or perhaps mainly) a matter of more scientific education and more expenditure on research, but of higher quality business management which is more alert in searching for technical improvements and less resistant to their introduction.

Cambridge.   NICHOLAS KALDOR.

JAMES A. MIRRLEES.

APPENDIX

We must enquire whether the solution of the equations for a state of steady growth is unique. Equation (25) is a linear equation for $e^{\gamma T}$ in terms of $\frac{1}{r}$; it can be represented on a diagram, with $\frac{1}{r}$ measured along one axis and $e^{\gamma T}$ along the other, by a straight line.

Equation (26), on the other hand, represents a curve of increasing slope (as shown in the diagram). The curve representing equation (26), BB', passes through the point $e^{\gamma T} = 1$, $\frac{1}{r} = 0$; AA', which represents equation (25), has $e^{\gamma T} < 1$ when $\frac{1}{r} = 0$.

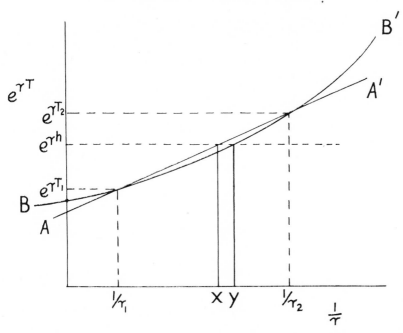

We shall prove that (1) AA', in fact cuts BB', and cuts it in two points, to which correspond the values r_1 and r_2 of r, and T_1 and T_2 of T; (2) $T_1 < h$, so that this case is in fact impossible (for entrepreneurs will make losses). It follows that there is a single possible steady growth state.

(1) To prove that AA' does not fail to cut BB', we show that there are points of BB' lying *below* AA'. Let x be the value of $\dfrac{1}{r}$ corresponding to $T = h$ on the curve AA' (*i.e.*, found by solving equation (25)); and let y be the value of $\dfrac{1}{r}$ corresponding to $T = h$ on the curve BB' (i.e., found by solving equation (26)).

Then

$$\gamma x = e^{\gamma h} \left[1 - \frac{h(\gamma + \lambda + \delta)}{s} \right] + \frac{h(\gamma + \lambda + \delta)}{s} \frac{e^{\gamma h} - 1}{\gamma h} - 1$$

$$= e^{\gamma h} - 1 - \frac{(\gamma + \lambda + \delta)}{\gamma s} [\gamma h . e^{\gamma h} - e^{\gamma h} + 1]$$

$$= \gamma h + \tfrac{1}{2} (\gamma h)^2 + \tfrac{1}{6} (\gamma h)^3 + \ldots$$

$$- \frac{\gamma + \lambda + \delta}{\gamma s} [\tfrac{1}{2} (\gamma h)^2 + \tfrac{1}{3} (\gamma h)^3 + \tfrac{1}{8} (\gamma h)^4 + \ldots]$$

$$= \gamma h + \tfrac{1}{2} (\gamma h)^2 \left[1 - \frac{\gamma + \lambda + \delta}{\gamma s} \right] + \tfrac{1}{6} (\gamma h)^3 \left[1 - 2 \frac{\gamma + \lambda + \delta}{\gamma s} \right]$$

$$+ \tfrac{1}{24} (\gamma h)^4 \left[1 - 3 \frac{\gamma + \lambda + \delta}{\gamma s} \right] + \dots$$

Clearly $\gamma + \lambda + \delta > \gamma s$, so that all the terms in square brackets are negative. Hence:

$$\gamma x < \gamma h - \tfrac{1}{2}(\gamma h)^2 \left[\frac{\gamma + \lambda + \delta}{\gamma s} - 1 \right],$$

so that $\gamma x < \gamma h - \tfrac{1}{2} \gamma h^2 . (\lambda + \delta),$ (28)

since $s \leq 1$

Also, $\gamma y \quad = \dfrac{\gamma}{\lambda + \delta} (\lambda + \delta) y = \dfrac{\gamma}{\lambda + \delta} [1 - e^{-(\lambda + \delta)h}]$

$$> \frac{\gamma}{\lambda + \delta} [(\lambda + \delta)h - \tfrac{1}{2} (\lambda + \delta)^2 h^2]$$

$$= \gamma h - \tfrac{1}{2} \gamma h^2 (\lambda + \delta),$$

which, as we have just shown, $> \gamma x$.

Hence $y > x$;

which is to say, that when $T = h$, the curve BB' lies to the right of AA'. Hence AA' meets BB'; for AA' cuts the $e^{\gamma T}$-axis below BB', and BB' eventually rises above AA'.

(2) It also follows from the fact that BB' lies to the right of AA' when $T = h$ that one of the points at which AA' and BB' cut has $t < h$; i.e., $T_1 < h$. Thus only T_2 (which is $> h$) is a possible value for T.

What we have shown is that there exists a single possible solution to our equations for the state of steady growth at rate γ. [The case $\lambda + \delta = 0$ follows in the same way; from (28), $\gamma x < \gamma h$; and $h = y$ in this case.]

IV

Two-Sector Models

INTRODUCTION

Part IV, together with Part V, represent perhaps the two fastest growing areas of research in growth theory. The two-sector growth model — comprising a consumption goods sector and a capital goods sector — differs from the one-sector model in that it is assumed that consumption and investment goods are produced by different sectors (different production functions).

For the short-run analysis of the model, this means that the production possibilities schedule, instead of being a straight line, is now curvilinear. If different proportions of income out of wages and profits

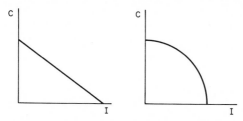

are saved, this in turn means that there may be more than one point along the production possibilities schedule at which the economy can operate at any point of time. In particular, if consumption goods are labor intensive, and workers consume a higher proportion of their income than capitalists, the workers may be able to perform a "bootstrap" operation — by demanding more consumption they increase their own incomes; there may be two or more equilibria, one where consumption is high and wage income is high, and one where investment is high and capital income is high. Solow shows in the article included here that whether there is more than one equilibrium may depend also on the elasticity of substitution of the production functions.

For the long-run analysis of the model, new problems are also introduced. The possibility of several balanced growth paths becomes much more important. Again, the interaction between distribution (with different aggregate savings rates, depending on the distribution of income) and production is crucial. In the first Uzawa article (only the second is reprinted here) where some fraction of profits are saved but all of wages are consumed, uniqueness of the balanced growth path is easily assured. On the other hand, if a constant fraction of income is saved, there may not be a unique balanced growth path, as the article by Uzawa demonstrates.

Finally, there is the problem of stability. Does the economy converge to balanced growth? Again, the answer depends on the combination of savings and production assumptions made.

It may be worthwhile to summarize the most important results on the conditions for existence of momentary equilibrium, stability, and uniqueness of momentary equilibrium.

I. All of wages consumed, constant fraction of profits saved
   A. Sufficient conditions for uniqueness of momentary equilibrium
      1. capital intensity in consumption goods sector ≥ capital intensity in capital goods sector
      2. sum of elasticities of substitution greater than 1
   B. Balanced growth always uniquely determined
   C. System stable if (sufficient conditions)
      1. capital intensity in consumption goods sector ≥ capital intensity in capital goods sector; or
      2. sum of elasticities of substitution greater than 1
II. Some of wages saved, but a smaller proportion than out of profits
   A. Same sufficiency conditions for uniqueness of momentary equilibrium as I.A
   B. Sufficient conditions for uniqueness and stability of balanced growth
      1. capital intensity in consumption goods sector ≥ capital intensity in capital goods sector
      2. elasticity of substitution in each section ≥1
III. Same proportion of profits as wages saved (constant fraction of income)
   A. Momentary equilibrium always uniquely determined

    B. Uniqueness and stability of balanced growth (sufficient conditions)
- 1. elasticity of substitution in each sector greater than or equal to 1
- 2. capital intensity in capital goods sector $\leq$ capital intensity in consumption goods sector

IV. Proportion of savings of capitalists greater than that of workers (Pasinetti savings assumption)

    A. Same sufficiency conditions for uniqueness of momentary equilibrium as I.A

    B. If it exists, two-class balanced growth path is always unique

    C. Necessary and sufficient conditions for existence of two-class balanced growth path:
- 1. ratio of workers' savings propensity to capitalists' less than share of profit
- 2. ratio of investment to income greater than savings rate of workers

    D. Sufficient condition for local stability of two-class balanced growth path: capital intensity in capital goods sector $\leq$ capital intensity in consumption goods sector

Note on Uzawa's Two-Sector Model of Economic Growth

Robert M. Solow

1. This Note has two objectives: one expository and one analytical. I am afraid that many readers will be put off by the apparent mathematical difficulty of Uzawa's paper. I say " apparent " advisedly, because the paper is in part very easy; it requires only a little arithmetic and the bare elements of the calculus of functions of one variable. Any economist who cannot read it ought at least to insist that his students do so. My first objective is to describe in plain English how the model works, because I think it is an interesting extension of earlier work in this branch of macro-economics.

2. My second objective is to try to elucidate the role of the crucial capital-intensity condition in Uzawa's model. He finds that his model economy is always stable (in the sense that full employment requires an approach to a state of balanced expansion) if the consumption-goods sector is more capital-intensive than the investment-goods sector. It seems paradoxical to me that such an important characteristic of the equilibrium path should depend on such a casual property of the technology. And since this stability property is the one respect in which Uzawa's results seem qualitatively different from those of my 1956 paper on a one-sector model, I am anxious to track down the source of the difference. Fortunately, I think plain English suffices for this too.

3. Uzawa's model works like this. There are two productive inputs: the services of a single grade of labor and of a single type of capital good depreciating at a rate μ. These two inputs are smoothly substitutable for each other in the production of consumer goods and in the separate industry which produces new machines; and labor and machines are freely transferable from one sector to the other. At any moment of time, an exogenously determined supply of labor is inelastically offered for employment. At any moment of time, the irrevocably existing stock of machines is inelastically offered for employment. What happens? The auctioneer calls off a value of the wage/rental ratio w/r. Each separate industry has a corresponding optimal machine/labor ratio: K_1/L_1 for the I-sector, K_2/L_2 for the C-sector. Since all the machines and all the labor must find employment,

and since $\dfrac{K}{L} = \dfrac{K_1 + K_2}{L_1 + L_2} = \dfrac{L_1}{L_1 + L_2}\left(\dfrac{K_1}{L_1}\right) + \dfrac{L_2}{L_1 + L_2}\left(\dfrac{K_2}{L_2}\right) = \dfrac{L_1}{L_1 + L_2}\left(\dfrac{K_1}{L_1}\right)$

$+ \left(1 - \dfrac{L_1}{L_1 + L_2}\right)\dfrac{K_2}{L_2}$, the given value of w/r determines the division of the labor force

between the two sectors and thus also the division of machines and the two outputs. Both industries make optimal adjustments and these yield unit costs; competition then sets the price ratio P_2/P_1 for the two commodities equal to the ratio of unit costs. Thus any w/r determines an equilibrium P_2/P_1.

Reprinted from *XXIX* (October 1961) 48–50 of *Review of Economic Studies* by permission of *Review of Economic Studies* published by Oliver & Boyd Ltd., Edinburgh and London. © 1962 The Economic Society.

Uzawa makes the new-old assumption that wages are all spent on consumer goods and rentals (= profits) all spent on machines. Now given the auctioneer's w/r, given history's K/L, and given the just-deduced outputs Y_1 and Y_2, equilibrium on the commodity market also requires that $\dfrac{wL}{rK} = \dfrac{P_2 Y_2}{P_1 Y_1}$. This provides another independent relation between w/r and P_2/P_1. The auctioneer finds the unique wage/rental ratio for which both equilibrium conditions are satisfied. This miniature Walrasian general equilibrium fixes, among other things, the output of machines and hence the stock available in the next period. Since the labor supply is exogenous, the process can repeat itself.

4. The stability proposition says that if this process repeats itself (with the labor supply growing geometrically at rate λ), it will eventually approach a situation in which $k = \dfrac{K}{L}$ is constant, so that the stock of machines is also growing at rate λ, and indeed the whole economy changes only in scale. Now the basic law of motion of the system is easily deduced. By assumption $\dfrac{\triangle L}{L} = \lambda$. Since all rentals are spent on gross investment, $\triangle K = rK/P_1 - \mu K$. From competition r/P_1, the product-rental of machines in the machine sector, is equal to the marginal product of machines in the machine sector (Uzawa's $f_1'(k_1)$), since under constant returns to scale it depends only on $k_1 = K_1/L_1$). Combining these assertions, we find $\triangle k/k = \triangle K/K - \triangle L/L = f_1'(k_1) - \lambda - \mu$, Uzawa's equation (41). The stability proposition asserts that both sides of this equation tend to zero and to prove it we must prove that when k gets very high, $\triangle k/k$ becomes negative and when k gets very low, $\triangle k/k$ becomes positive.

Now the marginal product $f_1'(k_1)$ is of course a *decreasing* function of k_1. So what we must show is that k and k_1 always move in the same direction (for then when k rises, k_1 also rises, and $f_1'(k_1)$ decreases and ultimately becomes equal to or less than $\lambda + \mu$). There would seem to be a strong presumption that k and k_1 do always move in the same direction: not only does k_1 increase when and only when w/r increases, but so does k_2. That is, the machine-labor ratio rises in each industry whenever the wage/rental ratio rises. There is one way and only one way in which the association between k and k_1 can be broken and that is if, while the separate machine/labor ratios should be rising, the less machine-intensive industry should gain enough at the expense of the more machine-intensive one to permit a fall in the overall machine/labor ratio.

5. Enter the assumption that the C-sector is more machine-intensive than the I-sector. Suppose that at any w/r ratio, $K_2/L_2 > K_1/L_1$; then also $rK_2/wL_2 > rK_1/wL_1$. Under constant returns to scale and competition, it is rigorously provable (and everyone should know) that when w/r increases, the price ratio P_2/P_1 will increase or decrease according as the relative share of wages in Sector 2 is greater or smaller than in Sector 1. Thus in Uzawa's model, P_2/P_1 falls when w/r rises and *vice-versa*. Now from the assumption that wages are consumed and profits saved, we have $\dfrac{wL}{rK} = \dfrac{P_2 Y_2}{P_1 Y_1}$ and so $\dfrac{K}{L} = \dfrac{w}{r} \dfrac{P_1}{P_2} \dfrac{Y_1}{Y_2}$. Suppose w/r rises; so does P_1/P_2. Then K/L must rise unless Y_1/Y_2 falls. But if Y_1/Y_2 falls, there is a shift of output in favor of consumption goods, the *more* machine-intensive commodity. But from my earlier argument, with the machine/labor ratio increasing in both sectors and the machine-intensive sector gaining at the expense of the other, we know that K/L *must* rise. There is no way out: k_1 and k must move together and the stability proposition holds.

6. Note that the crucial condition about the C-sector being more machine-intensive is a *sufficient* condition for stability in this model, not a necessary one. Here is an example in which that condition is violated but stability occurs. Suppose both sectors have Cobb-Douglas production functions with elasticities of α_1 and $1-\alpha_1$ for K_1 and L_1, and α_2 and $1-\alpha_2$ for K_2 and L_2. Then $rK = \alpha_1 P_1 Y_1 + \alpha_2 P_2 Y_2$. But also $rK = P_1 Y_1$. Then

$$P_1 Y_1 = \frac{\alpha_2}{1-\alpha_1} P_2 Y_2 \text{ and } \frac{P_1 Y_1}{P_2 Y_2} = \frac{\alpha_2}{1-\alpha_1}. \text{ But } \frac{P_1 Y_1}{P_2 Y_2} = \frac{rK}{wL}. \text{ So } \frac{rK}{wL} = \frac{\alpha_2}{1-\alpha_1}.$$

The right-hand side is a constant. Hence whenever r/w falls (so k_1 rises), K/L must rise. Once again k_1 and k move together and stability occurs, regardless of which sector is more machine-intensive (whether α_1 is bigger or smaller than α_2).

7. It is obvious from this mode of argument that the model works the way it does only because wages are spent entirely on consumption and profits on machines. This is an extraordinarily powerful assumption, more powerful than many of its users realize. Here is a cute example of just how powerful it is: Constant returns to scale, competition, machines produced by labor alone, consumables produced by machines alone, wages consumed, profits saved. Exercise: prove that the relative share of wages in national income is exactly 1/2!

8. In my 1956 paper (and in Swan's) this assumption is not made. We took saving as a fraction of aggregate income (at one point I permitted the savings ratio to depend on the rate of return on capital). If this assumption is carried into Uzawa's two-sector model, stability is no longer assured and the results become qualitatively more like the one-sector model.

Suppose that workers save a fraction S_w of their income and capitalists a fraction S_p of theirs. Then $P_1 Y_1 = S_w wL + S_p rK$ and $\triangle K = Y_1 - \mu K = S_w L \dfrac{w}{P_1} + S_p K \dfrac{r}{P_1} - \mu K$.

Using marginal productivity relations, $r/P_1 = f_1'(k_1)$ and $w/P_1 = f_1(k_1) - k_1 f_1'(k_1)$, we find $\dfrac{\triangle K}{K} = \dfrac{S_w}{k}(f_1 - k_1 f_1') + S_p f_1' - \mu$ and regrouping:

$$\frac{\triangle k}{k} = \frac{S_w}{k} f_1(k_1) + \left(S_p - S_w \frac{k_1}{k}\right) f_1'(k_1) - \lambda - \mu.$$

If $S_w = 0$, $S_p = 1$, this reduces to Uzawa's (41). If $S_w = S_p = S$, this reduces to
$$\triangle k = Sf_1(k_1) - (\lambda + \mu)k + S(k - k_1)f_1'(k_1).$$

This is more complicated than Uzawa's (41) and also than my analogous 1956 equation. If $k = k_1$ it reduces to something almost exactly like my 1956 equation. (Now that $P_1 Y_1 = S(wL + rK)$, it follows that $P_1 Y_1 / P_2 Y_2 = S/1-S$ and from this we can already deduce that k and k_1 go up and down together. Because an increase in w/r will increase k_1 and k_2 and also increase P_1/P_2 if Sector 1 is more labor-intensive, hence decrease Y_1/Y_2, hence increase relatively the output of the machine-intensive sector.)

It would not be easy to give a complete analysis of equilibrium paths for this model. But it seems highly likely from the first two terms on the right-hand side that it can give rise to behavior like that of the one-sector model; there may be equilibrium paths in which K/L increases without limit, for instance. It is also interesting to see the consequences if it should happen that the C-sector is more machine-intensive than the I-sector. Then $k - k_1$ would be positive. As k gets larger (along with k_1), $f_1'(k_1)$ would decrease. Whether the third term decreases or increases (thus contributing to stability or the reverse) would depend on whether $k - k_1$ increases faster or slower than $f_1'(k_1)$ and this in turn would depend on the shape of the two production functions.

Cambridge, Mass.   ROBERT M. SOLOW.

On a Two-Sector Model
of Economic Growth II [1]

Hirofumi Uzawa

1. *Introduction*

In a previous paper [9], I have analyzed the structure of a two-sector model of neo-classical growth, in which it has been assumed that labor consumes all, while capital only saves. The present paper is concerned with replacing this hypothesis with one which postulates that the propensity to save depends upon the rate of interest and the gross income per capita currently received.[2] The fundamental character of the model remains the same as in [9], except for the determination of investment and of rate of interest. At any moment of time, capital goods will be newly-produced at the rate at which the marginal efficiency of that capital is equated to the prevailing rate of interest. The prospective rentals to capital goods, which together with expected rates of discount determine the marginal efficiency of capital, are assumed to depend upon current rentals and quantities of newly-produced and existing capital goods. The rate of interest, on the other hand, is determined at the level which equates the value, at the current market price, of newly-produced capital goods to the amount of savings forthcoming at that level of the rate of interest.

It is assumed that prospective rentals to capital are positively correlated with current rentals, while they decrease as the quantity of new capital goods increases (with the elasticity less than unity). The average propensity to save is assumed to increase as rate of interest or current income per capita increases, and the marginal propensity to save is assumed less than or equal to unity.

Section 2 below investigates the structure of such a two-sector growth model when the average propensity to save is fixed at a certain level. It will be shown in particular that for arbitrarily given quantities of capital and labor, equilibrium quantities of consumption and capital goods currently produced, equilibrium prices of factors and goods, and rate of interest are all uniquely determined, and capital and labor both are fully employed. Any path of growth equilibrium will also be shown to approach a certain long-run steady state of balanced growth.

In later sections, the simple two-sector growth model will be extended to allow for a variably propensity to save, being dependent upon rate of interest and gross income per capita, and then to have the amount of new investment determined by the schedule of marginal efficiency of capital. The model preserves the main conclusions concerning the existence of short-run equilibrium and stability of the long-run growth equilibrium after such modification .

[1] This work was supported in part by the Office of Naval Research under Task NR-047-004 by the National Science Foundation under Grant GS-51, both at Stanford University and by the Center for Advanced Study in the Behavioral Sciences. Reproduction in whole or in part is permitted for any purpose of the United States Government.

I have benefitted from Robert M. Solow's comments, appearing as [7], on which the present version of the two-sector model is largely based. I also wish to acknowledge valuable comments and criticism by Ken-ichi Inada and Mordecai Kurz of Stanford University.

[2] Thus, the model presented here is an extension of the aggregate models of Solow and Swan ([6] and [8]) to the two-sector economy. It is a slightly different version of Meade's two-product economy without technical progress (see [5], Appendix II, pp. 83-133). The structure of a similar two-sector growth model has been analyzed by Kurz [4], where the elasticities of substitution in both sectors are assumed unity and the perfect foresight hypothesis is postulated.

Reprinted from *XXX*, No. 2 (June 1963) pp. 105–118 of *Review of Economic Studies* by permission of *Review of Economic Studies* published by Oliver & Boyd Ltd., Edinburgh and London. © 1963 The Economic Society.

Finally, we shall briefly analyze the structure of growth equilibrium in a model in which factor prices are not instantaneously adjusted to marginal products and 'involuntary' unemployment of either labor or capital may result at each moment of time. It will be shown that if the investment goods are more capital-intensive than the consumption goods, then the path of growth equilibrium approaches the state of balanced growth. On the other hand, if the consumption goods are more capital-intensive than the investment goods, the stability of growth equilibrium is not necessarily guaranteed, but the case of limit cycles may be observed.

2. *A Neoclassical Model of Economic Growth*

At the risk of repetition, the basic structure of the model will be described briefly. We consider an economy in which there exist two productive sectors, one producing consumption goods and another producing capital goods, respectively labelled C and I. Both consumption goods and capital goods are assumed to be composed of homogeneous quantities and to be produced by two homogeneous factors of production: labor and capital. Consumption goods are instantaneously consumed, while capital goods depreciate at a fixed rate μ. Let $L(t)$ be the total supply of labor at time t, and $K(t)$ the quantity of capital goods existing at time t. If we assume that labor forces grow at a constant rate, λ, and new capital goods are produced by the rate $Y_I(t)$ at the moment of time t, then the path of $K(t)$ and $L(t)$ is described by the following dynamic equations:

$$(1) \qquad \dot{L}(t)/L(t) = \lambda,$$

$$(2) \qquad \dot{K}(t) = Y_I(t) - \mu K(t).$$

In each sector, production is subject to constant returns-to-scale and diminishing marginal rates of substitution. Joint products are excluded and external (dis-) economies do not exist. The quantity of consumption goods, $Y_C(t)$, produced at time t is then related to the quantities of labor and capital employed in the C-sector, $L_C(t)$ and $K_C(t)$, respectively:

$$(3) \qquad Y_C(t) = F_C(K_C(t),\, L_C(t)),$$

where F_C is the C-sector's production function. Similarly, for the quantity of capital goods, $Y_I(t)$, produced at time t:

$$(4) \qquad Y_I(t) = F_I(K_I(t),\, L_I(t)).$$

The gross national product in terms of consumption goods, $Y(t)$, is measured by

$$(5) \qquad Y(t) = Y_C(t) + p(t)\, Y_I(t),$$

where $p(t)$ is the ratio of the price of the new capital good over that of the consumption good at time t. In what follows, prices are all measured in terms of the consumption good.

We assume that labor and capital are freely transferred from one sector to another[1] and both are fully employed;[2] namely,

$$(6) \qquad K_I(t) + K_C(t) = K(t),$$

$$(7) \qquad L_I(t) + L_C(t) = L(t).$$

The allocation of the two factors of production existing at any moment of time is assumed perfectly competitive, so that in each sector the wage $w(t)$ is equal to the marginal

---

[1] Namely, capital goods are perfectly malleable in Meade's terminology (see [5], e.g., p. 45).

[2] Under the hypotheses made on the production functions, (21) and (22), it is possible to show that both labor and capital are always fully employed.

product of labor and the rentals $r(t)$ of capital goods to the marginal product of capital:

$$(8) \qquad w(t) = \frac{\partial F_C}{\partial L_C} = p(t) \frac{\partial F_I}{\partial L_I},$$

and

$$(9) \qquad r(t) = \frac{\partial F_C}{\partial K_C} = p(t) \frac{\partial F_I}{\partial K_I},$$

where partial derivatives are evaluated at $(K_C(t), L_C(t))$ or $(K_I(t), L_I(t))$.

The price, $p(t)$, of the new capital good, satisfying equations (8) and (9), is considered as the supply price of capital; i.e., $p(t)$ is equal to the price of the new capital good which is just enough to induce each manufacturer in the I-sector to produce an additional unit of such a capital good.

Let us now assume that at any moment of time a constant fraction is saved out of the current gross national product.[1] If s stands for the average propensity to save $(0 < s < 1)$, we have an equation which determines the quantity of new capital goods:

$$(10) \qquad p(t) Y_I(t) = s Y(t).$$

The model above completely describes the path of growth equilibrium. At any moment of time t, the existing capital stock $K(t)$ is a result of past accumulation, and labor forces $L(t)$ are exogenously given. The equilibrium amount of new capital goods, $Y_I(t)$, is determined by solving equilibrium equations (3-10), and the dynamic equations (1) and (2) prescribe the path of growth equilibrium. The model will be conveniently referred to as *a neoclassical model of economic growth*.

3. *The Determination of Short-Run Equilibrium*

We shall first discuss the determination of equilibrium quantities and prices at each moment of time, given capital stock, $K(t)$, and available labor forces, $L(t)$. For brevity, all variables are denoted without explicitly referring to time t.

Let k and y be, respectively, the capital-labor ratio and the gross national product per head at time t:

$$k = K/L, \quad y = Y/L.$$

We also define:

$$k_i = K_i/L_i, \quad y_i = Y_i/L, \quad l_i = L_i/L, \quad i = I,C,$$

$$\omega = w/r.$$

The relations (3) and (4) are reduced to:

$$(11) \qquad y_i = f_i(k_i)l_i, \quad i = I,C,$$

where

$$f_i(k_i) = F_i(k_i, 1), \quad i = I,C.$$

---

[1] Throughout the paper, the propensity to save refers to that including depreciation, thus making its constancy or a variable version discussed below somewhat out of traditional formulation. The main reason for adopting gross instead of net propensity is due to the separation of entrepreneurs and owners of factors of production in my model. The interest of entrepreneurs is in maximizing their profits net of factor payments, while owners of productive factors are concerned not with keeping intact the means of production they own, but instead with achieving the highest level in their intertemporal preference scale. To analyze such a model fully would require the introduction of a new commodity, namely a bond, through which the saving behavior of the economy would be explicitly formulated.

It is assumed that, for each i, the function $f_i(k_i)$ is continuously twice differentiable for all $k_i > 0$, and

(12)
$$f_i(k_i) > 0, \quad f'_i(k_i) > 0, \quad f''_i(k_i) < 0,$$

$$\text{for all } k_i > 0,$$

(13)
$$f_i(0) = 0, \quad f_i(\infty) = \infty,$$

(14)
$$f'_i(0) = \infty, \quad f'_i(\infty) = 0.$$

A procedure similar to one used in [9] reduces the equilibrium conditions (3-10) to the following:

(15)
$$\omega = \frac{f_i(k_i)}{f'_i(k_i)} - k_i, \quad i = C, I,$$

(16)
$$p = \frac{f_C(k_C)}{f'_I(k_I)},$$

(17)
$$y = y_C + p \, y_I,$$

(18)
$$y_I = f_I(k_I) \frac{k_C - k}{k_C - k_I}, \qquad Y_C = f_C(k_C) \frac{k - k_I}{k_C - k_I},$$

(19)
$$p \, y_I = s \, y.$$

Given an arbitrary wage-rentals ratio ω, the optimum capital-labor ratio $k_i = k_i(\omega)$ in each sector is uniquely determined from equation (15). Differentiate (15) with respect to ω to get:

(20)
$$\frac{dk_i}{d\omega} = \frac{-[f'_i(k_i)]^2}{f_i(k_i) \, f''_i(k_i)} > 0, \quad i = C, I.$$

Substituting (15-18) into (19), we have:

(21)
$$[k + \omega] = \frac{[k_C(\omega) + \omega] \, [k_I(\omega) + \omega]}{s[k_C(\omega) + \omega] + (1-s) \, [k_I(\omega) + \omega]}.$$

Equation (21) uniquely determines the wage-rentals ratio ω. To see this, let us introduce the new variables:

(22)
$$Z = k + \omega, \quad Z_i = k_i(\omega) + \omega, \quad i = C, I.$$

Equation (21) then becomes

(23)
$$Z = \frac{Z_C Z_I}{sZ_C + (1 - s)Z_I}.$$

The right-hand side of equation (23) is a function of ω, which will be denoted by $g(\omega)$. Differentiate $g(\omega)$ to get:

$$g'(\omega) = \frac{sZ_C^2 Z'_I + (1 - s) \, Z_I^2 Z'_C}{[sZ_C + (1 - s) \, Z_I]^2},$$

which, in view of (20), yields:

$$g'(\omega) < \frac{[sZ_C^2 + (1 - s) \, Z_I^2]}{[sZ_C + (1 - s) \, Z_I]^2} \geq 1 \ .$$

[At the bottom of the page, the expression $g'(\omega) <$ should read: $g'(\omega) >$. The Editors.]

The function $g(\omega)$ takes all positive values and has a derivative greater than unity everywhere. Therefore, for any given positive k, equation (23) is uniquely solvable for ω, and ω increases as k increases. Thus we have:

Let us consider a neoclassical model of economic growth where the average propensity to save s remains constant, $0 < s < 1$. Then, for any positive capital-labor ratio, k, the equilibrium wage-rentals ratio $\omega = \omega(k)$ is uniquely determined by solving the fundamental equation (21). The higher the capital-labor ratio k, the higher the equilibrium wage-rentals ratio ω.

Let us now, in more detail, analyze the determination of short-run equilibrium in a neoclassical model. In most subsequent discussions we shall assume that the C-sector is always more capital-intensive than the I-sector; namely,

(24) $$k_C(\omega) > k_I(\omega), \text{ for all positive wage-rentals ratio } \omega,$$

which is required mainly for reasons of a mathematical nature and for which it seems to be difficult to give any economic justification (see [7]). Such a hypothesis was made in its extreme form by Wicksell in his analysis of Åkerman's problem ([10, pp. 274-299]), and an empirical evidence in the case of the United States economy was suggested by Professor Gordon in his recent paper ([2, p. 948]).

Let us first observe that *if the capital-intensity hypothesis (24) is satisfied, the supply price, p, of the capital good increases as the wage-rentals ratio ω increases.* In fact, differentiating (16) logarithmically with respect to ω and substituting (20) and (15), we obtain:

(25) $$\frac{1}{p}\frac{dp}{d\omega} = \frac{1}{\omega + k_I(\omega)} - \frac{1}{\omega + k_C(\omega)}.$$

Hence, by the hypothesis (24), $dp/d\omega$ is positive for an arbitrary wage-rentals ratio ω. In other words, as labor becomes relatively more expensive than capital, the capital good, in the production of which relatively more labor is employed than the consumption good, becomes relatively more expensive.

We next analyze the effect of a change in the wage-rentals ratio upon the gross national product. The gross national product per capita, y, defined by (17) with (16), (18), and (19), represents the level of the gross national product that corresponds to the full employment of labor and capital at a given wage-rentals ratio ω.

Substituting (16) and (18) into (17), and using (15), we get Walras' law:

(26) $$y = f_C'(k_C)\,(\omega + k).$$

Differentiating (26) logarithmically with respect to ω, we get

$$\frac{1}{y}\frac{dy}{d\omega} = \frac{f_C''(k_C)}{f_C'(k_C)}\frac{dk_C}{d\omega} + \frac{1}{\omega + k},$$

which, together with (20) and (15), yields:

(27) $$\frac{1}{y}\frac{dy}{d\omega} = \frac{1}{\omega + k} - \frac{1}{\omega + k_C(\omega)}.$$

415

The right-hand side of equation (27) is positive if and only if the hypothesis (24) is satisfied at ω; namely, we have shown that *the gross national product per capita is an increasing function of the wage-rentals ratio if and only if the capital-intensity hypothesis (24) is satisfied.*

A similar method may be used, e.g., to see the effect of a change in the wage-rentals ratio on the quantity of capital goods corresponding to full employment of labor and capital. Differentiating the first equation in (18) logarithmically and noting (15), we have:

$$(28) \quad \frac{1}{y_I} \frac{dy_I}{d\omega} = \left(\frac{1}{\omega + k_I(\omega)} + \frac{1}{k_C(\omega) - k_I(\omega)} \right) \frac{dk_I}{d\omega} + \left(\frac{1}{(k_C(\omega) - k)} \right.$$

$$\left. - \frac{1}{k_C(\omega) - k_I(\omega)} \right) \frac{dk_C}{d\omega}.$$

which has a positive value if $k_C(\omega) > k > k_I(\omega)$.

Hence, *if the capital-intensity hypothesis is satisfied, the higher the wage-rentals ratio ω, the larger the amount of new capital goods y_I.*

Let us see, finally, how the short-run equilibrium is related to the average propensity to save. We start with the following equation which is derived from the fundamental equation (21):

$$(29) \qquad \frac{1}{Z} = \frac{s}{Z_I} + \frac{1-s}{Z_C},$$

where Z, Z_I, Z_C are defined by (22).

Differentiating (29) with respect to s and noting that $\dfrac{\partial Z}{\partial \omega} = 1$, we get

$$(30) \qquad \frac{\partial \omega}{\partial s} = \frac{\dfrac{1}{Z_I} - \dfrac{1}{Z_C}}{\dfrac{sZ_I'}{Z_I^2} + \dfrac{(1-s)Z_C'}{Z_C^2} - \dfrac{1}{Z^2}}.$$

Then under the capital-intensity hypothesis (24), both the numerator and the denominator in the right-hand side of (30) are positive. Hence, *the equilibrium wage-rentals ratio $\omega(s)$ increases as the average propensity to save s increases.*

We have from (30) and (20) that

$$(31) \qquad \frac{\partial \omega}{\partial s} < \frac{\dfrac{1}{Z_I} - \dfrac{1}{Z_C}}{\dfrac{s}{Z_I^2} + \dfrac{1-s}{Z_C^2} - \dfrac{1}{Z^2}}.$$

4. *The Determination of Long-Run Equilibrium*

The dynamic equations (1) and (2) are reduced to

$$(32) \qquad \frac{\dot{k}}{k} = \frac{y_I}{k} - \lambda - \mu,$$

where $k = K(t)/L(t)$ and $y_I = Y_I(t)/L(t)$.

Since

$$y = rk + w = r(k + \omega) = pf'_I(k_I)(k + \omega),$$

we have from (18) that

$$y_I = s \frac{y}{p} = sf'_I(k_I)(k + \omega),$$

where ω is the equilibrium wage-rentals ratio and k_I is the corresponding optimum capital-labor ratio in the I-sector.

Equation (32) then becomes

$$(33) \qquad \frac{\dot{k}}{k} = sf'_I(k_I) \frac{k + \omega}{k} - \lambda - \mu,$$

where the right-hand side is a continuous function of ω. It is assumed that the differential equation (33) with any positive initial condition possesses a solution continuous with respect to the initial condition.

Let k^* be a capital-labor ratio such that

$$(34) \qquad sf'_I(k^*_I) \frac{k^* + \omega^*}{k^*} = \lambda + \mu,$$

where ω^* is the equilibrium wage-rentals ratio for k^* and k_I is the optimum capital-labor ratio in the I-sector. Such a k^* may be referred to as a *balanced capital-labor ratio*.

Let us first observe that *if the capital-intensity hypothesis (24) is satisfied, there always exists a uniquely determined balanced capital-labor ratio k*, corresponding to each level of the average propensity to save s.* To see this, define

$$(35) \qquad \phi(\omega) = f'_I(k_I(\omega)) \frac{k(\omega) + \omega}{k(\omega)},$$

where $k(\omega)$ satisfies

$$(36) \qquad k(\omega) + \omega = \frac{[k_C(\omega) + \omega](k_I(\omega) + \omega)}{s[k_C(\omega) + \omega] + (1 - s)[k_I(\omega) + \omega]}.$$

Differentiate (35) logarithmically and substitute (20) to get

$$\frac{1}{\phi(\omega)} \frac{\partial \phi}{\partial \omega} = - \frac{1}{\omega + k_I(\omega)} + \frac{1}{k(\omega) + \omega} + \left(\frac{1}{k(\omega) + \omega} - \frac{1}{k(\omega)} \right) \frac{dk(\omega)}{d\omega},$$

which, together with (24) and $dk(\omega)/d\omega > 0$, implies that

(37) $$\frac{\partial \phi(\omega)}{\partial \omega} < 0, \quad \text{for all } \omega.$$

Hence, for any λ and μ, there exists one and only one wage-rentals ratio ω^* for which

$$\phi(\omega^*) = \lambda + \mu.$$

The corresponding capital-labor ratio $k^* = k(\omega^*)$ is a balanced capital-labor ratio, which is uniquely determined by $\lambda + \mu$.

The relation (37) and $dk(\omega)/d\omega > 0$ yield the following stability theorem:

Let the capital-intensity hypothesis (24) *be satisfied, and let the propensity to save be kept constant at a certain positive level s ($0 < s < 1$). Then, along an arbitrary path of growth equilibrium $(K(t), L(t))$, the capital-labor ratio $k(t) = K(t)/L(t)$ asymptotically approaches the uniquely determined balanced capital-labor ratio k^*. The convergence of the growth equilibrium $k(t)$ is monotone; i.e., if $k(0)$ is greater than k^*, $k(t)$ decreasingly approaches k^* and if $k(0)$ is less than k^*, $k(t)$ increasingly approaches k^*, and similarly all the other equilibrium variables.*

In the general case where the capital-intensity hypothesis (24) is not necessarily satisfied, the balanced growth capital-labor ratio may be no longer uniquely determined, but there may be multiple balanced capital-labor ratios. However, *the growth path described by* (1-2), *or by* (32), *is globally stable; namely, the capital-laobr ratio $k(t)$ satisfying* (32) *converges monotonically to some balanced capital-labour ratio*. This is proved as follows:[1]

In view of the Arrow-Block-Hurwicz theorem,[2] it suffices to show that the right-hand side of the equation (33) tends to infinity as k goes to zero, and to zero as k goes to infinity. But k lies between $k_C(\omega)$ and $k_I(\omega)$, both of which tend to infinity (or zero) as k tends to infinity (or zero). Hence, it may suffice to show the following:

(38) $$\lim_{\omega \to 0} \phi(\omega) = \infty, \quad \lim_{\omega \to \infty} \phi(\omega) = 0,$$

where $\phi(\omega)$ is defined by (35).

---

[1] In Section 7 of [9], I have stated that the equilibrium growth is globally stable, as derived by the Arrow-Block-Hurwicz theorem. However, as Ken-ichi Inada pointed out to me, the steady state of balanced growth in the model of [9] is uniquely determined, but the differential equation describing the path of growth equilibrium may not have a continuous solution unless the capital-intensity hypothesis is satisfied. The Arrow-Block-Hurwicz theorem is not applicable to such a differential equation, which has no continuous solution. Hence, the original two-sector model as introduced in [9] may have a uniquely determined *unstable* steady state of growth equilibrium, and such is in fact the case with the example given in Section 6 of [9].

[2] The theorem referred to here is concerned with the global stability of a differentiable equation; namely, any solution to a differential equation $\dot{k} = \phi(k)$ converges to *some* equilibrium if $\lim_{k \to 0} \phi(k) > 0$ and $\lim_{k \to \infty} \phi(k) < 0$. See Arrow, Block, and Hurwicz [1, p. 108].

The first relation in (38) is easily derived from (14). To see the second relation, substitute (15) and (36) into (35) to get:

$$\phi(\omega) = \frac{f_I[k_I(\omega)]}{(1-s)\omega + k_I(\omega) - \dfrac{(1-s)\omega[\omega + k_I(\omega)]}{\omega + k_C(\omega)}} < \frac{1}{s} \frac{f_I[k_I(\omega)]}{k_I(\omega)},$$

which implies the second relation in (38).

5. The Propensity to Save and the Inducement to Invest

The neoclassical growth model as described in the previous sections will now be refined to allow for a variable propensity to save and for an adjustment in the amount of new capital goods to equate the rate of interest to the marginal efficiency of capital.

It will be assumed that the average propensity to save, $s(t)$, is dependent upon the current rate of interest, $\rho(t)$, as well as upon the gross national income per capita, $y(t)$:

$$(39) \qquad\qquad s(t) = g(\rho(t), y(t)).$$

The function $g(\rho, y)$ is assumed to be continuously differentiable, and

$$(40) \qquad\qquad 0 < \underline{g} < g(\rho, y) < \bar{g} < 1,$$

with some $\underline{g}$ and $\bar{g}$,

$$(41) \qquad\qquad \frac{\partial g}{\partial \rho} \geq 0, \quad \frac{\partial g}{\partial y} \geq 0.$$

It is assumed that the marginal propensity to save does not exceed unity, which may be in terms of function $g(\rho, y)$ forumlated as:

$$(42) \qquad\qquad \partial g/\partial y \leq \frac{1-s}{y} \quad \text{for all } \rho \text{ and } y > 0.$$

At each moment of time, new capital goods are produced up to the rate at which the marginal efficiency of that capital is equal to the prevailing rate of interest. The prospective rentals, which together with the expected rates of discount determine the marginal efficiency of capital, are assumed to be dependent on the current rentals, on the existing capital stock, and on the rate at which capital goods are newly-produced.

Let $\hat{r}(t, v)$ be the prospective returns v years ahead to the capital good newly-produced at time t. The prospective returns $\hat{r}(t, v)$, $0 < v < \infty$, are assumed to be dependent only on the current returns $r(t)$, the amounts of current capital stock $K(t)$, and of newly-produced capital goods $Y_I(t)$, and the existing labor forces $L(t)$. Let us assume that

$$(43) \qquad\qquad \hat{r}(t, v) = \varphi(t, v; r(t), k(t), y_I(t)),$$

where $k(t) = K(t)/L(t)$ is the aggregate capital-labor ratio and $y_I(t) = Y_I(t)/L(t)$ is the investment per head.

The function φ, which relates prospective returns of the newly-produced capital goods to current conditions of the economy, summarizes the state of long-term expectation[1] and will be assumed to satisfy:

(44) $$\frac{\partial \varphi}{\partial r} > 0, \quad \frac{\partial \varphi}{\partial y_I} < 0.$$

If for the sake of simplicity we assume that the expectation on future rates of interest is stationary, i.e., the current rate of interest, $\rho(t)$, is expected to prevail indefinitely, then the present value, $p_D(t)$ of prospective returns to newly-produced capital goods is given by

(45) $$p_D(t) = \int_0^\infty \hat{r}(t, v) \, e^{(-\mu + \rho(t)) v} \, dv.$$

The quantity $Y_I(t)$ of capital goods to be produced at time t is determined so as to satisfy the equation:

(46) $$p(t) = p_D(t),$$

where $p(t)$ is the supply price of capital and $p_D(t)$ the demand price of capital defined by (45).

As for the determination of the current rate of interest, $\rho(t)$, let us postulate that the rate of interest is so determined as to equate the value, evaluated at the prevailing market price, of the newly-produced capital goods to the savings.

For any given amounts of capital stock $K(t)$ and labor forces $L(t)$, equations (3-10) and (46), together with (39), (43), and (45), determine the equilibrium prices and quantities, in particular the rate at which capital goods are constructed, $Y_I(t)$. The dynamic equations (1) and (2) then characterize the path of growth equilibrium $(K(t), L(t))$ in the enlarged growth model.

The method used in section 3 may be slightly modified to discuss the determination of the short-run equilibrium in the enlarged growth model. For any given aggregate capital ratio $k(t) = K(t)/L(t)$, the equilibrium conditions are reduced to (15-18), (21), (39), and (46). Let the propensity to save be temporarily fixed at an arbitrary level $s(0 < s < 1)$; then the fundamental equation (21) uniquely solves the wage-rentals ratio $\omega = \omega(s)$ corresponding to the arbitrary fixed propensity to save s. The equations (16-18) then determine equilibrium price ratio $p = p(s)$, rentals $r = r(s)$, gross national produce $y = y(s)$, and the new capital construction $y_I = y_I(s)$, both per capita. The expected rentals $\hat{r}(t, v)$ are also determinate. The equilibrium rate of interest, $\rho = \rho(s)$, is hence uniquely solved by the equation (46).

Let the function $\psi(s)$ be defined by

(47) $$\psi(s) = s - g(\rho(s), y(s)), \qquad 0 < s < 1,$$

where $\rho(s)$ and $y(s)$ are the equilibrium rate of interest and gross national product corresponding to the level s of the propensity to save. We shall show that *the function $\psi(s)$ thus defined is an increasing function of s, provided the capital intensity hypothesis (24) is satisfied.*

---

[1] Chapter 12, pp. 147-164, in Keynes [3] is devoted to a discussion of the state of long-term expectation. Conditions (44) are based on Chapter 11, in particular Section II [3, pp. 141-144].

We have seen in Section 3 that $\omega(s)$ is an increasing function of s and $d\omega/ds$ satisfies the inequality (31). The supply price $p(s)$ and the quantity $y_I(s)$ of capital goods are then both increasing functions of s, as seen from (25) and (28), while current rentals $r(s)$ is a decreasing function. Hence, in view of the assumptions (44) and (45), *the rate of interest $\rho(s)$ satisfying equation (46) is a decreasing function of s.* Now let us differentiate (47) with respect to s:

$$(48) \qquad \frac{d\psi}{ds} = 1 - \frac{\partial g}{\partial \rho}\frac{d\rho}{ds} - \frac{\partial g}{\partial y}\frac{dy}{d\omega}\frac{d\omega}{ds}.$$

Substituting (27), (31) into (48) and using (41), we get:

$$\frac{d\psi}{ds} \geqq 1 - \frac{1}{y}\frac{\partial g}{\partial y}\left(\frac{1}{Z}-\frac{1}{Z_C}\right)\frac{\dfrac{1}{Z_I}-\dfrac{1}{Z_C}}{\dfrac{s}{Z_I^2}+\dfrac{1-s}{Z_C^2}-\dfrac{1}{Z^2}}.$$

which, together with (29) and (42), yields

$$(49) \qquad \frac{d\psi}{ds} > 1 - \frac{(1-s)\,s\left(\dfrac{1}{Z_I}-\dfrac{1}{Z_C}\right)^2}{\dfrac{s}{Z_I^2}+\dfrac{1-s}{Z_C^2}-\dfrac{1}{Z^2}} = 0.$$

The value of the function $\psi(s)$ becomes negative as s approaches zero, and positive as s approaches unity. Hence, there exists a uniquely determined level s of the propensity to save at which $\psi(s) = 0$. Such a level of the propensity to save and the corresponding equilibrium prices and quantities satisfy the equilibrium conditions (15-18), (21), (39), and (46). We have thus proved the following existence theorem:

Let the capital-intensity hypothesis (24) be satisfied in the extended neoclassical model of economic growth, in which the average propensity to save depends on the rate of interest and gross income, while the marginal efficiency of capital is equated to the prevailing rate of interest. Then, for any arbitrary given capital-labor ratio k, the average propensity to save, $s = s(k)$, is uniquely determined, and the equilibrium prices and quantities are accordingly determined,

The equations (1) and (2), as discussed in Section 4, may be reduced to equation (3) with s equal to the equilibrium average propensity to save corresponding to the capital-labor ratio k:

$$s = s(k).$$

An argument similar to the one given in Section 4 yields the following stability theorem:

In the extended neoclassical model of economic growth, for given rates of labor growth λ and of capital depreciation μ, there exists at least one balanced capital-labor ratio k^*. If the capital-intensity hypothesis (24) is satisfied, the dynamic equations (1) and (2) describe a continuous path, and along any path of growth equilibrium $(K(t), L(t))$, the capital-labor ratio $k(t) = K(t)/L(t)$ converges to some balanced capital-labor ratio k^*.

6. *Inflexibility of Factor Prices and ' Involuntary ' Unemployment*

The method we have developed in the previous sections may be extended without much difficulty to analyze the impact of the factor price inflexibility upon the behavior of growth equilibrium. In this section, we shall consider the two-sector model in which the rate of adjustment in real wage is inversely related to the quantity of ' involuntary ' unemployment, and the stability of growth equilibrium will be investigated.

At each moment of time, the quantities we take as given are the amounts of capital and labor available to the economy as a whole and the real wage prevailing in the economy at that moment. For the sake of simplicity, the average propensity to save, s, is assumed to be constant, and the basic premises of the model are identical with those described in the previous sections. We may then, without loss of generality, take as independent variables the aggregate capital-labor ratio $k = K/L$, and the wage-rentals ratio $\omega = w/r$. The full employment conditions (6) and (7), however, are not necessarily satisfied; instead, they are replaced by the following inequalities:

$$(50) \qquad\qquad K_I(t) + K_C(t) \leqq K(t),$$

$$(51) \qquad\qquad L_I(t) + L_C(t) \leqq L(t),$$

where either one is satisfied with equality. The remaining equilibrium conditions (3-5) and (8-10) are preserved without change.

The method discussed in Section 3 above may be slightly modified to determine the short-run equilibrium in such a model; namely, let the optimum aggregate capital-labor ratio $k(\omega)$, corresponding to given wage-rentals ratio ω, be defined by the equation:

$$(52) \qquad \frac{1}{k(\omega) + \omega} = \frac{s}{k_I(\omega) + \omega} + \frac{1 - s}{k_C(\omega) + \omega}.$$

It is easily seen that, if $k \geqq k(\omega)$, labor is fully employed and the equilibrium quantity of newly-produced capital goods per capita, y_I, is determined by:

$$(53) \qquad\qquad y_I = sf_I'[k_I(\omega)] \ (k(\omega) + \omega).$$

On the other hand, if $k < k(\omega)$, labor is not fully employed and y_I is given by:

$$(54) \qquad\qquad y_I = sf_I'[k_I(\omega)] \ (k(\omega) + \omega) \ \frac{k}{k(\omega)}.$$

The dynamic path of $k(t)$ and $\omega(t)$ is then described by the following differential equations:

$$(55) \qquad\qquad k = y_I - (\lambda + \mu)k,$$

$$(56) \qquad\qquad \omega = H[k - k(\omega)],$$

where H is a continuous sign-preserving function. In what follows, it will be assumed that, for any positive initial condition (k_0, ω_0), the pair of differential equations (55) and (56) has a positive solution $(k(t), \omega(t))$, for all $t > 0$, which is unique and continuous with respect to initial condition (k_0, ω_0).

Let us first consider the case where investment goods are more capital-intensive than consumption goods; *i.e.*,

$$k_I(\omega) > k_C(\omega) \text{ for all } \omega > 0.$$

Then, differentiating (53) logarithmically with respect to ω, we get

$$\frac{1}{y_I}\frac{dy_I}{d\omega} = -\frac{1}{k_I(\omega) + \omega} + \frac{\dfrac{dk(\omega)}{d\omega} + 1}{k(\omega) + \omega} > 0;$$

hence, if $k \geqq k(\omega)$, y_I is an increasing function of ω. The optimum aggregate capital-labor ratio $k(\omega)$ is also an increasing function of ω, but

$$y_I < k(\omega) \text{ for sufficiently small } \omega,$$

and

$$y_I < k(\omega) \text{ for sufficiently large } \omega,$$

therefore, the path described by the differential equations (55) and (56) behaves as those illustrated in Fig. 1, and any solution $(k(t), \omega(t))$ approaches the state of balanced growth (k^*, ω^*); or, in the case of multiple balanced growth equilibria, $(k(t), \omega(t))$ approaches *a* state of balanced growth.

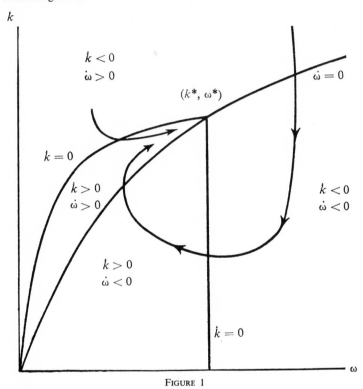

FIGURE 1

If consumption goods are always more capital-intensive, i.e.,

$$k_I(\omega) < k_C(\omega), \text{ for all } \omega > 0,$$

then the investment per capita, y_I, may not be an increasing function of ω, although the state of balanced growth equilibrium is uniquely determined. In this case, it is easily established (by using the Poincaré-Bendixon Theory) that the solution $(k(t), \omega(t))$ of differential equations (55) and (56) approaches either the state of balanced growth equilibrium or a periodic orbit. The case of limit cycles may be illustrated by Fig. 2.

Stanford.   H. UZAWA.

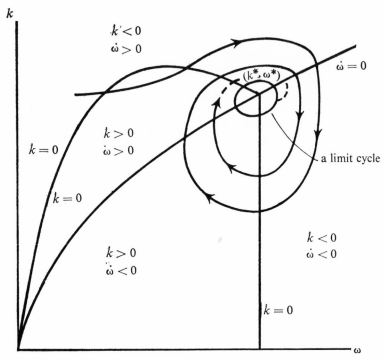

k

$k' < 0$
$\dot{\omega} > 0$

$\dot{\omega} = 0$

(k^*, ω^*)

$k > 0$
$k = 0$ $\dot{\omega} > 0$

$k = 0$

a limit cycle

$k < 0$
$\dot{\omega} < 0$

$k > 0$
$\ddot{\omega} < 0$

$k = 0$

ω

FIGURE 2

REFERENCES

[1] Arrow, K. J., H. D. Block, and L. Hurwicz, " On the Stability of Competitive Equilibrium, II," *Econometrica*, Vol. 27 (1959), 82-109.
[2] Gordon, R. A., " Differential Changes in the Prices of Consumers' and Capital Goods," *American Economic Review*, Vol. 51 (1961), 937-957.
[3] Keynes, J. M., *The General Theory of Employment, Interest and Money*, London: Macmillan, 1936.
[4] Kurz, M., " Patterns of Growth and Valuation in a Two-Sector Model," *Yale Economic Essays*, forthcoming.
[5] Meade, J. E., *A Neo-Classical Theory of Economic Growth*, New York: Oxford University Press, 1961.
[6] Solow, R. M., " A contribution to the Theory of Economic Growth," *Quarterly Journal of Economics*, Vol. 32 (1956), 65-94.
[7] Solow, R. M., " Note on Uzawa's Two-Sector Model of Economic Growth," *Review of Economic Studies*, Vol. 29 (1961-62), 48-50.
[8] Swan, T., " Economic Growth and Capital Accumulation," *Economic Record*, Vol. 66 (1956), 334-361.
[9] Uzawa, H., " On a Two-Sector Model of Economic Growth," *Review of Economic Studies*, Vol. 29 (1961-62), 40-47.
[10] Wicksell, K., *Lectures on Political Economy, I: General Theory*, London: Routledge and Kegan Paul, 1934.

V

Foundations of Optimal Economics

INTRODUCTION

Part V differs from the preceding parts in one important respect: in the previous parts, the consumption function is specified as a behavioral rule. The central problem of this section, on the other hand, is how income should be allocated between investment and consumption. This part serves, in this way, as a bridge between growth theory and planning. We are brought into the realm of welfare economics, of normative versus positive or descriptive economics. The criterion function used in the Ramsey article is the maximization of intertemporal utility

$$\text{Max} \int U[c(t), t]dt \quad \text{where } c \text{ is consumption, and } t \text{ is time.}$$

In Ramsey, $U[c(t), t]$ takes on the simple form of $U(c)$. In Koopmans [110] on the other hand, $U(c,t)$ takes on the form $(c)e^{-\delta t}$; that is, Koopmans introduces a rate of time preference. Although Ramsey has argued that there is no socially justifiable reason for introducing a pure discount factor, this is a moot question.

The Ramsey and Koopmans models are full dynamic models. There has been, on the other hand, a large literature on normative comparative dynamics; in particular, Solow, in the article reprinted here, as well as Phelps, Swan, Robinson, and von Weizsacker have all addressed themselves to the question of along which of the possible balanced growth paths is consumption per capita maximized. It is shown that the "Golden Rule" path, as Phelps has called it, is the one along which the marginal product of capital is equal to the rate of growth, $r = n$. To sustain a higher capital-labor ratio, investment must go up by $n\Delta k$, but output goes up by $r\Delta k$, and since r is a decreasing function of k, $r\Delta k - n\Delta k$ is negative; hence what is left over for consumption is reduced. Similarly, it can be shown that smaller capital-labor ratios reduce output by less than investment. If we multiply both sides of the equation $r = n$ by K, and observe that $rK = $ profits, and $nK = \dot{K} = $ investment, we obtain the result that along the Golden Rule path, investment $=$ profits, a result known as the neoclassical theorem. For planning, comparative dynamics is, of course, of little value or interest, since the essence of development is changing capital-labor ratios. Moreover, the focus on steady states may be misleading. For instance, there are situations where the path which is most preferred of all steady state paths, is not (without some intertemporal redistribution) sustainable by a competitive equilibrium; but there is no reason to limit choices to steady state paths, and it would be incorrect to conclude that the classic welfare theorems no longer hold.

Another outgrowth of the Ramsey work is the development of descriptive models of economic behavior where individuals take into consideration explicitly intertemporal considerations. In this sense, for instance, the Ramsey model can be thought of as how a competitive Robinson Crusoe economy, or a competitive economy with identical individuals living infinitely long, might behave. The undesirable assumption of infinite lifetime is eliminated in the life-cycle model formulated by Samuelson. Individuals live a finite number of periods (in his version, three), working in the first periods and saving for retirement in the latter periods. Samuelson shows that although the maximum level of steady state utility per capita requires (as in the Golden Rule theorem, see above) the rate of growth to equal the rate of interest, a competitive economy may have a rate of interest falling short of that; this can be shown to be intertemporally inefficient, in the sense that some generations could be better off without making any other generation worse off [117]. But through the introduction of money, or appropriate intertemporal redistributions, such inefficient paths can be avoided.

The final article, by Malinvaud, clarifies some of the relations between atemporal and intertemporal theories of resource allocation; in particular, it focuses on the problems of the choice criteria and the difficulties raised by infinity.

A MATHEMATICAL THEORY OF SAVING

F. P. Ramsey

I

THE first problem I propose to tackle is this : how much of
its income should a nation save ? To answer this a simple rule
is obtained valid under conditions of surprising generality; the
rule, which will be further elucidated later, runs as follows.

The rate of saving multiplied by the marginal utility of money
should always be equal to the amount by which the total net
rate of enjoyment of utility falls short of the maximum possible
rate of enjoyment.

In order to justify this rule it is, of course, necessary to make
various simplifying assumptions : we have to suppose that our
community goes on for ever without changing either in numbers
or in its capacity for enjoyment or in its aversion to labour; that
enjoyments and sacrifices at different times can be calculated
independently and added ; and that no new inventions or improvements in organisation are introduced save such as can be regarded
as conditioned solely by the accumulation of wealth.[1]

One point should perhaps be emphasised more particularly;
it is assumed that we do not discount later enjoyments in comparison with earlier ones, a practice which is ethically indefensible
and arises merely from the weakness of the imagination; we
shall, however, in Section II include such a rate of discount in
some of our investigations.

We also ignore altogether distributional considerations,
assuming, in fact, that the way in which consumption and labour
are distributed between the members of the community depends
solely on their total amounts, so that total satisfaction is a
function of these total amounts only.

Besides this, we neglect the differences between different
kinds of goods and different kinds of labour, and suppose them to
be expressed in terms of fixed standards, so that we can speak
simply of quantities of capital, consumption and labour without
discussing their particular forms.

Foreign trade, borrowing and lending need not be excluded,
provided we assume that foreign nations are in a stable state, so

[1] *I.e.* they must be such as would not occur without a certain degree of
accumulation, but could be foreseen given that degree.

Reprinted by permission of the publisher from *The Economic Journal*, XXXVIII, No. 152
(December 1928), pp. 543–559. London: Macmillan and Co. Limited, and New York: The
Macmillan Company.

that the possibilities of dealing with them can be included on the constant conditions of production. We do, however, reject the possibility of a state of progressive indebtedness to foreigners continuing for ever.

Lastly, we have to assume that the community will always be governed by the same motives as regards accumulation, so that there is no chance of our savings being selfishly consumed by a subsequent generation; and that no misfortunes will occur to sweep away accumulations at any point in the relevant future.

Let us then denote by $x(t)$ and $a(t)$ the total rates of consumption and labour of our community, and by $c(t)$ its capital at time t. Its income is taken to be a general function of the amounts of labour and capital, and will be called $f(a,c)$; we then have, since savings plus consumption must equal income,

$$\frac{dc}{dt} + x = f(a,c) \quad . \quad . \quad . \quad . \quad . \quad (1)$$

Now let us denote by $U(x)$ the total rate of utility of a rate of consumption x, and by $V(a)$ the total rate of disutility of a rate of labour a; and the corresponding marginal rates we will call $u(x)$ and $v(a)$;

so that
$$u(x) = \frac{dU(x)}{dx}$$

$$v(a) = \frac{dV(a)}{da}.$$

We suppose, as usual, that $u(x)$ is never increasing and $v(a)$ never decreasing.

We have now to introduce a concept of great importance in our argument. Suppose we have a given capital c, and are going neither to increase nor decrease it. Then $U(x) - V(a)$ denotes our net enjoyment per unit of time, and we shall make this a maximum, subject to the condition that our expenditure x is equal to what we can produce with labour a and capital c. The resulting rate of enjoyment $U(x) - V(a)$ will be a function of c, and will, up to a point, increase as c increases, since with more capital we can obtain more enjoyment.

This increase of the rate of enjoyment with the amount of capital may, however, stop for either of two reasons. It might, in the first place, happen that a further increment of capital would not enable us to increase either our income or our leisure; or, secondly, we might have reached the maximum conceivable rate of enjoyment, and so have no use for more income or leisure. In either case a certain finite capital would give us the greatest rate of enjoyment economically *obtainable*, whether or not this was the greatest rate *conceivable*.

On the other hand, the rate of enjoyment may never stop increasing as capital increases. There are then two logical possibilities : either the rate of enjoyment will increase to infinity, or it will approach asymptotically to a certain finite limit. The first of these we shall dismiss on the ground that economic causes alone could never give us more than a certain finite rate of enjoyment (called above the maximum conceivable rate). There remains the second case, in which the rate of enjoyment approaches a finite limit, which may or may not be equal to the maximum conceivable rate. This limit we shall call the maximum *obtainable* rate of enjoyment, although it cannot, strictly speaking, be obtained, but only approached indefinitely.

What we have in the several cases called the maximum obtainable rate of enjoyment or utility we shall call for short *Bliss* or *B*. And in all cases we can see that the community must save enough either to reach *Bliss* after a finite time, or at least to approximate to it indefinitely. For in this way alone is it possible to make the amount by which enjoyment falls short of bliss summed throughout time a finite quantity; so that if it should be possible to reach bliss or approach it indefinitely, this will be infinitely more desirable than any other course of action. And it is bound to be possible, since by setting aside a small sum each year we can in time increase our capital to any desired extent.[1]

Enough must therefore be saved to reach or approach bliss some time, but this does not mean that our whole income should be saved. The more we save the sooner we shall reach bliss, but the less enjoyment we shall have now, and we have to set the one against the other. Mr. Keynes has shown me that the rule governing the amount to be saved can be determined at once from these considerations. But before explaining his argument it will be best to develop equations which can be used in the more general problems which we shall consider later.

---

[1] As it stands this argument is incomplete, since in the last case considered above bliss was the limiting value, as capital tends to infinity, of the enjoyment obtainable by spending our *whole income*, and so making no provision for increasing capital further. The lacuna can easily be filled by remarking that to save $£\frac{1}{n}$ in the nth year would be sufficient to increase capital to infinity (since $\Sigma\frac{1}{n}$ is divergent), and that the loss of income $\left(£\frac{1}{n}\right)$ would then decrease to zero, so that the limiting values of income and expenditure would be the same.

o o 2

The first of these comes from equating the marginal disutility of labour at any time to the product of the marginal efficiency of labour by the marginal utility of consumption at that time,

i.e.
$$v(a) = \frac{\partial f}{\partial a} u(x) \quad \cdot \quad \cdot \quad \cdot \quad \cdot \quad \cdot \quad (2)$$

The second equates the advantage derived from an increment $\varDelta x$ of consumption at time t, to that derived by postponing it for an infinitesimal period $\varDelta t$, which will increase its amount to $\varDelta x\left(+ \frac{\partial f}{\partial c}\varDelta t \right)$, since $\frac{\partial f}{\partial c}$ gives the rate of interest earned by waiting. This gives

$$u\{x(t)\} = \left\{1 + \frac{\partial f}{\partial c}\varDelta t\right\} u\{x(t + \varDelta t)\}$$

or in the limit

$$\frac{d}{dt}u(x(t)) = -\frac{\partial f}{\partial c} \cdot u(x(t)) \quad \cdot \quad \cdot \quad \cdot \quad \cdot \quad (3)$$

This equation means that $u(x)$, the marginal utility of consumption, falls at a proportionate rate given by the rate of interest. Consequently x continually increases unless and until either $\frac{\partial f}{\partial c}$ or $u(x)$ vanishes, in which case it is easy to see that bliss must have been attained.

Equations (1), (2) and (3) are sufficient to solve our problem provided we know c_0, the given capital with which the nation starts at $t = 0$, the other "initial condition" being supplied by considerations as to the behaviour of the function as $t \to \infty$.

To solve the equations we proceed as follows : noticing that x, a and c are all functions of one independent variable, the time, we have

$$\frac{d}{dx}\{u(x) \cdot f(a,c)\} = \frac{du}{dx} \cdot f(a,c) + u(x)\frac{\partial f}{\partial a}\frac{da}{dx} + u(x)\frac{\partial f}{\partial c}\frac{dc}{dt}\frac{dt}{dx}$$

$$= \frac{du}{dx}f(a,c) + v(a)\frac{da}{dx} - \frac{du(x)}{dt}\{f(a,c) - x\}\frac{dt}{dx}$$

$$= x\frac{du}{dx} + v(a)\frac{da}{dx}. \quad \text{(Using (2), (3) and (1).)}$$

Consequently, integrating by parts

$$u(x) \cdot f(a,c) = xu(x) - U(x) + V(a) + \text{a constant } K,$$

or
$$\frac{dc}{dt} = f(a,c) - x = \frac{K - \{U(x) - V(a)\}}{u(x)}. \quad \cdot \quad \cdot \quad (4)$$

We have now to identify K with what we called B, or bliss. This is most easily done by starting in a different way.

$\int_0^\infty (B - U(x) + V(a))dt$ represents the amount by which enjoyment falls short of bliss integrated throughout time; this is (or can be made) finite, and our problem is to minimise it. If we apply the calculus of variations straight away, using equation (1), we get equations (2) and (3) again; but if, instead of this, we first change the independent variable to c, we get a great simplification. Our integral becomes

$$\int_{c_0}^\infty \frac{B - U(x) + V(a)}{dc/dt} \, dc \,^1$$

or $$\int_{c_0}^\infty \frac{B - U(x) + V(a)}{f(a,c) - x} \, dc. \quad \text{Using (1).}$$

Now in this x and a are entirely arbitrary functions of c, and to minimise the integral we have simply to minimise the integrand by equating to zero its partial derivatives. Taking the derivative with respect to x we obtain :

$$\frac{-u(x)}{f(a,c) - x} + \frac{B - U(x) + V(a)}{\{f(a,c) - x\}^2} = 0;$$

consequently $$\frac{dc}{dt} = f(a,c) - x = \frac{B - (U(x) - V(a))}{u(x)} \quad . \quad . \quad (5)$$

or, as we stated at the beginning,

rate of saving multiplied by marginal utility of consumption should always equal bliss minus actual rate of utility enjoyed.

Mr. Keynes, to whom I am indebted for several other suggestions, has shown me that this result can also be obtained by the following simple reasoning.

Suppose that in a year we ought to spend £x and save £z. Then the advantage to be gained from an extra £1 spent is $u(x)$, the marginal utility of money, and this must be equated to the sacrifice imposed by saving £1 less.

Saving £1 less in the year will mean that we shall only save £z in $1 + \frac{1}{z}$ years, not, as before, in one year. Consequently, we shall be in $1 + \frac{1}{z}$ year's time exactly where we should have been in one year's time, and the whole course of our approach

---

[1] The upper limit will not be ∞, but the least capital with which bliss can be obtained, if this is finite. c steadily increases with t, at any rate until the integrand vanishes, so that the transformation is permissible.

to bliss will be postponed by $\frac{1}{z}$ of a year, so that we shall enjoy $\frac{1}{z}$ of a year less bliss and $\frac{1}{z}$ of a year more at our present rate. The sacrifice is, therefore,

$$\frac{1}{z}\{B - (U(x) - V(a)\}.$$

Equating this to $u(x)$, we get equation (5) again, if we replace z by $\frac{dc}{dt}$, its limiting value.

Unfortunately this simple reasoning cannot be applied when we take account of time-discounting, and I have therefore retained my equations (1)–(4), which can easily be extended to deal with more difficult problems.

The most remarkable feature of the rule is that it is altogether independent of the production function $f(a, c)$, except in so far as this determines bliss, the maximum rate of utility obtainable. In particular the amount we should save out of a given income is entirely independent of the present rate of interest, unless this is actually zero. The paradoxical nature of this result will to some extent be mitigated later, when we find that if the future is discounted at a constant rate ρ and the rate of interest is constant and equal to r, the proportion of income to be saved is a function of the ratio ρ/r. If $\rho = 0$ this ratio is 0 (unless r be 0 also) and the proportion to be saved is consequently independent of r.

The rate of saving which the rule requires is greatly in excess of that which anyone would normally suggest, as can be seen from the following table, which is put forward merely as an illustration.

Family income per annum.					Total utility.
£150	.	.	.	.	. 2
£200	.	.	.	.	. 3
£300	.	.	.	.	. 4
£500	.	.	.	.	. 5
£1000	.	.	.	.	. 6
£2000	.	.	.	.	. 7
£5000	.	.	.	.	. 8 = Bliss.

If we neglect variations in the amount of labour, the amount that should be saved out of a family income of £500 would be about £300. For then bliss minus actual rate of utility = 8 − = 5. Savings = £300 and marginal utility of consumption at

£200 = about $\dfrac{1}{£60}$. (From £150 to £300 $U(x) = \dfrac{13x}{300} - 3 -$

$\dfrac{x^2}{15,000}$, approximating by fitting a parabola, so that $u(x) = \dfrac{13}{300} -$

$\dfrac{x}{7,500} = \dfrac{1}{60}$ if $x = 200$.)

It is worth pausing for a moment to consider how far our conclusions are affected by considerations which our simplifying assumptions have forced us to neglect. The probable increase of population constitutes a reason for saving even more, and so does the possibility that future inventions will put the bliss level higher than at present appears. On the other hand, the probability that future inventions and improvements in organisation are likely to make income obtainable with less sacrifice than at present is a reason for saving less. The influence of inventions thus works in two opposite ways : they give us new needs which we can better satisfy if we have saved up beforehand, but they also increase our productive capacity and make preliminary saving less urgent.

The most serious factor neglected is the possibility of future wars and earthquakes destroying our accumulations. These cannot be adequately accounted for by taking a very low rate of interest over long periods, since they may make the rate of interest actually negative, destroying as they do not only interest, but principal as well.

II

I propose now to assume that returns to capital and labour are constant and independent,[1] so that

$$f(a,c) = pa + rc,$$

where p, the rate of wages, and r, the rate of interest, are constants. This assumption will enable us

(a) To represent our former solution by a simple diagram;
(b) To extend it to the case of an individual who only lives a finite time;
(c) To extend it to include the problem in which future utilities and disutilities are discounted at a constant rate.

[1] It is worth noting that in most of (a) we only require independence of returns, and not constancy, and that nowhere do we really require *wages* to be constant, but these assumptions are made throughout to simplify the statement. They are less absurd if the state is one among others which are only advancing slowly, so that the rates of interest and wages are largely independent of what our particular state saves and earns.

On our new hypothesis the income of the community falls into two clearly defined parts, pa and rc, which it will be convenient to call its *earned* and *unearned* income respectively.

(*a*) Equation (2), which now reads

$$v(a) = pu(x),$$

determines a as a function of x only, and we can conveniently put

$$y = x - pa = \text{consumption} - \text{earned income}$$
$$w(y) = u(x) = v(a)/p$$
$$W(y) = \int w(y)dy = \int (u(x)dx - v(a)da) = U(x) - V(a).$$

$W(y)$ may be called the total and $w(y)$ the marginal utility of unearned income, since they are the total and marginal utilities arising from the possession of an unearned income y available for consumption.

Equation (5) now gives

$$rc - y = f(a,c) - x = \frac{B - W(y)}{w(y)} \quad . \quad . \quad . \quad (6)$$

or

$$B - W(y) = \frac{dW}{dy}(rc - y),$$

which means that the point (rc, B) lies on the tangent at y to the curve $z = W(y)$.

Figure (1) shows the curve $z = W(y)$, which either attains the value B at a finite value y_1 (the case shown in the figure) or else approaches it asymptotically as $y \to \infty$.

In order to determine how much of a given unearned income rc should be saved, we take the point P, (rc, B), on the line $z = B$, and from it draw a tangent to the curve (not $z = B$, which will always be one tangent, but the other one). If the abscissa of Q, the point of contact, is y, an amount y of the unearned income should be consumed, and the remainder, $rc - y$, should be saved. Of course y may be negative, which would mean that not only would the whole unearned income be saved, but part of the earned income also.

It is easy to see that there must always be such a tangent, because the curve $z = W(y)$ will have a tangent or asymptote $y = -\eta$, where η is the greatest excess of earnings over consumption compatible with continued existence.

This rule determines how much of a given income should be spent, but it does not tell us what our income will amount to after a given lapse of time. This is obtained from equation (3), which now gives us

$$\frac{d}{dt}w(y) = -rw(y)$$

or
$$w(y) = Ae^{-rt} \quad . \quad . \quad . \quad . \quad . \quad . \quad (7)$$

Here $A = w(y_0)$, where y_0 is the value of y for $t = o$ determined as the abscissa of Q, where P is (rc_0, B).

Supposing, then, we want to find the time taken in accumulating a capital c from an initial capital c_0, we take P to be the

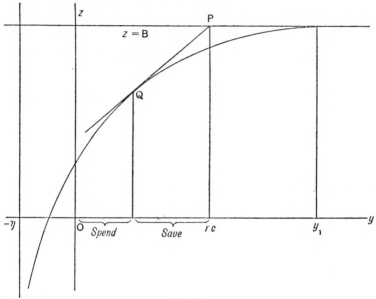

Fig. 1.

point (rc, B) and P_0 to be (rc_0, B). $w(y)$ is then the slope of the tangent from P, and $w(y_0)$ the slope of the tangent from P_0, so that the time in question

$$= \frac{1}{r} \log_e \frac{w(y_0)}{w(y)} = \frac{1}{r} \log_e \frac{\text{slope of tangent from } P_0}{\text{slope of tangent from } P}.$$

(b) Suppose now that we are concerned with an individual who lives only for a definite time, say T years, instead of with a community which lives for ever. We still have equation (4)

$$f(a,c) - x = \frac{K - (Ux - V(a))}{u(x)}$$

or
$$rc - y = \frac{K - W(y)}{w(y)} \quad . \quad . \quad . \quad . \quad . \quad (8)$$

but K is no longer equal to B, and has still to be determined. In order to find it we must know how much capital our man feels it necessary to leave his heirs; let us call this c_3.

Equation (8) means, as before, that y can be found as the abscissa of the point of contact Q of a tangent drawn from (rc, K) or P to the curve. P always lies on $z = K$, and its abscissa begins by being rc_0 and ends by being rc_3. K we can take as being less than B, since a man who lives only a finite time will save less than one who lives an infinite time, and the greater K is, the greater will be the rate of saving. Consequently $z = K$ will meet the curve, say at P_4.

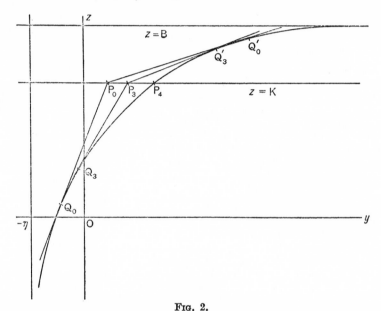

Fig. 2.

From both P_0 and P_3 there will be two tangents to the curve, of which either the upper or the lower can, for all we know, be taken as determining y_0 and y_3. If, however, $c_3 > c_0$ as in Fig. 2, we can only take the lower tangent from P_0, since the upper tangent gives a value of y_0 greater than either of the values of y_3, which is impossible, as y continually increases. Taking, then, Q_0 as the point of contact of the lower tangent from P_0, there are two possible cases, according as we take as giving y_3 either Q_3, the lower, or Q_3', the upper value. If we take Q_3, P_0 moves straight to P_3, and there is saving all the time; this happens when T is small. But if T is large, Q_0 moves right along to Q_3', and P_0 goes first up to P_4, and then back to P_3;

to begin with there is saving, and subsequently splashing. Similarly, if $c_0 > c_3$, there are two possible cases, and in this case it is the lower tangent from P_3 that cannot be taken.

In order to determine which tangents to take and also the value of K we must use the condition derived from equation (7)

$$\frac{\text{slope of tangent taken from } P_0}{\text{slope of tangent taken from } P_3} = \frac{w(y_0)}{w(y_3)} = e^{rT}.$$

This, together with the fact that the abscissae of P_0 and P_3 are c_0, c_3, and that they have the same ordinate K, suffices to fix both K and the tangents to be taken.

(c) We have now to see how our results must be modified when we no longer reckon future utilities and disutilities as equal to present ones, but discount them at a constant rate ρ.

This rate of discounting future *utilities* must, of course, be distinguished from the rate of discounting future sums of money. If I can borrow or lend at a rate r I must necessarily be equally pleased with an extra £1 now and an extra £$(1 + r)$ in a year's time, since I could always exchange the one for the other. My marginal rate of discount for money is, therefore, necessarily r, but my rate of discount for utility may be quite different, since the marginal utility of money to me may be varying by my increasing or decreasing my expenditure as time goes on.

In assuming the rate of discount constant, I do not mean that it is the same for all individuals, since we are at present only concerned with one individual or community, but that the present value of an enjoyment at any future date is to be obtained by discounting it at the rate ρ. Thus, taking it to be about $\frac{3}{4}$ per cent., utility at any time would be regarded as twice as desirable as that a hundred years later, four times as valuable as that two hundred years later and so on at a compound rate. This is the only assumption we can make, without contradicting our fundamental hypothesis that successive generations are actuated by the same system of preferences. For if we had a varying rate of discount—say a higher one for the first fifty years—our preference for enjoyments in 2000 A.D. over those in 2050 A.D. would be calculated at the lower rate, but that of the people alive in 2000 A.D. would be at the higher.

Let us suppose first that the rate of discount for utility ρ is less than the rate of interest r.

Then equations (1) and (2) are unchanged, but equation (3) becomes

$$\frac{d}{dt}u(x) = -u(x)\left\{\frac{\partial f}{\partial c} - \rho\right\}$$
$$= -u(x)(r - \rho) \quad . \quad . \quad . \quad . \quad (9)$$

as we are now assuming $\frac{\partial f}{\partial c}$ constant and equal to r;

consequently $\qquad w(y) = u(x) = Ae^{-(r-\rho)t}$ . . . . (9a)

and $\qquad rc - y = \frac{dc}{dt} = \frac{dc}{dw} \cdot \frac{dw}{dt} = -(r - \rho)w\frac{dc}{dw}$

so $\qquad \frac{dc}{dw} + \frac{rc}{(r - \rho)w} = \frac{y}{(r - \rho)w},$

where $\qquad cw^{r/(r-\rho)} = \int\frac{yw^{\rho/(r-\rho)}}{r - \rho}dw + \frac{K}{r}$

$$= \frac{1}{r}yw^{r/(r-\rho)} - \frac{1}{r}\int_b^y w^{r/(r-\rho)}(y)dy + \frac{K}{r}$$

(K, b constants.)

and $\qquad \frac{dc}{dt} = rc - y = \frac{K - \int_b^y w^{r/(r-\rho)}(y)dy}{w^{r/(r-\rho)}(y)}$ . . . (10)

This equation is the same as (8) except that instead of $w(y)$ and $W(y)$, which is $\int w(y)dy$, we have $w^{r/(r-\rho)}(y)$ and $\int w^{r/(r-\rho)}(y)dy$. The method of solution both for a community and for an individual is therefore the same as before, except that instead of the real utility of unearned income we have to consider what we can call its modified utility, obtained by integrating the marginal utility to the power $r/(r - \rho)$. This has the effect of accelerating the decrease of marginal utility and lessening the relative importance of high incomes. We can in this way translate our discounting of the future into a discounting of high incomes. The rate at which this is done is governed solely by the ratio of ρ to r, so that if ρ is 0 it is independent of the value of r, provided this is not also 0. The main conclusion of section I is thus confirmed.

There is, however, a slight difficulty, because we have not really shown yet that if we are considering an infinite time, the constant K is to be interpreted as what might be called " modified bliss," i.e. the maximum value of $\int_b^y w^{r/(r-\rho)}(y)dy$. This modified bliss would require the same income as bliss does, the modification being solely in the value set on it. This result can, however, be deduced at once from equation (9a), which shows that y increases until bliss is reached, so that $\frac{dc}{dt}$ can never become negative and K cannot be less than modified bliss.   On the other hand, provided this condition is fulfilled, $9(a)$ shows that the larger y is initially, the smaller will be A, and the larger will be y throughout future time.   Hence K must be as small as possible (provided it is not so small as to make $\dfrac{dc}{dt}$ ultimately negative); so that K cannot be greater than modified bliss.   Hence as it is neither less nor greater it must be equal.

As in (b), we can adapt our solution to the case of an individual with only a finite time to live, in this case drawing tangents to the modified utility curve.

An interesting special case is that of a community for which

$$w(y) = Dy^{-a} \qquad\qquad (a > 1)$$

we shall have $w^{r/(r-\rho)}(y) = Ey^{-\beta},\ \beta = \dfrac{r\alpha}{r-\rho},\ E = D^{r/(r-\rho)}$

$$\text{savings} = \frac{K - \int w^{r/(r-\rho)}(y)dy}{w^{r/(r-\rho)}(y)dy} = \frac{K - K_1 + \dfrac{Ey^{1-\beta}}{\beta-1}}{Ey^{-\beta}}.$$

It is clear that corresponding to $K = B$ in the case when $\rho = 0$

we have here $K = K_1$

and savings $= \dfrac{y}{\beta - 1}$

i.e., a constant proportion $\dfrac{r - \rho}{r(\alpha - 1) + \rho}$ of unearned income should be saved, which if $\rho = 0$ is $\dfrac{1}{\alpha - 1}$, and independent of r.

If the rate of interest is less than the rate of discounting utility, we shall have similar equations, leading to a very different result.   The marginal utility of consumption will rise at a rate $\rho - r$, and consumption will fall towards the barest subsistence level at which its marginal utility may be taken as infinite, if we disregard the possibility of suicide.   During this process all capital will be exhausted and debts incurred to the extent to which credit can be obtained, the simplest assumption on this point being that it will be possible to borrow a sum such that it is just possible to keep alive after paying the interest on it.

III

Let us next consider the problem of the determination of the rate of interest.

(α) In the first place we will suppose that everyone discounts future utility for himself or his heirs, at the same rate ρ.

Then in a state of *equilibrium* there will be no saving and

$$\frac{dx}{dt} = \frac{dc}{dt} = 0,$$

so that we have

$$x = f(a,c)$$

$$v(a) = \frac{\partial f}{\partial a} u(x)$$

$$\frac{\partial f}{\partial c} = \rho;$$

three equations to determine x, a and c.

The last equation tells us that the rate of interest as determined by the marginal productivity of capital, $\frac{\partial f}{\partial c}$, must be equal to the rate of discounting ρ.[1]

But suppose that at a given time, say the present, $\frac{\partial f}{\partial c} > \rho$. Then there will not be equilibrium, but saving, and since a great deal cannot be saved in a short time, it may be centuries before equilibrium is reached, or it may never be reached, but only approached asymptotically; and the question arises as to how, in the meantime, the rate of interest is determined, since it cannot be by the ordinary equilibrium equation of supply and demand.

The difficulty is that the rate of interest functions as a demand price for a whole quantity of capital, but as a supply price, not for a quantity of capital, but for a rate of saving. The resulting state of affairs is represented in Fig. 3, in which, however, variations in the amount of labour are neglected. This shows the demand curve for capital $r = \frac{\partial f}{\partial c}$, the ultimate supply curve $r = \rho$ and the temporary supply curve $c = c_0$. It is clear that the rate of interest is determined directly by the intersection of the demand curve with the temporary supply curve $c = c_0$. The ultimate supply curve $r = \rho$ only comes in as governing the rate at which c_0 approaches its ultimate value OM, a rate which depends roughly on the ratio of PM to QN. We see, therefore, that the rate of interest is governed primarily by the demand price, and may greatly exceed the reward ultimately necessary to induce abstinence.

[1] Equilibrium could, however, also be obtained either at bliss with $\rho < \frac{\partial f}{\partial c}$, or at the subsistence level with $\rho > \frac{\partial f}{\partial c}$. Cf. (γ) below.

Similarly, in the accounting of a Socialist State the function of the rate of interest would be to ensure the wisest use of existing capital, not to serve in any direct way as a guide to the proportion of income which should be saved.

(β) We must now try to take some account of the fact that different people discount future utility at different rates, and, quite apart from the time factor, are not so interested in their heirs as in themselves.

Let us suppose that they are not concerned with their heirs

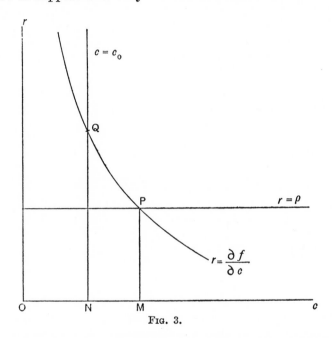

FIG. 3.

at all; that each man is charged with a share of the maintenance of such children as are necessary to maintain the population, but starts his working life without any capital and ends it without any, having spent his savings on an annuity; that within his own lifetime he has a constant utility schedule for consumption and discounts future utility at a constant rate, but that this rate may be supposed different for different people.

When such a community is in equilibrium, the rate of interest must, of course, equal the demand price of capital $\frac{\partial f}{\partial c}$. And it will also equal the "supply price," which arises in the following way. Suppose that the rate of interest is constant and equal to

r, and that the rate of discount for a given individual is ρ.   Then if $r > \rho$, he will save when he is young, not only to provide for loss of earning power in old age, but also because he can get more pounds to spend at a later date for those he forgoes spending now.   If we neglect variations in his earning power, his action can be calculated by modifying the equations of IIc to apply to a finite life as in IIb.   He will for a time accumulate capital, and then spend it before he dies.   Besides this man, we must suppose there to be in our community other men, exactly like him except for being born at different times.   The total capital possessed by n men of this sort whose birthdays are spread evenly through the period of a lifetime will be n times the *average* capital possessed by each in the course of his life.   The class of men of this sort will, therefore, possess a constant capital depending on the rate of interest, and this will be the amount of capital supplied by them at that price.   (If $\rho > r$, it may be negative, as they may borrow when young and pay back when old.)   We can then obtain the total supply curve of capital by adding together the supplies provided at a given price by each class of individual.

If, then, we neglect men's interest in their heirs, we see that capital has a definite supply price to be equated to its demand price.   This supply price depends on people's rates of discount for utility, and it can be equated to the rate of discount of the " marginal saver " in the sense that someone whose rate of discount is equal to the rate of interest will neither save nor borrow (except to provide for old age).

But the situation is different from the ordinary supply problem, in that those beyond this " margin " do not simply provide nothing, but provide a negative supply by borrowing when young against their future earnings, and so being on the average in debt.

(γ) Let us now go back to case (α) by supposing men, or rather families, to live for ever, and discount future utility at a constant rate, but let us try this time to take account of variations in the rate of discount from family to family.

For simplicity let us suppose that the amount of labour is constant, so that the total income of the country can be regarded as a function $f(c)$ of the capital only.   The rate of interest will then be $f'(c)$.   Let us also suppose that every individual could attain the maximum *conceivable* utility with a finite income x_1, and that no one could support life on less than x_2.

Now suppose equilibrium [1] is obtained with capital c, income $f(c)$ and rate of interest $f'(c)$ or r. Then those families, say $m(r)$ in number, whose rate of discount is less than r must have attained bliss or they would still be increasing their expenditure according to equation (9a). Consequently they have between them an income $m(r) \cdot x_1$. The other families, $n - m(r)$ in number (where n is the total number of families), must be down to the subsistence level, or they would still be decreasing their expenditure. Consequently they have between them a total income $\{n - m(r)\}x_2$,

whence
$$f(c) = m(r)x_1 + \{n - m(r)\}x_2$$
$$= n \cdot x_2 + m(r)\{x_1 - x_2\},$$

which, together with $r = f'(c)$, determines r and c. $m(r)$ being an increasing function of r, it is easy to see, by drawing graphs of r against $f(c)$, that the two equations have in general a unique solution.[2]

In such a case, therefore, equilibrium would be attained by a division of society into two classes, the thrifty enjoying bliss and the improvident at the subsistence level.

F. P. RAMSEY

King's College, Cambridge.

[1] We suppose each family in equilibrium, which is the only way in which that state could be maintained, since otherwise, although the savings of some might at any moment balance the borrowings of others, they would not continue to do so except by an extraordinary accident.

[2] We have neglected in this the negligible number of families for which ρ is exactly equal to r.

Comment on the Golden Rule

Robert M. Solow

In their different ways, Mrs. Robinson and Messrs. Black, Champernowne and Meade deal with the proposition (due also to Phelps) that a constant-returns-to-scale economy undergoing balanced geometric growth at its " natural " rate achieves its highest possible geometric consumption path when the share of investment in output equals the share of profits in output (or the rate of profit equals the rate of accumulation of capital). I would like to add three variations on this theme. First, I shall show that the proposition holds in the model described in my own contribution to this Symposium. Second, I shall prove the proposition in the context of a somewhat more general model of production than those discussed so far; this proof has the advantage of revealing the *entirely technological character* of the proposition itself. No amount of circumstantial story-telling should be permitted to becloud the fact that this is a theorem about production functions. The " rate of profit " plays a role only as an alias for the marginal product of capital. Third, I shall try to clarify the inwardness of the proposition by explaining its economic meaning in words of one syllable.

1. In my paper I did not record the steady-growth properties of the model because they are neither difficult nor novel. If the economy has somehow or other achieved a state of balanced growth, all machines built will be of a particular type λ; comparative statements about economies growing at the same rate, but with different values of λ, will not differ essentially in this fixed-coefficient model from analogous statements about a variable-proportions model. It is only in the process of getting from one such steady-growth path to another that the special properties of the model have any importance.

Suppose the labor force has been growing for a long time like $N_0(1 + n)^t$. In the absence of technical progress, the output of consumer goods (which will be equal to the number of machines in existence) will grow at the same rate and so will the annual output of machines. Let the latter be $M_0(1 + n)^t$. Then the total number of machines in existence

at time t is $\sum_{t-L}^{t-1} M_0(1 + n)^t = M_0(1 + n)^t \dfrac{1 - \dfrac{1}{(1 + n)^L}}{n} = M_0(1 + n)^t\, \varphi(n)$, where φ

is the same annuity function that appears in equation (1) of my paper. Since all machines in existence and being built of are of type λ, employment in the consumer-goods sector is $\lambda M_0(1 + n)^t \varphi(n)$ and employment in machine-building is $M_0(1 + n)^t c(\lambda)$. Total employment must add up to $N_0(1 + n)^t$, and this yields the equation:

(a) $\qquad N_0 = \lambda M_0\, \varphi(n) + M_0\, c(\lambda) = M_0(\lambda\varphi(n) + c(\lambda)\,)$.

The output of consumer goods is $M_0 (1 + n)^t \varphi(n)$ (the number of machines, each of which has unit capacity). Since n is given by nature, finding the highest feasible consumption path amounts to finding the highest possible value of M_0. But from (a), remembering that N_0 is another constant, the highest value of M_0 occurs if λ is chosen to minimize $\lambda\varphi(n) + c(\lambda)$. This in turn entails that:

(b) $\qquad c'(\lambda) = -\varphi(n)$.

* J. Robinson, "A Neo-classical Theorem," J. Meade, "The Effect of Savings on Consumption in a State of Steady Growth," D. G. Champernowne, "Some Implications of Golden Age Conditions when Savings Equal Profits," and J. Black, "Technical Progress and Optimum Savings," REStud, 29 (June, 1962). [The Editors.]

† "Substitution and Fixed Proportions in the Theory of Capital," REStud, 29 (June, 1962), reprinted on pp. 349–360. [The Editors.]

Comparing (b) with (1) of the original paper, one sees that along a maximal consumption path $\rho = n$, the rate of growth and the rate of interest (or the rate of profit or the marginal product of capital—see equation (4) of the paper) are equal. The key to the existence of a maximum is the fact that a reduction in λ permits a given consumption-sector labor force to produce more output, but only by requiring a larger investment-sector labor force to support the growth of capacity.

2. To get at the proposition in this way involves too many of the details of the particular model and may fail to separate the essential from the inessential. Suppose we eliminate all contextual detail and imagine an economy in which m different consumer goods are produced, according to any constant-returns-to-scale diminishing-returns technology, from s different kinds of capital goods and labor. At any instant of time—given the existing stocks of concrete goods and the supply of labor—there is a production-possibility surface listing the menu of maximal bundles of consumer goods and net increments to the capital stocks which can be made available. In a self-explanatory notation, one can write:

(c) $$C_1 = T(C_2, \ldots, C_m; \dot{K}_1, \dot{K}_2, \ldots, \dot{K}_s; K_1, K_2, \ldots, K_s; L).$$

The function T is homogeneous of degree one in all its arguments. Now suppose the supply of labor grows (and has grown) like $1e^{nt}$, and everything else grows (and has grown) to match: $C_i = c_i e^{nt}$, $K_i = k_i e^{nt}$, $\dot{K}_i = n k_i e^{nt}$. Then by substitution in (c) and use of homogeneity, one finds;

(d) $$c_1 = T(c_2, \ldots, c_m; nk_1, nk_2, \ldots, nk_s; k_1, k_2, \ldots, k_s; 1).$$

Fix the composition of the consumption bundle $c_2, \ldots, c_m$, and try to maximise c_1 (a symmetrical formulation is of course possible), by changing the k_i, which is all there is to change. One finds :

$$n \frac{\partial T}{\partial \dot{K}_i} + \frac{\partial T}{\partial K_i} = 0 \quad \text{or:}$$

(e)
$$n = -\frac{\dfrac{\partial T}{\partial K_i}}{\dfrac{\partial T}{\partial \dot{K}_i}}.$$

The righthand side in (e) is $\dfrac{\partial \dot{K}_i}{\partial K_i}$ (with all else in (c) held constant); it is in fact the rent on a dollar's worth of the i'th variety of capital goods, or the own-rate-of-interest of the i'th kind of capital good, or the marginal productivity of the i'th kind of capital good in producing itself. In any case, (e) says that along a maximal consumption path, the rate of growth equals the own-rate-of-interest or marginal product on each kind of capital good —and these must therefore all themselves be equal. This result depends *only* on the technology and the marginal equivalences that go into (c), on nothing else.

3. In loose commonsense terms, what is happening is this. Consumption, output, capital stocks and everything else are growing geometrically at the same rate, a rate independent of the ratio of capital accumulation to output. They have always been doing so. Consider these (logarithmically) parallel paths as they pass a given check point, say time zero. Had the rate of capital accumulation been higher all along, the level of output would have been higher. How much higher? That depends on the marginal product of capital. Suppose the marginal product of capital is r; then having a bit more capital $\triangle K$ at this time would yield $r \triangle K$ more in output—to be specific, $r \triangle K$ extra output of capital

itself. But not all of this is available for consumption. Having a bit more capital now commits the economy (under the steady-growth rules of the game) to some additional investment now and in the future, to *keep* the slightly larger capital stock growing at the fixed rate g. We are talking about (virtual) movements from one geometric path to another. In particular, an extra bit of capital $\triangle K$ now means that an output of $g\triangle K$ of capital goods is required simply to keep the new little bit growing at rate g. Clearly, if $r\triangle K > g\triangle K$ or $r > g$, having a bit more capital now will yield some extra consumption now (and forever). If $r < g$, having a bit more capital now would actually siphon off enough productive capacity to the investment sector to reduce consumption. Consumption is at a maximum when $r = g$, when the marginal product of capital equals the rate of growth. Profit, as a kind of income receipt, has nothing to do with it; neither does it matter who saves what. The rate of profit enters only as we take it to be a measure of the value of the marginal product of a dollar's worth of capital goods. A careful reader of Mrs. Robinson's article would realise this.

ROBERT M. SOLOW.

AN EXACT CONSUMPTION-LOAN MODEL OF INTEREST WITH OR WITHOUT THE SOCIAL CONTRIVANCE OF MONEY*

PAUL A. SAMUELSON

M Y FIRST published paper[1] has come of age, and at a time when the subjects it dealt with have come back into fashion. It developed the equilibrium conditions for a rational consumer's lifetime consumption-saving pattern, a problem more recently given by Harrod the useful name of "hump saving" but which Landry, Böhm-Bawerk, Fisher, and others had touched on long before my time.[2] It dealt only with a single individual and did not discuss the mutual determination by all individuals of the

* Research aid from the Ford Foundation is gratefully acknowledged.

[1] "A Note on Measurement of Utility," *Review of Economic Studies*, IV (1937), 155–61.

[2] As an undergraduate student of Paul Douglas at Chicago, I was struck by the fact that we might, from the marginal utility schedule of consumptions, deduce saving behavior exactly in the same way that we might deduce gambling behavior. Realizing that, watching the consumer's gambling responses to varying odds, we could deduce his numerical marginal utilities, it occurred to me that, by watching the consumer's saving responses to varying interest rates, we might similarly measure his marginal utilities, and thus the paper was born. (I knew and pointed out, p. 155, n. 2; p. 160, that such a cardinal measurement of utility hinged on a certain refutable "independence" hypothesis.)

market interest rates which each man had to accept parametrically as given to him.

Now I should like to give a complete general equilibrium solution to the determination of the time-shape of interest rates. This sounds easy, but actually it is very hard, so hard that I shall have to make drastic simplifications in order to arrive at exact results. For while Böhm and Fisher have given us the essential insights into the pure theory of interest, neither they nor other writers seem to have grappled with the following tough problem: in order to define an equilibrium path of interest in a perfect capital market endowed with *perfect certainty*, you have to determine *all* interest rates between now and the end of time; every finite time period points beyond itself!

Some interesting mathematical boundary problems, a little like those in the modern theories of dynamic programming, result from this analysis. And the way is paved for a rigorous attack on a simple model involving money as a store of value and a medium of exchange. My essay concludes with some provocative remarks about the field of social collusions, a subject of vital importance for political economy and of great analytical interest to the modern theorist.

THE PROBLEM STATED

Let us assume that men enter the labor market at about the age of twenty. They work for forty-five years or so and then live for fifteen years in retirement. (As children they are part of their parents' consumptions, and we take no note of them.) Naturally, they want to consume in their old age, and, in the absence of comprehensive social security—an institution which has important bearing on interest rates and saving—men will want to consume less than they produce during their working years so that they can consume something in the years when they produce nothing.

If there were only Robinson Crusoe, he would hope to put by some durable goods which could be drawn on in his old age. He would, so to speak, want to trade with Mother Nature current consumption goods in return for future consumption goods. And if goods kept perfectly, he could at worst always make the trade through time on a one-to-one basis, and we could say that the interest rate was zero ($i = 0$). If goods kept imperfectly, like ice or radium, Crusoe might have to face a negative real interest rate, $i < 0$. If goods were like rabbits or yeast, reproducing without supervision at compound interest, he would face a positive rate of interest, $i > 0$. This last case is usually considered to be technologically the most realistic one: that is, machines and round-about processes (rather than rabbits) are considered to have a "net productivity," and this is taken to be brute fact. (Böhm himself, after bitterly criticizing naïve productivity theorists and criticizing

Thünen and others for assuming such a fact, ends up with his own celebrated third cause for interest, which also asserts the fact of net productivity. Contrary to much methodological discussion, there is nothing circular about assuming brute facts—that is all we can do; we certainly cannot deduce them, although, admittedly, we can hope by experience to refute falsely alleged facts.)

For the present purpose, I shall make the extreme assumption that nothing will keep at all. Thus no intertemporal trade with Nature is possible (that is, for all such exchanges we would have $i = -1!$). If Crusoe were alone, he would obviously die at the beginning of his retirement years.

But we live in a world where new generations are always coming along. Formerly we used to support our parents in their old age. That is now out of fashion. But cannot men during their productive years give up some of their product to bribe other men to support them in their retirement years? Thus, forty-year-old A gives some of his product to twenty-year-old B, so that when A gets to be seventy-five he can receive some of the product that B is then producing.

Our problem, then, is this: In a stationary population (or, alternatively, one growing in any prescribed fashion) what will be the intertemporal terms of trade or interest rates that will spring up spontaneously in ideally competitive markets?

SIMPLIFYING ASSUMPTIONS

To make progress, let us make convenient assumptions. Break each life up into thirds: men produce one unit of product in period 1 and one unit in period 2; in period 3 they retire and produce nothing. (No one dies in midstream.)

In specifying consumption preferences,

I suppose that each man's tastes can be summarized by an ordinal utility function of the consumptions of the three periods of his life: $U = U(C_1, C_2, C_3)$. This is the same in every generation and has the usual regular indifference-curve concavities, but for much of the argument nothing is said about whether, subjectively, men systematically discount future consumptions or satisfactions. (Thus Böhm's second cause of interest may or may not be operative; it could even be reversed, men being supposed to overvalue the future!)

In addition to ignoring Böhm's second cause of systematic time preference, I am in a sense also denying or reversing his first cause of interest, in that we are *not* supposing that society is getting more prosperous as time passes or that any single man can expect to be more prosperous at a later date in his life, since, on the contrary, during his years of retirement he must look forward to producing even less than during his working years.

Finally, recall our assumption that no goods keep, no trade with Nature being possible, and hence Böhm's third technological cause of interest is being denied.

Under these assumptions, what will be the equilibrium time path of interest rates?

INDIVIDUAL SAVING FUNCTIONS

The simplest case to tackle to answer this question is that of a stationary population, which has always been stationary in numbers and will always be stationary. This ideal case sidesteps the difficult "planning-until-infinity" aspect of the problem. In it births are given by $B_t = B$, the same constant for all positive and negative t.

Now consider any time t. There are B men of age one, B men of age two, and B retired men of age three. Since each

producer produces 1 unit, total product is $B + B$. Now, for convenience of symbols, let $R_t = 1/(1 + i_t)$ be the discount rate between goods (chocolates) of period t traded for chocolates of the next period, $t + 1$. Thus, if $R_t = 0.5$, you must promise me two chocolates tomorrow to get me to part with one chocolate today, the interest rate being 100 per cent per period. If $R_t = 1$, the interest rate is zero, and tomorrow's chocolates cost 1.0 of today's. If $R_t > 1$, say $R_t = 1.5$, the interest rate is negative, and one future chocolate costs 1.5 of today's. (Clearly, R_t is the price of tomorrow's chocolates expressed in terms of today's chocolates as numeraire.)

We seek the equilibrium levels of . . . R_t, R_{t+1}, . . . , that will clear the competitive markets in which present and future goods exchange against each other.

At time t each man who is beginning his life faces[3] the budget equation,

$$C_1 + C_2R_t + C_3R_tR_{t+1}$$
$$= 1 + 1R_t + 0R_tR_{t+1}. \tag{1}$$

This merely says that the total discounted value of his life's consumptions must equal the discounted value of his productions. Subject to this constraint, he will, for each given R_t and R_{t+1}, determine an optimal (C_1, C_2, C_3) to maximize $U(C_1, C_2, C_3)$, which we can summarize by the "demand" functions,

$$C_i = C_i(R_t, R_{t+1}) \qquad (i = 1, 2, 3). \tag{2}$$

---

[3] I rule out, as I did explicitly in my 1937 paper (p.160), the Ulysses-Strotz-Allais phenomenon whereby time perspective distorts present decisions planned for the future from later actual decisions. Thus, if at the end of period 1 his ordinal preference follows $V(C_1, C_2, C_3)$ rather than $U(C_1, C_2, C_3)$, I am assuming $(\partial V/\partial C_i)/(\partial V/\partial C_j) \equiv (\partial U/\partial C_i)/(\partial U/\partial C_j)$. Hence all later decisions will ratify earlier plans. For a valuable discussion of this problem see R. H. Strotz, "Myopia and Inconsistency in Dynamic Utility Maximization," *Review of Economic Studies*, XXIII (1956), 165–80.

It might be convenient for us to work with "net" or "excess demands" of each man: these are the algebraic differences between what a man consumes and what he produces. Net demands in this sense are the negative of what men usually call "saving," and, in deference to capital theory, I shall work with such "net saving" as defined by

$$S_1 = S_1(R_t, R_{t+1}) = 1 - C_1(R_t, R_{t+1}),$$

$$S_2 = S_2(R_t, R_{t+1}) = 1 - C_2(R_t, R_{t+1}), \quad (3)$$

$$S_3 = S_3(R_t, R_{t+1}) = 0 - C_3(R_t, R_{t+1}).$$

In old age presumably S_3 is negative, matched by positive youthful saving, so as to satisfy for all (R_t, R_{t+1}) the budget identity,

$$S_1(R_t, R_{t+1}) + R_t S_2(R_t, R_{t+1})$$
$$+ R_t R_{t+1} S_3(R_t, R_{t+1}) = 0. \quad (4)$$

Of course, these functions are subject to all the restrictions of modern consumption theory of the ordinal utility or revealed preference type. Thus, with consumption in every period being a "superior good," we can infer that $\partial C_3/\partial R_{t+1} < 0$ and $\partial S_3/\partial R_{t+1} > 0$. (This says that raising the interest rate earned on savings carried over into retirement must increase retirement consumption.) We cannot unambiguously deduce the sign of $\partial S_1/\partial R_t$ and other terms, for the reasons implicit in modern consumption theory.

We can similarly work out the saving functions for men born a period later, which will be of the form $S_i(R_{t+1}, R_{t+2})$, etc., containing, of course, the later interest rates they will face—likewise for earlier interest rates facing men born earlier. Finally, our fundamental condition of clearing the market is this: Total net saving for the community must can-

cel out to zero in every period. (Remember that no goods keep and that real net investment is impossible, all loans being "consumption" loans.)

At any time t there exist B_t men of the first period, B_{t-1} men of the second period, and B_{t-2} men of the third period. The sum of their savings gives us the fundamental equilibrium condition:

$$0 = B_t S_1(R_t, R_{t+1}) + B_{t-1} S_2(R_{t-1}, R_t)$$
$$+ B_{t-2} S_3(R_{t-2}, R_{t-1}), \quad (5)$$

for every t. Note that in S_2 we have the interest rates of one earlier period than in S_1, and in S_3 we have still earlier interest rates (in fact, interest rates that are, at time t, already history and no longer to be determined.)

We have such an equation for every t, and if we take any finite stretch of time and write out the equilibrium conditions, we always find them containing discount rates from before the finite period and discount rates from afterward. We never seem to get enough equations: lengthening our time period turns out always to add as many new unknowns as it supplies equations, as will be spelled out later in equations (14).

THE STATIONARY CASE

We can try to cut the Gordian knot by our special assumption of stationariness, namely,

$$\ldots B_{t-1} = B_t = B_{t+1} = \ldots$$

$$= B, \text{ a given constant for all time}$$
$$\ldots R_{t-1} = R_t = R_{t+1} = \ldots \quad (6)$$

$$= R, \text{ the unknown discount rate.}$$

The first of these is a demographic datum; the second assumption of non-changing interest rates is a conjecture whose consistency we must explore and verify.

Now substituting relations (6) in equation (5), we get one equilibrium equation to determine our one unknown R, namely,

$$0 = BS_1(R, R) + BS_2(R, R) \\ + BS_3(R, R) . \tag{7}$$

By inspection, we recognize a solution of equation (7) to be $R = 1$, or $i = 0$: that is, zero interest must be one equilibrium rate under our conditions.[4]

Why? Because

$$B[S_1(1, 1) + 1S_2(1, 1) + 1S_3(1, 1)] = 0$$

by virtue of the budget identity (4).

Can a common-sense explanation of this somewhat striking result be given? Let me try. In a stationary system everyone goes through the same life-cycle, albeit at different times. Giving over goods now to an older man is figuratively giving over goods to *yourself* when old. At what rate does one give over goods to one's later self? At $R > 1$, or $R < 1$, or $R = 1$? To answer this, note that a chocolate today *is* a chocolate today, and when middle-aged A today gives over a chocolate to old B, there is a one-to-one *physical* transfer of chocolates, none melting in the transfer and none sticking to the hands of a broker. So, heuristically, we see that the hypothetical "transfer *through time*" of the chocolates must be at $R = 1$ with the interest rate i exactly zero.

Note that this result is quite independent of whether or not people have a systematic subjective preference for present consumption over future. Why? Because we have assumed that if *anyone* has such a systematic preference, *everyone* has such a systematic preference. There is no one any different in the system, no outsider—so to speak—to exact

a positive interest rate from the impatient consumers.[5]

A BIOLOGICAL THEORY OF INTEREST AND POPULATION GROWTH

A zero rate of population growth was seen to be consistent with a zero rate of interest for a consumption-loan world. I now turn to the case of a population growing exponentially or geometrically. Now

$$B_t = B(1 + m)^t, \quad \text{with}$$

$$B_{t+1} = (1 + m)B_t = (1 + m)^2 B_{t-1} \ldots .$$

For $m > 0$, we have growth; for $m < 0$, decay; for $m = 0$, our previous case of a stationary population. As before, we suppose

$$\ldots R_{t-1} = R_t = R_{t+1} = \ldots$$

$$= R, \text{ a constant through time.}$$

Now our clearing-of-the-market equation is

$$0 = B(1 + m)^t S_1(R, R) \\ + B(1 + m)^{t-1} S_2(R, R) \quad (8) \\ + B(1 + m)^{t-2} S_3(R, R) ;$$

or, cancelling $B(1 + m)^t$, we have

$$0 = S_1(R, R) + (1 + m)^{-1} S_2(R, R) \\ + (1 + m)^{-2} S_3(R, R) . \tag{9}$$

Recalling our budget identity (4), we realize $R = (1 + m)^{-1}$ or $i = m$ is one root satisfying the equation, giving

$$0 = S_1(R, R) + RS_2(R, R) + R^2 S_3(R, R) .$$

We have therefore established the following paradoxical result:

[4] We shall see that $R = 1$ is not the only root of equation (7) and that there are multiple equilibriums.

[5] If productive opportunities were to exist, Mother Nature would operate as an important outsider, with whom trade could take place, and our conclusion would be modified. But recall our strong postulate that such technological opportunities are non-existent.

THEOREM: Every geometrically growing consumption-loan economy has an equilibrium market rate of interest exactly equal to its biological percentage growth rate.

Thus, if the net reproductive rate gives a population growth of 15 per cent per period, $i = 0.15$ is the corresponding market rate of interest. If, as in Sweden or Ireland, $m < 0$ and population decays, the market rate of interest will be negative, with $i < 0$ and $R > 1$!

OPTIMUM PROPERTY OF THE BIOLOGICAL INTEREST RATE

The equality of the market rate of interest in a pure consumption-loan world to the rate of population growth was deduced solely from mechanically finding a root of the supply-demand equations that clear the market. Experience often confirms what faith avers: that competitive market relations achieve some kind of an optimum.

Does the saving-consumption pattern given by $S_1(R, R)$, $S_2(R, R)$, $S_3(R, R)$, where $R = 1/(1 + m)$, represent some kind of a social optimum? One would guess that, if it does maximize something, this equilibrium pattern probably maximizes the "lifetime (ordinal) well-being of a representative person, subject to the resources available to him (and to every other representative man) over his lifetime." Or, what seems virtually the same thing, consider a cross-sectional family or clan that has an unchanging age distribution because the group remains in statistical equilibrium, though individuals are born and die. Such a clan will divide its available resources to maximize a welfare function differing only in scale from each man's utility function and will achieve the same result as the biological growth rate.

To test this optimality conjecture, first stick to the stationary population case. The representative man is thought to maximize $U(C_1, C_2, C_3)$, subject to

$$C_1 + C_2 + C_3 = 1 + 1, \quad (10)$$

$1 + 1$ being the lifetime product available to each man. The solution to this technocratic welfare problem (free in its formulation and solution of all mention of prices or interest rates) requires

$$\frac{\partial U/\partial C_2}{\partial U/\partial C_1} = \frac{\partial U/\partial C_3}{\partial U/\partial C_1}. \quad (11)$$

But this formulation is seen to be identical with that of a single maximizing man facing market discount rates $R_1 = R_2 = 1$. Hence the solution of equations (10) and (11) is exactly that given earlier by equation (3): that is, our present welfare problem has, for its optimality solution,

$$1 - C_1 = S_1(1, 1),$$
$$1 - C_2 = S_2(1, 1),$$
$$0 - C_3 = S_3(1, 1).$$

Now that we have verified our conjecture for the stationary $m = 0$ case, we can prove it for population growing like $B(1 + m)^t$, where $m \gtrless 0$. As before, we maximize $U(C_1, C_2, C_3)$ for the representative man. But what resources are now available to him? Recall that in a growing population the age distribution is permanently skewed in favor of the younger productive ages: society and each clan has an age distribution proportional to $[1, 1/(1 + m), 1/(1 + m)^2]$ and has therefore a per capita output to divide in consumption among the three age classes satisfying

$$C_1 + \frac{1}{1 + m} C_2 + \frac{1}{(1 + m)^2} C_3$$
$$= 1 + \frac{1}{1 + m}. \quad (12)$$

By following a representative man throughout his life and remembering that there are always $(1 + m)^{-1}$ just older than he and $(1 + m)^{-2}$ two periods older, we derive this same "budget" or availibility equation. Subject to equation (12), we maximize $U(C_1, C_2, C_3)$ and necessarily end up with the same conditions as would a competitor facing the biological market interest rate $R_1 = R_2 = 1/(1 + m)$: namely,

$$1 - C_1 = S_1(R, R),$$
$$1 - C_2 = S_2(R, R),$$
$$0 - C_3 = S_3(R, R), \quad (13)$$

$$R = \frac{1}{1 + m}.$$

Hence the identity of the social optimality conditions and the biological market interest theory has been demonstrated.[6]

COMMON-SENSE EXPLANATION OF BIOLOGICAL MARKET INTEREST RATE

Productivity theorists have always related interest to the biological habits of rabbits and cows. And Gustav Cassel long ago developed a striking (but rather nonsensical) biological theory relating

---

[6] If U has the usual quasi-concavity, this social optimum will be unique—whether U does or does not have the time-symmetry that is sometimes (for concreteness) assumed in later arguments. Not only will the representative man's utility U be maximized, but so will the "total" of social utility enjoyed over a long period of time: specifically, the divergence from attainable bliss

$$[U(C_1, C_2, C_3) - U^*] + [U(C_1, C_2, C_3)$$
$$- U^*] + \ldots$$

over all time will be miminized, where U^* is the utility achieved when $R_1 = 1 = R_2$ and $S_i = S_i(1, 1)$. This theorem may require that we use an ordinal utility indicator that is concave in the C_i, as it is always open to us to do.

Of course, this entire footnote and the related text need obvious modifications if $m \neq 0$.

interest to the life-expectancy of men of means and their alleged propensity to go from maintaining capital to the buying of annuities at an allegedly critical positive i. I seem to be the first, outside a slave economy, to develop a biological theory of interest relating it to the reproductivity of human mothers.

Is there a common-sense market explanation of this (to me at least) astonishing result? I suppose it would go like this: in a growing population men of twenty outnumber men of forty; and retired men are outnumbered by workers more than in the ratio of the work span to the retirement span. With more workers to support them, the aged live better than in the stationary state—the excess being positive interest on their savings.

Such an explanation cannot be deemed entirely convincing. Outside of social security and family altruism, the aged have no claims on the young: cold and selfish competitive markets will not teleologically respect the old; the aged will get only what supply and demand impute to them.

So we might try another more detailed explanation. Recall that men of forty or of period 2 bargain with men of twenty or period 1, trying to bribe the latter to provide them with consumption in their retirement. (Men of over sixty-five or of period 3 can make fresh bargains with no one: after retirement it is too late for them to try to provide for their old age.) In a growing population there are more period 1 men for period 2 men to bargain with; this presumably confers a competitive advantage on period 2 men, the manifestation of it being the positive interest rate.

So might go the explanation. It is at least superficially plausible, and it does qualitatively suggest a positive interest rate when population is growing, although perhaps it falls short of explaining the remarkable quantitative identity between the growth rates of interest and of population.

THE INFINITY PARADOX REVEALED

But will the explanation survive rigorous scrutiny? Is it true, in a growing or in a stationary population, that twenty-year-olds are, in fact, overconsuming so that the middle-aged can provide for their retirement? Specifically, in the stationary case where $R = 1$, is it necessarily true that $S_1(1, 1) < 0$? Study of $U(C_1, C_2, C_3)$ shows how doubtful such a general result would be; thus, if there is no systematic subjective time preference so that U is a function *symmetric* in its arguments, it would be easy to show that $C_1 = C_2 = C_3 = \frac{2}{3}$, with $S_1(1, 1) = S_2(1, 1) = +\frac{1}{3}$ and $S_3(1, 1) = -\frac{2}{3}$. Contrary to our scenario, the middle-aged are *not* turning over to the young what the young will later make good to them in retirement support.

THE TWO-PERIOD CASE

The paradox is delineated more clearly if we suppose but two equal periods of life—work and retirement. Now it becomes *impossible* for *any* worker to find a worker younger than himself to be bribed to support him in old age. Whatever the trend of births, there is but one equilibrium saving pattern possible: during working years, consumption equals product and saving is zero; the same during the brutish years of retirement. What equilibrium interest rate, or R, will prevail? Since no transactions take place, $R = 0/0$, so to speak, and appears rather indeterminate—and rather academic. However, if men desperately want *some* consumption at *all* times, only $R = \infty$ can be regarded as the (virtual) equilibrium rate, with interest equal to -100 per cent per period.[7]

We think we know the right answer just given in the two-period case. Let us test our previous mathematical methods. Now our equations are much as before and can be summarized by:

Maximize $U(C_1, C_2) = U(1 - S_1, 0 - S_2)$

subject to $S_1 + R_t S_2 = 0$.

The resulting saving functions, $S_1(R_t)$ and $S_2(R_t)$, are subject to the budget identity,

$$S_1(R_t) + R_t S_2(R_t) \equiv 0 \text{ for all } R_t. \quad (4')$$

Clearing the market requires

$$0 = B_t S_1(R_t) + B_{t-1} S_2(R_{t-1}) \quad \text{for} \quad (5')$$
$$t = 0, \pm 1, \pm 2, \ldots.$$

If $B_t = B(1 + m)^t$ and $R_t = R_{t+1} = \ldots = R$, our final equation becomes

$$0 = B\left[S_1(R) + \frac{1}{1 + m} S_2(R)\right]. \quad (8')$$

The budget equation $(4')$ assures us that equation $(8')$ has a solution:

$$R = \frac{1}{1 + m} \quad \text{or} \quad m = i.$$

$$\text{with} \quad 0 < S_1(R) = -RS_2(R).$$

So the two-period mathematics appears to give us the same answer as before—a biological rate of interest equal to the rate of population growth.

Yet we earlier deduced that *there can be no voluntary saving in a two-period world*. Instead of $S_1 > 0$, we must have $S_1 = 0 = S_2$ with $R = +\infty$. How can we reconcile this with the mathematics?

---

[7] A later numerical example, where $U = \log C_1 + \log C_2 + \log C_3$, shows that cases can arise where no positive R, however large, will clear the market. I adopt the harmless convention of setting $R = \infty$ in every case, even if the limit as $R \to \infty$ does not wipe out the discrepancy between supply and demand.

We substitute $S_1 = 0 = S_2$ in equation (5′) or equation (8′), and indeed this does satisfy the clearing-of-the-market equation. Apparently our one equilibrium equation in our one unknown R has more than a single solution! And the relevant one for a free market is *not* that given by our biological or demographic theory of interest, even though our earlier social optimality argument does perfectly fit the two-period case.

THE PARADOX CONTEMPLATED

The transparent two-period case alerts us to the possibility that in the three-period (or n-period) case, the fundamental equation of supply and demand may have multiple solutions. And, indeed, it does.[8] We see that

$$\lim_{R \to \infty} S_1(R, R) = -\infty$$

is indeed a valid mathematical solution. This raises the following questions:

Is a condition of no saving with dismal retirement consumption and interest rate of -100 per cent per period thinkable as the economically correct equilibrium for a free market?

Surely, the non-myopic middle-aged will do almost anything to make retirement consumption, C_3 non-zero?[9]

One might conjecture that the fact that, in the three-period model, workers can always find younger workers to bargain with is a crucial difference from the two-period case.[10] To investigate the

[8] There is nothing surprising about multiple solutions in economics: not infrequently income effects make possible other intersections, including the possibility of an infinite number where demand and supply curves coincide.

[9] Before answering these questions, it would be well to decide what the word "surely" in the previous sentence means. Surely, no sentence beginning with the word "surely" can validly contain a question mark at its end? However, one paradox is enough for one article, and I shall stick to my economist's last.

problem, we must drop the assumption of a population that is, always has been, and always will be stationary (or exponentially growing or exponentially decaying). For within that ambiguous context $R = 1 (R < 1, R > 1)$ was indeed an impeccable solution, in the sense that no one can point to a violated equilibrium condition. (Exactly the same can be said of the two-period case, even though we "know" the impeccable solution is economically nonsense.)

We must give mankind a beginning. So, once upon a time, B men were born into the labor force. Then B more. Then B more. Until what? Until . . . ? Or until no more men are born? Must we give mankind an end as well as a beginning? Even the Lord rested after the beginning, so let us tackle one problem at a time and keep births forever constant. Our equilibrium equations, with the constant B's omitted, now become

$$S_1(R_1, R_2) + 0 + 0 = 0\,,$$

$$S_2(R_1, R_2) + S_1(R_2, R_3) + 0 = 0\,,$$

$$S_3(R_1, R_2) + S_2(R_2, R_3)$$
$$+ S_1(R_3, R_4) = 0\,,$$

$$S_3(R_2, R_3) + S_2(R_3, R_4) \qquad (14)$$
$$+ S_1(R_4, R_5) = 0\,,$$

. . . . ,

$$S_3(R_{t-2}, R_{t-1}) + S_2(R_{t-1}, R_t)$$
$$+ S_1(R_t, R_{t+1}) = 0\,,$$

. . . .

We feel that $S_1 \equiv 0 \equiv S_2 \equiv S_3$, while a mathematical solution, is not the economically relevant one. Since $S_1(1, 1)$, $S_2(1, 1)$, and $S_3(1, 1)$ do satisfy the last

[10] By introducing overlap between workers of different ages, the three-period model is essentially equivalent to a general n-period model or to the continuous-time model of real life.

of the written equations, we dare hope[11] that the Invisible Hand will ultimately work its way to the socially optimal biological-interest configuration—or that the solution to equation (14) satisfies

$$\lim_{t\to\infty} R_t = 1, \quad S_i(R_t, R_{t+1})$$
$$= S_i(1, 1), \quad (i = 1, 2, 3). \tag{15}$$

THE IMPOSSIBILITY THEOREM

But have we any right to hope that the free market will even ultimately approach the specified social optimum? Does not the two-period case rob us of hope? Will not all the trade that the three-period case makes possible consist of middle-aged period 2 people giving consumption to young period 1 people in return for getting consumption back from them one period later? Do not such voluntary mutual-aid compacts suggest that, if R_t does approach a limit x, it must be such as to make $S_1(x, x) < 0$? Whereas, for many men[12] not too subject to systematic preference for the present over the future (not too affected by Böhm's second cause of interest), we expect $S_1(1, 1) > 0$.

A colleague, whose conjectures are

[11] Our confidence in this would be enhanced if the linear difference equation relating small deviations $r_t = R_t - 1$ had characteristic roots all less than 1 in absolute value. Thus $a_0 r_{t+3} + a_1 r_{t+2} + a_2 r_{t+1} + a_3 r_t = 0$, where the a_i are given in terms of the $S_i(R_t, R_{t+1})$ functions and their partial derivatives, evaluated at $R_t = 1 R_{t+1}$. Logically, this would be neither quite necessary nor sufficient: not sufficient, since the initial R_0, R_1, R_2 might be so far from 1 as to make the linear approximations irrelevant; not necessary, since, with one root less than unity in absolute value, we might ride in toward $R = 1$ on a razor's edge. In any case, as our later numerical example shows, our hope is a vain one.

[12] There is admittedly some econometric evidence that many young adults do dissave, to acquire assets and for other reasons. Some modifications of exposition would have to be made to allow for this.

often better than many people's theorems, has suggested to me that in the three-period or n-period case I am taking too bilateral a view of trade. We might end up with $S_1 > 0$ and encounter no contradictions to voluntary trade by virtue of the fact that young men trade with *anyone* in the market: they do not know or care that all or part of the motive for trade with them comes from the desire of the middle-aged to provide for retirement. The present young are content to be trading with the present old (or, for that matter, with the unborn or dead): all they care about is that their trades take place at the quoted market prices; and, if some kind of triangular or multilateral offsetting among the generations can take place and result in $S_1(R_t, R_{t+1})$ positive and becoming closer and closer to $S_1(1, 1) > 0$, why cannot this happen?

I, too, found the multilateral notion appealing. But the following considerations—of a type I do not recall seeing treated anywhere—suggest to me that the ultimate approach to $R = 1$ and $S_1(1, 1) > 0$ is quite impossible.

List all men from the beginning to time t. All the voluntary trades ever made must be mutually advantageous. If A gives something to B and B does nothing for A directly in return, we know B must be doing something for some C, who does do something good for A. (Of course, C might be more than one man, and there might be many-linked connections within C.)

Now consider a time when $S_1(R_t, R_{t+1})$ has become positive, with $S_2(R_{t-1}, R_t)$ also positive. Young man A is then giving goods to old man B. Young man A expects something in return and will actually two periods later be getting goods from someone. From whom? It certainly cannot be directly from B: B will be dead then. Let it be from someone called C. Can B ever do anything good for such a C, or have in the past done so? No. B only has produce during his first two periods of life, and all the good he can do anyone must be to people who were born before him or just after him. That *never* includes C. So the postulated pattern of $S_1 > 0$ is logically impossible in a free market: and hence $R_t = 1 = R_{t+1}$, as an exact or approximate relation, is impossible. (Note that, for some special pattern of time preference, the competitive solution *might* coincide with the "biological optimum.")

A concrete case will illustrate all this. The purest Marshallian case of unitary price and income elasticities can be characterized by $U = \log C_1 + \log C_2 + \log C_3$, where all systematic time preference is replaced by *symmetry*.

A maximum of

$$\sum_1^3 \log C_i \text{ subject to} \qquad (16)$$
$$C_1 + R_1 C_2 + R_1 R_2 C_3 = 1 + R_1$$

implies

$$R_1 = \frac{\partial U / \partial C_2}{\partial U / \partial C_1} = \frac{1/C_2}{1/C_1},$$

$$R_1 R_2 = \frac{\partial U / \partial C_3}{\partial U / \partial C_1} = \frac{1/C_3}{1/C_1};$$

and, after combining this with the budget equation, we end up with saving functions,

$$S_1(R_1, R_2) = \frac{2}{3} - \frac{R_1}{3},$$

$$S_2(R_1, R_2) = \frac{2}{3} - \frac{1}{3R_1}, \qquad (17)$$

$$S_3(R_1, R_2) = 0 - \frac{1}{3R_1 R_2} - \frac{1}{3R_2}.$$

Equations (14) now take the form

$$\frac{2}{3} - \frac{R_1}{3} + 0 + 0 = 0,$$

$$\frac{2}{3} - \frac{1}{3R_1} + \left(\frac{2}{3} - \frac{R_2}{3}\right) + 0 = 0,$$

$$-\frac{1}{3R_1 R_2} - \frac{1}{3R_2} + \left(\frac{2}{3} - \frac{1}{3R_2}\right)$$
$$+ \left(\frac{2}{3} - \frac{R_3}{3}\right) = 0,$$

$$\left(-\frac{1}{3R_2 R_3} - \frac{1}{3R_3}\right) + \left(\frac{2}{3} - \frac{1}{3R_3}\right) \qquad (18)$$
$$+ \left(\frac{2}{3} - \frac{R_4}{3}\right) = 0,$$

$$\cdots \cdots \cdots \cdots \cdots$$

$$\left(-\frac{1}{3R_{t-1}R_{t-2}} - \frac{1}{3R_{t-1}}\right)$$
$$+ \left(\frac{2}{3} - \frac{1}{3R_{t-1}}\right) + \left(\frac{2}{3} - \frac{R_t}{3}\right) = 0,$$

$$\cdots \cdots \cdots \cdots \cdots$$

Aside from initial conditions, this can be written in the recursive form,

$$R_t = 4 - \frac{1}{R_{t-1}R_{t-2}} - \frac{2}{R_{t-1}}. \qquad (19)$$

Note that $\partial S_3(R_1, R_2) \equiv 0$ made our third-order difference equation degenerate into a second-order difference equation.

If we expand the last equation around $R_{t-2} = 1 = R_{t-1}$, retaining only linear terms and working in terms of deviations from the equilibrium level, $r_t = R_t - 1$, we get the recursive system,

$$r_{t+2} = 3r_{t+1} + r_t. \qquad (20)$$

which obviously explodes away from $r = 0$ and $R = 1$ for all small perturbations from such an equilibrium. This confirms our proof that the *social optimum configuration can never here be reached by the competitive market, or even be approached in ever so long a time.*

Where does the solution to (18) eventually go? Its first few R's are numerically calculated to be $[R_1, R_2, R_3, \ldots] = [2, 3\frac{1}{2}, 3\frac{2}{7}, \ldots]$. It is plain that the limiting R_t exceeds 1; hence a negative interest rate i is being approached by oscillations. Substituting $R_{t+2} = R_{t+1} = R_t = x$ in equation (19), we get the following cubic equation to solve for possible equilibrium levels:[13]

$$x = 4 - \frac{1}{x^2} - \frac{2}{x} \quad \text{or}$$

$$\hspace{4cm} (21)$$

$$x^3 - 4x^2 + 2x + 1 = 0 \, .$$

We know that $x = 1$, the irrelevant optimal level, is one root; so, dividing it out, we end up with

$$(x - 1)(x^2 - 3x - 1) = 0 \, .$$

Solving the quadratic, we have

$$x = \frac{3 \pm \sqrt{9 + 4}}{2}$$

or

$$x = \frac{3}{2} + \frac{\sqrt{13}}{2} = 3.3028 \text{ approx.}$$

for the asymptote approached by the free competitive market. The other root, $(3 - \sqrt{13})/2$, corresponds to a negative R, which is economically meaningless, in that it implies that the more we give up of today's consumption, the more we must give up of tomorrow's.

Our meaningful positive root, $R = 3.303$, corresponds to an ultimate negative interest rate,

$$i = \frac{1 - R}{R} = -\frac{2.303}{3.303} \, ,$$

[13] Martin J. Bailey has pointed out to me that the budget equation and the clearing-of-the-market equations do, in the stationary state, imply $S_1 = RS_3$ whenever $R \neq 1$, a fact which can be used to give an alternative demonstration of possible equilibrium values.

which implies that consumption loans lose about two-thirds of their principal in one period. This is here the competitive price to avoid retirement starvation.[14]

RECAPITULATION

The task of giving an exact description of a pure consumption-loan interest model is finished. We end up, in the stationary population case, with a negative market interest rate, rather than with the biological zero interest rate corresponding to the social optimum for the representative man. This was proved by the impossibility theorem and verified by an arithmetic example.

A corresponding result will hold for changing population where $m \gtrless 0$. The actual competitive market rate i_m will always be negative and always less than the biological optimality rate m.[15] And

[14] In other examples, this competitive solution would not deviate so much from the $i = m$ biological optimum. But it is important to realize that solutions to equations (14) that come from quasi-concave utility functions—with or without systematic time preference—*cannot* be counted on to approach asymptotically the biological optimum configuration of equation (13).

In this case the linear approximation gives for $r_t = R_t - 3.297$ the recursion relation

$$r_{t+2} = \frac{1}{(3.297)^3} r_{t+1} + \frac{2}{(3.297)^2} r_t \, .$$

This difference equation has roots easily shown to be less than 1 in absolute value, so the local stability of our competitive equilibrium is assured.

[15] Writing $\lambda = 1/(1 + m)$, our recursion relation (14) becomes

$$0 = S_1(R_t, R_{t+1}) + \lambda S_2(R_{t-1}, R_t)$$
$$+ \lambda^2 S_3(R_{t-2}, R_{t-1}) \, .$$

For the case where $U = \Sigma \log C_i$, our recursion relation (18) becomes

$$R_t = 2(1 + \lambda) - \frac{\lambda^2}{R_{t-1}R_{t-2}} - \frac{\lambda^2}{R_{t-1}} - \frac{\lambda}{R_{t-1}} \, .$$

Then $x = R_t = R_{t-1} = R_{t-2}$ gives a cubic equation with biological root corresponding to $x = \lambda$ and

increasing the productive years relative to the retirement years of zero product would undoubtedly still leave us with a negative interest rate, albeit one that climbs ever closer to zero.

Is this negative interest rate a hard-to-believe result? Not, I think, when one recalls our extreme and purposely unrealistic assumptions. With Böhm's third technological reason for interest ruled out by assumption, with his second reason involving systematic preference for the present soft-pedaled, and with his first reason reversed (that is, with people expecting to be *poorer* in the future), we should perhaps have been surprised if the market rate had not turned out negative.

Yet, aside from giving the general biological optimum interest rate, our model is an instructive one for a number of reasons.

1. It shows us what interest rates would be implied if the "hump saving" process were acting alone in a world devoid of systematic time preference.[16]

2. It incidentally confirms what modern theorists showed long ago but what is still occasionally denied in the literature, that a zero or negative interest rate is in no sense a *logically* contradictory thing, however bizarre may be the *em-*

$i = m$. The relevant competitive market root is given by

$$x = \frac{2+\lambda}{2} + \sqrt{\frac{(2+\lambda)^2 + 4\lambda}{2}}.$$

Where $m = 0$, $\lambda = 1$, we have $x = 3.303$; for $m \to \infty$, $\lambda \to 0$, $x \to 2$ and $i \to -\frac{1}{2}$; for $m \to -1$, $\lambda \to \infty$, $x \to \infty$ and $i \to -1$. Thus the market rate of interest is always between -1 and $-\frac{1}{2}$, growing as m grows, in agreement with the small husk of truth in our earlier "common-sense explanation."

[16] T. Ophir, of the Massachusetts Institute of Technology and Hebrew University, Jerusalem, has done unpublished work showing how systematic time preference will tend to alter the equilibrium interest rate pattern.

pirical hypotheses that entail a zero or negative rate.

3. It may help us a little to isolate the effects of adding one by one, or together, (*a*) technological investment possibilities, (*b*) innovations that secularly raise productivity and real incomes, (*c*) strong biases toward present goods and against future goods, (*d*) governmental laws and more general collusions than are envisaged in simple laissez faire markets, or (*e*) various aspects of uncertainty. To be sure, other orderings of analysis would also be possible; and these separate processes interact, with the whole not the simple sum of its parts.

4. It points up a fundamental and intrinsic deficiency in a free pricing system, namely, that free pricing gets you on the Pareto-efficiency frontier but by itself has no tendency to get you to positions on the frontier that are ethically optimal in terms of a social welfare function; only by social collusions—of tax, expenditure, fiat, or other type—can an ethical observer hope to end up where he wants to be. (This obvious and ancient point is related to 3*d* above.)

5. The present model enables us to see one "function" of money from a new slant—as a social compact that can provide optimal old age social security. (This is also related to 3*d* above.)

For the rest of this essay, I shall develop aspects of the last two of these themes.

SOCIAL COMPACTS AND THE OPTIMUM

If each man insists on a *quid pro quo*, we apparently continue until the end of time, with each worse off than in the social optimum, biological interest case. Yet how easy it is by a simple change in the rules of the game to get to the optimum. Let mankind enter into a Hobbes-Rousseau social contract in which the

young are assured of their retirement
subsistence if they will today support
the aged, such support to be guaranteed
by a draft on the yet-unborn. Then the
social optimum can be achieved within
one lifetime, and our equations (14) will
become

$$S_1(1, 1) + S_2(1, 1) + S_3(1, 1) = 0$$

from $t = 3$ on.

We economists have been told[17] that
what we are to economize on is love or
altruism, this being a scarce good in our
imperfect world. True enough, in the
sense that we want what there is to go as
far as possible. But it is also the task of
political economy to point out where
common rules in the form of self-imposed
fiats can attain higher positions on the
social welfare functions prescribed for us
by ethical observers.

The Golden Rule or Kant's Cate-
gorical Imperative (enjoining like people
to follow the common pattern that makes
each best off) are often not self-enforc-
ing: if all but one obey, the one may gain
selfish advantage by disobeying—which
is where the sheriff comes in: we po-
litically invoke force on ourselves, attempting to make an unstable equilibrium a stable one.[18]

Once social coercion or contracting is
admitted into the picture, the present
problem disappears. The reluctance of
the young to give to the old what the old
can never themselves directly or indirectly repay is overcome. Yet the young
never suffer, since their successors come
under the same requirement. Everybody
ends better off. It is as simple as that.[19]

[17] D. H. Robertson, *What Does the Economist
Maximize?* (a keynote address at the Columbia
bicentennial celebrations, May, 1954), published by
the Trustees of the University in the *Proceedings of
the Conference, 1955* (New York: Doubleday & Co.)
and reprinted as chap. ix in D. H. Robertson,
Economic Commentaries (London: Staples, 1956).

The economics of social collusions is a
rich field for analysis, involving fascinat-
ing predictive and normative properties.
Thus, when society *acts as if* it were
maximizing certain functions, we can
predict the effect upon equilibrium of
specified exogenous disturbances. And
certain patterns of thought appropriate
to a single mind become appropriate,

[18] Now, admittedly, there is usually lacking in
the real world the axis of symmetry needed to make
all this an easy process. In a formulation elsewhere,
I have shown some of the requirements for an
optimal theory of public expenditure of the Sax-
Wicksell-Lindahl-Musgrave-Bowen type, and the
failure of the usual voting and signaling mechanisms to converge to an optimum solution (see "The
Pure Theory of Public Expenditure," *Review of
Economics and Statistics*, XXXVI [November,
1954], 387–89, and "Diagrammatic Exposition of
Public Expenditure," *ibid.*, XXXVII [November,
1955], 350–56). Such a model is poles apart from
the pure case in which Walrasian laissez faire happens to be optimal. I should be prepared to argue
that a good deal of what is important and interesting
in the real world lies between these extreme poles,
perhaps in between in the sense of displaying properties that are a blending of the polar properties.
But such discussion must await another time.

[19] How can the competitive configuration with
negative interest rates be altered to everyone's advantage? Does not this deny the Pareto optimality
of perfect competition, which is the least (and most)
we can expect from it? Here we encounter one more
paradox, which no doubt arises from the "infinity"
aspect of our model. If we assume a large finite span
to the human race—say 1 million generations—
then the final few generations face the equations

$$S_1(R_{T-1}, \infty) + S_2(R_{T-2}, R_{T-1})$$
$$+ S_3(R_{T-3}, R_{T-2}) = 0 ,$$
$$S_2(R_{T-1}, \infty) + S_3(R_{T-2}, R_{T-1}) + 0 = 0 ,$$
$$S_3(R_{T-1}, \infty) + 0 + 0 = 0 ,$$
$$\text{where} \quad T = 1,000,000 .$$

If we depart from the negative interest rate pattern,
the final young will be cheated by the demise of the
human race. Should such a cheating of one generation 30 million years from now perpetually condemn
society to a suboptimal configuration? Perfect
competition shrugs its shoulders at such a question
and (not improperly) sticks to its Pareto optimality.

even though we reject the notion of a group mind. (Example: developed social security could give rise to the same bias toward increasing population that exists among farmers and close family groups, where children are wanted as a means of old age support.)

The economics of collusion provides an important field of study for the theorist. Such collusions can be important elements of strength in the struggle for existence. Reverence for life, in the Schweitzer sense of respecting ants and flowers, might be a handicap in the Darwinian struggle for existence. (And, since the reverencer tends to disappear, the ants may not be helped much in the long run.) But culture in which altruism abounds—because men do not think to behave like atomistic competitors or because men have by custom and law entered into binding social contracts—may have great survival and expansion powers.

An essay could be written on the welfare state as a complicated device for self- or reinsurance. (From this view, the graduated income tax becomes in part a device for reducing *ex ante* variance.) That the Protestant Ethic should have been instrumental in creating individualistic capitalism one may accept; but that it should stop there is not necessarily plausible.[20] What made Jeremy Bentham a Benthamite in 1800, one suspects, might in 1900 have made him a Fabian (and do we not see a lot in common in the personalities of James Mill and Friedrich Engels?).

Much as you and I may dislike government "interferences" in economic life, we must face the positive fact that the motivations for higher living standards that a free market channels into Walrasian equilibrium when the special conditions for that pattern happen to be favorable —these same motivations often lead to social collusions and myriad uses of the apparatus of the state. For good or evil, these may not be aberrations from laissez faire, but theorems entailed by its intrinsic axioms.

CONCLUSION: MONEY AS A SOCIAL
CONTRIVANCE

Let me conclude by applying all these considerations to an analysis of the role of money in our consumption-loan world. In it nothing kept. All ice melted, and so did all chocolates. (If non-depletable land existed, it must have been superabundant.) Workers could not carry goods over into their retirement years.

There is no arguing with Nature. But what is to stop man—or rather men—from printing oblongs of paper or stamping circles of shell. These units of money can keep.[21] (Even if ink fades, this could be true.) With ideal clearing arrangements, money as a medium of exchange might have little function. But remember that a money medium of exchange is itself a rather efficient clearing arrangement.

So suppose men officially through the state, or unofficially through custom, make a grand consensus on the use of these greenbacks as a money of exchange. Now the young and middle-aged do have something to hold and to carry over into their retirement years. And note this: as long as the new current generations of

---

[20] Recall the Myrdal thesis that the austere planned economies of Europe are Protestant, the Catholic countries being individualistic.

[21] I have been asked whether introducing durable money does not violate my fiat against durable goods and trades with Nature. All that I must insist on is that the new durable moneys (or records) be themselves quite worthless for consumption. The essence of them as money is that they are valued only for what they will fetch in exchange.

workers do not repudiate the old money, this gives workers of one epoch a claim on workers of a later epoch, even though no real *quid pro quo* (other than money) is possible.

We then find this remarkable fact: without legislating social security or entering into elaborate social compacts, society by using money will go from the non-optimal negative-interest-rate configuration to the optimal biological-interest-rate configuration. How does this happen? I shall try to give only a sketchy account that does not pretend to be rigorous.

Take the stationary population case with $m = 0$. With total money M constant and the flow of goods constant, the price level can be expected very soon to level off and be constant. The productive invest their hump savings in currency; in their old age they disinvest this currency, turning it over to the productive workers in return for sustenance.

With population growing like $(1 + m)^t$, output will come to grow at that rate. Fixed M will come to mean prices falling like $1/(1 + m)^t$. Each dollar saved today will thus yield a *real* rate of interest of exactly m per period—just what the biological social-optimality configuration calls for. Similarly, when $m < 0$ and population falls, rising prices will create the desired negative real rate of interest equal to m.

In short, the use of money can itself be regarded as a social compact.[22] When economists say that one of the functions of money is to act as a store of wealth and that one of money's desirable properties is constancy of value (as measured by constancy of average prices), we are entitled to ask: How do you know this? Why *should* prices be stable? On what tablets is that injunction written? Perhaps the function of money, if it is to serve as an optimal store of wealth, is so to change in its value as to create that optimal pattern of lifetime saving which could otherwise be established only by alternative social contrivances.[23]

I do not pretend to pass judgment on the policies related to all this. But I do suggest for economists' further research the difficult analysis of capital models which grapple with the fact that each and every today is followed by a tomorrow.

[22] In terms of immediate self-interest the existing productive workers should perhaps unilaterally repudiate the money upon which the aged hope to live in retirement. (Compare the Russian and Belgium calling-in of currencies.) So a continuing social compact is required. (Compare, too, current inflationary trends which do give the old less purchasing power than many of them had counted on.)

[23] Conversely, with satisfactory social security programs, the necessity for having secular stable prices so that the retired are taken care of can be lightened. Even after extreme inflations, social security programs can re-create themselves anew astride the community's indestructible real tax base.

The Analogy Between Atemporal and Intertemporal Theories of Resource Allocation[1]

E. Malinvaud

Two main motives led me to write this article.

On the one hand, after the great advance gained during the last years in the field of resource allocation and in the study of growth models, it seems advisable to look critically at the main features of the theory we have built. With this aim in view, I shall try to review, in its broad outline, the theory of resource allocation as applied to growth programs. I shall not attempt a complete presentation, that would involve a rather heavy formalisation. Indeed, I shall allow myself to rely boldly on the intuition of the reader, or on his prior knowledge of the subject. More specifically, my purpose will be to stress the points of departure between the static theory and its dynamic[2] counterpart, and to make a few remarks on the points which, in my opinion, should deserve some further discussion.

On the other hand, in a very stimulating article published last year by this journal [7], J. R. Hicks opened up the exploration of comparative dynamics. He showed how the relations of comparative statics may be generalized to dynamic models. While I feel myself in complete agreement with the basic findings of that article, I wonder whether, after the neat exposition of Professor Hicks, his readers will not view the question as more simple than it actually is. In the last part below, I shall try to show that the relations of comparative dynamics may lead to various, and sometimes opposite, conclusions according to the assumptions made on the similarities of the programs to be compared.

I. THE STATIC THEORY APPLIED TO DYNAMIC PROGRAMS[3]

1. *The Static Theory*

To fix our notation and terminology, let us first restate the results of the static theory.

There are n commodities in our economy, each one being characterized by an index i ($i = 1, 2 \ldots n$). The net output of commodity i from the whole production sphere is denoted by x_i. A "production program", or more simply a "program", is defined by the values ($x_1, x_2 \ldots x_n$) of the n net outputs. It may be viewed as a vector x in the n

---

[1] This article is based on a memorandum which was discussed at Professor J. R. Hicks' seminar at Oxford in November 1959. I have greatly benefited from this discussion, and from comments made by Gerard Debreu and Robert Solow. The present formulation of the last part owes much to an extensive exchange of views with Professor Hicks.

[2] I shall take the word "dynamic" as synonymous to intertemporal. This is a very loose but common practice.

[3] For a complete presentation of the subject of this paragraph, see for instance Koopmans [8].

Reprinted from *XXVIII* (June 1961) 143–160 of *Review of Economic Studies* by permission of *Review of Economic Studies* published by Oliver & Boyd Ltd., Edinburgh and London.
© 1961 The Economic Society.

dimensional Euclidean space. Technology imposes some limitations on the production programs. For the program to be technically feasible, it is necessary that the n-vector x be in some set X; or, if one prefers a more analytical approach, that it satisfies some production function:

$$f(x_1, x_2 \ldots x_n) = 0$$

A particular program x^1 is said to be " *efficient* ", if it is feasible and if there is no other feasible program x such that:

$$x_i \geqslant x_i^1 \quad \text{for} \quad i = 1, 2 \ldots n$$

Assuming that X or f fulfils some general hypotheses, among which convexity is particularly important, one proves that, to each efficient program x^1, is associated a price vector $p = (p_1, p_2 \ldots p_n)$ such that $p\,x = \sum_{i=1}^{n} p_i\,x_i$ is maximum at $x = x^1$ among all feasible programs. Conversely, if, for some p, $p\,x$ is maximum at x^1, then x^1 is efficient[1].

If production is decentralized, let x_{hi} be the net output of commodity i by firm h, and x_h the n-vector with components x_{hi}. In order to be technically feasible, x_h must be in a particular set X_h, or satisfy a particular production function. For the economy as a whole, the production program x is clearly the sum of the vectors x_h. One shows that decentralization does not affect the above result. To each efficient program x^1, is associated a price vector such that $p\,x_h$ is maximum at x_h^1 among all x_h technically feasible for firm h and conversely. This brings some support to decentralization rules based on a price system, since x_h^1 maximizes the profit $p\,x_h$ which is possible for firm h, with the given prices p_i.

The efficiency criterion deals only with allocation inside the production sphere. To consider problems raised by the distribution of commodities, one represents the preferences of consumer k with a utility function $U_k(x_{k1}, x_{k2} \ldots x_{kn})$ of the quantities x_{ki} consumed by him. A program is then defined by the net output vector x_h of each firm and the consumption vector x_k of each consumer. A program x^1 is said to be " Pareto optimal ", or more simply " optimal ", if there is no feasible program such that

$$U_k(x_k) \geqslant U_k(x_k^1) \quad \text{for all } k$$

with strict inequality holding for at least one consumer.

Similarly to what was mentioned for efficiency, to each Pareto optimal program x^1, is associated a price vector p such that the profit $p\,x_h$ obtained by firm h is maximum at x_h^1, and any consumption program x_k which would have a utility higher than x_k^1 for consumer k is more expensive (i.e., $U(x_k) > U(x_k^1)$ implies $p\,x_k > p\,x_h^1$). Conversely, given a production and distribution program x^1, if there is a price vector p with the above properties, then x^1 is Pareto optimal.[2]

---

[1] This is strictly true only if all components p_i are positive. Here, and again later on, we shall assume that whenever necessary.

[2] If there are some scarce primary resources, the net output x is computed after deduction of the inputs of these resources. For a program to be optimal, it is then also necessary that all available quantities be consumed except perhaps for those resources whose price is zero. For simplicity, we shall not insist on this point.

2. *Transposition to a dynamic model*

In principle, this theory is easily generalized to programs extending over time for a finite number of periods ($t = 1, 2 \ldots T$). Let x_{it} be the net output of commodity i during period t. A dynamic production program specifying all net outputs is represented by a vector x with nT components x_{it}. The technological limitations now impose that x be in some set X, since not all dynamic programs are feasible. We may still say that a particular program x^1 is efficient, if it is feasible and if there is no other feasible program x that would bring a larger net output of some commodity for some period, without implying a smaller net output of any commodity during any period:

(1) $$x_{it} \geqq x_{it}^1 \quad \text{for} \quad i = 1, 2 \ldots n; \quad t = 1, 2 \ldots T.$$

It is then clear that the static and dynamic theories are formally equivalent. One transposes the first to the second, by substituting a nT — dimensional model for the n— dimensional original one. But this substitution is trivial since n could be any number. Economists have always thought that the usefulness of a good depended on the time at which it is made available. Our transposition amounts to dealing with two quantities of the same good available during different periods as if they were quantities of two different commodities.

As the same kind of general hypotheses may be made on X, whether it is viewed in an atemporal or in an intertemporal setting, the results of the static theory apply to the dynamic model. In particular, to each efficient program x^1, is associated a nT-dimensional price vector p specifying the price p_{it} of a unit quantity of commodity i to be delivered during period t. Decentralization of production raises no new problem, each firm choosing its own dynamic program x_h within the technological set X_h, x_h and X_h being now nT- dimensional. Pareto optimality may also be brought into the picture, if the preferences of consumer k are defined according to a utility function $U_k(x_k)$ on the nT-dimensional vector x_k of his consumptions during the T periods.

3. *The Rate of Interest*

The developments made below will show that it may be interesting to go beyond this straightforward transposition of the static theory. Three general comments are already in order.

First, the theory of resource allocation over time is concerned with the choice among different programs extending into the future. The chosen program will be implemented during all future periods; only part of it will materialize from the start. One might therefore think that a sequential procedure could be appropriate, since it would lead to a progressive determination of the program. Our theory does not take this point of view. We want to know today how to allocate future resources, and intend to determine completely our program. The results outlined above deal with some characteristics of this immediate choice.

As a consequence, the price p_{it} defines the *present* value of a unit quantity of commodity i to be delivered at period t. It should be interpreted as a discounted price. This fact explains why the (present) value of the program is written as:

(2) $$p \, x = \sum_{t=1}^{T} \sum_{i=1}^{n} p_{it} \, x_{it}$$

One should also notice that no unique set of interest rates is associated with an efficient program.   Indeed, in order to define the rate of interest for period t, one needs to fix the general level of prices for this period.   For instance, one may assume that the undiscounted price $\bar{p}_{nt}$ of the last commodity will be constant and equal to 1.   The undiscounted price of commodity i should then be:

$$\bar{p}_{it} = \frac{p_{it}}{p_{nt}}$$

More generally, any normalization or monetary rule on the (undiscounted) prices will give $p_{it} = \beta_t\,\bar{p}_{it}$ with some appropriate proportionnality factor β_t.   The value of the program will then be written as:

$$\sum_{t=1}^{T} \beta_t \sum_{i=1}^{n} \bar{p}_{it}\,x_{it}$$

The corresponding rate of interest r_t for period t will accordingly be:

(3) $$r_t = \frac{\beta_t}{\beta_{t+1}} - 1$$

It depends in general on the normalization rule, like the β_t's.

Finally, the dynamic theory is subject to the same limitations as the static theory. Some of them may even look more restrictive in this new context.   A case in point is the assumption of perfect foresight which becomes necessary if one wants to find in the results a justification for a decentralized market system.[1]

II. CHOICE CRITERIA FOR GROWTH PROGRAMS

1. Relevance of Pareto-Optimality

Thus far, the choice criteria adopted for growth programs generalize those introduced for the static analysis.   Efficiency provides a minimum requirement for the arrangement of economic activities inside the production sphere.   Pareto optimality is intended to apply simultaneously to both problems of production and distribution.

In order to make this second criterion precise, we need to list all consumers $k = 1, 2 \ldots m$ and to know, for each one of them, a utility function $U_k(x_k)$.   This function summarizes his *present* preferences among programs defining all his future consumptions. We then accept the utility functions of the m consumers as providing the basis for the present social choices.   This approach raises two difficulties which should not be overlooked.

Firstly, if we are dealing with programs extending into the future for more than a few years (and we often have to), the list of consumers must include those who are not yet existing today.   The preferences of each one of them must already be taken into account

---

[1] A generalization of the theory to a model taking explicit account of uncertainties has been presented by K. Arrow [2] and by G. Debreu [5].   The market mechanism that is then implied may be considered as an idealization of the one existing in our societies, but a very remote idealization indeed.

by an appropriate utility function. This implies in particular that a competitive economy will realize a Pareto optimum only if, among other conditions, the future consumers are already well represented on the marked.

Secondly, it is easy to see that, in our societies, we do not usually rely on the present preferences of consumers to evaluate the relative importance of present and future needs. The part played by public savings in many countries and the existence of legal old age pension schemes show, on two different levels, that one often fears the consumers would under-value the future. This raises a question about the usefulness of Pareto-optimality as applied to dynamic programs. It seems that this criterion puts too much reliance on the consumers' present preferences. On the other hand, efficiency does not seem to be selective enough since it neglects all distribution problems.

2. *Allais-Optimality*

These thoughts lead M. Allais [1] to consider an intermediate criterion, which, in my opinion, has not received enough attention. He suggested that we take into account consumer preferences only for the distribution of production within each period. He then announced an interesting result that I may try to present briefly.

Considering, for the moment, a single consumer, let us drop the subscript k. The letter x will then refer to the consumption program of the consumer for all T periods. Let us designate by x_t the consumption program for period t, and by $_tx$ the consumption program for all periods after t. With this notation, we may write:

$$x = \{x_1 \ldots x_t \ldots x_T\}$$
$$_tx = \{x_{t+1} \ldots \ldots \ldots x_T\}$$

and

$$_{t-1}x = (x_t, \,_tx)$$

Changing somewhat Allais' formulation, I shall represent the consumer preferences by a set of T utility functions $U_t(_tx)$, one for each period. The function $U_t(_tx)$ defines in the usual way the choices which would be made by the consumer at time t among the consumption programs $_tx$ for the following periods.

I shall then assume that U_t is consistent with U_{t-1}, i.e. that, if the consumer prefers at time t the program $_tx^1$ to the program $_tx^2$, then he would have preferred at time $t-1$ the program $(x_t, \,_tx^1)$ to the program $(x_t, \,_tx^2)$, and conversely[1]:

(4) $\qquad U_t(_tx^1) \geqq U_t(_tx^2)$ if and only if $U_{t-1}(x_t, \,_tx^1) \geqq U_{t-1}(x_t, \,_tx^2)$

---

[1] It follows from (4) that, if $(x'_t, \,_tx^1)$ is preferred to $(x'_t, \,_tx^2)$, then also $(x'_t, \,_tx^1)$ is preferred to $(x'_t, \,_tx^2)$. Hence, even in the choices made at time $t-1$, the consumption program after t may be determined independently of the consumption program for period t. (For a similar hypothesis, see Postulate 3.b in Koopmans [9]). This restrictive assumption could be avoided if the utility function U_t was made dependent on the consumptions up to t. But it would then become necessary to say how two programs, which are not identical up to t, may be compared at time t. One may think that this comparison has no meaning in the theory of consumer choices, since this theory ignores preferences which could not be actually observed. From such a point of view, it is impossible to give a meaning to Allais-optimality, unless assumption (4) holds. Even if one is willing to bypass this objection, the whole theory becomes much more difficult when (4) does not hold. I shall not try here to go into it further.

In these conditions, one easily sees that utility at time $t - 1$ depends only on x_t and on the level of utility at time t. In other words, there exist functions $V_{t-1}(x_t, U_t)$ such that $U_{t-1} = V_{t-1}(x_t, U_t)$.

Writing again, from now on, the indices k, we shall designate the consumption of commodity i by consumer k during period t as x_{kti}, his consumption program for period t as x_{kt} and his utility function at time t as $U_{kt}(_tx_k)$.

Allais suggests that a production and distribution program x^1 should be considered as optimum if it is feasible and there is no feasible program x such that:

$$U_{kt}(_tx_k) \geqq U_{kt}(_tx_k^1) \text{ for all } k \text{ and } t$$

with strict inequality holding for at least one couple (k, t). In other words, a program is an Allais-optimum, if it is not possible to make any consumer better off in any period, without making him worse off during some other period, or some other consumer worse off during some period.

Clearly, an Allais-optimum program x^1 for an economy Σ with m consumers corresponds to a Pareto-optimum for a fictitious economy Σ' defined with the same production units, but with mT consumers, each one living for one period only, and choosing his consumption program x_{kt} according to the utility function $V_{k,t-1}(x_{kt}, U_{kt}^1)$ where U_{kt}^1 is the value reached by U_{kt} in x^1.

Hence, associated with x^1, there is a set of discounted prices p_{it} such that px_h is maximum at x_h^1 for each firm h, and $V_{k,t-1}(x_{kt}, U_{kt}^1)$ is maximum at x_{kt}^1 among all x_{kt} which satisfy $p_t x_{kt} \leqq p_t x_{kt}^1$.

For producers, the same decentralization rule applies as with efficiency or Pareto-optimality. But there is a difference for consumers. Each one of them will be allocated an income $r_{kt} = p_t x_{kt}^1$ for each period t, and will not be allowed to spend in any one period more than his income for this period. Lending and borrowing by consumers will no longer operate freely on the capital market. Under these new restraints, the consumers are, however, still supposed to maximize their utilities. There is still in the production sector a unique marginal rate of substitution between any commodity i delivered at time t and any other commodity j delivered at time θ. But this marginal rate of substitution agrees with the consumer preferences only if $\theta = t$.

3. Maximizing the Rate of Growth

The literature on economic development usually refers to a different criterion for choosing among growth programs. The best program is then supposed to be that one which maximizes the rate of expansion. This point of view is also adopted in some recent contributions which undoubtedly belong to the mathematical theory of resource allocation. They were initiated by J. von Neumann who presented his model of proportional growth in 1937 [12]. At first, this criterion may look quite sensible for judging problems of production; but it loses much of its value, if one thinks over it a little more closely.

On the one hand, the criterion is not really sufficient. Indeed, one should also make sure that the growing productions are economically useful. (An economy which would specialize in breeding rabbits, could reach a very high expansion rate). Thus, we have somehow to take into account the needs of final consumers.

On the other hand, for our theory of resource allocation, we want a criterion defined independently of any particular prices.   Usually, various productions increase at different rates.   They must be weighted in any measure of the overall growth rate.   It is not clear how the weights could be defined a priori.

The latter difficulty may be bypassed if we apply the criterion only to programs of proportional growth, in which all productions are increasing at the same rate.   (This limitation was adopted quite clearly by von Neumann and his followers).   We then have to assume that the consumptions of different commodities are also increasing at the same rate; i.e. to stick to an a priori given pattern of consumption.

We may assume, for our present purpose, that different programs of proportional growth with the same consumption pattern all imply the same consumptions during the first period.   They then may differ either by their expansion rate, or by their initial capital.[1]   It is almost obvious, and may be proved more rigorously, that raising the amount of initial capital while maintaining the same initial consumptions, will usually make possible the achievement of a higher expansion rate.   But the practical problem is not only to increase the growth rate, but also to do it with a limited amount of capital.

Taking this latter requirement into account makes the approach a little more difficult. One needs to assume a priori a fixed proportionality relation between the consumption of each commodity and the aggregated amount of capital.   Various programs of proportional growth then differ only by their expansion rate and the *composition* of their capital.

But the a priori definition of the capital becomes very important.   If it is properly chosen, one may show, with few additional assumptions, that the program with the maximum expansion rate is also " efficient " in the usual sense.   The prices associated to it are then also those used to compute the capital aggregate.   In other words, one should know the prices associated to an efficient proportional growth program; one could then define with these prices a relation between consumptions and capital in such a way that this relation be fulfilled by the efficient program; this program would then appear as the one with the maximum expansion rate.   The circularity of the argument makes the suggested procedure of little interest.

On the other hand, if the prices used to define the capital aggregate do not fulfil the above condition, then the program with the highest growth rate will usually not be efficient. The trouble arises from the fact that two different capital bundles giving the same value to the aggregate will really not imply an equivalent use of scarce resources.   Starting from the program with the maximum growth rate, it would then be possible to define a program with the same initial capital but a changing composition of capital, in such a way that consumption be raised for at least one couple (*it*) and lowered for no such couple.   This would imply an increase on the (unappropriately defined) capital aggregate, but no real increase in the amount of invested scarce resources.   (These questions are dealt more rigorously in [11]).

After these considerations, one does not see how in practice one could rely only on the growth rate criterion for choosing among production programs.   Of course, one may find very good reasons for selecting among the many *efficient* (or Allais-optimal) programs,

---

[1] Although we did not mention it in our general presentation, it is clear that the x_{i1} concerning the first period are equal to the difference between the consumptions of that period and the initial stock of capital goods.   Similarly the x_{iT} are equal to the sum of the consumptions of the last period and the final stock of capital goods.

one which brings about a high rate of expansion.   But one cannot get away without taking into account efficiency or some such " classical " criterion.

III. UNLIMITED GROWTH PROGRAMS

1. *Avoiding End Conditions*

In our generalization of the static theory to dynamic programs, we assumed a finite number T of periods. This implies a discrete representation of time as against the more common continuous one; but it does not bring about any real limitation since the length of the unit period may be chosen as short as one wishes. Much less satisfactory is the fact that we need to fix a terminal date to the future which we shall consider. According to our model we shall have to ignore what will happen beyong the " horizon " T. We, indeed, take into account the terminal capital stock into the consumption bundle (x_{iT}) of the last period. But, how could we make sure that it is efficient in its composition and amount? This capital stock will participate in production beyond the horizon. We cannot judge its usefulness since, by hypothesis, we ignore all economic activity that will take place after T. Thus, when we limit ourselves to some finite horizon, we cannot fully solve the problem of resource allocation.

Such is the reason for considering dynamic programs which would extend indefinitely into the future.   If we denote by x_t the n-dimensional vector with components x_{it} (for $i = 1, 2 \ldots n$), the consumptions will be represented by the sequence of vectors: $\{x_1, x_2 \ldots x_t \ldots\}$, that we shall sometimes write more shortly as x.   Then, one may generalize without difficulty the T period model.   There will be a set X of all sequences x which are technically feasible.   A particular unlimited program x^1 will be said to be efficient if it is feasible and if there is no other feasible program x such that

$$x_{it} \geq x_{ti}^1 \text{ for } i = 1, 2 \ldots n; \quad t = 1, 2 \ldots \ldots$$

Decentralization and Pareto-optimality may also be brought into the picture. Assumptions very similar to those made in the T period case may be introduced.   All this transposition only requires the kind of imagination and boldness that modern mathematics has taught us.

2. *A Suggested Mathematical Approach*

At first, it seems that the results of the static theory are also easily generalized to the new model. These results are, indeed, applications of mathematical properties which are not only true for finite dimensional vector spaces, but also for general linear spaces. One could therefore think of using directly the known theorems on linear spaces. For another generalization, the suggestion proved to be quite fruitful. Debreu [4] showed in particular that prices $p_i(t)$ are associated to any efficient continuous program in a model with a continuous representation of time $(0 \leq t \leq T)$. If the flow of consumption of commodity i between t and $t + dt$ is equal to $x_i(t)dt$, and if the functions $x_i(t)$ are integrable on [0.T], the value of the consumption program is

$$\int_0^T \left[\sum_{i=1}^n p_i(t) \, x_i(t) \right] dt$$

This value is found as a " linear functional " on the space of all n-dimensional integrable functions $x(t)$ defined for $0 \leq t \leq T$. For feasible programs, it is maximum when the $x_i(t)$ are equal to the consumption flows of the efficient program.

Coming back to our problem with a discrete representation of time, we may remark that the space L of all sequences $\{x_t\}$ is linear. We may therefore hope that, given any efficient program x^1, there is a value (i.e. a linear functional on L) which achieves its maximum at x^1 as among all feasible programs. But, this time, the suggestion leads to a blind alley. One of the conditions necessary for the relevant mathematical property is not fulfilled in our model.[1] That is after all not surprising. The linear functionals on spaces of sequences would imply rather queer valuation rules (that being true whether we consider spaces of all sequences, or spaces of sequences fulfilling some general mathematical property such as boundedness).[2]

3. Prices for Unlimited Programs

Using a more pedestrian mathematical approach, I was, however, able to generalize the results obtained for the T period model [10].[3] Given any efficient program x^1, there is an infinite sequence of discounted price vectors p_t. This sequence does *not* define a "value" which would be maximum for x^1 among all feasible programs. As far as my general result goes, the p_{it} should be used only for comparing the efficient program with other feasible programs which are identical with it after some horizon T (T being as large as one wishes). In such comparisons, the following inequality applies:

$$\sum_{i=1}^{T} \sum_{i=1}^{n} p_{it}\,(x_{it} - x_{it}^1) \leqq 0$$

In other words, x^1 has *up to* T the highest value as among all feasible programs which are identical with it after T, this being true for any T.

As before, analogous results apply for a decentralized production system and for Pareto-optimality. There is just a small difficulty with the converse property. When there are several independent producers, when each of them has chosen a program x_h^1 having highest value up to T among all feasible programs identical after T, then the aggregate program x^1 is not necessarily efficient. This lack of efficiency may, however, be excluded in the more relevant case, i.e., if, for x^1, the present discounted value of the capital stock that will be available at time T decreases to zero when T increases to infinity.

4. Competitive Equilibrium

Although I have only been concerned so far with the allocation of resources, a word may be in order now on the twin problem, that of defining a model of perfect competition and of studying its equilibrium. One knows the state of the theory for the static case. A general formalisation has been given. It has been proved, using the converse properties mentioned in our first paragraph, that any competitive equilibrium is efficient and Pareto-optimal. With some further assumptions, the existence of an equilibrium was established; and, with again some new assumptions, its stability.

---

[1] As an indication for the mathematical reader, I shall point out that, given any sequence x^1, the set P, of all sequences x such that $x_{it} \geqq x_{it}^1$ for all i and t, does not contain any interior point. (An interior point x^0 of P being defined as a point such that, given any x in the space, there is a scalar $\alpha > 0$ for which $\alpha x + (1 - \alpha) x^0$ is in P). It is not appropriate either to assume that the set X of all feasible sequences contains an interior point.

[2] For the forms of linear functionals on spaces of sequences, see [3].

[3] The mathematical proof given in [10] contains a gap which I have filled up in a mimeographed note, available on request.

All these results generalize to an intertemporal model obtained in the same spirit as for resource allocation.   They generalize at least to a model with a finite horizon.   There might be some difficulty with stability since time must then enter both the definition of equilibrium, and the process of convergence towards equilibrium.   I am not aware that anyone has really looked into the matter.   But it seems to me that the problem is just to find a proper definition of stability.

An intertemporal model of competitive equilibrium with a finite horizon will look somewhat artificial since it will necessarily contain consumers for the terminal capital stock. Thus, one may also look for a model with an infinite horizon.   To my knowledge, this model has not even been formulated so far.   I suspect that one will encounter there some mathematical difficulties.   But, the question really requires more thought than I have been able to put into it.

IV. The Recursive Character of Production

1. *Production Inside Each Period*

Thus far, I have considered production as being a general process of transformation of sequences of goods into other sequences of goods.   Such a point of view already leads to the general results on efficient dynamic programs.   As a matter of fact, production has also a recursive character.   Each operation consumes some inputs, many of them obtained in preceding operations; brings some outputs, many of them for use in subsequent operations; and requires some time.   One may therefore look for a more specific model of production which would take this fact into account and might perhaps lead to more precise results.

We shall still represent time by a sequence of periods $t = 1, 2 \ldots$, and assume that each productive operation starts at the beginning of a period and is carried through at the end of the same period.   Hence, each process is supposed to have a unit period of production.   In a theoretical model, that is not a serious limitation, since we may choose a short period as a unit, and admit the existence of as many intermediate operations and as many intermediate commodities as may be necessary.   A productive transformation which requires a long time between the main inputs and the output may be viewed as a sequence of shorter operations.

Let us write a_{it} for the input of commodity i at the beginning of period t, and $b_{j,t+1}$ for the output of commodity j at the end of period t, or the beginning of period $t + 1$. The net output available at the beginning of period t will be, as before, $x_{it} = b_{it} - a_{it}$ From now on, we shall speak of " time t " as being the beginning of period t, and use in our notation the n-dimensional vectors a_t, b_t and x_t.   For simplicity we shall not take into account the decentralization of production.

As before, production is limited by some technological constraints.   To represent them, we introduce a production function (or a technological set) for the inputs a_t and outputs b_{t+1} of each period.   We write for instance

$$(5) \qquad f_t(a_{1t} \ldots a_{nt}; \ b_{1,t+1} \ldots b_{n,t+1}) = 0$$

This production function is a direct generalization of the one used in the static case.   If technology does not change, all functions f_t are identical.   But, we need not assume that.

2. Maximizing the Period Profit

Of course, all results on efficient dynamic programs apply with this new representation. But, we may wonder whether there is not now any more definite criterion for the operations inside each period. The usual static concept of efficiency apply for each period. We may say that a feasible program (a_t^1, b_{t+1}^1) is " efficient for period t ", if there is no other feasible program such that:

$$a_{it} \leqq a_{it}^1 \text{ and } b_{i,t+1} \geqq b_{i,t+1}^1 \text{ for } i = 1, 2 \ldots . n$$

One may show without difficulty that if a dynamic program is efficient (in the sense of the preceding paragraph), then it is also efficient for any period t. But, the converse is not true in general. A program may be efficient for each period, without being efficient as a whole. Roughly speaking, other necessary conditions for efficiency imply that the marginal rate of substitution at time t between two commodities be the same whether we consider them as outputs of period $t - 1$, or as inputs of period t. (This point was studied by Dorfman, Samuelson and Solow [6]).

We have seen that to each efficient program, corresponds a sequence of discounted price vectors p_t. With these prices, the net discounted value of production during period t

$$(6) \qquad p_{t+1}\, b_{t+1} - p_t\, a_t$$

is maximum for the efficient program (a_t^1, b_{t+1}^1) as among all feasible programs. This result is in accordance with the efficiency of the program for period t.

Conversely, let us suppose that, given a dynamic program $(a_t^1, b_{t+1}^1; \ t = 1, 2 \ldots)$, there is a sequence of price vectors such that, for each t, (6) be maximum at (a_t^1, b_{t+1}^1), as among all feasible (a_t, b_{t+1}). The program is then efficient for each period. Moreover, the marginal rate of substitution is the same at time t for outputs of period $t - 1$ as for inputs of period t. (Indeed, the same price vector p_t appears in the two maximands $p_t\, b_t - p_{t-1}\, a_{t-1}$ and $p_{t+1}\, b_{t+1} - p_t\, a_t$). Can we then assert that the program is also efficient as a whole? The answer is " yes " if we limit ourselves to programs with a finite horizon.

For unlimited programs, it is also necessary that, at any time T, the value of inputs $p_T\, a_T$ be minimum for a_T^1, among all feasible programs such that $b_t - a_t = b_t^1 - a_t^1$ for $t > T$. If this last condition is fulfilled for T, and the maximum requirement on (6) satisfied for $t \leqq T$, then it is also fulfilled for any $t < T$. We therefore need only take into account this additional condition after some future date, as far remote as we may want. But we cannot dispense with it completely.

3. Proportional Growth Programs

One often considers programs of proportional growth, in which the input and outputs of all commodities increase (or decrease) at the same constant rate. Such programs are defined by two vectors a and b, together with a scalar g (the rate of growth per period). The input and output vectors are then:

$$a_t = (1 + g)^t\, a \qquad b_t = (1 + g)^t\, b$$

The first question is to know whether such programs are feasible. To study this and other points, one often assumes that the production function (5) (or the technological set) remains the same through time and obeys the law of constant returns to scale.[1] We shall make this hypothesis here. Under these conditions, if the program is feasible in any one period, then it is also feasible as a whole.

Let us now suppose that a given program of proportional growth $(a^1, b^1; g^1)$ is efficient. The results of the preceding sections take a simple form. Indeed, one may show that there exists a price vector p and a rate of interest r (or a sequence of discounted price vectors $p_t = (1 + r)^{-t} p$) such that

$$\text{(7)} \qquad \frac{1 + g}{1 + r}\, p\, b - p\, a$$

is maximum for $(a^1, b^1; g^1)$ as among all feasible $(a, b; g)$. Simultaneously, $p\, a$ is minimum for $(a^1, b^1; g^1)$ among all feasible $(a, b; g^1)$ such that $a - a^1 = (1 + g^1)(b - b^1)$. Conversely, if there is a price vector and an interest rate such that the two above conditions are fulfilled, then $(a^1, b^1; g^1)$ is efficient.

Assuming constant returns to scale, the maximum of (7) is necessarily zero. Thus we may write:

$$\text{(8)} \qquad \frac{1 + r}{1 + g^1} = \frac{p\, b^1}{p\, a^1} \quad \text{or} \quad \frac{r - g^1}{1 + g^1} = \frac{p\, x^1}{p\, a^1}$$

with $x^1 = b^1 - a^1$. Hence, the difference between the rate of interest and the rate of growth has the same sign as the value of net consumption (consumption of goods and services outside the production sphere, minus inputs of labor and primary resources). Although nothing in our model makes $r < g^1$ logically impossible, we may see that in reality $r > g^1$ must be the rule.

Indeed, let us denote by z the vector of commodities consumed outside the production sphere, by y the vector of inputs of labor and primary resources, and by c the vector of commodities which remain in the production sphere from one period to the next (the capital vector). Then:

$$\text{(9)} \qquad \begin{cases} b = z + c & \qquad a = y + c \\[2mm] x = b - a = z - y \end{cases}$$

With this new notation, (7) may be written as:

$$\text{(10)} \qquad pz - py - \frac{r - g}{1 + r} p(z + c)$$

If the efficient program were such that $r \le g^1$, all terms in this sum except $-py^1$ would be non negative for that program. Maintaining y and g constant and increasing any components of the capital vector c should not raise the value of (10), i.e. should not lead to any increase of the consumption vector (except perhaps for those commodities with zero prices).[2] It is clear that in reality some improvements to equipment may bring about a higher permanent production of desired consumption goods; hence, we can safely assume $r > g^1$.

---

[1] Once convexity is assumed, the law of constant returns to scale does not seem to bring any significant additional restriction. Diminishing returns to scale may only appear if some scarce primary factors of production are not taken into account of explicitly in the inputs. But we may assume that inputs cover all primary resources.

[2] According to the minimum condition on $p\, a$, it should not be possible either to decrease some components of c (with positive prices), while maintaining the same vectors for consumptions and primary inputs.

V. COMPARATIVE DYNAMICS

1. *General Formulas*

Given two efficient programs and their associated prices, what relations exist between differences in the two sets of prices and differences in the quantities produced and consumed in the two programs? The inequalities of comparative statics answer this question for static models. In a recent article, J. R. Hicks [7] shows how they may be generalized to dynamic models. As a matter of fact, a large part of classical capital theory was devoted to comparative dynamics. But attention was then limited to stationary programs. In contrast Professor Hicks directly attacks the comparative study of programs developing at different growth rates.

I shall look again at this question on the basis of the conditions reviewed during the preceding section. I shall derive general formulae which lead to the one found by J. R. Hicks, and try to see how far we can go in drawing more specific conclusions on a particular model. From now on, I shall assume that production obeys the law of constant returns to scale, an hypothesis that is already practically implied by the convexity of the technological sets.

Let us consider two efficient programs, with upper indices 1 and 2, and denote their associated price vectors respectively by p_t^1 and p_t^2; let $\triangle a_t$ stand for $a_t^2 - a_t^1$, $\triangle p_t$ for $p_t^2 - p_t^1$, ... and so on.

The maximum condition on (6) implies:

$$(11) \qquad p_{t+1}^1 \triangle b_{t+1} - p_t^1 \triangle a_t \leqq 0$$

$$(12) \qquad (p_{t+1}^1 + \triangle p_{t+1}) \triangle b_{t+1} - (p_t^1 + \triangle p_t) \triangle a_t \geqq 0$$

Hence:

$$(13) \qquad \triangle p_{+1} \triangle b_{t+1} - \triangle p_t \triangle a_t \geqq 0$$

Moreover, with the law of constant returns to scale, the maximum value of the profit is zero; hence:

$$(14) \qquad p_{t+1}^1 b_{t+1}^1 - p_t^1 a_t^1 = 0$$

$$(15) \qquad (p_{t+1}^1 + \triangle p_{t+1}) (b_{t+1}^1 + \triangle b_{t+1}) - (p_t^1 + \triangle p_t) (a_t^1 + \triangle a_t) = 0$$

Taking (12) and (14) into account, we see that (15) implies:

$$(16) \qquad \triangle p_{t+1} \cdot b_{t+1}^1 - \triangle p_t \cdot a_t^1 \leqq 0$$

The inequalities (11), (13) and (16) may be considered as the three basic laws of comparative dynamics.[1]

---

[1] It is sometimes easier to work with differentials than with finite differences. If one can assume that the differences between the two programs are infinitely small, for discounted prices as well as for quantities, then one may write:

$$(17) \qquad \begin{cases} p_{t+1} \, db_{t+1} & - \, p_t \, da_t & = 0 \\ dp_{t+0} \, db_{t+1} & - \, dp_t \, da_t & \geqq 0 \\ dp_{t+1} \cdot b_{t+1} & - \, dp_t \cdot a_t & = 0 \end{cases}$$

the equality signs in the first and last relations following from the fact that the left hand sides of (11) and (16) are now equal to zero to the first order.

We may sum up similar relations for various periods, and take account of the equality $b_t - a_t = x_t$. For instance, the relation (13) written for all periods from 1 to T lead to:

$$\sum_{t=1}^{T} \triangle p_t \, \triangle x_t + \triangle p_{T+1} \, \triangle b_{T+1} \geqq 0$$

(It is assumed here that $\triangle a_1 = -\triangle x_1$ since the vector of present outputs b_1 is given). If the first term converges, and the second decreases to zero, we may also write:

$$\sum_{t=1}^{\infty} \triangle p_t \, \triangle x_t \geqq 0$$

Such is the form of the basic relation used by Professor Hicks. Here, I shall rather work directly with the inequalities (11) to (16), since this leads to a somewhat simpler treatment.

2. *Comparative Dynamics in a Three Commodity Model*

The above relations are still too general to bring about very significant results in the fields of capital theory or resource allocation over time. One would like to know how the prices of capital goods, the real wages, or the interest rates change from one program to another. The answer to this question does not follow directly from our formulas. In order to throw some light on the subject, I shall try to explore the relations between proportional growth programs in a simplified model analogous to the one used by J. R. Hicks.

Let us suppose there are only three commodities, a consumption good, a primary input (labor), and a capital good. The rate of growth per period being g, a quantity $(1 + g)^t z$ of the consumption good will be available at time t, while a quantity $(1 + g)^t y$ of labor and a quantity $(1 + g)^t c$ of capital will be used. Let the undiscounted prices be recorded in terms of consumption goods, and be denoted by w for labor and q for capital, the rate of interest being r as before. Let us also write for simplicity in the relations to be found:

$$(1 + g) z = z' \qquad\qquad (1 + r) w = w'$$
$$(1 + g) c = c' \qquad\qquad (1 + r) q = q'$$

With these assumptions, the profit (6) for period t is proportional to:

$$(1 + g)(z + qc) - (1 + r)(wy + qc) = z' + qc' - w'y - q'c$$

(That would be the profit for period $t = -1$). We may also write it as

$$[(1 + g) z + gqc] - [r q c] - [(1 + r) wy]$$

The first bracket gives the value of the net production during the period, the second the capitalist income (available at the end of the period), the third the labor income (assumed to be paid at the end of the period). If wage earners do not save, $(1 + g) z - (1 + r) w y$ is the consumption by the capitalists. We may write it as $(1 - s) r q c$, s being the average propensity to save of capitalists. With constant returns to scale, it is also equal to $r q c - g q c$. Hence, the growth rate g is equal to $s r$, as it should be.

We may apply the relations (11) to (16) to a change from one proportional growth program to another proportional growth program.

We find[1]:

$$\triangle z' + q\triangle c' - q'\triangle c \qquad\qquad - w'\triangle y \qquad\qquad \leqq 0$$
$$(18)\quad (c' + \triangle c')\triangle q - (c + \triangle c)\triangle q' - (y + \triangle y)\triangle w' \geqq 0$$
$$c'\triangle q - c\triangle q' \qquad\qquad - y\triangle w' \qquad\qquad \leqq 0$$

the first and third inequalities being direct applications of (11) and (16), whereas the second follows from (15), (11) and (14).

For our purpose, the second and third inequalities will be the most relevant. We may deduce from them other relations with a more direct economic meaning. Dividing the second by $y + \triangle y$, the third by $-y$ and adding, we find:

$$(19)\qquad \triangle q \cdot \triangle \left(\frac{c'}{y}\right) - \triangle q' \cdot \triangle \left(\frac{c}{y}\right) \geqq 0$$

Alternatively, dividing the second and third inequalities in (18) by $y(y + \triangle y)$, multiplying the second by c and the third by $-(c + \triangle c)$, adding and noting that $c\triangle c' = c'\triangle c + c(c + \triangle c)\triangle g$, we obtain:

$$(20)\qquad k\triangle g\triangle q + \triangle \left(\frac{c}{y}\right)\triangle w' \geqq 0$$

in which k denotes the positive quantity $\dfrac{c(c + \triangle c)}{y(y + \triangle y)}$.

The two relations (19) and (20) do not provide the kind of clearcut law which we should like to reach. In order to arrive at more significant inequalities, we need to impose further restrictions either on the model, or on the differences between the two programs x^1 and x^2.

(i) Let us first restrict the generality of the model assuming *the capital good is identical with the consumption good.* (Such an assumption was often made in capital theory). The price q of the capital good is now equal to 1 in both models

$$\triangle q = 0 \qquad\qquad \triangle q' = \triangle r \cdot q$$

The inequalities (19) and (20) then become:

$$\triangle r \cdot \triangle \left(\frac{c}{y}\right) \leqq 0 \qquad\qquad \triangle w' \cdot \triangle \left(\frac{c}{y}\right) \geqq 0$$

Hence, *the programme with the higher level of capital per worker is associated with the lower interest rate and with the higher capitalized real wage rate.* This has a classical flavor. But it is interesting to see that we can reach this conclusion, in this model, without any assumption on the growth rates in the two programs.

The first inequality in (18) shows that there is a relation between the growth rate and other physical characteristics of the program. But this relation also involves the con-

[1] In a many commodity model in which z, c and y would be the vectors of consumption goods, capital goods and primary inputs, analogous relations would hold under the condition that the differences between the two programs be proportional inside each commodity group (with, for instance, $\dfrac{\triangle z_i}{z_i} = \dfrac{\triangle z_j}{z_j}$ for all i and j). Thus, our results are a little more general than the model on which they are based.

sumption z. The growth rate of the program with the lower interest rate may be higher or lower depending on the levels of consumption[1] in x^1 and x^2.

(ii) Let us, from now on, come back to our three commodity model, the capital good being distinct from the consumption good. The classical approach to capital theory assumed stationary programs. Let us be a little more general and suppose that *x¹ and x²* *expand at the same rate* $(\triangle g = 0)$. Then $\triangle c' = (1 + g) \triangle c$, (19) and (20) may be written:

$$\triangle[(r - g)q] \cdot \triangle \left(\frac{c}{y}\right) \leqq 0 \quad \triangle w' \cdot \triangle \left(\frac{c}{y}\right) \geqq 0$$

The program with the higher level of capital per worker is associated with the higher capitalized real wage rate, and with the smaller value of $(r - g)q$. It is noteworthy that this latter quantity differs from the rent rq of the capital good and is equal to it only when stationary programs are compared.

(iii) For the comparison of programs with different rates of growth, a natural first hypothesis would be that *x¹ and x² are capital intensive to the same extent*, i.e. $\triangle \left(\frac{c}{y}\right) = 0$. Then, from (20), $\triangle q \cdot \triangle g \geqq 0$. *The price of the capital good is higher in the program with the higher growth rate.* This does not imply a definite relation between the interest rate and the growth rate. Indeed, the relation between changes in the price of the capital good and changes in the interest rate, the last inequality in (18), also involves changes in the wage rate.

(iv) Taking now the last simple case, the one in which *the real capitalized wage rate w' is the same for both programs*, we see that (20) directly implies $\triangle g \cdot \triangle q \geqq 0$. Moreover, the last inequality in (18) may then be written $(r - g) \triangle q + q \triangle r \geqq 0$. Hence, whenever r exceeds g, $\triangle r \leqq 0$ implies $\triangle q \geqq 0$ and $\triangle g \geqq 0$. *The program associated with the lower interest rate grows faster*

Assuming wages to be paid at the end of the period, this last case applies to the comparison between prospective programs for an economy where the labor supply is perfectly elastic. With the emphasis now laid on unemployment, disguised or not, this case may be considered as particularly relevant. We must also recognize that the restriction to proportional growth programs will then look less drastic than for other situations. These may be good reasons for accepting the conclusion proposed by Professor Hicks, i.e. that the lower interest rate corresponds to the higher growth rate.[2]

I cannot avoid feeling, however, that the other cases also have a real interest. On the one hand, they show that the relation between the growth rate and the interest rate is not a simple one, even when the two programs use the same technology, as we have assumed throughout. On the other hand, they help to understand to what extent the results of

---

[1] Of course, if $\triangle y = \triangle z = 0$, one sees that $\triangle r \geqq 0$, which implies $\triangle c \leqq 0$, also implies $\triangle g \leqq 0$. The program with the lower interest rate has the higher growth rate.

[2] The careful reader may wonder how the formal result of Professor Hicks' article relates to the ones presented above. His mathematical approach is, indeed, somewhat different. To transpose his reasoning into our model, it suffices to start from his hypotheses, i.e. to assume that the ratio $\frac{z}{c}$ between the quantity of the consumption good and that of the capital good is the same in the two programs, that the noncapitalized real wage rate w is also the same, and that the programs are infinitely close so that differentials may be used. One may then see that the relations (18) imply $dg \cdot dr \leqq 0$, at least as long as $r > g$.

classical capital theory may be transposed to models which were not considered by the classics. One conclusion emerges: these results followed from the study of stationary programs and do not seem to lend themselves to easy generalizations, especially so when the growth rate varies.

*   *   *   *   *

May I end this article with a methodological comment on capital theory? Fundamentally, capital theory is part of the general theory of value. But, in order to reach a better understanding of those features which relate more specifically to intertemporal valuation, special models were built by most of those who wrote on the subject. We ought to go now beyond this stage, since we have found ways of formulating general models which take care of all difficulties at once, and bring a much better understanding of all interrelationships.

From the point of view of a general model, I find the recursive formulation (already proposed by Walras) much better than those where each input is said to " mature " at some later date, the output depending on the period of maturation.[1] If capital theory has something to say on the real working of our economies, why should it be presented with the help of such artificial hypotheses? The " period of production " may remain a useful characteristic for some questions on comparative dynamics. But that is another matter which I have not yet been able to clarify to my own satisfaction.

Paris. E. MALINVAUD.

REFERENCES

[1] M. Allais, *Economie et intéret* (Imprimerie Nationale, Paris, 1947), Chap. VI, p. 162-7 and Annexe III, notably p. 757-9.

[2] K. Arrow, " Roles des valeurs boursières pour la répartition la meilleure des risques " (*Econométrie*, Colloques dy C.N.R.S., Paris, C.N.R.S., 1953).

[3] S. Barnach, *Théorie des opérations linéaires* (Hafner, New-York), Chap. IV.

[4] G. Debreu, *Valuation Equilibrium and Pareto Optimum* (Proceedings of the National Academy of Science of the U.S.A., Vol. 40, pp. 588-592, 1954).

[5] G. Debreu, *Theory of Value—An Axiomatic Analysis of Market Equilibrium* (Wiley, New-York, 1959).

[6] R. Dorfman, P. A. Samuelson and R. Solow, *Linear Programming and Economic Analysis*, Chapter 12 (McGraw Hill, New-York, 1958).

[7] J. R. Hicks, " A ' Value and Capital ' Growth Model ", (*Review of Economic Studies*, June 1959).

---

[1] One frequently objects to the recursive approach that it assumes fixed delay periods between input and output. This is formally true of each elementary operation. But, if the length of a productive process may actually vary, nothing prevents us from representing this process by many elementary operations, each one describing the conditions corresponding to a definite production period. Thus, the concrete features of the technology will be present in our recursive model.

[8] T. Koopmans, *Three Essays on the State of Economic Science* (Chap. I), (New-York, 1957).

[9] T. Koopmans, " Stationary Ordinal Utility and Impatience," (*Econometrica*, April 1960).

[10] E. Malinvaud, " Capital Accumulation and Efficient Allocation of Resources ", (*Econometrica*, April 1953).

[11] E. Malinvaud, " Programmes d'expansion et taux d'intéret " (*Econometrica*, April 1959).

[12] J. Von Neumann, " A Model of General Economic Equilibrium ", (*Review of Economic Studies*, 1945-46).

Selected Bibliography

SELECTED BIBLIOGRAPHY

Abbreviations

AER	American Economic Review
EJ	Economic Journal
ER	Economic Record
Ec	Economica, New Series
Em	Econometrica
IER	International Economic Review
JB	Journal of Business
JPE	Journal of Political Economy
OEP	Oxford Economic Papers
QJE	Quarterly Journal of Economics
REStat	Review of Economics and Statistics
REStud	Review of Economic Studies
YB	Yorkshire Bulletin of Economic and Social Research

Part I. The Basic Aggregative Growth Models

Harrod-Domar Models

1. Alexander, S. S., "The Accelerator as a Generator of Steady Growth," *QJE, 63* (May 1949), 124–197.
2. Alexander, S. S., "Mr. Harrod's Dynamic Model," *EJ, 60* (December 1950) 724–739.

3. Domar, E. D., *Essays in the Theory of Growth*. London: Oxford University Press, 1957.
4. Harrod, R. F., *Towards a Dynamic Economics*. London: Macmillan, 1948.
5. Harrod, R. F., "Domar and Dynamic Economics," *EJ, 69* (June 1960), 451–464.
6. Harrod, R. F., "Second Essay in Dynamic Theory," *EJ, 70* (June 1960), 277–293.
7. Jorgenson, D. W., "On Stability in the Sense of Harrod," *Ec, 28* (August 1960), 243–248.
8. Rose, H., "The Possibility of Warranted Growth," *EJ, 69* (June 1959), 313–332.

Growth and Cycles

9. Duesenberry, J. S., *Business Cycles and Economic Growth*. New York: McGraw-Hill, 1958.
10. Goodwin, R. M., "The Problem of Trend and Cycle," *YB, 5* (August 1953) 89–97.
11. Goodwin, R. M., "A Model of Cyclical Growth," in E. Lundberg, ed., *The Business Cycle in the Postwar World*, Proceedings of International Economic Association Conference. London: Macmillan, 1955, pp. 203–221.
12. Harrod, R. F., *The Trade Cycle*. London: Oxford University Press, 1936.
13. Matthews, R. C. O., "Duesenberry on Growth and Fluctuations," *EJ, 69* (December 1959), 749–765.
14. Phillips, A. W., "A Simple Model of Employment, Money and Prices in a Growing Economy," *Ec, 28* (November 1961), 360–370.
15. Rose, H., "On the Non-Linear Theory of the Employment Cycle," *REStud, 34* (April 1967), 153–174.

Other General Essays

16. Bensusan-Butt, D. M., *On Economic Growth: An Essay in Pure Theory*. London: Oxford University Press, 1960.
17. Hicks, J. R., *Capital and Growth*. London: Oxford University Press, 1965.
18. Meade, J. E., *A Neo-Classical Theory of Economic Growth*. London: Allen and Unwin, 1961.
19. Robinson, J., *The Accumulation of Capital*. London: Macmillan, 1956.
20. Solow, R. M., *Capital Theory and the Rate of Return*. Chicago: Rand McNally, 1963.

Part II. Technical Progress and the Theory of Capital

Section A. Theory of Technical Progress

On the Classification of Inventions

21. Diamond, P. A., "Disembodied Technical Change in a Two Sector Model," *REStud, 32* (April 1965), 161–168.

22. Fei, J. C. H., and G. Ranis, "Innovational Intensity and Factor Bias, in the Theory of Growth," *IER, 71* (1951), 305–308.
23. Jones, R. W., "Neutral Technological Change and the Isoquant Map," *AER, 55* (1965), 848–855.
24. Salter, W. E. G., *Productivity and Technical Change*. London: Cambridge University Press, 1960.

On the Theory of Induced Innovation

25. Ahmad, S., "On the Theory of Induced Innovation," *EJ, 76* (June 1966), 344–357.
26. Arrow, K., "Economic Welfare and the Allocation of Resources for Invention," in Richard R. Nelson, ed., *The Rate and Direction of Inventive Activity*. Princeton: Princeton University Press, 1962, pp. 609–624.
27. Atkinson, A., and J. E. Stiglitz, "A New View of Technical Change," *EJ, 79* (1969).
28. Drandakis, E. M., and E. S. Phelps, "A Model of Induced Invention, Growth, and Distribution," *EJ, 76* (December 1966), 832–840.
29. Fellner, W. J., "Appraisal of the Labour-Saving and Capital-Saving Character of Innovations," Chapter 4 in F. A. Lutz and D. C. Hague, eds., *The Theory of Capital*, Proceedings of International Economic Association Conference. London: Macmillan, and New York: St. Martin's, 1961.
30. Fellner, W. J., "Does the Market Direct the Relative Factor-Saving Effects of Technological Progress," in Universities — National Bureau Committee for Economic Research, *The Rate and Direction of Inventive Activity*. Princeton: Princeton University Press, 1962.
31. Fellner, W., "Technological Progress and Recent Growth Theories," *AER, 57* (December 1967), 1073–1098.
32. Kennedy, C., "Samuelson on Induced Innovation," *REStat, 48* (1966), pp. 442–444.
33. Nordhaus, W., "The Optimal Rate and Direction of Technical Change," in K. Shell, ed., *Essays on the Theory of Optimal Economic Growth*. Cambridge, Mass.: M.I.T. Press, 1967.
34. Phelps, E. S., "Models of Technical Progress and the Golden Rule of Research," *REStud, 33* (April 1966), 133–146.
35. Samuelson, P. A., "A Theory of Induced Innovation along Kennedy-Weizsacker Lines," *REStat, 47* (November 1965), 343–356.
36. Samuelson, P., "Rejoinder . . ." (to Kennedy) *REStat, 48* (1966), 444–448.
37. Uzawa, H., "Optimal Technical Changes in an Aggregative Model of Economic Growth," *IER, 6* (January 1965), 12–31.

Section B. Vintage Models and Embodied Technological Change

38. Green, H. A. J., "Embodied Progress, Investment, and Growth," *AER, 56* (March 1966), 138–151.
39. Inada, K., "Economic Growth under Neutral Technical Progress," *Em, 32* (January–April 1964), 318–327.

40. Jorgenson, D. W., "The Embodiment Hypothesis," *JPE, 74* (February 1966), 1–17.
41. Kemp, M. C., and P. C. Thanh, "On a Class of Growth Models," *Em, 32* (April 1966), 257–282.
42. Nelson, R., "Aggregate Production Functions and Medium Range Growth Projections," *AER, 54* (September 1964), 575–606.
43. Salter, W. E. G., *Productivity and Technical Change.* London: Cambridge University Press, 1960.
44. Solow, R. M., J. Tobin, M. E. Yaari, and C. von Weizsacker, "Neoclassical Growth with Fixed Factor Proportions," *REStud, 33* (April 1966), 79–116.
45. Stiglitz, J. E., "Allocation of Heterogeneous Capital Goods in a Two Sector Model of Economic Growth," *IER, 10* (1969).
46. Uzawa, H., "A Note on Professor Solow's Model of Technical Progress," *Economic Studies Quarterly, 14* (June 1964), pp. 63–68.

Section C.   Smooth Substitutability *Ex Ante* but Rigid Complementarity *Ex Post*

47. Akerlof, G., "Stability, Marginal Products, Putty and Clay," Chapter 25 in K. Shell, ed., *Essays on the Theory of Optimal Economic Growth.* Cambridge, Mass.: M.I.T. Press, 1967.
48. Cass, D., and J. E. Stiglitz, "Implications of Alternative Savings and Expectations Hypotheses for Choices of Technique and Patterns of Growth," *JPE, 77* (1969).
49. Inada, K., "Economic Growth and Factor Substitutions," *IER, 5* (September 1964), 318–327, and "Comment" by M. C. Kemp, E. Sheshinski, and P. C. Thanh, *8* (June 1967), pp. 243–251.
50. Kurz, M., "Substitution versus Fixed Production Coefficients: A Comment," *Em, 31* (January–April 1963), 209–217.
51. Sheshinski, E., "Balanced Growth and Stability in the Johansen Vintage Model," *REStud, 34* (April 1967), 239–248.

Section D.   Learning-by-Doing and Technical Progress Functions

52. Black, J., "The Technical Progress Function and the Production Function," *Ec, 29* (May 1962), 166–170.
53. Levhari, D., "Further Implications of Learning by Doing," *REStud, 33* (January 1966), 31–38, and "Extensions of Learning by Doing," *REStud, 33* (April 1966), 117–133.
54. See also Kaldor and Mirrlees, reprinted below, pp. 384–402 and other articles by Kaldor listed at the end of the next section.

Section E.   Aggregation of Capital

55. Champernowne, D. G., and R. F. Kahn, "The Value of Invested Capital," *REStud, 21* (1953–1954), 107–111.
56. Diamond, P. A., "Technical Change and the Measurement of Capital and Output," *REStud, 32* (October 1965), 289–298.

57. Fisher, F. M., "Embodied Technical Change and the Existence of an Aggregate Capital Stock," *REStud, 32* (October 1965), 263–288.
58. Robinson, J., "The Production Function and the Theory of Capital," *REStud, 21* (1953–1954), 81–106.
59. Samuelson, P. A., "The Evaluation of 'Social Income': Capital Formation and Wealth," Chapter 3 in F. A. Lutz and D. C. Hague, eds., *The Theory of Capital*. London: Macmillan, and New York: St. Martin's Press, 1961.
60. Samuelson, P. A., "Parable and Realism in Capital Theory: The Surrogate Production Function," *REStud, 30* (June 1962), 193–206.
61. Samuelson, P. A., *et al.*, "Symposium on Switching of Techniques," *QJE, 81* (November 1967).
62. Sraffa, P., Part III of *Production of Commodities by Means of Commodities*. Cambridge: Cambridge University Press, 1960.

Section F.   Money and Growth

63. Johnson, H., "The Neo-Classical One-Sector Growth Model: A Geometrical Exposition and Extension to a Monetary Economy," *Ec, 33* (August 1966), and "Comment" by J. Tobin, *33* (February 1967), 265–287.
64. Shell, K., M. Sidrauski, and J. E. Stiglitz, "Capital Gains, Income, and Savings," *REStud, 36* (1969).
65. Sidrauski, M., "Rational Choice and Patterns of Growth in a Monetary Economy," *AER, 58* (May 1967), 534–544.
66. Sidrauski, M., "Inflation and Economic Growth," *JPE, 75* (December 1967), 796–810.

Other Related Topics

Durability of Capital Goods
67. Solow, R., "Notes Toward a Wicksellian Model of Distributive Shares," Chapter 12 in F. A. Lutz and D. C. Hague, eds., *The Theory of Capital*. London: Macmillan and New York: St. Martin's Press, 1961.
68. Wicksell, K., "Mathematical Analysis of Akerman's Problem," reprinted in *Lectures on Political Economy* (London, 1935), vol. I, pp. 274–299.

Heterogeneous Capital Goods
69. Hahn, F. H., "Equilibrium Dynamics with Heterogeneous Capital Goods," *QJE, 80* (November 1966), 633–646.
70. Shell, K., and J. E. Stiglitz, "The Allocation of Investment in a Dynamic Economy," *QJE, 81* (November 1967), 592–609.

Part III.   Cambridge Growth and Distribution Theory

General Discussions
71. Champernowne, D. G., "Capital Accumulation and the Maintenance of Full Employment," *EJ, 68* (June 1958), 211–244.

72. Champernowne, D. G., "A Dynamic Growth Model Involving a Production Function," Chapter 11 in F. A. Lutz and D. C. Hague, eds., *The Theory of Capital*, Proceedings of International Association Conference. London: Macmillan, and New York: St. Martin's, 1961.

73. Findlay, R., "The Robinsonian Model of Accumulation," *Ec, 30* (February 1963), 1–12.

74. Findlay, R., "A Reply (to J. Robinson, 'Findlay's Robinsonian Model of Accumulation: A Comment')," *Ec, 30* (November 1963), 411–412.

75. Robinson, J., "Findlay's Robinsonian Model of Accumulation: A Comment," *Ec, 30* (November 1963), 408–411.

76. Kaldor, N., "A Model of Economic Growth," *EJ, 68* (December 1957), 591–624.

77. Kaldor, N., "Economic Growth and the Problem of Inflation," *Ec, 26* (August, November, 1959), 212–226, 287–298.

78. Kaldor, N., "Capital Accumulation and Economic Growth," in F. A. Lutz and D. C. Hague, eds., *The Theory of Capital*, Proceedings of International Economic Association Conference, London: Macmillan, and New York: St. Martin's, 1961.

79. Kaldor, N., "A Rejoinder to Mr. Atsumi and Professor Tobin," *REStud, 27* (February 1960).

80. Kaldor, N., "Comment" (in Symposium on Production Function and Economic Growth), *REStud, 29* (June 1962), 249–250.

81. Kalecki, M., *Essays in the Theory of Economic Fluctuations*. London: Allen and Unwin, 1939.

82. Robinson, J., *The Accumulation of Capital*. London: Macmillan, 1956.

83. Robinson, J., *Essays in the Theory of Economic Growth*. London: Macmillan, 1962.

84. Tobin, J., "Towards a General Kaldorian Theory of Distribution," *REStud, 27* (February 1960), 119–120.

Pasinetti's Paradox

85. Kaldor, N., "Marginal Productivity and the Macro-Economic Theories of Distribution," *REStud, 33* (October 1966), 309–320.

86. Meade, J. E., "The Rate of Profit in a Growing Economy," *EJ, 73* (December 1963), 665–674.

87. Pasinetti, L., "Rate of Profit and Income Distribution in Relation to the Rate of Economic Growth," *REStud, 29* (October 1962), 267–279.

88. Pasinetti, L., "New Results in an Old Framework," *REStud, 33* (October 1966), 303–306.

89. Robinson, J., "Comment on Samuelson and Modigliani," *REStud, 33* (October 1966), 307–308.

90. Samuelson, P. A., and F. Modigliani, "The Pasinetti Paradox in Neoclassical and More General Models," *REStud, 33* (October 1966), 269–302.

91. Samuelson, P. A., and F. Modigliani, "Reply to Pasinetti and Robinson," *REStud, 33* (October 1966), 321–330.

92. Stiglitz, J. E., "A Two Sector-Two Class Model of Economic Growth," *REStud, 34* (April 1967), 227–238.

Part IV. Two-Sector Models

93. Amano, A., "A Further Note on Professor Uzawa's Two-Sector Model of Economic Growth," *REStud, 31* (April 1964), 97–102.
94. Corden, W., "The Two-Sector Growth Model with Fixed Coefficients," *REStud, 33* (July 1966), 253–262.
95. Drandakis, E. M., "Factor Substitution in the Two-Sector Growth Model," *REStud, 30* (October 1963), 217–228.
96. Hahn, F. H., "On Two-Sector Growth Models," *REStud, 32* (April 1964), 127–142.
97. Harcourt, G. C., "A Two-Sector Model of the Distribution of Income and the Level of Employment in the Short Run," *ER, 41*:103–117 (May 1965).
98. Inada, K., "On a Two-Sector Model of Economic Growth: Comments and a Generalization," *REStud, 30* (June 1963), 119–127.
99. Inada, K., "On the Stability of Two-Sector Growth Models," *REStud, 31* (April 1964), 127–142.
100. Inada, K., "Investment in Fixed Capital and the Stability of Growth Equilibrium," *REStud, 33* (January 1966), 19–30.
101. Shinkai, Y., "On Equilibrium Growth of Capital and Labor," *IER, 1* (May 1960), 107–111.
102. Stiglitz, J., "Allocation of Heterogeneous Capital in a Two-Sector Model of Economic Growth," *IER, 10* (1969).
103. Takayama, A., "On a Two-Sector Model of Economic Growth: A Comparative Statics Analysis," *REStud, 30* (June 1963), 95–104.
104. Uzawa, H., "On a Two-Sector Model of Economic Growth: I," *REStud, 29* (October 1961), 40–47.

Part V. Foundations of Optimal Economics

The Golden Rule (The Neo-neoclassical Theorem)

105. Champernowne, D. G., "Some Implications of Golden Age Conditions when Savings Equal Profits," *REStud, 29* (July 1962), 235–237.
106. Phelps, E., "The Golden Rule of Accumulation," *AER, 51* (September 1961), 638–643.
107. Phelps, E., "Second Essay on the Golden Rule of Accumulation," *AER, 55* (September 1965), 783–814.
108. Robinson, J., "A Neo-Classical Theorem," *REStud, 29* (June 1962), 219–226.

Aggregative Models

109. Cass, D., "Optimum Growth in an Aggregative Model of Capital Accumulation," *REStud, 32* (July 1965), 233–240.
110. Koopmans, T., "On the Concept of Optimal Economic Growth," *Semaine d'Etude sur le Role de l'Analyse Econometrique dans la Formulation de Plans de Development* (Study Week on the Econometric Approach to Planning), Pontificiae Scientiarum Scripta Varia *28* (published by Rand McNally and Co., 1965), 225–287.

111. Koopmans, T., "Intertemporal Distribution and 'Optimal' Aggregate Economic Growth," in *Ten Economic Studies in the Tradition of Irving Fisher*. New York: Wiley, 1967.
112. Srinivasan, T. N., "Optimal Savings in a Two-Sector Model of Growth," *Em, 32* (July 1964), 358–373, and errata *33* (April 1965), 424.
113. Uzawa, H., "Optimal Growth in a Two-Sector Model of Capital Accumulation," *REStud, 31* (January 1964), 1–24.
114. Von Weizsacker, C., "Existence of Optimal Programs of Accumulation for an Infinite Time Horizon," *REStud, 32* (April 1965), 85–104.

Life Cycle Model

115. Cass, D., and M. E. Yaari, "A Re-Examination of the Pure Consumption Loans Model," *JPE, 74* (1966), 353–367.
116. Cass, D., and M. E. Yaari, "Individual Saving, Aggregate Capital Accumulation, and Efficient Growth," in Chapter 13, K. Shell, ed., *Essays on the Theory of Optimal Economic Growth*. Cambridge, Mass.: M.I.T. Press, 1967.
117. Diamond, P. A., "National Debt in a Neoclassical Growth Model," *AER, 55* (December 1965), 1126–1150.
118. Meade, J. E., "Life-Cycle Savings, Inheritance and Economic Growth," *REStud, 33* (1966), 61–78.

Turnpike Theorems

119. Cass, D., "Optimum Growth in an Aggregative Model of Capital Accumulation: A Turnpike Theorem," *Em, 34* (October 1966), 833–850.
120. Dorfman, R., P. A. Samuelson, and R. M. Solow, *Linear Programming and Economic Analysis*. New York: McGraw-Hill, 1958.
121. Inada, K., "Some Structural Characteristics of Turnpike Theorems," *REStud, 31* (January 1964), 43–58.
122. Koopmans, T., "Economic Growth at a Maximal Rate," *QJE, 78* (August 1964), 355–394.
123. McKenzie, L., "Three Turnpike Theorems for a Generalized Leontief Model," *Em, 31* (January–April 1963), 165–180.
124. Morishima, M., "Proof of a Turnpike Theorem: The No Joint Production Case," *REStud, 28* (February 1961), 89–97.
125. Radner, R., "Paths of Economic Growth that Are Optimal with Regard only to Final States," *REStud, 28* (February 1961), 98–104.
126. Samuelson, P. A., "A Catenary Turnpike Theorem Involving Consumption and the Golden Rule," *AER, 55* (1965), 486–496 (errata, 864–866).

AUTHOR INDEX

493

SUBJECT INDEX

Accelerator, 14, 45, 380
"Adding-up problem," 335
Åkerman's problem, 112 ff., 336, 415
Allais-optimality, 469
"Animal spirits," 326, 361
Asset preferences, 46
Average age of capital, *see* Capital, average age

Balanced growth, 5, 200, 368, 475, 476, *see also* Comparative dynamics; Golden age
  in Cobb-Douglas economy, 90
  in economy with capital-labor substitution, 62 ff.
  in fixed coefficients technology, 38–42
  in Harrod model, 16
  in monetary economy, 49, 302
  uniqueness in two-sector model 403–406, 417
  in vintage model, 179
Biased technical change, *see* Technical progress, factor bias
Biological market interest rate, 453 ff.
Bliss, 431

Calculus of variations, 433
Capacity in fixed coefficients technology, 37
Capital, aggregation, 97 ff., 357, *see also* Wicksell effect

  aggregation with embodied technichange, 125, 160
  Champernowne chain index, 105, 261 ff
  J. R. units, 102, 261
  Leontief aggregation theorem, 286
  Solow aggregation theorem, 286
Capital, average age, 182, 192 ff., 205, *see also* Embodied technical change
  in *ex post* fixed coefficients model, 195
Capital, durability, 112, 124, *see also* Åkerman's problem; Depreciation
Capital intensity hypothesis, 409, 415
Causality, definition, 7
Causation, 350
Chain index of capital, 105, 261 ff.
Classical savings, *see* Savings functions, classical
Cobb-Douglas production function, 13, 69, 77, 88 ff., 157 ff., 172 ff., 260, 289
  and technical change, 140
Cohen, Ruth curiosom, 267
Comparative dynamics, def., 6, 477 ff., *see also* Balanced Growth; Golden age
Constant elasticity of substitution production function, 70, 193 ff.,